RESEARCH ADVANCES IN ALCOHOL AND DRUG PROBLEMS

Volume One

ADVISORY PANEL

J. C. BALL,

K. BRUUN,

D. C. CAMERON,

G. EDWARDS,

L. E. HOLLISTER,

O. IRGENS-JENSEN,

J. H. JAFFE,

K. F. KILLAM,

C. M. LEEVY,

J. MARDONES,

W. H. McGLOTHLIN,

H. McILWAIN,

J. H. MENDELSON,

W. D. M. PATON,

H. POPPER,

R. W. RUSSELL,

J. R. SEELEY,

M. H. SEEVERS,

C. R. SCHUSTER,

H. SOLMS,

R. STRAUS,

RC 565 .R37

81540
V.1

Research Advances in Alcohol and Drug Problems

RESEARCH ADVANCES IN ALCOHOL AND DRUG PROBLEMS

Volume One

Edited by

ROBERT J. GIBBINS
YEDY ISRAEL
HAROLD KALANT
ROBERT E. POPHAM
WOLFGANG SCHMIDT
REGINALD G. SMART

A WILEY-BIOMEDICAL HEALTH PUBLICATION

JOHN WILEY & SONS, New York • London • Sydney • Toronto

Copyright © 1974, by John Wiley & Sons, Inc.

All rights reserved. Published simultaneously in Canada.

No part of this book may be reproduced by any means, nor transmitted, nor translated into a machine language without the written permission of the publisher.

Library of Congress Catalog Card Number: 73-18088

ISBN 0-471-29737-2

Printed in the United States of America

10 9 8 7 6 5 4 3 2 1

CONTRIBUTORS

MONIQUE C. BRAUDE, *Center for Studies of Narcotic Addiction and Drug Abuse Studies, National Institute of Mental Health, Rockville, Maryland*

GEORGE M. HENRY, *Department of Psychiatry, University of Kentucky College of Medicine, Lexington, Kentucky*

LEO E. HOLLISTER, *Veterans Administration Hospital and Department of Medicine, Stanford University School of Medicine, Palo Alto, California*

CHRIS E. JOHANSON, *University of Chicago, Chicago, Illinois*

WERNER K. LELBACH, *Department of Internal Medicine, University Clinics of Bonn, Bonn, West Germany*

JOAN A. MARSHMAN, *Addiction Research Foundation, Toronto, Canada*

G. W. MERCER, *Department of Psychology, York University, Toronto, Canada*

KAI PERNANEN, *Addiction Research Foundation, Toronto, Canada*

CHARLES R. SCHUSTER, *University of Chicago, Chicago, Illinois*

R. G. SMART, *Addiction Research Foundation, Toronto, Canada*

EDWARD B. TRUITT, JR., *Department of Pharmacology, The George Washington University School of Medicine, Washington, D.C.*

PREFACE

During the last decade most parts of the world have experienced a growing interest in problems associated with the nonmedical use of drugs—specifically drug dependence. In part, this heightened awareness has corresponded to a real growth in the extent, diversity, and social impact of the use of drugs in many societies. Public concern, both reflected in and enhanced by the mass media of communication, has led to greater demands on experts of all types for information about the causes and consequences of drug use and about methods of coping with the perceived problems.

As a result, the amount of research and writing on the subject of drug problems has increased greatly. Thus as many clinical and scientific papers on the amphetamines have appeared since 1965 as were published from 1929 to 1965. This explosive growth of the scientific and clinical literature is not unique to the area of drug research. There is, however, an added difficulty—this field is an interdisciplinary one. It is almost a platitude to point out that the field of drug problems spans the entire range of investigation in social, behavioral, basic biological, and clinical disciplines. This means that the person who wishes to keep well informed about drug problems faces the difficulty of an expanding literature multiplied manyfold.

It is therefore impossible for one individual to keep up to date with all the relevant literature pertaining to the diverse aspects of the "drug problem." There is a particularly acute need in this field for critical reviews that assess the current developments, interpret them for the reader who is not expert in the particular area, and provide orientation in related areas of study. There are already a number of annual review publications, which have a well-established place in the continuing education of scientists. In general, however, they confine their attention to individual disciplines, such as biochemistry, physiology, psychology, medicine, and other traditionally defined fields of study. Many researchers and practicing professionals have felt a need for a single publication that would review the many aspects contributing to our understanding of drug use and drug problems. The present series, beginning with this volume, is intended to fill such a need.

Although one volume is to be published annually, the series is not intended to be an "annual review" in the usual sense. The aim is not to cover all the work reported during the preceding year in relation to a fixed selection of themes or disciplines. Rather, it is to present each year a number of critically evaluative papers dealing with selected topics in which enough recent progress has been made to warrant a review, or in which debate or confusion are such as to require an analysis and clarification of concepts. Consequently it is anticipated that a different selection of topics will be covered each year. Each paper will discuss the work appearing during a period of several years, the length of the period being determined by the relevance and amount of the material. The frequency with which any one topic is reexamined in later years will depend on the rate of progress of research on that topic.

Because of the multidisciplinary nature of problems of drug use and dependence, the papers published in each volume will be drawn from several disciplines or areas of research. It is our hope that in future volumes there will be an increasing emphasis on truly interdisciplinary reviews intended to correlate and integrate information derived from different types of investigation bearing on a specific problem. It is even conceivable that an entire volume might be devoted to a particular problem, with individual reviews and papers examining various aspects of it. The desirability of such an approach will undoubtedly be easier to assess as the series evolves.

The composition of the editorial board and the international advisory board reflects these objectives of the series. The editors are members of the senior scientific staff of the Addiction Research Foundation of Ontario. Their own areas of special interest include the fields of biochemistry, pharmacology, anthropology, experimental and clinical psychology, sociology, and jurisprudence. The members of the international advisory panel are well known in this field. Their interests range over the relevant disciplines, and, they represent seven countries in Europe, North and South America, and Australia. On the basis of their knowledge of the relevant fields, and their reading of the literature in various languages, they propose to the editors each year a list of the subjects that are most appropriate for review, as well as the names of investigators in different parts of the world who might be best qualified to write the reviews. Obviously no publication can guarantee that it will fill the needs of all its readers with respect to sorting out fact from conjecture, the important from the trivial, or the permanent from the transitory. Nevertheless, we hope that this series will provide a lead in the desired direction and will stimulate the type of interdisciplinary inquiry that is widely advocated but seldom practiced. To this end the editorial board and the advisory panel will be happy to consider suggestions submitted by readers for reviews on subjects that they would like to see covered in future issues of the series.

ROBERT J. GIBBINS
YEDY ISRAEL
HAROLD KALANT
ROBERT E. POPHAM
WOLFGANG SCHMIDT
REGINALD G. SMART

July 1973
Toronto, Canada

CONTENTS

**CHAPTER 1 THE USE OF ANIMAL MODELS FOR THE STUDY OF 1
DRUG ABUSE**

Charles R. Schuster and Chris E. Johanson

1. General Methodology, 3
2. Self-Administration Procedures as a means for Preclinical Assessment of a Drug's Abuse Liability, 10
3. Pharmacological Variables Affecting Drug Self-Administration, 17
4. Environmental Variables Affecting Drug Self-Administration, 21
5. Consequences of Drug Self-Administration, 23

**CHAPTER 2 CHEMICAL AND BIOCHEMICAL METHODS OF DRUG 33
DETECTION AND MEASUREMENT**

Joan A. Marshman

1. Cleanup Procedures 34

   Ion-Exchange Resins, 35
   A Nonionic Resin, Amberlite XAD-2, 36
   Other Cleanup Methods, 39

2. Gas Chromatographic Methods 40

   Detectors, 41
   Derivative Formation For Gas Chromatographic Detection,
   44 Barbiturates, 44 Narcotic analgesics, 46 Amphetamines
   and related compounds, 47 Cannabinoids, 52

3. Fluorescence Measurements, 52
4. Mass Spectrometry, 59

   Direct Inlet Mass Spectrometry, 59
   Gas Chromatography/Mass Spectrometry, 61
   GC/MS Application to Drugs per se, 61
   GC/MS Application to Drugs in Biological Samples, 63
   Mass Fragmentography, 65

5. Immunochemical Methods, 68

CHAPTER 3 ORGANIC PATHOLOGY RELATED TO VOLUME AND PATTERN OF ALCOHOL USE — 93
Werner K. Lelbach

1. Moderate Drinking and Heavy Drinking, 95
2. Capacity of Ethanol Elimination, 102
3. Controlled Studies of the Quantitative Effect of Alcohol Intake, 106

   Effect of Single Doses, 106
   Effects of Controlled Prolonged Ethanol Administration, 110

4. Influence of Duration and Dose of Alcohol Abuse as Evidenced by Retrospective Studies, 118
   Liver Pathology, 118
   Other Organic Lesions, 140

5. Influence of Pattern of Drinking: Effects of Abstinence, 142

   Pattern of Drinking, 142
   Abstinence, 145

6. Genetic Predisposition and Susceptibility, 147
7. Organic Pathology and Various Alcoholic Beverages, 151

   Influence of Congeneric Substances, 151
   Influence of Ingredients Other than Congeneric Substances, 162

8. Conclusion, 167

CHAPTER 4 PRECLINICAL PHARMACOLOGY OF MARIHUANA — 199

Edward B. Truitt, Jr., and Monique C. Braude

1. Pharmaceutics and Routes of Administration, 200
2. Metabolism, 201

   Absorption, 202
   Distribution, 202
   Biotransformation, 203
   Excretion, 205
   Metabolic Interactions, 205

3. Toxicity Studies, 206

   Acute Toxicity, 206
   Chronic Toxicity, 208
   Special Toxicity Studies, 211

4. Pharmacologic Actions, 212

   Central Nervous System Effects, 212 *Neurochemical effects,* 213 *Neuropharmacological and EEG effects,* 214 *Neuroendocrine effects,* 219 *Behavioral effects,* 219 *Interactions with other CNS drugs,* 222 *Possible therapeutic applications,* 223

   Cardiovascular Effects, 223

   Effects on Other Systems, 224 *Respiratory function,* 224 *Thermal regulation,* 225 *Gastrointestinal function,* 225 *Drug interactions,* 225

5. Summary and Conclusions, 226

CHAPTER 5 CLINICAL PHARMACOLOGY OF MARIHUANA — 243

Leo E. Hollister

1. Human Experimentation with Marihuana, 243

   Legal and Regulatory Constraints, 243
   Problems in Dosing, 243

Problems in Selecting Subjects, 244
Difficulties in Maintaining Blind Controls, 244

2. Constituents, Metabolites, and Homologs, 245

   Natural Cannabinoids, 245
   Metabolites, 245
   Homologs, 245

3. Pharmacokinetics, 246

   Absorption, 246 *Smoking,* 246 *Oral doses,* 247
   Distribution, Biotransformation, and Excretion, 247

4. Clinical Syndromes, 248

   General Considerations, 248
   Specific Effects, 248
   Relevance of Clinical Effects in Laboratory to Social Use, 249
   Placebo Effects, 249

5. Physiological Effects, 250

   General, 250 *Cardiovascular,* 250 *Eyes,* 250 *Neuromuscular,* 251 *Miscellaneous effects,* 251
   Neurophysiological, 251 *Electroencephalographic studies,* 251
   Sleep studies, 252 *Evoked potentials,* 253

6. Biochemical Effects, 253

7. Psychological Tests, 253

   Cognitive Functions, 253
   Perceptual Tests, 255
   Motor Tests, 256

8. Therapeutic Uses, 257

   Hypnotic, 257
   Analgesia, 257
   Withdrawal from Other Drugs, 258
   Antidepressant, 258
   Appetite Stimulant, 258
   Antihypertensive, 259
   Anticonvulsant, 259
   Other Uses, 259

9. Adverse Effects, 259

   Somatic, 259
   Psychiatric, 260

10. Marihuana and Other Drugs, 261

    Comparisons, 261   *LSD*, 261   *Dextroamphetamine and ethanol*, 262   *Ethanol*, 262

    Interactions, 262

CHAPTER 6   TREATMENT AND REHABILITATION OF NARCOTIC ADDICTION   267

George M. Henry

1. Detoxification, 267

2. Maintenance on Opioid Drugs, 273

   Examples of the Maintenance Approach, 274   *Morphine*, 274
   Heroin, 274   *Methadone*, 275   *Other narcotic drugs*, 277
   Inherent Problems in Opioid Maintenance, 278

3. Opioid Antagonists, 279

   Examples of Specific Antagonists, 279
   Therapeutic Uses of Opioid Antagonists, 281

4. Psychosocial Management, 283

5. Results of Treatment for Narcotic Addiction, 289

6. Conclusions, 292

CHAPTER 7   THE EPIDEMIOLOGY OF PSYCHOACTIVE AND HALLUCINOGENIC DRUG USE   303

G. W. Mercer and R. G. Smart

1. General Methodological Difficulties in Epidemiological Drug Research, 305

2. An Overview of Morbidity and Mortality, 308

   Cannabis, 309
   LSD, 310
   Amphetamines, 310
   Barbiturates and Tranquilizers, 310
   Overall Considerations, 311

3. Epidemiology in the Americas, 311

   Canada and the United States, 311   Secondary school drug use, 311   University and college studies, 315   Other populations studies, 321   Some noteworthy overviews, 326
   Mexico, 327
   Chile, 327

4. Epidemiology in Britain and Europe, 328

   Britain, 328
   France, 330
   Scandinavia, 330
   Switzerland, 332
   Holland, 332
   Germany, 333
   Czechoslovakia, 333

5. Epidemiology in Africa, 333

6. Epidemiology in Asia and Asia Minor, 333

   Mideast, 333
   India, 334

7. Epidemiology in Australia, 334

8. World Epidemiology: Summary with Suggestions for Further Research, 335

CHAPTER 8   VALIDITY OF SURVEY DATA ON ALCOHOL USE   355

K. Pernanen

1. Data from Family Expenditure Surveys, 356

2. Data from the Ontario Drinking Survey, 357

3. Factors Affecting Coverage, 359

   Sample Frames and Cluster Effects, 359
   Nonresponse, 360
   Response Error, 361   *Forgetting,* 362   *Selective reporting,* 365

4. Possible Consequences of Noncoverage 370

INDEX   375

RESEARCH ADVANCES IN ALCOHOL AND DRUG PROBLEMS

Volume One

Chapter One

THE USE OF ANIMAL MODELS FOR THE STUDY OF DRUG ABUSE*

CHARLES R. SCHUSTER, *University of Chicago, Chicago, Illinois*
CHRIS E. JOHANSON, *University of Chicago, Chicago, Illinois*

This paper outlines a conceptual framework for an animal model of drug abuse and selectively reviews some of the investigations utilizing this approach. Further, any implications of such investigations for the human problem of drug abuse are presented.

We believe it is important to distinguish four potentially separable problems in the study of drug abuse (for a fuller discussion of this see ref. 46): (1) physical dependence, (2) behavioral or psychological dependence, (3) self-administration of a compound for nonmedical purposes, and (4) the physiological and behavioral consequences of the self-administered drug. It is our contention that physical and behavioral dependence are relevant in the present context only to the extent that they predispose the organism to self-administer a drug. To clarify this issue, we will define these terms as we are using them in this paper.

Physical dependence can be defined as a state produced by chronic drug administration, which is revealed by the occurrence of signs of physiological dysfunction when the drug is withdrawn; further, this dysfunction can be reversed by the administration of the drug. The definition of behavioral (psychological) dependence has unfortunately been couched in motivational terms such as a "craving for the drug," the assumption being that if a drug is self-administered, this is due to some underlying psychological need. We feel that in the interest of operational clarity, it is preferable to define behavioral dependence in an analogous manner to physical dependence. We

---

* The preparation of this manuscript was supported by NIMH Grants MH-18,245 and MH-11,042 to Charles R. Schuster.

would therefore define *behavioral dependence* as a condition revealed when drug administration is terminated and measurable behavioral disruptions occur, which are reversed by the administration of the drug. These two forms of dependence are relevant to the concept of drug abuse to the extent that they lead to an organism's self-administration of a drug at sufficient dosages or frequency that physiological or behavioral toxicity occurs as a consequence. Thus we define drug abuse not only by the self-administration of a drug, but further require the demonstration that this practice leads to toxic consequences. We acknowledge, of course, that there will be some degree of disagreement as to what constitutes "toxicity," particularly behavioral toxicity. It is not always clear when a particular behavioral change should be viewed as a "toxic" manifestation of a drug. Nevertheless, we feel it is important to make these distinctions in order to distinguish drug abuse from drug use.

In the present review, we are limiting ourselves to studies of intravenously self-administered drugs. These studies are based on the general principles of operant conditioning (52) in which behavior is controlled by its consequences. Such consequences are called *reinforcers*. The investigations reviewed here were designed to determine whether a pharmacological agent will act as a reinforcer for an operant response (i.e., will be self-administered), and how various pharmacological and environmental variables alter this behavior.

The relevance of data from animal studies to the human problem of drug abuse is based upon the validity of two assumptions: (1) drugs that are reinforcers in infrahuman organisms can serve this same function in man, and (2) humans and the infrahuman test subject are comparable in their sensitivity to the toxic effects of the self-administered drug. The validity of these assumptions is an empirical question dependent on the accrual of large amounts of data. While such data are being collected, we will assume the relevance of animal studies and exploit their advantages in the study of drug abuse.

The use of infrahuman organisms in the study of physical dependence on opiates and barbiturates has been extremely useful for the preclinical assessment of a new compound's physical dependence liability as well as for investigating the basic mechanisms underlying this phenomenon. Techniques for studying the behavioral aspects of drug dependence and abuse in infrahuman organisms have only recently evolved. The advantages of an animal model encompassing both the behavioral and physiological aspects of drug dependence and abuse are many. First, the range of experimental manipulations ethically possible with animal subjects allows studies that could not be carried out in man. As has been stated elsewhere (49), the use of infrahuman subjects in the study of behavioral aspects of drug abuse has one special advantage in that it forces the investigator to divest himself of oversimplified preconceptions. The laboratory investigator is less prone to project vaguely defined personality or character disorders into his infrahuman subjects as an explanation of their drug intake.

1. GENERAL METHODOLOGY

To study drugs as a class of reinforcers, methods for their delivery had to be developed. Drugs can be delivered by several routes: (1) oral, (2) intravenous, (3) inhalation, (4) intracerebral, (5) intraperitoneal, and (6) intramuscular. Only the first two routes have been studied extensively in reinforcement research. In the present review, however, the intravenous route is the primary route considered. The experimental setups using the oral route are relatively inexpensive and simple, but the technique suffers from a confounding of several variables, including: (1) the taste of solutions, (2) the necessity of water deprivation [except in the case of adjunctive drinking (11)], (3) the delay in the time of onset of the pharmacological actions of the drug, and (4) the inability to specify the pharmacologically active dose. Lester (34) and Schuster and Thompson (48) give a fuller explanation of these problems and a review of the literature regarding oral self-administration studies.

Many studies of drug self-administration in rats and in monkeys have used the intravenous route of administration. This technique is described for rats by Weeks (58, 59) and Davis (4) and for rhesus monkeys by Yanagita, Deneau, and Seevers (75) and Wilson (65). Since drugs of high abuse liability such as heroin and cocaine are administered principally by this route (alcohol is an exception), its use has more face validity than the oral route as a model of drug abuse.

The intravenous system has several fundamental aspects: (1) the chronic implantation of a venous catheter into the organism to provide immediate delivery of a drug, (2) a restraining device which allows the organism relatively unrestricted movement within the experimental space yet still protects the catheter, and (3) an automatic programming system for the delivery of drug, contingent upon some response by the animal. Individual investigators have introduced modifications of these basic aspects in their work.

Figure 1 presents the system used by Schuster and his associates at the University of Chicago. The animal is fitted with a tubular steel harness which is connected to the wall of the cubicle by a metal spring. The cathe-

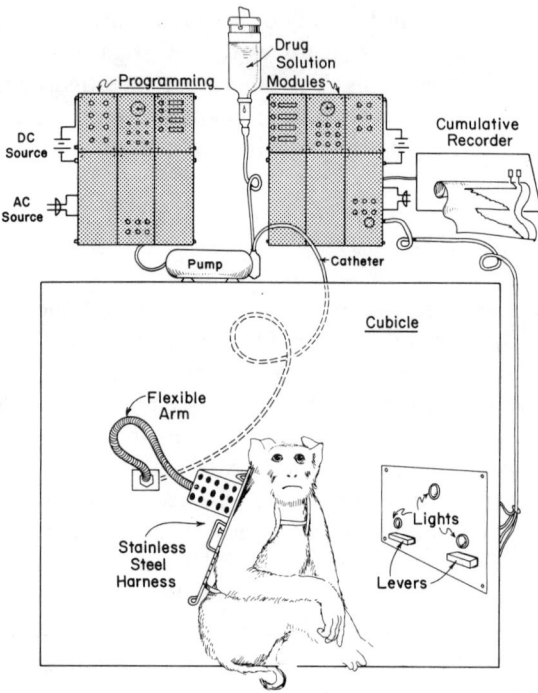

Fig. 1. System (used by Schuster at the University of Chicago) for automatic intravenous infusions into the rhesus monkey. The monkey is fitted with a tubular steel harness which is connected to the wall of the cubicle by a metal spring. The catheter runs through the metal spring and eventually to an infusion pump. Drug availability is controlled by electrical programming equipment and the relevant responses made by the monkey are automatically recorded by this same equipment.

ter runs through the metal spring to an infusion pump controlled by electrical programming equipment.

In addition to utilizing this technique the model employs the principles of behavior analysis (52). The fundamental principle is that the frequency or pattern of operant behavior is controlled by events that follow it. These consequences or stimulus events are known as *reinforcers*. An event is considered a positive reinforcer if it either increases the frequency of behavior it follows or decreases the frequency of a behavior that results in its removal. An event is considered a negative reinforcer if it either increases the frequency of behavior that avoids it or decreases the frequency of behavior which it follows. Drug self-administration as a class of responses can be analyzed in this manner. A drug would be considered a positive reinforcer if it increased the frequency of a response it followed; it would be considered a negative reinforcer if the frequency of a response that avoided or terminated its infusion increased. Drugs, however, in addition to having reinforcing properties, have other pharmacological effects that can indirectly modify their ability to act as a reinforcer. For instance, organisms administering opiates develop physical dependence to this drug; that is, discontinuation of the drug regimen results in disruption of a variety of physiological systems so that the organism becomes sick (i.e., undergoes withdrawal). Drug administration rapidly terminates the withdrawal syndrome. Therefore, the development of physical dependence may modify an opiate's reinforcing efficacy.

To understand drugs as reinforcers it is necessary to briefly review some additional concepts of behavior analysis. One of the more important of these is stimulus control. Reinforcement usually occurs under a particular set of environmental circumstances or stimulus events. If an animal is reinforced for responding only in the presence of a green light, the probability of his responding when the green light is on increases. The green light, known as the *discriminative stimulus*, is said to exert *stimulus control* over responding. Drug abusers are more likely to self-administer a drug in the presence of other addicts only because they have done so in the past and experienced the reinforcing pharmacological actions of the drug. Further, it has been demonstrated that such discriminative stimuli may also act as conditioned reinforcers (32).

A second concept of behavior analysis is the schedule relating responding and reinforcement. In the simplest schedule, *continuous reinforcement* (CRF), every response is followed by a reinforcer. However, the relationship between responding and reinforcement may be more complex. A response may be reinforced on the basis of the time elapsed since the last reinforcement, that is, on an *interval schedule*, or on the basis of the number of responses emitted since the termination of the previous reinforcement, which is a *ratio schedule*. An interval or ratio schedule may either be fixed or vary in number or time. The four basic schedules, then, are fixed interval, variable interval, fixed ratio, and variable ratio. In addition to these, there exist numerous other possibilities for relating responding and reinforcement, i.e. schedules of reinforcement (12). The schedule relating responding and drug reinforcement is a significant variable in determining both rate and pattern of responding.

Two other concepts are essential in the understanding of the behavioral analysis of drugs as reinforcers. These are the concepts of the operant level and extinction. *Operant level* is the rate of responding on some manipulandum when there are no programmed consequences, for example, a drug infusion. Most animals are likely to hit or press the manipulandum at some low level before any experimental manipulations. Any subsequent changes in rate are then compared to this operant level rather than zero. *Extinction* occurs when a response which has previously been followed by a reinforcement goes unreinforced. Typically, rate of responding increases dramatically at the beginning of extinction and then gradually declines to the operant level of responding. The magnitude of the increase in rate and the length of time before responding declines to the operant level is directly proportional to the efficacy of the reinforcing stimulus. In drug self-administration studies, responding during both the determination of operant level and extinction is usually followed by an infusion of saline, a neutral stimulus. This is done to compare response rates which are generated under identical situations *except* for the presence or absence of the drug.

The first drug studied using the self-administration technique and principles of behavior analysis was morphine. It was assumed that morphine and morphinelike drugs (e.g., heroin, codeine), since they produced physical dependence, derived their positive reinforcing properties at least in part from their ability to alleviate the withdrawal syndrome as well as from their euphoric effects. Therefore in these original studies the animals were made physically dependent on morphine prior to any opportunity for self-administration. Weeks (58) found that physically dependent rats would regularly press a lever when the response was followed immediately by a 10 mg/kg injection of morphine. Further, Weeks and Collins (60) found that lowering the dose of morphine increased the rate of responding but decreased overall intake. Similarly, Thompson and Schuster (57) found that monkeys who were first made physically dependent on morphine could be trained to respond on a complex schedule of reinforcement for morphine delivered intravenously. They also found that manipulating antecedent conditions modified response rate for morphine reinforcement. Antecedent conditions with more conventional reinforcers, like food, include manipulations such as deprivation or satiation. The greater the degree of deprivation (unless carried to an extreme where inanition results) for a particular reinforcer such as food, the greater the response rate; similarly, the greater the degree of satiation, the lower the response rate. Morphine deprivation can be accomplished in two ways: (1) by removing the opportunity for self-administration for a period of time (e.g., 24-hr deprivation), or (2) by injecting an opiate antagonist (e.g., nalorphine or naloxone). Morphine satiation can be accomplished by injecting the organism with morphine prior to an experimental session. In the study by Thompson and Schuster (57) an injection of 1.0 mg of nalorphine or 24-hr morphine deprivation increased response rate; on the other hand, noncontingent pretreatment with various doses of morphine decreased rate of responding.

The results of these early studies demonstrated the possibilities of using the methodology for the study of drug abuse, but in no way established whether morphine would be self-administered in the absence of physical dependence. Most humans who become opiate addicts have not been treated with the drug to establish prior physical dependence. It was essential, therefore, for the validation of the self-administration animal model to demonstrate that morphine may act as a reinforcer in the absence of physical dependence.

A variety of studies have shown that physical dependence is not a necessary condition in order for morphine to serve as a positive reinforcer. Deneau, Yanagita, and Seevers (8) showed that it was not necessary for animals to be made physically dependent on morphine for them to self-administer the drug. Similarly, Schuster (47) found that over a 30-day period, originally naive monkeys steadily increased their self-administration of 1.0 mg/(kg)(injection) morphine. However, in both studies rates of responding for morphine during the first 6 to 10 days were not greater than baseline responding for saline, yet were high enough at the dosages employed to produce physical dependence. Therefore it still was not clear whether morphine was a positive reinforcer in the absence of physical dependence. Woods and Schuster (70) showed, however, that a dose of morphine too small to produce physical dependence (as measured by observation and disruption in food-reinforced behavior) maintained rates of responding above saline baseline. Rates of responding during extinction, though, were higher in animals that were reinforced with higher dosages of morphine and as a consequence were physically dependent. It was concluded that (1) morphine is a positive reinforcer independently of its ability to terminate the withdrawal syndrome and (2) the reinforcing efficacy of morphine is increased if animals are physically dependent on it (47, 72).

Several drugs subsequently were tested with this procedure to verify whether mere availability of a drug is sufficient for its self-administration. Table 1 summarizes these studies. Cocaine, d-amphetamine, methamphetamine, nicotine, and other psychomotor stimulants (methylphenidate, phenmetrazine, pipradrol, and SPA) are positive reinforcers in the psychomotor stimulant class. The only stimulants unable to maintain lever-pressing were magnesium pemoline and chlorphentermine. Most opiates and opioids tested were found to be positive reinforcers. In the barbiturate class amobarbital, secobarbital, pentobarbital, and hexobarbital are positive reinforcers. In addition, chlordiazepoxide, a minor tranquilizer, and alcohol are positive reinforcers. On the other hand, mescaline and chlorpromazine are not reinforcing under these experimental conditions. As can be seen there is a tremendous range of drugs with diverse pharmacological

TABLE 1 LIST OF TESTED DRUGS

Drug	Species	Reference	Self-Administered
Cocaine	Rat	37, 41, 42	Yes
	Monkey	8, 70, 74, 75	Yes
d-Amphetamine	Rat	37, 38, 41	Yes
	Monkey	8, 25, 74	Yes
Methamphetamine	Rat	37, 40	Yes
	Monkey	8, 73	Yes
Nicotine	Monkey	7	Yes
Chlorphentermine	Monkey	74	No
Magnesium pemoline	Monkey	66	No
Caffeine	Monkey	74	No
Other psychomotor stimulants	Monkey	10, 51, 67, 70, 73, 74	Yes
Amobarbital	Rat	5, 6	Yes
	Monkey	71	Yes
Secobarbital	Monkey	13	Yes
Pentobarbital	Monkey	18, 45, 71	Yes
Hexobarbital	Rat	5	Yes
Thiopental	Rat	5	No
Morphine	Rat	58–60	Yes
	Monkey	3, 8, 26, 57, 70, 73	Yes
Codeine	Monkey	3, 26, 45	Yes
Meperidine	Monkey	73	Yes
Pentazocine	Monkey	26	Yes
Propiramfumarate	Monkey	26	Yes
Propoxyphene	Monkey	3, 26	Yes
Chlordiazepoxide	Monkey	13	Yes
Mescaline	Monkey	8	No
Chlorpromazine	Monkey	8, 25	No
Alcohol	Monkey	8	Yes

actions, not necessarily including physical dependence (e.g., the stimulants), which share the common property of serving as positive reinforcers.

Although these compounds all share the common pharmacological property of serving as reinforcers, there are important differences in their pattern of self-administration. If animals are given unlimited access (i.e., 24 hr/day) to opiates, the rate of self-administration on a fixed-ratio1(FR1) schedule of reinforcement increases each day over a 4- to 6-week period

(47). Although there are diurnal fluctuations, intake then becomes stable (71). However, both unit dosage and availability modify total daily intake. As unit dosage is increased daily intake also increases, even though rate of responding decreases (70, 60). The effect on total intake of limiting drug intake to particular hours of the day is unclear; Goldberg, Woods, and Schuster (22) found limited access had no effect, whereas Woods and Schuster (70) found intake lowered with restricted access. However, in the first study a ratio schedule was used, whereas in the second study an interval schedule was used.

The daily intake of ethanol is not stable; the fluctuations are so great that animals alternate between periods of severe intoxication accompanied by ataxia and periods of abstinence accompanied by signs of withdrawal (71). Similar patterns of intake have been found in humans who abuse ethanol (35). Barbiturate self-administration, like the opiates, increases daily until a stable asymptote is reached. The pattern of responding is dependent on dosage. At high doses single injections are regularly spaced; at lower doses bursts of responding occur which are separated by long pauses (70).

Unlimited access to psychomotor stimulants results in day-to-day variability in intake with periods of high intake alternating with periods of low intake (8, 38, 40, 44, 70). Similar results have been reported with humans (15, 33). Limiting access to a few hours a day, however, results in very stable daily intake. This stability is unaffected by unit dosage (38, 40–41, 67, 70). As unit dosage is decreased, rate of responding increases enough to keep total intake relatively stable. Volume and duration of infusion have also been manipulated. Pickens and Thompson (43) found that neither manipulation had any effect on rate of responding in rats on a ratio schedule; however, Balster and Schuster (2) using a fixed interval schedule and a wider range of values did find that longer infusion durations generated lower rates of responding by rhesus monkeys. It is important to note that increased rates of responding on ratio schedules result in increased drug intake, whereas with an interval schedule increased rates of responding do not increase reinforcement frequency.

Taken as a whole, two important generalizations can be drawn from these studies: (1) mere drug availability of a wide variety of pharmacological agents is sufficient for self-administration, and (2) monkeys self-administer the same drugs that are abused by man (9, 29) with the possible exception of the hallucinogens. These findings suggest the possible usefulness of the self-administration model in the study of drug abuse for predicting liability as well as for elucidating the underlying mechanisms controlling intake.

2. SELF-ADMINISTRATION PROCEDURES AS A MEANS FOR PRECLINICAL ASSESSMENT OF A DRUG'S ABUSE LIABILITY

We will now review some of the studies utilizing these procedures as predictors of a drug's abuse liability. Each year thousands of new compounds are synthesized by pharmaceutical companies; these compounds are subjected to a wide range of efficacy and toxicity tests to satisfy the standards of the federal government. Of the drugs screened, only about 1.6% reach clinical trials, and of these 2.3% are released to the public (27). One aspect of a drug's pharmacological properties which has received increasing attention is its abuse potential. For drugs producing physical dependence there are adequate preclinical screening procedures. There are, however, no valid and reliable screening procedures available for drugs that do not produce physical dependence. Because of the observed correlation between a drug's ability to act as a positive reinforcer in infrahuman subjects and its abuse by humans, self-administration procedures are being developed to predict a drug's abuse potential in humans.

When testing a new compound the investigator is faced with two immediate problems: Is the drug soluble in water? Is the dose appropriate? The use of the intravenous route of administration limits the procedure to drugs that are water soluble. The only alternative is the use of elaborate suspensions in vehicles which themselves may have some effect on behavior. If an experimenter has no idea of dose range it may first be necessary to use a procedure which can rapidly screen a wide range of doses without confounding acquisition of drug-taking in naive animals with drug dosage effects per se. One of the most useful methods in this regard is the substitution procedure first described by Yanagita, Ando, Takihashi and Ishida (74). In this procedure, monkeys are allowed to lever press for a known reinforcing drug, such as cocaine, on a fixed-ratio schedule until responding is stable. Next, responding is extinguished by substituting saline for cocaine until responding declines. Finally, an unknown agent is made available. Figure 2 shows the possible results of the substitutions. If the unknown drug is a positive reinforcer at the dosage tested, responding will increase and be maintained at some level above saline (Fig. 2A); the exact level, of course, is dose dependent. If a drug is a negative reinforcer or a nonreinforcer, responding will remain at a low rate or lower rate than the saline extinction level (Fig. 2B). Several standard drugs were used to validate this procedure before it could be used for new drugs. Yanagita et al. (74), using 0.1 mg/kg per injection l-1,2-diphenyl-ldimethylaminoethane (SPA) as the baseline drug, tested several doses each of cocaine (0.025 to 0.4 mg/kg per injection), chlorphentermine [0.025 to 0.4 mg/kg per injection], d-amphetamine (0.0025 to 0.04 mg/kg per injection), and caffeine (0.25 to 4.0 mg/kg per injection); each substitution test was separated by a return to 0.1 mg/kg per injection) SPA baseline and then saline. All doses of cocaine and d-amphetamine were self-administered at a rate higher than saline. However, there was an inverse relationship between rate and dosage. In fact, the difference between the rate of saline self-administration and the rate of self-administration of 0.4 mg/kg per injection cocaine was small. No doses of chlorphentermine and caffeine were taken significantly more than saline. Yanagita Ando and Takihashi (73), using the same procedure, found that pipradol, phenmetrazine, methamphetamine, morphine, and meperidine maintained responding above saline levels at intermediate and low doses. However, the highest dose tested for each drug could not be distinguished on the basis of rate from saline. Pentobarbital and chlordiazepoxide were not self-administered above the level of saline at any of the doses tested. Hoffmeister Goldberg, Schlichting and Wuttke (25) demonstrated essentially the same results using 0.05 mg/kg cocaine as the baseline drug. Unit doses of 0.05 to 0.1 mg/kg d-amphetamine maintained responding. Low doses of morphine (0.025 to 0.1 mg/kg) were also self-administered above saline levels, whereas the high morphine dose (0.5 mg/kg) was not. In addition, none of the unit doses of chlorpromazine (0.05 to 0.5 mg/kg) were self-administered above saline levels.

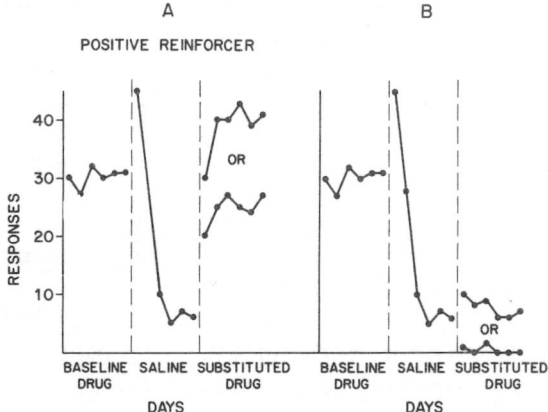

Fig. 2. Possible outcomes of the substitution procedure. The abscissa represents days of the experiment and the ordinate represents number of responses. When responding becomes stable for the baseline drug, saline is substituted (extinction) until responding declines to operant levels. Next, the test compound is substituted. If it is a positive reinforcer (A), responding will be maintained at a level above operant levels; the exact level is dose dependent. If the compound is not a positive reinforcer (B), responding will remain low.

Balster, Schuster, and Wilson (3) also used the substitution procedure with rhesus monkeys maintained on 0.2 mg/kg cocaine, but they substituted test agents directly without an intervening saline extinction period. Morphine (0.01, 0.025, and 0.05 mg/kg), propoxyphene (0.05, 0.1, 0.2, and 0.4 mg/kg), and codeine (0.05, 0.1, and 0.2 mg/kg) were tested; for each drug, rate of self-administration decreased as a function of unit dosage, but in all cases it was higher than saline. However, the results gave no evidence that morphine would generate a greater response rate than either propoxyphene or codeine. The fact that higher dosages of these compounds were not self-administered at a higher frequency than saline highlights one of the major problems with the use of response rate as a measure of reinforcing efficacy. Clearly, these drugs have a number of behavioral effects in addition to acting as reinforcers. These other effects may very well include effects upon lever-pressing rate independent of the nature of the reinforcer. This problem will be dealt with in greater detail in a subsequent section of this chapter.

A potential problem of this procedure is the choice of the baseline drug. Schlichting, Goldberg, Wutte and Hoffmeister (45) showed that different drug class histories have an effect on subsequent self-administration of a particular drug. Three monkeys were allowed to respond for 3 hr on a fixed ratio schedule for 0.05 mg/kg per injection cocaine, 0.05 mg/kg per injection codeine, or 0.25 mg/kg per injection pentobarbital until responding was stable. These doses of codeine and pentobarbital under such limited access do not produce discernible physical dependence. After saline substitution, d-amphetamine was tested in each group. All groups, regardless of their history, self-administered d-amphetamine. However, monkeys with a history of cocaine self-administration responded at higher rates for the higher dose of amphetamine (0.05 mg/kg per injection) and tended to extinguish at the lowest dose (0.005 mg/kg per injection) compared to the other two groups. In addition, the pentobarbital group self-administered more amphetamine than the codeine group. Patterns of amphetamine self-administration tended to be similar to the pattern of the previous drug; that is, the cocaine group took amphetamine at regular intervals whereas the other two groups had both long and short interresponse times (i.e., irregular patterns).

Hoffmeister and Schlichting (26) substituted several opiates (morphine and codeine) and opioids (pentazocine, propiramfumarate, d-propoxyphene, and nalorphine) in monkeys trained with 0.05 mg/kg per injection codeine or 0.05 mg/kg per injection cocaine as the baseline drug. Under the conditions of the experiment such a dose of codeine does not produce physical dependence. At doses of the substituted drugs self-administered above saline rates, the codeine group self-administered more of each of the drugs than the cocaine group; the only exception was nalorphine, which neither group self-administered. In addition, lower doses of the drugs tested were found to be reinforcers, i.e., they maintained behavior above saline levels, in the codeine group than in the cocaine group. The variables responsible for these differences are not known. Regardless of the mechanism, however, two conclusions can be drawn from the work of Hoffmeister and his associates: (1) regardless of prior drug history the same drugs that are abused by man are self-administered above saline by monkeys, and (2) the rate of self-administration is influenced by an animal's prior drug history.

The substitution procedure is an efficient and economical way to determine the range of dosages of an unknown compound that might serve as a positive reinforcer. In addition, it can identify drugs or particular doses of a drug which are not reinforcing or are aversive. However, a careful examination of the data demonstrates that in no way can this procedure be used to rank order drugs in terms of abuse liability. For instance, the data presented by Balster et al. (3) showed that propoxyphene and codeine were self-administered at higher rates than morphine, which clearly does not correlate with their abuse potential. In addition, since prior drug history is such an important variable, the choice of a baseline drug is difficult and makes interpretation of the results ambiguous. In the study by Yanagita et al. (73), pentobarbital, a known drug of abuse, was not self-administered at rates above saline baseline levels. It is not clear whether this result was due to the range of doses studied (0.25 to 0.4 mg/kg) or to the use of a stimulant as the baseline drug. Moreover, if a wide range of doses of a new pharmacological agent is not tested, a qualitative error in potential liability assessment is possible. However, given the efficiency of this procedure it is a highly useful first step in any screening program. Since it takes so little time to test a drug at a particular dose, an appropriate dose range can quickly be determined for use in more quantitative procedures.

The principal problem of the substitution procedure is the use of rate as the dependent variable. Any procedure which hopes to predict the abuse liability of an unknown agent must first be shown to be sensitive to differences in dosage of some standard well-described drug. Rate, either as a dependent variable in substitution studies or in studies using naive animals, is at best an ambiguous measure in this regard. An inverted U-shaped function has been found between dosage and rate of self-administration for all drugs which are positive reinforcers for rats and monkeys (37, 38, 40–42, 58, 60, 67, 70). Clearly there are dosages which are below the threshold for reinforcement. Further, high doses of a drug are often self-administered at rates no higher than saline. Drugs, in addition to possessing reinforcing efficacy, have other pharmacological effects that may modify rate in a dose-dependent fashion. Pickens and Thompson (42), for instance, found that dosages of cocaine (in a range which is self-administered by monkeys) given noncontingently on a food-reinforced baseline produced pauses comparable to those seen when the drug is self-administered; that is, the length of the pauses after food reinforcement was directly correlated with the dosage of the noncontingent cocaine infusion. Woods and Schuster (72), using a similar procedure, found that morphine, codeine, and methadone each suppressed food-reinforced behavior in a similar dose-dependent fashion (the higher the dose the greater the suppression) when compared to other doses of the same drug. However, when making comparisons between drugs, the degree of suppression of the food-reinforced baseline did not correlate with rates of self-administration. Undoubtedly there are many variables controlling pausing after drug infusion; such multiple control makes the use of rate as a measure of reinforcing efficacy difficult and likely to lead to inaccurate predictions.

To bypass the problems of using rate as a measure of reinforcing efficacy, preference procedures are presently being developed by several investigators (1, 13, 30). Although the details of these three procedures differ greatly, two aspects are important: (1) the organism is given a simultaneous pairwise choice between different drug solutions, and (2) the organism is offered this choice at a time when it is *relatively* free of the rate-modifying effects of a drug.

Although it is very difficult to validate a choice procedure which is able to differentiate the reinforcement efficacy of two different drugs, any procedure that ranks higher dosages of a known drug of abuse as having higher reinforcement efficacy relative to lower doses is potentially useful in comparisons of unknown drugs.

Johanson (30), using cocaine as a standard drug, described a procedure that utilized a sampling component preceding choice trials each daily session. Briefly, in sampling trials the subject had the opportunity to sample each drug solution paired with a different color stimulus light, contingent upon completion of a fixed ratio 5 (FR 5) on the appropriate lever. The correct lever alternated after each reinforcement. Drug solution *A* was available for the first five injections; following a 30-min time-out drug solution *B* was available for the next five injections. After the 10 sampling injections and a second 30-min time-out, the animal was presented with a choice trial. The first response on either lever terminated the stimulus light over the other lever and inactivated that lever for that trial. The completion of an FR 5 produced an injection of the drug solution appropriate to the stimulus light color above the lever. The position of the stimulus lights alternated randomly. A 15-min time-out separated each choice trial. After the development of a clear preference for one solution over the other, the stimulus lights were reversed and the animal was retrained to criterion. Using this procedure, dosages of cocaine from 0.05 to 1.5 mg/kg per injection have been tested. In almost every comparison the higher dose of cocaine was chosen over the lower dose on 80% or more of the trials. In addition, 0.5 mg/kg cocaine was preferred to unit doses of methylphenidate from 0.075 to 0.15 mg/kg. Although the results to date seem promising, the procedure does present some problems to the investigator who has to screen a large number of compounds the pharmacological activity of which is not entirely known. The time (sometimes as long as 3 months) and expense required for each comparison is a disadvantage for a screening device. In addition, if drugs of longer duration of action are tested, the time-out between trials may have to be lengthened, thereby again increasing the time required for each comparison. Balster, Johanson, and Schuster (1) described a choice procedure which eliminated the problem of other pharmacological effects influencing choice behavior. The procedure involved initially training animals to associate different drug solutions with different discriminative stimuli (S^D). When the S^D was red, the animal self-administered one drug, whereas when the S^D was green the animal self-administered a different drug. Daily sessions were conducted with only one color discriminative stimulus; thus only one drug solution was available during any one session. The schedule of reinforcement was a second-order schedule which generates high rates of responding during extinction. Training sessions were designed to give an opportunity for the colored discriminative stimuli to acquire conditioned reinforcing properties appropriate to the drug solution with which they were associated. After training was complete, test sessions were conducted. During these sessions, both stimulus lights were turned on, but drug injections were withheld. When two doses of cocaine were compared, animals pressed the lever below the stimulus previously associated with the high dose of cocaine more than the lever below the stimulus associated with the low dose. When cocaine and morphine were compared, the stimulus light associated with 0.2 mg/kg cocaine was preferred to the stimulus associated with 0.025 mg/kg morphine. These doses were chosen because they generated equal rates of self-administration during 1-hr discrimination training sessions. Although this procedure eliminates the problems of confounding the reinforcing effects of a drug with its other pharmacological effects, it has proven to be time consuming, sometimes requiring 3 months for one comparison. In addition, responding during extinction is likely to be controlled by nuisance variables, such as lever preference, thereby masking the main effects. Further, the use of test sessions precludes obtaining data on the development of the preference.

Findley, Robinson, and Peregrino (13) developed a forced choice procedure. To avoid shock, animals must choose between avoidance schedules signaled by two different discriminative stimuli. The only difference between the two schedules is the drug which is infused following the avoidance requirements. Infusions are followed by several hours of time-out so that the drug is metabolized. Using this procedure, the investigators found that both secobarbital and chlordiazepoxide were preferred to saline. In addition, secobarbital seemed to be preferred over chlordiazepoxide, although the latter was still self-administered substantially. However, the procedure, as was the case in the other procedures, is exceedingly time-consuming. It might be added that chlordiazepoxide in substitution procedures (73) never maintained self-administration above saline baselines.

In general, the choice procedures reviewed are more quantitative than the substitution procedure and eliminate many of the problems encountered in other procedures designed to assess abuse liability of a new compound. Their major disadvantage is the length of time required for completion. However, efficacy and toxicity tests normally conducted by pharmaceutical companies on any new compound also take an enormous length of time; given the consequences of releasing a drug of high abuse liability to the public, the extra time required by these procedures may be justified.

None of the preclinical procedures designed to assess abuse liability are adequate unless they are used under a variety of environmental situations. Any drug with central nervous system activity will probably be abused under some combination of circumstances. However, the frequency of occurrence of this set of environmental variables must be assessed before any drug, particularly one with great therapeutic value, is kept off the market. In fact, it may be easier to try to change the environment, particularly if its occurrence is infrequent. For instance, if a drug of therapeutic usefulness is abused only under conditions of food deprivation, it would be better to eliminate the deprivation. However, as long as the abuse liability of a drug is assessed under only one set of environmental variables, it will never be possible to make such rational decisions.

If preclinical screening programs are successful, new compounds with high abuse potential could be prevented from appearing on the market. However, given the fact that drugs of abuse are already available, the drug abuse problem will not be solved in this manner. So, in addition to being used for prediction, animal models should also be developed for assessing the variables that control drug-reinforced behavior. An understanding of these variables is essential for prevention and treatment of the problem. Basically there are three relevant classes of variables: environmental, pharmacological, and organismic.

3. PHARMACOLOGICAL VARIABLES AFFECTING DRUG SELF-ADMINISTRATION

Some of the pharmacological variables that have already been discussed are type of drug, dosage, and prior drug history. In the present section other variables which control rate of self-administration will be discussed. Given the multiplicative sources of control, only representative examples will be reviewed.

An important pharmacological variable that controls rate of drug self-administration is the injection of a second drug before the experimental session. This second drug may interact with the self-administered drug in two ways: (1) by substituting for its reinforcing effects, or (2) by blocking them. In the first case, rate of self-administration will decline to some lower level of responding as if the animal were satiated. In the second case, the block may be either partial or complete. If it is partial, responding will increase as if the effective dose had been lowered. If the block is complete, extinction will occur and responding will increase for a time and then decline to operant levels.

The effect of other drugs on opiate self-administration has been extensively studied. In the study of morphine self-administration, other opiates and opioids have been tested for their ability to substitute for morphine, that is, to produce satiation. This work is particularly interesting given the use of methadone, an opioid, in the treatment of heroin addiction.

Weeks and Collins (60) continuously infused morphine, codeine, or meperidine at various doses into rats allowed to self-administer 10 mg/kg morphine; in all cases responding for morphine decreased in a dose-dependent fashion. That is, the higher the dose of the noncontingent drug, the greater the suppression in responding for morphine. Surprisingly, with morphine as the noncontingent drug, there were no consistent results indicating whether voluntary intake plus automatic infusion intake was the same as, greater than, or less than voluntary intake during baseline conditions. There may be quantitative and qualitative differences between the effects of a drug which is self-administered and its effects when given noncontingently. Thompson and Schuster (57) also reported a decrease in responding with morphine pretreatment in monkeys on a chained fixed-interval, fixed-ratio schedule of morphine reinforcement. Thompson (53) reported that pretreatment with methadone resulted in a decrease in morphine self-administration.

Despite the fact that these studies seem to indicate that medicating an opiate-dependent person with some other opiate, such as methadone, will be effectual in terminating the self-administration of drugs, some caution should be used. Not enough quantitative work has been done to demonstrate how much of one drug must be given to completely eliminate drug-taking of a second drug. The work of Thompson (53) is a start; however, this experiment investigated only the acute effects of methadone on morphine self-administration. Further, pretreatment drugs must be concurrently assessed on behaviors other than self-administration to determine the specificity of the effects. Complete parametric studies are necessary to determine what drugs at particular doses decrease rate of drug self-administration the most without affecting other behaviors.

Beside methadone substitution, opiate antagonists have been used in the treatment of opiate abuse to block the reinforcing effects of opiates. Considerable work done with animals seems relevant clinically. Goldberg, Woods, and Schuster (24) found that low doses of nalorphine and naloxone, when given either acutely or chronically, increased the rate of morphine self-administration. This was true regardless of whether morphine was available for 1 or 24 hr./day. In the latter case, maximal increases usually occurred within the first 2 hr after injection of the antagonist. High doses of nalorphine suppressed self-administration when the doses were given either chronically or acutely in descending order; it had no effect on self-administration when the doses were given acutely in ascending order. This was only true when morphine was available one hour a day; when there was unlimited access, not only did no suppression occur but, in fact, after a relatively long time delay an actual increase in self-administration occurred. The fact that suppression did not occur immediately after the injection is most likely due to the fact that suppression is hard to demonstrate in already low rates of responding. The complexity of these results demonstrates that clinicians must be very careful in the use of narcotic antagonists. They must pay attention to how much and how often it is given as well as the patient's past drug history. It is not enough merely to give an antagonist at some arbitrary dose and assume opiate abuse will decrease. In fact, as this study has shown, under many circumstances antagonists may actually increase morphine intake. It may be argued that the amount of euphoria has not increased (being antagonized by the nalorphine), but since the amount of the drug the addict must buy and the social ills that can result are still greater than before treatment, the issue of euphoria is irrelevant.

The use of a narcotic antagonist in treatment must also be considered in light of its possible aversive effects. Goldberg et al. (17) demonstrated, using morphine-dependent monkeys, that responses which terminated either a stimulus associated with nalorphine or naloxone injections (avoidance), or the injections themselves (escape), were maintained at high rates. Nalorphine and naloxone, then, can be considered negative reinforcers under these circumstances. Since opiate antagonists are given clinically to postdependent former addicts, it must be determined whether postdependent monkeys would also avoid or escape opiate antagoists. Although these results are only suggestive, it has been found that monkeys formerly dependent on morphine had increased sensitivity to nalorphine's effect of suppressing operant responding for food as compared to monkeys without a history of morphine exposure (20). If opiate antagonists are aversive in postdependent organisms, it may be difficult to use these compounds in voluntary treatment programs.

Drug interaction experiments with psychomotor stimulants have received little attention relative to the opiates. This has primarily been due to the fact that no specific antagonists have been found for the stimulants. As a result, little attention has been given to the development of treatment programs using drugs that block the reinforcing effects of stimulants. In addition, since physical dependence does not develop to stimulants, treatment programs using drugs which substitute for stimulants also have not been developed. However, some research has been directed toward understanding the regularity of psychomotor stimulant intake. The outcome of such research may lead ultimately to the discovery of suitable pharmacotherapy for psychomotor stimulant abuse.

As has been discussed previously, rate of self-administration decreases with increases in dosage per injection for both psychomotor stimulants and opiates. However, with opiates there is a direct relationship between total daily intake and dosage; that is, although rate decreases with increasing dose, total intake still increases (60, 70). On the other hand, total daily intake of psychomotor stimulants does not change over a wide range of dosages when the drugs are available only a few hours a day (37, 67, 70); the decrease in rate with increasing dosages of stimulants is great enough to compensate for the dose increase. In addition, the pattern of psychomotor stimulant self-administration is very regular, particularly compared to the opiates.

It seems that some mechanism is involved in regulating or limiting drug intake of psychomotor stimulants. Wilson, Hitomi, and Schuster (67) suggested three mechanisms to explain this regulation. The first possibility is that rate of self-administration is adjusted to maintain an optimal blood level of the compound. A second possible mechanism is that all ongoing behavior, regardless of the reinforcer, is suppressed following the infusion of a given amount of the drug. Pickens and Thompson (42) offered some support for this. They showed that noncontingent intravenous infusions of cocaine disrupted lever-pressing behavior in rats working for food; the duration of the disruption was directly related to the size of the dose. However, this may have been due to the known anorexic effects of cocaine. Finally, it may be that additional infusions of the compounds produce aversive effects when a sufficient amount has already been self-administered. To date, there is not enough evidence to differentiate these possibilities. However, some attempts have been made to elucidate the mechanism. Wilson and Schuster (69) studied the effect of pretreating animals self-administering cocaine, pipradrol, phenmetrazine, d-amphetamine, and methyphenidate with chlorpromazine. Chlorpromazine, a phenothiazine, has been shown to antagonize many behavioral and physiological effects of psychomotor stimulants. Centrally, as well as peripherally, chlorpromazine is an alpha-adrenergic blocking agent. In the present study, chlorpromazine, across a wide range of dosages, produced increases in self-administration of cocaine. Similar results were seen with the other psychomotor stimulants. At high doses of chlorpromazine responding was greatly depressed and there was grossly observable central nervous system depression. In an effort to elucidate chlorpromazine's mechanism of action, Wilson and Schuster (68) pretreated monkeys self-administering cocaine with morphine, pentobarbital, trifluoperazine, phentolamine, and phenoxybenzamine. Trifluoperazine, like chlorpromazine, is a phenothiazine. Phentolamine and phenoxybenzamine are peripheral alpha-adrenergic blocking agents. Morphine and pentobarbital, like the phenothiazines, produce central nervous system depression. Trifluoperazine increased rate of cocaine self-administration at intermediate doses and resulted in suppression at the high doses just like chlorpromazine. Since the phenothiazines generally produce a dose-related depression in behavior maintained by other reinforcers, such as food and water (49), these results appear to be uniquely related to cocaine as a reinforcer. It may be that the phenothiazines partially antagonize the reinforcement effect of cocaine and thereby functionally lower its unit dose. Both morphine and pentobarbital decrease rate of self-administration of psychomotor stimulants in a dose-related manner. Therefore, the effect seen with phenothiazines is not a general property of drugs producing central nervous system depression. The failure of phentolamine and phenoxybenzamine to alter the intake of cocaine indicates that the effects observed with the phenothiazines are not based upon their peripheral alpha-adrenergic blocking properties. There is a great deal of evidence that cocaine and other psychomotor stimulants exert their effect on central catecholamine systems of the brain. It has not been determined whether the reinforcing effects of these drugs is mediated by these systems. With this hypothesis in mind, Pickens, Meisch, and Dougherty (39) pretreated rats self-administering methamphetamine with alpha-methylparatyrosine (AMPT) and L-DOPA given i. p. When given alone, AMPT decreases the levels of whole brain dopamine and norepinephrine by blocking their synthesis; L-DOPA on the other hand increases the levels of whole brain catecholamines (14). Five milligrams per kilogram of AMPT slightly increased rate of responding while doses of 10, 20, 40, and 80 mg/kg produced changes in the previously steady interresponse times; that is, responding was characterized by bursts alternating with pauses. L-DOPA at all the doses tested had no effect on responding for methamphetamine. Although these effects are interesting, no firm conclusions can be made about the role of catecholamines in mediating the reinforcing effect of psychomotor stimulants from this one study. However, there is clinical evidence that AMPT antagonizes the euphoric effects of stimulants. Jönsson, Anggard, and Gunne (31) administered oral doses of AMPT (2 or 4 g) prior to the intravenous administration of 200 mg of *dl*-amphetamine; they found euphoria, as measured by a self-rating scale, to be reduced for approximately 24 to 48 hr. However, tolerance to the AMPT blocking effect developed with chronic administration. This tolerance disappeared when AMPT administration was discontinued for 3 days.

4. ENVIRONMENTAL VARIABLES AFFECTING DRUG SELF-ADMINISTRATION

One environmental variable that can effect drug self-administration is the condition under which the drug is available. Several investigators have studied the role of stressful conditions such as unavoidable shock delivered concurrently with drug availability. Some of this work has used the oral route of administration and is reviewed elsewhere (48). Davis and Miller (6) and Davis, Lulenski, and Miller (5), using an intravenous route of administration, found that rats self-administered barbiturates (amobarbital) in the presence of unavoidable shock, but not in its absence. Monkeys, on the other hand, will self-administer barbiturates in the absence of stressful conditions (18, 45, 71). Another current environmental condition that has been investigated is the presence of other animals during self-administration. In almost every study of drug self-administration animals are totally isolated. However, Thompson, Bigelow, and Pickens (54, 55) found that a monkey housed with a second monkey could learn a complex chain of behaviors to self-administer morphine; these behaviors included making a cooperative response (simultaneous activation of switches) with the second monkey, who was working for food or water but not morphine. It can be concluded, therefore, that isolation is not a necessary condition for morphine self-administration. Needless to say, far more work is needed to delineate current conditions which can modify drug self-administration.

Schedules of reinforcement have been shown to be important environmental variables controlling frequency and pattern of responding for a variety of reinforcers. Thus schedules of reinforcement are likely to be important variables in the control of drug self-administration.

Most early self-administration studies used a fixed ratio 1 (FR 1: one response required for reinforcement) schedule of reinforcement. Weeks (58) found that increasing the ratio requirement to 5 (FR 5) for morphine lowered net morphine intake; that is, rate was not increased fivefold. However, a further increase to a fixed ratio 10 (FR 10) schedule did not further lower net morphine intake. Weeks and Collins (60) used a progressive ratio schedule; that is, each day they increased the ratio requirement up to a maximum of fixed ratio 400 (FR 400). As the ratio increased, less and less morphine was self-administered; in addition, pausing was increased. In some cases, animals ceased responding completely. Goldberg, Hoffmeister, Schlichting and Wuttke (18) found that at a dose of pentobarbital (0.25 mg/kg) which did not produce anesthesia, responding and total intake decreased as the ratio requirements were gradually raised from 1 to 10.

Increasing the ratio requirements for psychomotor stimulants does not result in a decrease in overall intake. Pickens and Harris (38) found that responding for *d*-amphetamine was a direct function of the ratio requirement, until values were reached where the behavior became erratic. Similar results were found by Pickens (37) for cocaine and methamphetamine. In addition, this author (37) found that the highest ratio able to maintain responding was a direct function of the dosage of cocaine. Above this ratio, responding was erratic or ceased. For psychomotor stimulants, it seems possible that the highest ratio requirement which sustains responding can be used as a measure of reinforcing efficacy and is therefore useful in predicting a drug's abuse liability.

Little work has been done with other schedules. What has been done, however, demonstrates that drugs as reinforcers generate responding patterns similar to those of other reinforcers (12, 42, 44, 48, 57, 70). In 1972, investigations were begun with drugs as reinforcers using more complex schedules. Although most of this work is just being prepared for publication, work in this laboratory by Balster and Schuster (2) can serve as an illustration. In this study, monkeys performed daily on a multiple fixed-interval schedule for food and cocaine reinforcement. Between each fixed-interval component, a time-out period was programmed to minimize the rate-modifying effects of cocaine, other than its reinforcing efficacy. Under this schedule, response rate in the fixed-interval component for cocaine reinforcement was a direct function of dosage. Responding for food, however, remained constant, or at higher doses of cocaine, was inversely related. This is in contrast to ratio schedules where rate of responding for cocaine reinforcement is an inverse function of dosage. Thus the schedule of reinforcement is an important variable relating rate of responding to the magnitude of reinforcement.

5. CONSEQUENCES OF DRUG SELF-ADMINISTRATION

As has been shown, a multitude of pharmacological and environmental variables control rate of self-administration. An understanding of these variables can be useful in designing an adequate prevention and treatment program. However, the fact that a drug is self-administered by animals does not necessarily mean that it is a dangerous drug for humans. As has been said, the social, behavioral, and physiological consequences of drug-taking are equally important aspects of the study of drug abuse. If a drug that is self-administered at a high frequency does not alter the social, behavioral, or physiological functioning of an individual, it should not be of concern. However, little work has been done on elucidating the consequences of drug-taking in animals. Such research requires the cooperation of a multidisciplinary team including psychologists, psychiatrists, pathologists, endocrinologists, biochemists, immunologists, and pharmacologists, to mention a few. Despite the difficulties of gathering such a team, it is essential for a complete understanding of drug abuse.

One consequence of opiate self-administration is the development of physical dependence. Although physical dependence has been shown to be neither sufficient nor necessary for opiate self-administration, it can be shown to be a variable affecting the rate of self-administration. Drug deprivation in physically dependent organisms can be achieved in two ways: (1) by withdrawing the opportunity for opiate intake for some period of time, or (2) by injecting some opiate antagonist such as nalorphine or naloxone. Regardless of its etiology, opiate deprivation leads not only to physiological and behavioral disruptions but also to changes in rate of opiate self-administration. Both Thompson and Schuster (57) and Goldberg, Woods, and Schuster (23) found that deprivation in physically dependent monkeys resulted in an increase in morphine self-administration. This fact becomes extremely relevent in light of the theory of Wikler (62–64), who proposed a two-factor theory of relapse to opiate self-administration. Relapse is defined as the reinitiation of drug self-administration after a drug-free period. Wikler postulates that the withdrawal syndrome (the physiological disruptions) is classically conditioned to stimuli in the environment through repeated association. These stimuli are capable of eliciting the syndrome even when the organism is no longer physically dependent. This alone, however, would not result in relapse. In addition, the organism must have learned how to avoid the withdrawal syndrome by self-administering an opiate. As a result, if classically conditioned stimuli elicit withdrawal, the probability of the drug-taking response will be increased. A great deal of research has been conducted to verify this theory.

Nichols, Headlee, and Coppock (36) demonstrated the importance of operant conditioning; postdependent rats, with a history of maintaining their dependence by drinking a morphine solution, returned to such drinking, whereas postdependent rats without this drinking history did not drink this solution. Weeks and Collins (61) showed that both prior opiate dependence and prior operant conditioning are important factors in the relapse of postdependent rats. Postdependent rats originally trained to self-administer morphine took more morphine upon return to the experimental situation than did postdependent rats made dependent by programmed infusions but trained to lever-press for water. However, the latter group took more morphine than rats only trained to lever-press for water but with no prior exposure to morphine. Therefore it may be necessary for treatment programs to provide a means for extinguishing these operantly conditioned responses.

As has previously been suggested, stimuli associated with drug reinforcement may acquire conditioned reinforcing properties. When the human addict "fixes" his heroin, he goes through a long chain of behaviors terminated by the actual injection of the drug. The environmental and interoceptive stimuli accompanying the injection may acquire significance derived from their temporal pairing with the pharmacological actions of the drug. Schuster and Woods (50) showed that a stimulus, associated with morphine reinforcement in the rhesus monkey, generated increased response rates in extinction. Further, the ability of this stimulus to act as a conditioned reinforcer remained even after an interpolated period of 20 days of drug abstinence. Thus the conditioned reinforcer's efficacy was independent of the organism's state of physical dependence.

One of the first investigations (28) that demonstrated the possibility of classically conditioning abstinence used nalorphine, an opiate antagonist. An injection of nalorphine in animals physically dependent on opiates will elicit signs and symptoms almost identical to the opiate withdrawal syndrome. These investigators found that in monkeys dependent on methadone, keto-bemidone, or racemorphan, who had experienced repeated nalorphine-induced abstinence, an injection of saline elicited the withdrawal syndrome even after a drug-free period of one or two months. They interpreted these findings as showing that the injection procedure had acquired the ability to elicit the withdrawal response because of its association with nalorphine.

Goldberg and Schuster (19) provided a further demonstration that at least certain aspects of the morphine withdrawal syndrome could be classically conditioned. Nalorphine (a UCS), when given to morphine-dependent monkeys working for food on an FR 10 schedule of reinforcement, caused a disruption in behavior. When a tone (the CS) was repeatedly presented 5 min before and after such an injection, it alone became capable of suppressing food-reinforced behavior. In addition, when saline injections were substituted for nalorphine, suppression during the tone persisted for up to 40 days. Bradycardia, emesis, and salivation were also conditioned. This study demonstrates that stimuli in an addict's environment can elicit reactions similar to those elicited by withdrawal. Goldberg, Woods, and Schuster (23) increased the generality of this finding by showing that the list of conditionable reactions included increased self-administration of morphine. Injections of certain dosages of nalorphine in morphine-dependent monkeys increase their rate of self-administration of morphine. When a flashing red light (CS) was paired with the nalorphine injections, eventually injections of saline accompanied by the light also resulted in increased self-administration.

These studies by Goldberg and his associates are relevant for explaining some of the variables contributing to the continual use of opiates in dependent persons. However, they say little about the relevance of conditioning in relapse. Goldberg and Schuster (21) have extended their work successfully in this area, using the same paradigm as in their original study (19). They again found that a neutral stimulus, this time a red light, when paired with nalorphine injections, could produce, when presented alone, suppression of food-reinforced behavior. Next they discontinued morphine injections for 30 days and allowed animals to undergo withdrawal. When they returned the animals to the experimental situation, the red light alone suppressed food responding; the effect persisted for 60 to 120 days and when finally extinguished was rapidly reconditioned. However, one important part of this study remains to be done. To adequately show the relevance of conditioning in reinitiated drug-taking, it must be demonstrated that opiate intake will increase in *postdependent* animals in the presence of conditioned stimuli.

Thompson and Ostlund (56) have shown the relevance of both the addiction and withdrawal environments in relapse. Postdependent rats returned to the same environment as the one in which they were addicted in showed a higher recidivism rate than postdependent rats returned to a different environment. Additionally, rats extinguished in the same environment as the one in which they were addicted in had a lower rate of recidivism than those extinguished in a different environment. The implications of all this research for treatment of addicts is clear. It may not be enough to merely force a person to undergo withdrawal, as is done in prisons, and expect him to never return to drug-taking behavior when returned to his home environment. Even methadone maintenance cannot by itself extinguish the effect of environmental stimuli. Far more attention must be paid to both operant and classical conditioning factors in the design of any rehabilitation program. Goldberg (16) offers several suggestions for criteria of treatment programs: (1) continued exposure to the drug-taking environment to facilitate extinction of classically conditioned stimuli, (2) continued drug self-administration, but in conjunction with other drugs which block the reinforcing effects to extinguish the operantly conditioned response of self-administration, and (3) the conditioning of new socially acceptable behaviors which are incompatible with drug-taking.

Besides physical dependence and its conditioning, which can lead to continuous opiate use, there has been little work on the consequences of drug-taking. In an assessment of the possible toxic consequences, all of the traditional techniques for evaluating functional and morphological changes can be brought to bear on the problem. The only distinction from the usual toxicity testing is that the dosage of the drug is determined by the subject rather than arbitrarily by the experimenter. In this regard, Fischman and her colleagues (13a) are in the process of studying the chronic effects of methamphetamine on behavioral, biochemical, and morphological indices of toxicity. Such experimentation, in addition to determining the consequences of a self-administered drug, may allow the correlation of functional and morphological changes.

To summarize, the present paper has attempted to review the conceptual framework for analyzing the behavior of self-administering drugs. This conceptual framework of behavior analysis views drugs as reinforcers and allows the utilization of data gathered using other reinforcers in an attempt to understand the variables controlling drug self-administration. The relevance of these animal studies to the problem of human drug abuse is an empirical question that can be resolved only when the implications of these studies are used in treatment programs.

REFERENCES

1. Balster, R. L., C. E. Johanson, and C. R. Schuster, The development of choice procedures for the evaluation of abuse liability of psychoactive drugs, Paper presented at the 34th Annual Meeting of the Committee on Problems of Drug Dependence, NAS-NRC, 1972.
2. Balster, R.L. and C. R. Schuster, Fixed-interval schedule of cocaine reinforcement: Effect of dose and infusion duration, *J. Exp. Anal. Behav.*, **20**, 119–129 (1973).
3. Balster, R.L., C.R. Schuster, and M.C. Wilson, The substitution of opiate analgesics in monkeys maintained on cocaine self-administration, Paper presented at the 33rd Annual Meeting of the Committee on Problems of Drug Dependence, NAS-NRC, 1971.
4. Davis, J.D., A method for chronic intravenous infusion in freely moving rats, *J. Exp. Anal. Behav.*, **9**, 385 (1966).
5. Davis, J.D., G.C. Lulenski, and N.E. Miller, Comparative studies of barbiturate self-administration, *Int. J. Addict.*, **3**, 207–214 (1968).
6. Davis, J.D., and N.E. Miller, Fear and pain: Their effect on self-injection of amobarbital sodium by rats. *Science*, 141, 1286–1287 (1963).
7. Deneau, G. A. and R. Inoki, Nicotine self-administration in monkeys, *Ann. N.Y. Acad. Sci.*, **142,** 277 (1967).
8. Deneau, G., T. Yanagita, and M. H. Seevers, Self-administration of psychoactive substances by the monkey. A measure of psychological dependence, *Psychopharmacologia*, **16,** (1), 30–48 (1969).
9. Eddy, N. B., H. Halbeck, H. Isbell, and M.H. Seevers, Drug dependence: Its significance and characteristics, *Bull. WHO*, **32**, 721 (1965).
10. Estrada, U., J. E. Villarreal, and C. R. Schuster, Self-administration of stimulant drugs as a function of the dose per injection, Paper presented at the 29th Annual Meeting of the Committee on Problems of Drug Dependence, NAS-NRC, 1967.
11. Falk, J. L., Production of polydipsia in normal rats by an intermittent food schedule, *Science*, **133**, 195–196 (1961).
12. Ferster, C. B. and B.F. Skinner, *Schedules of Reinforcement*, Appleton-Century-Crofts, New York, 1957.
13. Findley, J. D., W. W. Robinson, and L. Peregrino, Addiction, to secobarbital and chlordiazepoxide in the rhesus monkey by means of a self-infusion preference, *Psychopharmacologia*, in press (1972).
13a. Fischman, Personal communication.
14. Glowinski, J. and R. J. Baldessarini, Metabolism of norepinephrine in the central nervous system, *Pharm. Rev.*, **18,** 1201–1238 (1966).
15. Goldberg, L., Drug abuse in Sweden, *Bull. Narcotics*, **20** (1), 1–36 (1968).

16. Goldberg, S. R., Relapse to opioid dependence: The role of conditioning, in *Advances in Mental Science,* Vol. 2, *Drug Dependence,* pp. 170–197, R. T. Harris, W. M. McIsaac, and C. R. Schuster, University of Texas Press Austin, 1970.
17. Goldberg, S. R., F. Hoffmeister, U. Schlichting, and W. Wuttke, Aversive properties of nalorphine and naloxone in morphine-dependent rhesus monkeys, *J. Pharmacol. Exp. Ther.,* **179,** 268–276 (1971).
18. Goldberg, S. R., F. Hoffmeister, U. U. Schlichting, and W. Wuttke, A comparison of pentobarbital and cocaine self-administration in rhesus monkeys: Effects of dose and fixed-ratio parameter, *J. Pharmacol. Exp. Ther.,* **179,** 277–283 (1971).
19. Goldberg, S. R. and C. R. Schuster, Conditioned suppression by a stimulus associated with nalorphine in morphine-dependent monkeys, *J. Exp. Anal. Behav.,* **10,** 235–242 (1967).
20. Goldberg, S.R. and C.R. Schuster, Nalorphine: Increased sensitivity of monkeys formerly dependent on morphine, *Science,* **166,** 1548–1549 (1969).
21. Goldberg, S.R. and C.R. Schuster, Conditioned nalorphine-induced abstinence changes: Persistence in post morphine-dependent monkeys, *J. Exp. Anal. Behav.,* **14,** 33–46, (1970).
22. Goldberg, S. R., J. H. Woods, and C. R. Schuster, Nalorphine-induced changes in morphine self-administration, Paper presented at the 30th Annual Meeting of the Committee on Problems of Drug Dependence, NAS-NRC, 1968.
23. Goldberg, S. R., J. H. Woods, and C. R. Schuster, Morphine: Conditioned increases in self-administration in rhesus monkeys, *Science,* **166,** 1306–1307 (1969).
24. Goldberg, S.R., J.H. Woods, and C.R. Schuster, Nalorphine-induced changes in morphine self-administration in rhesus monkeys, *J. Pharmacol. Exp. Ther.,* **176,** 464–471 (1971).
25. Hoffmeister, F., S.R. Goldberg, U. Schlichting, and W. Wuttke; Self administration of *d*-amphetamine, morphine and chlorpromazine by cocaine "dependent" rhesus monkeys, *Naunynschmiedebergs Arch. Pharmarkol,* **266,** 359–360 (1970).
26. Hoffmeister, F. and U. U. Schlichting, Reinforcing properties of some opiates and opioids in rhesus monkeys with histories of cocaine and codeine self-administration, *Psychopharmacologia,* **23,** 55–74 (1972).
27. Irwin, Samuel, Drug screening and evaluative procedures, *Science,* **136,** 123–128 (1962).
28. Irwin, S. and M.H. Seevers, Comparative study of regular and *N*-allylnormorphine induced withdrawal in monkeys addicted to morphine, 6-methylhydromorphine, dromoran, methadone and keto-bemidone, *J. Pharmacol. Exp. Ther.,* **106,** 397 (1952).

29. Jaffe, J. H., Narcotic analgesics, in *The Pharmacological Basis of Therapeutics*, pp. 237-275, L. S. Goodman and A. Gilman (Eds.), Macmillan, New York. 1970.
30. Johanson, C., Choice of cocaine by rhesus monkeys as a function of dosage. *Proc. 79th Ann. Conv. APA* 751-752 (1971).
31. Jonsson, Lars-Erik, E. Anggard, and Lars-M. Gunne, Blockade of intravenous amphetamine euphoria in man, *Clin. Pharmacol. Ther.*, **12**, (6), 889-896 (1971).
32. Kelleher, R. T. and L.R. Gollub, A review of positive conditioned reinforcement, *J. Exp. Anal. Behav.*, **5**, 543-597 (1962).
33. Kramer, J. C., V. s. Fischman, and D.C. Littlefield, Amphetamine abuse, *J. Am. Med. Assoc.*, **201**, 89 (1967).
34. Lester, D., Self-maintenance of intoxication in the rat, *Qt. J. Stud. Alcohol*, **22**, 223-231 (1961).
35. Mello, N.K. and J.H. Mendelson, Experimentally induced intoxication in alcoholics: A comparison between programmed and spontaneous drinking, *JPET*, **173**, 101-116 (1970).
36. Nichols, J. R., C. P. Headlee, and H.W. Coppock, Drug addiction I. Addiction by escape training, *J. Am. Pharm. Assoc.* (science edition), **45**, 788-791 (1956).
37. Pickens, Roy, Self-administration of stimulants by rats, *Int. J. Addict.* **3**, 215-221 (1968).
38. Pickens, R. and W. Harris, Self-administration of *d*-amphetamine by rats, *Psychopharmacologia* (Berl.), **12**, 158-163 (1968).
39. Pickens, R., R.A. Meisch, and J.A. Dougherty, Jr., Chemical interactions in methamphetamine reinforcement, *Psychol. Rep.* **23**, 1267-1270 (1968).
40. Pickens, R., R. Meisch, and L. McGuire, Methamphetamine reinforcement in rats, *Psychonomic Sci.*, **8**, 371-372 (1967).
41. Pickens, R. and T. Thompson, Self-administration of amphetamine and cocaine by rats, Paper presented at the 29th Annual Meeting of the Committee on Problems of Drug Dependence, NAS-NRC, 1967.
42. Pickens, R. and T. Thompson, Cocaine-reinforced behavior in rats: Effects of reinforcement magnitude and fixed-ratio size, *JPET*, **161**, 122-129 (1968).
43. Pickens R. and T. Thompson, Reinforcement by stimulant drugs, Paper presented at APA (1968).
44. Pickens, R. and T. Thompson, Characteristics of stimulant drug reinforcement, in *Stimulus Properties of Drugs*, T. Thompson and R. Pickens (eds), Appleton-Century-Crofts, New York, 1971.
45. Schlichting, U. U., S. R. Goldberg, W. Wuttke, and F. Hoffmeister, *d*-Amphetamine self-administration by rhesus monkeys with different self-administration histories, Proceedings of the European Society for the Study of Drug Toxicity (1970), *Excerpta Med. Int. Congr. Ser.*, **220**, 62-69 (1971).

46. Schuster, C. R., Variables affecting the self-administration of drugs by rhesus monkeys, in *Use of Nonhuman Primates in Drug Evaluation*, pp. 283–299, H. Vagtborg (Ed.), University of Texas Press, Austin, 1968.
47. Schuster, C.R., Psychological approaches to opiate dependence and self-administration by laboratory animals, *Fed. Proc.*, **29** (1), 2–5 (1970).
48. Schuster, C. R. and T. Thompson, Self-administration of and behavioral dependence on drugs, *Ann. Rev. Pharm.*, **9**, 483, (1969).
49. Schuster, C.R. and J.E. Villarreal, The experimental analysis of opioid dependence, in *Psychopharmacologia: A Review of Progress*, pp. 811–828, D. Efron (Ed.) 1968.
50. Schuster, C. R. and J.H. Woods, The conditioned reinforcing effects of stimuli associated with morphine reinforcement, *Int. J. Addict.*, **3**, 223–230 (1968).
51. Schuster, C.R., J.H. Woods, and M.H. Seevers, Self-administration of central stimulants by the monkey, in *Abuse of Central Stimulants*, F. Sjoquist and M. Tottie (Eds.), Raven Press, New York, 1969.
52. Skinner, B.F., *The Behavior of Organisms*, Appleton-Century-Crofts, New York, 1938.
53. Thompson, T., Drugs as reinforcers: Experimental addiction, *Int. J. Addict.*, **3**, 199–206 (1968).
54. Thompson, T., G. Bigelow, and R. Pickens, Morphine self-administration by unrestrained monkeys in a complex programmed environment, Paper presented at the 31st Annual Meeting of the Committee on Problems of Drug Dependence, NAS-NRC, 1969.
55. Thompson T., G. Bigelow, and R. Pickens, Environmental variables influencing drug self-administration, in *Stimulus Properties of Drugs*, T. Thompson and R. Pickens (Eds.), Appleton-Century-Crofts, New York, 1971.
56. Thompson, T. and W. Ostlund, Susceptibility to re-addiction as a function of the addiction and withdrawal environment, *JCPP*, **59**, 388–392 (1965).
57. Thompson, T. and C. R. Schuster, Morphine self-administration, food-reinforced and avoidance behavior in rhesus monkeys. *Psychopharmacologia*, **5**, 87–94 (1964).
58. Weeks, J. R., Experimental morphine addiction: Method for autonomic intravenous injections in unrestrained rats, *Science*, **138**, 143–144 (1962).
59. Weeks, James R., Experimental narcotic addiction, *Sci. Am.*, **210** (3), 46–52 (1964).
60. Weeks, J. R., and R. J. Collins, Factors affecting voluntary morphine intake in self-maintained addicted rats, *Psychopharmacologia*, **6**, 267–279 (1964).
61. Weeks, J.R. and R. J. Collins, Patterns of intravenous self-injection by morphine-addicted rats, *Res. Publ. Assoc. Res. Nerv. Ment. Disord.*, **46**, 288 (1968).
62. Wikler, A., On the nature of addiction and habituation, *Br. J. Addict.*, **57**, 73 (1961).

63. Wikler, A., Conditioning factors in opiate addiction and relapse, in *Narcotics*, D. M. Wilner and G. G. Kassebaum (Eds.), McGraw-Hill, New York, 1965.
64. Wikler, A., Some implications of conditioning theory for problems of drug abuse, *Behav. Sci.*, **16**, 92–97 (1971).
65. Wilson, Marvin C., Variables which influence the reinforcing properties of cocaine in the rhesus monkey, Unpublished doctoral dissertation, University of Michigan (1970).
66. Wilson, M., M. Hitomi, and C.R. Schuster, Further studies of the self-administration of psychomotor stimulants in the rhesus monkey, Paper presented at the 31st Annual Meeting of the Committee on Problems of Drug Dependence, NAS-NRC, 1969.
67. Wilson, M. C., M. Hitomi, and C. R. Schuster, Psychomotor stimulant self administration as a function of dosage per injection in the rhesus monkey. *Psychopharmacologia*, **22**, 271–281 (1971).
68. Wilson, M.C. and C.R. Schuster, Pharmacological modification of the self-administration of cocaine and SPA in the rhesus monkey, Paper presented at the 30th Annual Meeting of the Committee on Problems of Drug Dependence, NAS-NRC, 1968.
69. Wilson, M. C. and C. R. Schuster, The effects of chlorpromazine on psychomotor stimulant self-administration in the rhesus monkey, *Psychopharmacologia*, **26**, 115–126 (1972).
70. Woods, J. H. and C. R. Schuster, Reinforcement properties of morphine, cocaine and SPA as a function of unit dose, *Int. J. Addict.* **3**, 231–237 (1968).
71. Woods, J. H. and C.R. Schuster, Regulation of drug self-administration, in *Advances in Mental Science II: Drug Dependence*, R.T. Harris, W.M. McIsaac, and C.R. Schuster (Eds.), University of Texas Press, Austin, 1970.
72. Woods, J.H. and C. R. Schuster, Opiates as reinforcing stimuli, in *Stimulus Properties of Drugs*, T. Thompson and R. Pickens (Eds.), Appleton-Century-Crofts, New York, 1971.
73. Yanagita, T., K. Ando, and S. Takihashi, A testing method for psychological dependence liability of drugs in monkeys, Paper presented at the 32nd Annual Meeting of the Committee on Problems of Drug Dependence, NAS-NRC, (1970).
74. Yanagita, T., K. Ando, S. Takihashi, and K. Ishida, Self-administration of barbiturates, alcohol (intragastine) and CNS stimulants (intravenous) in monkeys, Paper presented at the 31st Annual Meeting of the Committee on Problems of Drug Dependence, NAS-NRC, 1969.
75. Yanagita, T., G. Deneau, and M. Seevers, Evaluation of pharmacological agents in the monkey by long-term intravenous self-or programmed administration, *Excerpta Med. Int. Congr. Ser.*, **87**, 453–457 (1965).

Chapter Two

CHEMICAL AND BIOCHEMICAL METHODS OF DRUG DETECTION AND MEASUREMENT

JOAN A. MARSHMAN, *Addiction Research Foundation, Toronto, Canada*

During the 1960s much drug-related research depended on adequate means of detection and quantitation of drugs and their biotransformation products. While the pharmaceutical industry and government inspection services have developed adequate quality control procedures for dosage forms of conventional therapeutic agents, "street drug" products containing new or unusual drugs or combinations of drugs have presented new challenges to researchers and law enforcement agencies concerned with the phenomenon of nonmedical drug use. In addition, investigations into the incidence and treatment of "bad trips," monitoring of drug use to modify performance in sports events, and the evaluation of treatment modalities for drug-dependent patients have been facilitated by appropriate techniques for the detection of drugs in biological fluids. Studies of drug distribution and metabolism, tolerance development and the joint action of drugs have required methods not only for detection, but also for reliable quantitation, especially for blood level determinations; indeed since such studies frequently involve repeated sampling from small laboratory animals or human subjects (including neonates), they have presented severe restrictions in the size of individual blood samples, requiring analytical techniques of extremely high sensitivity. Finally, the development of rational emergency treatment techniques for drug overdose patients has imposed a further requirement of rapidity in these determinations.

New and improved analytical methods for drugs of abuse are therefore of interest to many disciplines, and each type of investigator may properly select a different method or devise a new method suitable for his particular circumstances. A method appropriate to mass screening of urine samples which may be adequate to provide a "yes-no" answer as part of a methadone maintenance program will be totally inadequate for the forensic toxicologist; a much simpler approach may suffice for the behavioral scientist who desires blood level data for a specific drug than for the clinical toxicologist faced with a comatose patient as a result of multiple drug use. Thus the individual investigator must decide on a method or group of methods based on his own particular requirements of specificity, sensitivity, and rapidity.

It is not intended in this chapter to comprehensively review the methods of analysis for psychoactive drugs. Recently Kaisha (163) and Mulé (208) reviewed methods of detection and identification of drugs of abuse, and the viewpoint of the forensic toxicologist has been presented by Finkle (104) and Robinson (235), while Curry has considered both forensic and clinical toxicological viewpoints (81). Rather, this chapter is intended to consider some selected advances in methodology which have facilitated research into problems associated with nonmedical drug use, drug dependence, and related phenomena.

1. CLEANUP PROCEDURES

There have been many approaches to the separation of drugs and drug metabolites from extracts of plants, dosage forms, and biological fluids, in order to facilitate unequivocal identification of these compounds. Appropriate "cleanup" of crude extracts reduces interference by nondrug components not only in spectroscopic methods of analysis but also in analytical chromatographic methods. Without such preliminary separation thin layer chromatograms may show confusing additional nondrug spots, the presence of nondrug components at the same rf values as drugs or drug metabolites (thus precluding simple confirmation after elution), or rf values for extracted drug components somewhat different from those of reference standards; with gas chromatographic techniques, extraneous components in crude extracts may cause masking of drug component peaks, substantial shortening of column life, or considerable fouling of the detector.

Classically the techniques of selective liquid-liquid extraction, column chromatography, and preparative thin layer chromatography have served to reduce the relative concentrations of nondrug materials and to permit at least partial separation of drugs into groups according to their physicochemical properties. However, recent years have seen increased utilization of resins in cleanup procedures. The utility of such techniques, particularly in drug-screening of biological fluids, depends on the balance between the separation of the drug(s) from nondrug components, and the loss of drug(s) which accompanies the process; for a "cleanup" technique is of little value if the quantity of drug recovered lies below the minimum level of detection.

Ion-Exchange Resins

Ion-exchange resins have been used extensively for the binding of drugs both in the formulation and analysis of dosage forms. Their application to urine screening for drugs became widespread following the 1966 report of Dole et al. (94), who employed a cation-exchange paper (Reeve-Angel SA-2, containing Amberlite IR-120, Na^+ form) with sequential elutions at pH 2.2, 9.3, and 11.0 for acidic, weakly basic, and strongly basic drugs, respectively, with subsequent analysis of the eluates by thin layer chromatography (TLC). Shortly thereafter Jaffe and Kirkpatrick (157) confirmed the utility of this technique for a variety of basic drugs; however, their studies using an anion-exchange paper (Reeve-Angel SB-2 paper containing Amberlite IRA-400) for the extraction of barbiturates from urine showed a low sensitivity.

In 1969 Mulé (206) reported that because of recovery limitations the cation-exchange paper technique was unacceptable for barbiturates, amphetamines, and certain other psychoactive drugs, although it was adequate for the detection by TLC of narcotics 24 hours after the last administration. Mulé found methadone difficult to extract using this technique, noting a lower limit of detection of 5 to 10 μg/ml urine, whereas direct extraction permitted detection at levels of 1 μg/ml urine. In the hands of Heaton and Blumberg (138) the technique presented problems in recovery both for small concentrations of barbiturates and for amphetamines, and Montavo et al. (204) similarly reported a low sensitivity of the method for methadone, phenobarbital, and d-amphetamine, with a minimum detectable level for methadone of 6 μg/ml urine. Baselt and Casarett (22) confirmed the utility of the ion-exchange approach for the detection of opiates in urine in a methadone treatment program, while preferring direct extraction procedures for amphetamines and barbiturates; they too pointed out the unreliability of the technique for detection of methadone, preferring to make use of a methadone metabolite as an indicator of methadone usage. Kaistha and Jaffe (164), in comparing ion-exchange and direct extraction methods, concluded that the ion-exchange method is satisfactory in clinical monitoring when urine volumes of at least 40 ml are available at 48- to 72-hr intervals. This conclusion has been substantiated by their more recent work (165, 166) in which they reported detection of morphine, methamphetamine, and various barbiturates at urinary concentrations as low as 0.5 μg/ml and methadone at 1μg/ml both by ion-exchange extraction using 50-ml urine volumes and by direct extraction uing 15-ml urine volumes with subsequent TLC analysis on silica gel glass microfiber sheets. They also provided data concerning the time period following a single dose of drug during which urinary concentrations are adequate to allow detection by this method. Recently Dole et al. (93) noted some modifications which they have made since the introduction of their method and have pointed out some potential sources of error that may account for problems of sensitivity encountered by other workers.

Other workers have recently employed somewhat different ion-excahnge techniques. Frings and Queen (115) employed Rexyn 101 (H^+ form) and found it to be a suitable substitute for the SA-2 resin paper employed by Dole. Fenimore and Davis (101) passed urine samples through a short column of Dowex 50W X 2 cation-exchange resin (Na^+ form), and subsequently applied Marquis reagent to the resin to test for the presence of narcotic alkaloids; they concluded that this was an efficient extraction procedure. Routh et al. (236) extracted mixtures of drugs including barbiturates, opiates, and amphetamines from small volumes of biological fluids using a column of mixed-bed ion-exchange resins (Dowex -50 Na^+ form and Rexyn-201 Cl^- form). Combinations of charcoal adsorption and ion exchange chromatography have also proven useful, as in the studies of Yoshimura et al. (292) who employed Dowex 50 W-X8 (H^+ form) and Dowex 1-X2 (formate form) in the concentration and purification of morphine glucuronides in urine and bile of rabbits.

Certainly the use of ion-exchange techniques in cleanup procedures introduces an element of selectivity, apparently at the expense of recovery yields. The technique would appear to have utility in routine urine monitoring for patients on a regular medication regimen (as in methadone maintenance programs) provided that samples are collected frequently (every 24 to 48 hr), urine volumes available are large enough (at least 40 ml), and the techniques employed for the detection of drugs show a high sensitivity.

A Nonionic Resin, Amberlite XAD-2

Amberlite XAD-2 resin has been described (133) as a nonionic copolymer of styrene-divinylbenzene of macroreticular structure; because of its high surface area it effectively adsorbs many water-soluble organic species from aqueous solution by means of van der Waal's interactions. It was successfully employed by Fujimoto and his collaborators in 1969 (116, 117, 119) in the isolation of metabolites of morphine, nalorphine, and naloxone from the urine of several species of animals, as well as by Yeh and Woods (290) in a study of codeine metabolism in the rat. In 1970 Fujimoto and Wang (118) reported on the incorporation of this technique into a method for identifying narcotic analgesics in human urine after the administration of therapeutic doses. After the urine had been passed through the resin column, the adsorbed drug and its metabolites were eluted with methanol nonselectively into the same fraction as some highly colored urinary pigments; these pigments served as a guide to the fractions appropriate for collection. The eluate was then analyzed by TLC using silica gel glass microfiber sheets. A study using ^{14}C-labeled morphine showed that use of the resin column effectively separated the urinary residue from the drug, concentrating the drug approximately threefold; it was thus possible to detect 6 μg of morphine sulfate in 10 ml urine. Use of this technique with urine samples collected from persons receiving therapeutic doses of narcotic analgesics showed that the column eluates contained relatively complex mixtures of intact drug and drug metabolites, and these provided the basis for "fingerprinting," that is, comparisons with urine standards were based not solely on the presence on TLC of a spot corresponding to a particular drug, but on the whole complex pattern of drug plus metabolites.

Mulé et al. (209) studied the feasibility of using the XAD-2 resin system in the routine identification of drugs in urine. They noted that the volume of the eluting solvent, the flow rate of urine and eluting solvent, aqueous washing of the resin, and the organic solvent mixture used for elution were all very significant in obtaining good recoveries for psychoactive drugs. Using chloroform-isopropanol (3:1), determined to be the most efficient solvent for elution of ^{14}C-morphine, and washing the eluate with a saturated aqueous solution of sodium bicarbonate, they carried out recovery studies for ^{14}C-labeled drugs; the recoveries obtained ranged from 49.3% for d-amphetamine to 91.6% for cocaine when drug concentrations in urine ranged from 1 to 30 mg/ml. These workers noted that the urine effluent contained a relatively large percentage of the drugs, that is, the major source of loss lay in the inefficient uptake by the resin of certain drugs rather than in inefficient desorption. Overall, however, they considered that the recoveries obtained with this method were satisfactory in comparison to other methods, and suggested that depending on the requirements of the program it is feasible to analyze urine for drugs of abuse using the XAD-2 resin method, without preliminary acid hydrolysis or spectrofluorometry, which have been found useful for the detection of morphine in very low concentrations.

Much greater recoveries were reported by Weissman et al. (284), who employed methanol for elution from the resin column; recoveries for phenobarbital, amphetamine (20 µg), and morphine (100 µg) added to control urine were reported to be, respectively, 90 to 100%, 90%, and "essentially quantitative." These authors noted that the pigments that accompany the drug eluate from the column are increased in the urines of drug abusers, as compared with normal urines, and may present a problem in overloading the application zone on the thin layer plate, thus distorting the patterns obtained. More recently Hetland et al. (141) applied this approach to the screening of aqueous standard solutions using methanol as the eluting solvent; their overall screening method was sensitive to "at least" 2 µg/ml of each drug tested when a 30-ml aliquot of solution was used. Their results for urines from hospitalized patients following therapeutic dose regimens led them to conclude that "the method is sufficiently sensitive to detect therapeutic drug levels in human urine and should therefore be adequately sensitive for detection and tentative identification in cases of drug overdoses."

To determine whether there is a substantial difference in the binding capacity of XAD-2 resin for unionized and ionized forms of weak organic acids and bases, Hetland et al. (141) studied the effect of pH alteration over the range pH 3 to 9.5 for standard aqueous drug solutions applied to the column. Since pH adjustment for the drugs studied (morphine, amphetamine, phenobarbital, and glutethimide) effected no major alterations in elution pattern, the researchers concluded that pH adjustment of urine specimens was unnecessary. Contrary to this view, Finkle (104) pointed out pH dependence of the resin method, noting optimum pH values of 8.5 to 9.5 for morphine, 7 to 9 for amphetamine, and 5 to 7 for barbiturates. He noted that a compromise pH in the range 6 to 9 will permit recovery of 75 to 80% of various drugs including barbiturates. Finkle also noted that the eluting solvent ethylene dichloride-ethyl acetate recommended for commercially prepared columns has the advantage over methanol-containing systems of removing less water.

Sohn et al. (252) compared an Amberlite XAD-2 column eluted with methanol with a direct extraction method, using as test material 5-ml aliquots of urine from patients receiving methadone, to which a barbiturate was added. They found little difference in the total number of peaks seen on gas chromatographic analysis of the resulting solutions; however, the relative peak heights for barbiturates, methadone, and methadone metabolite in the column eluate were three times or more those of the direct extracts, whereas unknown peaks were no higher than the corresponding peaks in the extract. They concluded that this approach to cleanup, employing smaller urine samples and correspondingly smaller volumes of solvent, will effectively reduce the concentration of interfering substances and provide an adequate cleanup prior to gas chromatographic analysis. Davidow and Quame (86), evaluating the utility of a commercial disposable column, found it equivalent in sensitivity to the conventional extraction procedure.

Peters and Tocci (229) reported the use of Amberlite XAD-2 resin impregnated into plastic sheets. They extracted the drugs from urine by shaking the sheets with the urine sample for 5 min, then subsequently washing with water, and eluting with methanol prior to TLC analysis.

Unlike the ion-exchange resins, Amberlite XAD-2 resin does not effect significant separation of various drug groups, although there is evidence to suggest an influence of pH on relative drug recoveries. This lack of separation has been turned to advantage in the monitoring of urinary drug and drug metabolite profiles. Although both types of resin effectively reduce the relative concentrations of some water-soluble nondrug components of urine, the drug-containing eluate from the nonionic resin contains urinary pigments, and Weissman et al. (284) suggested that increased concentrations of these pigments in the urine of drug abusers may introduce difficulties in analysis. Widely varying recovery efficiencies reported for various drugs suggest that recovery is highly dependent on experimental conditions; where optimum conditions exist the procedure appears to be satisfactory for screening procedures both for patients receiving drugs in therapeutic doses and for those whose dose levels are much higher. The availability of disposable columns and resin-impregnated sheets has made it possible for clinicians remote from an analytical laboratory to conveniently mail urine samples for drug screening.

Other Cleanup Methods

Preparative gas chromatography was used by McAuley and Kofoed (193) as a cleanup procdure for tissue extracts for toxicological investigation. They employed relatively short columns (3 m) of 7 mm diameter with packings of OV-1 or OV-17 10% on Chromosorb A to achieve separation in relatively short times. Whereas most neutral and acidic drugs could be collected without cooling of the effluent, a cooling procedure was necessary for nearly all basic drugs.

Broich, Hoffman, et al. (56) reported the application of lyophilization to urine samples for detection of drugs of abuse. They noted that extraction of the freeze-dried samples resulted in significant increases in recovery because of the elimination of partition of the drug, and in the recovery of water-soluble drugs which tend to escape detection with conventional liquid-

liquid extraction. The lyophilized material was extracted with methanol, and acetone was used to precipitate inorganic salts, thus yielding a much cleaner extract. More recently this group successfully applied this approach to the detection of drugs in bile samples (145). This technique may eventually make a substantial contribution to the study of water-soluble drug metabolites.

In 1970, Bastos et al. (23) reported the use of a salting-out technique for separation of basic drugs and their metabolites from urine. After the addition of ethanol and potassium carbonate to urine, followed by mixing and centrifugation, the highly colored ethanol phase was removed and concentrated. The addition of ether and pH 8.5 buffer solution gave rise to two layers, the ethanol-buffer layer containing the water-soluble fraction including morphine glucuronides and the ethanol-ether layer containing basic organic drugs. Although the ethanol-ether layer yielded relatively clean residues, suitable for thin layer analysis, the recoveries reported for methamphetamine and morphine were only 52 and 74%, respectively; nevertheless, most drugs could be detected at concentrations of 2 μg/ml urine, and the utility of the technique was validated using urine samples from patients on known drug therapy. Horning et al. (151) adapted this salting-out procedure for isolation of drugs and drug metabolites from plasma; the addition of isopropanol and potassium carbonate to diluted plasma followed by centrifugation yielded an isopropanol layer containing drugs and drug metabolites, with proteins precipitated at the interface. The resulting extracts were analyzed by TLC or GLC, and recoveries for ^{14}C-labeled phenobarbital and caffeine were reported to be 100 ± 5%. The authors suggested that where fatty acids extracted from plasma interfere with gas chromatographic analysis, they may be removed by an additional extraction step. This "salting-out" technique has a number of advantages: it is applicable to a wide range of drugs; it permits the use of small samples of biological fluid; and for at least some drugs it provides virtually quantitative yields. Although it is less adaptable to mass screening applications, it could be profitably employed in clinical laboratories and research settings where multiple samples are handled.

2. GAS CHROMATOGRAPHIC METHODS

Recent years have seen many advances in gas chromatographic equipment and methods. These have culminated in automatic injection systems coupled with automatic integration and printout, which permit unattended round-the-clock sample handling, and systems composed of a gas chromatograph interfaced to a mass spectrometer and computer. This degree of sophistication is available to a limited number of laboratories; other advances have been more widely adopted. The need to measure extremely low concentrations of drugs in biological fluids has brought a requirement for detectors of higher sensitivity; the need to determine the presence of drugs in relatively complex mixtures has promoted the search for detectors of greater specificity; and to realize the full analytical potential of gas chromatography (GC) derivative formation has been found useful for various classes of drugs.

Detectors

The flame ionization detector (FID), which has been substantially improved to provide high sensitivity (of the order of 100^{-11} µg), has long been recognized as the "workhorse" detector for studies of drugs; its properties, which have been reviewed by Gough and Walker (128), include a wide linear dynamic range, making it extremely useful for quantitative analysis.

Although the greater specificity and sensitivity shown by the electron capture detector (ECD) in pesticide work are highly desirable for drug studies, only a few psychoactive drugs (e.g., chloral hydrate, bromisoval, chlorpromazine, ethchlorvynol) bear halogen atoms or other structural features of extremely high electron affinity and therefore can be studied per se using ECD either alone or in combination with FID (48, 80). Thus the application of ECD to the study of psychoactive drugs has been largely confined to those drugs where appropriate halogen-containing derivatives can be prepared (see section following on derivatives). However, the ECD does have limitations, including somewhat unpredictable response and a relatively small linear dynamic range; thus its applicability to quantitative studies is restricted (128).

One useful modification of the FID is the thermionic detector, which is sensitized to chlorine, bromine, iodine, phosphorus, or nitrogen by heating an alkali metal salt in the flame. Karmen (171) noted that the increased volatility of the alkali metal in the presence of the effluent compound's combustion products contributes substantially to the increased sensitivity for chlorine-, bromine-, or iodine-containing compounds; however, such modifications have not yielded detectors of adequate fluorine sensitivity. Because of the advantages of using fluorine-containing derivatives of some drugs [e.g., methyprylon (98) and amphetamines (see section following on derivatives)], attempts have been made to devise comparable fluorine-sensitive detectors. Karmen and Kelly (172) reported a detector design in which the hydrogen fluoride generated by combustion of fluorine-containing species is passed through calcium chloride to release hydrogen chloride, which then reacts with the alkali metal of the detector as in the case of chlorine-containing compounds; this design makes it impossible to distinguish fluorine-containing compounds from compounds containing other halogens. Kojima et al. (176) recently designed a system for selective detection of fluorine-containing compounds; detection is based on hydrogenolysis of the compound to yield hydrogen fluoride, absorption of the hydrogen fluoride in solution, and monitoring of the fluoride ion concentration in the solution by means of a fluoride ion electrode. The limit of detection for the system was 5×10^{-1} mole for fluorobenzene, and although the response time was relatively slow, peak distortion was reported to be negligible when retention time exceeded 5 min. Significant improvement in sensitivity seems to be necessary before such detectors become useful for studies of drugs in biological fluids.

A highly sensitive nitrogen-specific version of the thermionic detector has been developed. It was reported that combustion of nitrogen-containing compounds results in increased ionization of the alkali metal (171), and the choice of alkali salt and the geometry of the detector are considered important design factors (95). Donike et al. (95) studied the applicability of this detector to various drugs including amphetamine, methamphetamine, and ephedrine. For drug-screening of urine, using a temperature programming technique as might be required for forensic purposes, they found it necessary to prepare an ether extract of urine; this prevented extraneous urinary components from causing problems arising through cleavage of residues in the injector port at high temperatures. However, they were able to determine optimum conditions for direct analysis of aqueous solutions, including urine samples per se, containing drugs in concentrations as low as 1 to 5 ppm. This type of detector probably will make a significant contribution to future studies of psychoactive drugs.

The sequence of separation by GC, trapping of the eluate fractions, and determination of the infrared spectra for the trapped microsamples has been used extensively to facilitate identification (83). In 1964 Bartz and Ruhl (21) and Wilks and Brown (288) proposed systems to permit direct infrared analysis of column effluent; although the scan speeds were greatly increased over conventional instruments, they remained relatively slow (16 to 45 sec) and required relatively large samples (minimally 0.3 to 0.5 mg). Low and Freeman (189) employed a multiple scan inference spectrometer, reducing the scanning time to 1 sec for the 2500- to 250-cm^{-1} region, although multiple scans were necessary for good sensitivity. Krakow (177) employed a system that continually produced spectra from 2.7 to 9μ at the rate of 1.6 spectra/sec, and with samples as small as 25 μg functional group analysis was possible. The system discussed by Brown et al. (58) reduces the required sample size even further, with good quality spectra determined over 5 to 20 sec using as little as 20-μg sample, and observation of functional groups being possible with 3-μg sample. This approach to "on-line" infrared identification of GC fractions has been developed commercially, with sample size and scan speed limitations of the same order as those noted by Brown et al., and has been tested with a wide variety of compounds including barbiturates (233). Obviously the applicability of such systems to the study of drugs of abuse is limited by sample size requirements of the system; this limitation is particularly significant with respect to detection in biological fluids. It may, however, become a useful tool in the analysis of dosage forms; in such cases its use might minimize sample handling time required for the more conventional sequence of separation followed by spectrophotometric analysis.

Fluorescence detection has been proposed as a suitable means of providing high sensitivity and selectivity for GC analysis. While Bowman and Beroza (47) extracted the effluent into a flowing liquid solvent, the system of Burchfield et al. (63) carried out fluorimetric analysis directly on the gas phase, thus eliminating the extraction step but sacrificing sensitivity. More recently Freed and Faulkner (113) effected direct coupling of a fast-scanning spectrophotofluorometer to a gas chromatograph; this system proved superior to the earlier gas phase system in generating both emission and excitation spectra of the emerging components, which can be displayed on a storage oscilloscope until the chromatogram is completed, and in showing sensitivity comparable to the Bowman and Beroza system, with detection limits for polycyclic aromatic hydrocarbons in the nanogram and subnanogram range. Freed and Faulkner noted that gas phase emission at high temperature is almost always restricted to molecules with some degree of aromatic character; although this appears to impose a severe restriction on the applicability of such a system to psychoactive drugs, it seems reasonable that the formation of fluorescent derivatives will permit widespread use of such a technique.

Recently Tsuda et al. (270) reported the development of a system combining gas chromatography with nuclear magnetic resonance (NMR) spectroscopy. The effluent vapor was mixed with carbon tetrachloride vapor, the combined vapors were condensed, and the resulting liquid was fed continuously into a NMR flow-cell of small volume. The requirement of minimum sample size of 1 μl restricts the present applicability of the system with respect to drugs. However, it is to be expected that subsequent refinement of the system may make this technique useful in drug and drug metabolite identification.

The ultimate GC detector in providing structural information concerning the separated compounds is the mass spectrometer (MS). The widespread application of GC/MC systems to drugs of dependence is discussed in a later section.

Derivative Formation for Gas Chromatographic Detection

Barbiturates

Early gas chromatographic studies of barbiturates, which have a relatively high polarity as a result of their cyclic ureide structure, showed that these compounds tend to be adsorbed to the column packing. This adsorptive loss of drug on the column packing led to contamination of the column, severe tailing of peaks, ineffectiveness of the technique at submicrogram concentrations, and limited applicability for quantitation. While some workers such as Street (196, 259) attempted to minimize these disadvantages by "deactivating" the column supports, others attempted to modify the barbiturate molecule to reduce its polarity and thus its tendency to be absorbed.

N,N-dimethyl barbiturate derivatives, less polar than the parent drugs, have been prepared by various methods. Reaction with diazomethane was the approach employed by Cook et al. (75), by Gilbert, Millard, and Powell (122) in their study of barbiturate metabolites, and by Horning et al. (149, 151) in their study of barbiturates in plasma and urine. In 1966 Martin and Driscoll (192) reported on methylation of barbiturates using dimethyl sulfate with potassium carbonate; this method was also used by Stewart et al. (257), Fiereck and Tietz (103), Baselt and Casarett (22), and Baylis et al. (24) in their studies of barbiturates in biological fluids. Whereas most workers extracted the barbiturate before derivatization, Stewart et al. (257) carried out the methylation reaction directly in serum, tissue, or water, then separated the methylated barbiturate by extraction; they reported that this rapid procedure eliminated much of the interfering material and showed detection limit of 0.01 to 0.05 μg drug. Baylis et al. (24) were concerned with simultaneous determination of phenobarbitone and diphenylhydantoin, both of which are susceptible to alkaline hydrolysis; therefore the methylation conditions selected by these investigators were not optimal for either drug, but they provided a reasonably satisfactory compromise.

Stevenson (256) introduced "flash heater" methylation of barbiturates, based on thermal decomposition of quaternary ammonium salts; thus, reaction in the injector port of barbiturate with tetramethylammonium hydroxyde gave rise to the methylated barbiturate. The sensitivity of this reaction to the experimental conditions prompted Brochmann-Hanssen and Oke (52) to replace this methylating agent with trimethylphenylammonium hydroxide (i.e., trimethylailinium hydroxide) with the expectation that the reaction would proceed at lower injector port temperatures since the dimethylaniline formed as a by-product of the reaction is a better "leaving group" than the trimethylamine formed in Stevenson's reaction. They reported that most barbiturates gave single symmetrical peaks when the methylation was carried out with trimethylanilinium hydroxide, whereas minor second peaks occurred when tetramethylammonium hydroxide was used. This approach to methylation was applied to barbiturates in biological fluids by Kupferberg (178), Kallberg et al. (167), Street (261), and Kananen et al. (169). Kallberg pointed out that it is necessary to carry out the quantitation relatively rapidly to minimize hydrolysis of the barbiturates in the strongly alkaline solution. Street (261) reported some variability in results, including the appearance of extra peaks and inconsistent relative peak heights, for which the causes were not apparent; he therefore recommended that quantitative determinations be carried out on unmodified drug, and that derivative formation be used in confirmation of the drug's identity. MacGee (190) proposed that ethylation of barbiturates was superior to methylation in producing fewer side products from mephobarbital and phenobarbital, in eliminating a second peak from secobarbital, and in permitting differentitation of phenobarbital and mephobarbital. However, Kananen et al. (169) pointed out that use of trimethylanilinium hydroxide produced sharper peak symmetry and shorter retention times without any loss of resolution.

Both NMR (52, 217) and MS techniques (122, 149, 167) have provided confirmation that the N,N-dimethyl barbiturate is formed in these methylation procedures. Gilbert et al. (122) used GC analysis to show that the N,N-dimethylation using diazomethane proceeded with 85 to 90% yield. On the basis of NMR studies Neville (217) concluded that methylation of the common barbiturates using dimethyl sulfate or diazomethane, or the on-column procedure using tetramethylammonium hydroxide or trimethylanilinium hydroxide, yields N,N-dimethyl derivatives; however, there was evidence of a small amount of O-methyl derivative with the use of diazomethane. The formation of N,O-dimethyl isomer has been reported by Horning and Horning (149) on the basis of MS data.

Trimethylsilyl (TMSi) derivatives of barbiturates seem to be much less useful than the methylated derivatives. Street (260) prepared TMSi derivatives using an on-column method and considered that the product was silylated on only one nitrogen atom. Brochmann-Hanssen and Oke (52) noted that TMSi derivatives of barbiturates are unstable. Nevertheless, TMSi derivatives of hydroxylated barbiturate metabolites have been extensively used (168, 224, 267) and Horning (149, 151) found the preparation of Me-TMSi derivatives of barbiturate metabolites quite satisfactory for analysis using GC/MS.

It has been the experience of this laboratory in both clinical service and research studies that barbiturate samples of at least 0.1 μg yield symmetrical peaks satisfactory for quantitation without derivatization when modern column packings such as OV-7 or OV-17 on Chromosorb W High Performance are used. However, studies requiring quantitation of smaller samples might usefully employ a methylation technique.

Narcotic Analgesics

In a study of the gas chromatographic behavior of opiates as pure substances Anders and Manning determined that acetylated derivatives of codeine and norcodeine were more easily separated than were the free base forms; they subsequently initiated a peak-shift technique for a variety of bases including codeine, morphine, and dihydromorphinone whereby acylated derivatives were formed on the column following injection of the parent compound and acetic, propionic, or trifluoroacetic anhydride (6). This approach to derivatization of morphine was more successful than silylation. Brochmann-Hanssen and Svendsen (54), in their quantitative determination of morphine in opium samples, employed hexamethyldisilazane (HMDS) with trimethylchlorosilane (TMCS) in pyridine to form the bistrimethylsilyl ether of morphine prior to injection, and they reported that this reaction proceeded quantitatively. The TMSi derivative was eluted from the column as a symmetrical peak, unlike the free base, which had shown considerable tailing, and was therefore suitable for quantitative estimation. Formation of the TMSi derivatives was found appropriate by Martin and Swinehart (191) for the estimation of both morphine and codeine in opium samples and by Grooms (130) in the study of illicit samples containing heroin. This latter study made use of the more powerful silylating agent BSA [*N,O*-bis-(trimethylsilyl)-acetamide], which permitted the detection and identification of various adulterants including lactose, mannitol, and procaine using the same column employed for alkaloid determination. However, Miller (200) preferred to use trifluoroacetyl derivatives for characterization of sugars present in illicit preparations of heroin in order to minimize any interference by heroin and its associated adulterants. His studies indicated that heroin, procaine, and quinine react with the trifluoroacetic anhydride but the nature of these derivative by-products was not determined.

Mulé (205) employed the on-column acylation technique for the analysis of a wide range of narcotic analgesics extracted from biological material and reported gas chromatographic retention data for both acetyl and propionyl derivatives. Drugs such as heroin, methadone, propoxyphene, and meperidine, which do not form esters, showed unaltered retention times using this technique, whereas a number of compounds including codeine and *l*-acetylmethadol reacted partially with acetic and propionic anhydrides. Although the technique was readily applied to extracts of plasma and urine that had not been subjected to preliminary acid hydrolysis, hydrolyzed samples gave rise to extracts which yielded extraneous peaks, thus requiring that similarly prepared control extracts be run concurrently.

In their studies of morphine excretion in the urine of human subjects Ikekawa et al. (154) and Fish and Wilson (107) formed the TMSi derivative using BSA which effected silylation very rapidly at room temperature. Ikekawa et al. reported that their method involving charcoal adsorption and solvent extraction followed by gas chromatographic analysis of the TMSi derivative permitted the detection of morphine 96 hr after subcutaneous injection of a 10-mg dose of morphine hydrochloride. The BSA method has also been employed by Parker et al. (227).

For the determination of morphine in plasma and cerebrospinal fluid at concentrations as low as 25 ng per sample Wilkinson and Way (287) prepared the TMSi derivative using BSTFA [*N,O*-bis-(trimethylsilyl) trifluoroacetamide] with 1% TMCS both as the silylating agent and solvent; silylation occurred very rapidly at room temperature. The reduced response of the flame ionization detector to this reagent relative to that for BSA coupled with the small total volume of solution permitted detection of very small amounts of morphine. Elliott et al. (99) employed BSTFA in pyridine for silylation of morphine and 6-monoacetyl morphine in their determination of heroin metabolites in urine.

While recognizing the value of acetylation of morphine for purposes of its measurement by gas chromatography, Fish and Wilson (107) preferred the silylation procedure for routine measurements of urinary output in drug-dependent persons. However, Wallace, Biggs, and Blum (282) selected the acetylation procedure for nanogram quantities of morphine isolated from blood, urine, liver, and bile, because of its less stringent requirements for purification and dryness of the extract.

Amphetamines and Related Compounds

Although GC analysis of amphetamines per se has been shown to be useful for routine studies when Carbowax-KOH (25, 26, 28, 33, 183, 225), SE-30 (183, 247), or one of the Apiezon series (269, 276) is used as the liquid phase, derivative formation involving the amine function has been extensively used in the analysis of amphetamine and its analogs. This approach has been particularly valuable in providing a second criterion of identity when preliminary identification has been made using the free base (i.e., use of the peak-shift approach). In addition, the reduction in polarity of the compound reduces adsorptive losses, thus minimizing tailing and increasing sensitivity (27, 53), and the reduced volatility of the derivatives may permit more accurate estimations of concentration.

Brochmann-Hanssen and Svendsen (53) made use of the condensation reaction between amines and simple ketones such as acetone in applying the peak shift approach to separation and identification of sympathomimetic amines. Primary amines may be expected to react with acetone to yield the corresponding eneamines; secondary amines would be expected to be nonreactive, although when a β-hydroxyl group is present (e.g., ephedrine) formation of the oxazolidine might be anticipated; and tertiary amines remain unreacted (31, 53, 68). This technique was used by Beckett and his co-workers in drug excretion and metabolism studies of amphetamine (27-29), methamphetamine (30), and ephedrine (33); this group has also pointed out the value of this technique in general urine screening for drugs that may be used to modify performance in sport (31). Analogously, Lebish et al. (183) reported the use of benzaldehyde reagent for confirmation of amphetamine in urine in a method appropriate for clinical and forensic purposes.

Although the peak shift approach is useful in providing additional qualitative data, formation of the acetone adduct is a relatively slow reaction, and its utility in quantitative studies is limited by the fact that derivative formation is incomplete (27, 31). A useful alternative procedure is formation of the N-acetyl or N-propionyl derivative by reaction of the amine with the appropriate acid anhydride (17, 22, 31, 105, 183, 242, 277), acyl chloride (269), or N-acylimidazole (153). Toseland and Scott (269) preferred this approach because derivative formation occurs more rapidly than does Schiff base formation with acetone, and the chromatographic conditions for the N-acetyl derivative permitted consecutive determinations of other drugs. Acetylation has been used extensively for confirmation of identity of amphetamines extracted from blood or urine both for routine clinical and forensic purposes (11, 17, 22, 105, 183, 242), and Angrist et al. (11) used the acetylation approach in quantitation of urinary amphetamine levels.

Reaction of amines with carbon disulfide has served to distinguish among primary, secondary, and tertiary amines; whereas both primary and secondary amines react with carbon disulfide to form the dithiocarbamate, only in the case of primary amines is this derivative converted to the isothiocyanate. This reaction of primary amines with carbon disulfide permitted Brandenberger and Hellback (49) to use the peak shift technique to distinguish between amphetamine and methamphetamine in urine. These authors, as well as Beckett et al. (31), noted the potential applicability of the technique to urine screening associated with sports competitions. Brandenberger (48) recommended the toxicological study of amphetamine based on its conversion to the isothiocyanate derivative because of this derivative's relative simplicity for GC (as compared with the free base form), and because of its suitability for mass spectral study. Study of the reaction of primary amines of the tryptamine group with carbon disulfide led Narasimhachari et al. (214) to conclude similarly that the isothiocyanates are superior to the Schiff's bases for separating the primary amines because of their greater stability, excellent GC properties, and their suitability for mass spectral study. Recently Narasimhachari and Vouros (216) made use of this approach in their GC/MS study of a variety of biogenic amines and amphetamine-type compounds including mescaline, 3,4-dimethoxyamphetamine (3,4-DMA), 2,5-dimethoxyamphetamine (2,5-DMA), 2,3,4-trimethoxyamphetamine (TMA-2), and 2,4,6-trimethoxyamphetamine (TMA-6), and they noted the potential applicability of isothiocyanate derivatization in quantitative analysis of such amines in biological samples.

The use of halogenated acyl derivatives of amphetamines for GC analyses has become increasingly widespread for the following reasons: they tend to be readily formed; they have been shown to yield excellent peak shapes with general purpose packings conventionally used for GC/MS; their mass spectra are frequently more complex, yielding more information to facilitate identification; and their high affinity for electrons results in a high electron-capture response (10). The early work of Vanden Heuvel, Horning, et al. (277, 150) included GC separation of the pentafluoropropionyl derivative of various amines including amphetamine, and subsequently Horning et al. (153) and Beckett et al. (31) noted the utility for GC of heptafluorobutyryl derivatives. More recent trifluoroacetyl derivatives of amines have been prepared for GC analysis using the FID (8, 9, 143, 156, 223). Anggard et al. (8, 9) applied this method to the determination of amphetamine and phenmetrazine in urine; using a 2-ml urine sample, the minimum detectable concentration of drug was 0.1 μg/ml; thus the method was adequately sensitive for pharmacokinetic studies. To enhance the sensitivity of the method sufficiently for determinations in blood these authors changed to the trichloracetyl derivative with an ECD. However, O'Brien et al. (223), using 5-ml blood samples, retained the use of the FID with the trifluoroacetyl derivative; they found it adequate provided that precautions were taken (e.g., use of the scavenger amine diethylamine) to minimize losses. In particular they noted the high risk of loss of amphetamine either as free base or as the trifluoroacetyl derivative when samples are concentrated under a stream of nitrogen at room temperature. Their data showed a linearity of response over the concentration range 10 to 40 ng/ml blood with deviation from linearity at lower concentrations.

In 1968 Walle (283) quantitatively determined amphetamine in urine in concentrations as low as 5 ng/ml by preparing the 2,4-dinitrophenyl derivative and using an ECD. The limitations of this method included the nonselectivity of the 2,4-dinitrofluorobenzene reagent (and the resulting need for selective extraction of amphetamine from urine) and the need for selective extraction of amphetamine for urine) and need for frequent reconditioning of the column. In addition, Anggard and Hankey (10) pointed out that the relatively long retention times of these derivatives might preclude the application of this approach to higher molecular weight species.

For studies of amphetamine-type compounds using an ECD Bruce and Maynard (60) selected the heptafluorobutyramide as the best derivative. This approach was shown to be effective in determining blood levels of a number of compounds including amphetamine, methamphetamine, fenfluramine and chlorphentermine at concentrations as low as 60 ng/ml for the nonhalogenated amphetamines and somewhat lower for fenfluramine and chlorphentermine. In this method preconditioning of the column with heptafluorobutyric anhydride was found to be critical, as was the need for frequent reconditioning of the column.

Anggard and Hankey (10) studied a variety of derivatives of amphetamine and phenmetrazine with respect to GC behavior, response to ECD, and GC/MS properties. The perfluorooctanamide, maleamide, and pentafluorobenzamide showed less than ideal peak shape, especially at lower concentration levels, and although the isothiocyanate derivative showed satisfactory peak shape, its ECD response was not significantly better than its FID response. The trichloroacetyl derivative was found to be superior to the heptafluorobutyramide in being less volatile (and therefore less subject to losses) and in yielding a higher ECD response. Therefore the trichloroacetyl derivative was selected as best on the basis of its facile formation, narrow and symmetrical peak shape, and high ECD response. Anggard and his co-workers (8, 9) subsequently employed the trichloroacetamide of amphetamine and phenmetrazine in their quantitation of these drugs in plasma, cerebrospinal fluid, brain, and other tissues. The trichloroacetamide derivative approach has also been used by Noonan et al. (222, 234) for the detection of amphetamines in plasma, saliva, and urine of horses, and by Baggott and Davis (18, 19) in a comparative study of amphetamine pharmacokinetics in various species. In all of these studies an ECD was employed. In their studies with methamphetamine in blood following therapeutic doses, Driscoll et al. (97) confirmed the superiority of the trichloroacetyl derivative on the basis of its higher ECD sensitivity (as compared with the heptafluorobutyramide and pentafluorobenzamide) and its lower volatility (as compared with the heptafluorobutyramide), which eliminated a need for temperature programming. The ECD response to pure methamphetamine trichloroacetamide was linear over the range 0 to 1.0 ng and quantities as small as 25 pg were detectable.

Using pure compounds Wilkinson (286) prepared a variety of fluorinated derivatives of β-phenylethylamine and established that for GC analysis using an ECD the pentafluorobenzamide was preferable because of its sensitivity to EC detection; this approach yielded linear responses in the subnanogram range with detection limits of 10, 25, and 60 pg for amphetamine, ephedrine and pseudoephedrine, and norephedrine, respectively. The author pointed out the greater sensitivity observed for the ^{3}H-ECD relative to the ^{63}Ni-ECD in these studies.

Recently Moffat et al. (203) studied a variety of perfluorobenzene derivatives of phenylethylamine and N-methylphenethylamine using GC with ECD and determined that the best derivatizing agent for secondary amines was pentafluorobenzoyl chloride, whereas for primary amines either pentafluorobenzaldehyde or pentafluorobenzoyl chloride was suitable. The pentafluorobenzaldehyde-phenylethylamine Schiff's base showed the greater electron-capturing response, followed by the pentafluorobenzoyl derivative. However, pentafluorobenzaldehyde did not react quantitatively with N-methylphenethylamine to give the eneamine, but it gave a mixture of two products; this reflects the relative versatility of pentafluorobenzaldehyde in condensing with various types of amine to form different products. The authors noted that the gas chromatographic properties of all of perfluorobenzene derivatives prepared were excellent.

N-Trifluoroacetyl-l-prolyl chloride (TPC) has been used as a resolving agent in the GC analysis of optical isomers of amphetamine (126) and the method has been applied to the determination of amphetamine stereoisomers in body tissues (127) and in dosage forms (285). In their study of the stereoselective metabolism of amphetamine in rats Gunne and Galland (132) prepared the O-methyl ether of the excreted hydroxyamphetamine and subsequently used the TPC technique to resolve the optical isomers of the p-methoxyamphetamine. Preliminary methylation was required since the unmethylated hydroxyamphetamine was not sufficiently resolved by this method.

Cannabinoids

In studies of cannabis preparations derivatization has been useful in protecting tetrahydrocannabinolic acids (THCA) and related carboxylated species against thermal decarboxylation under gas chromatographic conditions. Prior to GC analysis of a petroleum ether extract of marihuana Lerner (185) reacted the extract with diazomethane to produce methyl esters of the constituent carboxylic acids, while cannabidiol (CBD), tetrahydrocannabinol (THC), and cannabinol (CBN) remained unreacted. This procedure was subsequently used by Claussen et al. (70) in their gas chromatographic study of cannabidiolic acid; Skinner (248) used trimethyl anilinium hydroxide as a methylating agent.

By silylation of both the acidic and phenolic cannabinoids present in a cannabis extract Davis et al. (87), Fetterman et al. (102), and DeZeeuw et al. (92) separated Δ^9-THC and Δ^9-THCA; quantitation of these two species was possible by comparison of the relative "apparent" THC present in the extract before and after silylation. Other workers have prepared TMSi derivatives of cannabinoids (e.g., 37, 64, 70, 72, 108, 139, 226) and cannabinoid metabolites (e.g., 110, 199, 281) for gas chromatographic studies. This approach has been useful in providing an additional criterion of identity (peak-shift), in permitting the use of lower operating temperatures, and in providing improved resolution.

Although they found TMSi ethers to be satisfactory cannabinoid derivatives, Caddy et al. (64) considered trifluoroacetyl esters to be a suitable alternative, potentially detectable in low concentration in biological fluids by the ECD, and free from silicone, which leads to fouling of the FID. Skinner (248) has suggested that, in addition to the trifluoroacetate, the heptafluorobutyrate would be suitable for use with the ECD. In their studies of cannabinoid detection in urine Andersen et al. (7) treated urinary extracts with *p*-toluenesulfonic acid and detected two components by means of TLC. With a view to GC investigation of these compounds for identification and quantitation using a ^{63}Ni-ECD they prepared the trichloroacetyl derivatives (241) and determined that as little as 0.04 ng Δ^9-THC could be measured (218). This sensitivity suggests that the method may have considerable potential for pharmacological studies provided that the linearity of detector response is adequate.

3. FLUORESCENCE MEASUREMENTS

The increasing use of spectrophotofluorometry for analysis of drugs is due in part to the fact that it permits acquisition of two criteria for characterization, an excitation spectrum and a fluorescence emission spectrum. In addition the sensitivity of fluorescence methods is generally very high, with the detection limit for a particular drug reflecting that drug's fluorescence intensity. As pointed out by DeSilva and D'Arconte (90), the practical application of spectrophotofluorometry to the analysis of drugs in biological materials has been facilitated by recent advances in selective extraction and separation techniques. For example, TLC may serve not only to appropriately separate the component(s) of interest but also to permit *in situ* scanning for quantitative fluorescence estimation; thus the advantages of high sensitivity and specificity are combined with rapidity of analysis (12), and indeed Janchen and Pataki (158) consider such measurements of fluorescence to be the most advantageous of all optical scanning techniques. Lauffer et al. (181) studied a group of 60 psychoactive substances using spectrophotofluorometric analysis on thin-layer plates and reported that some of these drugs showed fluorescence in quantities as low as 0.01 µg; they therefore proposed the utilization of this approach for clinical pharmacological and toxicological investigations.

DeZan et al. (91) recently summarized data relating to the fluorometric analysis of various narcotics and dangerous drugs. In a spectrofluorometric study of a variety of hallucinogens Gillespie (124) reported that, with the appropriate choice of solvent, strongly fluorescent compounds including N,N-diethyltryptamine (DET), N,N-dimethyltryptamine (DMT), psilocybin, 3,4-methylenedioxyamphetamine (MDA), and 4-methyl-2,5-dimethoxyamphetamine (STP) had practical detection limits of 0.5 to 1 ppm, whereas detection limits for weakly fluorescent compounds including mescaline, phencyclidine (PCP), benactyzine, and N-methyl-3-piperidylbenzilate (LBJ,JB-336) were 20 to 50 ppm. [Lysergic acid diethylamide (LSD), which shows extremely intense fluorescence, was detected at levels as low as 0.05 ppm.] The different fluorescent characteristics (excitation and emission peak wavelengths) of STP and MDA provided Canaff (66) with the basis for differentiation between these two compounds. Antun et al. (14) studied the fluorescence intensity of various methoxylated amphetamines and noted a generally good correlation between the degree of native fluorescence and hallucinogenic potency, except for the 3,4-, 2,4,6,- and 2,3,4,5- methoxylated species; this relationship was somewhat analogous to that between HOMO energy and hallucinogenic activity which had been noted previously.

The relatively weak native fluorescence characteristics of codeine and morphine were observed by Brandt et al. (51) to be very similar at pH 1 to 3; however at pH 10 to 12 that of morphine was markedly reduced, whereas that of codeine remained unchanged. Thus, using a differential approach, these workers carried out spectrophotofluorometric detection and estimation of each of these drugs in the presence of the other in the submicrogram range. More recently this approach was adapted by Chalmers and Wadds (69) to the detection and determination of morphine, codeine, narcotine, and papaverine in mixtures, with the use of trichloroacetic acid to simultaneously quench the fluoroscence of papaverine and intensify that of narcotine; they proposed the applicability of this method to the analysis of single dosage forms.

It has long been recognized that appropriate treatment of weakly fluorescent morphine with concentrated sulfuric acid results in the formation of highly fluorescent material (120, 212); using this approach, Nadeau and Sobolewski (212) were able to estimate quantities of morphine as low as 0.02 µg. Kupferberg et al. (180) effected the oxidation of morphine to the highly fluorescent species pseudomorphine using potassium ferricyanide in weakly alkaline solution. They found fluorometric quantitation of the resulting pseudomorphine adequate for the determination of morphine in plasma and brain tissue at levels as low as 0.1 µg drug; thus the method permitted the determination of plasma levels of free morphine following administration of a therapeutic dose of morphine sulfate. This method is applicable not only to morphine but also to closely related species bearing a free phenolic hydroxyl function (e.g., 6-aminoacetylmorphine and nalorphine), and it does not suffer from interference by compounds such as codeine, heroin, meperidine, and methadone, which lack the appropriate structural features. Subsequently Takemori (266) modified this oxidative procedure to achieve a tenfold increase in sensitivity in the method, which he employed for the determination of plasma and cerebrospinal fluid levels of morphine in dogs after administration of small doses intravenously, and also in the study of morphine transport by rabbit choroid plexus *in vitro*.

The increasing demand in recent years for rapid and sensitive screening tests to detect the presence of morphine in urine has resulted in adaptation of these conventional techniques. Thus Broich (55) evaporated small volumes of urine to dryness and made use of the reaction of morphine and morphine glucuronide with concentrated sulfuric acid followed by the addition of alkali and heat to form fluorescent species; this screening approach eliminated the need both for hydrolytic cleavage of the glucuronide and for extraction from the urine (unless quantitative estimates for free and conjugated morphine were required, in which case an extraction procedure was employed to separate the two species). This method was sensitive in the microgram range.

Retaining this approach to fluorophore development, Mulé and Hushin (210) increased the sensitivity of the method to permit detection of morphine in urine in concentrations as low as 0.22 µg/ml. As in the work of Broich (55), the fluorescence of quinine, a frequently encountered diluent for heroin, served as confirmatory evidence for heroin use. While Mulé and Hushin carried out their fluorescence studies on urinary extracts (as opposed to evaporated urine samples as used by Broich), they too shunned preliminary acid hydrolysis, which would be expected to destroy quinine and produce erratic analytical results. A further gain in rapidity was achieved by use of an automated turret spectrofluorometer, which permitted the routine screening of large numbers of urine samples daily (207, 210)

Goldbaum et al. (125) extended the ferricyanide oxidation procedure to the determination of morphine in urine; these workers, too, considered acid hydrolysis undesirable because of its destruction of quinine and its increased interference and unnecessary because of the very high sensitivity of the method (0.2 μg/ml), which made it quite adequate for detection of heroin-dependent persons. This method has been incorporated into a routine scheme for mass drug screening as reported by Santinga (239). These procedures have been reviewed by Passwater (228).

The oxidation of morphine to pseudomorphine has permitted its facile detection on thin layer chromatograms in concentrations of 0.1 μg and greater; oxidizing spray reagents such as potassium ferricyanide (179) or potassium platinum iodide reagent (291) have been employed in this approach. However, the application of this method to the detection of morphine in urine was reported by Yoshimura et al. (291) to be feasible only when morphine concentrations exceeded 0.2 to 1 μg/ml; this limitation is the result of interference by other fluorescing urinary constituents.

Other narcotic analgesics that have been detected in biological fluids using fluorescence techniques include meperidine and methadone. Dal Cortivo et al. (85) established that meperidine extracted from urine or plasma reacted with a formaldehyde-concentrated sulfuric acid reagent to yield a fluorophore which permitted detection of the drug at levels as low as 300 ng/ml in urine or plasma as well as in post-mortem tissue samples. Quinine, quinidine, and methapyrilene were found to interfere because of their similar fluorescence. Using the same reagents under slightly different conditions McGonigle (195) was able to detect microgram quantities of methadone and showed linearity of fluorescence intensity as a function of methadone concentration over the range 1 to 10 μg. Whereas meperidine, quinine, and amphetamine, which fluoresce similarly, would be expected to interfere with the detection of methadone by this method, various narcotics including morphine, codeine, heroin, and cocaine did not give rise to any interfering fluorescence, nor did they produce any quenching; thus methadone could be determined in the presence of an equal concentration of any of these compounds without prior separation.

The intense native fluorescence of LSD has provided the basis for highly sensitive and specific methods for its detection and quantitation. Genest and Farmilo (121) found the spectrophotofluorometric estimation of LSD in dosage forms to be sufficiently specific that preliminary thin layer chromatographic separation was unnecessary except when other lysergic acid derivatives were present. Fluorometric assay methods have also been reported by Dal Cortivo et al. (84) and Canaff and DeZan (67). Estimation of LSD on thin layer plates by *in situ* fluorometry has been reported by Dal Cortivo et al. (84), and more recently by Niwaguchi and Inoue (220). The latter workers found that a plot of LSD concentration against either LSD emission intensity or the ratio of LSD emission intensity to quinine (internal standard) emission intensity was linear over the range 0.2 to 1.5 μg LSD.

In 1957 Axelrod et al. (16) introduced a spectrofluorometric method for the estimation of LSD in biological samples; a slightly modified procedure was employed by Aghajanian and Bing (2) for its estimation in plasma samples from subjects to whom the drug had been administered intravenously at a dose level of 2 μg/kg. The method was reported to show linearity over the range 0 to 40 ng LSD and to be sensitive to 1 ng drug; thus it was possible to measure plasma levels for an 8-hr period following drug administration. The potential applicability of this method to clinical and toxicological situations has been widely discussed (e.g., ref. 173) and Curry has commented, "Clearly if it is assumed that LSD has been taken, levels of fluorescence can be ascribed to it; unhappily this often cannot be assumed and there seems to be a grey area . . . " (82).

Recently Upshall and Wailling (271) reported a spectrofluorometric method for the quantitation of LSD in human plasma; this method permitted the estimation of LSD in plasma samples up to 5 hr after oral administration of 160 μg drug. Making use of the ultraviolet catalyzed transformation of LSD to a nonfluorescent lumiderivative, these authors used the difference in fluorescence of plasma extracts before and after ultraviolet radiation as a measure of LSD concentration.

Various 1,4-benzodiazepine derivatives, including chlordiazepoxide, diazepam, and oxazepam, develop an intense fluorescence in acid media. This property has provided the basis for their detection and/or quantitation in solution and in dosage forms (65, 181), as well as their detection in biological fluids (90). Other drugs of abuse potential that have been determined in biological fluids using fluorometric methods include pentazocine (36), methyprylon (90), and barbiturates (88, 146, 265).

Many classes of drugs, however, do not have sufficient native fluorescence to permit adequate measurement by fluorometric techniques, and the formation of fluorescent derivatives has proven a useful approach for such compounds. A wide variety of nonfluorescent or extremely weakly fluorescent compounds bearing a primary or secondary amino function or phenolic hydroxyl function have been reacted with 1-dimethylaminonaphthalene-5-sulfonyl chloride (dansyl chloride) to yield fluorescent "dansyl" derivatives. These extremely stable derivatives are reported to be readily detectable on TLC plates and can be eluted and characterized spectrophotofluorometrically (112, 246). Seiler (246) reviewed the advantages of this approach for amines and its applicability to the determination and identification of amines in tissue, and he noted that *in situ* fluorescence measurements show linear relationships over a wide range of concentrations. Cohen and Vogel (74) applied the dansylation approach to the determination of mescaline in rat brain, liver, and plasma and reported the sensitivity of the procedure to be 0.5 μg/g or ml of sample.

Recently Ho et al. (144) reported a thin layer method of greatly improved sensitivity for the detection of morphine and other drugs of abuse in urine or tissue. Their use of "mini" thin layer plates (3 × 3 cm) together with derivatization of the extracted drug(s) using dansyl chloride provided a very rapid screening method, capable of detecting morphine, amphetamine, methamphetamine, and mescaline in quantities of the order of 1 ng. *In situ* scanning of these plates showed a linear relationship of fluorescence intensity over drug concentrations of 1 to 10 ng for the β-phenylethylamine derivatives studied. Although the minimal detectable concentrations of drugs in urine were not reported, the method was shown to be appropriate for monitoring of patients on a methadone maintenance program.

Nix and Hume (221) described a spectrophotofluorometric procedure for the determination of amphetamine in aqueous solutions either alone or in combination with other drugs. The procedure was based on the reaction of amphetamine and acetylacetone to produce a fluorescing lutidine derivative. The authors noted the possibility of interference by methamphetamine (in high concentrations) and phenylethylamine. Stewart and Lotti (258) also reported a fluorometric procedure for determination of amphetamine, methamphetamine, and a variety of amphetamine analogs in dosage forms. Their method, based on the reaction between the amphetamine and 3-carboxy-7-hydroxycoumarin to yield a highly fluorescent salt, was found to give results comparable to other methods, including a dansylation procedure and the acetylacetone method, and was applicable to a wide variety of amines.

Brown and Smart (59) devised a fluorometric method for the assay of methaqualone in plasma at levels characteristic of therapeutic regimens. Methaqualone, selectively extracted from plasma, was reduced by lithium borohydride to the tetrahydroquinazolinone which shows intense fluorescence. This highly sensitive method permitted the use of very small samples of blood (50 to 150 µl).

The growing need for methods of detection of cannabinoids and cannabinoid metabolites in biological samples has generated a number of attempts to employ fluorescence techniques, in the hope that these will provide adequate sensitivity which has been lacking with conventional methods.

Bowd et al. (46) reported on the fluorescence properties of cannabinoids in ethanol solution, noting that all cannabinoids tested (i.e., Δ^8- and Δ^9-THC, CBD, and CBN) showed closely similar behavior; they were characterized by a single prominent peak at 318 nm. On prolonged radiation the spectra changed rapidly, yielding new peaks at 366 and 383 nm. Provided corrections were made for reflected light and intrinsic fluorescence of the solvent, detection of these cannabinoids was possible at levels as low as 10 mg/ml. King and Forney (174) reported the fluorometric determination of CBN and THC in biological samples after administration of these drugs to rats at dose levels of 125 mg/kg.

Other workers have prepared cannabinoid derivatives with a view to obtaining compounds of increased fluorescence intensity, thus increasing the sensitivity of fluorometric assay methods. Bullock et al. (62) condensed these four cannabinoids with malic acid to yield derivatives that were very similar with respect to excitation and emission maxima; hence the method was not useful for distinguishing among the compounds, although CBD gave rise to the most intense fluorescence. This approach permitted quantitation of 0.6 µg Δ^9-THC isolated from a blood plasma sample.

More recently Forrest et al. (111) reported the conversion of various cannabinoids to their dansyl derivatives; all cannabinoids studied (including those noted above and 11-hydroxy- Δ^8-THC) yielded monodansylated species, except for CBD which additionally formed the di-dansyl compound. Mixtures of these derivatives were separated by TLC and individual components were detectable at the 0.5-ng level. This dansylation approach was also studied by Just et al. (161, 162) with respect to Δ^8- and Δ^9-THC. Following multiple-development TLC they used a direct fluorometric estimation procedure for dansyl-THC and carried out mass spectral studies on the eluted compounds. The minimum detectable quantities were 10^{-12} and 10^{-10} moles for fluorometry and mass spectrometry, respectively. Extracts prepared from urine, blood, and saliva samples from subjects who had smoked hashish either in an experimental situation or on a regular basis were reacted with dansyl chloride, separated by two-dimensional TLC, and studied fluorometrically. This technique permitted the detection of THC in saliva and blood of volunteer subjects for periods of at least 2 hrs and in urine for at least 6 hr, with detection being possible in saliva of chronic users for considerably longer periods, even after rinsing the mouth.

4. MASS SPECTROMETRY

Mass spectrometry (MS) has provided the researcher with an unparalleled tool for structure elucidation studies as well as drug identification studies, yielding up very rapidly a vast amount of information about molecular structure from minute samples. To date the majority of the mass spectral data for drugs has originated in electron impact (EI) mass spectrometry, although chemical ionization (CI) mass spectrometry has seen limited use, as exemplified by the work of Fales et al. (100). This latter technique was recently reviewed by Munson (211).

Direct Inlet Mass Spectrometry

Mass spectra obtained by a direct inlet procedure have been reported for many classes of psychoactive drug, studied either as pure compounds or in extracts prepared from dosage forms [e.g., barbiturates (77, 78, 100, 131, 194); methamphetamine (148); hallucinogens including LSD (34, 155, 219), DMT (34, 35) DET (35) MDA (35), various dimethoxyamphetamines (20), STP (34, 231), mescaline (34), LBJ (35), psilocin (34), ditran (148), and benactyzine (35)]. Although this technique has certainly facilitated drug identification, Bellman et al. (35) and more recently Sobol et al. (251) have justifiably noted the usefulness of a combined spectral technique. Bellman et al. pointed out the similarity of the mass spectra of DMT and N-ethyltryptamine and of LBJ (JB-336, N-methyl-3-piperidylbenzilate) and JB-8191 (N-methyl-4-piperidylbenzilate), warning that MS is not generally useful in differentiating such isomers and that reliance on MS alone could lead to errors in identification.

In 1965 Budzikiewciz et al. (61) reported mass spectral data for a number of cannabinoids, including CBN, CBD, Δ^8-THC, and cannabigerol; both these workers and Claussen et al. (71) have discussed cannabinoid fragmentations rearrangement reactions. Over recent years MS has been routinely employed to assist in structure elucidation of cannabinoids of natural or synthetic origin (73, 123, 159, 175, 197, 198, 230, 289) after their isolation by classical techniques, by countercurrent distribution, or by preparative thin layer chromatography.

Mass spectrometry as a tool for structure elucidation has also been important in the study of *Argyreia nervosa* (baby Hawaiian woodrose). Crawford (79) presented and discussed the mass spectra of lysergic acid amide and iso-lysergic acid amide which were isolated from this plant.

Direct insertion MS has also been employed for the analysis of drugs and drug metabolites isolated from body fluids by means of separation techniques such as TLC. Thus Bohn and Rucker (42) were able to identify various barbiturates, carbromal, and bromisoval from autopsy material when the amount present exceeded 20 to 25 µg. Using simliar techniques they determined glutethimide qualitatively in stomach contents and its metabolite α-phenylglutarimide in urine in quantities as small as 15 µg (41). Arnold and Grutzmacher (15) and Palmer et al. (224) isolated products of barbiturate metabolism and used MS in their identification studies. Alfes and Clasing (4) identified d-methamphetamine in urine samples by formation of the dansyl derivative followed by TLC separation and MS investigation. In their studies of the metabolism of diazepam (243), chlordiazepoxide (244), and flurazepam (245) Schwartz and his co-workers used thin layer chromatography for isolation of metabolites, and the eluted metabolites were studied by means of high-resolution MS. Thus MS has been adopted as a routine tool for identification and structure elucidation of isolated drugs and their metabolites.

The direct probe insertion technique has proven extremely useful for the study of relatively pure drugs, but the complexity of the EI spectra of most drugs precludes the use of this sample introduction technique for extracts prepared from biological samples. However, Althaus et al. (5) were able to use the direct insertion technique with high-resolution MS for the investigation of urine extracts for the presence of chlordiazepoxide since this analysis was directed to the detection of chlorine, which is known to be retained in the chlordiazepoxide metabolite structures. Except for such unusual cases there are two general approaches to this problem: (1) separate the extract components before their introduction into the mass spectrometer or (2) use the CI technique. Milne et al. (201) have made use of the CI approach with methane as the carrier gas. This technique results in proton transfer to the drug molecule, resulting in formation of the MH^+ ion of m/e $(M + 1)$ where M is the molecular weight of the drug. This ion is more stable than the odd-electron molecular ion derived via the electron impact technique, and it gives relatively few fragment ions; thus a relatively simple spectrum is obtained. These authors reported CI spectra for a wide range of psychoactive drugs (201, 202) and have shown the application of the technique to total crude gastric extract. Fales et al. (100) discussed the CI mass spectra of various barbiturates when methane is employed as the reactant gas. While noting that intense quasimolecular ions at m/e $(M + 1)^+$ were present for all barbiturates investigated, they were unable to distingish between isomeric barbiturates such as amobarbital and pentobarbital by this method. However, when methane was excluded and the EI spectrum was recorded, the distinction was apparent. The CI technique has also been used by Le Clerc et al. with reference to drug metabolites (184).

Gas Chromatography/Mass Spectrometry

The utility of the mass spectrometer has been greatly enhanced by employing it as a highly sensitive detector for a gas chromatograph, thus permitting the acquisition of detailed structural information for each of the compounds appearing in the column effluent. The nature of appropriate interfacings for such combination units was recently reviewed by Freedman (114). The combination is feasible since the mass spectrometric scan is accomplished in a fraction of the time of emergence of a GC peak and sample sizes appropriate to GC are generally appropriate for MS. The minimal sample size for identification by the gas chromatography/mass spectrometry (GC/MS) technique (total spectrum) has been estimated to be as low as 10^{-10} g (160, 170), significantly less than for other spectroscopic techniques, although Hammar et al. (136) noted that the required sample size is higher for packed columns than for capillary columns.

Repeated analyses using different stationary phases would provide additional criteria of identity. However, column packings of good thermal stability at the relatively high temperatures employed for analysis of drugs are required to avoid excessive background signals. Liquid phases employed in GC/MS systems for analysis of drugs of abuse have included SE-30 (10, 39, 44, 48, 50, 106, 148, 149, 152, 199, 216, 232); Se-52 (122); OV-1 (10, 250); OV-101(119); OV-17 (43, 76, 182, 188, 213); OV-225(216); UC W-98 (263); Carbowax (45) and Carbowax - KOH (31, 39, 44); Apiezon L-KOH (280); and Dexil 300 polycarborane-siloxane (119); in addition, Porapak Q has been used for volatile compounds (250). Thus the phases most commonly employed in current GC studies of psychoactive drugs have proven adequate for use in combined GC/MS systems.

The utility of GC/MS systems is greatly enhanced by the addition of computer capabilities. The principles, design, and applications of GC/MS/ computer systems were recently reviewed by Junk (160) and Karasek (170). Hammer et al. (136) discussed the application of combined systems in the identification of drugs and metabolites.

GC/MS Application to Drugs Per Se

The value of the GC/MS combination in the identification of "street drugs" has been discussed by Holmstedt (147), who reported the sequence of work that led to structure determinations of STP and PCP. Holmstedt and Linnarson (148) presented mass spectra, obtained by means of this combined technique, for LSD, Δ^9 THC, atropine, and scopolamine, while Nakamura et al. (213) reported on heroin in illicit preparations. In their study of amphetamines and closely related compounds using GC, Anggard and Hankey (10) pointed out that, compared with the free bases, amine derivatives could be more readily introduced into the mass spectrometer in small amounts via a GC inlet system, and the mass spectra of the derivatives assumed a more complex character with more abundant peaks at high mass numbers, thus giving more structural information and facilitating positive identification. They considered that the trichloroacetamide was the best overall derivative. In their GC/MS studies of ring-methoxylated amphetamines and mescaline, Narasimhachari and Vouros (216) made use of isothiocyanate derivatives; they reported gas chromatographic and mass spectral data for the isothiocyanate derivatives of mescaline, 3,4- and 2,5-dimethoxyamphetamines, and 2,3,4- and 3,4,6-trimethoxyamphetamines. Narasimhachari (215) recently reported on further studies of these isothiocyanate derivatives. Sadée and van der Kleijn (238) employed GC/MS in the study of the thermolysis at GC temperatures of 1,4-benzodiazepine derivatives including diazepam, oxazepam, and chlordiazepoxide.

A new approach to the use of GC/MS for structure elucidation of cannabinoids is that of Vree et al. (278). They established that the combination of the electron energy and the ion source temperature is an important determinant for the mass spectra of labile cannabis constituents. For various effluent peaks obtained from cannabis extracts they plotted electron voltage versus mass fragment intensity for particular mass fragments. Comparison of these plots for the various extract components provided evidence for the presence in some hashish samples of n-propyl homologs of CBD, Δ^9-THC, and CBN (i.e., cannabidivarin, tetrahydrocannabidivarin, and cannabivarin, respectively) (278, 279). In their study of a Brazilian marihuana sample, they obtained evidence for the methyl homologs of Δ^9-THC and CBN, and a Lebanese hashish sample contained, in addition, the methyl homolog of CBD. For these methyl homologs there have been proposed the trivial names Δ^9-tetrahydrocannabirocol, cannabiorcal, and cannabidiorcol, respectively.

While GC/MS has indeed proven useful in these studies of specific classes of drugs, such systems have the potential for even greater impact in the area of "drug screening" functions, that is, the detection and identification of any of the possible thousands of drugs which might be found on both the licit and illicit markets. Obviously, in such a screening function, the demands on mass spectral data analysis are greatly increased, and manual operation is much more difficult, if not impossible. Law et al. (182) generated a master file of mass spectral data for 58 commonly used psychoactive drugs; they used the five biggest peaks in the mass spectrum, listed in order of decreasing abundance. A computer program provided the means of comparison of experimental data with the file entries. More recently Finkle et al. (106) described a GC/MS reference system for identification of drugs of abuse, reporting mass spectral data for 133 drugs. Each drug was numerically coded by means of the amu value of the base peak, followed in sequence by the m/e of the most intense peak in each group of 14 amu beginning at mass 34 and continuing through mass 453; thus a maximum of 30 peaks is possible for identification of a compound of molecular weight less than 453. A computer program was developed to facilitate the matching of unknowns against the coded library and the selected matches were ranked in order of similarity.

This approach to identification was somewhat less sophisticated than the technique reported by Biemann's laboratory (140). This method included selection of the two largest peaks in each mass unit interval throughout the entire spectrum, selection by the computer of the most similar mass spectra in the library, and calculation of a similarity index as a measure of the degree of match. Application of this technique to drug identification has been reported by Althaus et al. (5) and Costello et al. (76).

GC/MS Application to Drugs in Biological Samples

The identification of drugs in biological samples such as blood, urine, stomach contents, and tissue is frequently made difficult by extremely low concentrations of the drugs together with variable amounts of drug metabolites, and by the presence of normal fluid or tissue components which may contribute to very complex gas chromatographic profiles; this is particularly so when flame ionization detectors are employed, for they couple high sensitivity with very low specificity. Thus the mass spectrometer has been an important advance in the study of such samples, particularly when computer search systems are employed. The applications and advantages of this approach in forensic toxicology have been described by Blomquist et al. (39) and Skinner et al. (250); Law et al. (182), Costello et al. (76), and Milne and Vanden Heuvel (202) have discussed the technique with reference to emergency clinical treatment situations. Althaus et al. (5) have noted that only mass spectrometric analysis of gas chromatographic effluents can provide the necessary structural identification of drugs and their metabolites in approximately 20% of patients comatose after ingestion of unknown drugs; in the remaining 80% of such patients they consider comparison of gas chromatographic retention times to be satisfactory.

Recently Bonnichsen et al. (43) reported a method for identification of barbiturates isolated from less than 50-mg samples of blood or tissue from intoxicated patients. The identification procedure employed a computer program with a master file containing only 43 mass numbers chosen to be characteristic of the spectra of 14 barbiturates. For purposes of general emergency toxicological analysis it is desirable to include in the master file potentially toxic nondrugs (76) as well as normal fluid or tissue components or their artifacts which may be encountered in sample extracts, to minimize potential confusion of these materials with drugs or drug metabolites (182, 202). The inclusion of drug metabolites is, of course, essential because they are frequently found in the fluid together with the unaltered drug. Since the time between drug ingestion and blood sampling is frequently unknown, the concentration ratio of drug to drug metabolites for some psychoactive agents may fall within a very broad range. Moreover, Costello et al. (76) noted that in overdose cases, the distribution of metabolites is often different from that normally encountered after therapeutic dosage. Bonnichsen and Ryhage (45) described a very small GC/MS system constructed specifically for determination of alcohols in aqueous solution. They consider that this approach to determination of blood alcohol levels is highly desirable because it provides greater specificity than other available methods including GC with FID.

Beckett et al. (31) reported the use of GC/MS to provide confirmatory evidence for the presence of amphetamine and methamphetamine in urine samples; they pointed out the utility of this approach in detection of the misuse of these stimulants in sport, noting that these drugs were readily detected at levels of 10 to 20 μg per sample, levels significantly lower than the 50 to 100 μg per sample required for linked GC-infrared systems. Brandenberger (48) reported a rapid method for detection of amphetamine in urine using sodium carbonate to release amphetamine into the vapor phase above the urine sample, and GC/MS for analysis of the vapor phase. A more refined approach to amphetamine detection in urine involved ether extraction of the amphetamine, formation of the isothiocyanate, which is superior to the free base for gas chromatographic determination, and analysis of the resulting material by GC/MS. Bonnichsen et al. (44) reported GC/MS determination of amphetamine and phenometrazine in blood samples taken from impaired drivers; they were able to detect characteristic peaks even when the amount of drug presented to the mass spectrometer was of the order of 5 ng.

Studies of metabolic transformations of a wide variety of drug molecules are being facilitated by GC/MS. Milne and Vanden Heuvel noted that following the administration of ^{14}C-labeled drugs, duplicate gas chromatographic analyses using both radioactivity monitoring and mass spectrometer monitoring may provide a means for the detection and identification of drug metabolites in biological fluids (202). They also noted the potential advantage of stable isotope labeling of drugs for biotransformation investigations in providing readily detectable doublets in the mass spectra.

Gilbert et al. (122) found that a number of barbiturate metabolites could be separated and characterized by the application of GC/MS when analysis was carried out in the N,N-dimethyl derivatives. In their study of phenobarbital metabolism in the rat, Horning and Horning (149) treated the isolated materials with diazomethane and then BSTFA, so that barbiturates would be present as N,N-dimethyl derivatives while hydroxylated metabolites would be present as N,N-dimethyl-TMSi ethers. Palmer et al. (224) also employed GC/MS in their studies of canine metabolism of pentobarbital.

Vree et al. (280) used the technique in their study of deuterium isotope effects in the metabolism of N-alkyl-substituted amphetamines in man. The determination of the ratio of deuterated to nondeuterated amphetamine in a mixture of compounds was accomplished by taking the ratio of the base peaks and relating this to a calibration curve (base peak ratio versus concentration ratio) prepared using known mixtures.

Ahlborg et al. (3) employed GC/MS in their study of the fate and metabolism of some hallucinogenic indoleakylamines. Urine extracts collected from rats after administration of dimethyltryptamine, 5-hydroxydimethyltryptamine, and 5-methoxydimethyltryptamine were examined, and it was determined that the main excretion products were the corresponding indoleacetic acids.

The increasing use of methadone in the treatment of heroin dependence has generated renewed interest in its distribution, metabolism, and excretion. In their investigations of this drug Pohland and his co-workers (232, 263) employed GC/MS for the identification of two major metabolites 2-ethylidene-1,5-dimethyl-3,3-diphenyl pyrrolidine and its N-demethylation product, 2-ethyl-5-methyl-3,3-diphenyl-1-pyrroline. Recent GC/MS studies of Sullivan et al. (264) extended this work, providing evidence for the presence of a ring-hydroxylated derivative of each of these compounds present as a glucuroxide or sulfate conjugate, as well as the compound 4-dimethylamino-2,2-diphenylpentanoic acid. Studies by Beckett et al. (32) resulted in the identification of yet another metabolite, methadone-N-oxide.

A number of authors have reported the use of GC/MS systems for investigations of psychoactive drugs and/or drug metabolites in blood and/or urine from neonatal patients (76, 142, 152). Such studies have permitted clarification of the significance of transplacental drug distribution and diffusion of drugs and/or drug metabolites into milk, and they have increased our understanding of neonatal drug metabolism. Thus Horning et al. (152)

found differences between the neonate's capacity to hydroxylate barbiturates and the ability to effect N-demethylation of caffeine. Billets et al. (38) noted that the limited ability of many infants to effect glucuronide conjugation of drugs and drug metabolites emphasizes the need for qualitative and quantitative analysis of these intact glucuronides as an aid in rational adjustment of therapeutic dosages. Both of these reports noted the application of mass spectrometry to intact glucuronide detection.

Mass Fragmentography (Specific Ion Detection)

Although the normal mode of GC/MS use involves the scanning of the entire mass (spectral) range for each peak to be investigated in the effluent, the mass spectrometer has been adapted to monitor only fragments of particular m/e values, either a single m/e value (hence the term "single ion detection") or two or three different m/e values. This is feasible because of the availability of an accelerating voltage alternator unit which makes possible the recording of the ion intensities of three mass numbers within a short time interval when these mass numbers fall within a fairly narrow mass range. This technique of mass fragmentography uses the mass spectrometer as an extremely selective and highly sensitive detector for the gas chromatograph. The high sensitivity is achieved by amplification of the signals by an electron multiplier. It thus permits the detection of components present in very low concentration or those present together with large amounts of other materials which would swamp the component(s) of interest if a conventional detector were employed. Thus this technique frequently permits use of a simplified isolation procedure.

The technique of mass fragmentography was introduced by Hammar et al. in 1968 (137) in their study of the metabolites of chlorpromazine in human blood. From their study of the mass fragmentation patterns of a series of chlorophenothiazines, these workers were able to select appropriate mass numbers for monitoring extracts of plasma and red blood cells and succeeded in detecting chlorpromazine in quantities as low as 10^{-12} g (as compared with 10^{-9} g by ECD and 10^{-8} g when "total ion current" was used for detection of the gas chromatograph effluent).

Recent advances in this technique have been reported by Hammar (134), who also discussed its application to the study of the tricyclic antidepressant nortriptyline and some of its metabolites in plasma, urine, and cerebrospinal fluid (134, 135). Other drugs whose detection and metabolism have been studied in this manner include amphetamine (39, 44, 48, 280), methamphetamine (48), dimethylamphetamine (272), phenmetrazine (39,

44), trichloroethylene (39), phenobarbital (149), and diazepam (250). Skinner et al. (250) noted the application of this technique to chlordiazepoxide, d-propoxyphene, meperidine, methadone, atropine, dilaudid, and morphine, and Bogentoft et al. (40) sought to apply this approach to the identification and determination of methaqualone metabolites in blood.

Brandenberger and Schnyder (50) made use of the isothiocyanate derivatives of amphetamine, mescaline, and STP for detection of picogram quantities of these compounds in biological systems using mass-specific detection. The isothiocyanate derivatives provided much simpler mass spectra with few intensive ions as compared with the free bases.

Recently Mikes et al. (199) used mass fragmentography as well as conventional GC/MS in their study of the metabolism and excretion of Δ^9-THC in the rat. They noted that whereas the total ion current detection limit for Δ^9-THC is about 10 ng, the detection limit for this compound using mass fragmentography is about 20 pg. In their use of mass fragmentography for the detection of Δ^9-THC, these authors focused on mass numbers known to be typical for THC: $m/e = 314$, molecular peak; $m/e = 231$, base peak; and $m/e = 313$, M^+-H. In screening for monohydroxylated Δ^9-THC, they selected $m/e = 330, 231, 313$, and for an O-methylated metabolite $m/e = 328$. They were able to detect unchanged Δ^9-THC in urine and feces, and after glucuronidase treatment of feces, they detected CBN and Δ^9-THC. Dihydroxy- Δ^9-THC was obtained in bile. Skinner (249) also reported the use of mass fragmentography for the detection of Δ^9-THC and its metabolites in urine and blood from rats receiving Δ^9-THC and in urine from marihuana smokers. He found that the best results were obtained by monitoring m/e 299, with the sensitivity being in the picogram range.

Brooks and Middleditch (57) explored the practicability of GC/MS for quantitative estimations using single ion monitoring, that is, the process in which ions of one characteristic m/e value are selectively detected during chromatography. In their study of ethylestrenol and ethynylestrenol they noted limits of detection of 10 and 40 pg, respectively, with direct correlation of peak height and sample size over the range 50 to 1000 pg. Recently Draffan et al. (96) used single ion monitoring of the GC effluent as a quantitative detector for barbiturates and their metabolites at levels of less than 50 ng. They sought to apply the method to the study of the neonatal metabolism of amylobarbitone using plasma samples and to a study of the mixed function oxidases of human liver by means of microscale incubations of barbiturate using liver tissue obtained by needle biopsy.

5. IMMUNOCHEMICAL METHODS

In 1970 Spector and Parker (255) reported the development of a radioimmunoassay procedure for morphine. Morphine was converted to 3-O-carboxymethylmorphine, which was coupled to bovine serum albumin in the presence of a carbodiimide; the resulting carboxymethylmorphine-BSA was used to immunize rabbits, from whom antiserum was subsequently collected. It was determined that ^{3}H-labeled dihydromorphine would bind to the antibody, and this complex could be precipitated using ammonium sulfate; the radioactivity of the precipitate, reflecting the amount of bound ^{3}H-dihydromorphine, could then be measured by means of a liquid-scintillation spectrometer. However, the addition of morphine to a preparation of antiserum and ^{3}H-dihydromorphine resulted in competitive inhibition of the ^{3}H-dihydromorphine for the formation of antibody-hapten complex; hence the antibody-bound radioactivity measured in the resulting precipitate was decreased compared with the control. The preparation of a standard curve using varying quantities of morphine permitted the method to be used for quantitation of morphine in an unknown sample. This radioimmunoassay method was shown by Spector (253) to detect morphine at a level of 100 pg with a variability of ± 10%, and it was used for quantitative estimations of morphine plasma levels in pharmacokinetic studies of morphine in rats. In a study of the specificity of this reaction a comparison was made of the concentrations of various morphine congeners required to effect 50% inhibition of the antibody-^{3}H-dihydromorphine complex formation; codeine, normorphine, and heroin were found to be effective inhibitors with efficacy similar to that of morphine, while morphine-3-glucuronide, methadone, and nalorphine required a concentration 500 times greater, and dextromethorphan and levallorphan showed no effect at levels 500 times that of morphine. The low efficacy of morphine-3-glucuronide suggests that estimates of morphine levels in plasma would include a small contribution from this major morphine metabolite.

Using the same immunization technique Adler and Liu (1) confirmed the efficacy of Spector and Parker's radioimmunoassay technique. They also developed a hemiagglutination-inhibition test for morphine using sheep erythrocytes coated with carboxymethylmorphine conjugated to rabbit serum albumin, and they showed that this test was sensitive to morphine concentrations as low as 1 ng/ml. Since methadone was a much less effective inhibitor than morphine (by a factor of 10^3 to 10^4), it appears that this rapid and inexpensive test could be potentially applicable for the detection of heroin use by patients on a methadone maintenance regimen.

For their studies of antibodies to morphine Van Vunakis et al. (275)

conjugated carboxymethylmorphine to poly-L-lysine with carbodiimide and used the resulting conjugate complexed to succinylated hemocyanin for immunization. Since the rabbit antibodies produced showed relatively weak binding constants with ^{14}C-morphine, these workers developed a radioimmunoassay for morphine, utilizing a multivalent copolymer-carboxymethylmorphine conjugate in which the tyrosine of the copolymer was labeled with ^{125}I. In addition to their investigation of this assay technique for the detection of "morphine-related" compounds in autopsy blood samples, they initiated studies aimed at the detection of antibodies to morphine. Serum samples taken from rats injected with polylysine-carboxymethylmorphine conjugates or with human serum albumin-morphine conjugates were shown to have antimorphine activity as reflected in their capacity to compete with the calibrated anticarboxymethylmorphine for the ^{125}I-copolymer-carboxymethylmorphine.

Spector and Flynn (254, 255) extended radioimmunoassay techniques to the determination of barbiturates. They converted 5-allyl-(1-carboxyisopropyl) barbituric acid to 5-allyl-5-(1-*p*-nitrophenyloxycarbonylisopropyl) barbituric acid, which was then coupled to bovine gamma globulin (BGG) in the presence of dicyclohexylcarbodiimide, and the resulting barbiturate-BGG was used for immunization of albino rabbits. Antiserum produced was shown to bind ^{14}C-pentobarbital or ^{14}C-barbital. The radioimmunoassay was based on the competition between unlabeled barbiturate and a standard of ^{14}C-barbiturate for combination with barbiturate antibodies in rabbit antisera, in a procedure analogous to Spector's radioimmunoassay for morphine. This technique permitted detection of barbiturate at levels as low as 500 pg and was applicable to quantitation of barbiturate in aqueous solution, plasma, urine, and brain homogenate. Studies of the specificity of the barbiturate-antibody reaction indicated that structural requirements for the drug molecule include a six-membered ring containing a urea moiety (without *N*-substitution) together with carbonyl functions at the 4 and 6 positions; replacement of the urea moiety by a thiourea moiety resulted in decreased affinity for antibody. Although differences in substitution at position 5 of the ring were tolerated, the inactivity of the 5,5-dihydrogen analog (barbituric acid) suggested that the substituents at position C_5 contribute to binding to the antibody. From these findings it seems that barbiturate metabolites in which a C^1 side chain is oxidized to yield a hydroxylated or carboxylated species (and may be subsequently conjugated) would also react with antibody. Therefore it is possible that accurate estimation of unmetabolized barbiturate might require a preliminary extraction procedure.

Van Vunakis and her co-workers studied production of antibodies to other hallucinogenic compounds including mescaline and STP (273) as well as to lysergic acid (274) and developed a radioimmunoassay procedure based on this latter reaction. Their studies indicated that the specificity of the lysergamide-antilysergamide reaction is relatively low, since LSD and several ergot alkaloids were more potent competitors than lysergic acid, whereas tryptamine analogs bearing N,N-dimethyl substitution and mescaline were somewhat less effective competitors. Although a number of these competitive species do show hallucinogenic activity, the relatively low specificity raises some question about the potential utility of this technique in clinical situations. Nevertheless, there has been a recent report of the detection of LSD in human subjects using a radioimmunoassay technique (13).

The possibility of an immunological approach to the assay of cannabinoids in biological samples led Grant et al. (129) to couple Δ^9-THC to paraminobenzoic acid to form a hapten, which was purified and coupled using cyclohexycarbodiimide to keyhole limpet hemocyanin (KLH). The resulting THC-azobenzoyl-KLH conjugate, injected into rabbits, gave rise to antibodies. It was shown that THC-azobenzoic acid (ATHC) and its reduced fluorescent hydrazo derivative have excitation spectra which overlap with the emission peak of the antibody, thus permitting efficient energy transfer as a result of specific binding. Since Δ^9-THC was shown to effect quantitative competitive displacement of ATHC from the ATHC-antibody conjugate, thus inhibiting the ATHC quenching of antibody fluorescence, these workers suggested that this conjugate might prove to be a useful reagent for fluorometric or isotopic methods of analysis for Δ^9-THC.

Leute and his co-workers (186,187) recently reported the development of a spin immunoassay or free radical assay technique (FRAT^{tm}) for the determination of morphine. They sensitized rabbits to morphine by injection of carboxymethylmorphine-bovine serum albumin, and they used ammonium sulfate precipitation to isolate the γ-globulin fraction of serum. A spin-labeled analog of morphine (I) was prepared by introducing a stable nitroxide radical at position C_3 of the morphine molecule, the position of the haptene used to couple albumin in the preparation of the antigen. When this spin-labeled morphine was complexed with antibody, the electron spin resonance spectrum showed very broad peaks reflecting the relatively slow tumbling of the free radical because of its immobilization by the antigen. When morphine (in solution, urine, or saliva) was added it effected displacement of the spin-labeled hapten; this free spin-labeled morphine, now free to tumble rapidly in solution, gave rise to three sharp spectral peaks, whose amplitude reflected the number of free spin-labeled molecules. Studies of specificity indicated that codeine, hydrocodone, and ethylmorphine had a greater affinity for antibody than did morphine, while

[Chemical structure labeled I, showing a pyrrolidine ring with -HNOC-CH₂-O- linker attached to a morphine-like structure with HO, O, and NCH₃ groups]

I

binding of the 3-O-glucuronide metabolite of morphine was slightly less than that for the parent compound; methadone and propoxyphene did not effect significant displacement of the spin-labeled species. Leute et al. (186) noted that there are few cross-reacting drugs of other families and that barbiturates, amphetamines, and cocaine do not cross-react. However, the data presented suggest that the commonly used cough suppressant dextromethorphan might be expected to yield false positives, and that other classes of drugs used at extremely high dose levels by drug abusers might be difficult to distinguish from extremely low levels of morphine. Nevertheless, in a study of normal subjects there was a wide separation of results between those who had recently used codeine and the remainder of the group. This technique made it possible to determine morphine at levels as low as 0.285 μg/ml.

Rubinstein, Schneider, et al. (237, 240) reported the use of homogeneous enzyme immunoassay based on the principle presented in Eq. 1.

$$\underbrace{\text{(enzyme-drug): antibody}}_{\text{enzyme-inactive}} + \text{drug} \rightleftarrows \underbrace{\text{(enzyme-drug)}}_{\text{enzyme active}} + \text{antibody: drug} \quad (1)$$

When an enzyme labeled with a drug was complexed with an antibody against the drug, the enzyme was rendered inactive. However, free drug present in a sample such as urine displaced from the antibody a corresponding quantity of enzyme-drug, with consequent reactivation of this enzyme. In the presence of an appropriate substrate this reactivated enzyme could be measured and related back to the quantity of drug present in the sample. Screening of a large number of urine samples from patients in a methadone maintenance program indicated that the method has greater sensitivity for opiates than does TLC. However, the reported background level for urine samples from a normal population (< 0.3 μg/ml opiate) raises some doubt concerning the applicability of the technique to situations outside of a methadone program, or indeed in those programs in which urine screening is carried out less frequently than daily and in which it is important to detect extremely low concentrations of morphine residual from much earlier use.

The immunoassay techniques show sufficiently high sensitivity that the time-consuming preliminary hydrolysis and/or extraction procedures used with TLC methods are unnecessary. As compared with radioimmunoassay techniques, spin immunoassay and homogeneous enzyme immunoassay eliminate the need for precautions appropriate for the handling of radiolabeled materials as well as the need for a separation procedure for displaced labeled compounds. In addition, this latter technique offers the relative simplicity of a spectrophotometric measurement for transformed substrate. In general these techniques show a much lower sensitivity to methadone than to morphine, thus making them appropriate for detection of heroin use by patients participating in methadone maintenance programs; in such a situation a positive response resulting from the presence of a morphine metabolite could also constitute an advantage. In his discussion of testing for drugs as part of clinical programs, de Angelis (89) noted that both positive and negative urine screening results may be important in the interaction between counselor and patient; the possibility of immediate feedback of results using the spin immunoassay technique should facilitate better utilization of screening results in this context. However, in many programs urine screening serves not only to detect heroin use but also to detect use of amphetamines and barbiturates and to monitor the patient's continuing use of prescribed methadone. Thus there remains further developmental work in the immunoassay techniques to permit this broader range screening.

REFERENCES

1. Adler, F. L. and C.-T. Liu, Detection of morphine by hemagglutination-inhibition, *J. Immunol.*, **106,** 1684 (1971).
2. Aghajanian, G. K. and O. H. L. Bing, Persistence of lysergic acid diethylamide in the plasma of human subjects, *Clin. Pharmacol. Ther.*, **5,** 611 (1964).
3. Ahlborg, U., B. Holmstedt, and J.-E. Lindgren, Fate and metabolism of some hallucinogenic indolealkylamines, *Adv. Pharmacol.*, **6,** Suppl. B, 213 (1968).
4. Alfes, H. and D. Clasing, Identifizierung geringer Mengen Methamphetamins nach Korperpassage dürch Kopplung von Dunnschichtchromatographie und Massenspektrometrie, IV. Mitteilung zum Problem des Doping, *Deut. Z. Gericht. Med.*, **64,** 235 (1969).
5. Althaus, J. R., K. Biemann, J. Biller, P. F. Donaghue, D. A. Evans, H. J. Forester, H. S. Hertz, C. E. Hignite, R. C. Murphy, G. Preti, and V. Rein-

hold, Identification of the drug Darvon and its metabolites in the urine of a comatose patient using a gas chromatograph-mass spectrometer-computer system, *Experientia,* **26,** 714 (1970).
6. Anders, M. W. and G. J. Mannering, New peak-shift technique for gas-liquid chromatography, *Anal. Chem.,* **34,** 730 (1962).
7. Andersen, J. M., E. Nielsen, J. Schou, A. Steentoft, and K. Worm, A specific method for the demonstration of cannabis intake by TLC of urine, *Acta Pharmacol. Toxicol.,* **29,** 111 (1971).
8. Anggard, E., L.-M. Gunne, L.-E. Jonsson, and F. Niklasson, Pharmacokinetic and clinical studies on amphetamine dependent subjects, *Eur. J. Clin. Pharmacol.,* **3,** 3 (1970).
9. Änggärd, E., L. M. Gunne, and F. Niklasson, Gas chromatographic determination of amphetamine in blood, tissue, and urine, *Scand. J. Clin. Lab. Invest.,* **26,** 137 (1970).
10. Änggärd, E. and A. Hankey, Derivatives of sympathomimetic amines for gas chromatography with electron capture detection and mass spectrometry, *Acta Chem. Scand.,* **23,** 3110 (1969).
11. Angrist, B. M., J. Schweitzer, A. J. Friedhoff, S. Gershon, L. J. Hekimian, and A. Floyd, The clinical symptomatology of amphetamine psychosis and its relationship to amphetamine levels in urine, *Int. Pharmacopsychiat.,* **2,** 125 (1969).
12. Anonymous, Direct fluorometric and spectrofluorometric quantification of TLC plates, *Fluorescence News,* 3, 3 (1968).
13. Anonymous, *Microgram,* **5,** 83 (1972).
14. Antun, F., J. R. Smythies, F. Benington, R. D. Morin, C. F. Barfknecht, and D. E. Nichols, Native fluorescence and hallucinogenic potency of some amphetamines,*Experientia,* **27,** 62 (1971).
15. Arnold, W. and H. F. Grützmacher, Identification of barbiturate metabolites by means of mass-spectrometry and infrared-spectroscopy, *Arch. Toxikol.,* **25,** 200 (1969).
16. Axelrod, J., R. O. Brady, B. Witkop, and E. V. Evarts, The distribution and metabolism of lysergic acid diethylamide, *Ann. N.Y. Acad. Sci.,* **66,** 435 (1957).
17. Baden, M. M., N. N. Valanju, S. K. Verma, and S. N. Valanju, Confirmed identification of biotransformed drugs of abuse in urine, *Am. J. Clin. Pathol.,* **57,** 43 (1972).
18. Baggot, J. D. and L. E. Davis, Pharmacokinetic study of amphetamine elimination in dogs and swine, *Biochem. Pharmacol.,* **21,** 1967 (1972).
19. Baggot, J. D., L. E. Davis, and C. A. Neff, Extent of plasma protein binding of amphetamine in different species, *Biochem. Pharmacol.,* **21,** 1813 (1972).
20. Bailey, K., The mass spectra of dimethoxyamphetamine hydrochlorides, *Anal. Chim. Acta,* **60,** 287 (1972).

21. Bartz, A. M. and H. D. Ruhl, Rapid scanning infrared-gas chromatography instrument, *Anal. Chem.*, **36**, 1892 (1964).
22. Baselt, R. C. and L. J. Casarett, Detection of drugs in urine for methadone treatment programs, *J. Chromatog.*, **57**, 139 (1971).
23. Bastos, M. L., G. E. Kananen, R. M. Young, J. R. Monforte, and I. Sunshine, Detection of basic organic drugs and their metabolites in urine, *Clin. Chem.*, **16**, 931 (1970).
24. Baylis, E. M., D. E. Fry, and V. Marks, Micro-determination of serum phenobarbitone and diphenylhydantoin by gas-liquid chromatography, *Clin. Chim. Acta.*, **30**, 93 (1970).
25. Beckett, A. H. and L. G. Brookes, The absorption and urinary excretion in man of fenfluramine and its main metabolite, *J. Pharm. Pharmacol.*, **19**, 42S (1967).
26. Beckett, A. H., A. C. Moffat, M. Rowland, G. T. Tucker, and G. R. Wilkinson, Observations on the gas chromatographic behaviour of some amines used in anorectic formulations, *J. Chromatog.*, **30**, 199 (1967).
27. Beckett, A. H. and M. Rowland, A specific method for the determination of amphetamine in urine, *J. Pharm. Pharmacol.*, **16**, 27T (1964).
28. Beckett, A. H. and M. Rowland, Determination and identification of amphetamine in urine, *J. Pharma. Pharmacol.*, **17**, 59 (1965).
29. Beckett, A. H. and M. Rowland, Urinary excretion kinetics of amphetamine in man, *J. Pharm. Pharmacol.*, **17**, 628 (1965).
30. Beckett, A. H. and M. Rowland, Urinary excretion kinetics of methylamphetamine in man, *J. Pharm. Pharmacol.*, **17**, 109S (1965).
31. Beckett, A. H., G. T. Tucker, and A. G. Moffatt, Routine detection and identification in urine of stimulants and other drugs, some of which may be used to modify performance in sport, *J.Pharm. Pharmacol.*, **19**, 273 (1967).
32. Beckett, A. H., D. P. Vaughn, and E. E. Essien, N-Oxidation—An important route in the metabolism of methadone in man, *J. Pharm. Pharmacol.*, **24**, 244 (1972).
33. Beckett, A. H. and G. R. Wilkinson, Identification and determination of ephedrine and its congeners in urine by gas chromatography, *J. Pharm. Pharmacol.*, **17,,** 104S (1965).
34. Bellman, S. W., Mass spectral identification of some hallucinogenic drugs, *J. Assoc. Off. Anal. Chem.*, **51**, 164 (1968).
35. Bellman, S., J. Turczan, and T. Kram, Spectrometric forensic chemistry of hallucinogenic drugs, *J. Forensic Sci.*, **15**, 261 (1970).
36. Berkowitz, B. A., J. H. Asling, S. M. Shnider, and E. L. Way, Relationship of pentazocine plasma levels to pharmacological activity in man, *Clin. Pharmacol. Ther.*, **10**, 320 (1968).
37. Betts, T. J. and P. J. Holloway, Chromatographic identification of cannabis, *J. Pharm. Pharmacol.*, **19**, 97S (1967).

38. Billets, S., P. S. Lietman, and C. Fenselau, Structurally significant fragmentation of urinary glucuronides, paper presented at the 20th Annual Conference on Mass Spectrometry and Allied Topics, Dallas. Texas, June 4–9, 1972.
39. Blomquist, M., R. Bonnichsen, C.-G. Fri, Y. Mårde, and R. Ryhage, Gas chromatography-mass spectrometry in forensic chemistry for identification of substances isolated from tissue, *Z. Rechtsmed.,* **69,** 52 (1971).
40. Bogentoft, C., Ö. Ericsson, B. Danielsson, J.-E. Lingren, and B. Holmstedt, Mass spectrometry of methaqualone metabolites. Fragmentation of the monohydroxy derivatives, *Acta Pharm. Suec.,* **9,** 151 (1972).
41. Bohn, G. and R. Rücker, Use of a combination of thin layer chromatography and mass spectrometry in the determination of glutethimide in organ material, *Arch. Toxikol.,* **23,** 221 (1968).
42. Bohn, G. and G. Rücker, Detection of barbituric acid derivatives by mass spectrometry in autopsy material after separation by thin layer chromatoraphy, *Arch. Toxikol.,* **25,** 95 (1969).
43. Bonnichsen, R., C.-G. Fri, B. Hedfjäll, and R. Ryhage, Identification of barbiturates by computerized mass spectrometry, *Z. Rechtsmed.,* **70,** 150 (1972).
44. Bonnichsen, R., A. C. Maehly, Y. Marde, R. Ryhage, and B. Schubert, Determination and identification of sympathomimetic amines in blood samples from drivers by a combination of gas chromatography and mass spectrometry, *Z. Rechtsmed.,* **67,** 19 (1970).
45. Bonnichsen, R. and R. Ryhage, Determination of ethyl alcohol using gas chromatography-mass spectrometry as a routine method, *Blutalkohol,* **8,** 241 (1971).
46. Bowd, A., P. Byron, J. B. Hudson, and J. H. Turnbull, Ultraviolet absorption and luminescence properties of some cannabis constituents, *Talanta,* **18,** 697 (1971).
47. Bowman, M. C. and M. Beroza, Apparatus combining gas chromatography with spectrophotofluorometry by means of a flowing liquid interface, *Anal. Chem.,* **40,** 535 (1968).
48. Brandenberger, H., Die Gaschromatographie in der toxikologischen Analytik. Verbesserung von Selektivität und Empfindlichkeit dürch einsatz multipler Detektoren, *Pharm. Acta Helv.,* **45,** 394 (1970).
49. Brandenberger, H. and E. Hellbach, Gaschromatographic determination of amphetamine as (1-phenyl-iso-pr)-isothiocyanate, *Helv. Chim. Acta,* **50,** 958 (1967).
50. Brandenberger, H. and D. Schnyder, Trace analysis of biological active amines (amphetamines, catechol amines, halluzinogenes), in the body by gas chromatography with mass specific detection (multiple ion detection), *Z. Anal. Chem.,* **259,** 210 (1972).

51. Brandt, R., S. Ehrlich-Rogozinsky, and N. D. Cheronis, Spectrophotofluorometric method for the microdetection and estimation of morphine and codeine, *Microchem. J.,* **5,** 215 (1961).
52. Brochmann-Hanssen, E. and T. A. Oke, Gas chromatography of barbiturates, phenolic alkaloids and xanthine bases: Flash-heater methylation by means of trimethylanilinium hydroxide, *J. Pharm. Sci.,* **58,** 370 (1969).
53. Brochmann-Hanssen, E. and A. B. Svendsen, Separation and identification of sympathomimetic amines by gas-liquid chromatography, *J. Pharm. Sci.,* **51,** 938 (1962).
54. Brochmann-Hanssen, E. and A. B. Svendsen, Quantitative determination of morphine in opium by gas-liquid chromatography, *J. Pharm. Sci.,* **52,** 1134 (1963).
55. Broich, J. R., Simultaneous spectrophotofluorometric determination of morphine and quinine from biological specimens, *Fluorescence News,* **4,** 7 (1969).
56. Broich, J. R., D. B. Hoffman, S. J. Goldner, S. Andryauskasis, and C. J. Umberger, Liquid-solid extraction of lyophilized biological material for forensic analysis, I. Application to urine samples for detection of drugs of abuse, *J. Chromatog.,* **63,** 309 (1971).
57. Brooks, C. J. W. and B. S. Middleditch, The mass spectrometer as a gas chromatographic detector, *Clin. Chim. Acta,* **34,** 145 (1971).
58. Brown, R. A., J. M. Kelliher, J. J. Heigl, and C. W. Warren, Rapid scan infrared spectrometer for operation with support coated open tubular or packed column gas chromatographs, *Anal. Chem.,* **43,** 353 (1971).
59. Brown, S. S. and G. A. Smart, Fluorimetric assay of methaqualone in plasma by reduction to 1,2,3,4-tetrahydro-2-methyl-4-oxo-3-*o*-tolylquinazoline, *J. Pharm. Pharmacol.,* **21,** 466 (1969).
60. Bruce, R. B. and W. R. Maynard, Jr., Determination of amphetamine and related amines in blood by gas chromatography, *Anal. Chem.,* **41,** 976 (1969).
61. Budzikiewicz, H., R. T. Alpin, D. A. Lightner, C. Djerassi, R. Mechoulam, and Y. Gaoni, Massenspektroskopie und ihre Anwendung auf strukturelle und stereochemische Probleme—LXVIII, *Tetrahedron,* **21,** 1881 (1965).
62. Bullock, F. J., R. J. Bruni, and E. Werner, A fluorescence assay of submicrogram amounts of cannabis constituents in biological fluids, paper presented to the American Chemical Society, September 1970.
63. Burchfield, H. P., R. J. Wheeler, and J. B. Bernos, Fluorescence detector for analysis of polynuclear arenes by gas chromatography, *Anal. Chem.,* **43,** 1976 (1971).
64. Caddy, B., F. Fish, and W. D. C. Wilson, Gas chromatography of Indian hemp *(Cannabis sativa L), J. Pharm. Pharmacol.,* **19,** 851 (1967).
65. Caille, G., J. Braun, and J. A. Mockle, Spectrofluorometric and polarographic analysis of pharmaceutical dosage forms of 1,4-benzodiazepine derivatives, *Can. J. Pharm. Sci.,* **5,** 78 (1970).

66. Canaff, R. F., Fluorimetric determination of STP and MDA, *Microgram,* **3,** 123 (1970).
67. Canaff, R. E. and P. De Zan, Determination of LSD in illicit preparations by fluorescence spectroscopy, *Microgram,* **3,** 194 (1970).
68. Capella, P. and E. C. Horning, Separation and identification of derivatives of biologic amines by gas-liquid chromatography, *Anal. Chem.,* **38,** 316 (1966).
69. Chalmers, R. A. and G. A. Wadds, Spectrofluorimetric analysis of mixtures of the principal opium alkaloids, *Analyst.,* **95,** 234 (1970).
70. Claussen, U., W. Borger, and F. Korte, Gaschromatographische Analyse der Inhaltsstoffe des Hanfes, *Ann. Chem.,* **693,** 158 (1966).
71. Claussen, U., H. W. Fehlhaber, and F. Korte, Massenspektrometrische Bestimmung von Haschisch-Inhaltsstoffen-II, *Tetrahedron,* **22,** 3535 (1966).
72. Claussen, U. and F. Korte, Herkunft, Wirkung und Synthese der Inhaltsstoffe des Haschisch, *Naturwiss.,* **21,** 541 (1966).
73. Claussen, U., F. V. Spulak, and F. Korte, Zur chemischen Klassifizierung von Pflanzen, XXXI, Haschisch—X. Cannabichromen, ein neuer Haschish —Inhaltsstoff, *Tetrahedron,* **22,** 1477 (1966).
74. Cohen, I. and W. H. Vogel, An assay procedure for mescaline and its determination in rat brain, liver and plasma, *Experientia,* **26,** 1231 (1970).
75. Cook, J. G. H., C. Riley, R. F. Nunn, and D. E. Budgen, Gas chromatography of methyl derivatives of some barbiturates, *J. Chromatog.,* **6,** 182 (1961).
76. Costello, C. D., T. Sakai, and K. Biemann, Identification of drugs in body fluids, particularly in emergency cases of acute poisoning, Paper presented at the 20th Annual Conference on Mass Spectrometry and Allied Topics, Dallas, Texas, June 4–9, 1972.
77. Costopanagiotis, A. and H. Budzikiewicz, Massenspektroskopie in der Drogenanalyse die Massenspektren von Barbitursäurederivaten, *Monatsch. Chem.,* **96,** 1800 (1965).
78. Coutts, R. T. and R. A. Locock, Identification of medicinal barbiturates by means of mass spectrometry, *J. Pharm. Sci.,* **57,** 2096 (1968).
79. Crawford, K. W., The identification of lysergic acid amide in baby Hawaiian woodrose by mass spectrometry, *J. Forenic Sci.,* **15,** 588 (1970).
80. Cummins, L. M., Y. C. Martin, and E. E. Scherfling, Serum and urine levels of ethchlorvynol in man, *J. Pharm. Sci.,* **60,** 261 (1971).
81. Curry, A. S., *Advances in Forensic and Clinical Toxicology,* The Chemical Rubber Co. Press, Cleveland, 1972.
82. Curry, A. S., *Advances in Forensic and Clinical Toxicology,* Chemical Rubber Co. Press, Cleveland, 1972, p. 49.
83. Curry, A. S., J. F. Read, C. Brown, and R. W. Jenkins, Micro infra-red spectroscopy of gas chromatographic fractions, *J. Chromatog,* **38,** 200 (1968).
84. Dal Cortivo, L. A., J. R. Broich, A. Dihrberg, and B. Newman, Identifica-

tion and estimation of lysergic acid diethylamide by thin-layer chromatography and fluorometry, *Anal. Chem.*, **38**, 1959 (1966).
85. Dal Cortivo, L. A., M. M. De Mayo, and S. B. Weinberg, Fluorometric determination of microgram amounts of meperidine, *Anal. Chem.*, **42**, 941 (1970).
86. Davidow, B. and B. Quame, Extraction of drugs from urine using disposable chromatographic columns, *Pharamacologist*, **13**, 309(1971).
87. Davis, K. H., Jr., N. H. Martin, C. G. Pitt, J. W. Wildes, and M. E. Wall, The preparation and analysis of enriched and pure cannabinoids from marihuana and hashish, *Lloydia*, **33**, 453 (1970).
88. Dayton, P. G., J. M. Perel, M. A. Landrau, L. Brand, and L. C. Mark, The relationship between binding of thiopental to plasma and its distribution into adipose tissue in man, as measured by a spectrophotofluorometric method, *Biochem. Pharmacol.*, **16**, 2321 (1967).
89. De Angelis, G. G., Testing for drugs—Advantages and disadvantages, *.Int. J. Addict.*, **7**, 365 (1972).
90. De Silva, J. A. F., and L. D'Arconte, The use of spectrophotofluorometry in the analysis of drugs in biological materials, *J. Forensic Sci.*, **14**, 184 (1969).
91. De Zan, P., R. F. Canaff, and R. Bianchi, Fluorimetric characteristics of some narcotic and dangerous drugs, *J. Assoc. Off. Anal. Chem.*, **54**, 925 (1971).
92. De Zeeuw, R. A., Th. M. Malingré, and F. W. H. M. Merkus, Δ^1-Tetrahydrocannabinolic acid, an important component in the evaluation of cannabis products, *J. Pharm. Pharmacol.*, **24**, 1 (1972).
93. Dole, V. P., A. Crowther, J. Johnson, M. Monsalvatge, B. Biller, and S. S. Nelson, Detection of narcotic, sedative and amphetamine drugs in urine, *N.Y. State J. Med.*, **72**, 471 (1972).
94. Dole, V. P., W. K. Kim, and I. Eglitis, Detection of narcotic drugs, tranquilizers, amphetamines and barbiturates in urine, *JAMA*, **198**, 349 (1966).
95. Donike, M., L. Jaenicke, D. Stratmann, and W. Hollmann, Gas chromatographic detection of nitrogen-containing drugs in aqueous solutions by means of the nitrogen detector, *J. Chromatog*, **52**, 237 (1970).
96. Draffan, G. H., R. A. Clare, F. M. Williams, B. Krauer, D. S. Davies, and C. T. Dollery, Measurement of barbiturates and their metabolites in small volumes of biological fluids by quantitative gas chromatography-mass spectrometry, Paper presented at the 20th Annual Conference on Mass Spectrometry and Allied Topics, Dallas, Texas, June 4–9 1972.
97. Driscoll, R. C., F. S. Barr, B. J. Gragg, and G. W. Moore, Determination of therapeutic blood levels of methamphetamine and pentobarbital by GC, *J. Pharm. Sci.*, **60**, 1492 (1971).
98. Ehrsson, H. and B. Mellström, Gas chromatographic determination of amides after perfluoroacylation. Preparations and properties of the trifluo-

roacetyl and pentafluorobenzoyl derivatives, *Acta Pharm. Suec.,* **9,** 107 (1972).

99. Elliott, H. W., K. D. Parker, J. A. Wright, and N. Nomof, Actions and metabolism of heroin administered by continuous intravenous infusion to man, *Clin. Pharmacol. Ther.,* **12,** 806 (1971).
100. Fales, H. M., G. W. A. Milne, and T. Axenrod, Identification of barbiturates by chemical ionization mass spectrometry, *Anal. Chem.,* **42,** 1432 (1970).
101. Fenimore, D. C. and C. M. Davis, Rapid screening of urine for detection of narcotic drugs, in *Drug Dependence,* R. T. Harris, W. N. McIsaac, and C. R. Schuster, Jr., (Eds), University of Texas Press, Austin, 1970.
102. Fetterman, P. S., N. J. Doorenbos, E. S. Keith, and M. W. Quimby, A simple gas liquid chromatography procedure for determination of cannabinoidic acids in *Cannabis sativa L., Experientia,* **27,** 988 (1971).
103. Fiereck, E. A. and N. W. Tietz, A gas-chromatographic method for separating and measuring barbiturates and glutethimide in blood, *Clin. Chem.,* **17,** 1024 (1971).
104. Finkle, B. S., Forensic toxicology of drugs, *Anal. Chem.,* **44,** 18A (1972).
105. Finkle, B. S., E. L. Cherry, and D. M. Taylor, A GLC based system for the detection of poisons, drugs and human metabolites encountered in forensic toxicology, *J. Chromatog. Sci.,* **9,** 393 (1971).
106. Finkle, B. S., D. M. Taylor, and E. J. Bonelli, A GC/MS reference data system for the identification of drugs of abuse, *J. Chromatog. Sci.,* **10,** 312 (1972).
107. Fish, F. and W. D. C. Wilson, Gas chromatographic determination of morphine and cocaine in urine, *J. Chromatog.,* **40,** 164 (1969).
108. Fish, F. and W. D. C. Wilson, Identification of cannabis constituents in the particulate matter of smoke, *J. Forensic Sci., Soc.,* **9,** 37 (1969).
109. Flynn, E. J. and S. Spector, Determination of barbiturate derivatives by radioimmunoassay, *JPET,* **181,** 547 (1972).
110. Foltz, R. L., A. F. Fentiman, E. G. Leighty, J. L. Walter, H. R. Drewes, W. E. Schwartz, T. F. Page, Jr., and E. B. Truitt, Jr., Metabolite of (-) trans- Δ^8-tetrahydrocannabinol: Identification and synthesis, *Science,* **168,** 844 (1970)
111. Forrest, I. S., D. E. Green, S. D. Rose, G. C. Skinner, and D. M. Torres, Fluorescent-labeled cannabinoids, *Res. Commun. Chem. Path. Pharmacol.,* **2,** 787 (1971).
112. Forrest, I. S., S. D. Rose, L. G. Brookes, B. Halpern, V. A. Bacon, and I. A. Silberg, Fluorescent labelling of psychoactive drugs, *Agressol.,* **11,** 127 (1970).
113. Freed, D. J. and L. R. Faulkner, Characterization of gas chromatographic effluents via scanning fluorescence spectrometry, *Anal. Chem.,* **44,** 1194 (1972).

114. Freedman, A. N., The gas chromatograph-mass spectrometer interface, *Anal. Chim. Acta,* **59,** 19 (1972).
115. Frings, C. S. and C. Queen, Critical evaluation of Dole's method for screening alkaloids, narcotics and other organic bases in urine, *Clin. Chem.,* **17,** 664 (1971).
116. Fujimoto, J. M., Isolation of two different glucuronide metabolites of naloxone from the urine of rabbit and chicken, *JPET,* **168,** 180 (1969).
117. Fujimoto, J. M. and V. B. Haarstad, the isolation of morphine ethereal sulfate from urine of the chicken and cat, *JPET,* **165,** 45 (1969).
118. Fujimoto, J. M. and R. I. H. Wang, A method of identifying narcotic analgesics in human urine after therapeutic doses, *Toxicol. Appl. Pharmacol.,* **16,** 186 (1970).
119. Fujimoto, J. M., W. M. Watrous, and V. B. Haarstad, Isolation of nalorphine ethereal sulfate and nalorphine glucuronide from urine of cat and rabbit, *Proc. Soc. Exp. Biol. Med.,* **130,** 546 (1969).
120. Fulton, C. C., Sulfomorphid; and the purple fluorescence test, a new derivative test for morphine, *J. Am. Pharm. Assoc.,* **26,** 726 (1937).
121. Genest, K. and C. G. Farmilo, the identification and determination of lysergic acid diethylamide in narcotic seizures, *J. Pharm. Pharmacol.,* **16,** 250 (1964).
122. Gilbert, J. N. T., B. J. Millard, and J. W. Powell, Combined gas-liquid chromatography-mass spectrometry in the study of barbiturate metabolism, *J. Pharm. Pharmacol.,* **22,** 897 (1970).
123. Gill, E. W., Propyl homologue of tetrahydrocannabinol: Its isolation from cannabis, properties and synthesis, *J. Chem. Soc. (Org.),* **3,** 579 (1971).
124. Gillespie, A. M., A spectrofluorometric study of selected hallucinogens, *Anal. Lett.,* **2,** 609 (1969).
125. Goldbaum, L., P. H. Santinga, and A. M. Dominguez, Rapid procedure for the mass screening of urine for morphine, Paper presented to the 23rd Annual Meeting, American Academy of Forensic Sciences 1971.
126. Gordis, E., Gas chromatographic resolution of optical isomers in microgram samples of amphetamine, *Biochem. Pharmacol.,* **15,** 2124 (1966).
127. Gordis, E. and V. P. Dole, Gas-chromatographic resolution of optical isomers in microgram samples of amphetamine, *Federation Proc.,* **25,** 690 (1966).
128. Gough, T. A. and E. A. Walker, Techniques in gas chromatography. Part III. Choice of detectors, *Analyst, 95,* 1 (1970).
129. Grant, J. D., S. J. Cross, P. Lomax, and R. Wong, Antibody detection of marihuana, *Nature New Biology.,* **236,** 216 (1972).
130. Grooms, J. O., Quantitative gas chromatographic determination of heroin in illicit samples, *J. Assoc. Off. Anal. Chem.,* **51,** 1010 (1968).

131. Grützmacher, H. F. and W. Arnold, Massenspektren von Barbitursaurederivaten, *Tetrahedron Lett.,* **13,** 1365 (1966).
132. Gunne, L.-M. and L. Galland, Stereoselective metabolism of amphetamine, *Biochem. Pharmacol,* **16,** 1374 (1967).
133. Gustafson, R. L., R. L. Albright, J. Heisler, J. A. Lirio, and O. T. Reid, Adsorption of organic species by high surface area styrene-divinylbenzene copolymers, *Ind. Eng. Chem. Prod. Res. Develop.,* **7,** 107 (1968).
134. Hammar, C.-G., Mass fragmentography and elemental analysis by means of a new and combined multiple ion detector-peak matcher device, *Acta Pharm. Suec.,* **8** 129 (1971).
135. Hammar, C.-G., B. Alexanderson, B. Holmstedt, and F. Sjöqvist, Gas chromatography-mass spectrometry of nortriptyline in body fluids of man, *Clin. Pharmacol. Therap.,* **12,** 496 (1971).
136. Hammar, C.-G., B. Holmstedt, J.-E. Lindgren, and R. Tham, The combination of gas chromatography and mass spectrometry in the identification of drugs and metabolites, in *Advances in Pharmacology and Chemotherapy,* S. Garattini, A. Goldin, F. Hawking, and I. J. Kopin (Eds.), Vol. 7, Academic Press, New York, 1969.
137. Hammar, C.-G., B. Holmstedt, and R. Ryhage, Mass fragmentography identification of chlorpromazine and its metabolites in human blood by a new method, *Anal. Biochem.,* **25,** 532 (1968).
138. Heaton, A. M. and A. C. Blumberg, Thin-layer chromatographic detection of barbiturates, narcotics, and amphetamines in urine of patients receiving psychotropic drugs, *J. Chromatog.,* **41,** 367 (1969).
139. Heaysman, L. T., E. A. Walker, and D. T. Lewis, the application of gas chromatography to the examination of the constituents of *Cannabis sativa L., Analyst.,* **92,** 450 (1967).
140. Hertz, H. S., R. A. Hites, and K. Biemann, Identification of mass spectra by computer-searching a file of known spectra, *Anal. Chem.,* **43,** 681 (1971).
141. Hetland, L. B., D. A. Knowlton, and D. Couri, A method for the detection of drugs at therapeutic dosages in human urine using adsorption column chromatography and thin layer chromatography, *Clin. Chem. Acta,* **36,** 473 (1972).
142. Hill, R. M., M. G. Horning, E. C. Horning, L. D. Waterbury, and M. M. Desmond, Identification in the newborn infant of transplacentally acquired anticonvulsant drugs and drug metabolites, *Southern Med. J.,* **62,** 1554 (1969).
143. Hirtz, J. and A. Gérandin, Séparation et Dosage des Amphétamine dans les Milieux Biologiques par Chromatographie en Phase Gazeuse de Leurs Dérivés Trifluoroacétylés, *Ann. Pharm. Franc.,* **27,** 581 (1969).
144. Ho, I. K., H. H. Loh, and E. L. Way, Mini thin layer chromatography in the

detection of narcotics in the urine, *Proc. West. Pharmacol. Soc.,* **14,** 183 (1971).

145. Hoffman, D. B., C. J. Umberger, S. Goldner, S. Andryauskas, D. Mulligan, and J. R. Broich, Liquid-solid extraction of lyophilized biological materials for forensic analysis, II. Application to bile samples for the detection of drugs, *J. Chromatog.,* **66,** 63 (1972).

146. Hollister, L. E., S. L. Kanter, and D. J. Clyde, Studies of prolonged-action medication, III. Pentobarbital sodium in prolonged-action form compared with conventional capsules: Serum levels of drug and clinical effects following acute doses, *Clin. Pharmacol. Therap.,* **4,** 612 (1963).

147. Holmstedt, B., Gas chromatography-mass spectrometry as a tool to elucidate the structure of unknown psycho-active drugs, in *Abuse of Central Stimulants,* F. Sjöqvist and M. Tottie (Eds.), Almqvist and Wiksell, Stockholm, 1968, p. 357.

148. Holmstedt, B. and A. Linnarson, Chemistry and means of determination of hallucinogens and marihuana, in *Drug Abuse Proceedings of the International Conference,* C. J. D. Zarafonetis (Ed.), Lea and Febiger, 1972, p. 291.

149. Horning, E. C. and M. G. Horning, Metabolic profiles: Gas phase methods for analysis of metabolites, *Clin. Chem.,* **17,** 802 (1971).

150. Horning, E. C., M. G. Horning, W. J. A. Vanden Heuvel, K. L. Knox, B. Holmstedt, and C. J. W. Brooks, Part II. Tryptamine-related amines and catecholamines, *Anal. Chem.,* **36,** 1546 (1964).

151. Horning, M. G., E. A. Boucher, M. Stafford, and E. C. Horning, A rapid procedure for the isolation of drugs and drug metabolites from plasma, *Clin. Chim. Acta,* **37,** 381 (1972).

152. Horning, M. G., D. J. Harvey, and E. C. Horning, The use of mass spectrometry in the study of urinary metabolites, Paper presented at the 20th Annual Conference on Mass Spectrometry and Allied Topics, Dallas, Texas, June 4-9, 1972.

153. Horning, M. G., A. M. Moss, E. A. Boucher, and E. C. Horning, The GLC separation of hydroxyl-substituted amines of biological importance including the catecholamines. Preparation of derivatives for electron capture detection, *Anal. Lett.,* **1,** 311 (1968).

154. Ikekawa, N., K. Takayama, E. Hosoya, and T. Oka, Determination of morphine in urine by gas chromatography, *Anal. Biochem.,* **28,** 156 (1969).

155. Inoue, T., Y. Nakahara, and T. Niwaguchi, Studies on lysergic acid diethylamide and related compounds, II. Mass spectra of lysergic acid derivatives, *Chem. Pharm. Bull.,* **20,** 409 (1972).

156. Irvine, W. J. and M. J. Saxby, Gas chromatography of primary and secondary amines as their trifluoracetyl derivatives, *J. Chromatog.,* **43,** 129 (1969).

157. Jaffe, J. H. and D. Kirkpatrick, The use of ion-exchange resin impregnated

paper in the detection of opiate alkaloids, amphetamines, phenothiazines and barbiturates in urine, *Psychopharmacol. B0ll.*, **3**, 49 (1966).

158. Janchen, D. and G. Pataki, Quantitative *in situ* fluorometry of thin-layer chromatograms, *J. Chromatog.*, **33**, 391 (1968).

159. Jen, T. Y., G. A. Hughes, and H. Smith, Total Synthesis of Δ^8 $\Delta^{1(6)}$-tetrahydrocannabinol, a biologically active constituent of hashish (marijuana), *J. Am. Chem. Soc.*, **89**, 4551 (1967).

160. Junk, G. A., Gas chromatograph-mass spectrometer combinations and their applications, *Int. J. Mass Spectrom. Ion Phys.*, **8**, 1 (1972).

161. Just, W. W., and G. Werner, Quantitative determination of Δ^8 - and Δ^9-tetrahydrocannabinol in nanomol range, *Z. Anal. Chem.*, **259**, (1972).

162. Just, W. W., G. Werner, and M. Wiechmann, Bestimmung von Δ^1- und $\Delta^{1(6)}$-tetrahydrocannabinol in Blut, Urin und Speichel von Haschish-Rauchern, *Naturwiss.*, **59**, 222 (1972).

163. Kaistha, K. K., Drug abuse screening programs: Detection procedures, development costs, street-sample analysis, and field tests, *J. Pharm. Sci.*, **61**, 655 (1972).

164. Kaistha, K. K. and J. H. Jaffe, Extraction techniques for narcotics, barbiturates, and central nervous system stimulants in a drug abuse urine screening program, *J. Chromatog.*, **60**, 83 (1971).

165. Kaistha, K. K. and J. H. Jaffe, Reliability of identification techniques for drugs of abuse in a urine screening program and drug excretion data, *J. Pharm. Sci.*, **61**, 305 (1972).

166. Kaistha, K. K. and J. H. Jaffe, TLC techniques for identification of narcotics, barbiturates, and CNS stimulants in a drug abuse urine screening program, *J. Pharm. Sci.*, **61**, 679 (1972).

167. Kallberg, N., S. Agurell, B. Jalling, and L. O. Boréus, Rapid gas chromatographic determination of phenobarbital in small plasma samples, *Eur. J. Clin. Pharmacol.*, **3**, 185 (1971).

168. Kamm, J. J., and E. J. Von Loon, Amobarbital metabolism in man: A gas chromatographic method for the estimation of hydroxyamobarbital in human urine, *Clin Chem.*, **12**, 789 (1966).

169. Kananen, G., R. Osiewicz, and I. Sunshine, Barbiturate analysis—A current assessment, *J. Chromatog. Sci.*, **10**, 283 (1972).

170. Karasek, F. W., GC/MS/Computers, *Anal. Chem.*, **44**, 32 (1972).

171. Karmen, A., Differential specificity in detecting phosphorous, nitrogen, and halogens with alkali flames, *J. Chromatog. Sci.*, **7**, 541 (1969).

172. Karmen, A. and E. L. Kelly, Flame ionization detection of fluorine in gas-liquid chromatography effluents, *Anal. Chem.*, **43**, 1992 (1971).

173. Ketchum, J. S., Detection of LSD, *Am. J. Psychiat.*, **125**, 1447 (1969).

174. King, L. J. and R. B. Forney, The absorption and excretion of the marihuana constituents, cannabinol and tetrahydrocannabinol, *Fed. Proc.,* **26,** 540 (1967).

175. Klein, F. K., H. Rapoport, and H. W. Elliott, Cannabis alkaloids, *Nature,* **232,** 258 (1971).

176. Kojima, T., M. Ichise, and Y. Seo, Selective gas-chromatographic detection using an ion-selective electrode, II. Selective detection of fluorine compounds, *Talanta,* **19,** 539 (1972).

177. Krakow, B., Continual analysis of gas chromatographic effluents by rapid repetitive infrared scanning, *Anal. Chem.,* **41,** 815 (1969).

178. Kupferberg, H. J., Quantitative estimation of diphenylhydantoin, primidone and phenobarbital in plasma by gas-liquid chromatography, *Clin. Chim. Acta,* **29,** 283 (1970)

179. Kupferberg, H. J., A. Burkhalter, and E. L. Way, Fluorometric identification of sub-microgram amounts of morphine and related compounds on thin-layer chramatographs, *J. Chromatog.,* **16,** 558 1964).

180. Kupferberg, H., A. Burkhalter, and E. L. WAy, A sensitive fluorometric assay for morphine in plasma and brain, *JPET,* **145,** 247 (1964).

181. Lauffer, S., E. Schmid, and F. Weist, Dünnschichtchromatographische Trennung und Spektrophoto-Fluometrischer Nachweis Psychotroper Pharmaka, *Arzneimittel-Forsch.,* **19,** 3 (1969).

182. Law, N. C., V. Aandahl, H. M. Fales, and G. W. A. Milne, Identification of dangerous drugs by mass spectrometry, *Clin. Chim. Acta,* **32,** 221 (1971).

183. Lebish, P., B. S. Finkle, and J. W. Brackett, Jr., Determination of amphetamine, methamphetamine, and related amines in blood and urine by gas chromatography with hydrogen-flame ionization detector, *Clin. Chem.,* **16,** 195 (1970).

184. Leclercq, P. A., K. Hagele, B. Middleditch, R. Thompson, and D. M. Desiderio, Chemical ionization mass spectrometry of biologically active compounds, Paper presented at the Annual Conference on Mass Spectrometry and Allied Topics, Dallas, Texas, June 4–9, 1972.

185. Lerner, M., Marihuana: Tetrahydrocannabinol and related compounds, *Science,* **140,** 175 (1963).

186. Leute, R., E. F. Ullman, and A. Goldstein, Spin immunoassay of opiate narcotics in urine and saliva, *JAMA,* **221,** 1231 (1972).

187. Leute, R. K., E. F. Ullman, A. Goldstein, and L. A. Herzenberg, Spin immunoassay technique for determination of morphine, *Nature New Biology,* **236,** 93 (1972).

188. Lindgren, J.-E., C.-G. Hammar, R. Hessling, and B. Holmstedt, The chemical identity of "hog"—A "new" hallucinogen, *Am. J. Pharm.,* **141,** 86 (1969)

189. Low, M. J. D. and S. K. Freeman, Measurement of infrared spectra of gas-

liquid chromatography fractions using multiple-scan interference spectrometry, *Anal. Chem.*, **39**, 194 (1967).

190. MacGee, J., Rapid identification and quantitative determination of barbiturates and glutethimide in blood by gas-liquid chromatography, *Clin. Chem.*, **17**, 587 (1971).

191. Martin, G. E. and J. S. Swinehart, Use of silyl derivatives in the quanttative gas chromatographic determination of morphine and codeine, *Anal. Chem.*, **38**, 1789 (1966).

192. Martin, H. F. and J. L. Driscoll, Gas chromatographic identification and determination of barbiturates, *Anal. Chem.*, **38**, 345 (1966).

193. McAuley, F. and J. Kofoed, Preparative gas chromatography as a clean-up procedure in toxicology, *J. Chromatog.*, **50**, 513 (1970).

194. McChesney, J. D., D. K. Beal, and R. M. Fox, Rapid qualitative identification of barbiturates by mass spectrometry, *J. Pharm. Sci.*, **61**, 310 (1972).

195. McGonigle, E. J., Determination of microgram quantities of methadone by fluorescence, *Anal. Chem.*, **43**, 966 (1971).

196. McMartin C., and H. V. Street, Gas-liquid chromatography of submicrogram amounts of drugs, II. Analysis of barbiturates and related drugs in biological media, *J. Chromatog.*, **23**, 232 (1966).

197. Mechoulam, R. and Y. Gaoni, A total synthesis of *dl*- Δ^1-tetrahydrocannabinol the active constituent of hashish, *J. Am. Chem. Soc.*, **87**, 3273 (1965)

198. Merkus, F. W. H. M., Cannabivarin and tetrahydrocannabivarin, two new constituents of hashish, *Nature*, **232**, 579 (1971).

199. Mikes, F., A. Hofmann, and P. G. Waser, Identification of (-)- Δ^9-6a, 10a-trans-tetrahydro-cannabinol and two of its metabolites in rats by use of combination gas chromatography-mass spectrometry and mass fragmentography, *Biochem. Pharmacol.*, **20**, 2469 (1971).

200. Miller, M. D., The determination of excipient sugar diluents in illicit preparations containing heroin by gas chromatography, *J. Forensic Sci.*, **17**, 150 (1972).

201. Milne, G. W. A., H. M. Fales, and T. Axenrod, Identification of dangerous drugs by isobutane chemical ionization mass spectrometry, *Anal. Chem.*, **43**, 1815 (1971).

202. Milne, G. W. A. and W. J. A. Vanden Heuvel, General problems in the identification of drugs and drug metabolites by mass spectrometry, Paper presented at the 20th Annual Conference on Mass Spectrometry and Allied Topics, Dallas, Texas, June 4–9, 1972.

203. Moffat, A. C., E. C. Horning, S. B. Matin, and M. Rowland, Perfluorobenzene derivatives as derivatising agents for the gas chromatography of primary and secondary amines using electron capture detection, *J. Chromatog.*, **66**, 255 (1972).

204. Montalvo, J. G., E. Klein, D. Eyer, and B. Harper, Identification of drugs of abuse in urine, I. A study of the Dole technique, *J. Chromatog.*, **47**, 542 (1970).
205. Mulé, S. J., Determination of narcotic analgesics in human biological materials application of ultraviolet spectrophotometry, thin layer and gas liquid chromatography, *Anal. Chem.*, **36**, 1907 (1964).
206. Mulé, S. J., Identification of narcotics, barbiturates, amphetamines, tranquilizers and psychotomimetics in human urine, *J. Chromatog.*, **39**, 302 (1969).
207. Mulé, S. J., Routine identification of drugs of abuse in human urine, 1. Application of fluorometry, thin-layer and gas-liquid chromatography, *J. Chromatog.*, **55**, 255 (1971).
208. Mulé, S. J., Detection and identification of drugs of dependence, in *Chemical and Biological Aspects of Drug Dependence*, S. J. Mulé and H. Brill (Eds.), 1972, p. 277.
209. Mulé, S. J., M. L. Bastos, D. Jukofsky, and E. Saffer, Routine identification of drugs of abuse in human urine, II. Development and application of the XAD-2 resin column method, *J. Chromatog.*, **63**, 289 (1971).
210. Mulé, S. J. and P. L. Hushin, Semiautomated fluorometric assay for submicrogram quantities of morphine and quinine in human biological material, *Anal. Chem.*, **43**, 708 (1971).
211. Munson, B., Chemical ionization mass spectrometry, *Anal. Chem.*, **43**, 28A (1971).
212. Nadeau, G. and G. Sobolewski, Une Nouvelle Méthode de Dosage de Trés Petites Quantités de Morphine, *Can. J. Biochem. Physiol.*, **36**, 625 (1958).
213. Nakamura, G. R., T. T. Noguchi, D. Jackson, and D. Banks, Forensic identification of heroin in illicit preparations using integrated gas chromatography and mass spectrometry, *Anal. Chem.*, 44, 408 (1972).
214. Narasimhachari, N., J. Spaide, and B. Heller, Gas liquid chromatographic and mass spectrometric studies on trimethylsilyl derivatives or *N*-methyl- and *N,N*-dimethyltryptamines, *J. Chromatog. Sci.*, **9**, 502 (1971).
215. Narasimhachari, N. and P. Vouros, Gas-liquid chromatography and mass spectrometry of biogenic amines and amphetamines as their isothiocyanate derivatives, Paper presented at the 20th Annual Conference on Mass Spectrometry and Allied Topics, Dallas, Texas, June 4-9, 1972.
216. Narasimhachari, N. and P. Vouros, Gas-liquid chromatography and mass spectrometry of biogenic amines and amphetamines as their isothiocyanate derivatives, *Anal. Biochem.*, **45**, 154 (1972).
217. Neville, G. A., Gas chromatographic and nuclear magnetic resonance spectroscopic studies of 1,3-dimethylbarbiturates obtained by various methylation techniques, *Anal. Chem.*, **42**, 347 (1970).
218. Nielsen, E., J. Schou, A. Steetoft, K. Worm, and J. M. Andersen, A new gas

chromatographic method for the demonstration of cannabis intake by analysis of biological fluids, *Acta Pharmacol. Toxicol.,* **29** (Suppl. 4), 50 (1971).

219. Nigam, I. C. and J. L. Holmes, Mass spectrometry of lysergic acid diethylamide, *J. Pharm. Sci.,* **58**, 507 (1969).

220. Niwaguchi, T. and T. Inoue, Studies on quantitative *in situ* fluorometry of lysergic acid diethylamide (LSD) on thin-layer chromatograms, *J. Chromatog.,* **59**, 127 (1971).

221. Nix, C. R. and A. S. Hume, A spectrophotofluorometric method for the determination of amphetamine, *J. Forensic Sci.,* **15**, 595 (1970).

222. Noonan, J. S., P. W. Murdick, and R. S. Ray, A method for detecting amphetamine using gas chromatography of a halogenated derivative, *JPET,* **168**, 205 (1969).

223. O'Brien, J. E., W. Zazulak, V. Abbey, and O. Hinsvark, Determination of amphetamine and phentermine in biological fluids, *J. Chromatog. Sci.,* **10** 336 (1972).

224. Palmer, K. H., M. S. Fowler, M. E. Wall, L. S. Rhodes, W. J. Waddell, and B. Baggett, The metabolism of $R(+)$-and RS-pentobarbital, *JPET,* **170**, 355 (1969).

225. Parker, K. D., C. R. Fontan, and P. Kirk, Separation and identification of tranquilizers by gas chromatography, *J. Chromatog.,* **34**, 757 (1962).

226. Parker, K. D., J. A. Wright, A. F. Halpern, and C. H. Hine, Preliminary report on the separation and quantitative determination of cannabis constituents present in plant material, and when added to urine, by thin-layer and gas chromatography, *Bull. Narcotics,* **20**, 9 (1968).

227. Parker, K. D., J. A. Wright, A. F. Halpern, and C. H. Hine, Preliminary report on the detection and quantitation of opiates and certain other drugs of abuse as trimethylsilyl derivatives by gas liquid chromatography, *J. Forensic Sci. Soc.,* **10**, 17 (1970).

228. Passwater, R. A., Fluorometric procedures for illicit drug detection, *Fluorescence News,* **6**, 8 (1971).

229. Peters, A. A. and P. M. Tocci, A simple method for the separation and identification of barbiturates, alkaloids and amphetamines in urine, *Fed. Proc.,* **30**, 443 (1971).

230. Petrzilka, T., W. Haefliger, and C. Sikemeier, Synthese von Haschisch—Inhaltasstoffen, *Helv. Chim. Acta,* **52**, 1102 (1969).

231. Phillips, G. and R. Mesley, Examination of the hallucinogen 2,5-dimethoxy-4-methylamphetamine, *J. Pharm. Pharmacol.,* **21**, 9 (1969).

232. Pohland, A., H. E. Boaz, and H. R. Sullivan, Synthesis and identification of metabolites resulting from the biotransformation of dl-methadone in man and in the rat, *J. Med. Chem.,* **14**, 194 (1971).

233. Product Bulletin. Model RS-1 GC Identifier, Norcon Instruments, Inc., South Norwalk, Conn.

234. Ray, R. S., J. S. Noonan, P. W. Murdick, and V. L. Tharp, Detection of methylphenidate and methamphetamine in equine body fluids by gas chromatographic analysis of an electron-capturing derivative, *Am. J. Vet. Res.*, **33**, 27 (1972).
235. Robinson, A. E., Forensic toxicology of psychoactive drugs, *Chem. Bri.*, **8**, 118 (1972).
236. Routh, J. I., L. Stoll, and R. E. Bannow, A scheme for separation and detection of toxicologically significant drugs in biological fluids, *Clin. Chem.*, **17**, 637 (1971).
237. Rubenstein, K. E., R. S. Schneider, and E. F. Ullman, Homogeneous enzyme immunoassay: A new technique for the quantitative determination of abused drugs, *Clin. Chem.*, **18**, 714 (1972).
238. Sadée, W. and E. Van der Kleijn, Thermolysis of 1,4-benzodiazepines during gas chromatography and mass spectroscopy, *J. Pharm. Sci.*, **60**, 135 (1971).
239. Santinga, P. H., Application of fluorescence and gas chromatography to mass drug screening, *Fluorescence News*, **6**, 1 (1971).
240. Schneider, R. S., K. E. Rubenstein, S. Myers, E. Wong, and P. Lindquist, Homogeneous enzyme immunoassay for opiates in urine, *Clin. Chem.*, **18**, 714 (1972).
241. Schou, J., A. Steentoff, J. M. Andersen, and E. Nielsen, A highly sensitive method for gas chromatographic measurement of tetrahydrocannabinol (THC) and cannabinol (CBN), *Acta Pharmacol. Toxicol.*, **30**, 480 (1971).
242. Schubert, B., Detection and identification of methylphenidate in human urine and blood samples, *Acta Chem. Scand.*, **24**, 433 (1970).
243. Schwartz, M. A., P. Bommer, and F. M. Vane, Diazepam metabolites in the rat:Characterization by high-resolution mass spectrometry and nuclear magnetic resonance, *Arch. Biochem. Biophys.*, **121**, 508 (1967).
244. Schwartz, M. A., F. M. Vane, and E. Postma, Chlordiazepoxide metabolites in the rat. Characterization by high resolution mass spectrometry, *Biochem. Pharmacol.*, **17**, 965 (1968).
245. Schwartz, M. A., F. M. Vane, and E. Postma, Urinary metabolites of 7-chloro-1-(2-diethylaminoethyl)-5-(2-fluorophenyl)-1,3-dihydro-2H-1,4-benzodiazepin-2-one dihydrochloride, *J. Med. Chem.*, **11**, 770 (1968).
246. Seiler, N., Identification and quantitation of amines by thin-layer chromatography, *J. Chromatog.*, **63**, 97 (1971).
247. Setchell, K. D. R. and J. D. H. Cooper, A routine method for the detection and quantitation of amphetamine in urine, *Clin. Chem. Acta*, **35**, 67 (1971).
248. Skinner, R. F., The state of the art in the analysis of marihuana, *Proc. West. Pharmacol. Soc.*, **14**, 4 (1971).
249. Skinner, R. F., The determination of submicrogram amounts of ^{9}-THC and its metabolites, *Proc. West. Pharmacol. Soc.*, **15**, 136 (1972).
250. Skinner, R. F., E. J. Gallaher, J. B. Knight, and E. J. Bonelli, The gas

chromatograph-mass spectrometer as a new and important tool in forensic toxicology, *J. Forensic Sci.*, **17**, 189 (1972).
251. Sobol, S. P., R. P. Barron, and T. C. Kram, The use of NMR and mass spectral data in the forensic laboratory, *J. Assoc. Offic. Anal. Chem.*, **55**, 866 (1972).
252. Sohn, D., J. Simon, M. Hanna, and G. Ghali, Preparatory procedures in screening for drugs of abuse: "Clean-up" methods in current use, *J. Chromatog. Sci.*, **10**, 294 (1972).
253. Spector, S., Quantitative determination of morphine in serum by radioimmunoassay, *JPET*, **178**, 253 (1971).
254. Spector, S. and E. J. Flynn, Barbiturates: Radioimmunoassay, *Science*, **174**, 1036 (1971).
255. Spector, S. and C. W. Parker, Morphine: Radioimmunoassay, *Science*, **168**, 1347 (1970).
256. Stevenson, G. W., On-column methylation of barbituric acid, *Anal. Chem.*, **38**, 1948 (1966).
257. Stewart, J. T., G. B. Duke, and J. E. Willcox, Rapid micromethod for the gas chromatographic determination of methylated barbiturates in biological samples, *Anal. Lett.*, **2**, 449 (1969).
258. Stewart, J. T. and D. M. Lotti, Fluorometric determination of amphetamines with 3-carboxy-7-hydroxycoumarin, *J. Pharm. Sci.*, **60**, 461 (1971).
259. Street, H. V., Forensic problems in the gas chromatography of amines and alkaloids, *J. Chromatog.*, **37**, 162 (1968).
260. Street, H. V., Gas-liquid chromatography of submicrogram amounts of drugs, IV. Identification of barbiturates, hydantoins, amides, imides, carbamates, phenylbutazone, carboxylic acids, and hydrazine derivatives by direct derivative formation within the gas chromatograph, *J. Chromatog.*, **41**, 358 (1969).
261. Street, H. V., Determination of barbiturates in blood by GLC, *Clin. Chim. Acta*, **34**, 357 (1971).
262. Stromberg, L., Minor components of cannabis resin, II. Separation by gas chromatography, mass spectra and molecular weights of some components with shorter retention times than cannabidiol, *J. Chromatog.*, **68**, 248 (1972).
263. Sullivan, H. R. and D. A. Blake, Quantitative determination of methadone concentrations in human blood, plasma, and urine by gas chromatography, *Res. Comm. Chem. Pathol. Pharmacol.*, **3**, 467 (1972).
264. Sullivan, H. R., S. L. Due, and R. E. McMahon, The identification of three new metabolites of methadone in man and in the rat, *J. Am. Chem. Soc.*, **94**, 4050 (1972).
265. Swagzdis, J. E. and T. L. Flanagan, Spectrophotofluorometric determination of low concentrations of amobarbital in plasma, *Anal. Biochem.*, **7**, 147 (1964).

266. Takemori, A. E., An ultrasensitive method for the determination of morphine and its application in experiments *in vitro* and *in vivo, Biochem. Pharmacol.*, **17**, 1627 (1968).
267. Toki, S. and E. W. Maynert, Species differences in dihydroxysecobarbital excretion, *Fed. Proc.*, **25**, Pt. I, 531 (1966).
268. Tompsett, S. L., Interference from the presence of other substances in detecting and determining barbiturates in biological material, *J. Clin. Pathol..* **22**, 291 (1969).
269. Toseland, P. A. and P. H. Scott, Determination of amphetamine as its N-acetyl derivative by gas-liquid chromatography, *Clin. Chim. Acta,* **25**, 75 (1969).
270. Tsuda, T., Y. Ojika, M. Izuda, I. Fujishima, and D. Ishii, The combination of gas chromatography and nuclear magnetic resonance spectroscopy, *J. Chromatog.*, **69**, 194 (1972).
271. Upshall, D. G. and D. G. Wailling, The determination of LSD in human plasma following oral administration, *Clin. Chim. Acta,* **36**, 67 (1972).
272. Van Rossum, J. M., D. D. Breimer, G. A. M. Van Ginneken, J. M. G. Van Kordelaar, and T. B. Vree, Gas-liquid chromatography in pharmacology and toxicology. Pharmacokinetic analysis limited by the sensitivity of the analytical technique, *Clin. Chim. Acta,* **34**, 311 (1971).
273. Van Vunakis, H., H. Bradvica, P. Benda, and L. Levine, Production and specificity of antibodies directed toward 3,4,5-trimethoxyphenylethylamine, 3,4-dimethoxyphenylethylamine and 2,5-dimethoxy-4-methylamphetamine, *Biochem. Pharmacol.*, **18**, 393 (1969).
274. Van Vunakis, H., J. T. Farrow, H. B. Gjika, and L. Levine, Specificity of the antibody receptor site to D-lysergamide: Model of a physiological receptor for lysergic acid diethylamide, *Proc. Nat. Acad. Sci.*, **68**, 1483 (1971).
275. Van Vunakis, H., E. Wasserman, and L. Levine, Specificities of antibodies to morphine, *JPET,* **180**, 514 (1972).
276. Van Zwol, D. E., Gas chromatographic separation and identification of some sympathomimetic amines in use in anorexigenic drugs, *J. Chromatog.*, **24**, 26 (1966).
277. Vanden Heuvel, W. J. A., W. L. Gardiner, and E. C. Horning, Characterization and separation of amines by gas chromatography, *Anal. Chem.*, **36**, 1550 (1964).
278. Vree, T. B., D. D. Breimer, C. A. M. Van Ginneken, J. M. Van Rossum, R. A. De Zeeuw, and A. H. Witte, Identification of cannabivarins in hashish by a new method of combined gas chromatography-mass spectrometry, *Clin. Chim. Acta,* **34**, 365 (1971).
279. Vree, T. B., D. D. Breimer, C. A. M. Van Ginneken, and J. M. Van Rossum, Identification in hashish of tetrahydrocannabinol, cannabidiol and cannabinol analogues with a methyl side-chain, *J. Pharm. Pharmacol.*, **24**, 7 (1972).

280. Vree, T. B., J. P. M. C. Gorgels, A. Th. J. M. Muskens, and J. M. Van Rossum, Deuterium isotope effects in the metabolism of N-alkylsubstituted amphetamines in man, *Clin. Chim. Acta,* **34**, 333 (1971).
281. Wall, M. E., The *in vitro* and *in vivo* metabolism of tetrahydrocannabinol (THC), *Ann. N.Y. Acad. Sci.,* **191**, 23 (1971).
282. Wallace, J. E., J. D. Biggs, and K. Blum, Gas-liquid and thin-layer chromatographic determination of morphine in biologic specimens, *Clin. Chim. Acta,* **36**, 85 (1971).
283. Walle, T., Quantitative gas chromatography of picogram quantities of amines as 2,4-dinitrophenyl derivatives, *Acta Pharm. Suec.,* **5**, 367 (1968).
284. Weissman, N., M. L. Lowe, J. M. Beattie, and J. A. Demetriou, Screening method for detection of drugs of abuse in human urine, *Clin. Chem.,* **17**, 875 (1971).
285. Wells, C. E., G.L.C. Determination of the optical isomers of amphetamine, *J. Assoc. Off. Anal. Chem.,* **53**, 113 (1970).
286. Wilkinson, G. R., The GLC separation of amphetamine and ephedrines as pentafluorobenzamide derivatives and their determination by electron capture detection, *Anal. Lett.,* **3**, 289 (1970).
287. Wilkinson, G. R. and E. L. Way, Sub-microgram estimation of morphine in biological fluids by gas-liquid chromatography, *Biochem. Pharmacol.,* **18**, 1435 (1969).
288. Wilks, P. A. and R. A. Brown, Construction and performance of an infrared chromatographic fraction analyzer, *Anal. Chem.,* **36**, 1896 (1964).
289. Yamauchi, T., Y. Shoyama, Y. Matsuo, and I. Nishioka, Cannabigerol monomethyl ether, a new component of hemp, *Chem. Pharm. Bull.,* **16**, 1164 (1968).
290. Yeh, S. Y. and L. A. Woods, Isolation of morphine-3-glucuronide from urine of rats injected with codeine, *Pharmacologist,* **11**, 240 (1969).
291. Yoshimura, H., K. Oguri, and H. Tsukamoto, Detection of morphine in urine, II. An improved method by thin-layer chromatography utilizing potassium platinum iodine as the reagent for both coloration and fluorescence, *Chem. Pharm. Bull.,* **14**, 1286 (1966).
292. Yoshimura, H., K. Oguri, and H. Tsukamoto, Metabolism of drugs, LXII. Isolation and identification of morphine glucuronides in urine and bile of rabbits, *Biochem. Pharmacol.,* **18**, 279 (1969).

Chapter Three

ORGANIC PATHOLOGY RELATED TO VOLUME AND PATTERN OF ALCOHOL USE

WERNER K. LELBACH, *Department of Internal Medicine, University Clinics of Bonn, Bonn, West Germany*

It is commonly accepted that prolonged heavy intake of alcoholic beverages may lead to organic lesions in liver, pancreas, myocardium, and peripheral muscles. However, only in a certain percentage of those who are heavy users of alcoholic beverages do organic changes become manifest. Whatever type of causal relationship between alcohol intake and organic pathology may be believed to exist, there can be no doubt that this relationship is not a simple one. This will be readily understood if the ambivalent nature of ethanol* is taken into consideration. On the one hand, this relatively small, neutral, water-soluble molecule (M.W. 46.07) can be regarded as a source of energy providing 7.1 Kcal/g to be fully utilized in the process of metabolic degradation by specific enzyme systems localized predominantly in the hepatocytes. On the other hand, owing to the limited capacity of the metabolic pathways, the toxic nature of this pharmacologically active compound manifests itself in its depressant action on the central nervous system as soon as the influx of this substance exceeds the individual's capacity for metabolism and excretion. Therefore insight into the nature of this relationship will not be possible without considering volume and pattern of alcohol use and also other factors that may modify the turnover of this substance.

By studying the epidemiology of alcoholic beverage use and its consequences it has become evident that especially after World War II alcohol

---

* "Alcohol" and "ethanol" are used synonymously pertaining to absolute alcohol (1 liter = 793.9 g) (107) unless otherwise stated.

consumption was on a steady rise in all "civilized" countries. It has been customary to express total consumption in a given country in liters of absolute alcohol per capita (either of total population or of "drinking" population, e.g., beyond age 15) per year. Bättig (19) considers an annual consumption of less than 5 liters per capita (e.g., Holland) as low, 5 to 10 liters as moderate (e.g., Great Britain and Scandinavian countries), and more than 10 liters (the extreme is France, 30 liters) as high. Consumption is dependent on several factors, such as volume and type of indigenous production as well as traditional beverage use, revenue laws, and import taxation, and price of beverages in relation to per capita income.

A number of surveys concerning the effects of an increase in overall consumption have been carried out in those regions of the world where sale and consumption of alcoholic beverages are of socioeconomic relevance. Their results strongly suggest that fluctuations in per capita consumption of alcoholic beverages are correlated to secular trends not only in the number of patients hospitalized with alcoholic psychoses (383) and in mortality from acute alcoholism (18, 19) but also in cirrhosis mortality for individual countries (55, 115, 119, 178, 215, 235, 268, 318, 319, 341, 380, 381, 414, 475), though variations and exceptions should be subject of further investigations (115). Even price of beverage alcohol in relation to per capita income was shown by Seeley (441) to be inversely related to mortality from cirrhosis of the liver. Similar trends for a rise in alcohol consumption concomitant with that of income were reported for Denmark by Nielsen (364, 365) and for West-Germany by Wurzbacher (537). Bättig (19) presented evidence that the death rate from alcoholism increases in proportion to the square of the increase in consumption.

However, annual per capita consumption is only a very crude indicator of the incidence of alcoholism because the frequency distribution of alcohol use is highly skewed and its curve actually follows the logarithmic normal law as was shown by Ledermann (252). His theoretical model was later confirmed by De Lint and Schmidt (283, 435) who found their empirically derived distribution curve of alcohol buying in Ontario to fit very smoothly to Ledermann's equation. Thus a high percentage of the total consumption is used by only a small fraction of the drinking population. This was already pointed out by Jellinek (208) in 1955 who stated that not more than 2% of the population in the United States drank 25% of the whole production. Similar were Bättig's (20) results for Switzerland. Postulating that at the most only 50% of the population drink regularly, Müting (345) calculated that in West Germany daily consumption in 1971 had already reached an amount of 60 g of absolute alcohol for this half of the population. Methodological problems in describing drinking practices were outlined by Knupfer (239), who emphasized the importance of obtaining data on both frequency and quantity, if one was to regard the amount of intake as "intensity" factor related to some time unit.

However, a look at Ledermann's highly skewed distribution curve makes it evident that alcoholism is not solely a question of quantity.

1. MODERATE DRINKING AND HEAVY DRINKING

It has been repeatedly pointed out (50, 316, 524) that alcoholism cannot be defined in terms of quantity consumed per time unit. Moreover, excessive drinking is by no means necessarily identical with addiction to alcohol. For example, Prys-Williams (392) states that according to statistics from England and Wales most regular heavy drinkers and most of those arrested for drunkenness are not alcoholics. But for the sake of classifying drinking behavior in connection with various pathologic conditions thought to be associated with alcohol abuse, quite a number of investigators found it convenient to define some quantitative limit of (daily) consumption, however arbitrary, that would be consistent with the concept of "moderate drinking" or beyond which it might be justified to allot an individual to the class of "heavy drinkers."

How much criteria for "moderate drinking" may vary from generally accepted standards of today can be inferred from the rules set up by the so-called *Mässigkeitsvereine* [temperance societies; in the fifteenth and sixteenth centuries in Germany (112); different, however, from the temperance movements of later centuries, which insisted on total abstinence (461)]. During this time, wine consumption in Germany seemed to have reached a peak, so that imperial decrees were issued against excessive drunkenness, though without any effect. The statutes of such temperance societies, founded by several knightly orders in wine-growing Germany and Austria, prescribe exactly the number of *Ordensbecher* ("cups") per day their members were allowed to drink; for instance, not more than 14 *Ordensbecher* per day. In retrospect the contents of these cups can only be estimated within a minimum-maximum range from specimens still exhibited in municipal historic collections. The average content of such cups seems to have been 0.2 liter, so that in the name of "temperance" 2.8 liters of wine were permitted to be ingested during meals. The alcohol content of wine in those times is not known. It was not allowed to fill this number of cups with "Spanish or Italian spiced wine" or with "brandy" (burned wine). As to brandy, not more than 120 to 300 ml/day were thought to be in compliance with the rules of "moderate drinking."

Table 1 gives an idea of what today is thought to be consistent with the concept of "moderate use" of alcohol. For the sake of relating amount of intake to a time unit a daily consumption is assumed. The lowest figure of about 6 g ethanol per day is mentioned by Sackett et al. (423), who, in an investigation pertaining to lifetime use of tobacco and alcohol of 1019 consecutively interviewed white patients, distinguished two categories within the class of "alcohol users": those who drink less or more than the equivalent of 0.5 fl oz of 100 proof whiskey. Dölle (108) recommended as "moderate" use not more than 250 ml wine or 0.5 liter beer on not more than 3 days/week (corresponding to 120 to 150 g/week). A well-documented definition of "moderate use of alcohol" was given in a study by the Joint Committee of the Actuarial Society of America and the Association of Life-Insurance Directors carried out in 1914 and again in 1929 covering over 2 million policies. This term was applied to persons who took an average of two glasses of beer or one glass of whiskey or their equivalent per day (corresponding to 7 to 18 g ethanol per day if as typical servings 7-oz glasses of beer and 1- to 1.5-oz of 86 to 100 proof whiskey are used for calculation); this use was connected with a slightly raised relative mortality of 115% for those who were accepted at standard rates of premium (6).

From the nutritional aspect 20% of total daily caloric requirement is the largest proportion that should be derived from alcoholic beverages (316, 72). The Food and Agricultural Organization of the United Nations (FAO) recommended not more than 10% (224). Ugarte et al. (490) defined excessive drinking as consumption of more than 20% of calories as ethanol. On the basis of statistics of the Federal Republic of Germany for 1964 to 1965 Wirths (533) calculated that the average potential consumer derived 5.5% of a total of 3083 kcal/day from ethanol, a proportion that seems to be still increasing. Le Breton and Trémolière (249) calculated that for the average male consumer in France alcohol covers 10 to 15% of daily calories, for some up to 30%. In a survey of the calorie and nutrient contribution from alcoholic beverages to the diet of 155 nonalcoholic male and female "nondrinkers" and "social drinkers" in Cleveland, Ohio, subdivided into four groups according to their drinking habits, Bebb et al. (34) found that the highest daily alcohol calorie intake on drinking days was 16.5% for men and 10.9% of total calories for women. Hartroft (183) described a hypothetical "executive drinker" who may consume as much as 1800 kcal as alcohol distributed in numerous small portions over the day and still not fall into the sociomedical category of an alcoholic because he continues to function well socially.

Hayman (184), attacking the "myth of social drinking," stressed that "moderation" is as difficult to define as "social drinking." General consensus holds that drinking while maintaining a low blood alcohol concentration (BAC less than 50 mg/100 ml) is not harmful, but Hayman points out that innumerable so-called social drinkers exceed this level regularly or on many occasions. Indeed, using BAC levels for defining desirable limits of alcohol consumption in keeping with social propriety might result in actually recommending a considerable alcohol intake, as Forney and Hughes (130) made clear; 57 young adult subjects who consumed hourly 1 oz of 100 proof bourbon whiskey per 68 kg of body weight did not reach blood alcohol concentrations exceeding 50 mg/100 ml until they had been drinking 5 hr, that is, after an intake of 45 g ethanol. In a different study, blood alcohol concentrations (BAC) were determined in 19 members of a dining club who had each consumed 62 to 67 g of ethanol as wine (interspersed with food) over a period of about 2 1/2 hrs (391); BAC varied within a wide range of 30 to 95 mg/100 ml for the majority, reaching 117 and 138 mg/100 ml in two individuals. There was no correlation between BAC and subjective assessment of alcohol impairment.

In a viticultural country like France distributing large quantities of wine in small installments over 16 hr of the day is not unusual. According to Bastide (32) the French regard a daily intake of nearly 2 qt of wine (1893 ml = 150 g ethanol) as not harmful to either body or mind of the working man. In a large metropolitan area (Bordeaux) interviews with a small sample of the population revealed that three-quarters of them think one who consumes less than 2 liters of wine per day is immune to alcoholism (135). An intake of this magnitude lies within the range compatible with the concept of "heavy drinking" or "alcoholism" in Table 2. This table also makes it clear that there is no generally accepted hard and fast quantitative limit between moderate and heavy drinking or abuse but that ranges are overlapping. An illustration of what might still be thought to fall into the category of so-called "social drinking" is William's report quoted by Hayman (184): In a social party setting with free whiskey 90 fraternity men consumed within one hour on the average 11 oz of 86 proof whiskey equalling 111 g of ethanol.

However, most authors agree that in heavy drinkers average intake exceeds 80 g/day. Thaler (476) notes that data on consumption obtained from alcoholics in his series should usually be multiplied by the factor 2 or 3 to arrive at the true figures. Recently, data were collected from groups of alcoholics of different nationality for the specific purpose of establishing the average daily alcohol consumption. Comparison of estimates from these samples shows that they are surprisingly similar, with means lying between 176 and 220 g/day (Table 3). What Ledermann (251) calls the "terrain éthylique" (i.e., the range of 160 to 240 g/day) seems to be a good

TABLE 1 RANGE OF ETHANOL INTAKE PER DAY THOUGHT TO BE CONSISTENT WITH "DRINKING IN MODERATION"

Author	Definition of Drinking Habits	Equivalent to Grams of Ethanol per Day (if daily consumption is assumed)[a]	Country
Sackett et al. (423)	Alcohol "users"	(a) <5.8 g (b) >5.8 g (see text)	USA
Joint Committee (6)	Moderate use	7–18 g (see text)	USA
Goldberg (157)	Moderate consumer	8–12 g (see text)	Sweden
Prys-Williams (392)	Regular light drinker	9 g	England
	Moderate steady drinker	18 g	
Dölle (108)	Moderate use	17–21 g (see text)	West Germany
Carey et al. (72)	Moderate alcohol intake	47–75 g (20% of total calories)	USA
Ugarte et al. (488)	Moderate drinking	Less than 80 g	Chile

Bättig (20)	Moderate use to Moderate drinking	Less than 80 g	Switzerland
Marconi (316)	Moderate drinking	Up to 80 g	Chile

[a] All liquid measures (continental, Imperial, U.S.) were converted to milliliter or liter. Quantities consumed will preferably be given in grams ethanol with calculations based on the following average alcohol contents:

Beer: 4% v/v = 31.8 g/liter
Must: 5 to 6% v/v = 39.7 to 47.6 g/liter
Wine: 10% v/v = 79.3 g/liter
Fortified wines: 15 to 20% v/v = 119.0 to 158.7 g/liter
Spirits: 38% v/v (Germany, Australian whiskey) to 50% v/v = 301.6 to 396.9 g/liter
Whiskey (U.S.): 86 to 100 proof (U.S.) = 43 to 50% v/v
Whisky (U.K.): 70 proof (U.K.) = 40% v/v

For customary measures, "typical servings," standards for converting measures, concentrations of alcohol in different beverages and converting % v/v to g/100 ml the following literature was used: Wallgren and Barry (506), Bahr (23), Mellor (325) Ledermann (250), Documenta Geigy (107).

TABLE 2 RANGE OF ETHANOL INTAKE PER DAY FOUND IN "HEAVY DRINKERS" OR "ALCOHOLICS"

Author	Definition of Drinking Habits	Beverage	Equivalent to Grams of Ethanol per Day (if daily consumption is assumed)	Country
1. Kager et al. (219)	"Strong consumer"	Spirits	33 g or more	Norway
2. Mannhardt (315)	Considerable consumption	Beer; wine	40 g	Switzerland
3. McDonald et al. (300)	Excessive consumption	Beer; wine; whiskey	>21–45 g	USA
4. Jellinek (209)	Alcoholics, moderate drinking	—	Not more than 50–60 g	USA
5. Ratnoff and Patek (399)	Alcoholic	Beer; wine; whiskey	>50–75 g	USA
6. Baumberger (33)	Alcoholic	Beer; wine; spirits (for several years)	>80 g	Switzerland
7. Kuster et al. (246)	Continuous immoderate drinking	Wine	>80 g	Chile
8. Armas-Cruz et al. (16)	Continuous excessive drinking Alcoholic	Wine	Daily up to inebriation >80 g	Chile
9. Nakamura et al. (355)	Heavy drinker	Saké (15.5% v/v)	>66–110 g	Japan
10. Wilkinson et al. (531)	Alcoholics, excessive drinking	Beer; wine; spirits	>100 g	Australia
11. Tofler et al. (482)	High consumption Very high consumption	Beer or equivalent	72–135 g >135 g	Australia
12. Eppinger (117)	Alcoholic	Beer; wine	>60–120 g	Austria

13. Gros (170)	Alcoholic	Wine or equivalent	>120 g	West Germany
14. von Oldershausen (371)	Alcoholic	Wine or equivalent	>120 g	West Germany
15. Thaler (476)	Excessive drinking	Beer; wine; spirits	80–120 g (multiplied by 2 to 3)	Austria
16. MacKay (310)	High alcohol consumption	Beer; wine	>120 g	Australia
17. Gigglberger (151, 152)	Alcoholic	Beer; wine; spirits	>120 g (plus once/twice weekly consid. more)	South Germany
18. Goldberg (Wien) (157)	Average alcoholic	Beer; wine; spirits	160 g	Sweden
19. Menghini (332)	Chronic alcohol abuse	Wine	>160 g	Italy
20. Wilens (528)	Chronic excessive alcoholism	Whiskey or equivalent	>160–188 g	USA
21. Vetter (495)	Average chronic alcoholic	Wine; spirits	176 ± 132 g ($\bar{x} \pm 2s$)	Switzerland
22. Lelbach (260)	Chronic alcoholics	Beer; must; wine; spirits	Average: 180 g	West Germany
23. Lutterotti (296)	Chronic alcoholic	Wine	Average: 180 g	Italy (Alto Adige)
24. Bättig (20)	Heavy drinking Excessive drinking	Absolute alcohol	160–240 g >240 g	Switzerland
25. Ledermann (251)	"Terrain éthylique"	Absolute alcohol	160–240 g	France
26. Baggenstoss and Stauffer (21)	Alcoholic	Whiskey	80–376 g	USA
27. Baggenstoss (22)	"Active alcoholic"	Whiskey	160–300 g (up to terminal illness)	USA
28. Hällen and Krook (174)	Heavy drinker	Spirits	Up to 320–400 g	Sweden

TABLE 3 ESTIMATES OF *AVERAGE* DAILY ETHANOL INTAKE IN ALCOHOLICS OF DIFFERENT NATIONALITY

Author	Number of Patients	Average Daily Ethanol Consumption (g)	Nationality of Patients
Lutterotti (296)	210	180	Austro-Italian (Alto Adige)
Lelbach (260)	417	178.5 (range: 99–266)	West German
Jaross (207)	41	186.6 ± 75.5	East German
Vetter (495)	101	176 ± 132	Swiss
Schmidt and Popham (433)	100	195	Canadian
Grünberger et al. (172)	99	192.0 ± 92.7	Austrian
Wilkinson et al. (532)	179 (male) 41 (female)	220 155	Australian

average estimate throughout the world. Of course, superimposed on this average intake, there will be limited periods (bouts) with ingestion of larger quantities. Alling et al. (12) described such drinking bouts in 14 Swedish patients with advanced alcoholic habits of long standing (more than 10 to more than 25 years' duration; average: 16.8 years). These patients reported that during their last drinking bout prior to admission (duration: 3 days to 1 month; average: 18 days) they had had an intake between 200 and 400 g/day; the authors, however, point out that the real intake might have been less.

2. CAPACITY OF ETHANOL ELIMINATION

Based on the data gathered from experiments of 19 authors, Elbel (116) stated that after oral (in four of the statistics intravenous) administration the rate of ethanol oxidation in relation to body weight varies in the human between 70 and 132 mg/(kg)(hr), with an average of almost exactly 100 mg/(kg)(hr). Data by other workers are also within this range: Barnes et al. (31) [75 mg/(kg)(hr)], Lundsgaard (291) [105 mg/(kg)(hr)], Goldberg (156) (for 9 nondrinkers, 16 moderate drinkers, and 14 heavy drinkers: 87.9 ± 10.3, 95.5 ± 7.7, and 110.0 ± 4.6 mg/(kg)(hr), respectively]. Trémolières et al. (483) [105 mg/(kg)(hr)], Bernstein and Staub (36) [107 ± 16 mg /(kg)(hr)], Liebermann (277) [for 11 cirrhotics with jaundice, 10 cirrhotics without jaundice, and 10 controls: 73, 98, and 102 mg/(kg)(hr), respectively; note: increase in water compartment in the cirrhotics], Reynolds et al. (408) [72 to 121 mg/(kg)(hr) in 10 patients with decompensated alcoholic cirrhosis], and recently Greenberg (167) [100 mg/(kg)(hr)].

Weatherall (512) reports a somewhat larger range between 60 and 150 mg/(kg)(hr), Thompson (480) a range of 50 to 180 mg/(kg)(hr). Westerfeld and Schulman (518) estimated alcohol metabolism to vary between 100 and 200 mg/(kg)(hr), the upper limit being equal to the intake of about 1/5 gal of 100 proof liquor per day for a man of 70 kg body weight. Widmark (521) mentions a hypothetical subject with exceptionally high individual constants who would be able to eliminate ethanol at a rate of 203 mg/(kg)(hr). After oral ingestion, hourly elimination ranges between 4.1 and 11.0 g /hr (48, 116, 520). Bonnichsen et al. (49), reviewing Widmark's constants r and β, found hourly elimination to be 5 to 9 g/hr for adolescents, 8 to 11 g/hr for adult "normal drinkers," and up to 14 to 16 g/hr for alcoholics. But they state that even a heavy drinker accustomed to large quantities cannot eliminate more than $15 \times 24 = 360$ g ethanol per day as an absolute maximum limit once a blood alcohol concentration of between 200 and 300 mg/100 ml has been reached. Filip and Hoenigova (127) calculated the hourly rate of ethanol oxidation after intravenous infusion to be 7.61 ± 1.6 g/hr for 10 controls and 5.45 ± 1.64 g/hr for 10 cirrhotics.

Based on results of prolonged feeding experiments in dogs Newman (362) arrived at a hypothetical maximum rate in the human of about 224 mg/(kg)(hr) (1 qt of 100 proof whiskey per day at 70 kg body weight). Later, direct determinations (363) of maximal daily elimination in four subjects (two moderate, two heavy drinkers), however, showed that under hourly oral administration for up to 52 hr the peak elimination was about 185 mg/(kg)(hr) (760 ml of 100 proof whiskey per day in a male alcoholic weighing 68.2 kg). They point out that this figure pertains to the sum of all factors responsible for disposal of ingested alcohol, that is, ethanol oxidation and elimination by breath and urine; furthermore, for oral ingestion together with meals a certain deficit in absorption of at least 10 to 20% and/or a retarded absorption (47, 116, 176, 242, 453, 458, 485) has to be taken into consideration. Mendelson et al. (328) reported a mean maximum rate of 181 mg/(kg)(hr) in seven alcoholics. De Lint and Schmidt (282), employing a sociological method of estimating maximal alcohol consumption applicable to a drinking population at large, arrived at a figure of 195 mg/(kg)(hr), which is surprisingly close to the elimination rates found in the experimental studies.

When alcohol was given by intravenous infusion, Wilkinson et al. (530) saw an elimination rate of 136 ± 23 mg/(kg)(hr) in 16 alcoholics. Studying the rate of removal of alcohol from the blood in 8 moderate drinkers and in 20 alcohol addicts with normal liver, 18 with fatty liver, and 15 with cirrhosis, Ugarte et al. (489, 491) observed higher values but failed to find significant differences between the groups [162 ± 45, 178 ± 48, 184 ± 75, and 193 ± 41 mg/(kg)(hr), respectively]. Fenna and co-workers (121) found a highly interesting racial difference in the rate of alcohol metabolism after intravenous infusion between 17 whites [144.9 ± 39.0 mg/(kg)(hr)] and 26 Indians or 21 Eskimos, respectively [101.3 ± 2.7 or 109.8 ± 33.7 mg/(kg)(hr), respectively]. Alcohol degradation rate following intravenous infusion in persons possessing typical [mean: 111.4 mg/(kg)(hr) for men; 95.5 mg/(k(hr) for women] and atypical liver alcohol dehydrogenase [man: 113.6 mg/(kg)(hr); woman: 125.4 mg/(kg)(hr)] was not essentially different. The finding did not confirm the theory that liver-ADH is a rate-limiting factor in ethanol metabolism in man (114).

During short-term experiments, even larger amounts have been ingested (204, 326, 328), for which it would be necessary to postulate an elimination rate of about 180 to 220 mg/(kg)(hr). This intake was always accompanied by a more or less steep rise in blood alcohol concentration with moderate to severe symptoms of intoxication and could not be continued for more than a very limited period of time. Forney and Hughes (130) investigated alcohol accumulation after prolonged drinking and determined blood alcohol levels by breathalyzer. Their 25 male and 75 female subjects ingested hourly 1 oz of 100 proof bourbon whiskey per 68 kg of body weight [requiring an elimination rate of 172.5 mg/(kg)(hr)] together with light meals; blood alcohol concentration slowly rose and reached 53 to 60 mg/100 ml at the end of 7 hr. However, doubling the amount ingested resulted in a sharp rise in blood alcohol concentration exceeding 50 mg/100 ml after 1 1/2 hr and reaching 160 to 220 mg/100 ml at 5 to 5 1/2 hr. Following Widmark's (521) original definition of maximal daily alcohol consumption, that is, neither entailing an appreciable accumulation of alcohol in the blood with concomitant signs of intoxication, if intake is accordingly spaced, nor allowing for intervals in which pathways of alcohol metabolism are not completely saturated, a range of about 100 to 130 mg/(kg)(hr) would still be a good average estimate to be safely used for clinical and medicolegal purposes (167). For a 70-kg man this would be equivalent to an intake of 168 to 218 g ethanol per day.

In prolonged heavy drinking it would be unrealistic to base calculations on a 24-hr drinking day and on figures for maximal possible daily elimination. In drinking practice, the alcoholic has to take his daily intake within the 16 waking hours of the day. Unless he belongs to the pleasure-seeking type of drinker, found, for instance, in France, he is not interested in spacing his drinks evenly to keep his alcohol degradation systems fully saturated without allowing his blood alcohol level to rise more than slightly, which would prevent him from losing control. Instead, he wants the tension-relieving effect of intoxicating levels of blood alcohol concentration on the CNS.

Within medicolegally recognized limits, temporary enhancement of clearance of ethanol from the blood (as well as that of meprobamate and pentobarbital) was observed in alcoholics and nonalcoholics after experimental consumption of large amounts of ethanol (140 to 300 g/day) over prolonged periods (more than 2 weeks) by Misra et al. (340) and by Mezey and Tobon (337). Under controlled dietary conditions alcohol was given either as isocaloric substitution for carbohydrates or in addition to normal adequate diets. Rates of disappearance of intravenously administered ethanol from the blood rose from control values of 13.6 ± 2.4, 13.8 ± 2.0 (alcoholics, nonalcoholics; 340), and 14.9 ± 2.5 mg/(100 ml)(hr) (controls; 337) to 18.5 ± 2.0, 23.8 ± 2.0, and 19.7 ± 3.4 mg/(100 ml)(hr), respectively, Increased clearance rates rapidly returned to pre-ethanol values as early as 7 days after cessation of continuous alcohol ingestion. Since activity of liver alcohol dehydrogenase did not appreciably increase (but merely returned to normal values under adequate protein intake), this acceleration might result, at least in part, from an induction of NADPH-dependent ethanol-oxidizing enzyme systems (276), as became evident from simultaneous induction of other drug-metabolizing systems (340, 418) or to other mechanisms.

Nutritional factors also can alter the rate of alcohol metabolism. As was recently shown by Bode et al. (44), a short period of protein malnutrition can result in a significant retardation of ethanol metabolism. At the end of 1 week on a low-protein diet (20 g/day), elimination of intravenously administered ethanol from the blood was reduced, in all of eight human volunteers, by $35 \pm 8\%$, in comparison to initial rates under an isocaloric standard diet containing 80 g of protein per day. Prolonging this period for another 10 days with reduction of protein intake to 10 g/day had an even more pronounced effect. Clearance rates returned to normal after 3 to 4 days of a high protein (120 g/day) diet. Differences found in the ADH-activity of the liver as well as in ethanol metabolism between fed and fasted rats (65, 499) and the significant reduction of ADH-activity and alcohol oxidation produced by controlled protein malnutrition in the same species (42, 43, 229) had led to the assumption that the same would be valid for the human. The role played by mechanisms of ethanol breakdown other than

ADH, including the hepatic microsomal ethanol-oxidizing system (276), under protein malnutrition is not known. It is well known that in actual drinking practice intake of excessive amounts of alcohol may readily entail an absolute or relative decrease in the percentage of protein calories, though this is not necessarily so (360).

3. CONTROLLED STUDIES OF THE QUANTITATIVE EFFECT OF ALCOHOL INTAKE

Investigators have given various amounts of ethanol under controlled conditions once or over prolonged periods to groups of volunteers with different previous drinking habits.

Effect of Single Doses

Bang et al. (28) found elevated SGOT-levels 1 to 10 hr after the last consumption in 27 out of a group of 35 heavy drinkers without clinical or biochemical evidence of hepatic disease, all admitted to the hospital in a state of acute intoxication. A rough positive correlation existed between blood alcohol concentrations on admission and maximum SGOT-values, the latter returning to normal within 1 to 11 days. Two weeks after admission one of these alcoholics was challenged with 100 g of ethanol as aquavit; this resulted in a prompt typical rise of SGOT for 48 hr. An even more pronounced elevation of enzyme levels with slower return to normal could be provoked in the same patient after 5 weeks of an adequate diet with a larger test dose of 135 g ethanol. SGOT in 12 healthy nonalcoholic volunteers, on the other hand, remained within normal limits when a dose of about 85 g of ethanol was given to them. Results observed in the alcoholics were believed to be indicative of alcohol-induced cell damage to the liver.

No alterations in transaminases, bromosulfalein-retention, and serum alkaline phosphatase levels were observed in seven out of a group of 104 hospitalized alcoholics who were given a single dose of 113 g of ethanol by continuous nasogastric drip (1). Neither could Childs et al. (82) detect a rise in SGOT-levels in 12 nonalcoholics after intravenous infusion of 0.6 to 0.7 g ethanol per kilogram of body weight, with maximum blood alcohol levels ranging between 78 and 135 mg/100 ml. However, a significant reduction of the rate of BSP-clearance was found in 8 of 11 subjects and was attributed to impairment of liver function. Brohult and Reichard (58) gave a much higher single dose of 200 to 300 g of ethanol to 10 healthy volunteers as whiskey or wine and determined serum-ornithine-carbamoyl-transferase (SOCT) values for the next 11 days. They saw elevations of SOCT-values in all those who had been given 300 g as whiskey, with a maximum around the seventh day, but not in two subjects who had taken only 200 g as wine. The authors believed that the reason why serum enzyme levels rose in healthy individuals—contrary to the results of Bang et al.—should be sought in the fact that they had used a very large single dose of alcohol, a probably almost liver-specific enzyme together with a sensitive method for its determination, and they had extended daily blood examinations over a period of 11 days. SOCT-values after a much smaller dose of ethanol determined only up to 96 hr did not rise (405).

Müting (345) determined the levels of a number of serum enzymes, lactate, ammonia, free phenols, glucose, and lipids before and 2, 4, 8, and 24 hr after an oral load of 70 g of ethanol as wine in 6 healthy subjects, 12 patients with alcohol-induced fatty infiltration of the liver, and 1 patient with residual damage after infectious hepatitis. While a slight rise in glutamate-dehydrogenase (GLDH) and sorbitol-dehydrogenase (SDH) values as well as levels of ammonia, lactate, and free phenols remained within normal limits for the healthy subjects, GLDH, SDH, and blood ammonia values became markedly abnormal in the patients with alcohol-induced fatty infiltration of the liver and in the patient with residual posthepatitic damage. In another study (155) oral alcohol taken over a 4-hr period in a single dose of 1.7 g/kg of body weight (about one-half bottle of whiskey) by 8 healthy volunteers also resulted in a significant elevation of serum isocitric dehydrogenase (SICD) at 4 hr and of SOCT at 15 hr after ingestion, whereas no significant change in SGOT and SGPT or bromsulfalein retention was noted. The authors point out that minor elevations of SOCT and SICD might be found in the absence of changes in other serum enzymes, since SOCT seems a more sensitive index of liver damage than the transaminases, as was also, if to a lesser extent, SICD (35, 238, 406). With a much smaller dose of about 28 g (0.5 ml of ethanol per kilogram administered intravenously) to 42 patients with active hepatocellular injury and 22 patients without liver disease, Galambos et al. (142) failed to exert a significant effect on either the mean level of activity for SGOT, SGPT, SLDH, and SOD or on the diurnal variability of enzyme activities in both groups. Wiebe et al. (522) studied the time course of hepatic lipid accumulation in three healthy young male subjects who were given a single dose of about 190 g (3 g/kg of body weight of ethanol within 5 hr) together with a light meal. Fine-needle aspiration biopsy was performed five times during the 48-hr period of the study. In all three subjects a slight but constant rise of SGOT and SGPT up to 48 hr was found, though remaining within normal limits. Maximal hepatic triglyceride accumulation occurred within 24 hr (expressed as molar ratio of triglyceride over phospholipids); values returned to normal at 48 hr. A significant, dose-related enhancement of postprandial lipemia after rapid ingestion of 12, 24, or 48 g of ethanol prior to a meal of moderate or high fat content was observed by Friedman et al. (137), Swartz et al. (471), and Barboriak and Meade (29). The increase was of a higher order than could have been expected from a merely additive effect of the meal and alcohol.

Extrahepatic effects of single doses of ethanol were also recorded; the following selection cannot claim to be complete.

A transient drop in platelet counts was provoked three times in a female alcoholic without evidence of liver disease after intravenous infusion of 80 g of ethanol (388) and in three alcoholics after an oral dose of 72 g, probably due to a peripheral effect on platelets (422).

Symptoms of glucose intolerance, absent under abstinence, were induced after a dose of 200 to 215 g of ethanol given to one female and one male alcoholic over one day (384). Of four apparently healthy young adults challenged similarly with alcohol over several days (a total of 344 to 387 g of ethanol spaced unevenly over 3 to 4 days) glucose intolerance became manifest in one subject. On the other hand, the clinical syndrome of "alcohol hypoglycemia" has been experimentally reproduced after appropriate periods of dietary deprivation (18 to 74 hr fast) in normal subjects, patients with clinical episodes of alcohol hypoglycemia, and juvenile-type diabetics from whom insulin and food had been withheld (134). Alcohol was given over a 6- to 8-hr period either by gastric tube or as intravenous infusion in total doses of between 86 and 120 g. Hypoglycemia was produced after an overnight fast in patients with prior episodes of hypoglycemia, but it was more pronounced when antecedent periods of fasting were longer. In normal subjects an infusion after an overnight fast did not lower blood sugar but infusions after up to 74 hr of fasting invariably led to significant reduction of plasma glucose values. Results seen in juvenile-type diabetics precluded the possibility that "alcohol hypoglycemia" is mediated by increases in the absolute availability of insulin. Fields and William (125) proved that this type of hypoglycemia is refractory to glucagon. The syndrome seems to originate principally from a direct inhibition of gluconeogenesis within the liver. Vulnerability in normals is especially great for those who have diminished gluconeogenic reserve owing to adrenocortical insufficiency, whereas in diabetic and thyrotoxic subjects an accelerated diversion from the postprandial metabolism of carbohydrate and protein to the starvation metabolism of fat seems to predispose to alcohol-induced inhibition of gluconeogensis.

Lowenfels et al. (286) observed an increase in both the volume and the amylase content of secretion collected from a pancreatic fistula in a 79-year-old nonalcoholic woman 3 hr after maximum blood alcohol concentration (70 mg/100 ml) was reached by intravenous infusion of about 22 g of ethanol over a 1-hr period. As opposed to this, Madding et al. (311) stated that neither oral ingestion of 16 g of ethanol within 10 min nor intravenous infusion of 22 g during 1 hr in a young patient with pancreatic fistula had any effect on volume or amylase level of the collected secretion. Dreiling et al. (111) gave 10 to 30 g of ethanol as intravenous infusion to 12 patients (7 with pancreatic disease, 5 without) within 10 min to the point of inebriation and collected duodenal secretion by double-lumened tube; volume, bicarbonate, and amylase content of external pancreatic secretion were not augmented. The authors point out, however, that larger doses of alcohol might have been necessary to produce an effect. Neither did instillation of 3 to 12 g of ethanol (as 50% v/v solution) into the duodenum, blocked by double-ballon catheter, in 20 volunteers convincingly change volume output, bicarbonate content, or enzyme activities of pancreaticoduodenal secretion (411). But even with a higher oral dose of 86 g of ethanol Baker (25) could not see any change in secretion in three patients with traumatic external pancreatic fistula.

In relation to the acute effects of ethanol on cardiovascular phenomena, Riff et al. (409) observed a significant increase in cardiac output due to an accelerated heart rate without change of stroke volume in 10 young nonalcoholic subjects after they had taken 81 g as bourbon whiskey within 10 min. Juchems and Klobe (218) found that 52 to 67 min after an oral dose of 0.73 to 1.52 g of ethanol per kilogram of body weight, given to 14 healthy volunteer subjects and ingested within 5 min, heart rate and cardiac output significantly increased, whereas peripheral resistance decreased. Alterations proved to be correlated to maximum levels of blood alcohol concentration. Stroke volume was not significantly changed, indicating that increase in cardiac output was mainly dependent on the increased pulse rate. It was concluded that these hemodynamic alterations were due to CNS-reflex mechanisms. Wendt et al. (515) failed to detect significant hemodynamic changes in chronic alcoholics after ingestion of 81 g as chilled vodka. Regan et al. (402, 404), evaluating the dose-response relationship of ethanol in the production of cardiac malfunction, found that in noncardiac alcoholics left-ventricular function, myocardial blood flow, and metabolism did not significantly change after oral administration of about 60 g of ethanol (6 oz of 42% v/v whiskey) within 2 hr. However, after 120 g of ethanol there was a progressive decrease of stroke output and rise of end-diastolic left-ventricular pressure with mean blood alcohol levels reaching 150 mg/100 ml, returning to normal after 4 hr. Leakage of cell constituents into coronary blood suggested a direct reversible myocardial injury. On the other hand, the smaller dose of 60 g of ethanol given to an alcoholic with heart failure was sufficient to reveal a depressant effect of ethanol on the left ventricle. Gould et al. (161), by employing cardiac catheterization, also found that even small amounts of alcohol can impair cardiac function in patients with cardiac disease. Two ounces of Canadian whiskey (about 18 to 20 g of ethanol) given to 10 patients with various kinds of heart disease and to 4 normal subjects resulted in a fall in cardiac index (liter/minute $\times$ meter^2) and stroke index (milliliter/meter^2) in all cardiac cases, whereas these parameters increased in the normals.

Effects of Controlled Prolonged Ethanol Administration

A number of experiments were conducted with the aim of assessing the effects of controlled continuous administration of alcohol over periods of several days to several months. Usually care was taken to space alcohol intake evenly over the 24 hours of the day and to ensure a nutritious diet with adequate vitamin and mineral content. Results obtained have proved to be largely dependent on dose and duration as well as on the choice of parameters sensitive enough to detect incipient or early functional and structural derangement caused by ethanol administration.

The fact that several workers have given alcohol to patients with well-established cirrhosis of the liver, under controlled conditions, for limited periods of time, together with a well-balanced diet, and that they claim that in spite of continuous alcohol administration no further deterioration of the clinical condition occurred, makes it clear how controversial results can be (Table 4). However, Table 4 shows that three of these experiment periods were relatively short and/or dosage did not exceed 90 g of ethanol per day. Yet Erenoglu et al. (118) gave a dose of 157 g of ethanol daily over 2 months and Reynolds et al. (408) even adjusted daily quantities of grain alcohol to increasing maximum capacity of ethanol elimination, or raised the dose finally 25% above the calculated rate of elimination, respectively, for periods of 10 to 11 weeks with maximum daily intake reaching 226 to 332 g of ethanol. But even under these conditions in the presence of an excellent calorie and protein intake, clinical, biochemical, and histologic data revealed improvement. Patients selected for this experiment were all incorrigible alcoholics, who had been repeatedly admitted for complications of alcoholism. Alcohol administration was not begun until a controlled period of 1 to 3 weeks' duration had made it clear that they were not going to develop progressive hepatic failure.

TABLE 4 CONTROLLED SHORT-TERM ADMINISTRATION OF ETHANOL TO CIRRHOTICS WITHOUT APPARENT ADVERSE EFFECTS ON CLINICAL CONDITION OR COURSE OF CLINICAL IMPROVEMENT

Author	Number of Cases (sex)	Ethanol Dose (g/day)	Duration of Experiment	Histological (and clinical) Diagnosis
Volwiler et al. (503)	1 (m)	48	30 days	Cirrhosis
Patek and Post (376)	4 (m)	84	6–18 months (6, 6, 14, 18)	Cirrhosis
Summerskill et al. (468)	6 (m)	70–90	10–32 days (10, 14, 20, 21, 21, 24, 32)	Cirrhosis (6)
	1 (f)			Fatty vacuolization (1)
Erenoglu et al. (118)	17 (m)	157	2 months	Cirrhosis
	4 (f)			
Reynolds et al. (408)	13	154 (at 150 lb) (2.26 g/kg body wt.)	10 weeks	
	10	Up to 245 (150 lb) adjusted to increasing maximum elimination rates	11 weeks	"Decompensated" cirrhosis (all jaundiced; majority with ascites)
	4	226–332 (25% above calculated maximum elimination rates)		

Under metabolic ward conditions, Mendelson et al. (326, 328) gave increasing doses of whiskey for 24 days to 10 chronic spree drinkers of long standing (skid-row alcoholics) who were in good health, had previously experienced withdrawal symptoms, and had been abstinent for 10 to 37 days before the onset of the study. During the first 5 days, doses were increased to 300 g of ethanol per day and this dosage was continued for 14 days, resulting in surprisingly moderate levels of intoxication at blood alcohol concentrations varying between 100 and 150 mg/100 ml. For the last 5 days intake was increased to about 400 g/day, resulting in a steep rise of blood alcohol levels to 200 to 350 mg/100 ml and signs of severe intoxication. Alcohol was abruptly discontinued on day 24. Only during the last 5 days of the experiment all subjects had slightly raised bromsulfalein retention, 9 developed proteinuria, 4 significant glucosuria, and ketonuria was observed in all 10. Serum uric acid, triglycerides, phospholipids, and cholesterol rose in all of the patients, serum free fatty acids only during the last 5 days. At blood alcohol levels below 200 mg/100 ml serum triglycerides increased two- to threefold unaccompanied by changes in free fatty acids. At levels of 200 to 400 mg/100 ml, however, triglycerides fell to or below normal values, whereas free fatty acids increased up to fivefold (430). However, no enzyme activities were measured in this series, nor were liver biopsies performed, which reduces the import of these experiments insofar as hepatic pathology is concerned.

In a similar experiment (204), 10 healthy morphine addicts were held in a maximum state of alcohol intoxication compatible with safe ambulatory management for 7 to 87 days by daily doses of ethanol ranging on the average from 200 to 370 g with a maximum intake (4 to 79 days) between 286 and 392 g/day. As long as patients were ingesting up to 300 to 350 g of ethanol per day, blood alcohol concentrations determined by breathalyzer in 3 patients did not exceed 50 mg/100 ml; elevation of intake to between 325 and 361 g/day resulted in blood alcohol levels between 150 and 250 mg/100 ml, accompanied by marked intoxication. Three months after the end of this experiment no residual clinical or laboratory impairment could be detected (blood count, urinalysis, thymol turbidity, cephalin flocculation, blood glucose, BUN). Again, no enzyme determinations, BSP-tests, or liver biopsies were done in this series.

In five alcoholics with a history of alcoholic fatty liver but without clinical or histologic evidence of liver disease at the time of the study, consecutive liver biopsies showed that isocaloric replacement of carbohydrates by ethanol, in an otherwise adequate diet, or addition of alcohol to such a diet, promtply resulted in hepatic fat accumulation (272). Alcohol was built into the diet as either whiskey or laboratory ethanol in increasing doses up to between 141 and 300 g/day for periods of 8 to 21 days. It is noteworthy that in the individual given the highest amount (300 g/day) with peak blood alcohol levels of 200 mg/100 ml, fat accumulation was already visible after 8 days, whereas subjects given about half this amount, which resulted in only moderately increased blood alcohol levels (30 to 100 mg/100 ml), fatty changes became evident only after longer administration (14 to 21 days). Liver function tests, including determinations of SGOT-activity, remained unaltered.

In another experiment (273), two alcohol-feeding periods, each lasting 16 to 18 days with only moderate doses of alcohol (increasing up to 98 to 131 g/day), which produced only mild euphoria without overt intoxication in three male and two female alcoholics, also resulted in histologically visible fat accumulation at the end of each period. Beside individual variations, the degree of steatosis depended partly on the different fat content of the diets fed in each of the two periods.

To test the possibility that a low-fat diet containing an excess of protein might protect the liver from alcohol-induced steatosis, Lieber and Rubin (275) gave 25% as protein and 25% as fat in a total of 2100 to 2700 cal/day to five alcoholic subjects. After a control period, carbohydrates in this diet were replaced by increasing doses of ethanol (for 4 days: 24% = 72 to 93 g; during subsequent 2 days: 36% = 108 to 139 g; during the last 12 days: 46% = 138 to 177 g/day). In spite of protein being given in quantities of more than twice the recommended amounts, minimal fat accumulation was seen after 8 days of alcohol (2 days of full dose) in three subjects, and moderate to extensive fatty metamorphosis after the full 18 days in four subjects. After 1 month of withdrawal, fat had completely disappeared in two alcoholics. Striking ultrastructural changes in endoplasmic reticulum and mitochondria were already conspicuous after 2 days of the full dose (416). Again, there was great individual variation in degree of steatosis as well as in ultrastructural changes. The authors concluded that, although deficient diets may potentiate the effects of ethanol, even an excess of dietary protein proved to be incapable of preventing the assumed direct toxic effect of alcohol on the human liver.

Rubin and Lieber (417) also demonstrated that even a 2-day administration of alcohol (mimicking "weekend" drinking) to seven nonalcoholic volunteers in doses of 180 to 270 g on the first and 245 to 270 g on the second day—irrespective of the diet (standard or high-protein and minimal-fat diet)—rapidly resulted in a significant increase in hepatic triglyceride content, although blood alcohol levels did not exceed 80 mg/100 ml. With lower doses (increasing from 68 g to a maximum of 170 g/day) given to another five nonalcoholics it took 6 to 14 days of continuous intake for a four- to thirteen-fold increase in triglycerides and for the previously mentioned ultrastructural changes to develop. There was also a rise in SGOT-values and serum uric acid concentration while BSP-retention remained within normal limits. Large supplements of vitamins, choline, and folic acid could not prevent these changes. It is pointed out that with a blood alcohol concentration of around 50 mg/100 ml the subjects showed, at the most, episodes of mild euphoria without being grossly intoxicated; this seems pertinent in view of the fact that a so-called social drinker who is not considered an alcoholic by his equals and who successfully conducts his business, apparently without ever being drunk, may nevertheless incur the whole range of alcohol-induced liver damage if he spaces his drinking accordingly.

Leevy (257, 259) gave exceptionally high doses of alcohol in the form of vodka added to a diet sufficient in calories, protein, vitamins, and minerals to seven alcoholics under metabolic ward conditions. Liver morphology and function had returned to normal in these alcoholics before the experiment began. In two patients 150 to 200 g of ethanol for 10 to 12 days produced fatty liver; increasing the dose to 300 to 600 g ethanol for 30 to 45 days resulted in alcoholic hepatitis in three patients accustomed to drinking large quantities of alcohol; in some of these patients alcohol had to be discontinued because of severe behavioral or gastrointestinal disturbances. With uncontrolled alcohol consumption, preexisting hepatic steatonecrosis in 26 patients developed eventually into cirrhosis of the liver within 8 to 120 months.

It is of interest to see that Chey et al. (81), using six mongrel dogs prepared with an esophagostomy, gastric fistula, and Heidenhain pouch, succeeded in producing fatty metamorphosis of the liver and, in all animals, degenerative as well as inflammatory and proliferative lesions histologically comparable to those of alcoholic hepatitis in man. Large doses of alcohol were administered for periods ranging from 10 to 18 months; the animals, weighing 13.6 to 20.5 kg, were given 4.4 g of ethanol per kilogram body weight from Monday through Friday with a small maintenance dose on weekends together with a well-balanced diet. Peak blood ethanol concentrations, usually seen at the sixth hour, ranged from 315 to 477 mg/100 ml, and the animals showed symptoms of severe intoxication. Fatty metamorphosis, which was found in only four of the animals, took a relatively long time to develop, at least 2 to 12 months. Biochemically, there was significant increase of serum alkaline phosphatase levels and gradual decrease of serum total protein and albumin concentrations in all six dogs, whereas SGPT and SGOT activities were significantly elevated only during the second and third month of ethanol treatment. No significant changes were observed in serum globulin, bilirubin, or BSP retention. With a liquid diet in which 41% of the calories were derived from grain alcohol, Ruebner et al. (420) produced fatty liver in rhesus monkeys, demonstrable by light microscopy and ultrastructural changes after 10 days, in spite of a 15% protein content and additional choline chloride in this diet.

On the other hand, Carey et al. (72) report that 12 nonalcoholic volunteers given 47 to 75 g of ethanol per day (20% of total calories) for 12 days did not develop significant alterations in serum uric acid, lactate, pyruvate, cholesterol, triglycerides, phospholipid, or zinc. In testing the effects of the composition of a diet given together with alcohol on blood enzyme values, Dimberg et al. (104) treated 12 male alcoholics (none with clinical or biochemical evidence of alcoholic cirrhosis) with a daily dose of 160 g of ethanol for 5 days together with a normal hospital diet (six patients) or a diet extremely poor in carbohydrate (six patients). During alcohol administration or shortly after its termination four of the six patients given a diet poor in carbohydrates showed elevated serum-GOT, -GPT, and creatine phosphokinase levels, indicating cell damage in liver and muscle. None of the six patients given a normal hospital diet exhibited these changes. The authors discussed the possibility that alcohol-induced disturbances of carbohydrate metabolism might have been responsible for these alterations. Similarly, from a significant increase of serum activities of the isoenzymes LDH_1 and LDH_2 (without concomitant increase of GOT, GPT, and CPK) in healthy volunteer subjects given a lower dose of alcohol (63, 127, and 127 g, administered on 2 1/2 successive days) together with a diet poor in carbohydrates, Hed et al. (185) concluded that a lack of carbohydrates may be a factor involved in the pathogenesis of alcoholic myopathy.

In a recent study by Song and Rubin (456), three occasional consumers of nonintoxicating amounts of alcohol were given 225 g of ethanol for 28 days (42% of a total of 3900 Kcal/day with 15% as protein). All exhibited a rise in serum creatine phosphokinase activity, returning to normal two weeks after cessation of alcohol. In two subjects, there were also striking ultrastructural changes in biopsy specimens taken from peripheral muscle, whereas light microscopy showed no changes. Since no appreciable metabolism of ethanol occurs in muscle, the authors suggest that the damage produced by ethanol administration might be interpreted as a direct toxic effect of ethanol.

Sullivan and Herbert (467) found that suppression of erythropoiesis, leukopoiesis, and thrombopoiesis as well as conversion of bone marrow from normoblastic to megaloblastic occurred within 10 days in three alcoholic patients after controlled daily consumption of alcohol in amounts readily consumed by "heavy drinkers." Alcohol was given for repeated periods of 10 to 21 days either as whiskey, whiskey plus fortified wines, or pure 43% v/v USP ethanol in doses equivalent to 75 to 270 g/day. A dose of 75 g/day proved to be an only partially suppressive dose for reticulocyte response to folic acid, but 150 g or more was fully effective. However, alcohol-induced inhibition of folate utilization could be overcome by very high doses of folate, exceeding minimal requirements three- to tenfold in spite of continued alcohol administration. During alcohol consumption, serum iron content and saturation of iron-binding protein were also increased, irrespective of influence on reticulocyte count. All hematologic changes rapidly returned to normal after withdrawal of alcohol.

In a separate study by Lindenbaum and Lieber (279), nine chronic alcoholics (five given a diet with 12.5% of total calories as protein, four with 25% plus folic acid and other vitamins) were treated with alcohol doses, increased every 2 days, up to 46 to 66% of total calories isocalorically substituted for carbohydrate over periods from 17 to 63 days. Maximum daily doses were given for 5 to 55 days with a peak intake corresponding to 253 g of ethanol. In the absence of folate deficiency or other malnutrition, alcohol administration resulted in marked vacuolization of bone marrow pronormoblasts and, to a lesser degree, of promyelocytes. Vacuolization proved to be dose-related, occurring only with a larger doses of alcohol. There was also thrombocytopenia after the third to fifth week of alcohol ingestion, whereas changes in red or white blood parameters were not seen. During the ethanol period, slight increase of serum iron content occurred followed by a significant fall during withdrawal. Liver biopsies obtained in five individuals during alcohol administration showed varying degrees of fatty liver with triglyceride content of liver tissue raised four to fifteenfold over the baseline levels. Furthermore, Lindenbaum and Lieber (280) found an alcohol-induced malabsorption of vitamin B_{12} in four alcoholics maintained on a maximal dose of 158 to 253 g of ethanol substituting carbohydrates in a sufficient diet for 3 to 8 weeks.

Hines and Cowan (189) gave a daily basic dose of 205 g of ethanol to three alcoholic subjects without clinical or biochemical evidence of liver injury after a period of abstinence of at least 22 days. This dose was increased on alternate days to 307 to 374 g for 8 to 12 weeks; subjects were given a diet nutritionally adequate except for folate content, which was kept marginal. Folate deficiency, hypomagnesemia, and hypokalemia developed in all three alcoholics. Alcohol-induced bone marrow suppression was indicated by the appearance of a reversible dimorphic sideroblastic and megaloblastic anemia due to interference with vitamin B_6 and folate metabolism. Vacuolization of proerythroblasts and basophilic erythroblasts was observed in all three subjects. There was also hyperferremia, increased plasma iron turnover with decreased erythrocyte iron utilization, and in two subjects thrombocytopenia. Bone marrow sideroblastic abnormalities dramatically improved following parenteral administration of pyridoxal phosphate. Treatment with folate and pyridoxine had no effect. Definitely abnormal elevations of serum-GOT activity and increased BSP retention was seen in all three subjects during alcohol administration, and also marginal increases of serum alkaline phosphatase and SGPT values. A comment on these studies (5) notes the surprisingly short time needed for manifestation of the suppressive effect of ethanol on the bone marrow.

Jenkins and Connolly (211) studied the stimulatory effect of alcohol on pituitary-adrenal function in seven male and eight female healthy subjects given alcohol once intravenously in doses between 45 and 60 g; they found an increase in plasma cortisol levels only when plasma ethanol concentrations were elevated above 100 mg/100 ml. To determine the effect of alcohol on serum cortisol levels, Mendelson and Stein (329) extended the administration of alcohol, as 86 proof bourbon whiskey, over 4 days in an experiment with four alcoholics and four nonalcoholics. Ethanol could be ingested by the patients during the 4-day period up to 4 g/kg of body weight per day with doses evenly spaced over the 24-hr day. Nonalcoholic subjects consumed less alcohol (165 to 258 g/day) than did alcoholics (255 to 313 g/day) and reached lower blood alcohol concentrations (mean: 20.1 to 40.9 mg/100 ml or 52.3 to 111.6 mg/100 ml, respectively), owing to development of gastrointestinal disturbances, such as nausea, epigastric pain, and vomiting, symptoms which were absent in the alcoholic subjects. During alcohol ingestion serum cortisol levels increased for both nonalcoholic and alcoholic subjects, the increase being of a lesser degree in the nonalcoholics and here only in association with the appearance of gastrointestinal illness. In the nonalcoholics serum cortisol levels returned to predrinking values following cessation of ethanol intake, whereas values in the alcoholic subjects rose even more in the postdrinking phase associated with prodromal or overt symptoms of withdrawal.

Results of experiments with single doses of ethanol on cardiac function as described above do not necessarily imply that cumulative effects of ethanol after continued alcohol abuse may result in cardiomyopathy as seen in alcoholic addicts. To test this hypothesis, Regan et al. (403, 404) studied the cardiac effects of ethanol in one male alcoholic with a 15-year history of drinking who was given alcohol over a period of 23 weeks in quantities to which he had been accustomed formerly. The patient had already experienced a first episode of heart failure, which could readily be controlled by abstinence and medical management, and he remained compensated when cardiac glycosides and diuretics were discontinued.

After 4 weeks of recompensation, he was given ethanol in daily doses of whiskey corresponding to about 120 to 158 g added to an adequate 20% protein diet. After 6 weeks on alcohol, his resting heart rate began to rise, circulation time was prolonged, and venous pressure was elevated. After 4 months, a ventricular gallop rhythm appeared. Spontaneous restoration without specific cardiac therapy occurred after ethanol was discontinued, which suggests that alcohol plays a primary role independant of nutritional factors.

In view of the fact that most of the clinically relevant forms of alcohol-induced organic damage in man take years or decades to develop, the range of information that can be gained from such controlled short-term experiments is necessarily restricted to those fully reversible alterations that occur within a relatively short time. Insight into the factors responsible for the development of organic pathology in actual drinking practice could best be gained from prospective studies of representative groups of alcoholics. Since such studies, which would have to be extended over the greater part of an alcoholic's "drinking life," do not yet exist, fairly reliable information on the cumulative effects of long-continued alcohol abuse can only be gathered from well-documented retrospective analyses. Their notorious shortcomings have to be taken into consideration.

4. INFLUENCE OF DURATION AND DOSE OF ALCOHOL ABUSE AS EVIDENCED BY RETROSPECTIVE STUDIES

Liver Pathology

One of the earliest series large enough for statistical evaluation, was that of Voegtlin and co-workers (500–502), which comprises 300 cases (265 male and 35 female patients, aged 24 to 69 years, mean: 42.8 years) admitted consecutively to a private institution for the treatment of chronic alcoholic patients in Seattle, Washington. These patients from middle and upper classes of society were all in good general health and without evidence of alcoholic deterioration. Employing a battery of 11 tests, liver dysfunction of minor degree was found in about 70%, more serious disorders in an additional 17%, and severe hepatic disease in only about 3% of the cases, while 9.6% were entirely free of any laboratory evidence of functional hepatic derangement. Without presenting individual data, the authors could not establish any significant correlation between the incidence of liver dysfunction and the length of drinking history as estimated by age, type of beverage habitually consumed (beer, wine, whiskey), occurrence of psychiatric complications, decreased alcohol tolerance, or poor dietary habits. Careful nutritional histories showed that those who consistently ate poorly approximately equalled the number of those who ate well; 24.3% of the entire series were overweight, 15.0% underweight, but liver dysfunction was definitely more frequent and severe in the overweight group. Among steady drinkers, there was, however, a slight but significant tendency to more frequent and severe hepatic derangement than among periodical drinkers. This tendency was thought to be due to recovery during the abstinent phases in periodic drinking. The authors found the profile of liver dysfunction in this socioeconomic group not to be compatible with a clinical diagnosis of portal cirrhosis but indicative only of transient reversible hepatic changes. A shortcoming of this series was that no serum enzyme derangement (BSP retention, serum bilirubin, hippuric acid excretion) in 38 following two reports. In a preliminary communication on functional liver derangement (BSP retention, serum vilirubin, hippuric acid excretion) in 38 alcoholics with a drinking history of 2 to 30 years Rouleau and Nadeau (413) stated that there seemed to be a positive correlation between the duration of alcoholism and the degree of hepatic dysfunction; in addition, regular drinkers showed more severe liver derangement than did periodic drinkers. This could not be confirmed, however, in a later study of 133 heavy drinkers by Nadeau et al. (350), who solely employed BSP retention and a BSP clearance coefficient as the most reliable and sensitive index in screening for slight hepatic dysfunction. But data that revealed abnormal dye retention in more than 50% of the final number of 178 patients were interpreted as to indicate that decreased liver function was grossly related to the type of beverage in the order: ale and/or gin, ale and/or whiskey, indiscriminate drinking (including whiskey, wines, and liqueurs). Functional liver damage of the reversible type was also observed by Kay et al. (225) in 118 alcoholics with a drinking history of 10 to 15 years' duration and by Bersohn and Frame (37) in 40 South African alcoholics (age: 25 to 45 years; mean: 38.1 years) who had, on the average, commenced daily drinking 12.9 years prior to admission.

Knott and Beard (238) found that on inclusion of serum enzyme determinations, some degree of impairment of hepatic function was found in all of 30 apparently healthy chronic alcoholics examined at 24 hr subsequent to admission. They were well-nourished, nonintoxicated individuals (average age: 32 years) who had at least a 5-year but not more than 10-year history of alcoholism. Most frequently abnormal tests were BSP (97% of the patients), SGOT (80%), SICD (67%), SGPT (57%), and total serum bilirubin (23%). After abstinence, repeat examination three weeks later showed that all parameters had significantly ($p < 0.05$) reverted toward normal, but BSP and SICD values were still pathologic in 77 and 43%, respectively. Histopathology in one patient revealed minimal necrosis and centrolobular fatty infiltration.

Von Oldershausen (369), who examined 135 alcoholics without overt clinical symptoms of cirrhosis in Concepción, Chile (1953–1954) and 65 cases in West Berlin (1955–1960), reported a statistically significant positive correlation between duration of excessive drinking (less than 5 years as compared to more than 5 years) and pathologic results of biochemical tests (BSP retention, thymol turbidity, serum albumin level, albumin/gamma globulin/quotient). Values for SGOT, SGPT, aldolase, BSP retention, and hippuric acid excretion determined three or more weeks after the last debauch proved to be significantly less abnormal than those of the first week after admission, indicating the potential reversibility of these functional aberrations by abstinence. Cirrhosis of the liver could be diagnosed in this series by peritoneoscopy and biopsy in only 4% of the Chilean alcoholics, whereas this figure was 25% in the West Berlin group. It should be noted, however, that the latter group was on the average 10 years older and had had an alcohol abuse of usually more than 10 years' duration. Pronounced fatty infiltration, however, was about equally distributed in both groups. The drinking patterns of the Chilean alcoholics showed frequent binges lasting days to weeks superimposed on a mean daily consumption of wine exceeding the equivalent of 120 g of ethanol (up to 240 g and more), followed by periods of abstinence. In the West Berlin alcoholics, who preferred a combination of beer and spirits, drinking habits and quantities consumed were similar. Nutrition had been generally inadequate in the Chilean alcoholics, but signs of severe protein or vitamin deficiency were rare, this being also valid for the West Berlin group in which case histories indicated antecedent severe nutritional imbalance in less than one-fifth of the cases.

Nakamura et al. (354) were the first to demonstrate by liver biopsy a correlation between hepatic pathology and intensity of alcohol abuse, significant at a level of $p < 0.05$, in a very small group of 14 alcoholics not admitted for liver disease. All five cases in which fatty metamorphosis or fibrosis were detected had a history of drinking on the average 140 g of ethanol or more per day for 10 years or more, whereas none of the 9 cases without these histologic changes had imbibed alcohol to that degree or duration. Results of biochemical tests (including SGOT and SGPT) in 175 Japanese alcoholics and of liver biopsies performed in 70 heavy drinkers with or without complaints pertaining to liver disease (355) later showed that incidence of hepatic enlargement, abnormal BSP retention, and histological evidence of fatty liver, fibrosis, and cirrhosis was similar in patients who drank 66 to 110 g of ethanol per day and those whose consumption exceeded 110 g/day. No mention is made of duration of heavy alcohol intake. Ingestion of protein calories at more than 110 g of ethanol per day was significantly lower than at less than 110 g.

Liver biopsies revealed pathologic changes in all of 11 tasters employed in a large distillery establishment in East Germany for periods of 2 to 37 years who had, during this time, professionally consumed alcoholic beverages in quantities corresponding to 40 to 125 g of ethanol per day. Additional inhalative uptake was considered possible since air ethanol concentration at their working places exceeded MAC values up to sixfold. Diagnoses ranged from slight hemosiderosis in the two cases with the shortest period of employment to fatty liver and signs of moderate chronic inflammatory changes (438). None was without clinical or laboratory evidence of liver disease. Addiction could be ruled out in all, as could asymptomatic diabetes mellitus. Nutritional status was excellent. All of them denied additional alcohol intake, which was confirmed by others, but reported rather an aversion to spirits and liqueurs. The results raise the question of a potential specific occupational hazard for this type of work.

In an earlier survey, Leevy et al. (255) were unable to find a correlation between hepatic abnormalities and amount, duration, or type of alcohol intake in 66 alcoholics admitted for treatment of delirium tremens. Figures for length of drinking history or amounts consumed are not reported. Aspiration biopsy revealed normal liver in 29% of the cases, focal inflammation in 6%, fatty infiltration in 31%, and portal cirrhosis in 35%. Stigmata of vitamin deficiency were present in patients with both normal and abnormal hepatic histology. Repeat biopsies proved that fat disappeared from the liver within 4 to 6 weeks of abstinence and that there was also regression of hyaline necrosis and inflammatory lesions in patients with portal cirrhosis. It was, however, of interest to learn that histologic studies repeated in 25 patients 1 to 5 years after the initial observation revealed that improvement or further deterioration strictly paralleled discontinuation of alcohol intake or resumption of previous habits after discharge.

The exceptionally high mortality from cirrhosis of the liver in wine-drinking France induced Péquignot (379, 380) to study the question whether this is really connected with the high overall consumption of alcohol in this country. Aided by a team of dieteticians and a statistician, he carried out a carefully planned survey of alcohol consumption and dietary habits in cirrhotics treated at three hospitals (Paris, Marseilles, Nantes). The aim was to determine whether cirrhotics had really imbibed more alcohol up to onset of symptoms and eaten a nutritionally less balanced diet than control patients. A total of 116 patients with cirrhosis of the liver,

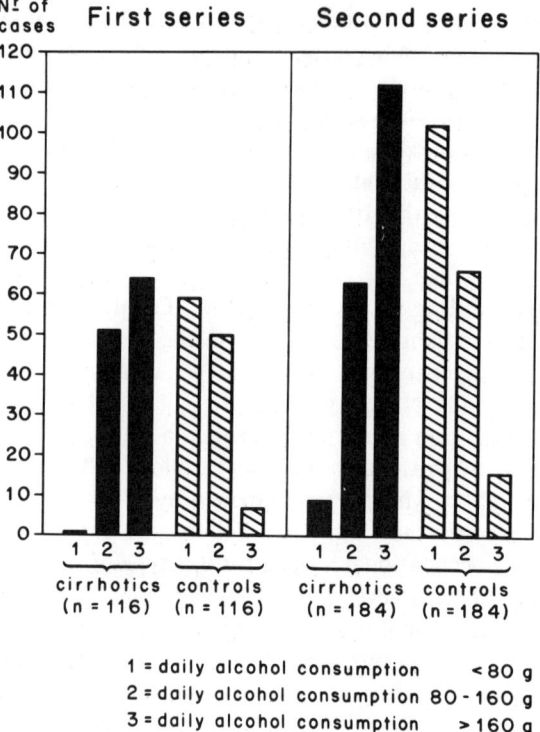

Fig. 1. Mean daily alcohol consumption in two comparable groups of French patients with and without (controls) cirrhosis of the liver. (Pequignot, 379, 380)

believed to be due to alcohol, were interrogated as far back into their past as possible and compared to a group of 116 noncirrhotic controls of the same age, sex, and social background. If alcohol intake during life had varied, the calculations were based on the maximum consumption during at least five consecutive years. The comparison showed that in the cirrhotics alcohol consumption had on the average ranged between 174 and 212 g/day for about 20 to 25 years and between 72 to 82 g/day in the controls, wine being the predominant alcoholic beverage in 79 to 91% of the cirrhotics. On the other hand, there was no significant difference between the two groups as regards duration of alcohol intake, protein and caloric content of the diet, body weight, physical activity, marital and social status. Neither had a reduction in food intake seemed to have been a predisposing factor for decompensation of the illness, since only 28 cirrhotics (24%) had reduced their dietary intake before onset of symptoms.

In a second series another group of 184 patients with cirrhosis of the liver (excluding only cases of unequivocally nonalcoholic etiology) from four hospitals (Bordeaux, Caen, Nantes, Franche Comté) were compared to 184 noncirrhotic patients. Here the average alcohol consumption had ranged from 185 to 212 g/day in the cirrhotics and from 46 to 88 g/day in the noncirrhotic patients while again there was no significant difference in the other parameters. Since both series showed that only in a small number of patients had mean daily alcohol intake been less than 80 g for the cirrhotics or exceeded 160 g for the noncirrhotic controls (Fig. 1), Péquignot thought it justified to distinguish three categories of alcohol consumption: (1) less than 80 g/day = innocuous; (2) 80 to 160 g/day = potentially cirrhogenic; (3) more than 160 g/day = involving a very high risk of cirrhosis. He inferred that the average cirrhogenic dose would be in the range of 170 to 210 g of ethanol per day if ingested over a period of approximately 25 years.

Bonnichsen (50) criticized Péquignot's categories and expressed doubts as to whether an intake of 80 g/day could be regarded as a practically safe consumption concerning the development of cirrhosis. He argued that drinking patterns differ from country to country and that social consequences of heavy drinking, invariably leading to less and inadequate intake of food, usually precede somatic damage so that other factors might play a decisive role. These points had already been subject to criticism by Péquignot's compatriots. Martini discussed the matter with Péquignot (320) and pointed out that since the figures had been collected from five different cities according to the same pattern of interrogation, including information provided by the individual's family and other sources, and had led to the same results, this appreciable thoroughness could well be expected to give at least comparable results.

Von Oldershausen (370, 371) has reported morphological results obtained by peritoneoscopy, biopsy, or autopsy in a second selected group of 250 alcoholics receiving clinical treatment at a West Berlin hospital between 1960 and 1963. Since drinking histories in the majority of these cases proved unreliable, histologic results were arranged according to age in order to arrive at an approximate assessment of the time necessary for the development of different stages of alcoholic liver disease (Table 5). This, of course, allows only a rough estimate of the influence which the duration of heavy drinking might have had. Successive stages of alcoholic liver disease (with or without pronounced steatosis) were seen to be associated with a distinct increase in mean age. Cases with advanced cirrhosis were on the average 20 years older than cases with normal hepatic histology. Mean age was not appreciably different when only cases with accom-

TABLE 5 CORRELATION BETWEEN MEAN AGE OF 250 ALCOHOLICS AND INCREASING SEVERITY OF ALCOHOLIC LIVER DISEASE

Histology	Number of cases	Percentage of Total	Mean age[a] (years)
Normal	22	9%	37.1 ± 1.9
Alcoholic "hepatosis"[b] or hepatitis	82	33%	48.2 ± 1.2
Incipient cirrhosis	46	18%	53.8 ± 1.6
Advanced cirrhosis	100	40%	58.5 ± 1.1
	N = 250	100%	

[a] Mean ± standard deviation of mean.
[b] Defined as "metabolic derangement of hepatic parenchyma" as evidenced by liver cell necrosis with or without accompanying fatty infiltration.
From von Oldershausen (371).

panying severe steatosis were selected, suggesting that fatty liver is not a special phase in the course of alcohol-induced hepatic pathology. With due caution, Von Oldershausen deduced that on the average it usually takes about 10 years of continuous heavy drinking for alcoholic "hepatosis" or hepatitis to develop, another 5 years for incipient cirrhosis, and altogether more than 20 years until advanced cirrhosis is established. Reliable drinking histories obtained from next of kin in 66 of these cases with advanced alcoholic cirrhosis seemed to confirm this notion. Duration of alcohol abuse had ranged from 4 to 15 years in only 25% of the cases, in another 25% it had been more than 30 years, but in half of the cases heavy drinking had lasted 15 to 30 years, with a mean duration of 22.4 years. As opposed to this, Von Oldershausen found mean length of time for development of 169 cases of hepatitic cirrhosis to be 4.8 years and for 117 cases of biliary cirrhosis 3.9 years.

In a group of 82 alcoholics examined by Cachera et al. (70), duration of alcoholism had also been about 20 years for the majority of 21 histologically diagnosed cases of cirrhosis of the liver. No fatty change was detected in the liver in two cases after a daily consumption of about 240 g (wine) for 5 years or 300 g (wine plus liqueur d'absinthe) for 4 years. An alcohol abuse of more than 10 or 20 years duration was found in 85 or 60%, respectively, of 130 Chilean cirrhotic drinkers (16) with 73.1% of them having had an intake of more than 2 liters of wine daily (more than 160 g). Similarly, Kuster et al. (246) observed a history of daily consumption of 80 g or more of ethanol for 10 to 30 years in 20 Chilean alcoholics with cirrhosis of the liver.

Relying on a vast body of data, Viel and co-workers (496, 498) chose a different approach to the problem of evaluating the cumulative influence of alcohol misuse. Autopsy material from the bodies of 1322 Chilean men and 340 women beyond 15 years of age who had come to a violent death was studied and information on drinking habits was obtained from interviews with next of kin one to three weeks after death. With respect to drinking habits, cases were allotted to five categories in the following order: (*a*) abstemious; (*b*) normal drinker; (*c*) heavy drinker; (*d*) intermittent alcoholic; (*e*) inveterate alcoholic. Blood alcohol levels at the moment of death indicated a high degree of consistency with information on drinking history obtained by interviews with relatives. Analysis revealed that 48.3% of the males and 11.4% of the females had been heavy drinkers or alcoholics. Excessive alcohol intake proved to be inversely related to socioeconomic status and level of education. The effect of a time factor in alcohol abuse was evaluated by dividing the total into two subgroups according to age: cases below 35 years of age were compared to those older than 35 years. When similar patterns of drinking behavior were compared, the two sexes presented almost the same proportion of cirrhosis of the liver. Beyond age 35, differences in the frequency of cirrhosis (both incipient and advanced) between abstemious persons and normal drinkers on the one hand, and heavy drinkers and alcoholics of both types on the other, were highly significant. In individuals younger than 35, the proportion of cirrhosis was almost equally distributed over the range of different drinking habits, indicating that cirrhosis in those under 35 years of age usually had a nonalcoholic etiology. Fatty liver with inflammatory reaction, thought to be a precursor of cirrhosis, was also significantly more frequent in alcoholics of both types than among normal or heavy drinkers of male sex older than 35 years of age, which was equally valid for both male and female alcoholics younger than 35 years. Finally, the incidence of moderate or abundant fat in otherwise normal livers, though being correlated with age, increased significantly with greater alcohol consumption. On the other hand, thickness of adipose panniculus, an index for obesity, did not increase with heavier drinking. Estimating the nutritional status by means of the admittedly crude index of the ratio real/ideal weight revealed that after 35 years of age there was a general tendency for this index to be above normal, whereas the proportion above normal diminished significantly as the degree of alcohol intake increased. With respect to the possible association of alcohol use and malnutrition, however, the authors state that although their data do not allow them to take a definite stand on this problem, they are led to think that alcohol is a factor in the etiology of cirrhosis independent of malnutrition.

Ugarte et al. (490) and Insunza et al. (198) investigated a group of 130 Chilean male alcoholic addicts (85 inveterate, 45 intermittent alcoholics) who had been admitted to an alcoholic ward and showed no clinical signs of advanced liver failure. All had a history of alcohol abuse of 6 or more years' duration (58%: more than 15 years; 30%: more than 20 years), and alcohol intake had ranged from 200 up to more than 500 g/day in 93% of the cases. Dietary surveys revealed that protein and fat consumption had been low during periods of abuse in 98% of the cases; for approximately one-fourth, diet was also deficient in protein during periods of abstinence. While normal liver or minor nonspecific abnormalities were found in only 25% of the cases by liver biopsy, cirrhosis of septal (portal) type was present in 12%, and minimal to severe steatosis in 63%; included were 12 cases (8 with cirrhosis) in which there were additional signs of alcoholic hepatitis. There was no difference in the incidence of cirrhosis between intermittent and inveterate drinkers.

In an earlier smaller sample of 75 alcoholics Ugarte et al. (491) observed cirrhosis in 21.6% of the cases, more frequently in the inveterate than in the intermittent drinkers (24.0 against 16.7%), whereas moderate to marked steatosis was more frequent in the intermittent drinkers. In the group reported upon by Insunza et al. cirrhosis was found only in those with a history of alcohol abuse of more than 10 years' duration and was significantly more frequent ($p < 0.05$) after more than 15 years of alcohol abuse (18%) than after less than 15 years (5%). Moreover, moderate to severe steatosis was significantly more frequent ($p < 0.05$) in biopsies performed during the first week after the last alcohol consumption (55%) as compared to biopsies after 8 to 29 days of abstinence (28%). So-called laboratory "liver tests" (serum total bilirubin, GOT, alkaline phosphatase, flocculation tests, total cholesterol), done immediately on admission, gave pathologic results only in a small percentage (up to 27%), with the exception of serum GOT activities, which were elevated predominantly in cases with alcoholic hepatitis and/or cirrhosis. The authors thought it surprising that in 24% of the cases with prolonged heavy alcohol intake of more than 15 years' duration no steatosis could be found. Since dietary histories pointed to a low protein intake in all, irrespective of histologic results, this was ascribed to the existence of a low susceptibility to alcohol-induced steatosis or liver damage. However, hepatomegaly was found in 20% of patients with histologically normal liver, indicating that liver cell hypertrophy related to adaptive ultrastructural changes probably produced by induction of drug-detoxifying enzyme systems might have played a role in both hepatic enlargement and absence of lesions demonstrable by light microscopy due to increased elimination capacity. In 1965, Kiessling et al. (234) had found a correlation between the number of enlarged mitochondria and degree of alcohol abuse by examining liver biopsies from 39 male alcoholics of long standing. The cases were subgrouped into six classes, extending from no alcohol intake at all (controls) to a consumption of 160 g or more of ethanol per day. On electron microscopy, a connection between the degree of ethanol intake and the mitochondrial size, as determined by measuring the longest axes of 500 mitochondria from each patient, was found with a correlation coefficient r equal to 0.80 ($p < 0.001$). No correlation was found between mitochondrial size and age of the patients. Grünberger et al. (172) could establish a significant correlation ($p < 0.05$) between the duration of alcoholism (mean $\pm$ SD: 12.85 $\pm$ 6.85 years) and serum GOT levels in 99 alcoholic inpatients with liver damage who were examined for the purpose of investigating possible connections between liver damage and CNS performance. The correlation between the average amount of daily ethanol intake (mean $\pm$ SD: 192 $\pm$ 92.2 g) and the degree of fatty degeneration as evidenced by liver biopsy and triglyceride determination was not significant ($0.1 > p > 0.05$). No correlation existed between BSP-retention and duration or daily intake. On the other hand, duration and daily intake correlated well with the results of certain tests chosen for estimating impeded brain function. It was concluded that in the alcoholic a direct connection between liver damage and impediment of brain function is most unlikely; the noxious agent seems to influence two differently structured organs in a different manner.

With the aim of assessing the influence of both duration and degree of excessive alcohol intake as well as of other predisposing factors on the incidence of chronic liver disease, Lelbach (260, 261, 267) studied a large group of chronic alcoholics from all social strata consecutively admitted between 1960 and 1963 to a special sanitarium for withdrawal treatment in West Germany. Preliminary results obtained from smaller initial samples (59, 60) suggested that both time and dose had a cumulative influence. Clinical, biochemical and histologic examination of the final unselected total of 526 male alcoholics yielded a body of data large enough for statistical evaluation of subgroups.

The institution admitted only patients who primarily required no special medical attention, who were free of symptoms of acute organic psychosis, and who stayed for the customary six-month period of withdrawal on a voluntary basis. Thus alcoholics in the end-stage and the skid-row-type were not included in this fairly homogenous group. The mean age was 40 $\pm$ 10.5

years (range: 19 to 64 years). All drinking histories were taken by the author according to a detailed questionnaire and, at a later date, a second history was obtained from each patient by the psychiatrist in charge of the institution. In addition, all quantitative data contained in the reports from social workers responsible for admission procedures, information furnished by family physicians and next of kin, as well as all available records of clinical treatment in the past were collected. If figures from different sources were divergent, final computation was based on the highest figures mentioned. In view of the alcoholic's tendency to belittle his actual intake, this procedure was thought to yield a fairly reliable body of data for subsequent analysis.

Mean duration of alcohol abuse proper was 9.1 ± 5.8 years; in one-third (177 cases) duration exceeded 10 years. Alcohol abuse had been preceded by a prodromal phase of increasing intake, lasting on the average 7 years. Though duration of abuse was related to age, liver damage proved to be less closely correlated with age than with calculated duration of heavy drinking. Each patient was questioned about his lowest and highest daily (weekly) ethanol consumption and its increase in the successive stages of his drinking history. For the final computation, only the individual minimal and maximal quantities reported for the period of the highest intake served as a basis for estimating the average range of consumption in the total or in subgroups. As to quantities consumed, records of only 417 patients appeared reliable enough to be included in the final evaluation. Mean daily ethanol intake in these 417 cases was 180 g (corresponding to 590 ml of 76 proof liquor), ranging from 145 (mean of all individual minimum quantities) to 212 g (mean of all maximum quantities). Of these patients, 231 reported a daily intake of more than 160 g (mean: 224 g; range: 182 to 266 g). More than one-half of the patients were steady daily imbibers, only 12% reported spree-drinking, the rest were "weekend" drinkers. Almost one-half (49.3%) drank exclusively beer, 10% took only spirits, 3% wine, the rest took alcohol in more than one form, preferably as beer plus spirits (23.6%). The cases were subdivided according to duration of alcohol abuse (1 to 5, 6 to 10, 11 to 15, and > 15 years) and to mean daily intake below or above 160 g. In general, mean daily intake tended to rise with increasing duration of abuse.

Enlargement of the liver, present in 67.5% on admission, decreased in frequency to 43% after an average of 41 days of abstinence. Liver function was assessed by employing a battery of 12 tests on blood samples taken after an average of 50 days of abstinence, with BSP retention, serum gamma globulin, erythrocyte sedimentation rate, serum albumin, and thymol turbidity being the most frequently pathologic tests (43, 33, 28, 20,

20%, respectively). The degree of liver dysfunction was graded semiquantitatively on a 0 to +++ scale. As can be seen from Tables 6 and 7, a statistically highly significant correlation was shown to exist between duration of alcoholism and frequency of hepatomegaly and of more severe liver dysfunction graded ++ and +++ after respective periods of abstinence. The cumulative effect of both factors, duration of abuse and daily intake, on laboratory results becomes evident in Table 8. With a mean daily consumption of 116 g of ethanol, the incidence of liver dysfunction grade ++ and +++ was 6% after 3.5 years of heavy drinking, but it rose to 73% after 21 years with a mean consumption of 246 g of ethanol. By contrast, no correlation could be found between the degree of hepatic dysfunction and antecedent episodes of potentially hepatotropic disease in the past history. For 338 patients (64%), alcoholism was the only etiological factor in the case histories, and 187 had in the past experienced illnesses that might have predisposed them to chronic liver disease. For instance, a history of infectious hepatitis, which had occurred on the average 20.4 years before the present examination, was given by only 60 patients (12%). Neither was underweight positively correlated with the degree of hepatic dysfunction. Clinical symptoms of vitamin deficiencies or laboratory evidence of hypoproteinemia indicating severe protein malnutrition were extremely rare.

Results of liver biopsies in 320 patients (mean duration of alcoholism: 9.9 ± 5.9 years), generally performed after a longer period of abstinence

TABLE 6 CORRELATION BETWEEN DURATION OF ALCOHOL ABUSE AND FREQUENCY OF LIVER ENLARGEMENT AFTER A PERIOD OF ABSTINENCE (MEAN: 41 DAYS)

Group	Duration (years)	Number of Cases	Hepatomegaly in percentage of Cases	Comparison between Different Groups. Levels of Significance $(2p<)$
I	(1–5)	158	31	0.05
II	(6–10)	191	41	0.025
III	(11–15)	119	45	0.0005 / 0.0005
IV	(over 15)	57	77	0.0005
		(N = 525)		

TABLE 7 CORRELATION BETWEEN DURATION OF ALCOHOL ABUSE AND FREQUENCY OF LIVER DYSFUNCTION GRADED ++ AND +++

Group	Duration (years)	Number of Cases	Percentage of Cases with Liver Dysfunction Grade ++/+++	Comparison between Different Groups. Levels of Significance ($2p <$)
I	1–5	158	8	0.0005
II	6–10	191	27	0.0005 / 0.0005
III	11–15	119	33	0.0005 / 0.0005
IV	over 15	57	65	0.0005
		N = 525		

From Lelbach (260).

(77 ± 54 days) and corresponding features of patient's drinking histories are shown in Table 9. Cirrhosis was found in 12% (39 cases); in addition a clinical diagnosis of cirrhosis could be established in another 14 cases of the total 526 patients, so that the estimated overall incidence was 10%, which agrees well with the figures reported by Jolliffe and Jellinek (215) and Klatskin (235). A histological diagnosis of severe liver damage (groups C–E) was made in 41% of the 320 cases. Figures for mean duration of alcohol abuse as well as of mean daily intake rose successively from "normal" to "cirrhosis." When calculated in relation to body weight and expressed as milligrams of ethanol per kilogram of body weight per hour, daily intake in those with liver damage more severe than simple steatosis was found to range at or above the accepted average rate of removal of ethanol from the blood [100 ±30 mg/(kg)(hr)].

Severe liver damage (exceeding in degree simple steatosis) and cirrhosis of the liver showed a highly significant correlation with the duration of alcoholism (Table 10). Since mean daily intake rose with length of drinking history, a comparison of two selected groups of 108 alcoholics each, identical in age, body weight, and duration of alcohol abuse but differing in daily intake, was necessary to elucidate the influence average amounts ingested had on liver pathology. As Table 11 indicates, a highly significant differ-

TABLE 8 INFLUENCE OF BOTH DURATION AND DAILY INTAKE ON LIVER DYSFUNCTION GRADED ++ AND +++ IN 417 PATIENTS

Group	Duration (years) (mean ± SD)	Below 160 g/day			Above 160 g/day		
		Number of Cases	Percentage of Cases with Liver Dysfunction Grade ++/+++	Mean Daily Intake (g) (min.-max.)	Number of Cases	Percentage of Cases with Liver Dysfunction Grade ++/+++	Mean Daily Intake (g) (min.-max.)
I	3.5 ± 1.3	74	6%	116.5 (91–142)	55	11%	207.5 (167–248)
II	7.8 ± 1.4	76	16%	124.5 (99–150)	79	37%	232.5 (192–273)
III	12.8 ± 1.5	30	17%	132.5 (108–157)	64	40%	217.0 (179–255)
IV	21.1 ± 5.4	6	17%	130.0 (111–149)	33	73%	246.5 (199–294)
		N = 186			N = 231		

From Lelbach (260).

TABLE 9 HISTOLOGICAL DIAGNOSIS IN 320 DRINKERS AND CORRESPONDING DATA ON DURATION AND DEGREE OF ALCOHOLISM

Group	Histology	Number of Cases	Percentage of Total	Duration of Alcoholism (years) (mean ± SD)	Average Ethanol Intake (g/day)		Average Ethanol Intake in Relation to Body weight [mg/(kg)(hr)]	
					Mean	Minimum-Maximum	Mean	Minimum-Maximum
A	Essentially normal or minor abnormalities	70	22.0	7.7 ± 4.1	139.5	106–173	90.5	69–112
B	Moderate to severe fatty infiltration	118	37.0	7.8 ± 4.7	172.0	142–201	109.0	91–128
C	Severe steatosis with fibrosis and inflammatory reactions	44	13.7	10.3 ± 5.5	216.0	174–258	127.0	102–152
D	Chronic hepatitis with or without fatty infiltration	48	15.0	11.9 ± 5.2	203.5	170–237	125.0	105–145
E	Cirrhosis with or without fatty infiltration	39	12.0	17.1 ± 6.8	245.5	197–294	146.5	118–175
—	Massive siderosis plus fibrosis	1	0.3	—	—	—	—	—
		N = 320	100					

From Lelbach (260).

TABLE 10 INCIDENCE OF SEVERE LIVER DAMAGE (EXCEEDING SIMPLE STEATOSIS) AND CIRRHOSIS OF THE LIVER IN RELATION TO THE DURATION OF ALCOHOL ABUSE (INCLUDED ARE 14 CASES WITH CLINICAL DIAGNOSIS OF CIRRHOSIS)

Group	Duration of Alcoholism (years) (mean)	Size of Sample	Severe Liver Damage (groups C–E)		Cirrhosis		Statistical Evaluation		
			Number of Cases	Percentage of Cases	Number of Cases	Percentage of Cases	Comparison of Groups	Severe Liver Damage	Cirrhosis
								(2p<)	
I	1–5 (3.6)	73	14	19.2	0	0.0	I:II	ns	0.05
II	6–10 (8.3)	129	41	31.8	10	7.8	II:III	0.0005	0.01
III	11–15 (12.9)	81	49	60.5	17	21.0	III:IV	0.025	0.001
IV	>15 (21.6)	51	42	82.4	26	51.0	I:III	0.0005	0.0005
		N = 334					II:IV	0.0005	0.0005

From Lelbach (260).

TABLE 11 INCIDENCE OF SEVERE LIVER DAMAGE AND CIRRHOSIS IN RELATION TO DAILY ETHANOL INTAKE IN TWO SELECTED GROUPS WITH IDENTICAL DURATION OF ABUSE

Selected Groups	Size of Sample	Duration of Alcoholism (years) (mean ± SD)	Daily Intake of Ethanol (g)		Severe Liver Damage (groups C–E)		Cirrhosis	
			Mean	Minimum to Maximum	Number of Cases	Percentage of Cases	Number of Cases	Percentage of Cases
<160 g	108	7.9 ± 4.1	126.5	101–152	15	13.9	0	0.0
>160 g	108	7.9 ± 3.8	227.0	188–266	51	47.2[a]	15	13.9[b]

[a] $2p < 0.0005$.
[b] $2p < 0.0005$.

From Lelbach (260).

ence regarding the incidence of severe liver damage and cirrhosis existed between the two groups. This suggests that both dimensions, length of drinking history and average intake, are additive factors and their influence on hepatic pathology can be demonstrated independently. Taking together all 157 cases of this series with an intake of more than 160 g/day (mean: 226.5 g; range: 185 to 286 g), for which the calculated mean duration of abuse was 11.4 ± 6.5 years, showed that the percentage of severe liver damage was 59% and that of cirrhosis 25%; thus cirrhosis was present in every fourth patient in this subgroup. Yet, after roughly 22 years of heavy drinking with a mean daily alcohol intake of 227 g (range: 179 to 275 g), as seen in group IV (Table 10), well-established cirrhosis of the liver could be diagnosed in every second alcoholic. However, in another 31.5% of group IV, potentially precirrhotic lesions were found. On the other hand, 4% still had normal hepatic histology even after an alcohol abuse of this duration and intensity, and in 13.5% there was only uncomplicated fatty infiltration. This suggests that a particularly low susceptibility to alcohol-induced liver damage can be expected to exist in a small percentage of any drinking population. In contrast to the well-documented pathogenic influence of alcohol, there was no evidence in this series that hepatotropic disease in the past, particularly infectious hepatitis, had in any way determined the severity of the lesions. Neither was there conclusive evidence that quantitative dietary deficiencies as indicated by body weight had had any significant influence. On the basis of these results, it can be assumed that an association exists between the total amount of alcohol ingested over the years of abuse and the final degree of liver damage—irrespective of other enhancing or additional factors. In other words, the incidence of liver lesions more severe in degree than uncomplicated fatty metamorphosis would be correlated with the total amount of alcohol consumed up to the date of diagnosis in a way that might resemble a dose-effect relationship. If total amounts ingested were calculated in relation to individual body weight, this association might be even closer. Data on drinking histories gathered from alcoholics are considered to be notoriously unreliable. Therefore it could be expected that the more quantitative data on duration and degree of alcohol abuse deviated from the real values in both directions, the less clear-cut would such a dose-effect relationship present itself.

For 265 alcoholics of this series histologic results as well as apparently reliable figures for duration of alcoholism and average alcohol intake were available (267). Of these alcoholics, 90% were regular daily imbibers, in 24 cases drinking pattern was that of "weekend" drinkers, and only two were "spree drinkers" with drinking episodes interrupted by short phases of abstinence. For each patient the dose-time-product; "mean daily intake in grams of ethanol per kilogram of body weight multiplied by duration of abuse in years," was computed [g/(kg)(day)] × [years]. Values obtained (range: 2.5680 to 118.1544) were grouped according to rank into 13 classes. For each class the percentage of severe liver damage and of cirrhosis was calculated and plotted against the mean total dose of ethanol ingested over the years. As is shown by analysis of regression (Figs. 2 and 3), there was an astonishingly high degree of correlation between alcoholism as expressed in terms of total amount of ethanol consumed per kilogram of body weight during life and the incidence of severe liver damage (n = 108) and even more so of cirrhosis of the liver (n = 39), with a coefficient of correlation r of 0.95 or 0.98, respectively, corresponding to a probability of error of less than 0.001. Total volumes ingested for different alcoholic beverages also were calculated. Since maximally possible daily ethanol intake has an individually determined upper limit, ranging from 80 to about 300 g/day, the individually consumed total quantity of ethanol is thus essentially a function of time. This is corroborated by the results of a survey in Australian alcoholics by Wilkinson et al. (531). In a large group of 800 problem drinkers, in which cirrhosis morbidity was 8.1% for the men and 16.8% for the women, they found the period of excessive drinking in 54 male alcoholics with cirrhosis to have been significantly longer (20.0 ± 9.5 years) than for alcoholic men without cirrhosis (15.8 ± 8.3 years), whereas average daily consumption (210 ± 80, or 220 ± 100 g of ethanol, respectively) did not differ. The difference in duration of excessive drinking was, however, not significant in alcoholic women with (13.5 ± 8.4 years; 140 ± 55 g of ethanol per day) or without cirrhosis (11.7 ± 8.0 years; 155 ± 55 g of ethanol per day).

Theoretically, Péquignot's estimation that a dose of 180 g of ethanol consumed daily for roughly 25 years would be an average cirrhogenic dose could therefore be specified by stating that after such a total dose a diagnosis of well-established cirrhosis of the liver could be expected in every second alcoholic of Lelbach's group. If one assumes that a primarily healthy subject weighing 70 kg would be capable of maintaining a daily intake of about 210 g of ethanol (roughly 21 oz of 86 proof whisky) for about 20 years, he would have a 50% chance of suffering from cirrhosis of the liver. However, any additional enhancing factor would reduce this length of time in an unpredictable manner.

These relatively long periods of time necessary for the development of alcohol cirrhosis—in comparison with the life span of alcohol-consuming age groups—might explain the apparent discrepancy between the high incidence of an alcohol etiology in cirrhosis of the liver (40 to 80%) and the relatively low cirrhosis morbidity in alcoholics (10 to 25%). It can be

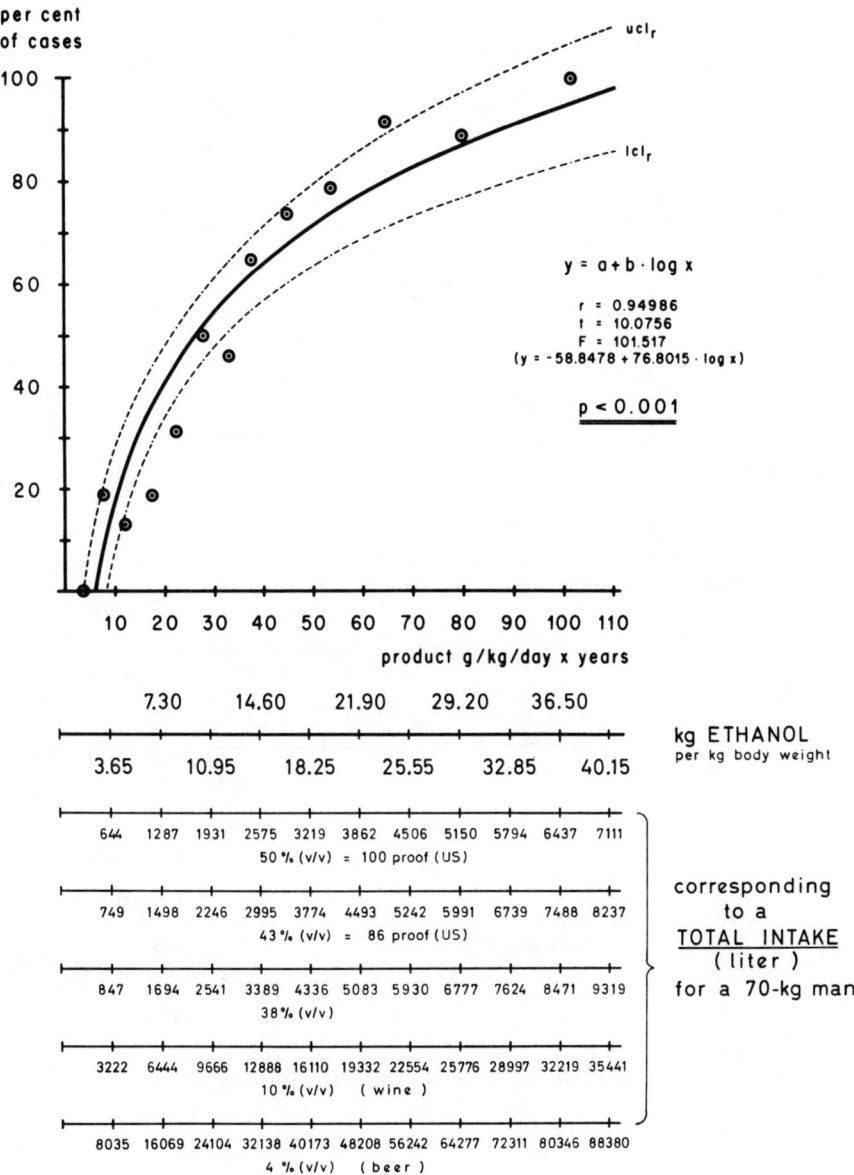

Fig. 2. Correlation between total amount of ethanol consumed per kilogram of body weight and incidence of histologically diagnosed severe liver damage (exceeding simple fatty liver) in 265 alcoholics (ucl_r and lcl_r = upper and lower confidence limits of regression, respectively).

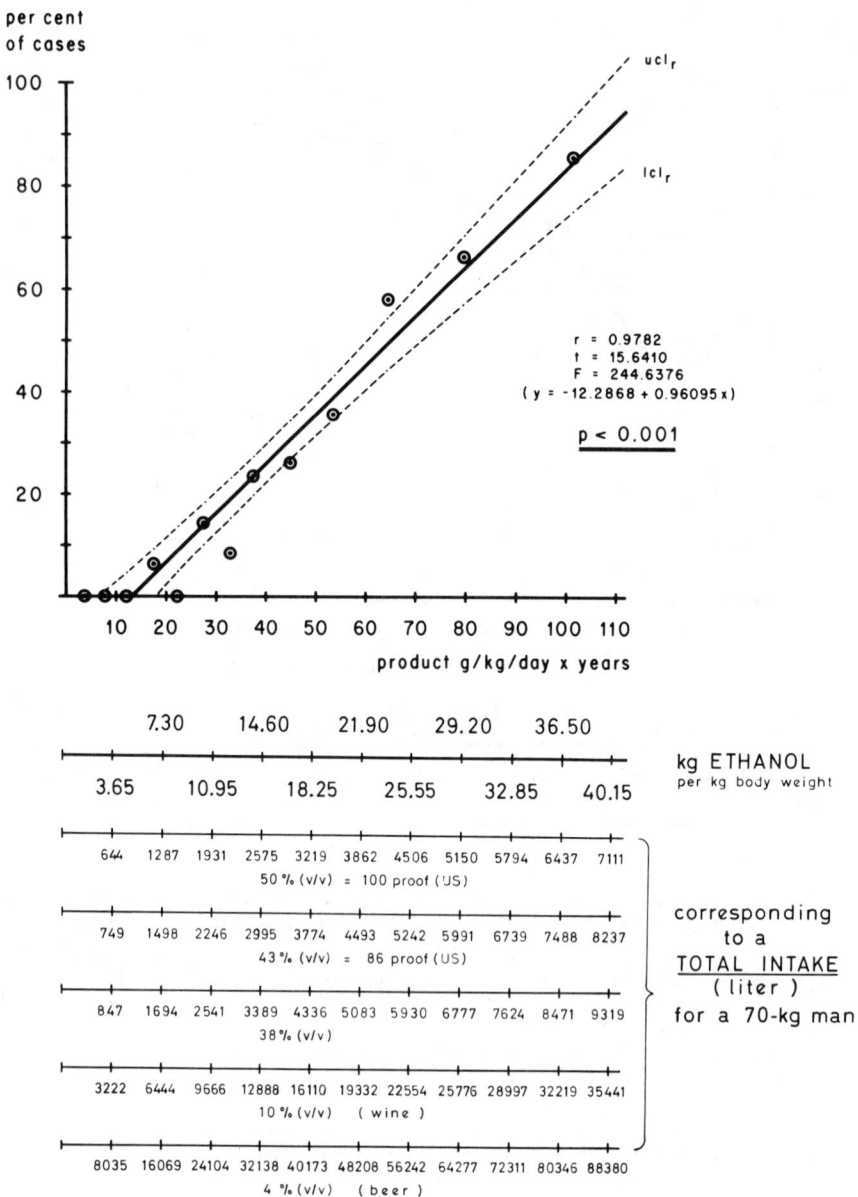

Fig. 3. Correlation between total amount of ethanol consumed per kilogram of body weight and incidence of histologically diagnosed cirrhosis of the liver in 265 alcoholics (ucl_r and lcl_r = upper and lower confidence limits of regression, respectively).

inferred that the surprisingly close association between total doses consumed, if calculated on a weight basis, and liver damage suggests a direct effect of alcohol on the human liver. Furthermore, it can be concluded that data on drinking history obtained from alcoholics are not as unreliable as might be expected, provided that they can be cross-checked by means of other sources of information. In view of the wide range of individual capacity for alcohol metabolism and of susceptibility for liver disease as well as the unpredictable influence of other factors, it would most certainly not be warranted to draw any predictive or retrospective conclusions for an individual case from these collective data.

As was rightly pointed out by Thaler and co-workers (100, 478), it would be incorrect and misleading to assume that the development of alcoholic cirrhosis is a continuous process which takes 10 or 20 or 25 years. Actually, this development sets in at some point along the time axis. The relatively benign stage of uncomplicated fatty metamorphosis, which is completely reversible by abstinence alone, may persist for many years as the only indication of the metabolic effects of alcohol abuse. This stage can at any time be complicated by degenerative and necrotizing processes followed by inflammatory and fibrogenic reactions. These transitional processes, which may occur either explosively after an extended bout of exceptionally high alcohol intake, or more furtively and gradually in socially functioning, often well-to-do persons, are the real precursors of the end-stage of structural derangement of hepatic architecture characteristic of cirrhosis (429). Such transitional hepatic processes are usually encountered after not less than 5 years of alcohol abuse and on the average after 10 to 13 years (260). In a group of 169 cases of acute alcoholic hepatitis in which there was lack of relationship between duration of drinking (range: 3 months to 36 years) and severity of parenchymal lesions, Lischner et al. (285) found the average duration of drinking to be 11.9 years but reported the shortest duration of excessive alcohol intake prior to onset of symptoms in a patient who had consumed large quantities during 3 months. Compared to the usual overall duration of alcohol abuse, the development of alcoholic hepatitis seems to take place within a relatively short time which ranges from several months to at most a few years, as Denk et al. (100) demonstrated by repeated liver biopsies. On the other hand, this intermediate stage (alcoholic hepatitis) can still be arrested by strict abstinence. Thus, due to the great regenerative capacity of hepatic parenchyma, only a relatively harmless and inactive fibrosis may ensue (100, 479). Although early ("young") collagen formation and hepatic fibrosis are reversible on discontinuation of the toxic agent (144, 196), continued exposure to alcohol not only enhances collagen formation (120) and leads to an irreversible phase of fibrosis but also impedes the regenerative power of the parenchyma.

Galambos (143) followed the development of alcoholic hepatitis into cirrhosis by repeated biopsies in 65 patients over a period of 1/2 to 12 years after the diagnosis of alcoholic hepatitis had been established histologically. In eighteen cases an increase in fibrosis leading to cirrhosis was seen to develop within 1 year in eight, within 2 to 4 years in six and in four patients within more than 4 years. Of 46 surviving patients, 41 had continued alcoholic hepatitis up to 12 years, a condition for which the term "chronic alcoholic hepatitis" was suggested. In 21 of these cases cirrhosis was not seen to develop after an average of 2.3 years. Rapid development of cirrhosis was reported to occur in children, whose necessary dose of alcohol appeared to be proportionally smaller than in the adult (216, 248).

Other Organic Lesions

The abundant literature covering the subject of the influence of volume and pattern of alcohol abuse on the liver has no counterpart in the study of other organs.

Only a few studies could be found in which mention is made of dose and duration of alcohol abuse in connection with chronic calcifying pancreatitis. In Southern France, where this type of chronic pancreatitis seems to be relatively frequent, Sarles et al. (425, 426) compared dietary habits and alcohol consumption of 35 patients with those in two groups of 35 control subjects each, matched in age, sex, racial origin, and occupation. They found that in the patients daily alcohol intake had on the average been about three times as high (158 g) as in the two control groups (35 or 77 g, respectively). Fat consumption was also significantly higher and protein content of the diet certainly not less than in the controls. The same difference (424) in alcohol consumption was true for another group of 50 patients, matched with two control groups of 50 cases each (175 g of ethanol per day, against 74 or 72 g, respectively) and for a third group of 16 patients (428) with nontraumatic cysts or pseudo-cysts of the pancreas, similarly matched with two groups of 16 controls each (160 g of ethanol per day, against 66 or 34 g, respectively). As opposed to this, in 16 patients with acute relapsing pancreatitis without calcification dietary surveys comparing them to two groups of 16 controls each revealed no such differences (76 g of ethanol per day, against 65 or 58 g, respectively). From the results of these dietary surveys, Sarles and co-workers (426) proposed an etiologic role of alcohol in the development of chronic calcifying pancreatitis, though not as a direct causative agent but acting on a genetic basis.

In West Germany, Koch (240) collected 16 cases in 10 years and found that alcohol abuse in 8 had commenced between age 20 and 25; first attacks of pain were not seen until 5 to 10 or even 20 years of abuse. In three cases development of calcification could be followed by x-ray examination; this development again took another 5 to 10 years of alcoholism. Herfort (187) in Czechoslovakia, who only found seven cases with an alcohol etiology among 151 patients, also states that pancreatic symptoms as a rule became manifest about 8 to 12 years after the patients had begun to consume regularly large amounts of alcohol. In 32 patients with calcifying pancreatitis and a history of chronic alcoholism the average time until attacks of pain set in was 9 years of alcoholism (194, 372). Attacks of pain usually began during an acute alcoholic bout; calcification appeared on an average of 15 years after the onset of alcohol abuse. Bode et al. (41) and Goebell et al. (154) used a standardized secretin-pancreozymin test to examine exocrine pancreatic function in 54 alcoholics without clinical symptoms of chronic pancreatitis who had maintained a mean daily intake of more than 120 g of ethanol for a number of years. Dividing the cases into two groups with or without a histological diagnosis of cirrhosis of the liver, they found excretory pancreatic function more often disturbed in alcoholics without cirrhosis; the difference could be attributed to the fact that the alcoholics with cirrhosis had either discontinued or drastically reduced their alcohol consumption at least one year before examination, whereas those without cirrhosis had maintained their usual alcohol intake up to hospitalization. Filippini and Löffler (128) could establish a dose-time dependency for abnormalities of exocrine pancreatic function in 85 patients with chronic alcoholism of more than 5 years' standing (in 24 more than 10 years) after at least 2 weeks of abstinence. The pancreozymin-secretin test revealed no abnormalities with a daily intake of less than 80 g. If daily intake had exceeded 80 g and particularly 160 g for more than 5 years, impairment of exocrine pancreatic function was seen in 68%.

In a summarizing paper on alcoholic cardiomyopathy not connected with exposure to cobalt, Regan (404) states that the duration of alcoholism reported by most authors was usually at least 10 years before cardiac symptoms appeared. Brigden (56) thought that alcoholic heart disease occurred earlier and was more severe in spirit drinkers (10 to 20 years) than in beer drinkers (10 to 40 years). But his spirit drinkers had usually taken about 240 g of ethanol per day, whereas the beer drinkers had usually consumed only 180 g of ethanol.

5. INFLUENCE OF PATTERN OF DRINKING; EFFECTS OF ABSTINENCE

Pattern of Drinking

From the foregoing discussion, it seems reasonable to assume that the development of alcohol-induced organic lesions is dependent on the maintenance of an individually varying alcohol intake per time unit high enough and over periods long enough either to permit the hypothetical organotoxic property of ethanol per se to become manifest or to serve as basis for equally hypothetical secondary influences to become effective. The height of this critical dose would be determined individually by the degree of absorption, the sum total of mechanisms responsible for ethanol elimination and their capability for adaptation. Theoretically, a pattern of continuous drinking would thus be more effective than periodic intermittent drinking, which allows for spontaneous remission and regenerative processes. This can be illustrated and supported by recalling the predominant type of drinking pattern and its consequences in countries with a more permissive society where a large part of the population is accustomed to the habitual use of alcoholic beverages. The outstanding example is France.

As Moeschlin and Righetti (341) pointed out, wine drinkers are usually daily drinkers. A continuous "alcohol impregnation" resulting in a state of persistent slight euphoria without overt drunkenness seems to be characteristic for the type of alcohol misuse found in viticultural regions (454, 455) corresponding to the delta-type of alcoholism described by Jellinek. Solms speaks of the "rarely intoxicated gratification-seeking habitual drinker" who maintains an uninterrupted intake of considerable quantities and is unable to abstain even for a short period because withdrawal symptoms would promptly set in. The particularly high incidence of alcoholic cirrhosis in France, Chile, Portugal, Italy, and Switzerland (319), where this type of alcoholism prevails, strongly supports the assumption that continuous alcohol ingestion is more deleterious to the liver than periodically repeated bouts. It seems obvious that only where this type of drinking prevails, cirrhosis morbidity can serve as an indication for the degree of alcoholism in a given region or social group (55). On the other hand, drinking habits with a trend to weekly alcohol excesses primarily on weekends, as seen in Russia, Poland, and the Scandinavian countries, give the liver a chance to repair between periods of heavy alcohol loading. Isselbacher and Greenberger (205) exemplified another aspect of the consequences of continuous ingestion as opposed to intermittent drinking by citing two typical cases. One, a severe chronic alcoholic, could consume 304 g of ethanol daily under experimental conditions for 18 days and continue to show a blood alcohol level of less than 150 mg/100 ml; he showed signs of intoxication only after the dose had been increased to 405 g with blood alcohol concentration rising above 300 mg/100 ml. As opposed to this, an intermittent moderate drinker, accustomed only to drink smaller amounts of alcohol, promptly developed a semistuporous state with BAC above 400 mg/100 ml within 2 days on the same experimental dose of 304 g of ethanol. This latter effect of a heavy alcohol load will unavoidably entail a period of complete abstinence of at least 2 days' duration, thus interrupting the ethanol influence. Furthermore, considering that acute alcohol gastritis developed in some of the subjects after particularly high experimental alcohol administration necessitating a dose reduction (327), gastrointestinal tolerance may be an important determinant for the amount and periodicity of ethanol ingestion in alcoholics (330).

Though little has been published in the way of controlled studies concerning strictly comparable groups of continuous versus intermittent or periodic drinkers, several workers have found functional hepatic derangement to be more frequent and/or more severe in steady drinkers than in those who went on periodic bouts (37, 413, 447, 501). The results of histologic studies have been divergent. Edmondson et al. (113) were particularly interested in the early stages of liver injury after a binge. They studied 100 cases addicted to alcohol for many years, without evidence of cirrhosis, who had recently been on a "spree." Though severe hepatic lesions were rare, over 90% of the patients showed fatty change; in about one-half of the cases some centrolobular intrasinusoidal collagen accumulation was observed. In more than one-third swollen hydropic liver cells were seen, characterized electronmicroscopically by organelle disorganization. Frank hyaline necrosis was rare, but small intracytoplasmic round hyaline bodies, whose significance remained undetermined, were seen somewhat oftener. Most of this type of liver injury, except frank necrosis, was still reversible even after repeated "binges" over several years. The severity of fatty change in these spree drinkers was well correlated with scarcity of food intake during the preceding last binge (see also ref. 160). Lischner et al. (285) could determine patterns of drinking in 155 patients with acute alcoholic hepatitis. In 77.5% of the cases drinking (in excess of 80 g/day) had been continuous; in only 14.2% it had occurred in sprees which terminated in hospital or recovery at home followed by varying periods of abstinence. Although drunkenness was not uncommon among these patients, many were capable of holding steady jobs without exibiting overt inebriation despite an intake of 1 pint of hard liquor or more on workdays and even more during weekends. Once the spree drinkers in this series started to drink they maintained as a rule a state of persistent inebriation as long as alcoholic beverages were available. It is now common knowledge that acute alcoholic hepatitis usually becomes manifest in close connection with a prolonged period of particularly high intake of alcohol (71, 84, 460, 477, 516, 540). Recurrent episodes of rhabdomyolysis after drinking bouts in a male alcoholic were reported by Douglas et al. (110); during the bouts about 250 to 280 g of ethanol (beer and brandy) were consumed daily with the last bout ending in death.

Leevy and Smith (258) believe that any periodic interruption of alcohol intake will significantly lower the incidence of chronic liver disease. In the large series studied by Wilkinson et al. (531) many more habitual excessive drinkers were found among 77 cirrhotic alcoholics than were "bender" drinkers. Only two of the cirrhotic male alcoholics (= 4%) and none of the women cirrhotics had alternated bouts of heavy drinking with periods of moderate drinking or complete abstinence. Of 21 histologically diagnosed cases of cirrhosis studied by Seife et al. (442), 17 had been steady drinkers, only 4 were intermittent drinkers. Chalmers et al. (77) compared two groups of 12 steady and 12 intermittent drinkers and determined that extent and character of liver injury seemed to depend on the drinking habits insofar as steady drinkers were more likely to show alcoholic cirrhosis. In Lelbach's group of 265 alcoholics (267), which revealed a strikingly close association between total doses consumed on a weight basis and incidence of histologically confirmed cirrhosis of the liver, 90% of the cases were steady daily drinkers. From epidemiologic data on alcoholic cirrhosis among the Hopi and Navajo tribes Kunitz et al. (245) also thought it justified to suggest that differences in cirrhosis rates between the two tribes reflected different drinking habits with continued drinking being likely to end in cirrhosis. In a group of 75 Chilean alcoholics (491) liver biopsies revealed cirrhosis to be more frequent among the inveterate steady drinkers (24 %) than in the intermittent drinkers (16.7%), whereas the reverse was true of moderate to marked steatosis (15.2 against 37.5%). However, in a later study with liver biopsies from 130 alcoholics, Ugarte et al. (198, 490) could not detect significant differences between continuous and periodic drinkers except that severe steatosis was more frequent in the periodic drinkers.

The problem has also been tackled by means of animal experiments. Unless ethanol is built into a completely liquid diet, it is technically difficult to maintain in rats a continuous alcohol load in quantities large enough to sufficiently occupy ethanol degradation systems, since the capacity of these systems is in the rat at least twice as great as in the human. Using a feeding technique described by Porta and Gomez-Dumm (387) with sucrose-sweetened 20% v/v alcohol solutions, Takeuchi et al. (472)

tried to simulate different drinking patterns in rats. Fatty change, production of hyaline bodies, and elevated plasma GOT levels were observed only in animals maintained on the alcohol solution as sole source of drinking fluid and in addition subjected to periodically repeated acute alcohol intoxication by means of gastric intubation. No such changes developed in animals kept on the alcohol solution without additional intoxicating doses nor in those fed tap water and given alcohol by stomach tube intermittently in intoxicating doses. A similar experiment was made by Wallgren et al. (505), who used special feeding techniques in long-term experiments on rats with the aim of exploring the roles of pharmacological and nutritional effects of ethanol in connection with a marginal diet.

In summing up, the bulk of evidence collected up to the present seems to be in favor of the assumption that in the human a more or less continuous saturation of the alcohol elimination systems for a sufficiently long period is most likely to result in severe irreparable chronic liver damage, which at a certain stage may start to become autonomous.

Abstinence

An indirect corroboration for the effectiveness of a continuous intake is the practically unanimous agreement that prognosis of alcohol-induced liver disease is to a large extent dependent on strict abstinence. This is borne out by results of studies concerned with the immediate effects of cessation of exposure on the more transient alterations as well as by long-term studies of the course of alcoholic cirrhosis. Blood ethanol clearance was found to return to normal (336, 340, 492) and functional impairment of the liver was proved to disappear rapidly after onset of abstinence by Small et al. (450), Knott and Beard (238), Von Oldershausen (369), McBroom and Smith (298), Lelbach (263, 264), Wilkinson et al. (529), Kay et al. (225), Jaross et al. (207), Smith and Layden (452), and Boivin et al. (45). Glucosuria and alcohol hyperuricemia following experimentally induced chronic alcoholic intoxication disappeared rapidly after cessation of drinking (327, 271). Significant decrease of blood levels of free fatty acids, phospholipids, cholesterol, and bile acids during abstinence was also demonstrated by Jaross et al. (207).

Parallel to this, a number of histologic studies based on repeat biopsies of the liver performed after varying intervals of complete abstinence have shown that at least fatty metamorphosis is rapidly reversible (63, 71, 199–201, 203, 207, 256, 263–265, 332, 333, 422, 490, 527). Seife et al. (442) proved that in 32 of 42 alcoholics (76%) with fatty metamorphosis some degree of reduction occurred within 1 week of abstinence; in five patients marked steatosis was completely restored to normal liver histology. Intracellular fat was seen to be mobilized within 3 weeks by Leevy et al. (255, 256), elimination of extracellular fat within fatty cysts required 4 to 6 weeks with focal areas of cellular infiltration remaining after removal of fat. On the other hand, portal cirrhosis developed within 1 1/2 to 5 years in seven patients with initial fatty liver who continued to consume large quantities of whisky and to eat poorly, as demonstrated by consecutive biopsies.

Goldberg and Thompson (159) presented evidence suggesting that in some alcoholics recurrent episodes of acute fatty metamorphosis that occur before and after development of cirrhosis are reversible on adequate therapy. Complete reversal of fatty liver on withdrawal plus a normal diet within 1 week to 1 month, depending on its severity, was also reported by Ugarte et al. (490). Effects of a 6-month withdrawal treatment in the absence of other therapeutic measures was studied in 526 alcoholics by Lelbach (263, 264, 266). Biochemical symptoms of acute alcohol-induced injury to the liver began to return to normal within 1 to 2 weeks. After an average abstinence of 41 days, reduction in liver size was less marked the more inflammatory and structural changes predominated. Histology in 333 cases revealed a significant correlation between length of withdrawal period and frequency of severe fatty infiltration as opposed to minimal or moderate degrees, becoming evident after 4 to 8 weeks of abstinence. Methods of investigation employed did not permit an evaluation of the influence of abstinence on additional degenerative or inflammatory processes. Serial biopsies spaced over 1/2 year in a patient with decompensated alcoholic cirrhosis (99) showed that strict abstinence, beside causing fatty change to disappear rapidly, resulted finally in the picture of a quiescent cirrhosis within this period. Serenyi and Devenyi (445) found a considerable decrease in the degree of portal fibrosis within 6 to 12 months on repeat biopsy of the liver in two patients who had reduced their alcohol intake, while in five patients who continued to drink heavily frank cirrhosis was seen in the second biopsy. Alexander et al. (11) proved that the mortality rate was significantly lower in those patients who either considerably reduced or completely discontinued their alcohol intake.

Concerning long-term prognosis, a prospective study of 283 patients with Laennec's cirrhosis carried out by Powell and Klatskin (390) provided unrefutable evidence that 5-year survival and prognosis of alcoholic cirrhosis improved significantly if alcohol was completely given up. Results agreeing well with the findings of Powell and Klatskin were reported by Sherlock et al. (448), who studied 150 patients with alcoholic liver disease, and by Tygstrup et al. (487) in a series of 187 cirrhotics. Similarly, in a prospective followup study Rankin et al. (397), comparing three groups of patients with alcoholic cirrhosis who either gave up alcohol completely, reduced their intake, or continued their alcoholic habits, concluded that a good prognosis can be expected only in those cases where the underlying alcoholism can be favorably influenced. In studies by Dagradi (94a) repeated esophagoscopy even revealed definite reduction in caliber or extent of esophageal varices in advanced cirrhosis, together with clinical and biochemical improvement, when alcohol was discontinued, whereas in a control group hemorrhage occurred from unimproved varices in a considerable percentage. Influence of abstinence on life span is also reflected in the relatively high incidence of hepatoma found by Lee (254) to develop in the coarse nodular type of cirrhosis, especially in patients who had given up alcohol a long time before death. The reason for this is probably to be sought in the increased survival rate, that is, patients live long enough to develop hepatoma.

With regard to pancreatic function in alcoholics, it was pointed out that discrepancies found between results of Dinoso et al. (105) and those of Mezey et al. (335) were due to the fact that most of the abnormalities of pancreatic secretion produced by alcoholism are of a transient nature and returned to normal by the third week of hospitalization. Correlation between abstention and waning of clinical severity and of persistent drinking and waxing of degree of clinical symptoms was likewise observed in alcohol-induced myocardial disease (481).

6. GENETIC PREDISPOSITION AND SUSCEPTIBILITY

Although a close positive correlation between total dose of alcohol consumed over the years and incidence of severe liver damage was shown to exist, an inversely decreasing percentage of chronic alcoholics still continues to exhibit normal liver histology despite maintenance of a high alcohol intake over years and decades (267). On the one hand, this suggests that alcohol has some direct effect on the liver, which must be seen against the background of the very selective hepatic metabolism of this compound (274); on the other hand, this suggests that manifestation of alcohol induced liver disease requires a certain constitutional (or acquired) predisposition (9, 257, 446, 476, 490, and others).

From a gerontologic point of view, Mars and Ingegnieros (321) compared two groups of 20 male patients each over 70 years of age, one group comprising alcoholics (mean age: 81.1 years; range: 67 to 86), the other nonalcoholics (mean age: 83.3 years; range: 72 to 91). Hepatomegaly was found in 50% of the alcoholics and in 10% of the nonalcoholics. Biochemically only serum albumin and gamma globulin levels differed significantly in both groups, whereas hepatic histology was practically identical. The authors laid stress on the fact that the study dealt with subjects who had proved by their age to be particularly resistent. A case of a centenarian who had all his life consumed considerable amounts of alcohol and even increased his intake to the point of needing special treatment at the age of 78 years but showed no cirrhosis at autopsy was reported by Steinmann (463). Thaler (477) and Wewalka (519) recently reassessed Chvostek's original annotation (85) that certain only vaguely defined constitutional characteristics (long torso, dense cranial hair, and relative lack of body hair) are found in male patients with alcoholic cirrhosis, which he believed pointed to an *Anlagefaktor*. Lack of pectoral hair in apparently well-nourished or even obese patients with acute alcoholic steatonecrosis was also mentioned by Zimmerman (540). However, no statistical data were furnished to confirm this clinical impression. Smith and Berk (451), who compared 50 patients with cirrhosis, 50 patients without symptoms of liver disease, and 50 apparently healthy male subjects, could not detect any significant difference in pectoral hair growth between the three groups. Neither could Ratnoff and Patek (399) observe any characteristic diathesis in a carefully studied group of 54 patients (376).

Attempts to correlate constitution and alcohol consumption (96) were unsuccessful except for a probable positive association between consumption and body weight among white women independent of age, and for a possible association between consumption and morphological masculinity, which, however, may have been fortuitous. Among alcoholics Lundquist (290), using the Rohrer index for "compactness of body," found no difference in physical build between deliriants and nondeliriants. Neither could an association of alcohol-induced liver disease with certain types of color blindness claimed by Cruz-Coke (88, 89, 90, 91) be confirmed, although an association of color blindness with alcoholism seems to exist (490). Ethnic differences in alcohol sensitivity between Mongoloids and Caucasoids were recently reported by Wolff (534), who compared alcohol flushing responses of Caucasoids and various Mongoloid groups by means of optical densitometry. Of Mongoloid adults 83% responded with a marked visible flush as compared to 6% of the Caucasoids, though intake (beer 5% v/v: 0.14 to 0.30 ml/kg body weight) was considerably less than in the latter group (0.36 to 0.45 ml/kg).

Lack of an analogous animal model in the past made it difficult to assess the relative importance of susceptibility and dose; an exception is perhaps Chey's (81) recent experimental design, which proved that with sufficiently high doses given long enough histologic alterations of the liver comparable to those observed in patients with alcoholic hepatitis can be produced in dogs. Senior (443) pointed out that the cellular or enzymatic basis for susceptibility to alcoholic liver disease in the human remains a most challenging enigma. Most probably, however, the basis for this susceptibility is in some way connected with the variable capacity for alcohol metabolism and its potentially adaptive adjustment (9, 257). Cherrick et al. (80) suggested that variations in susceptibility may in part derive from differences in capacity to oxidize alcohol. From determinations of ethanol disappearance rates and ADH, NAD, and NADH levels in liver tissue before and after an alcohol load in 15 alcoholics with and without alcoholic liver disease, they concluded that persons with abnormal hepatic NADH accumulation after alcohol appeared to be unusually susceptible to hepatotoxic effects of alcohol. An interesting aspect in this connection is the extraordinarily high rate of ethanol oxidation [460 mg/(kg body weight)(hr)] found in children with glycogen storage disease type I (375, 511) correlated to an increase in NADH reoxidation due to a high pyruvate concentration in these patients. Questioning the explanation that degree of liver damage may be correlated with limitations in metabolizing ethanol, Clark and Senior (86) could find no significant difference in peak levels, clearance rates, or blood lactate concentrations when studying alcohol users with and without liver disease of the Laennec type after oral and intravenous alcohol administration (0.5 to 0.75 g of ethanol per kilogram of body weight). They concede, however, that higher alcohol loads or a previous nutritional insult may be necessary to bring out the distinguishing differences between those prone or not prone to develop alcoholic cirrhosis.

Rankin et al. (397) pointed out that initial susceptibility and later progression of an established condition are not necessarily governed by the same factors. In an earlier communication (531) not only duration of alcohol consumption but also sex was found to be an important factor in the causation of cirrhosis insofar as women in this series seemed to be more susceptible to cirrhosis and to develop the disease after a shorter period of excessive drinking. Glatt (153) showed that the interval between first occurrence of inebriation (males: 20.1 years, females: 30.9 years) and first hospitalization for alcoholism or its consequences (males: 40.2 years; females: 43.3 years) was shorter for females than for males. Lischner et al. (285) reported a preponderance of Negro women in a group of unselected patients with alcoholic hepatitis which had not been described before. In a series of 768 cases of cirrhosis in one Swedish community Hällen and Krook (175) found alcoholic cirrhosis in ages below 40 years more common among women than among men, suggesting a quicker development of the disease in women. Caroli and Péquignot (73) likewise noted a higher frequency of cirrhosis in women alcoholics at a lower level of alcohol intake than men. Similarly, Lutterotti (296) found cirrhosis of the liver in over 50% of the females but only in 14% of the male drinkers in his group of 210 alcoholics (24 women, 186 men). In the later followup of 77 alcoholics with cirrhosis in the series of Wilkinson et al. (531) no significant difference in mortality or development of symptoms was seen between the two sexes (397); continuation or cessation of drinking were the most important factors. Hardison and Lee (181) reported mortality from severe acute alcoholic liver disease to have been the same for males and females in a group of 87 heavy drinkers. According to Schmidt and De Lint (434), the clinical impressions concerning sex differences in alcoholic use are not reflected in mortality data; they concluded that women alcoholics perhaps only appear more abnormal as they deviate more drastically from the expected social role. Viel et al. (497) found a greater proportion of cirrhosis in female normal drinkers older than 35 years than in the comparable male group. However, they attributed this finding to false information given by the interviewed relatives, considering the derogatory character of being an alcoholic woman in Chile.

Female alcoholics seem to have a higher frequency of psychic abnormalities, their prodromal phase is shorter, they suffer more from personal, familial, or social conflicts, are more evasive than men, and minimize their consumption. They are less likely to be periodic drinkers, more frequently drink distilled spirits and wine than beer, and are more reluctant to undergo a withdrawal treatment voluntarily, usually not until a relatively late stage with corresponding bad prognosis (92, 93, 192, 213, 342, 398, 494, 507, 508, 536, 539). Drinking rarely occurs in public, and women are seldom seen drunk but are often incapacitated by "sickness" (444). By the time they are hospitalized, alcoholism tends to be more severe in women (400) with more frequent symptoms of polyneuropathy (346). Studies reporting less hepatic and cerebral damage in women because of lower alcohol consumption and higher likeliness to seek treatment after five or fewer years of alcoholism were also published (440).

All this casts some doubt on the assumption that the observed higher frequency of cirrhosis in alcoholic women is only sex-linked; it may, at least in part, be due to the fact that apparently the stage of continuous alcoholization is more rapidly reached and less likely to be interrupted.

7. ORGANIC PATHOLOGY AND VARIOUS ALCOHOLIC BEVERAGES

Influence of Congeneric Substances

Opinions are widely divergent on the question of whether ethanol per se or the presence of various other ingredients in alcoholic beverages is of major importance in the production of organic lesions. On the one hand, the bulk of clinical experience tends to make it evident that the source of alcohol is of no importance (24, 166, 261, 334, 399, 447, 506). Alcoholic beverages of the most divergent origin and composition are drunk all over the world, but the stereotype character of organic lesions resulting from overindulgence is unanimously reported from all those regions where consumption of alcoholic beverages is of socioeconomic relevance. Though a number of substances other than ethanol have been incriminated, this makes it exceedingly unlikely that the cause for the ubiquitous phenomenon of organic complications, especially alcoholic liver disease (477), is to be found in certain components rather than in the ethanol content. To date, very little evidence has been forthcoming to support the hypothesis that in human pathology such impurities or contaminations are responsible for organic pathology safe for a few exceptions (discussed later).

An intermediate position concedes that small amounts of congeners present may play a role in the overall intoxicating effects of alcoholic beverages (177, 220, 351, 352, 353, 413), but their concentration is too low to be of anything but doubtful importance (343, 367, 509). The extreme opposite is a discussion remark by György (173), who goes to the extent of denying that ethanol has anything to do with "alcoholic cirrhosis."

The common denominator is that all alcoholic beverages constitute more or less dilute solutions of ethyl alcohol; they differ with respect to their content of a large number of chemically divergent additional components present in very low concentrations which are responsible for specific flavor and aroma. Such additional constituents are either contained in raw materials or result from mashing methods, fermentation processes, or distillation procedures or are added to or accumulate in the end-products, as in aging processes (278, 284, 459, 469, 470). In distilled spirits, part of them is eliminated during the distillation process (163), the fractional rectification, or the filtration procedures for which absorptive agents, such as charcoal, are used (e.g., vodka). The principal compounds are various aldehydes, ketones, ethers, esters, organic acids, methanol, and higher aliphatic and aromatic alcohols (177). Only the higher homologs of ethanol, also known as "fusel oils," should rightly be called "congeners." Of these, the most important are *n*-propyl, isopropyl, *n*-butyl, isobutyl, *n*-amyl, isoamyl, hexyl, and heptyl alcohol. From a toxicological point of view, the amyl alcohols seem to be the most dangerous type of higher alcohols.

By fermentation of different raw materials, fusel oil solutions of varying composition can be obtained. Typical compositions were described for the following raw materials: cane sugar, potatoes, grain, cellulose, xylose, stone fruit (129, 146, 148, 509). Congener solutions were also prepared from aged whiskey (401). The main ingredients of such solutions are *n*- and isoamyl alcohol (51 to 80% w/v), *n*- and isobutanol (1.3 to 24.0% w/v), and *n*- and isopropanol (0.3 to 26.7% w/v) (129, 146, 148, 509).

The acute toxicity of the first five primary alcohols (C_1 to C_5) increases with their molecular weight (338, 514) with an inverse linear relationship existing between the number of carbon atoms and the logarithm of the mean lethal doses (309). Increasing with chain length are also the affinity of enzymes or enzyme systems involved in the degradation processes of alcohols (312) and the inhibitory effects on oxygen consumption in rat liver slices (509). Kalant (222) and Kalant and Israel (221) have reviewed the direct pharmacologic effects of alcohols on cell membranes and have pointed out that short-chain alcohols reduce the membrane potential whereas longer-chain alcohols increase it, so that stronger stimuli are required for depolarization. The interaction of alcohols with protein and lipid constituents of cell membranes, in which hydrogen bonding and van der Waals' forces seem to play a role, is still open to discussion, but its elucidation will perhaps contribute to the comprehension of a number of observed functional changes.

In a carefully designed large-scale experiment, Haggard et al. (177) investigated the comparative acute toxicity of 64 different distilled spirits (commercial spirits, specially rectified commercial spirits, neutral spirits used in preparing spirit blends, highly purified spirits, several specimens of whiskey, applejack, cognac, and gin) after intraperitoneal administration to fasted male rats. They took special care to give consideration to the rate of administration, absorption and completion of absorption, distribution, and the amounts of alcohol lost by oxidation and elimination through lungs and kidneys. No attempts were made to identify particular congeners. In contrast to the virtual uniformity of the blood alcohol concentrations at respiratory failure (taken as measure of toxicity), the amounts of the different spirits required to produce these concentrations varied considerably. This was interpreted as an indication for a real and marked difference in the toxicity of distilled spirits. A high toxicity was found in samples of high-quality cognac and applejack and in the commercial spirits tested, although the latter contained only a small fraction of the amounts of known congeners found in low-toxicity whiskey (such as fusel oils). Furthermore, fractional redistillation of commercial spirits did not alter their toxicity, but a marked reduction in toxicity occurred after treatment with both charcoal and lime. Whatever congeners were present in the spirits tested, they did not add directly to the toxicity of the alcohol as measured by blood alcohol concentrations at respiratory failure. Differences in the acute toxicity could be attributed solely to a retardation in the rate of metabolization of the alcohol, which was found to be a function of the respective congeneric content. A human volunteer subject, given 176 g of ethanol to drink over different time periods either as highly purified or as commercial spirit, also exhibited the same marked difference in the rate of disappearance of alcohol from the blood. The authors concluded that the congeners, whatever their chemical nature, only reduced the rate of oxidation of alcohol without exercising a direct toxic action.

Differential effects of vodka and bourbon whiskey, in spite of identical blood alcohol concentrations on sleeping time of mice and related measures, attributable to different congener contents, were observed by Blum et al. (40). Walker and Shand (504), using an embryonic chick tibia preparation as an *in vitro* collagen-synthesizing system, concluded that certain proprietary alcoholic beverages with a higher congener content (Scotch whisky, brandy) may effect collagen biosynthesis in a more pronounced way than gin or pure ethanol.

Gaillard and Derache (140) determined the rate of removal from the blood of methanol and higher alcohols after oral administration to fasted Wistar rats. Methanol, isopropanol, and tertiary butanol disappeared from the blood much slower than ethanol after having reached blood concentrations similar to or higher than those seen after an equal dose of ehtanol; *n*-propanol, *n*-butanol, isobutanol, *n*-amyl, and isoamyl alcohol reached only very low levels as compared to ethanol, which was interpreted as being due either to a rapid rate of oxidation or to fixation in the peripheral tissues. However, the rate of removal of these higher alcohols is definitely modified by the presence of ethanol due to a competitive interference at different levels of metabolism, since these congeners share the same metabolic pathways with ethanol in the organism (2, 510). Greenberg (168) found that intraperitoneally injected isoamyl alcohol, though disappearing rapidly from the blood of rats when administered alone, remains detectable 10 hr when given jointly with ethanol. The same was valid for its first metabolite, isovaleraldehyde, which was at no time detectable when isoamyl alcohol had been given alone. The opposite was also true, although a single dose of 400 mg/kg body weight of fusel oil derived from stone fruit did not influence the rate of oxidation of $1-C^{14}$-ethanol to CO_2, a higher dose of 2 g/kg as well as pure propanol significantly inhibited ethanol oxidation (2).

Ethanol inhibited significantly the elimination of isopropanol and vice versa (1a). All this suggests that a competitive inhibition of common metabolic pathways may possibly lead to an accumulation of congeners contained in alcoholic beverages after prolonged and heavy drinking.

After 15 alcoholics engaged in a 10- to 15-day period of free choice drinking (mean daily intake: 258 g of ethanol), Majchrowitz and Mendelson (313, 331) found blood acetaldehyde concentrations to be twice as high in those who drank bourbon whiskey than in those who consumed pure grain ethyl alcohol; the difference was accounted for by the presence of acetaldehyde and congeners in bourbon and by a competitive inhibition of acetaldehyde dehydrogenase by higher acetaldehydes in bourbon. However, no dose or dose-time relationship between blood alcohol levels and blood acetaldehyde concentrations was seen. On the other hand, blood methanol concentrations rose steadily during an analogous experimental situation in both bourbon and grain alcohol drinkers; levels were only slightly higher in bourbon drinkers, so that methanol apparently came from endogenous sources (312). Effective inhibition of methanol oxidation by the presence of ethanol is well known (314). Further investigation of the still undetermined role that acetaldehyde may play in the development of tolerance (331) is recommended (484). Schüppel and Dürr (436, 437) also demonstrated an inhibitory effect of alcohols on microsomal N-demethylation of aminophenazone, which increases with chain length from methanol to n-butanol.

A number of animal experiments, in some of which vodka and whiskeys were used as examples for a very low and a high congener content have been conducted to determine the chronic toxicity of higher alcohols. Growth over a period of 150 days was identical in male white rats maintained on a 10% v/v solution of ethanol either without or with an addition of 4% v/v fusel oils derived from stone fruit (2). Similarly, no differences in weight gain were seen in male Long-Evans rats on wines (sherries, muscatels) and ethanol solutions over 32 weeks (361). In a long-term experiment with male Wistar rats maintained on alcohol solutions (12 to 15% v/v) derived from pure ethanol, cognac, Scotch whisky, vermouth, white and red wine as sole source of drinking fluid, Kiessling and Pilström (233) observed weight after 25 weeks to be 14% lower in ethanol and cognac drinkers, 20% lower in whiskey and vermouth drinkers, and 6% lower in white wine drinkers as compared to controls. No differences in weight were seen in red wine drinkers. The authors concluded that by-products present in alcoholic beverages intensify the effect of ethanol on certain of the functions studied but counteract its effect on others. Whiskey did not produce greater hepatic enzyme alterations than ethanol when given to female Sprague-Dawley rats for six weeks, although a depression of alcohol dehydrogenase activity seemed to occur more rapidly with whiskey than with ethanol (126). No difference in plasma or hepatic lipid responses was seen after a single dose of 6 g of ethanol per kilogram of body weight given either as purified laboratory alcohol or as various commercial alcoholic beverages to fasted female Holtzman rats (102); neither did rat liver triglyceride content increase differently after acute administration of cornoil plus either laboratory alcohol or two commercial beverages (vodka, bourbon) (102). However, chronic ingestion of ethanol built into a fat-rich formula diet as 35% of total calories over three weeks resulted in an increase of hepatic triglycerides twice as high on vodka and bourbon as source of ethanol as compared to absolute purified alcohol. Furthermore, whereas no mortality was seen after absolute alcohol and vodka, a 23% mortality occurred after bourbon. Both findings were interpreted as reflecting a possibly additive injurious effect of congeners (103).

Additives in anisated and mastic araq (volatile oils derived from the anis seed and fermentation products of grapes, or from mastic and fermentation products of dates, respectively) also differentially accentuated alcohol-induced accumulation of total lipids, triglycerides, and total cholesterol in the liver of male rats after 38 weeks when compared with the effect of ethanol solutions. However, no cellular infiltration, alcoholic hyalin, focal necrosis, fibrosis, or cirrhosis was evident. Mastic araq proved to be the most effective of both types in this respect (95). Gaillard et al. (141), believing that the concentration of higher aliphatic alcohols in alcoholic beverages is far from negligible, gave a mixture of higher alcohols in concentrations roughly similar to that in commercial beverages (*n*-propanol, isopropanol, *n*-butanol, isobutanol, tertiary butanol, *n*-amyl, isoamyl alcohol, and methanol, of each 0.02 g/100 ml) contained in a 10% w/v solution of ethanol to female Wistar rats for 6 months, while they were kept on a low-protein, high-fat diet. A rise in hepatic triglycerides, total fatty acids, and hydroxyproline content was more pronounced in animals receiving ethanol plus the mixture than in those given either ethanol alone or the mixture of fusel oil.

When, however, undiluted fusel oils are employed in animal experiments, the highly toxic nature of higher alcohols becomes indisputably manifest. Gibel et al. (146, 148–150) provided unequivocal evidence for a chronic hepatotoxicity in a number of experiments. They gave doses of fusel oils derived from grain or potatoes thrice weekly for prolonged periods to mice and Wistar rats by stomach tube or intramuscular or subcutaneous injection. Fatty infiltration of the liver was seen after 4 weeks. Grossly degenerative lesions similar to those of alcoholic hepatitis occurred within 4 to 6 months, and coarsely nodular cirrhosis developed in animals living longer than 6 months, with ascites and splenomegaly in some of them. Overall mortality was high. At the site of injection, severe tissue necrosis and in two cases sarcoma developed. A mutagenic and cancerogenic effect was also observed since multiple hyperkeratotic papillomata and in several animals carcinoma of the esophagus and forestomach were found. Remmer (407) commented on Gibel's studies as being an important contribution to the problem of fusel oil hepatotoxicity. Remmer thinks that from a toxicological point of view the usually low concentration of such congeners in alcoholic beverages could not be fully appreciated on the basis of a simple dose relationship, since cumulation due to competitive inhibition of breakdown may occur.

It would be highly desirable to define and standardize the toxicologically tolerable upper limits for fusel oil content in beverage alcohol. However, no generally accepted standards exist yet. According to Jarosch (206), the Codex Alimentarius Austriacus allows at present a maximum fusel oil content of 0.5% v/v. Jarosch pleads for legal enforcement of stricter control in the sale of alcoholic beverages with respect to statutory maximum values of fusel oil content. Congener content has been studied in various alcoholic beverages by methods of varying accuracy. Table 12 reviews values found for the main constituents, although it cannot claim to be complete. Gas liquid chromatography combined with mass spectrography seems at present the optimum method. According to total congener and isoamyl alcohol content (as reported from the literature), the commonly consumed alcoholic beverages can roughly be ranked in the following order: vodka, gin, beers, wines, distilled spirits other than vodka and gin. Although the congener content of high-quality vodka seems to be very low and is similar to that of neutral grain spirits, a cheap variety, known as "samogon," which is crudely distilled from grain, corn, sugar beet, or potatoes, is reported to contain much fusel oil and to be widely consumed in Russia in spite of its toxic effects and the high penalties imposed on its sale (241, 295, 344). Purchase (393) reports that Bantu beer brewed from kaffir corn on the Witwatersrand has a definitely higher fusel oil content (227 mg/liter) than ordinary beer; however, in an experiment with Wistar rats lasting up to 56 weeks no significant differences could be found when either a combination of ethanol with fusel oils from Bantu beer (twice the normal amount) or a 2% isoamyl-alcohol solution was fed as sole source of drinking fluid (212).

Uptake of congeners, however, is to be seen in relation to amounts of ethanol consumed as different alcoholic beverages. If calculations are based on a dose of 160 g of ethanol, amounts of total congener and of isoamyl alcohol ingested with different beverages are shown in Table 13.

As can be deduced from this table, beer consumption is associated with a relatively low, but, in comparison to vodka, still appreciable ingestion of congeners. Values for wines and spirits overlap.

In human pathology, however, no clear-cut evidence has been presented to prove that, if comparable quantities of ethyl alcohol are absorbed, any of the commonly consumed alcoholic beverages exert a more pronounced influence on the production of organic lesions than others. With beverages of low alcohol content such as beer, must, or cider (3 to 6% v/v) it is of course impossible to reach high degrees of intoxication rapidly. Furthermore, it takes about 10 times the volume of fluid if one is to maintain a certain daily ethanol intake as beer (4% v/v) than in the form of an 80 proof whiskey. Rates of passage into the intestines, rates of absorption from the gastrointestinal tract and distribution, rates of rise in blood alcohol concentration and maximum concentration attained in blood and tissues are to some degree proportional to the concentration of ethanol in the beverages drunk on an empty stomach (87, 176). Modifying factors are buffer capacity of beverages (157) and protective mechanisms of central nervous origin acting upon the emptying time of the stomach. They are missing in persons with gastrectomy who are therefore particularly sensitive, even to small doses of beer (57, 242–244). Beverages containing less than 1.5% v/v ethanol are incapable of producing inebriation (367) because ensuing water-diuresis eliminates alcohol too fast.

No consistent differences in behavior attributable to differences in congener content (vodka, bourbon) were noted during a 30-day drinking period in eight male volunteers (356). Hangover was demonstrated to be essentially dependent on the amount of alcohol ingested. If a certain basic amount of ethanol was consumed, a somewhat greater incidence of definite hangover symptoms was reported to occur from bourbon whiskey than from vodka; observed differences, however, could conceivably have been due merely to psychological suggestion (78). Murphree et al. (348, 349) concluded that the amounts of congeneric in the two extremes, commercially available vodka and bourbon whiskey, might be too small for a detectable effect of a single dose. They therefore prepared a "superbourbon" with four to eight times the congener content of commercial bourbon whiskey. This superbourbon produced some qualitatively different, but not uniformly occurring electroencephalographic effects, which in a way resembled the effects of barbiturates. Intensity of positional alcohol nystagmus (157, 347) and ataxic responses (133) is connected with different beverages only insofar as it seems to be in proportion to blood alcohol peaks, which are highest after distilled spirits and lowest after beers, provided the same amount of alcohol is given under standard conditions. As concerns roving

TABLE 12 CONGENER CONTENT OF VARIOUS ALCOHOLIC BEVERAGES DETERMINED BY DIFFERENT METHODS

Beverage	Total Congener Content	Isoamyl Alcohol	Isobutanol	n-Propanol	Ethyl Acetate
1. Vodka, gin, Canadian, Scotch, bourbon blend, cognac, bourbon (348)	2.65–245.5 (mg/100 ml)	0.40–120.0 (mg/100 ml)	1.05–33.5 (mg/100 ml)	0.00–11.0 (mg/100 ml)	0.00–82.5 (mg/100 ml)
2. Scotch, Irish, bourbon, rye, straight, blended, Canadian whiskey, rum, brandies (75)	40.54–761.65 (g/100 liters)	trace–501.5 (g/100 liters)	5.0–134.0 (g/100 ml)	1.9–146.0 (g/100 liters)	10.8–162.5 (g/100 ml)
3. Vodka, gin, whiskeys, rum, cognac (75)	3.30–285.56 (g/100 liters at 100 U.S. proof)	0.0–139.5 (g/100 liters at 100 U.S. proof)	1.35–39.60 (g/100 liters at 100 U.S. proof)	0.49–14.76 (g/100 liters at 100 U.S. proof)	0.0–96.00 (g/100 liters at 100 U.S. proof)

4. German fruit brandy (Zwetschgenwasser) (163)	—[a]	376 mg per 100 g ethanol	78 mg per 100 g ethanol	50 mg per 100 g ethanol	24.8 mg per 100 g ethanol
5. German wine (Sylvaner 1963)	—	179 mg/liter	78 mg/liter	—	—
Hybrid wine (269)	—	180 mg/liter	50 mg/liter	—	—
6. Italian grappa (509)	up to 1300 mg per 100 g ethanol	—	—	—	—
7. Cheap Austrian brandies (206)	1.25 ml/100 ml	76%	17%	4%	—
8. 42 red wines (149)	285–550 mg/liter	—	—	—	—
33 white wines	157–437 mg/liter	—	—	—	—
9. 20 types of German beer (410)	74 mg/liter	81.9%	11.1%	7.4%	—

[a] — = not determined.

TABLE 13 CALCULATED AMOUNTS OF TOTAL CONGENER AND ISOAMYL ALCOHOL CONTAINED IN A 160-g DOSE OF ETHANOL IF INGESTED IN THE FORM OF DIFFERENT ALCOHOLIC BEVERAGES (BASED ON VALUES REPORTED IN THE LITERATURE)

Beverage	Total Congener Content (mg/100 ml)	Isoamyl Alcohol (mg/100 ml)	Amount of Beverage Equivalent to 160 g of ethanol[c] (ml)	A Quantity of 160 g of Ethanol Would Contain:	
				Total Congener (mg)	Isoamyl Alcohol (mg)
Vodka (348)	2.65	0.40	540	13.6	2.02
German beers (410)	7.40	6.06	5,031	372.3	304.90
Red wines (149, 269)	28.5–55.0[a]	18.00[b]	2,018	575.1–1109.9	363.20
White wines (149, 269)	15.7–43.7[a]	18.00[b]	2,018	316.8–881.9	363.20
Bourbon whiskey	245.50	120.00	469	1151.4	562.8

[a] Source: ref. 149.
[b] Source: ref. 269.
[c] calculations were based on the following alcohol concentrations: beer = 4% v/v; wines = 10% v/v; vodka = 40% v/v; bourbon whiskey = 43% v/v.

ocular movements, however, wines seemed to bring about a somewhat higher intensity than other alcoholic beverages not proportional to the height of the blood alcohol curve, so that Goldberg (158) concluded this to be due to a modifying effect of constituents other than ethanol. No clinical difference was found between alcoholism induced by wine and that induced by liqueurs (24).

Delirium tremens is not connected with any special beverage, but choice of beverage follows local usage; it is seen in spirits drinkers as well as in wine and beer drinkers (39, 64, 122, 123, 138, 145, 186, 290, 294, 525). Neither has the preferred beverage any influence on the lethality of delirium tremens. Duration and intensity of previous overindulgence are the decisive factors for the development; it seems to be most frequent after continuous heavy drinking of certain minimum amounts over prolonged periods of definite length (3, 94, 124, 204, 214, 221, 281, 290, 385, 474, 523) with bouts of severe intoxication being rather rare (171a); it can become manifest in the absence of nutritional deficiencies (359) and of alcoholic liver disease (54, 202, 255).

In contrast to the well-documented influence of duration and dose on alcohol-induced liver disease, the choice of beverages is of secondary or no importance. Lelbach (261, 262) compared two groups of 52 alcoholics each, one drinking only beer, the other only spirits. Except for the choice of beverage, the two groups were practically identical as to duration of alcoholism, daily amounts of ethanol ingested, length of abstinence period, age, relative body weight, and previous illnesses. Neither the degree of functional hepatic derangement nor of histologically diagnosed liver damage was significantly different in the two groups. Considering the choice of beverage in the total group of 526 alcoholics, however, a statistically highly significant positive correlation was seen between increasing intensity of alcohol abuse and the number of those who preferred spirits to beer. This shift to more concentrated beverages instead of beer in the later stages of alcoholism is well known (157, 217, 526). From a comparison of amounts of ethanol consumed per capita per year in different countries and the percentage distribution to spirits, wine, and beer, Battig (18) concluded that a close association exists between alcoholism and consumption of spirits but only a loose correlation to beer or wine consumption. The previously mentioned comparison of the two groups of beer and spirits drinkers strongly suggests that the development of liver disease through different alcoholic beverages is predominantly due to the ethanol content itself and not to other ingredients (261, 262). Schmidt and Bronetto (432) demonstrated a statistically significant relationship between cirrhosis mortality and the consumption of cheap native wines, but not of beer or spirits. This, however, had nothing to do with a particular toxicity but was explained on sociological grounds, since these native wines were the cheapest source of alcohol (106, 419) for the socially displaced chronic alcoholic.

It was shown by Frank et al. (132) that, in the absence of nutritional deficiencies, long-continued heavy consumption of beer in 200 brewery workers (76% of them consuming at least 160 g, some reaching a peak of about 500 g of ethanol per day), as compared to control groups employed in the steel industry, leads to liver damage in the same way and to the same extent as other alcoholic beverages. Among patients with alcoholic cirrhosis in South Germany 30.7% drank beer exclusively (152). In the Australian group of patients with alcoholic cirrhosis studied by Rankin et al. (397) and Wilkinson et al. (531) the majority were beer drinkers; the same was valid for Green's study (165).

Similarly, alcoholic myopathy (366) and cardiomyopathy unrelated to cobalt was seen to develop after long-continued heavy beer consumption as well as through other more concentrated beverages (10, 13, 17, 46, 66, 83, 230, 297, 299, 300, 482).

Influence of Ingredients Other than Congeneric Substances

Certain pesticides containing arsenic (As_2O_3) widely used in German wine-growing regions following their introduction in 1923 were the cause of an increasing number of cases of chronic arsenic intoxication in wine growers and vintagers in the Kaiserstuhl and Moselle area and the Palatinate until the sale of these pesticides was prohibited by law in 1942 (67-69, 109, 139, 182, 270, 323, 368, 378, 493). Consumption of an inferior home-made wine from the pressed skins of grapes, not sold to the public, the so-called *Haustrunk* (alcohol content: 3 to 5% v/v), had led to a considerable uptake of arsenic over the years. From analysis of several specimens (less than 2.0 to 8.9 mg/liter) Roth (412) calculated an average total uptake of approximately 54 g of arsenic over a period of 12 years. Typical skin lesions (hyperkeratosis, melanosis, multiple epitheliomata, Bowen's disease) developed in these cases as well as a special type of "arsenical" cirrhosis and, many years later (latency periods of 13 to 15 years), multiple malignant tumors of the liver and bronchial system were found (101, 278, 288, 412). Up to about 1965, the conditions were acknowledged as occupational disease of wine growers (288). British statutory limits for arsenic in wines are 0.2 ppm and for lead 1 ppm, except for vintage port for which the limit was set at 2 ppm (197).

Prolonged consumption of illicitly distilled whiskey ["moonshine"; estimated production in 1966: 55,700,000 gal (26)] has resulted in lead poisoning (324, 377), appearing now to be limited to the "moonshine-belt" [12 southeastern U.S. states (26)] with a remarkable frequency of saturnine gout (26, 27, 236). In samples of Alabama moonshine 89% contained lead in amounts ranging from 1000 to 200,000 μg/liter (26). Nervous system disorders, intrauterine growth retardation, and perinatal failure to thrive were reported after consumption of moonshine (373, 374). Furthermore, absorption of lead from the intestinal tract is speeded by alcohol (136).

Widely varying iron contents of different alcoholic beverages are reported from a number of countries. The lowest content was found in beers and stout (0.1 to 0.9 mg/liter) as well as in distilled spirits like gin, vodka, whiskeys, rum (trace to 1.0 mg/liter) (301, 389, 449). Sherries, port, and fortified wines also have a relatively low iron content, ranging from 1.6 to 3.9 mg/liter (389, 449). Analysis of iron content in white and red wine from a large number of countries showed an enormous variation from 1.5 to 350 mg/liter (14, 74, 292, 293, 302, 303, 357, 382, 449). Amerine (14) found average values to be highest (12.1 to 22.0 mg/liter) in wines from Russia, Portugal, Italy, and Rumania in this order; for Californian, Swiss, German, and French wines average values ranged from 4.9 to 8.8 mg/liter. Average iron content in cheap wines commonly used by alcoholics in Göteborg, Sweden, was 11.9 mg/liter (7.6 to 14.3) for red and 8.6 mg/liter (6.0 to 14.6) for white wines (292). McDonald (301) calculated that the total amounts of iron absorbed from different wines in 20 years of drinking practice with an average consumption of 2 liters/day can well lie in the order of 12 to 50 g.

Highest iron contents have been found in a variety of fermented alcoholic beverages of the Bantu in the range of 5 to 160 (mean: 40) mg/liter (52, 53). Values of 72 to 324 mg/liter in illegally brewed Bantu beer with an average content of 166 mg were reported by Buchanan (62). A high frequency of considerable tissue siderosis in the adult African population of South Africa and Rhodesia is well known (51, 61, 98, 188) and is attributed to large amounts of iron absorbed during life from foodstuffs and, particularly, home-brewed beer. A mean iron concentration of 144 mg/100 g was found in the feces collected from males on Monday morning as compared to 34 mg/100 g on Thursday morning; the variation was thought to reflect the weekend drinking habits of the urban Bantu (52). Buchanan (62) succeeded in producing an experimental siderosis in guinea pigs by addition of such home-brewed African beer to a normal diet. Tissue iron distribution was identical to that found in uncomplicated siderosis in Africans, but no fibrosis of the liver ensued.

However, iron content of beverages seems not to be the only factor in the development of siderosis in the alcoholic (8). Apart from increased absorption of iron, Neame and Beck (358) think it possible that siderosis may, in part, be related to increased plasma iron concentration due to decreased utilization of iron for heme synthesis (193) in reversible alcoholic sideroblastosis (189, 190). Alcohol in the form of whiskey or brandy was found to potentiate considerably the absorption of ferric iron but had no effect on absorption of ferrous hemoglobin (79). Neither was absorption of ferrous radio-iron in rats increased after single large doses of blended whiskey or ethanol solution (473). Enhanced absorption of ferric iron may result from stimulation of hydrochloric acid production in the stomach (79). In 100 subjects who had suffered sudden unexpected death, hepatic iron concentration and total hepatic iron content were significantly higher in those who had had a "heavy alcohol consumption" (71 or more grams of ethanol per day) (389). Investigations made by Lundvall et al. (292, 293) and Lundin et al (289), however, did not show increased iron stores in individuals with long-standing alcohol abuse who were predominantly consumers of distilled spirits (at least 68 g of ethanol per day) with only a few consuming appreciable quantities of wine. Lundvall et al. (292) criticized the results of Powell (389) in several points and thought it probable that the males with "heavy alcohol intake" in Powell's study had been wine drinkers. Only in hepatic histiocytes did Lundvall et al. find increased iron deposition, which was attributed to a transfer of iron from injured parenchymal cells.

In 1965–1966 an almost epidemic outbreak of a particular nonobstructive type of cardiomyopathy with a high mortality occurred in chronic beer drinkers, in Canada (Quebec), in the United States (Omaha, Minneapolis), and in Belgium (Louvain), where it was preferably accompanied by pericardial effusion (180, 231, 232, 299, 394, 415, 464, 465, 466). A number of symptoms differing from the beri-beri type of alcoholic cardiomyopathy and that characterized by myocardial fibrosis suggested a common causative agent other than alcohol. Histology of the thyroid gland in fatal cases pointed to a cobalt intoxication (415). Fatal cases showed strikingly severe centrilobular hepatic necroses (299). The causative agent was found to be a foam-stabilizing cobalt compound added to local brands of beer. In those who survived, the condition had a relatively good prognosis; once the cobalt additive was omitted, no new cases were reported. A special edition of the *Canadian Medical Association Journal* (395) was exclusively devoted to publications of an ad hoc committee dealing with this at first mysterious disease. In animal experiments, cobalt itself had a significant effect on myocardial metabolism through enzyme inhibition; it might have potentiated the effects of alcohol on the myocardium (179) or vice versa, and it was rarely seen after heavy industrial exposure to this metal (30). Dietary deficiencies in sulfhydryl groups containing proteins were also incriminated (232). The reason why it appeared in only a small percentage of the population consuming beer with a high cobalt content and only rarely among metal workers is still a matter of speculation.

Soriano (457) described 32 cases of periostitis deformans, nearly all occurring in Barcelona, the cause of which was a high content of sodium fluoride in table wine added to halt fermentation and aid preservation.

Though the mechanism whereby heavy consumption of alcoholic beverages may be effective is not known, a significant positive association, independent of smoking habits, seems to exist between alcoholism and cancer of the mouth, pharynx, and particularly of the esophagus (223, 226, 227. 486, 538). Ledermann (253) states that a heavy chronic alcoholism is found in 80 to 90% of cases of esophageal cancer in France (see also ref. 228). At the turn of the century 80% of 134 cases with cancer of the esophagus and the cardia in a French sample were associated with "Absinthism" (247). Wynder and Bross (538) think it probable that alcohol merely promotes the effect of concomitant heavy smoking. Cancer of the esophagus seems to be exceptionally frequent with a patchy distribution in certain regions in South Africa, especially Zambia and Malawi. McGlashan et al. (304–308) found a statistically demonstrable degree of spatial coextensiveness with the consumption of an indigenous type of spirit (kachasu) distilled from a fermented beer of sugar and maize husks; in eight samples of Zambian kachasu, dimethylnitrosamine or a similar substance was found in concentrations of 1 to 3 ppm, an amount that would be carcinogenic in laboratory animals. British gin and whiskey contained no detectable nitrosaminelike substances. Whether kachasu had a carcinogenic effect in rats was not yet investigated, nor has its influence in human esophageal cancer been established. Gibel (147) demonstrated the syncarcinogenic effect of alcohol and dimethylnitrosamine in rats with production of multiple papillomata and epidermoid carcinoma of the esophagus, but no syncarcinogenesis was seen with respect to hepatic carcinoma (431). No evidence of illegal alcohol production but possible connections with particular ecological conditions was found in some Caspian littoral areas of Iran with an exceptional high incidence of esophageal cancer (237). Milham (339) speculated that carcinogenic substances in wines and spirits might have been dissolved from wooden containers during the process of production and aging. Presence of aflatoxin in 33 Baden (Southwest Germany) wines was investigated by Schuller et al. (439); in only two of them traces (less than 1 μg/liter) could be found by thin layer chromatography. No biological tests were made. Amounts of carcinogenic polycyclic aromatic hydrocarbons found in several brands of bourbon, Scotch, and Japanese whiskey were extremely small when compared to other known sources such as cigarettes or broiled meats (322).

Headache and flushing sometimes experienced after ingestion of certain alcoholic beverages may partly be due to their histamine content, if absorption of alcoholic histamine solutions from the intestine could be conceivable. Granerus et al. (164) found that red wines and sherries contained large amounts (208 to 1560 μg/100 ml) of free histamine base; Danish and Swedish beers, Moselle wines, white bordeaux, and port contain from 2.6 to 19 μg/100 ml. Marquardt and Werringloer (317) analyzed more than 200 European, North African, and Chilean wines and found a histamine content of up to 22 μg/ml. Distilled spirits, of course, contain no histamine. Sulfur dioxide is the only preservative permitted in wine up to 450 ppm in Great Britain (197). The Italian regulation allows a maximum of 200 mg/liter, in France the tolerated upper limit is 350 mg/liter (162). Gounelle et al. (162) found the following total SO_2 content in French wines: 48 white wines = 128 to 589 mg/liter; 15 rosé wines = 7 to 120 mg/liter; 25 red wines = 20 to 220 mg/liter; they pleaded for an alignment to Italian regulation. Steinhoff and Marquardt (462) found 25 to 200 mg of $K_2S_2O_5$ per liter in German wines; in a prolonged feeding experiment, no differential effect of toxicity was seen with the combination of $K_2S_2O_5$ and alcohol in rats as compared to the single components.

The production, import, and sale of one type of alcoholic beverage, Absinthe and kindred spirits, has been prohibited by law in Germany since 1923 because of its content of aromatic volatile oil (wormwood oil) derived from *Artemisia absinthium* (wormwood) and related plants of the genus *Artemisia* (191). The poisonous constituent of extract of wormwood is thujone (thanaceton), a ketone. Habitual consumption of Absinthe leads to particularly severe central nervous disturbances, especially epileptiform convulsions, with a high mortality. Bitters and vermouth wines contain essentially only the bitter principle and merely traces of the volatile oil of vermouth (191); an analysis of Swedish vermouth showed that the content of thujone did not exceed 1 mg/liter; according to the regulations of the U.S. Food and Drug Administration the upper limit for thujone in victuals and beverages is 10 ppm (97). Consumption of cheap vermouth wines, however, was associated with particularly severe and prolonged delirium tremens (97, 169, 535). Symptoms similar to delirium tremens were seen in the absence of alcohol abuse in a patient who for four weeks drank large quantities of strong vermouth tea daily during the initial phase of infectious hepatitis (171). In the manufacture of gin essential oil of juniper (*Juniperus communis*) is used. A related species, *Juniperus sabina*, contains sabinene and sabinol, which have a close structural relationship to thujan, thujol, and thujone, and a similar toxicity. In Spain batches of juniper berries contaminated with sabina berries are therefore subject to confiscation (76).

8. CONCLUSION

Considering the range of factors involved in the development of alcohol-induced organic complications, volume and pattern of alcohol abuse are most certainly the two decisive factors. Experimental work and retrospective as well as the few prospective studies have made it clear that organic damage can be expected to ensue from alcohol consumption if ingestion of sufficiently large quantities is maintained for sufficiently long periods of time, the latter being dependent on drinking pattern. The elucidation of the mechanisms involved is rendered difficult by the pathophysiologically ambivalent nature of ethanol.

Up to a certain influx, ethanol can be fully dealt with by metabolic pathways. Beyond this borderline, the pharmacological effects of ethanol become manifest and in turn may temporarily inhibit further ingestion until tissue levels have returned to values compatible with normal functioning. The critical quantities are mainly determined by the individually varying saturation point of the mechanisms of alcohol elimination, which is predominantly a metabolic problem.

Other factors that have been made responsible for the development of organic damage, such as genetic predisposition, nutritional imbalance, or influence of congeneric substances, have been shown to either determine or modify, that is, lower the individual capacity of ethanol degradation. Nutritional deficiencies can greatly enhance the deleterious effect of alcohol but their absence does not prevent alcohol-induced organic injuries. It can therefore be concluded that factors other than the intensity of alcohol misuse play essentially a secondary, auxiliary role.

REFERENCES

1. Abbott, R. R., J. L. Conboy, and A. C. Rekate, Liver function in alcoholism, *J. Mich. med. Soc.,* **62,** 990 (1963).
1a. Abshagen, U. and N. Rietbrock, Elimination von 2-Propanol und ihre Beeinflussung durch aliphatische Alkohole, *Arch. Pharmacol. (Berlin),* **264,** 212 (1969).
2. Aebi, H. and J. P. von Wartburg, Vergleichend-biologische Aspekte der

experimentellen Erforschung chronischer Alkoholwirkungen, *Bull. Schweiz. Akad. Med. Wiss.,* **16,** 25 (1960).
3. Ahlfors, U. G. and Saukkonen, M., Alkoholpsykoser is stad och på landsbygd; en finländsk fältundersöknig sommaren 1964, *Nord. psykiat. Tidsskr.,* **19,** 235 (1965).
4. Alcohol and Liver Disease. Summary of a Conference on Cirrhosis of the Liver and Alcoholism, N. Y. Acad. Med., *Gastroenterology,* **39,** 643 (1960).
5. Alcohol and the Blood, *Lancet,* **1969/II,** 675.
6. Alcohol Taken in Moderation, *JAMA,* **134,** 985 (1947).
7. Alcoholism and Cirrhosis of the Liver, *United Bureau of Census, Mortality Statistics,* **1923,** p. 53.
8. Alcoholism and Iron Metabolism, *Br. Med. J.,* **1965/I,** 1331.
9. Is Alcohol Hepatotoxic? Editorial, *N. Engl. J. Med.,* **278,** 905 (1968).
10. Alexander, C. S., Idiopathic heart disease, I. Analysis of 100 cases with special reference to chronic alcoholism, *Am. J. Med.,* **41,** 213 (1966).
11. Alexander, J. F., M. W. Lischner, J. T. Galambos, Alcoholic hepatitis: Factors influencing survival, *Gastroenterology,* **56,** 1210 (1969).
12. Alling, C., S. J. Dencker, L. Svennerholm, and J. Tichy, Serum fatty acid pattern in chronic alcoholics after acute abuse, *Acta Med. Scand.,* **185,** 99 (1969).
13. Amelung, D., Die alkoholische Kardiomyopathie, *Dtsch. Med. Wochenschr.,* **95,** 759 (1970).
14. Amerine, M. A., *Food Res.,* **8,** 176 (1958).
15. Amerine, M. A., The search for good wine, *Science,* **157,** 1621 (1966).
16. Armas-Cruz, R., R. Yazici, O. Lopez, E. Montero, J. Cabello, and G. Lobo, Portal cirrhosis: An analysis of 208 cases with correlation of clinical, laboratory and autopsy findings, *Gastroenterology,* **17,** 327 (1951).
17. Aufrecht, Die alkoholische Myocarditis mit nachfolgender Lebererkrankung und zeitweiliger Albuminurie, *Dtsch. Arch. Klin. Med.,* **54,** 615 (1895).
18. Bättig, K., Ausmass und Ursachen des Alkoholismus, *Z. Präventivmed.,* **9,** 133 (1964).
19. Bättig, K., Alkoholismus: Epidemiologische Zusammenhänge und Folgen, *Naturwiss. Rundsch.,* **20,** 200 (1967).
20. Bättig, K., Zum Problem des Alkoholismus in der Schweiz, *Volk und Alkohol,* issue No. 18, Blaukreuz Verlag, Bern, 1967.
21. Baggenstoss, A. H. and M. H. Stauffer, Posthepatic and alcoholic cirrhosis: Clinicopathologic study of 43 cases of each, *Gastroenterology,* **22,** 157 (1952).
22. Baggenstoss, A. H., Discussion to Popper et al., *Gastroenterology,* **39,** 669 (1960).
23. Bahr, H. M., Lifetime affiliation patterns of early- and late-onset heavy drinkers on skid row, *Q. J. Stud. Alcohol,* **30,** 645 (1969).

24. Bailly-Salin, P., Clinical forms of alcoholism prevalent among wine drinkers, in *Alcohol and Alcoholism*, R. E. Popham (Ed.), University of Toronto Press, Toronto and Buffalo, 1970, p. 117.
25. Baker, R. J., Effects of alcohol on the pancreas, *JAMA*, **206**, 376 (1968).
26. Ball, G. V. and L. B. Sorensen, Pathogenesis of hyperuricemia in saturnine gout, *N. Engl. J. Med.*, **280**, 1199 (1968).
27. Ball, G. V. and J. A. Morgan, Chronic lead ingestion and gout, *South. Med. J.*, **61**, 21 (1968).
28. Bang, N. U., K. Iversen, T. Jagt, and S. Madsen, Serum glutamic oxalacetic transaminase activity in acute and chronic alcoholism, *JAMA*, **168**, 156 (1958).
29. Barboriak, J. J., and R. C. Meade, Enhancement of alimentary lipemia by preprandial alcohol, *Am. J. Med. Sci.*, **255**, 245 (1968).
30. Barborik, M. and J. Dusek, Case report. Cardiomyopathy accompanying industrial cobalt exposure, *Br. Heart J.*, **34**, 113 (1972).
31. Barnes, E. W., N. J. Cooke, A. J. King, and R. Passmore, Observations on the metabolism of alcohol in man, *Br. J. Nutr.*, **19**, 485 (1965).
32. Bastide, H., Une Enquête sur l'opinion publique à l'égard de l'alcoolisme, *Population*, **9**, 13 (1954).
33. Baumberger, N., Alkoholische Leberschäden unter besonderer Berüksichtigung des Zieve-Syndroms, *Inaugural-Dissertation*, Zürich, Switzerland, 1967.
34. Bebb, H. T., H. B. Houser, J. C. Witschi, A. S. Littell, and R. K. Fuller, Calorie and nutrient contribution of alcoholic beverages to the usual diets of 155 adults, *Am. J. Clin. Nutr.*, **24**, 1042 (1971).
35. Bell, J. L., S. Shaldon, and D. N. Baron, Serum isocitric dehydrogenase in liver disease and some other conditions, *Clin. Sci.*, **23**, 57 (1962).
36. Bernstein, A. and H. A. Staub, Zur funktionellen Leberprüfung mit Alkohol, *Helv. Med. Acta*, **15**, 494 (1948).
37. Bersohn, I. and M. C. Frame, Alcoholism and liver-function tests, *S. Afr. Med. J.*, **35**, 664 (1961).
38. Besorgniserregende Zunahme des Frauenalkoholismus, *Ther. Gegenw.*, **109**, 130 (1970).
39. Bischof, H. L., Zur Pathogenese des Alkoholdelirs; dargestellt aufgrund von Beobachtungen an 209 Fällen, *Nervenarzt*, **40**, 318 (1969).
40. Blum, K., R. S. Ryback, and I. Geller, Effects of vodka and bourbon on sleeping time in mice, *Q. J. Stud. Alcohol*, Suppl. No. 5, 62 (1970).
41. Bode, Ch., H. Goebell, and R. Bastian, Zur Störung der exkretorischen Pankreasfunktion bei chronischen Alkoholikern mit und ohne Leberzirrhose, in *Modern Gastroenterology*, O. Gregor and O. Riedel (Eds.), F. K. Schattauer, Stuttgart-New York, 1969, p. 1291.

42. Bode, Ch., H. Goebell, and M. Stähler, Änderungen der Alkoholdehydrogenase-Aktivität in der Rattenleber durch Eiweissmangel und Äthanol, *Z. Gesamte Exp. Med.*, **152**, 111 (1970).
43. Bode, Ch., H. Kono, H. Goebell, Christiane Bode, and G. A. Martini, Zur Pathogenese der Fetteinlagerung in der Leber dürch Alkohol, III. Effekt von Äthanol auf Metabolite und Coenzyme des energieliefernden Stoffwechsels in der Leber und im Blut bei Standardkost und proteinarmer Ernährung, *Klin. Wschr.*, **48**, 1180 (1970).
44. Bode, Ch., B. Buchwald, and H. Goebell, Hemmung des Äthanolabbaues durch Proteinmangel beim Menschen, *Dtsch. Med. Wochenschr.*, **96**, 1576 (1971).
45. Boivin, P., P. Oudea, and R. Faubert, Acute alcoholic liver damage, in *Alcohol and Alcoholism*, R. E. Popham (Ed.), University of Toronto Press, Toronto and Buffalo, 1970, p. 252.
46. Bollinger, Über die Häufigkeit und Ursachen der idiopathischen Herzhypertrophie in München, *Dtsch. Med. Wochenschr.*, **10**, 180 (1884).
47. Bonnischsen, R., and L. Sjöberg, Alcohol absorption, *Publ. No. 12, Institutet för Maltdrycksforskning* (Stockholm), p. 3 (1964).
48. Bonnichsen, R., R. Dimberg, and L. Sjöberg, Oxidation of alcohol, *Publ. No. 12, Institutet för Maltdrycksforskning* (Stockholm), p. 37 (1964).
49. Bonnichsen, R., R. Dimberg, A. Maehly, and S. Åquist, Die Alkoholverbrennung bei Alkoholikern und bei übrigen Versuchsperonen, *Blutalkohol*, **5**, 301 (1968).
50. Bonnichen, R., Discussion of G. A. Martini and Ch. Bode, The epidemiology of cirrhosis of the liver, in *Alcoholic Cirrhosis and other Toxic Hepatopathias*, A. Engel and T. Larsson (Eds.), Nordisk Bokhandelns Förlag, Stockholm, 1970, p. 353.
51. Bothwell, T. H. and C. Isaacson, Siderosis in the Bantu, *Br. Med. J.*, **1962/I**, 522.
52. Bothwell, T. H., Iron overload in the Bantu, in *Iron Metabolism*, F. Gross, S. R. Naegeli, and H. D. Philps (Eds.), Springerverlag, Berlin-Göttingen-Heidelberg, 1964, p. 362.
53. Bothwell, T. H., H. Seftel, P. Jacobs, J. D. Torrance, and N. Baumslag, Iron overload in Bantu subjects; Studies on the availability of iron in Bantu beer, *Am. J. Clin. Nutr.*, **14**, 47 (1964).
54. Boudin, G., A. Lauras, M. Laniece, and H. Krebs, Le syndrome biologique du delirium tremens, *Presse méd.*, **68**, 1469 (1960).
55. Brésard, M., I. Consommation d'alcool et mortalité par Cirrhose du foie à Saint-Etienne et à Marseille. II. Consommation du Tabac et alcool, *Bull. Inst. Nat. Hyg.*, **14**, 367 (1959).
56. Brigden, W., Uncommon myocardial disease. The non-coronary cardiomyopathies, *Lancet*, **173**, 1179, 1243 (1957).

57. Brinkmann, B., W. Naeve, R. Eichen, and M. Rehner, Beziehungen zwischen Pylorustonus und Resorptionsgeschwindigkeit von getrunkenem Äthylalkohol, *Blutalkohol,* **7,** 358 (1970).
58. Brohult, J. and H. Reichard, Liver damage after a dose of alcohol, *Lancet,* **1965/II,** 78.
59. Broicher, H., A. Heymer, W. K. Lelbach, and O. Hermanns, Die Leber bei mittelschwerem chronischem Alkoholismus unter besonderer Berücksichtigung der Leberverfettung, in *2. Weltkongress für Gastroenterologie, München, 1962,* Vol. III, L. Demling, M. Demole, and H. Popper (Eds.), S. Karger, Basel-New York, 1963, p. 338.
60. Broicher, H., A. Heymer, O. Hermanns, and W. K. Lelbach, Chronischer Alkoholismus und Leber. Bioptische und klinische Befunde bei der alkolischen Fettleber, *Acta hepatosplenol.,* **9,** 37 (1962).
61. Buchanan, W. M., Siderosis in the Rhodesian Africans, *S. Afr. J. Med.,* **12,** 199 (1966).
62. Buchanan, W. M., Experimental production of "Bantu" siderosis using home-brewed beer, *S. Afr. J. Med. Sci.,* **35,** 15 (1970).
63. Buck, R. E., Observations on alcoholic fatty liver: The use of interval needle biopsy and liver function tests, *J. Lab. Clin. Med.,* **33,** 555 (1948).
64. Bührer, O. A., Über 200 Fälle von Delirium tremens, *Münch. Med. Wochenschr.,* **106,** 1016 (1964).
65. Büttner, H., Aldehyd- und Alkoholdehydrogenase-Aktivität in Leber und Nieren der Ratte, *Biochem. Z.,* **341,** 300 (1965).
66. Bulloch, R. T., M. L. Murphy, and M. B. Pearce, Fine structural lesions in the myocardium of a beer drinker with reversible heart failure, *Am. Heart J.,* **80,** 629 (1970).
67. Butzengeiger, K. H., Über periphere Zirkulationsstörungen bei chronischer Arsenvergiftung, *Klin. Wochenschr.,* **19,** 523 (1940).
68. Butzengeiger, K. H., Über die chronische Arsenvergiftung, I. EKG-Veränderungen und andere Erscheinungen am Herzen und Gefäss-System, II. Schleimhautsymptome und Pathogenese. *Dtsch. Arch. Klin. Med.,* **194,** 1 (1948).
69. Butzengeiger, K. H., Die chronische Arsenvergiftung der Winzer, *Ärztl. Wochenschr.,* **4,** 365 (1949).
70. Cachera, R., M. Lamotte, and S. Lamotte-Barillon, Etude clinique, biologique et histologique des stéatoses du foie chez les alcooliques, *Sem. Hôp. (Paris),* **26,** 3497 (1950).
71. Cardinal, J., M. Turgeon, F. Turcotte, J. Coté, J. Bernier, and A. Viallet, L'hépatite alcoolique. Etude clinique, biologique et histologique portant sur 105 observations, *Un. Méd. Can.,* **98,** 400 (1969).
72. Carey, M. A., J. D. Jones, and C. F. Gastineau, Effect of moderate alcohol intake on blood chemistry values, *JAMA,* **216,** 1766 (1971).

73. Caroli, J. and G. Péquignot, Enguête sur les circonstances diététiques de la cirrhose alcoolique en France, *Proc. World Congr. Gastroenterol.*, **1**, 661 (1958).
74. Caroli, J. and J. André, Surcharge ferrique dans les cirrhoses (á l'exclusion de l'hémochromatose idiopathique), in *Iron Metabolism*, F. Gross, S. R. Naegeli, and H. D. Philps (Eds.), Springerverlag, Berlin-Göttingen-Heidelberg, 1964, p. 326.
75. Carroll, R. B., Analysis of alcoholic beverages by gas-liquid chromatography, *Q. J. Stud. Alcohol*, Suppl. No. 5, 6 (1970).
76. Casares, R., Juniperus sabina, *Food, Cosmetics, Toxicol.*, **2**, 680 (1964).
77. Chalmers, T. C., T. L. Murphy, and E. B. Taft, The incidence, character and course of liver disease in chronic alcoholics as determined by needle biopsy, *J. Clin. Invest.*, **27**, 528 (1948).
78. Chapman, L. F., Experimental induction of hangover, *Q. J. Stud. Alcohol*, Suppl. No. 5, 67 (1970).
79. Charlton, R. W., P. Jacobs, H. Seftel, and T. H. Bothwell, Effect of alcohol on iron absorption, *Br. Med. J.*, **1964/II**, 1427.
80. Cherrick, G. R., M. M. Howard, W. Tenhove, and C. M. Leevy, The varying susceptibility of man to alcohol hepatotoxicity, *J. Clin. Invest.*, **43**, 1253 (1964).
81. Chey, W. Y., S. Kosay, H. Siplet, and S. H. Lorber, Observations on hepatic histology and function in alcoholic dogs, *Am. J. Digest. Dis.*, **16**, 825 (1971).
82. Childs, A. W., R. M. Kivel, and A. Lieberman, Effects of ethyl alcohol on hepatic circulation, sulfobromophtalein clearance, and hepatic glutamic oxalacetic transaminase production in man, *Gastroenterology*, **45**, 176 (1963).
83. Christmann, W., "Alkohol und Herz." Allgemeine Betrachtungen mit 2 kasuistischen Beiträgen, *Münch. Med. Wochenschr.*, **114**, 85 (1972).
84. Christoffersen, P., K. Iversen, K. Nielsen, and H. Poulsen, Alcoholic hepatitis. A comparative study of two groups of patients with Mallory bodies with and without liver cell necrosis and neutrophilic infiltration in liver biopsies, *Scand. J. Gastroenterol.*, **5**, 633 (1970).
85. Chvostek, F., Zur Pathogenese der Lebercirrhose, *Wien. klin. Wochenschr.*, **35**, 381, 408 (1922).
86. Clark, C. G. and J. R. Senior, Rates of ethanol metabolism in alcoholic-nutritional liver disease, *Gastroenterology*, **54**, 152 (1968).
87. Cooke, A. R. and A. Birchall, Absorption of ethanol from the stomach, *Gastroenterology*, **57**, 269 (1969).
88. Cruz-Coke, R., Asociación de defectos de visión de colores y cirrhosis hepática, *Rev. Med. Chile*, **93**, 519 (1965).
89. Cruz-Coke, R., Color blindness and cirrhosis of the liver, *Lancet*, **1965/I**, 1131.

90. Cruz-Coke, R. and A. Varela, Color blindness and alcohol addiction, *Lancet*, **1965/II**, 1348.
91. Cruz-Coke, R. and A. Varela, Inheritance of alcoholism, *Lancet*, **1966/II**, 1282.
92. Curlee, J., Alcoholism and the "empty nest," *Bull. Menninger Clin.*, **33**, 165 (1969).
93. Curlee, J., A comparison of male and female patients at an alcoholism treatment center, *J. Psychol.*, **74**, 239 (1970).
94. Cutshall, B. J., The Sounders-Sutton Syndrome: an Analysis of Delirium tremens. *Q. J. Stud. Alcohol* **26**, 423 (1965).
94a Dagradi, A. E., Esophageal varices grow smaller when alcoholics stop drinking, *JAMA*, **219**, 573 (1972).
95. Dajani, R. M., L. Chandour-Mnaymneh and F. Saadeh, Effect of Congeners in Araq on the Incidence of Alcoholic Fatty Liver in the Rat, *Q. J. Stud. Alcohol*, Suppl N°5, 34 (1970).
96. Damon, A., Constitution and alcohol consumption: Physique, *J. Chronic Dis.*, **16**, 1237 (1963).
97. Daugård, J., Kronisk vermouth-förgiftning med neurologiska och psykiska symtom, *Nord. Med.*, **75**, 710 (1966).
98. Davies, J. N. P. and H. C. Trowell, Hemosiderosis in the African, *Br. Med. J.*, **1951/I**, 1514.
99. Davis, W. D., Jr., and W. S. Culpepper, Cirrhosis of the liver associated with alcoholism: Report of acute exacerbation with serial liver biopsies, *Ann. Intern. Med.*, **29**, 942 (1948).
100. Denk, H., I. Leodolter, H. Schnack, and H. Thaler, Klinisch-bioptische Untersuchungen über den Verlauf der Fettleberhepatitis, *Wien. Klin. Wochenschr.*, **82**, 98 (1970).
101. Denk, R., H. Holzmann, H. J. Lange, and D. Greve, Über Arsenspätschäden bei obduzierten Moselwinzern, *Med. Welt*, **20**, 557 (1969).
102. Di Luzio, N. R., Comparative study of the effect of alcoholic beverages on the development of the acute ethanol-induced fatty liver, *Q. J. Stud. Alcohol*, **23**, 557 (1962).
103. Di Luzio, N. R., Effect of acute and chronic administration of ethanol and alcoholic beverages on tissue triglycerides, *Q. J. Stud. Alcohol,*, Suppl. No.5, 26 (1970).
104. Dimberg, R., R. Hed, G. Kallner, and A. Nygren, Liver-muscle enzyme activities in the serum of alcoholics on a diet poor in carbohydrates, *Acta Med. Scand.*, **181**, 227 (1967).
105. Dinoso, V. P., W. Y. Chey, and S. H. Lorber, Pancreatic exocrine function in chronic alcoholics, *Gastroenterology*, **61**, 559 (1971).
106. Docter, R. F., Drinking practices of skid row alcoholics, *Q. J. Stud. Alcohol*, **28**, 700 (1967).

107. *Documenta Geigy. Wissenschaftliche Tabellen,* 6th ed. J. R. Geigy AG. (Ed.), Basel, Switzerland, 1960, p. 284.
108. Dölle, W., Mass, Mässingkeit, Verbot beim Alkohol, in *Kongressbericht,* 74th Meeting of the Nordwestdeutsche Gesellschaft für Innere Medizin, A. Dönhardt (ed.), Hansisches Verlagskontor, Lùbeck, 1970, p. 29.
109. Dörle, M. and K. Ziegler, Schädigungen bei Rebschädlingsbekämpfung, *Z. Klin. Med.,* **112,** 237 (1930).
110. Douglas, R. M., J. D. Fewings, J. R. Casley-Smith, and R. F. West, Recurrent rhabdomyolysis precipitated by alcohol; A case report with physiological and electron microscopic studies of skeletal muscle, *Med. Mschr. Stuttgart,* **20,** 251 (1966); also in *Australas. Ann. Med.,* **15,** 251 (1966).
111. Dreiling, D. A., A. Richman, and N. F. Fradkin, The role of alcohol in the etiology of pancreatitis: A study of the effect of intravenous ethyl alcohol on the external secretion of the pancreas, *Gastroenterology,* **20,** 636 (1952).
112. Duka, N., Das Kriterium des mässigen Trinkens im 16. und 17. Jahrhundert, *Dtsch. Ärzteblatt,* **66,** 86 (1969).
113. Edmondson, H. A., R. L. Peters, H. H. Frankel, and S. Borowski, The early stage of liver injury in the alcoholic, *Medicine,* **46,** 119 (1967).
114. Edwards, J. A. and D. A. P. Evans, Ethanol metabolism in subjects possessing typical and atypical liver alcohol dehydrogenase, *Clin. Pharmacol. Ther.,* **8,** 824 (1967).
115. Egoz, N., M. A. Kendrick, and J. W. Mosley, Cirrhosis mortality in relation to alcohol consumption, *Gastroenterology,* **58,** 281 (1970).
116. Elbel, H. and F. Schleyer, *Blutalkohol,* Georg Thieme Verlag, Stuttgart, 1956.
117. Eppinger, H., *Die Leberkrankheiten,* Springer Verlag, Wien, 1937.
118. Erenoglu, E. J., G. Edreira, and A. J. Patek, Observations on patients with Laennec's cirrhosis receiving alcohol while on controlled diets, *Ann. Intern. Med.,* **60,** 814 (1964).
119. Etienne-Martin, P. and C. Klepping, *Le Foie Alcoolique de l'Hépatite à la Cirrhose Alcoolique,* Masson et Cie., Paris, 1960.
120. Feinman, L. and C. S. Lieber, Hepatic collagen metabolism: Effect of alcohol consumption in rats and baboons, *Science,* **176,** 795 (1972).
121. Fenna, D., L. Mix, O. Schaefer, and J. A. L. Gilbert, Ethanol metabolism in various racial groups, *Can. Med. Assoc. J.,* **105,** 472 (1971).
122. Feuerlein, W., Klinisch-statische Untersuchungen über die Entstehungsbedingungen und die Prognose des Alkoholdelirs, *Nervenarzt,* **38,** 206 (1967).
123. Feuerlein, W., Neuere Ergebnisse der Alkoholdelir-Forschung, *Nervenarzt,* **38,** 492 (1967).
124. Feuerlein, W., Zur Frage des Alkohol-Entzugssyndroms, *Nervenarzt,* **43,** 247 (1972).

125. Field, J. B., H. E. Williams, and G. E. Mortimore, Studies on the mechanism of ethanol-induced hypoglycemia, *J. Clin. Invest.*, **42**, 497 (1963).
126. Figueroa, R. B. and A. P. Klotz, The effect of whiskey and low-protein diets on hepatic enzymes in rats, *Am. J. Digest. Dis.*, **9**, 121 (1964).
127. Filip, J., and J. Hoenigová, Rychlost spalováni etanolu po intravenózni aplikaci u cirhotikú, *Čas. Lék.*, **104**, 1178 (1965).
128. Filippini, L. and A. Löffler, Exokrine Pankreasfunktion bei chronischem Alkoholüberkonsum, *Dtsch. Med. Wochenschr.*, **97**, 596 (1972).
129. Foerst, W. (Ed.), *Ullmann's Enzyklopädie der technischen Chemie*, 3rd ed., Urban & Schwarzenberg, München-Berlin, 1965.
130. Forney, R. B. and F. W. Hughes, Alcohol accumulation in humans after prolonged drinking, *Clin. Pharmacol. Ther. (St. Louis)*, **4**, 619 (1963).
131. Forsander, O. A., The effect of ethanol on liver metabolism, in *Alcoholic Cirrhosis and Other Toxic Hepatopathias*, A. Engel and T. Larsson (Eds.), Nordiska Bokhandelns Förlag, Stockholm, 1970, p. 77.
132. Frank, H., W. Heil, and I. Leodolter, Leber und Bierkonsum. Vergleichende Untersuchungen an 450 Arbeitern, *Münch. Med. Wochenschr.*, **109**, 892 (1967).
133. Fregly, A. R., M. Bergstedt, and A. Graybiel, Relationships between blood alcohol, positional alcohol nystagmus, and postural equilibrium, *Q. J. Stud. Alcohol*, **28**, 11 (1967).
134. Freinkel, N. and R. A. Arky, Effects of alcohol on carbohydrate metabolism in man, *Psychosom. Med.*, **28**, 551 (1966).
135. Fréour, P., M. Serise, P. Coudray, and J. Benier, Que pensent de l'alcoolisme les habitants des grands ensembles urbains? Résultats d'une enquête d'opinion, *Rev. Alcsme*, **15**, 97 (1969).
136. Fridman, V., Udruženo dejstvo alkohola i drugih alkoholnih supstancija: olova, žive i dr, *Alkoholizam (Beograd)*, **8**, 51 (1968).
137. Friedman, M., R. H. Rosenman, and S. O. Byers, Effect of moderate ingestion of alcohol upon serum triglyceride response of nomo- and hyperlipemic subjects, *Proc. Soc. Exp. Biol. Med.*, **120**, 696 (1965).
138. Fritschka, J. and M. Bergener, Behandlung des Delirium tremens mit Chlormethiazol, *Dtsch. med. Wochenschr.*, **89**, 1632 (1964).
139. Frohn, W., Über gewerbliche Arsenvergiftungen bei Winzern, *Münch. med. Wochenschr.*, **85**, 1630 (1938).
140. Gaillard, D. and R. Derache, Vitesse de la métabolisation de différents alcools chez le rat, *C. R. Soc. Biol. (Paris)*, **158**, 1605 (1964).
141. Gaillard, D., G. de Saint-Blanquat, and R. Derache, Effets hépatotoxiques des alcools des boissons au cours de l'administration d'un régime gras chez le rat, *Pathol. Biol.*, **17**, 385 (1969).
142. Galambos, J. T., M. Asade, and J. Z. Shanks, The effect of intravenous

ethanol on serum enzymes in patients with normal or diseased liver, *Gastroenterology*, **44**, 267 (1963).

143. Galambos, J. T., Chronic alcoholic hepatitis, *Gastroenterology*, **56**, 412 (1969).
144. Galambos, J. T., Collagen metabolism in chronic alcoholic liver injury, in *Alcohol and the Liver*, W. Gerok, K. Sickinger, and H. H. Hennekeuser (Eds.), F. K. Schattauer, Stuttgart-New York, 1971, p. 321.
145. Geréby, G., Delirium tremens; pathogeneticai és tünettani elemzés 223 delirium alapján, in *Tanulmányok az alkoholizmus pszichiátriai következményeiről*, I. Tariska and G. Geréby (Eds.), Alkoholizmus Elleni Országos Bizottság; Budapest, 1969, p. 147.
146. Gibel, W., G. P. Wildner, and Kh. Lohs, Untersuchungen zur Frage einer kanzerogenen und hepatotoxischen Wirkung von Fuselöl, *Arch. Geschwulstforsch.*, **32**, 115 (1968).
147. Gibel, W., Experimentelle Untersuchungen zur Synkarzinogenese beim Ösophaguskarzinom, *Arch. Geschwulstforsch.*, **30**, 181 (1967).
148. Gibel, W., Kh. Lohs, G. P. Wildner, S. Wittbrodt, E. Geissler, and H. Hilscher, Untersuchungen zur Frage einer möglichen mutagenen Wirkung von Fuselöl, *Arch. Geschwulstforsch.*, **33**, 49 (1969).
149. Gibel, W., Kh. Lohs, K. Schremmer, and G. P. Wildner, Experimentelle Untersuchungen über toxische Wirkungen von Alkoholbeistoffen, *Dtsch. Gesundheitsw.*, **25**, 573 (1970).
150. Gibel, W., G. P. Wildner, and Kh. Lohs, Experimentelle Untersuchungen über die hepatotoxische Wirkung von höheren Alkoholen (Fuselöl), *Gastroenterol.*, **7**, 108 (1969).
151. Gigglberger, H., Zur Ätiologie der Laennec'schen Cirrhose, *Münch. Med. Wochenschr.*, **101**, 858 (1959).
152. Gigglberger, H., Zur Ätiologie der Leberzirrhose. Klinisch-statistische Untersuchungen an 400 Kranken, *Acta hepatosplenol.*, **15**, 415 (1968).
153. Glatt, M. M., Gruppenbehandlung von Alkoholikern in ("offenen") englischen Spitälern, in *Arbeitstagung über Alkoholismus*, K. Kryspin-Exner (Ed.), Wien, 1962.
154. Goebell, H., Ch. Bode, R. Bastian, and G. Strohmeyer, Klinisch asymptomatische Funktionsstörungen des exokrinen Pankreas bei chronischen Alkoholikern, *Dtsch. Med. Wochenschr.*, **95**, 808 (1970)
155. Goldberg, D. M. and C. Watts, Serum enzyme changes as evidence of liver reaction to oral alcohol, *Gastroenterology*, **49**, 256 (1965).
156. Goldberg, L., Quantitative studies on alcohol tolerance in man, *Acta Physiol. Scand.*, **5**, Suppl. XVI, 128 (1943).
157. Goldberg, L., Research into the etiology, pathogenesis and therapy of chronic alcoholism, in *Arbeitstagung über Alkoholismus*, K. Kryspin-Exner (Ed.), Wien, 1962, p. XIII.

158. Goldberg, L., Physiological Research on Alcohol, 1960-1970, in *Proceedings of the 28th International Congress on Alcohol and Alcoholism*, Vol. 2, M. Keller and T. G. Coffey (Eds.), Hillhouse Press, Highland Park, N.J., 1969, p. 37.
159. Goldberg, M. and Ch. M. Thompson, Acute fatty metamorphosis of the liver, *Ann. Intern. Med.*, **55**, 416 (1961).
160. Gonçalves, C. S., F. E. L. Pereira, V. Buaiz, W. M. Zanotti, B. Zanandréa, and U. M. Santos, Biópsia hepática percutánea em alcoólatras crônicos internados em hospital psiquiátrico, *Arch. Gastroenterol. (Sao Paolo)*, **9**, 5 (1972).
161. Gould, L., M. Zahir, A. Demartino, and R. F. Comprecht, Cardiac effects of a cocktail, *JAMA*, **218**, 1799 (1971).
162. Gounelle, H., C. Boudene, A. Szakvary, and M. Fauchet, Contribution á l'étude des résidus d'anhydride sulfureux dans les denrées alimentaires: cas des boissons alcoolisées, *Bull. Inst. Nat. de la Santé*, **24**, 1431 (1969).
163. Grab, W., Pharmakologische Probleme bei Wein und Spirituosen, *Arzneim. Forsch.*, **11**, 73 (1961).
164. Granerus, G., S. E. Svensson, and H. Wetterquist, Histamine in alcoholic drinks, *Lancet*, **1969/I**, 1320.
165. Green J. R., Subclinical acute liver disease of the alcoholic, *Australas. Ann. Med.*, **24**, 111 (1965).
166. Greenberg, L. A., Alcoholintoxication, *JAMA*, **186**, 528 (1963).
167. Greenberg, L. A., The pharmacology of alcohol and its relationship to drinking and driving, *Q. J. Stud. Alcohol*, Suppl. No. 4, 252 (1968).
168. Greenberg, L. A., The appearance of some congeners of alcoholic beverages and their metabolites in blood, *Q. J. Stud. Alcohol*, Suppl. No. 5, 20 (1970).
169. Gros, H., Beitrag zur Alkoholverträglichkeit, *Dtsch. Med. Wochenschr.*, **78**, 1302 (1953).
170. Gros, H., Die Leber des Alkoholikers, *Physikal. Med. Rehabil.*, **7**, 264 (1966).
171. Grosser, L., Absinth-Delirium bei Hepatitis, *Med. Klinik*, **46**, 1364 (1951).
171a. Grünberger, J. and K. Kryspin-Exner, Die Restitution nach dem Alkoholdelir, *Wien. Klin. Wochenschr.*, **77**, 694 (1965).
172. Grünberger, J., K. Irsigler and K. Kryspin-Exner, Cronischer Alkoholismus: Beziehungen zurschen Hirnleistung und Leberschaden, *Wien. Z. Nervenheilk* **28**, 235 (1970).
173. György, P., Discussion of Klatskin, G., Experimental studies on the role of alcohol in the pathogenesis of cirrhosis, *Am. J. Clin. Nutr.*, **9**, 439 (1961).
174. Hällén, J. and H. Krook, Follow-up studies on an unselected ten-year material of 360 patients with liver cirrhosis in one community, *Acta Med. Scand.*, **173**, 479 (1963).
175. Hällén, J. and I. Linné, Cirrhosis of the liver in one community. A study of

768 cases of liver cirrhosis from a city with one hospital: Incidence, etiology and prognosis, in *Alcoholic Cirrhosis and Other Toxic Hepatopathias,* A. Engel and T. Larsson (Eds.), Nordiska Bokhandelns Förlag, Stockholm, 1970, p. 336.
176. Haggard, H. W., L. A. Greenberg, and L. H. Cohen, Quantitative differences in the effects of alcoholic beverages, *N. Engl. J. Med.,* **219,** 466 (1938).
177. Haggard, H. W., L. A. Greenberg, and L. H. Cohen, The influence of the congeners of distilled spirits upon the physiological action of alcohol, *Q. J. Stud. Alcohol,* **4,** 3 (1943).
178. Hall, J. L., A. Y. Olsen, and F. D. Davis, Portal cirrhosis. Clinical and pathologic review of 782 cases from 16, 600 necropsies, *Am. J. Pathol.,* **29,** 993 (1953).
179. Hall, J. L. and E. B. Smith, Cobalt heart disease, *Arch. Pathol.,* **86,** 403 (1968).
180. Hardewig, A., Kobalt als Ursache einer Herzerkrankung bei chronischen Biertrinkern, *Internist,* **10,** 29 (1969).
181. Hardison, W. G. and F. I. Lee, Prognosis in acute liver disease of the alcoholic patient, *N. Engl. J. Med.,* **275,** 61 (1966).
182. Harren, F. and H. Heinlein, Klinische und anatomische Untersuchungen zur Frage der arsenbedingten Leberschädigung der Winzer, *Dtsch. Arch. Klin, Med.,* **190,** 31 (1943).
183. Hartroft, W. S., Introductory remarks. Symposium on Alcohol, Metabolism and Liver Disease, Chicago, 1967. *Fed. Proc.,* **26,** 1432 (1967).
184. Hayman, M., The myth of social drinking, *Am. J. Psychiat.,* **124,** 585 (1967).
185. Hed, R., A. Nygren, and L. Sundblad, Muscle and liver serum enzyme activities in healthy volunteers given alcohol on a diet poor in carbohydrates, *Acta Med. Scand.,* **191,** 529 (1972).
186. Helbig, H., Das tödliche Alkoholdelir, *Nervenarzt,* **33,** 221 (1962).
187. Herfort, K., Contribution to the aetiology of chronic relapsing pancreatitis, in *Pancreatitis. Symposium Marseille 1963,* Facs.7, H. Sarles (Ed.), Bibliotheca Gastroenterologica, S. Karger, Basel-New York, 1965, p. 35.
188. Higginson, J., Th. Gerrisen, and A. R. P. Walker, Siderosis in the Bantu of Southern Africa, *Am. J. Pathol.,* **29,** 779 (1953).
189. Hines, J. D. and D. H. Cowan, Studies on the pathogenesis of alcohol induced sideroblastic bone-marrow abnormalities, *N. Engl. J. Med.,* **283,** 441 (1970).
190. Hines, J. D., Alcohol-induced vitamin B_6-responsive anemia. Letter to the Editor, *N. Engl. J. Med.,* **283,** 1173 (1970).
191. Holthöfer-Juckenack-Nüse, *Deutsches Lebensmittelrecht,* Vol. III, 4th ed., Carl Heymanns-Verlag, Berlin-Wien-München-Bonn, 1963.
192. Horn, J. L. and K. W. Wanberg, Symptom patterns related to excessive use of alcohol, *Q. J. Stud. Alcohol,* **30,** 35 (1969).

193. Hourihane, D. O'B. and D. G. Weir, Suppression of erythropoiesis by alcohol, *Br. Med. J.,* **1970/I,** 86.
194. Howard, J. M. and E. W. Ehrlich, The etiology of pancreatitis. A review of clinical experience, *Ann. Surg.,* **152,** 135 (1960).
195. Huhn, A., Folgekrankheiten des Alkoholismus, *Rheinisches Ärzteblatt,* **1969/11,** p. 358.
196. Hutterer, F., Collagen metabolism in chronic alcoholic liver injury, in *Alcohol and the liver,* W. Gerok, K. Sickinger, and H. H. Hennekeuser (Eds.), F. K. Schattauer, Stuttgart-New York, 1971, p. 315.
197. Impurities in wine. *Br. Med. J.,* **1971/I,** 533.
198. Insunza, I., H. Iturriaga, G. Ugarte, and H. Altschiller, Clinical and histological liver abnormalities in alcoholics, *Acta hepatosplenol.,* **18,** 460 (1971).
199. Irsigler, K., E. Keibl, K. Kryspin-Exner, and W. Mildschuh, Ernährungstherapie bei Patienten mit Fettleber, *Wien. klin. Wochenschr.,* **81,** 540 (1969).
200. Irsigler, K., E. Keibl, K. Kryspin-Exner, and W. Mildschuh, Rückbildungstendenzen der alkoholischen Leberschädigung unter Abstinenzbedingungen, *Acta hepatosplenol.,* **16,** 356 (1969).
201. Irsigler, K., K. Kryspin-Exner, and W. Mildschuh, Rückbildungstendenzen der alkoholischen Fettleber unter Diät; Änderung des Fettanteils der Kost, *Acta hepatosplenol.,* **17,** 103 (1970).
202. Irsigler, K., K. Kryspin-Exner, W. Mildschuh, H. Pointner, and P. Schmidt, Lebermorphologie und Leberfunktion im Delirium tremens, *Dtsch. Med. Wochenschr.,* **96,** 9 (1971).
203. Irsigler, K., K. Kryspin-Exner, and F. Wolzogen, Rückbildung der alkoholischen Leberschädigung durch Ernährungstherapie, *Leber-Magen-Darm,* **1,** 138 (1971).
204. Isbell, H., H. F. Fraser, A. Wikler, R. E. Belleville, and A. J. Eisenman, An experimental study of the etiology of "rum fits" and delirium tremens, *Q. J. Stud. Alcohol,* **16,** 1 (1955).
205. Isselbacher, K. J. and N. J. Greenberger, Metabolic effects of alcohol on the liver, *N. Engl. J. Med.,* **270,** 351, 402 (1964).
206. Jarosch, K., Die toxische Wirkung der Fuselöle, in *Arbeitstagung über Alkoholismus,* K. Kryspin-Exner (Ed.), Wien, 1962, p. 127.
207. Jaross, W., M. Hanefeld, K. U. Schentke, A. Trübsbach, H. Stötzner, W. Leonhardt, V. Herrmann, and R. Fuchs, Veränderungen von metabolischen Parametern, insbesondere des Fettstoffwechsels bei chronischen Alkoholikern unter klinischer Alkoholkarenz, *Z. Gesamte Inn. Med.,* **27,** 311 (1972).
208. Jellinek, E. M., Distribution of alcohol consumption and of calories derived from alcohol in various selected populations, *Proc. Nutr. Soc.,* **14,** 93 (1955).
209. Jellinek, E. M., *The Disease Concept of Alcoholism,* Hillhouse Press, New Haven, Conn., 1960.

210. Jellinek, E. M., Alcoholism, a genus and some of its species, *Can. Med. Assoc. J.*, **83**, 1341 (1960).
211. Jenkins, J. S. and J. Connolly, Adrenocortical response to ethanol in man, *Br. Med. J.*, **1968/II**, 804.
212. Johannsen, E. and I. F. H. Purchase, Kaffircorn malting and brewing studies, XXI. The effect of the fusel oils of Bantu beer on rat liver, *S. Afr. Med. J.*, **43**, 326 (1969).
213. Johnson, M. W., Physicians' views on alcoholism: With special reference to alcoholism in women, *Nebr. State Med. J.*, **50**, 378 (1965).
214. Johnson, R. B., The alcohol withdrawal syndromes, *Q. J. Stud. Alcohol*, Suppl. No. 1, 66 (1961).
215. Jolliffe, N. and E. M. Jellinek, Vitamin deficiencies and liver cirrhosis in alcoholism. Part VII. Cirrhosis of the liver, *Q. J. Stud. Alcohol*, **2**, 544 (1941).
216. Jones, E., *Br. J. Child. Dis.*, **4**, 1 (1907) (quoted from ref. 399).
217. Joske, R. A. and C. N. Turner, Studies in chronic alcoholism, I. The clinical findings in 78 cases of chronic alcoholism, *Med. J. Austr.*, **1952/I**, 729.
218. Juchems, R. and R. Klobe, Hemodynamic effects of ethyl alcohol in man, *Am. Heart J.*, **78**, 133 (1969).
219. Kager, L., S. Lindberg, and G. Ågren, Alkoholkonsumtion och pankreatit hos mänen intensivstudie av ett ettårsmaterial, *Nord. Med.*, **85**, 413 (1971).
220. Kalant, H., The pharmacology of alcohol intoxication, *Q. J. Stud. Alcohol*, Suppl. No. 1, 1 (1961).
221. Kalant, H. and Y. Israel, Effects of ethanol on active transport of cations, in *Biochemical Factors in Alcoholism*, R. P. Maickel (Ed.), Pergamon Press, London, 1967, p. 25.
222. Kalant, H., Cellular effects of alcohol in *Alcohol and Alcoholism*, R. E. Popham (Ed.), University of Toronto Press, Toronto and Buffalo, 1970, p. 22.
223. Kamionkowski, M. D. and Fleshler, B., The role of alcoholic intake in esophageal carcinoma, *Am. J. Med. Sci.*, **249**, 696 (1965).
224. Karvonen, M. J., Assessment of caloric requirements for different populations, *Duodecim*, **73**, 369 (1957).
225. Kay, W. W. and K. C. Murfitt, Liver damage in addictive alcoholics, *J. Mental Sci.*, **105**, 748 (1959).
226. Keller, A. Z. and M. Terris, The association of alcohol and tobacco with cancer of the mouth and pharynx, *Am. J. Publ. Health*, **55**, 1578 (1965).
227. Keller, A. Z., Cirrhosis of the liver, alcoholism and heavy smoking associated with cancer of the mouth and pharynx, *Cancer*, **20**, 1015 (1967).
228. Keller, M. and V. Efron, Selected statistics on alcoholic beverages and on alcoholism; with a bibliography of sources, *New Haven, Conn. J. Stud Alcohol, Inc.*, **1959**, 3, 9 (mimeographed).

229. Kerner, E. and W. W. Westerfeld, Effect of diet on rate of alcohol oxidation by the liver, *Proc. Soc. Exp. Biol. Med.*, **83**, 530 (1953).
230. Kerr, A., Jr., Myocardopathy, alcohol, and pericardial effusion, *Arch. Intern Med.*, **119**, 617 (1967).
231. Kesteloot, H., R. Terryn, P. Bosmans, and J. V. Joossens, Alcoholic perimyocardiopathy, *Acta Cardiol. (Brux.)*, **21**, 341 (1966).
232. Kesteloot, H., J. Roelandt, J. Willems, J. H. Claes, and J. V. Joossens, An enquiry into the role of cobalt in the heart disease of chronic beer drinkers, *Circulation*, **37**, 854 (1968).
233. Kiessling, K. H., and L. Pilström, Effect of ethanol on rat liver, V. Morphological and functional changes after prolonged consumption of various alcoholic beverages, *Q. J. Stud. Alcohol*, **29**, 819 (1968).
234. Kiessling, K. H., L. Pilström, B. Strandberg, and L. Lindgren, Ethanol and the human liver. Correlation between mitochondrial size and degree of ethanol abuse, *Acta Med. Scand.*, **178**, 533 (1965).
235. Klatskin, G., Alcohol and its relation to liver damage, *Gastroenterology*, **41**, 443 (1961).
236. Klinenberg, J. R., Saturnine gout—A moonshine malady, *N. Engl. J. Med.*, **280**, 1238 (1969).
237. Kmet, J. and E. Mahboubi, Esophageal cancer in the Caspian Littoral of Iran: Initial studies, *Science*, **175**, 846 (1972).
238. Knott, D. H. and J. D. Beard, Liver function in apparently healthy chronic alcoholic patients, *Am. J. Med. Sci.*, **252**, 260 (1966).
239. Knupfer, G., Some methodological problems in the epidemiology of alcoholic beverage usage: Definition of amount of intake, *Am. J. Publ. Health*, **56**, 237 (1966).
240. Koch, E., Verkalkende Pankreopathie und Alkoholabusus, *Diagnostik*, **2**, 39 (1969).
241. Korenevskaya, E., Combating alcoholism in the USSR. *Q. J. Stud. Alcohol*, **27**, 97 (1966).
242. Kürzinger, R., Zur Rückrechnung des Blutalkoholwerts, *Forum der Kriminalistik (Berlin-Ost)*, **1**, 5 (1969).
243. Kürzinger, R., Besonderheiten im resorptiven Teil der Blutalkoholkurve alkoholisierter Personen nach Magenresektion, *Dtsch. Gesundheitsw.*, **24**, 1646 (1969).
244. Kürzinger, R., Bemerkungen uber die Alkoholelimination magenresezierter Personen, *Dtsch. Gesundheitsw.*, **25**, 2022 (1970).
245 Kunitz, S. J., J. E. Levy, C. L. Odoroff, and J. Bollinger, The epidemiology of alcoholic cirrhosis in two southwestern Indian tribes, *Q. J. Stud. Alcohol*, **32**, 706 (1971).
246. Kuster, G., F. Biel, G. Gabrera, and H. Schultz, Habito alcohólico en pacientes con cirrhosis hepática, in *VIIth International Congress of Internal Medicine*, Vol. II, Georg Thieme Verlag, Stuttgart, 1963, p. 604.

247. Lamu, L., Etude de statistique clinique de 134 cas de cancer de l'oesophage et du cardia, *Arch. Mal. Appar. dig.*, **4**, 451 (1910).
248. Laplane, R., D. J. Duché, Dalion, D. Graveleau, and M. Seligmann, Cirrhose hypertrophique alcoolique chez un enfant de deux ans, *Arch. Fr. Pédiatr.*, **10**, 874 (1953).
249. Le Breton, E. and Trémolières, J., Part de l'alcool dans la dépense calorique, *Proc. Nutr. Soc.*, **14**, 97 (1955).
250. Ledermann, S., *Alcool, Alcoolisme, Alcoolisation*, Cahier 29, Presses Universitaires de France, Paris, 1956, p. 84.
251. *Ibid.*, p. 110.
252. *Ibid.*, p. 126.
253. Ledermann, S., *Alcool, Alcoolisme, Alcoolisation*, Cahier 41, Presses Universitaires de France, Paris, 1964, Chap. XXII, p. 377.
254. Lee, F. I., Cirrhosis and hepatoma in alcoholics, *Gut*, **7**, 77 (1966).
255. Leevy, C. M., I. Patrylo, and W. Doody, Hepatic abnormalities in alcoholics with delirium tremens, *Q. J. Stud. Alcohol*, **14**, 568 (1953).
256. Leevy, C. M., M. R. Zinke, T. J. White, and A. M. Gnassi, Clinical observations on the fatty liver, *Arch. Intern. Med.*, **92**, 527 (1953).
257. Leevy, C. M., Clinical diagnosis, evaluation and treatment of liver disease in alcoholics, *Fed. Proc.*, **26**, 1474 (1967).
258. Leevy, C. M. and F. Smith, Ethanol and the liver. *Excerpta Medica International Congress Series No. 213*, Proceedings of the 8th International Congress on Nutrition, Prague, p. 462 (1969).
259. Leevy, C. M. and M. F. Sorrell, Management of fatty liver and steatonecrosis in alcoholics, in *Alcohol and the Liver*, W. Gerok, K. Sickinger, and H. H. Hennekeuser (Eds.), F. K. Schattauer Verlag, Stuttgart-New York, 1971, p. 501.
260. Lelbach, W. K., Leberschäden bei chronischem Alkoholismus, I-IV. *Acta Hepatosplenol.*, **13**, 321 (1966); **14**, 9 (1967).
261. Lelbach, W. K., Zur leberschädigenden Wirkung verschiedener Alkoholika, *Dtsch. Med. Wochenschr.*, **92**, 233 (1967).
262. Lelbach, W. K. Liver damage from different alcoholic drinks, *Ger. Med. Mon.*, **13**, 31 (1968).
263. Lelbach, W. K., Alkoholischer Leberschaden und Alkoholentwöhnung, *Therapiewoche* **20**, 2400 (1970).
264. Lelbach, W. K., Alkoholischer Leberschaden und Alkoholentwöhnung, in *Alcohol and the Liver*, W. Gerok, K. Sickinger, and H. H. Hennekeuser (Eds.), F. K. Schattauer Verlag, Stuttgart-New York, 1971, p. 537.
265. Lelbach, W. K., "Leberverfettung" und "Fettleber" im Rahmen alkoholischer Leberschädigung, *Leber Magen Darm*, **1**, 130 (1971).
266. Lelbach, W. K., Die alkoholische Fettleber—Ihre Rückbildung durch Alkohol-Abstinenz, *Münch. Med. Wochenschr.*, **113**, 1549 (1971).

267. Lelbach, W. K., Dosis-Wirkungs-Deziehung bei Alkohol-Leberschäden, *Dtsch. Med. Wochenschr.*, **97** (1972) (in press).
268. Lereboullet, J. and J. N. Biraben, Bilan de l'alcoolisme en France, *Rev. Prat.*, **14** (Suppl. No. 4), I-XII (1964).
269. Leuschner, F. and A. Leuschner, Vergleichende tierexperimentelle Untersuchungen mit Weinen aus Hybriden- und Europäerreben, *Arzneim. Forsch.*, **17**, 59 (1967).
270. Liebegott, G., Pathologische Anatomie der chronischen Arsenvergiftung, *Dtsch. Med. Wochenschr.*, **74**, 855 (1949).
271. Lieber, C. S., J. H. Mendelson, and L. M. DeCarli, Experimentally induced chronic intoxication and withdrawal in alcoholics, Part 8. Serum lipids and uric acid, *Q. J. Stud. Alcohol*, **25**, 100 (1964).
272. Lieber, C. S., D. P. Jones, and L. M. DeCarli, Effects of prolonged ethanol intake: Production of fatty liver despite adequate diets, *J. Clin. Invest.*, **44**, 1009 (1965).
273. Lieber, C. S. and N. Spritz, Effects of prolonged ethanol intake in man: Role of dietary, adipose, and endogenously synthesized fatty acids in the pathogenesis of the alcoholic fatty liver, *J. Clin. Invest.*, **45**, 1400 (1966).
274. Lieber, C. S., Chronic alcoholic hepatic injury in experimental animals and man: Biochemical pathways and nutritional factors, *Fed. Proc.*, **26**, 1443 (1967).
275. Lieber, C. S. and E. Rubin, Alcoholic fatty liver in man on a high protein and low fat diet, *Am. J. Med.*, **44**, 200 (1968).
276. Lieber, C. S. and L. M. DeCarli, Ethanol oxidation by hepatic microsomes: Adaptive increase after ethanol feeding, *Science*, **162**, 917 (1968).
277. Liebermann, F. L., The effect of liver disease on the rate of ethanol metabolism in man, *Gastroenterology*, **44**, 261 (1963).
278. Liebmann, A. J. and M. Rosenblatt, Changes in whisky while maturing, *Industr. Engng. Chem. (Industr. Ed.)*, **35**, 994 (1943).
279. Lindenbaum, J. and C. S. Lieber, Hematologic effects of alcohol in man in the absence of nutritional deficiency, *N. Engl. J. Med.*, **281**, 333 (1969).
280. Lindenbaum, J. and C. S. Lieber, Alcohol, induced malabsorption of vitamin B_{12} in man, *Nature*, **224**, 806 (1969).
281. Lindinger, H., Beobachtungen über den Verlauf der Alkoholkrankheit am Krankengut einer Heilanstalt, *Münch. Med. Wochenschr.*, **105**, 982 (1963).
282. de Lint, J. and W. Schmidt, Maximum individual alcohol consumption, *Q. J. Stud. Alcohol*, **26**, 670 (1965).
283. de Lint, J. and W. Schmidt, The distribution of alcohol consumption in Ontario, *Q. J. Stud. Alcohol*, **29**, 968 (1968).
284. Linko, M., Side reactions of alcoholic fermentations, *Suom. Kemistil.*, **43A**, 103 (1970).
285. Lischner, M. W., J. F. Alexander, and J. T. Galambos, Natural history of alcoholic hepatitis, I. The acute disease, *Am. J. Dig. Dis.* **16**, 481 (1971).

286. Lowenfels, A. B., B. Masih, T. C. Y. Lee, and M. Rohman, Effect of intravenous alcohol on the pancreas, *Arch. Surg.*, **96**, 440 (1968).
287. Lüchtrath, H., Zu den Ursachen der chronischen Arsenvergiftung bei Kellereiarbeiten in Weinbaubetrieben, *Arbeitsmed., Sozialmed. Arbeitshygiene*, **2**, 228 (1967).
288. Lüchtrath, H., Die Leberzirrhose bei chronischer Arsenvergiftung der Winzer, *Dtsch. Med. Wochenschr.*, **97**, 21 (1972).
289. Lundin, P., O. Lundvall, and A. Weinfeld, Iron storage in alcoholic fatty liver, *Acta Med. Scand.*, **189**, 541 (1971).
290. Lundquist, G., Delirium tremens, *Acta Psychiatr. Scand.*, **36**, 443 (1961).
291. Lundsgaard, Le Taux d'Elimination de l'Alcool, in *Alcool, Alcoolisme, Alcoolisation*, Cahier 29, S. Ledermann, Annexe 2.1, Presses Universitaires de France, Paris, 1956.
292. Lundvall, O., A. Weinfeld, and P. Lundin, Iron stores in alcohol abusers, I. Liver iron, *Acta Med. Scand.*, **185**, 259 (1969).
293. Lundvall, O. and A. Weinfeld, Iron stores in alcohol abusers, II. As measured with the desferrioxamine test, *Acta Med. Scand.*, **185**, 271 (1969).
294. Lustig, B., Hinweise zur Behandlung des Alkoholdelirs, in *Arbeitstagung über Alkoholismus*, K. Kryspin-Exner (Ed.), Wien, 1962, p. 115.
295. Lustig, B., Alkoholismus und Suchtprobleme in der Sowjetunion, *Berichte des Osteuropa—Instituts an der Freien Universität Berlin, Reihe Medizin*, Heft 64, 1964.
296. Lutterotti, A. von, Frühsymptome des chronischen Alkoholismus, *Münch. Med. Wochenschr.*, **106**, 2203 (1964).
297. Lutterotti, A. von, Chronischer Alkoholismus als Ursache von Arrhythmien, *Z. Kreislaufforsch.*, **56**, 275 (1967).
298. McBroom, G. L. and H. W. Smith, Liver function studies on alcoholics, *Can. Med. Assoc. J.*, **69**, 32 (1953).
299. McDermott, P. H., R. L. Delaney, J. D. Egan, and J. F. Sullivan, Myocardosis and cardiac failure in men, *JAMA*, **198**, 163 (1966).
300. McDonald, C. D., G. E. Burch, and J. J. Walsh, Alcoholic cardiomyopathy managed with prolonged bed rest, *Ann. Intern. Med.*, **74**, 681 (1971).
301. McDonald, R. A., Idiopathic hemochromatosis, *Arch. Intern. Med.*, **112**, 184 (1963).
302. McDonald, R. A., Wine as source of iron in hemochromatosis, *Nature*, **199**, 922 (1963).
303. McDonald, R. A. and N. Baumschlag, Iron in alcoholic beverages; possible significance for hemochromatosis, *Am. J. Med. Sci.*, **247**, 649 (1964).
304. McGlashan, N. D., Esophageal cancer and contaminated alcoholic spirits, *Int. Pathol.*, **9**, 50 (1968).

305. McGlashan, N. D., C. L. Walters, and A. E. McLean, Nitrosamines in African alcoholic spirits and oesophageal cancer, *Lancet*, 1968/II, 1017.
306. McGlashan, N. D., Oesophageal cancer and alcoholic spirits in Central Africa, *Gut*, **10**, 643 (1969).
307. McGlashan, N. D., and C. L. Walters, Nitrosamines in South African alcoholic drinks in relation to oesophageal cancer, *S. Afr. Med. J.*, **43**, 800 (1969).
308. McGlashan, N. D., R. L. S. Patterson, and A. A. Williams, *N*-Nitrosamines and grain-based spirits, *Lancet*, 1970/II, 1138.
309. McGregor, D. C., E. Schönbaum, and W. G. Bigelow, Acute toxicity studies on ethanol, propanol and butanol, *Can. J. Physiol. Pharmacol.*, **42**, 689 (1964).
310. MacKay, I. R., The effects of alcohol on the gastro-intestinal tract, *Med. J. Aust.*, **2**, 372 (1966).
311. Madding, G. F., E. E. Tueller, and P. A. Kennedy, Oral and intravenous administration of alcohol and the pancreas, *JAMA*, **205**, 106 (1968).
312. Majchrowicz, E. and J. H. Mendelson, High blood ethanol levels appear to produce blood methanol build-up, *JAMA*, **212**, 1454 (1970).
313. Majchrowicz, E. and J. H. Mendelson, Blood concentrations of acetaldehyde and ethanol in chronic alcoholics, *Science*, **168**, 1100 (1970).
314. Makar, A. B., T. R. Tephly, and G. J. Mannering, Methanol metabolism in the monkey, *Mol. Pharmacol.*, **4**, 471 (1968).
315. Mannhart, M., Krankheiten in ihrer Beziehung zu Genussmitteln in der Bevölkerung von Basel. Enquête bei erwachsenen Personen 1956-1961, *Z. Klin. Med.*, **157**, 240 (1962).
316. Marconi, J. T., The concept of alcoholism, *Q. J. Stud. Alcohol*, **20**, 216 (1959).
317. Marquardt, P. and J. Werringloer, Wirkungen von Begleitstoffen des Alkohols in alkoholischen Getränken, in *Alkohol und Coffein*, K. Lang (Ed.), Steinkopff-Verlag, Darmstadt, 1970, p. 40.
318. Martini, G. A. and Ch. Bode, Zur Epidemiologie der Lebercirrhose, *Internist*, **11**, 84 (1970).
319. Martini, G. A. and Ch. Bode, The epidemiology of cirrhosis of the liver, in *Alcoholic Cirrhosis and Other Toxic Hepatopathias*, A. Engel and T. Larsson (Eds.), Nordiska Bokhandelns Förlag, Stockholm, 1970, p. 315.
320. Martini, G. A., Discussion of ref. 319.
321. Mars, G., and S. Ingegnieros, Liver bioptic features in patients over 70 with chronic alcoholism, *G. Gerontol.*, **12**, 247 (1964).
322. Masuda, Y., K. Mori, T. Hirohata, and M. Kuratsune, Carcinogenesis in the esophagus, III. Polycyclic aromatic hydrocarbons and phenols in whisky, *GANN*, **57**, 549 (1966).

323. Matras, A., Arsenvergiftungen bei Weinhauern, *Med. Klin.*, **36**, 1273 (1940).
324. Mehbod, H., Treatment of lead intoxication, *JAMA*, **201**, 972 (1967).
325. Mellor, C. S., Nomogram for calculating mass of alcohol in different beverages, *Br. Med. J.*, 1970/II, 703.
326. Mendelson, J. H. and J. LaDou, Experimentally induced chronic intoxication and withdrawal in alcoholics, Part I. Background and experimental design, *Q. J. Stud. Alcohol*, **25**, Suppl. No. 2, 1 (1964).
327. Mendelson, J. H. and J. LaDou, Experimentally induced chronic intoxication and withdrawal in alcoholics, Part II. Physiological findings, *Q. J. Stud. Alcohol*, **25**, Suppl. No. 2, 14 (1964).
328. Mendelson, J. H., Experimentally induced chronic intoxication and withdrawal in alcoholics, Part X. Conclusions and implications, *Q. J. Stud. Alcohol*, **25**, Suppl. No. 2, 117 (1964).
329. Mendelson, J. H. and S. Stein, Serum cortisol levels in alcoholic and nonalcoholic subjects during experimentally induced ethanol intoxication, *Psychosom. Med.*, **28**, 616 (1966).
330. Mendelson, J. H. and N. K. Mello, Mechanisms of physical dependence in alcoholism, in *Alcohol and alcoholism*, R. E. Popham (Ed.), University of Toronto Press, Toronto and Buffalo, 1970, p. 126.
331. Mendelson, J. H., Biologic concomitants of alcoholism, *N. Engl. J. Med.*, **283**, 24, 71 (1970).
332. Menghini, G., L'aspect morpho-bioptique du foie de l'alcoolique (noncirrhotique) et son évolution, *Bull. Schweiz. Acad. Med. Wiss.*, **16**, 35 (1960).
333. Menghini, G., C. Branciari, and D. Caporicci, Alcoholic fatty liver apropos of its treatment, in *Alcohol and the Liver*, W. Gerok, K. Sickinger, H. H. Hennekeuser (Eds.), F. K. Schattauer Verlag, Stuttgart-New York, 1971, p. 512.
334. Merry, J., Alcohol (Ethanol); Some facts and figures, *Practitioner*, **207**, 67 (1971).
335. Mezey, E., E. Jou, and R. Slavin, Pancreatic function and intestinal absorption in chronic alcoholism, *Gastroenterology*, **59**, 657 (1970).
336. Mezey, E., Changes in metabolism and ethanol oxidizing enzymes in chronic alcoholic patients following withdrawal from alcohol, *Gastroenterology*, **60**, 174 (1971).
337. Mezey, E. and F. Tobon, Rates of ethanol clearance and activities of the ethanol-oxidizing enzymes in chronic alcoholic patients, *Gastroenterology*, **61**, 707 (1971).
338. Mezey, K. and H. Staub, Giftwirkungen am isolierten Herzkammerstreifen des Frosches, *Naunyn-Schmiedeberg's Arch. Pharmacol.*, **180**, 12 (1936).
339. Milham, S., Alcoholic cancers and wood, *Lancet*, 1970/I, 1059.
340. Misra, P. S., A. Lefèvre, H. Ishii, E. Rubin, and C. S. Lieber, Increase of

ethanol, meprobamate and pentobarbital metabolism after chronic ethanol administration in man and in rats, *Am. J. Med.*, **51**, 346 (1971).

341. Moeschlin, S. and P. Righetti, Wine and cirrhosis, in *Alcoholic Cirrhosis and Other Toxic Hepatopathias*, A. Engel and T. Larsson (Eds.), Nordiska Bokhandelns Förlag, Stockholm, 1970, p. 301.

342. Mogar, R. E., W. M. Wilson, and S. T. Helm, Personality subtypes of male and female alcoholic patients, *Int. J. Addict.*, **5**, 99 (1970).

343. Muehlberger, C. W., Relative toxicological effects of synthetic ethanol and grain fermentation alcohol in blended whiskies, *Am. J. Publ. Health*, **25**, 1132 (1935).

344. Müller-Dietz, H., Gesundheitserziehung in der Sowjetunion, III. Schwerpunkt: Kampf gegen die Trunksucht, *Dtsch. Ärzteblatt*, 39/1967, 2031.

345. Müting, D., Alkohol und Leber, *Ärztl. Praxis*, **23**, 3699 (1971).

346. Murcia-Valcarcel, E., L'alcoolisme chez la femme, *Rev. Alcsme.*, **15**, 285 (1969).

347. Murphree, H. B., L. M. Price, and L. A. Greenberg, Effect of congeners in alcoholic beverages on the incidence of nystagmus, *Q. J. Stud. Alcohol*, **27**, 201 (1966).

348. Murphree, H. B., L. A. Greenberg, and R. B. Carroll, Neuropharmacological effects of substances other than ethanol in alcoholic beverages, *Fed. Proc.*, **26**, 1468 (1967).

349. Murphree, H. B., R. E. Schultz, and A. G. Jusko, Effects of high congener intake by human subjects on the EEG, *Q. J. Stud. Alcohol*, Suppl No. 5, **50** (1970).

350. Nadeau, G., Y. Rouleau, and J. Delage, The fate of the liver in chronic alcoholics, *Can. Med. Assoc. J.*, **70**, 665 (1954).

351. Nagaratnam, N., Alcohol and heart disease in Ceylon, *Cardiology*, **55**, 41 (1970).

352. Nagaratnam, N. and K. R. W. Gunawardene, Fatal and prolonged coma following indigenous distilled spirits, *J. Colombo Gen. Hosp.*, **2**, 74 (1971).

353. Nagaratnam, N. and D. C. Peiris, Acute alcoholic hepatitis in Ceylon, *Ceylon Med. J.*, **16**, 28 (1971).

354. Nakamura, T., S. Nakamura, K. Sugawara, Y. Katakura, T. Isono, T. Suzuki, T. Kaneko, and T. Takizawa, Studies on cirrhosis of the liver, III. Liver biopsy and liver function tests in alcoholics, *Tohoku J. Exp. Med.*, **67**, 105 (1958).

355. Nakamura, T., S. Nakamura, T. Alkawa, N. Karohi, O. Suzuki, and A. Onodera, Hepatic changes in heavy drinkers among in- and out-patients, *Tohoku J. Exp. Med.*, **93**, 191 (1967).

356. Nathan, P. E., N. C. Zare, E. W. Ferneau, Jr., and L. M. Lowenstein, Effects of congener differences in alcoholic beverages on the behavior of alcoholics, *Q. J. Stud. Alcohol*, Suppl. No. 5, 87 (1970).

357. Natvig, H. and Wilhelmsen, L. H., Innholdet av jern i rødvin m.m., *Tidsskr, norske Laegeforen.*, **84**, 1648 (1964).
358. Neame, P. B. and I. Beck, Recurrent alcoholic sideroblastosis and hepatic hemosiderosis, *N. Engl. J. Med.*, **283**, 1173 (1970).
359. Neurologic complications of alcoholism, *Am. J. Med.*, **46**, 118 (1969).
360. Neville, J. N., J. A. Eagles, G. Samson, and R. E. Olson, Nutritional status of alcoholics, *Am. J. Clin. Nutr.*, **21**, 1329 (1968).
361. Newell, G. W., T. E. Shellenberger, and D. R. Reinke, Chronic effects of alcohol, muscatel, and sherry on the growth and performance of male rats, *Toxicol. Appl. Pharmacol.*, **6**, 696 (1964).
362. Newman, H. W., Maximal consumption of ethyl alcohol, *Science*, **109**, 594 (1949).
363. Newman, H. W., R. H. L. Wilson, and E. J. Newman, Direct determination of maximal daily metabolism of alcohol, *Science*, **116**, 328 (1952).
364. Nielsen, J., Alkoholpriser, Alkoholforbrug, Delirium tremens og Mortalitet ved Kronisk Alkoholisme fra 1911 til 1961, *Usgekr. Laeg.*, **130**, 987 (1968).
365. Nielsen, J. and E. Strömgren, Über die Abhängigkeit des Alkoholkonsums und der Alkoholkrankheiten vom Preis alkoholischer Getränke, *Bibl. Psychiat. Neurol.*, **142**, 165 (1969).
366. O'Brien, E. T. and P. Goldstraw, Alcoholic myopathy, *Br. Med. J.*, 1969/IV, 785.
367. Oettel, H., Physiologie und Toxikologie, in W. Foerst (Ed.), *Ullmanns Encyklopädie der technischen Chemie*, 3. Aufl., 16. Band, Urban & Schwarzenberg, München-Berlin, 1965, p. 161.
368. Oettel, H., Toxische Gefässchäden und Durchblutungsstörungen, *Hippokrates*, **40**, 285 (1969).
369. Oldershausen, H. F. von, Zur Klinik und Pathogenese der alkoholischen Leberschäden. Eine Studie über funktionelle und morphologische Leberveränderungen nach akuter und chronischer Einwirkung von Alkohol und deren Abgrenzung von chronischen Leberschäden anderer Ätiologie, *Habilitationsschrift*, Freie Universität Berlin, 1962.
370. Oldershausen, H. F. von, Zur sozialmedizinischen Bedeutung und Pathogenese der alkoholischen Leberschäden, in *Leber, Haut und Skelett*, Georg Thieme Verlag, Stuttgart, 1964.
371 Oldershausen, H. F. von, Über die Pathogenese alkoholischer Leberschäden, *Dtsch. Med. Wochenschr.*, **89**, 867 (1964).
372. Owens, J. L. and J. M. Howard, Pancreatic calcification. A late sequel in the natural history of chronic alcoholism and alcoholic pancreatitis, *Ann. Surg.*, **147**, 326 (1958).
373. Palmisano, P. A., Moonshine danger, *JAMA*, **210**, 1386 (1969).
374. Palmisano, P. A., R. C. Sneed, and G. Cassady, Untaxed whiskey and fatal lead exposure, *J. Pediat.*, **75**, 869 (1969).

375. Papenberg, J., Ethanol metabolism, in *Alcohol and the Liver*, W. Gerok, K. Sickinger, and H. H. Hennekeuser (Eds.), F. K. Schattauer Verlag, Stuttgart-New York, 1971, p. 45.
376. Patek, A. J. and J. Post, Treatment of cirrhosis of the liver by a nutritious diet and supplement rich in vitamin B complex, *J. Clin. Invest.*, **20,** 481 (1941).
377. Patterson, M. and W. C. T. Jernigan, Lead intoxication from "moonshine," *Gen. Practit. Kansas City*, **40,** 126 (1969).
378. Pein, H. von, Untersuchungen über die chronische Arsenvergiftung der Weinbauern, *Dtsch. Arch. Klin. Med.*, **186,** 200 (1940).
379. Péquignot, G., Enquête par interrogatoire sur les circonstances diététiques de la cirrhose alcoolique en France, *Bull. Inst. Nat. Hyg.*, **13,** 719 (1958).
380. Péquignot, G., Die Rolle des Alkohols bei der Ätiologie von Lebercirrhosen in Frankreich, *Münch. Med. Wochenschr.*, **103,** 1464 (1961).
381. Péquignot, G., Les enquêtes par interrogatoire permettent elles de déterminer le fréquence de l'étiologie alcoolique des cirrhoses du foie?, *Bull. Acad. Natl. Med.*, **147,** 90 (1963).
382. Perman, G., Hemochromatosis and red wine, *Acta Med. Scand.*, **182,** 281 (1967).
383. Perrin, P., L'alcoolisme en Italie; son importance, ses causes, premières conclusions, *Rev. Alcsme.*, **11,** 45 (1965).
384. Phillips, G. B. and H. F. Safrit, Alcoholic diabetes. Induction of glucose intolerance with alcohol, *JAMA*, **217,** 1513 (1971).
385. Pieper, W. A., M. J. Skeen, H. M. McClure, and P. G. Bourne, The chimpanzee as an animal model for investigating alcoholism, *Science*, **176,** 71 (1972).
386. Popper, H., E. Rubin, St. Krus, and F. Schaffner, Postnecrotic Cirrhosis in alcoholics, *Gastroenterology*, **39,** 669 (1960).
387. Porta, E. A. and C. L. A. Gomez-Dumm, A new experimental approach in the study of chronic alcoholism, I. Effects of high alcohol intake in rats fed a commercial laboratory diet, *Lab. Invest.*, **18,** 352 (1968).
388. Post, R. M. and F. Desforges, Thrombocytopenic effect of ethanol infusion, *Blood*, **31,** 344 (1968).
389. Powell, L. W., Norman human iron storage and its relation to ethanol consumption, *Australas, Ann. Med.*, **15,** 110 (1966).
390. Powell, W. J., Jr., and G. Klatskin, Duration of survival in patients with Laennec's cirrhosis. Influence of alcohol withdrawal, and possible effects of recent changes in general management of the disease, *Am. J. Med.*, **44,** 406 (1968).
391. Pryor, W. J., Social drinking and blood alcohol levels, *N. Z. Med. J.*, **65,** 689 (1966).
392. Prys-Williams, G., The statistics of alcoholism, *J. Alcoholism London*, **4,** 116 (1969).

393. Purchase, I. P. H., Studies in Kaffircorn malting and brewing, *S. Afr. Med. J.*, **43,** 795 (1969).
394. Quebec beer-drinkers' cardiomyopathy, *JAMA*, **202,** 1145 (1967).
395. Quebec beer-drinkers' cardiomyopathy, *Can. Med. Assoc. J.*, **15,** 881-931 (1967).
396. Queries and minor notes, *JAMA*, **157,** 303 (1955).
397. Rankin, J. R., P. Wilkinson, and J. N. Santamaria, Factors influencing the prognosis of the alcoholic patient with cirrhosis, *Aust. Ann. Med.*, **3,** 232 (1970).
398. Rathod, N. H. and I. G. Thomson, Women alcoholics, a clinical study, *Q. J. Stud. Alcohol*, **32,** 45 (1971).
399. Ratnoff, D. D. and A. J. Patek, The natural history of Laennec's cirrhosis of the liver, *Medicine*, **21,** 207 (1942).
400. Raymondis, L. M., La morbidité par alcoolisme et sa signification pour l'étude comparative en criminologie d'après les résultats d'observations dans un service hospitalier, *Rev. int. Criminol.*, **21,** 33 (1967).
401. Raynes, A. E. and R. S. Ryback, Effect of alcohol and congeners on aggressive response in Betta splendens, *Q. J. Stud. Alcohol*, Suppl. No. 5, 130 (1970).
402. Regan, T. J., A. B. Weisse, C. B. Moschos, L. J. Lesniak, M. Nadimi, and H. K. Hellems, The myocardial effects of acute and chronic usage of ethanol in man, *Trans. Assoc. Am. Physicians*, **78,** 282 (1965).
403. Regan, T. J., G. E. Levinson, H. A. Oldewurtel, M. J. Frank, A. B. Weisse, and C. B. Moschos, Ventricular function in noncardiacs with alcoholic fatty liver: Role of ethanol in the production of cardiomyopathy, *J. Clin. Invest.*, **48,** 397 (1969).
404. Regan, T. J., Ethyl alcohol and the heart, *Circulation*, **44,** 957 (1971).
405. Reichard, H., Serum ornithine transcarbamylase activity in normal individuals, *Enzym. Biol. Clin.*, (Basel), **1,** 47 (1961).
406. Reichard, H., Studies on ornithine carbamyl transferase activity in blood serum: A methodologic, experimental and clinical investigation, *Acta Med. Scand.*, Suppl. 390, **172,** 723 (1962).
407. Remmer, H., Discussion of ref. 144.
408. Reynolds, T. B., A. G. Redeker, and O. T. Kuzma, Role of alcohol in pathogenesis of alcoholic cirrhosis, in *Therapeutic Agents and the Liver*, N. McIntyre and S. Sherlock (Eds.), Blackwell Scientific Publications, Oxford, 1965, p. 131.
409. Riff, D. P., A. C. Jain, and J. T. Doyle, Acute hemodynamic effects of ethanol on normal human volunteers, *Am. Heart J.*, **78,** 592 (1969).
410. Rinke, W., *Das Bier*, Parey Verlag, Berlin-Hamburg, 1967, p. 71.
411. Ritter, U., Zur Alkoholpankreatitis, *Dtsch. Med. Wochenschr.*, **90,** 382 (1965).

412. Roth, F., Über die chronische Arsenvergiftung der Moselwinzer unter besonderer Berücksichtigung des Arsenkrebses, *Z. Krebsforsch.*, **61**, 287 (1956).
413. Rouleau, Y. and G. Nadeau, Dysfonction du foie chez les alcooliques chroniques, *Laval Méd.*, **17**, 473 (1952).
414. Rowntree, L. G., Considerations in cirrhosis of the liver, *JAMA*, **89**, 1590 (1927).
415. Roy, P. E., Bonenfant, J. L., and Turcot, L., Thyroid changes in cases of Quebec beer drinkers' myocardosis, *Am. J. Clin. Path.*, **50**, 234 (1968).
416. Rubin, E. and C. S. Lieber, Early fine structural changes in the human liver induced by alcohol, *Gastroenterology*, **52**, 1 (1967).
417. Rubin, E. and C. S. Lieber, Alcohol-induced hepatic injury in non-alcoholic volunteers, *N. Engl. J. Med.*, **278**, 869 (1968).
418. Rubin, E. and C. S. Lieber, Studies in man and rat of the induction and inhibition of hepatic drug metabolizing enzymes by alcohol, *Gastroenterology*, **56**, 411 (1969).
419. Rubington, E., The bottle gang, *Q. J. Stud. Alcohol*, **29**, 943 (1968).
420. Ruebner, B. H., R. Kanayama, R. Freedland, M. Tsao, and M. A. Brayton, Production of fatty liver by ethanol in rhesus monkeys, *Gastroenterology*, **62**, 198 (1972).
421. Rum fits and DT'S, *JAMA*, **212**, 2112 (1970).
422. Ryback, R. and J. Desforges, Alcoholic thrombocytopenia in three inpatients drinking alcoholics, *Arch. Intern. Med.*, **125**, 475 (1970).
423. Sackett, D. L., R. W. Gibson, I. D. J. Bross, and J. W. Pickren, Relation between aortic atherosclerosis and the use of cigarettes and alcohol, *N. Engl. J. Med.*, **279**, 1413 (1968).
424. Sarles, H. and J. C. Sarles, Chronische alkoholische Pankreatitis, Chronische calcifizierende Pankreatitis, *Verh. Dtsch. Ges. Inn. Med., 70. Kongress*, B. Schlegel (Ed.), J. F. Bergmann Verlag, München, 1964, p. 773.
425. Sarles, H., R. Muratore, J. C. Sarles, M. Gaini, R. Camatte, J. Pastor, and C. Guien, Aetiology and pathology of chronic pancreatitis, in *Pancreatitis*, Facs. 7, H. Sarles (Ed.), Bibliotheca Gastroenterologica, S. Karger, Basel, 1965, p. 75.
426. Sarles, H., J. C. Sarles, R. Camatte, *Proc. 3rd World Congr. Gastroenterol., Tokyo*, **4**, 282 (1966).
427. Sarles, H., C. Figarella, F. Tasso, R. Camatte, and A. Gerolami, Pancréatites nutritionnelles (carence protéique, alcoolisme), in *Modern Gastroenterology*, O. Gregor and O. Riedl (Eds.), F. K. Schattauer Verlag, Stuttgart-New York, 1969, p. 1267.
428. Sarles, H., R. Camatte, M. Martin, and J. C. Sarles, Studie über 48 Kranke mit nichttraumatischen Zysten oder Pseudozysten des Pankreas, *Med. Welt (N.F.), 1968/I,* 550.
429. Schaffner, F. and H. Popper, Alcoholic hepatitis in the spectrum of ethanol-induced liver injury, *Scand. J. Gastroenterol.*, **5**, (Suppl. 7), 69 (1970).

430. Schapiro, R. H., G. H. Drummey, R. Scheig, J. H. Mendelson, and K. J. Isselbacher, Abnormalities of lipid transport accompanying prolonged alcohol ingestion in man, *Gastroenterology*, **44,** 849 (1963).
431. Schmähl, D., C. Thomas, W. Sattler, and G. F. Scheld, Experimentelle Untersuchungen zur Syncarcinogenese, 3.Mitteilung. Versuche zur Krebserzeugung bei Ratten bei gleichzeitiger Gabe von Diäthylnitrosamin und Tetrachlorkohlenstoff bzw. Äthylalkohol; zugleich ein experimenteller Beitrag zur Frage der "Alkoholcirrhose," *Z. Krebsforsch.*, **66,** 526 (1965).
432. Schmidt, W. and J. Bronetto, Death from liver cirrhosis and specific alcoholic beverage consumption: An ecological study, *Am. J. Publ. Health*, **52,** 1473 (1962).
433. Schmidt, W. and R. E. Popham, Alcohol consumption of alcoholics, *Addiction Research Foundation*, Ontario, 1968.
434. Schmidt, W. and J. De Lint, Mortality experiences of male and female alcoholic patients, *Q. J. Stud. Alcohol*, **30,** 112 (1969).
435. Schmidt, W. and J. De Lint, Estimating the prevalence of alcoholism from alcohol consumption and mortality data, *Q. J. Stud. Alcohol*, **31,** 957 (1970).
436. Schüppel, R. and W. Dürr, Die N-Demethylierung von Aminophenazon unter dem Einfluss verschiedener Alkohole, *Naunyn-Schmiedeberg's Arch. Pharmakol.*, **263,** 249 (1969).
437. Schüppel, R., Wirkungen von Alkohol auf den Arzneistoffwechsel, in *Alcohol and the Liver*, W. Gerok, K. Sickinger, H. H. Hennekeuser (Eds.), F. K. Schattauer Verlag, Stuttgart-New York, 1971, p. 227.
438. Schüttmann, Ch., W. Schüttmann, and L. H. Kettler, Berufliche Leberschäden dürch Alkohol, *Z. Gesamte Hyg.*, **14,** 337 (1968).
439. Schuller, P. L., Th. Ockhuizen, J. Werringloer, and P. Marquardt, Aflatoxin B_1 und Histamin in Wein, *Arzneim. Forsch.*, **17,** 888, (1967).
440. Sclare, A. B., The female alcoholic, *Br. J. Addict.*, **65,** 99 (1970).
441. Seeley, J. R., Death by liver cirrhosis and the price of beverage alcohol, *Can. Med. Assoc. J.*, **83,** 1361 (1960).
442. Seife, M., B. J. Kessler, and J. R. Lisa, Clinical, functional, and needle-biopsy study of the liver in alcoholism, *Arch. Intern. Med.*, **86,** 658 (1950).
443. Senior, J. R., Ethanol and liver disease, *Postgrad. Med.*, **41,** 65 (1967).
444. Sensemann, L. A., The housewife's secret illness; How to recognize the female alcoholic, *R. I. Med. J.*, **49,** 40 (1966).
445. Serenyi, G. and P. Devenyi, Portal fibrosis in alcoholic liver disease, *Am. J. Gastroenterol.*, **57,** 429 (1972).
446. Sherlock, S., *Diseases of the Liver and Biliary System*, 1st ed., Blackwell Scientific Publications, Oxford, 1955, Chap. 10.
447. Sherlock, S., *Diseases of the Liver and the Biliary System*, 3rd ed., Blackwell Scientific Publications, Oxford, 1963.
448. Sherlock, S., P. Brunt, and P. J. Scheuer, Clinical and pathological aspects

of alcoholic liver disease, in *Alcohol and the Liver*, W. Gerok, K. Sickinger, and H. H. Hennekeuser (Eds.), F. K. Schattauer Verlag, Stuttgart-New York, 1971, p. 383.

449. Sinniah, R., Environmental and genetic factors in idiopathic hemochromatosis, *Arch. Intern. Med.*, **124**, 455 (1969).

450. Small, M., A. Longarini, and N. Zamchek, Disturbances of digestive physiology following acute drinking episodes in "skid-row" alcoholics, *Am. J. Med.*, **27**, 575 (1959).

451. Smith, B. and J. E. Berk, Pectoral hair in cirrhosis, *Am. J. Gastroenterol.*, **55**, 387, (1971).

452. Smith, J. W. and T. A. Layden, Changes in psychological performance and blood chemistry in alcoholics during and after hospital treatment, *Q. J. Stud. Alcohol*, **33**, 379 (1972).

453. Soehring, K., Pharmakologie des Aethanols, in *Alcohol und Coffein*, K. Lang (Ed.), Steinkopff-Verlag, Darmstadt, 1970, p. 28.

454. Solms, H., Notwendige Abwandlungen der Behandlungsmethoden des chronischen Alkoholismus infolge regionaler Verschiedenheit der Trinksitten und Alkoholkrankheiten, in *Arbeitstagung über Alkoholismus*, K. Kryspin-Exner (Ed.), Wien, 1962, p. 142.

455. Solms, H., Soziologische, kulturelle, wirtschaftliche und regionale Verschiedenheiten des Alkoholkonsums und der alkoholischen Störungen, in *Sucht und Missbrauch*, F. Laubenthal (Ed.), Georg Thieme Verlag, Stuttgart, 1964, p. 573.

456. Song, S. K. and E. Rubin, Ethanol produces muscle damage in human volunteers, *Science*, **175**, 327 (1972).

457. Soriano, M., Periostitis deformans; un nuevo tipo de fluorosis ósea en el hombre; la fluorosis vinica, *Rev. Clin. Esp.*, **97**, 375 (1965).

458. Spann, W., Zuverlässigkeit der Blutalkoholbestimmung (Queries), *Münch. Med. Wochenschr.*, **109**, 201 (1968).

459. Specht, H. and C. C. Emeis, Alkoholische Gärung, in *Handbuch der Lebensmittelchemie: Alkoholische Genussmittel*, Springer Verlag, Berlin-Heidelberg, 1968, p. 36.

460. Steigmann, F. and M. H. Shah, Fatty liver with jaundice: A diagnostic enigma with surgical implications, *Am. J. Gastroenterol.*, **54**, 126 (1970).

461. Steinhilber, R. M., V. D. Kuluvar, D. J. Anderson, R. O. Heilman, and P. L. Hansen, Symposium on the problem of the chronic alcoholic, *Mayo Clin. Proc.*, **42**, 705 (1967).

462. Steinhoff, D. and P. Marquardt, Kombination von Kaliumpyrosulfit und Äthylalkohol im Tränkungsversuch an Ratten, *Arzneimittelforsch.*, **13**, 237 (1964).

463. Steinmann, B., Über Hundertjährige, *Gerontol. clin.*, **8**, 23 (1966).

464. Sullivan, J., J. Woodbury, J. Egan, and G. Mulcahy, Hepatic function and pathology in alcoholic myocardopathy, *Gastroenterology*, **54**, 170 (1968).

465. Sullivan, J., M. Parker, and S. B. Carson, Tissue cobalt content in "beer drinkers myocardiopathy", *J. Lab. Clin. Med.*, **71**, 893 (1968).
466. Sullivan, J., R. George, R. Bluvas, and J. D. Egan, Myocardiopathy of beer drinkers: Subsequent course, *Ann. Intern. Med.*, **70**, 277 (1969).
467. Sullivan, L. W. and V. Herbert, Suppression of hematopoiesis by ethanol, *J. Clin. Invest.*, **43**, 2048 (1964).
468. Summerskill, W. J., S. J. Wolfe, and C. S. Davidson, Response to alcohol in chronic alcoholics with liver disease, *Lancet*, 1957/I, 335.
469. Suomalainen, H., Penetration of some metabolic compounds into and from the yeast cell, *Suom. Kemistil.*, **41A**, 239 (1968).
470. Suomalainen, H. and L. Nikänen, Composition of whisky flavor, *Proc. Biochem.*, **5**, 13 (1970).
471. Swartz, M., A. Brewster, and J. Sullivan, The effect of ethanol on alimentary lipemia, *Clin. Res.*, **12**, 343 (1964).
472. Takeuchi, J., A. Takada, Y. Kato, Y. Hasumura, F. Ikegami, and Y. Matsuda, Hepatic changes in chronic alcoholic rats following periodic acute alcoholic intoxications, *Am. J. Clin. Nutr.*, **24**, 628 (1971).
473. Tapper, E. J., S. Bushi, R. D. Ruppert, and N. J. Greenberger, Effect of acute and chronic ethanol treatment on the absorption of iron in rats, *Am. J. Med. Sci.*, **255**, 46 (1968).
474. Tavel, M. E., A new look at an old syndrome: Delirium tremens. (Editorial), *Arch. Intern. Med.*, **109**, 129 (1962).
475. Terris, M., Epidemiology of cirrhosis of the liver: National mortality data, *Am. J. Publ. Health*, **57**, 2076 (1967).
476. Thaler, H., Die Fettleber und ihre pathogenetische Beziehung zur Leberzirrhose, *Virchows Arch.*, **335**, 180 (1962).
477. Thaler, H., Alkohol und Leberschaden, *Dtsch. Med. Wochenschr.*, **94**, 1213 (1969).
478. Thaler, H., Die Klinik der präzirrhotischen alkoholischen Leberschädigung, in *Aktuelle Hepatologie*, H. A. Kühn and H. Liehr (Eds.), G. Thieme Verlag, Stuttgart, 1969, p. 70.
479. Thaler, H., Morphologische Befunde bei chronischer Alkoholintoxikation, in *Alcohol and the Liver*, W. Gerok, K. Sickinger, H. H. Hennekeuser, (Eds.), F. K. Schattauer Verlag, Stuttgart-New York, 1971, p. 253.
480. Thompson, G. N., *Alcoholism*, C. C. Thomas, Springfield, Ill., 1956.
481. Tobin, J. R., J. F. Driscoll, M. T. Lim, G. C. Sutton, P. B. Szanto, and R. M. Gunnar, Primary myocardial disease and alcoholism. The clinical manifestation and course of the disease in a selected population of patients observed for three or more years, *Circulation*, **35**, 754 (1967).
482. Tofler, O. B., B. M. Saker, K. A. Rollo, M. J. Burvill, and N. Stenhouse, Electrocardiogram of the social drinker in Perth, Western Australia, *Br. Heart J.*, **31**, 306 (1969).

483. Trémolières, J., R. Lowy, and G. Griffaton, Physiologie de l'oxydation et de l'utilisation de l'éthanol à doses normales et toxiques, *Ann. Nutr. Aliment.* (Paris), **21**, 69 (1967).
484. Truitt, E. B., Jr., and G. Duritz, The role of acetaldehyde in the actions of ethanol, in *Biochemical Factors in Alcoholism*, R. P. Maickel (Ed.), Pergamon Press, New York, 1967, p. 61.
485. Tuovinen, P. I., Über den Alkoholgehalt des Blutes unter verschiedenen Bedingungen, *Scand. Arch. Physiol.*, **60**, 1 (1930).
486. Tuyns, A. J., Cancer of the oesophagus: Further evidence of the relation to drinking habits in France, *Int. J. Cancer*, **5**, 152 (1970).
487. Tygstrup, N., E. Juhl, and the Copenhagen Study Group for Liver Diseases, The treatment of alcoholic cirrhosis. The effect of continued drinking and prednisone on survival, in *Alcohol and the Liver*, W. Gerok, K. Sickinger, H. H. Hennekeuser (Eds.), F. K. Schattauer Verlag, Stuttgart-New York, 1971, p. 519.
488. Ugarte, G., Hepatic alcohol dehydrogenase in alcoholic addicts with and without hepatic damage, *Am. J. Digest. Dis.*, **12**, 589 (1967).
489. Ugarte, G., T. Pereda, M. E. Pino, F. Lorca, and B. Sepulveda, Velocidad metabolica del etanol y lactácidemia en bebedores moderados y adictos alcohólicos con y sin daño hepático, *Rev. méd. Chile*, **95**, 67 (1967).
490. Ugarte, G., H. Iturriaga, and I. Insunza, Some effects of ethanol on normal and pathologic livers, in *Progress in Liver Disease*, Vol. III, H. Popper, F. Schaffner (Eds.), Grune & Stratton, New York and London, 1970, Chap. 22.
491. Ugarte, G., I. Insunza, H. Altschiller, and H. Iturriaga, Clinical and metabolic disorders in alcoholic hepatic damage, in *Alcohol and Alcoholism*, R. E. Popham (Ed.), University of Toronto Press, Toronto, 1970, p. 229.
492. Ugarte, G., T. Pereda, M. E. Pino, and H. Iturriaga, Influence of alcohol intake, abstinence and meprobamate on the rate of ethanol metabolism in man, *Gastroenterology*, **60**, 727 (1971).
493. Uhlenhut, Ziegler, and Heger, Über die Arsenvergiftungen im Weinbaugebiet ("Kaiserstuhlkrankheit") mit Krankenvorstellungen, *Klin. Wochenschr.*, **13**, 1698 (1934).
494. Vanderperre, G., Over het alcoholisme bij de vrouw, *Tijdschr. Geneesk.*, **23**, 1497 (1967).
495. Vetter, D., *Das Verhalten der Serumlipide beim chronischen Alkoholismus*, Inaugural-Dissertation, Zürich, 1966.
496. Viel, B., S. Donoso, D. Salcedo, P. Rojas, A. Varela, and R. Alessandri, Alcoholism and socioeconomic status, hepatic damage, and arteriosclerosis, *Arch. Intern. Med.*, **117**, 84 (1966).
497. Viel, B., S. Donoso, D. Salcedo, and A. Varela, Alcoholic drinking habit and hepatic damage, *J. Chron. Dis.*, **21**, 157 (1968).
498. Viel, B., D. Salcedo, S. Donoso, and A. Varela, Alcoholism, accidents, ath-

erosclerosis, and hepatic damage, in *Alcohol and Alcoholism*, R. E. Popham (Ed.), University of Toronto Press, Toronto and Buffalo, 1970, p. 319.

499. Vitale, J. J., G. H. McGrath, J. Nay, and D. M. Hegsted, Alcohol oxidation in relation to alcohol dosage and the effect of fasting, *J. Biol. Chem.*, **204**, 257 (1953).

500. Voegtlin, W. L., W. R. Broz, and M. H. Moss, Liver function in chronic alcoholic patients, I. The incidence of liver disease as indicated by laboratory methods and suggested screening procedures, *Gastroenterology*, **12**, 184 (1949).

501. Voegtlin, W. L., W. R. Broz, W. E. Tupper, and M. W. Robinson, Liver function in chronic alcoholic patients, II. Correlation between elements of the history and presence of liver dysfunction as indicated by laboratory tests, *Gastroenterology*, **13**, 391 (1949).

502. Voegtlin, W. L., W. E. Tupper, and M. W. Robinson, Liver function in chronic alcoholic patients, III. Correlation between the presence of liver dysfunction as indicated by laboratory tests and objective findings of examinations, *Gastroenterology*, **14**, 485 (1950).

503. Volwiler, W., C. M. Jones, and T. B. Mallory, Criteria for the measurement of results of treatment in fatty cirrhosis, *Gastroenterology*, **11**, 164 (1948).

504. Walker, F. and J. Shand, Influence of alcohol on collagen synthesis *in vitro*, *Lancet*, 1972/I, 233.

505. Wallgren, H., J. Ahlquist, K. Åhman, and H. Suomalainen, Repeated alcoholic intoxication compared with continued consumption of dilute ethanol in experiments with rats on a marginal diet, *Br. J. Nutr.*, **21**, 643 (1967).

506. Wallgren, H. and H. Berry, III, *Actions of Alcohol*, Vol. I, Elsevier Publishing Company, Amsterdam-London-New York, 1970, p. 28.

507. Wanberg, K. W. and J. L. Horn, Alcoholism symptom patterns of men and women, *Q. J. Stud. Alcohol*, **31**, 40 (1970).

508. Wanberg, K. W. and J. Knapp, Differences in drinking symptoms and behavior of men and women alcoholics, *Br. J. Addict.*, **64**, 347 (1970).

509. Wartburg, J. P. von, M. Röthlisberger, and H. M. Eppenberger, Hemmung der Äthylalkoholoxydation durch Fuselöle, *Helv. Med. Acta*, **28**, 696 (1961).

510. Wartburg, J. P. von, and J. Papenberg, Alcohol dehydrogenase in ethanol metabolism, *Psychosom. Med.*, **28**, 405 (1966).

511. Wartburg, J. P. von, Alcohol dehydrogenase distribution in tissues of different species, in *Alcohol and Alcoholism*, R. E. Popham (Ed.), University of Toronto Press, Toronto and Buffalo, 1970, p. 13.

512. Weatherall, M., Alcohol in the diet, *Nature*, **175**, 702 (1955).

513. Wegmann, T. and W. Geiser, Gehäuftes Vorkommen von Dupuytren'scher Kontraktur bei chronischem Alkoholismus, *Schweiz. Med. Wochenschr.*, **24**, 719 (1961).

514. Welch, H. and G. G. Slocum, Relation of length of carbon chain to the

primary and functional toxicities of alcohols, *J. Lab. Clin. Med.*, **28,** 1440 (1943).

515. Wendt, V. E., C. Wu, R. Balson, G. Doty, and R. J. Bing, Hemodynamic and metabolic effects of chronic alcoholism in man, *Am. J. Cardiol.*, **15,** 175 (1965).

516. Wessler, St., and L. V. Avioli, Alcoholic hepatitis, *JAMA,* **203,** 145 (1968).

517. West German Agency for Addiction Control, Alcoholism increasing among German women, *JAMA,* **209,** 1914 (1969).

518. Westerfeld, W. W. and M. P. Schulman, Metabolism and caloric value of alcohol, *JAMA,* **170,** 197 (1959).

519. Wewalka, F., Konstitutionelle Faktoren bei Leberzirrhose, *Dtsch. Med. Wochenschr.*, **94,** 1827 (1969).

520. Widmark, E. M. P., *Die theoretischen Grundlagen und die praktische Verwendbarkeit der gerichtlich-medizinischen Alkoholbestimmung*, Urban & Schwarzenberg, Berlin-Wien, 1932.

521. Widmark, E. M. P., Die Maximalgrenzen der Alkoholkonsumption, *Biochem. Z.*, **259,** 285 (1933).

522. Wiebe, T., A. Lundquist, and P. Belfrage, Time-course of liver fat accumulation in man after a single load of ethanol, *Scand. J. Clin. Lab. Invest.*, **27,** 33 (1971).

523. Wieser, St., Zur Theorie und Klinik der Alkoholpsychosen, in *Arbeitstagung über Alkoholismus,* K. Kryspin-Exner (Ed.), Wien, 1962, p. 90.

524. Wieser, St., Alkoholismus 1940–1959, *Fortschr. Neurol. Psychiatr.*, **30,** 169 (1962).

525. Wieser, St., Alkoholismus, II: Psychiatrische und neurologische Komplikationen, *Fortschr. Neurol. Psychiatr.*, **33,** 349 (1965).

526. Wieser, St., Über das Trinkverhalten der allgemeinen Bevölkerung und Stereotype des Abstinenten und Trinkers, *Fortschr. Neurol. Psychiat.*, **36,** 485 (1968).

527. Wildhirt, E., Über die Rolle des Alkoholentzugs in der Therapie der alkoholischen Leberschäden, in *Alcohol and the Liver*, W. Gerok, K. Sickinger, and H. H. Hennekeuser (Eds.), F. K. Schattauer Verlag, Stuttgart-New York, 1971, p. 545.

528. Wilens, S. L., The relationship of chronic alcoholism to atherosclerosis, *JAMA*, **135,** 1136 (1947).

529. Wilkinson, P., D. M. O'Day, K. J. Breen, and J. G. Rankin, Bromsulphthalein metabolism in acute alcoholic liver disease, *Gut*, **9,** 707 (1968).

530. Wilkinson, P., D. M. O'Day, and J. G. Rankin, Alcohol degradation and bromsulphthalein metabolism in acute alcoholic liver disease, *Gut*, **10,** 241 (1969).

531. Wilkinson, P., J. N. Santamaria, and J. G. Rankin, Epidemiology of alcoholic cirrhosis, *Aust. Ann. Med.*, **18,** 222 (1969).

532. Wilkinson, P., J. N. Santamaria, J. G. Rankin, and D. Martin, Epidemiology of alcoholism: Social data and drinking patterns of a sample of Australian alcoholics, *Med. J. Aust.*, **1,** 1020 (1969).
533. Wirths, W., Zufuhr von Calorien aus alkoholischen Getränken ausgewählter Bevölkerungs- und Berufsschweregruppen, in *Alkohol und Coffein*, K. Lang (Ed.), Dietrich Steinkopff Verlag, Darmstadt, 1970, p. 56.
534. Wolff, P. H., Ethnic differences in alcohol sensitivity, *Science*, **175,** 449 (1972).
535. Wolfert, E., Das Wermutweindelir—eine schwere Verlaufsform des Alkoholdelirs, *Arch. Psychiat. Nervenkr. (Berlin)*, **200,** 230 (1960).
536. Wood, H. P. and E. L. Duffy, Psychological factors in alcoholic women, *Am. J. Psychiat.*, **123,** 341 (1966).
537. Wurzbacher, G., Die Alkoholfrage in soziologischer Sicht, *Kriminalbiol. Gegenwartsfr.*, **6,** 21 (1964).
538. Wynder, E. L. and I. J. Bross, A study of etiological factors in cancer of the esophagus, *Cancer*, **14,** 389 (1961).
539. Zelen, S. L., J. Fox, E. Gould, and R. W. Olsen, Sex-contingent differences between male and female alcoholics, *J. Clin. Psychol.*, **22,** 160 (1966).
540. Zimmerman, H. J., The evolution of alcoholic cirrhosis. Clinical, biochemical, and histologic correlations, *Med. Clin. North Am.*, **39,** 241 (1955).

Chapter Four

PRECLINICAL PHARMACOLOGY OF MARIHUANA

EDWARD B. TRUITT, JR., *Department of Pharmacology, The George Washington University School of Medicine, Washington, D.C.*
MONIQUE C. BRAUDE, *Center for Studies of Narcotic Addiction and Drug Abuse Studies, National Institute of Mental Health, Rockville, Maryland*

Stimulated by the unique nature of marihuana and the social impact of increasing use of the drug, accelerated research on the basic pharmacology of cannabis has been rapidly closing the gap in knowledge that formerly existed between marihuana and other drugs of abuse. Retrospectively, the major breakthrough enabling this has clearly been the isolation by column chromatography, structural elucidation and synthesis of the optically active forms of (1)-trans-delta-8- and (1)-trans-delta-9-tetrahydrocannabinol (Δ^8- and Δ^9-THC*) by Mechoulam and his collaborators (151). Further, the more facile syntheses of these compounds by Petrzilka, Taylor, Hively, or Razdan and their associates, reviewed by Neumeyer and Shagoury (168), and the availability of generous supplies of these compounds from NIMH have been a catalyst to research in this field.

So many reviews and books have appeared in the broad field of drug abuse and marihuana that it will be possible to mention here only those that are recent and deal directly or partly with the preclinical aspects. Several recent books have begun to catch up with the surge in preclinical research (15, 85, 162, 208), and a few conference monographs have now appeared (107, 176, 206, 230). In addition to reviews contained in these symposia proceedings, others may be cited that are general (22, 23, 77, 84, 145, 161, 162, 186) or specialized in various areas, such as botany (79, 200), chemistry and metabolism (6, 34, 127, 151, 153, 168, 191, 207), and pharma-

---

* According to a benzopyran-based numbering system. Also referred to as $\Delta^{1,6}$ and as Δ^1-THC in a monoterpene system, respectively.

cology (22, 105). In addition, many able reviews with extensive bibliographies are contained in the reports of various commissions and committees (7, 28, 83, 165, 225, 232). A number of cannabis bibliographies have also been compiled (74, 108, 159, 192, 229).

These reviews have reported the preclinical findings on the drug, but there has been little effort to present a critical analysis of the data. Many special problems exist in the design and conduct of successful and meaningful marihuana research. These include the marked water insolubility of most cannabinoids, difficulty in quantitating smoke administration, the biphasic nature of the temporal course of action, possible differences between THC and the complete crude drug, marked differences between acute and chronic effects, and problems associated with chronic administration of the drug such as local tissue irritation. Another unique factor not often considered in the design and interpretation of THC experiments is the possibility of an indirect mechanism of action of the drug through hydroxylated metabolites (4, 219, 220, 221). These and other considerations will be utilized in the following survey of the recent preclinical research on marihuana.

1. PHARMACEUTICS AND ROUTES OF ADMINISTRATION

A troublesome problem which often complicates and influences the quantitative outcome of cannabinoid research is the low solubility of these compounds in aqueous media. In a systematic study of various solvents and emulsifying agents it was found that sesame oil solutions (with up to 30% THC) provided the best means of administering the large oral doses required for toxicity studies (194). Stock solutions of THC in sesame oil were found to be stable for months and could be used directly for oral administration or for formulating injectables. For parenteral administration, the solubilization, microemulsification, or suspension of finely divided particles is a necessary but confounding factor (91, 220). The agents used have included various surfactants (Tween 80, Triton X-100, Pluronic F-68), solvents (ethanol, propylene glycol, dimethylsulfoxide, glycerin, and peanut, olive, or sesame oils) and suspending agents (bovine serum albumin, carboxymethyl cellulose, and gum arabic). Most of these agents may produce pharmacological actions themselves in large volumes and influence the rate of THC absorption.

The route of administration has proven to be critical in determining the time of onset, duration, and degree of cannabinoid action. Judging from toxicity studies and other quantitative data, intravenous injection yields the most rapid and potent effects and the rate of onset closely approximates that which follows smoking. Oral administration produces about one-third to one-half the intensity of effects of the same dose given I. V., and involves a delay of 30 to 60 min for attainment of maximum activity. Administration of THC by the intraperitoneal route is even less effective than oral administration (95, 103), and chronic dosage may produce severe irritation with possible behavioral consequences (134), although this effect is not always observed (185).

2. METABOLISM

Since adequate supplies of Δ^8- and Δ^9-tetrahydrocannabinols, cannabinol, cannabidiol, and other cannabinoids in purified form with ^{14}C or ^3H labels became available, the study of cannabis metabolism has been one of the most fruitful areas for the discovery of new information about the drug. This area has been the principal subject of three recent reviews (6, 127, 220). Findings in the metabolic area have included characterization and quantitation of the smoke-delivered dose, examination of pyrolysis effects on cannabinoids and other components during combustion, recognition of the rapid conversion of tetrahydrocannabinols in the liver and lung to possibly active metabolites, and the further metabolism of these to a variety of slowly excreted inactive products. The study of marihuana metabolism has been greatly assisted by the application of advanced methods of chemical analysis such as nuclear magnetic resonance, combined gas-liquid-chromatography and mass spectroscopy, and other techniques. Thus virtually the whole pattern of combustion, absorption distribution, biotransformation, and excretion has been explored to some degree, mostly since 1969.

The main form of marihuana use in the United States and in many other countries is by smoking. Recent studies have refuted the early claim that only 1 to 2% of the combusted tetrahydrocannabinol is available to the smoker (42). The amount transferred to the mainstream smoke and into the smoker varies from 14 to 60%, depending on the air flow rate, the size of the butt (roach) and thus the amount trappable there (2, 8, 49, 61a, 65, 136, 154). There are many possible explanations of the wide disparity between marihuana smoking studies, including the humidity of the plant material, particle size, packing density, cannabinoid content, air flow rate, and interval between puffs, but the burning temperature is probably the most important.

Another significant finding of recent smoke analysis studies is the recognition of pyrolysis as a means of converting the various precursor tetrahydrocannabinolic acids to THC's by decarboxylation (2, 42, 65, 154). Conversion by cyclization of cannabidiol to form additional THC has been reported by some (154) but denied as a significant factor by others (2, 42, 61a, 65). Most of these same investigators agree that there is little conversion of Δ^9- to Δ^8-THC by the smoking process.

Absorption

The poor solubility of most cannabinoids in water makes their experimental administration difficult without the use of unphysiologic vehicles or dispersing agents except for the smoking route. Rough estimates from dose-activity studies in animals and man show the intravenous route to be the most rapidly effective, closely followed by smoke inhalation (5 to 15 min), intraperitoneal [15 to 30 min, depending upon the vehicle (95)], oral (30 min to 2 hr), and finally subcutaneous (1 hr or longer). Smoke inhalation and oral administration are not economical delivery systems but are better suited to chronic use than the intravenous or intraperitoneal routes because of parenteral irritation.

Distribution

Tissue distribution and particularly brain distribution of THC's have been widely studied by radiochemical and radioautography methods (see review 220 for early references). These initial studies of distribution showed that the highest accumulations of radiolabeled drug occurred in the liver followed by concentrations greater than plasma levels in the lung, kidney, spleen, and adrenal glands. Many of these earlier studies as well as some that are recent did not differentiate unchanged ^{14}C or ^3H-THC from its hydroxylated metabolites (89, 109, 125, 146). More recent studies have recognized the rapid conversion of THC to hydroxylated metabolites and differentiated them from THC by a semiselective extraction process (70, 98, 126). One of the most striking observations from these studies has been the absence of high brain concentrations, which might be expected from a highly lipid-soluble drug. This may be due to its high rate of uptake and metabolism by the liver and the lung, but it also emphasizes the potent effect of the active metabolites directly on neuronal tissue (41, 219, 221). Another area of accumulation of the drug which appears significant is its persistence in the gastrointestinal tract, largely as a result of biliary excretion of metabolites and their reabsorption and reexcretion through the enterohepatic system (114). The drug persists in the adrenals, spleen, and body fat despite its slow accumulation in the latter reservoir. Although high chronic doses are required, some correlative toxicological evidence has been found in the form of adrenal and splenic hypoplasia (21).

Despite the relatively low initial concentrations, the drug persists in the brain as well, largely in the form of metabolites (98). The differential distribution of radioactivity within the brain shows similarities to the pattern for ^{14}C-ethanol and a predilection for the frontal cortex, cerebellar, hippocampal, amygdaloidal, and collicular areas, all of which suggest correlations with certain behavioral effects of THC (146).

In animal studies it has been found that the drug is transported across the blood-placenta barrier and it may accumulate in the fetus and the amniotic fluid (89, 103). However, probably because of a lack of enzymes for metabolic activation the concentrations found do not show a potentially dangerous degree of accumulation (89).

Biotransformation

The rapid disappearance of ^{14}C- or ^{3}H-THC and its high accumulation in the liver prompted an examination of the possible hepatic metabolism of first Δ^8-THC (10, 64) and then Δ^9-THC (4, 227) which led to the finding of the primary metabolites 11-OH- Δ^8-THC and 11-OH- Δ^9-THC, respectively. This pathway has also been shown in lung tissue with the formation of 11-OH- Δ^9-THC as well as minor amounts of unidentified metabolites (164). Further study of THC metabolism has suggested the diagram presented in Fig. 1 for the principal pathways, although it can be easily recognized that numerous yet unfound metabolites are theoretically possible.

Considerable interspecies variation exists in THC metabolism and those differences may eventually explain differences in reactivity. Early studies on ^{3}H-THC metabolism showed a pattern of higher enterohepatic concentrations of polar metabolites in the rat compared to the rabbit. In studies made *in vitro* with hepatic microsomal preparations, considerable interspecies variation has been reported in the primary metabolite. Rat liver preparations generally yield 11-hydroxy derivatives (64, 227), and these have been detected in rabbits and man. Side chain oxidations at positions 1' and 3' have been found from the metabolism of Δ^8-THC in the beagle dog liver preparations (143). Ring oxidation at positions 7 and 8 occurred for Δ^8- and Δ^9-THC, respectively, in similar fractions from squirrel monkey liver (87). Several of these compounds, with structures confirmed by synthesis, have also shown biological activity (152, 226).

Recent findings have indicated that the hydroxylations at positions 8 and 11 are both functions of microsomal monooxygenases and that *in vivo* SKF-525-A impedes the second hydroxylation step more than the first, causing an increase in the amount of 11-OH-THC in the brain (78). Δ^9-THC has a high affinity for hepatic microsomes especially from phenobarbital pretreated rats and gives a typical type I difference spectrum, support-

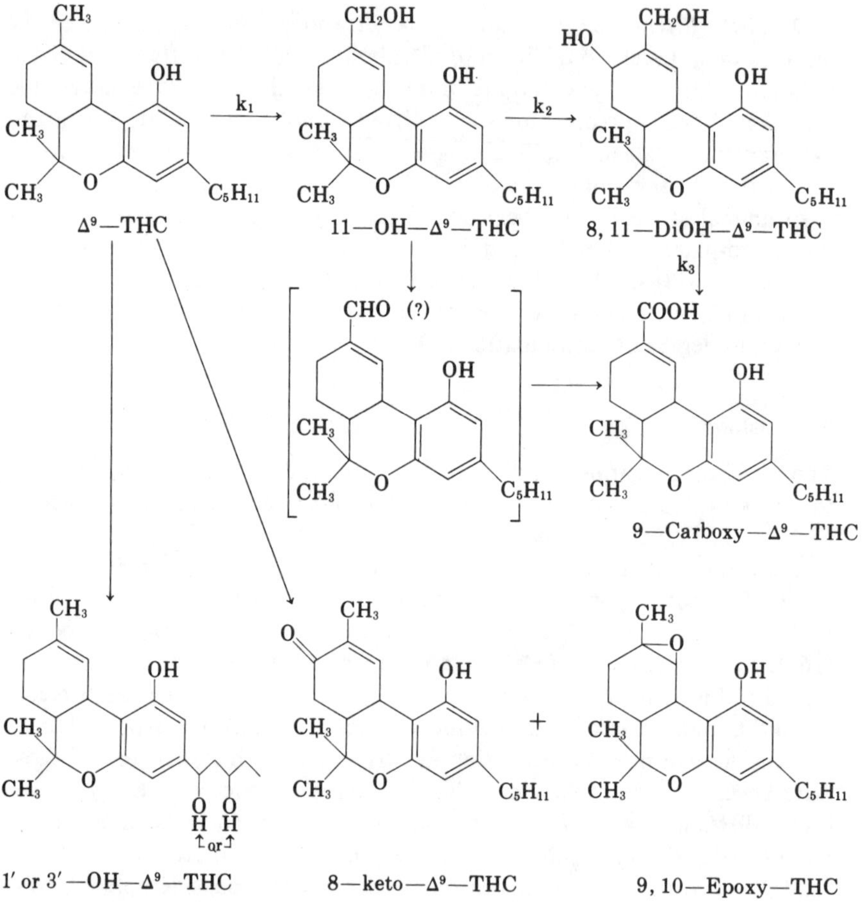

Fig. 1. Identified routes of metabolism of Δ^9-THC in various species including one postulated aldehyde intermediate (in brackets).

ing the view that it is metabolized by the hepatic mixed function oxidase system involving cytochrome P-450 (43). Large amounts of SKF-525-A ($3 \times 10^{-4} M$) can reduce 11-hydroxylation *in vitro* (26) and slow the onset of behavioral activity *in vivo* (181), but the amount needed to completely block activity by preventing 11-OH-THC formation is much greater (78). Upon the formation of dihydroxylated derivatives, Δ^8- and Δ^9-THC begin to show divergent pathways forming 7,11-dihydroxy-Δ^8-THC and 8,11-dihydroxy-Δ^9-THC derivatives, respectively. An aldehyde intermediate as shown in Fig. 1 is a logical possibility, but this has not been isolated.

Identification of the exact nature of the persistent polar metabolites appearing in the urine and feces has been difficult (3), but tentative evidence now supports the view that the isolated compounds are 9-carboxy-Δ^9-THC and its derivative with a hydroxylated side chain (27). Oxidation of the side chain without previous hydroxylation in position 11 has been shown in studies using Δ^8-THC (143) and Δ^9-THC (226). No single study has yet provided quantitative data on the relative amounts of each metabolite, but the 11-carboxy derivatives are persistent in large enough amounts to provide a possible means of detection of cannabis use.

Studies of cannabinol and cannabidiol, the other two principal cannabinoids, have shown these to be metabolized similarly to Δ^9-THC (5, 170). A study of the influence of the metabolism of these two compounds on that of simultaneously administered THC is needed because all three are present in marihuana smoke. No reports have appeared on the metabolic handling of tetrahydrocannabivarin (found only in some Asiatic strains), cannabichromene, and cannabigerol, which have slight pharmacological activity and are present in small amounts in the plasma after administration of cannabis.

Excretion

There is considerable species variation in the pattern of excretion of the cannabis metabolites, but the products are qualitatively similar. Very little unchanged THC is detectable in the urine (3, 27, 114). The long persistence of metabolites in the feces has been noted by many and attributed to recyclization through the enterohepatic system. Cannabinoids are also excreted into the saliva but have not yet been the basis of a reliable test for identification of users.

Metabolic Interactions

The implication of THC in the common pathway of hepatic microsomal monooxygenases involves the likelihood of interactions with the metabolism of many other drugs, some instances of which have already been noted (26, 43). Phenobarbital and 3-methylcholanthrene pretreatments have been shown to induce more rapid production of hydroxylated metabolites of THC in the liver (227) and lung (164), respectively. Accelerated THC metabolism by barbiturate pretreatment has been shown to reduce Δ^9-THC toxicity (137).

SKF-525-A, as reported by many investigators, can impede THC metabolism either weakly (k_2, Fig. 1) or strongly (k_1 and k_2) and thus potentiate or block THC action, respectively (56, 78, 181, 211). Although it has never been well established that ethanol interacts with microsomal enzymes, a cross-tolerance has been claimed to exist between alcohol and THC (169).

The active metabolites of two antidepressant drugs, nortriptyline and desmethylimipramine, have been shown to inhibit THC metabolism competitively *in vitro* (56). THC reciprocally interferes with microsomal metabolism of aminopyrine, hexobarbital, conjugation of estradiol, *p*-nitrophenol (56), and ethylmorphine (43). Doubtless other interactions of THC exist for which a metabolic basis cannot be advanced, and these will be discussed in a later section.

3. TOXICITY STUDIES

Irrespective of arguments concerning legalization, therapeutic utility, or mechanism of action of marihuana, the primary medical concern has been for the health and long-term safety of the user. Until recent years there had been no systematic evaluation of the possible toxicological hazards of the drug. Thus the initial priority in an overall program for examining the human health hazards of marihuana use was a preclinical toxicological evaluation of the acute and chronic risks to experimental animals.

A number of comprehensive reviews deal extensively with the problems of cannabinoid toxicity (21, 67, 68, 161, 163). However, the largest body of toxicity studies has been conducted under contracts by the National Institute of Mental Health and the results of these tests have been reported and reviewed only recently (21). A crude marihuana extract containing the alcohol-soluble, heat-decarboxylatable, and free cannabinoids has been employed in these tests to represent the mixture present in the whole plant. In addition, synthetic Δ^8- and Δ^9-THC were tested as the pure compounds. Most of these experiments have used parenteral and oral administration for acute toxicity and oral administration for chronic toxicity studies. However, it is recognized that smoke inhalation is the usual form of street use of marihuana and toxicity by this route needs comparative evaluation.

Acute Toxicity

Acute toxicity studies have been useful not only to quantitate lethality and study the mechanism of toxicity, but also to compare absorption by various routes. Several studies have reported the acute lethal doses for pure Δ^9-THC by various routes of administration (54, 184). Even by the intravenous route of administration, the ratio of lethal to pharmacologically effective dose for Δ^9-THC is large (54). This study also showed that quantitative differences in pharmacological and lethal effects may occur with the use of various suspending agents.

The recently reviewed NIMH toxicity studies have reconfirmed older observations that the acute oral toxicity of cannabinoid compounds is very low (21). Female rats are significantly more sensitive to the lethal effects (217-A) and also to the pharmacologic impairment of behavior (44). The isolation of mice in single cages also enhances Δ^9-THC toxicity (210). The acute toxicity of marihuana by smoke inhalation must be due mainly to carbon monoxide, since there is very little difference between the lethality of marihuana and that of its resin-free residue (50). In larger laboratory animals such as dogs and monkeys there is an even larger oral therapeutic index of about 1000 times the behavioral dose (21).

However, recently reported toxicity studies using a Russian hashish of unknown composition show that large doses (1.5 to 4.0 g/kg) affected the central nervous system of the dogs, leading to severe impairment of behavior and development of neurological symptoms (59, 60). These symptoms were most intense in the early days, after which their severity decreased. Morphological changes in the brain were distinguished by disorders of the vascular circulation, which were a main constituent of the histopathological process. Degenerative changes such as hydropic degeneration and karyocytolysis, which could lead to the death of the cells, were seen in the cerebral cortex, medulla oblongata, and cerebellum. The overall evaluation of histological experiments on acute *cannabis* resin poisoning is that the pathological process is of the nature of toxic encephalopathy. Analysis of EKGs also showed considerable and varied cardiovascular disturbance. Electrocardiographic and hemodynamic shifts which were observed during the first 1 to 2 hours—tachycardia, bradycardia, pronounced sinus arrythmia, symptoms of coronary insufficiencies, and reduced arterial pressure—were reportedly the results of damage to the vegetative centers and not to a direct toxic effect on the myocardium. Pathological changes were also observed in the liver, kidneys, and adrenal glands. Clinical chemistry showed a decrease in red blood cells and an increase in leucocytes. Blood sugar, cholinesterase activity, and blood plasma protein levels rose and fell at different times.

Although the authors mention that these effects are similar to those of Indian *cannabis* and that their results are in basic agreement with the much older findings of Chopra and Loewe, it is difficult to compare these findings with those of studies using American marihuana, since no analytical determination of the potency of the resin was made. Furthermore, the vehicle in which the resin was given is not mentioned and there do not seem to be any controls included in the experimental design of these studies.

Chronic Toxicity

The most striking characteristic of chronic marihuana toxicity studies has been the behavioral reversal from sedation to hyperactivity and aggressiveness, seen at psychoactive dose levels (10 to 50 mg/kg daily) in normally fed rats receiving Δ^9-THC orally for as short a period as one month (21). CNS depression seen in the first week of treatment was reduced as tolerance developed. With continued dosing, animals became irritable, hypersensitive, hyperactive, and exhibited hypnotic trances. Irritability and fighting occurred in the third week and the intensity of aggression was associated with the emergence of a dominant animal in each cage. Territorial aggression was manifested predominantly in male rats and was more apparent at 10 mg/kg than 50 mg/kg, probably due to the continuing tranquilizing effect of the higher dose. Fighting could become so severe that the animals had to be placed in separate single cages to avoid further wounding of their cagemates. A similar increase in aggressiveness has previously been reported (31) in animals that were food-deprived. As the hyperirritability increased over time, tremors and later clonic convulsions occurred in increasing numbers of animals in a dose related manner after at least 4 to 5 weeks of daily administration.

Initial weight losses and significant decrease in the rate of weight gain have been reported by many authors. The peak for these effects occurs within 2 to 8 days after the first administration. After a week, the animals resume gaining weight but at a lower rate than control groups. This effect on body weight gain has been correlated by some with a decrease in food consumption (134). However, in the NIMH experiments using higher dose levels, growth in all treated groups was persistently decreased (30 to 130%) by the three compounds despite an increased consumption of food after day 50 and of water at the end of the study. Abdominal fat stores were also depleted. Drug-related hypothermia and bradypnea were prevalent. There was evidence of cumulative toxicity during the first days of the study, but virtually all deaths occurred during the first 36 to 72 hours after initial treatment. A consistently higher incidence of mortalities occurred in females than in males. Hematological parameters were usually normal except for mild leukopenia, increased SGOT, and decreased coagulation time. Toxicity, which was similar for Δ^9-THC, Δ^8-THC, and a marihuana extract, suggested a prominent effect on endocrine systems. At autopsy, changes in organ weights showed decreases for uterus, prostate, ovary, and spleen and increases in adrenals. Histopathological changes observed included hypocellularity of bone marrow and spleen, and vacuolization and hypertrophy of the adrenal cortex (165).

In monkeys, the patterns of behavioral and organic changes were similar but not as severe as those seen in rats. Some tolerance to depression followed by hyperactivity was noted, but no increase in aggressiveness or presence of seizures were seen.

In interpreting the results of these chronic toxicity data, one must remember that the doses administered, although smaller than in acute studies, are still larger than the psychoactive human doses. For instance, the oral dose of marihuana which produces psychoactive effects in man varies from 200 to 500 μg/kg. Thus a 10 mg/kg dose in animals is about 20 to 100 times greater than the effective human dose.

Toxicity studies using parenteral routes of administration were usually limited to 28 to 30 days, and those performed by the oral route continued for 119 days. Two species, rats and monkeys, were used. Two NIMH-sponsored toxicity studies were performed using parenteral routes of administration. A 28-day study was made in monkeys giving Δ^9-THC intravenously. Another 28-day study was performed in rabbits, using the subcutaneous route of administration.

A subacute 28-day i.v. study was carried out in groups of rhesus monkeys (two males and two females per group) at doses of 1, 5, 15, and 45 mg/kg. The Δ^9-THC was suspended by sonication at a concentration of 40 mg/ml in 13% sesame oil and 1.0% Tween 80 in saline. Mortalities occurred only in the group treated with 45 mg/(kg/day); two out of four animals in this group succumbed to treatment on days 8 and 19 as a result of acute hemorrhagic pneumonia. Behavioral and clinical effects included lethargy, huddled posture, bradypnea, hypothermia, bradycardia, weight loss, anorexia, constipation, anemia, and increased BSP retention. The duration of these effects was extended by multiple treatments, but tolerance eventually developed. The delayed onset of mortalities, indicative of cumulative toxicity, and appearance of edema, ulceration, and fibrosis at injection sites in the 28-day study were the major toxicological differences between effects produced by single and 28 daily treatments. No ulceration or fibrosis was seen at injection sites in control monkeys receiving only the vehicle.

Oxygen uptake measurements on slices of cerebral cortex, midbrain, medulla, cerebellum, and lungs by conventional Warburg manometry showed that endogenous respiration increased 16 to 30% in the brain cortex from animals receiving doses above 5 mg/kg. No change occurred in the medulla, and an apparent decline in endogenous lung respiration was not significant. Exogenous succinate consistently stimulated oxygen uptake, more so for tissues with low endogenous respiration, indicating no impairment of oxidative capacity. This alteration in oxygen uptake was only related to chronic intoxication with high doses of THC. This study also confirmed an earlier report that chronic parenteral administration of Δ^9-

THC, either by the intravenous or the subcutaneous route, produce edema, ulceration, and fibrosis at the injection site, due to the caustic properties of cannabinoids (21, 217).

An irritation study was performed in rabbits to evaluate the effect of subcutaneous administration of Δ^9-THC. Groups of three New Zealand albino rabbits were injected subcutaneously for 28 days with isotonic saline, sesame oil, and 15.9, 45.0, and 153.4 mg/kg of Δ^9-THC, respectively, dissolved in sesame oil. The volume of injection was kept constant at 0.6 ml/kg for all formulations. The sites of injection were assessed daily for signs of erythema, edema, vesiculation, nodule formulation, and suppurative processes. Body weights were taken daily. At necropsy, animals were exsanguinated by cardiac puncture and the serum used for clinical chemistry and hematological examination. Livers were weighed and a biopsy used for determination of liver glycogen. Rabbits receiving Δ^9-THC displayed a dose related transient erythema, a progressively worsening focal edema, and persistent formation of nodules at the site of injection in high-dosed animals. The nodules were granulomatous with an oily core and exhibited liquefaction necrosis. It was also found that body weight, liver weight, and liver glycogen declined in a dose-related manner.

Since this route of administration was the most convenient in rodents, the intraperitoneal route was used extensively by the first investigators for acute administration of cannabinoids. Although measurable pharmacological and behavioral effects do occur after intraperitoneal administration of relatively large doses, autoradiographic studies have shown that radiolabeled Δ^9-THC administered intraperitoneally remains in the abdominal cavity, with little absorption and distribution to other tissues such as the central nervous system, while the same dose given intravenously or by inhalation was distributed rapidly throughout the body (95). The irritating properties of the Δ^9-THC when given intraperitoneally are still under debate. In a chronic study, reported recently, the authors did not observe an inflammatory response after administration of 30 daily doses of Δ^9-THC (185). In this study, the Δ^9-THC in doses ranging from 3 to 30 mg/kg was suspended in water, and injections were made at six different locations. The Δ^9-THC was probably well absorbed, as the animals showed typical signs of cannabinoid effects. Following each day's injection, the animals became ataxic, lacrimated, had diarrhea, and exhibited both depression and hyperexcitability. During the last days of this study, the hyperexcitability increased. At autopsy, there was no evidence of an inflammatory response. However, others, using the same or higher dose levels, reported chronic peritonitis in cannabinoid-treated animals (134).

Very recently, toxic effects of marihuana tar in the mouse have been found. Confiscated marihuana was rolled into cigarettes and artificially puffed in a smoking machine. The smoke was collected and condensed, producing a tar which was used for painting the skin of mice. A positive control group receiving benzo[α]pyrene, a known carcinogen, was included in the experimental design. Marihuana tar, like benzo[α]pyrene or cigarette smoke condensate in equal concentrations produced complete metaplasia of all sebaceous glands in the painted mouse skin. The authors conclude that "since metaplasia of all sebaceous glands in the target area correlates well with carcinogenicity, it may be an indication that Cannabis tar will prove to be carcinogenic" (48). These findings confirm an earlier report (132) and indicate that smoking crude marihuana produces tar which, like that of tobacco and other plant materials, can be demonstrated to be carcinogenic by this type of technique. This is potentially important for long-term toxicity in heavy smokers of cannabis, since a recent study (61a) indicated that marihuana smoke contained 50% more tar than smoke from a high-tar brand of tobacco cigarettes, when expressed per gram of starting material. On the other hand, a comparative evaluation of the carcinogenic potential of the major cannabinoids of marihuana in another test system (transformation of cultures of rat embryo cells by combined action of murine leukemia virus and cannabinoids) showed that these compounds, in contrast to the tar, have a weak oncogenic activity compared to that of methylcholanthrene (190).

Special Toxicity Studies

Perinatal Studies

Possible effects of marihuana on the fetus or newborn infant have led to conflicting results, with some authors reporting reduced fertility (158), stunting, fetal resorptions, or malformations after administration of marihuana extracts by various routes (75, 76, 89, 179, 180). Others, however, using dose levels ranging from 0.01 to 200 mg/kg for Δ^9-THC, 20 to 40 mg/kg for Δ^8-THC, and 200 to 300 mg/kg of a marihuana extract containing 17.1% Δ^9-THC, in a large number of experiments failed to find any abnormalities in offspring (173). In these studies, cannabinoids were dissolved in various solvents and administered at different times of gestation to rats and hamsters in attempts to replicate closely the experimental conditions of previously reported studies. However, the results were different. The only adverse effect noted was that, at high dose levels of 100 mg/kg and above, postnatal mortality was high in all groups as compared to controls. A cross-fostering experiment demonstrated that agalactia (i.e., lack of milk production in the mother) was primarily responsible for the death of pups. Some of the offspring that survived were bred; the data indicated that there was no fertility impairment in the F_1 and F_2 generations and no development of abnormalities in their offspring. Unfortunately, the drug was given by subcutaneous injection, which has been shown to be a rather poor route for repeated administration of cannabinoids in view of their caustic properties.

Using a different route and specie (mice), another study showed that at a high dose level of 200 mg/kg, i.p. (about half of the LD_{50} by that route), Δ^9-THC significantly increase fetal resorptions in mice, especially if administered during early organogenesis, on days 8 and 9 of gestation. The developing organism appears to be less sensitive to toxic effects of Δ^9-THC during late organogenesis or the period of fetal maturation (89). In the same study, Δ^9-THC also significantly reduced the body weight of the surviving fetuses, and this effect was most pronounced when the drug was administered between days 10 and 13.

In view of these conflicting reports, in 1972 the National Institute of Mental Health initiated a comprehensive study of the effects of Δ^9-THC and a crude marihuana extract in two species (rats and rabbits) to determine the teratogenic potential as well as the effects of these compounds given orally on reproductive functions and on the newborn. In these studies, animals received doses of 0.5 to 50 mg/kg, lower than those indicated in most of the previous studies but more comparable to human usage (1 to 100 times human dose). These doses produced dose-related behavioral effects but were nontoxic and did not markedly affect the body weight gain of the animals. In this type of study, this is an important consideration so that effects on reproduction and fetal development can be differentiated from general toxic effects. The results were as follows: mating and fertility indices as well as the number of implantation sites, live fetuses, and live pups were similar in control and treatment groups. Examinations of external, internal, and skeletal development disclosed no effects that could be related to prenatal exposure of fetuses to the cannabinoids (88, 110).

In summary, the NIMH studies confirm the previous report (173) that, at doses within and above human range, synthetic or natural marihuana does not appear to have serious deleterious effects during pregnancy on the fetus or the mother, or, after birth, on the newborn.

4. PHARMACOLOGIC ACTIONS

Central Nervous System Effects

The pharmacologic effects of marihuana produce an unusual pattern of central nervous system changes in animals and man that is unique among existing drugs. The temporal course of this action is also an important consideration because early, peak, and late effects differ considerably from each other. In the rat, Δ^9-THC produces the same pattern of activity as marihuana extracts (86) or smoke (104) and in turn 11-OH-THC reproduces the activity of THC (41, 219, 221). After an initial short period of hyperactivity, rat behavior is characterized by intermittent periods of arrested attention which become increasingly longer until a continuous trancelike state, variously labeled as catalepsy or catatonia, ensues. At the same time, large doses produce marked sensitivity to startle stimuli and often the animal will respond with inordinately long vocalization to almost any stimulus. Coordination, especially of the hind legs, is impaired. Another effect seen during early intoxication in the rat is an aggressive tendency to bite abnormally at projected objects and failure to release. The animal's body becomes flattened against the cage bottom and other neurological impairments appear at higher doses. Other animals exhibit similar behavioral changes, which may be more complex in higher species.

It is unlikely that any single simple neuropharmacologic effect may explain these behavioral changes. Nevertheless, many attempts have been made to provide the neurochemical, neuroendocrine, neurophysiological, and behavioral correlates for an explanation.

Neurochemical Effects

Because of the marked behavioral and emotional effects of marihuana it was logical for many early investigators to probe the action of crude marihuana extracts with studies of changes in the biogenic amine levels of the brain. These studies have been summarized in a number of reviews (22, 222). While completely consistent results have not been obtained because of the multiplicity of variables in methods, drugs, doses, and time of analysis, a general pattern can be observed. Substantial doses (generally larger than those producing threshold effects on behavior) produce a rise in brain serotonin (5-HT) and a slight but nonsignificant decrease in norepinephrine (NE) levels (99). The rise in 5-HT level is not the result of increased synthesis or decreased breakdown but could be explained by increased stability of the vesicular membrane (212, 213). Inhibition of 5-HT uptake into brain synatosomes can be demonstrated, but it is not a potent action of THC (212). A simultaneous increase in the amount of 5-hydroxyindoleacetic acid can be demonstrated with a large single dose of THC (100 mg/kg) or by moderate-sized doses for 7 days (97, 174). Although significant effects of THC can be demonstrated with these larger doses, no changes were found at a dose level of 1 mg/kg, which still produces distinct behavioral effects (73).

Despite the equivocal changes in NE levels demonstrated by several investigators, significant changes can be measured by using turnover analysis. These results have differed according to the methods used for turnover analysis, the dose of Δ^9-THC used, and the period selected after THC administration for estimation of the rate effect. Both by ^{3}H-tryosine conversion and ^{3}H-NE disappearance methods, the rate of NE turnover is accelerated at 2 to 3 hr after THC (72, 133, 199).

However, in the THC-pretreated rats the earliest effects seen are increased uptake and retention of NE by neurons and diminished production of the metabolite normetanephrine (222, 223). This effect is most strikingly seen in histochemical studies of hypothalamic neurons which show intense fluorescence in hashish-treated animals (72, 157). The metabolite, 11-hydroxy-THC, also shows the same effect as THC in causing early retention of intracisternally delivered ^{3}H-NE, but its effect is more prompt and shorter in duration than for THC (222, 223). It may be tentatively concluded that THC causes a mixed effect on adrenergic neurons. An early increase in NE uptake and diminished normetanephrine formation is then followed by a stimulation of NE turnover, possibly by means of an increased activity of tyrosine hydroxylase since dopamine turnover is accelerated also (72, 133).

Neuropharmacological and EEG Effects

The neurophysiological and neuropharmacological effects of marihuana in various species have been extensively investigated in the last few years. Results of some studies are presented in Table 1.

Evaluation of effects reported in the different studies is, as usual, difficult since various dose levels, routes, and experimental conditions were used. When one considers, however, the results obtained by the i.v. route, a typical pattern of marihuana effects on the EEG seems to emerge. It appears to consist of a triphasic EEG response characterized by an early stimulation and increase in arousal, then depression shown as cortical synchronization simultaneous with or followed by high-voltage spiking activity (201). Cortically, the effect seems to be more intense in the frontal than in the posterior areas. Subcortically, the cannabinoids produce definite changes in the "old brain" areas. In the hippocampus, changes in rhythm (128, 40), epileptiform spikes and slow waves (19, 128, 139), and fast high-amplitude spindles (40,100) have been reported. Spindles were also seen in the amygdala and hypothalamus (100). The effect of cannabinoids on the septal region is mixed, with stimulation occurring sometimes (fast spindling activity) and depression at other times (slowing with sharp waves) (40, 93). The marked effect of the cannabinoids on these areas is not surprising in view of the findings by autoradiography of the distribution of labeled cannabinoids in the monkey brain, that high concentrations of Δ^9-THC or its metabolites occur in the amygdala and hippocampus (146).

In rodents, Δ^8-THC produces the same effects as Δ^9-THC (12), but in the cat distinct differences have been found with Δ^8-THC producing EEG depression rather than activation as seen with Δ^9-THC (201).

Repeated daily administration led to development of some tolerance to the EEG changes in voltage but not to the spikelike activity (128, 187, 188). Although this spikelike activity has been a consistent finding in most studies, there has been no report of seizure activity after *acute administraion* of cannabinoids, even at high dose levels. It has even been shown (113) that small doses of 5 to 160 µg/kg of Δ^9-THC, which produce changes in spectral power density distribution of resting EEG patterns in the baboon, can block photomyoclonic evoked seizures. This is consistent with the findings of anticonvulsant effect of the cannabinoids (214).

In an attempt to understand the mechanism of action of marihuana in producing changes in sensory perception, a study was made of the effects of Δ^9- and Δ^8-THC on the responsiveness of the polysensory areas of the cortex (19). The authors stimulated the primary somatosensory cortex at first in the *cerveau isolé* squirrel monkey, then in further experiments, in an *encéphale isolé* preparation. Responses were recorded in the frontal and parietal lobes. In the *cerveau isolé* preparation, THC, like pentobarbital, increased the amplitude of the responses at low doses and decreased them at higher doses, reflecting a sedative action of THC. However, unlike pentobarbital, THC did not markedly reduce the facilitation seen in control recovery cycles. In the *encéphale isolé* preparation, the early response complex similar to that seen in the *cerveau isolé* preparation was followed by a later response. In contrast to sedative drugs like ethanol and pentobarbital, in this preparation the cannabinoids increased the amplitudes of early responses at all dose levels tested. An even more striking differential effect of the cannabinoids was observed on the late responses. Both Δ^9-THC and Δ^8-THC caused a dose-dependent increase in the late responses, followed by rhythmic activity, whereas all doses of pentobarbital and ethanol tested depressed the late responses.

It is suggested that these differential effects of the cannabinoids on the polysensory cortical areas may underlie the distortions of sensory perception or time estimation caused in humans by marihuana smoking and may also be implicated in the hyperreactivity to sensory stimuli reported in experimental animals after THC administration (20). Cannabis extract, THC, and a synthetic congener, Synhexyl, abolish the linguomandibular reflex in the dog even after atropine administration (196). In a comparable dose range, chlorpromazine produces the same effect, which can be antago-

TABLE 1 EFFECTS OF CANNABINOIDS ON THE EEG

Reference	Compound Studied	Species	Route and Dose (mg/kg)	Results
12	Racemic Δ^8 and Δ^9-THC	Rabbit	i.v.—8.0	Restlessness, decreased cortical arousal threshold to RF stimulation, EEG activation
128	Δ^9-THC, Δ^8-THC, CBD	Rabbit	i.v.—0.5–10.0	Suppression of hippocampal theta rhythm. Production of neocortical high voltage spikes and waves
16, 17	Cannabis extract	Rabbit	i.p.—15–30	Neocortical stimulation, then depression. Appearance of high voltage sharp waves at recovery
121	Cannabis tincture 1:10	Rabbit	i.v.—0.1 ml/kg	Depression of neocortical areas as shown by decreased responses to auditory and visual stimuli
71	Δ^9-THC	Rabbit	i.v.—0.1–2.0	EEG synchronization—slow waves, high amplitude in delta band
187, 188	Cannabis extract	Rat	i.v.—1.25–2.5 i.p.—20.0 p.o.—10.0–40.0 p.o.—20.0 (C)^a 55 days	Decrease in integrated voltage but tolerance develops to that effect after 5–12 doses. High-voltage spindlelike activity after acute and chronic treatment. No tolerance to that effect. Rebound in voltage after stop of chronic treatment
40	Δ^9-THC Cannabis extract	Rat Rat	p.o.—20.0–30.0 i.v.—1.2	Decrease in frequency and increase in magnitude of power spectrum of dorsal septem and hippocampus

160	Δ^9-THC	Rat	i.p.—5.0–10.0 (C)[a] 20 days	Decreased paradoxical and slow wave sleep and increased in wakefulness in non-deprived rats. Tolerance to this develops after 2 days
140	Cannabis extract	Rat	i.p.—10.0 (C-8 days)[a]	Polyspike discharges in awake and REM states after both acute and chronic administration
18	Δ^8-THC Δ^9-THC DMHP	Rat Rat Cat	i.p.—2.5 and 5.0 i.p.—Dose? i.v.—0.2	Increase in cortical arousal threshold to RF stimulation, decrease in EEG and behavioral arousal
100	Δ^9-THC	Cat (un-anesth.)	i.p.—0.5–4.0	Hypersynchrony with concomitant bizarre behavior followed by high-voltage activity and fast high-amplitude spindles from amygdala, hypothalamus, hippocampus
228	Δ^8-THC	Cat	i.v.—1.0 i.p.—10.0–20.0	Sedation, slow-wave sleep, sleeping posture. Polyphasic spiking both during control periods and following THC
201	Δ^9-THC Δ^8-THC	Cat	i.v.—2.0–20.0	Increase in reticular arousal threshold. Triphasic EEG response with Δ^9-THC marked arousal pattern, cortical synchronization, high-voltage spiking activity. With Δ^8-THC, EEG depression instead of activation
57	DMHP MOP Δ^9-THC	Dog Monkey	i.v.—0.05–1.0 i.v.—0.5–1.0 i.v.—0.5–1.0	Slow wave bursts changed to activation by afferent stimulation. High-voltage spikelike slow waves in more frontal portions antagonized by amphetamines.

TABLE I (Continued)

Reference	compound Studied	Species	Route and Dose (mg/kg)	Results
19, 20	Δ^8-THC Δ^9-THC	Squirrel monkeys	i.v.—0.25–1.5 (cumulative)	Dose-dependent reduction of high-frequency activity in the electrocorticogram replaced at first by spikes and then by both slow waves and spikes, quite different from the dose-dependent flattening and spindling at intermediate doses produced by pentobarbital
93	Marihuana	Monkeys	Smoking—Dose?	Mixed effect on septal region, either fast spindling or slowing with some sharp waves
139	Δ^9-THC	Monkeys	i.v.—0.05–12.8	Desynchronization in cortical areas, epileptoform slow waves in hippocampus, amygdala and superior cerebellar peduncul followed by rhythmic bursts
113	Δ^9-THC	Baboons	i.v.—0.005–0.16 (C-6 days)[a]	Changes in spectral power density distribution and blocking of photomyoclonic seizures. Some tolerance to the latter effect after six successive daily doses

[a] Chronic study.

nized by strychnine (196). Others, after administering DMHP to cats, concluded that this effect was exerted in the forebrain area, because facilitation of the linguomandibular reflex resulting from forebrain stimulation was also depressed (18). Cannabinoids were also found to depress the presynaptic potential in the trigeminal nerve, although the tibialis nerve was unaffected, suggesting a specific central depressant action (123).

Neuroendocrine Effects

Animal studies have now identified at least three possible neuroendocrine effects of THC on pituitary-controlled functions. However, confirmation of these actions has not been clearly evident in chronic marihuana smokers, except for anecdotal reports of menstrual dysfunction. Large doses of THC cause a stresslike depletion of adrenal ascorbic acid in rats (52) and this has been confirmed at lower doses by measurement of plasma corticosterone levels (118). However, in humans a corresponding elevation of plasma cortisol levels was not found in marihuana smokers, unless an overt panic reaction occurred (101).

An opposite inhibitory influence by THC has been demonstrated in the hypothalamic mechanisms regulating TSH (130) and LH secretion (138). The inhibition of TSH secretion reduces I^{131} release from the thyroid gland; studies in brain-lesioned animals suggest a hypothalamic site of action, which resembles that of morphine (130). Relatively small doses of THC (1 to 10 mg/kg) have a temporary depressing effect on LH levels measured in the rat by radioimmunoassay and, paradoxically, also antagonize similar depression caused by low doses of estrogen (138). In view of the interference by THC with biogenic amine function in the hypothalamus, it is not surprising that the drug may affect various pituitary hormone-releasing factors in this area. These data as well as adverse effects which have been shown on the adrenals and gonads in long-term, high-dose toxicity studies should prompt a more thorough examination of possible neuroendocrine irregularities in heavy marihuana smokers.

Behavioral Effects

Gross Observational Effects. The behavioral effects of marihuana are sufficiently distinctive that early investigators were perhaps justified in employing simple observational measurements such as descriptions of open-field behavior and the use of semiquantitative scale ratings. These methods continue to be the most sensitive available for detecting the effects of lower doses of THC, although they are more subjectively variable than other quantitative procedures. Many of the early investigations using descriptive techniques have been summarized (67, 68, 91). Semiquantitative scale ratings for spontaneous and evoked behavior were able to reveal the similarities in potency and behavioral profile between 11-OH- Δ^8-THC and its precursor in the rat (219), and between 11-OH- Δ^9-THC and its precursor in the mouse (41). In a similar set of scaled tasks it was found that female rats were more sensitive to THC effects (44). The open-field behavior of rats receiving THC shows greatest sensitivity in grooming, sniffing, defecation, and ambulation, but the direction of effect depends on the time after drug administration (58, 141).

Operant Behavior. Modern study of the behavioral effects of marihuana has been greatly facilitated by the application of a variety of standard operant tests to problems such as the effects of the drug on learning, eating, memory, and especially timing behavior. These methods can be divided into two main categories, responses to negative reinforcers such as shock or fear (avoidance or conditioned emotional responses) and responses to positive reinforcers such as food and water. Within these schedules, the effects of marihuana have been examined on acquisition (learning), tolerance, and retention or extinction (memory) and other parameters such as state-dependent learning.

1. Negative Reinforcement Studies. Conflicting results have been obtained so far from studies using negative types of reinforcement to produce either a conditioned avoidance response (CAR) or conditioned emotional response (CER). This may be due in part to differences in species, route of administration, doses, and experimental design. Most studies have been performed in rodents (9, 16, 17, 57, 80, 82, 94, 106, 175, 188, 189, 213); a few have used other species such as squirrel monkeys (9, 198), cats (166) and rhesus monkeys (92, 117). The effects of THC on avoidance behavior have not been consistent between these two species since the CAR is abolished in rats (9, 86, 94, 189, 231), whereas in the monkey it may be enhanced (117, 198) or suppressed (9). As noted with other behavioral effects of THC, female rats are more sensitive than males to CAR disruption (175). The drug retards both the learning (82, 94, 171) and unlearning (extinction) of conditioned responses (80, 106). When rats were trained under the influence of Δ^9-THC no transfer of the avoidance occurred to the nondrugged state (94). The pattern of effects on avoidance responding behavior resembled that produced by other hallucinogens (231). No loss of conditioned alimentary responses was produced by a small single dose of Δ^9-THC (166).

2. Positive Reinforcement Studies. Studies using food or water rewards for behavioral testing with marihuana have generally been more complex and sensitive than avoidance studies. Various schedules have been used and differential reinforcement of a low rate of response (DRL) has been particularly sensitive in chimpanzees to low doses comparable to the human psychoactive range (62). In addition, both stimulatory and depressant effects can be demonstrated by this pattern of reinforcement. The DRL response schedule has been employed to show that effects of synthetic Δ^9-THC are the same as those of a mixed distillate of cannabinoids from marihuana (63). This conclusion is also supported by a study in which rats were trained to respond specifically by discriminating their type of response depending upon the presence or absence of marihuana-like effects (119).

Low doses of Δ^9-THC also disrupted timing behavior (46, 47, 69) impaired recent memory (233), caused taste aversion to saccharin solutions (61), and altered auditory (116) or visual discrimination (66, 202, 203). The drug altered the social interaction between a bar-pressing and a nonworking rat (142). An operant behavioral task was employed to demonstrate the possible activity of a metabolite of Δ^9-THC (181). Some evidence of an anticholinergiclike activity of THC has been obtained from mouse behavioral studies (24).

Behavioral Tolerance Studies. Despite the lack of clearcut measurements of the development of tolerance in humans, there appears to be adequate demonstration of this characteristic in animals (reviewed in ref. 148). Decreasing effects of THC have been demonstrated in pigeons (14, 147, 149), rats (25, 30, 205), and dogs (53). The development of tolerance is quite rapid (6 to 10 doses) and persists for a considerable time, possibly owing to release of THC and metabolites from lipoidal tissues (38, 39, 55, 150). Nevertheless, no significant differences have been found in the distribution or metabolism of THC in tolerant and nontolerant animals (55, 150). Cross-tolerance to other active cannabinoids such as Δ^8-THC occurs (148, 149) and behavioral evidence for cross-tolerance to ethanol has been demonstrated (169). As behavioral tolerance develops to depressant effects of THC, some stimulant characteristics become unmasked and avoidance performance may be enhanced (160, 187).

Aggression. Popular interest in the speculated connections between marihuana use and aggressive criminal behavior has stimulated a large number of experimental tests of such a relationship in animals. Although the diverse results showing both increases and reduction in aggressive behavior at first appear contradictory, they now can be explained more rationally.

Single doses of cannabis extracts or THC have been shown to inhibit isolation-induced fighting behavior in mice (195, 197) and fights attributable to intermale dominance in small-sized mouse groups (204). Predatory attacks by rats on frogs or turtles are also attenuated by THC (111, 112, 144), as is the spontaneous aggressive behavior of the Siamese fighting fish, *Betta splendens* (81). However, chronic treatment may produce muricidal activity (224).

In the case of fighting elicited by foot shock, different results have been reported depending on the type of cannabinoids and methods employed. When graded intensities of shock were used, a sensitization to fighting has been reported for very low doses of a concentrated marihuana extract equivalent to (0.25 to 0.50 mg/kg of Δ^9-THC) and attenuation of fighting occurred with higher doses (>1.0 mg/kg) (29). However, the sensitization disappeared if the rats were familiarized with the test situation (29). If a fixed intensity of shock was given producing fighting in 50% of cases, no inhibition of aggressiveness was seen after doses of up to 6.4 mg/kg of pure Δ^9-THC intraperitoneally (135). Thus the conclusion seems evident that single doses of marihuana can attenuate most forms of aggressive behavior but that considerable variation in effectiveness occurs with different motivations and methodology.

In the case of chronic marihuana studies, in somewhat higher doses (equivalent to 5 to 10 mg/kg of Δ^9-THC) aggressiveness is evoked by repeated administration with or without starvation (21, 31, 171) or by morphine withdrawal (32). It is potentiated by cold stress (33) and by either serotonin depletion through *p*-chlorophenylalanine or by an increase in catecholamines after DOPA administration (167). Fighting has also occurred among grouped animals during chronic toxicity testing after several weeks at higher doses (25 to 50 mg/kg, Δ^9-THC) (218). This type of aggressive action may be relevant to long-term high consumption of marihuana but clearly requires additional stresses for faster development. It appears temporally correlated with the onset of tolerance to the sedative-depressant effects of THC, as discussed in the following section.

Interactions with Other CNS Drugs

Although THC and other cannabinoids may interact with certain barbiturates through their mutual hepatic metabolism, they may also influence the action of other CNS agents where a metabolic mechanism is less apparent. Barbital is not appreciably metabolized in the liver and yet this barbiturate is potentiated in its hypnotic effect by Δ^9-THC (211). However, mouse sleeping time following diethyl ether is not increased and this has been interpreted to suggest primarily a metabolic interaction (178). The prolongation of thiopental sleeping time follows both single and repeated large doses of THC if sufficient time for clearance of the active cannabinoid metabolites from the rabbits is allowed (177). Ethanol enhances the sleeping time of THC and also the combination of THC and a barbiturate (182). Thus the central sedative action of THC may synergize other CNS depressants.

The potentiation of amphetamine locomotor activity by THC (67, 183) is more difficult to explain on either a metabolic or neural interaction basis. Moreover, other stimulants such as caffeine and methamphetamine also increase or extend the duration of increased activity by THC (183). It is not clear whether this potentiation is related to the increased catecholamine turnover found 2 to 3 hr after THC doses (133, 199) or to some of the early THC effects of sensory afferent enhancement such as those shown by the startle reaction.

Possible Therapeutic Applications

Several of the CNS effects of THC have been considered for their possible therapeutic application, but none has received a critical comparison with prototype therapeutic drugs of the same class. The analgesic action of THC is, however, unique and not easily compared to that of morphine, since the effect varies in different tests of analgesia (54). The anticonvulsant effect of THC has also been examined and found to resemble that of diphenylhydantoin in pattern (113, 214). An interesting effect of marihuana in decreasing intraocular pressure has also been recently reported which may be of value in the treatment of glaucoma (68a).

Cardiovascular Effects

Although the effects of THC on the cardiovascular system do not necessarily reflect a primary action, they may contribute to the afferent sensory characteristics of the marihuana experience. Additionally, in cases of overdosage, these actions may become more important since their understanding may lead to more rational treatment of acute intoxication. The general cardiovascular observations for the effects of THC on animals have been reviewed in several of the early symposia (67, 90, 91). When injected intravenously into most laboratory animals, Δ^9-THC produces dose-related cardiac slowing and a fall in the systolic and diastolic pressures. This, unfortunately, is different from the human response, in which a tachycardia is one of the best clinical guides to severity of intoxication (104). The mechanism of this action is complex and is not dependent on the fact that most laboratory animals are studied while anesthetized; it occurs in conscious animals as well (122). The animal bradycardia is central in origin, is mediated vagally, and is partially responsible for the hypotension. However, it is only partially blocked by atropine and requires vagotomy or C-1 spinal transection for full attenuation (35, 122, 155, 156). The central locus of the THC depressor effect in laboratory animals has not been identified but is most likely in the hypothalamus (102) and involves depression of sympathetic cardiac and vascular efferent neural tone (172). No direct depressor effects of THC have been shown on the isolated myocardium (67), although the active metabolite, 11-OH-THC, has not yet been tested to rule out this possibility, nor have changes in cardiac catecholamine levels or uptake been associated with the effect of THC on heart rate (133). Some of the hypotensive action arises from peripheral vasodepression, as shown in isolated perfused limb studies (51).

The effects of chronic marihuana use on the cardiovascular system deserve equal or greater attention in comparison to those of single doses as a possible health hazard. The development of tolerance to THC makes the choice of dosage for a chronic study difficult. Nevertheless, chronic administration of marihuana smoke to rats for 10 min a day produced a significant hypotension in 5 to 6 weeks (96). With exponentially increasing doses in dogs, the initial bradycardiac response changed to tachycardia after the dose was increased to 16 mg/kg i.v., but there was no significant change in blood pressure (53). Certainly many more detailed examinations of chronic cardiovascular changes are needed before the consequences of repeated smoking of marihuana or THC use can be fully evaluated.

The hypotensive effects of Δ^9-THC, and especially that of the dimethylheptyl derivative of $\Delta^6(10)$-THC, suggest a possible application in the treatment of hypertension. Studies in genetically and artificially hypertensive rats show increased sensitivity to this hypotensive effect (13). The therapeutic potential of these compounds will undoubtedly be limited by psychic side effects.

Effects on other Systems

Respiratory Function

The lethal effects of marihuana are mediated by respiratory depression and some of the persistent chronic effects of smoking are also seen on respiratory function. Nevertheless, this system has received negligible attention in preclinical studies. In an isolated lung perfusion study, Δ^9-THC produced a pharmacologically unique effect of increased tidal volume accompained by a pulmonary vascular constriction (216). A transient hyperpnea and hypoxia has been observed in dogs receiving 5 mg/kg of Δ^9-THC intravenously and the suggestion has been made that this hypoxia masks the hypotensive effect of THC through the induction of a compensating rise in blood pressure (36). This respiratory effect, like the animal bradycardia, is attenuated by the same measures of vagal and sympathetic denervation.

Thermal Regulation

A fall in body temperature is one of the more consistent objective changes in animals following Δ^9-THC, but unfortunately for its utility it has not been noted in man (1, 90). There is a wide interspecies variation in this action (1), and the rat shows a paradoxical hyperthermia with low doses (209). Upon repeated administration, however, tolerance develops to the hypothermia and a hyperthermic effect is unmasked (129). Phenitrone, a compound once claimed to antagonize hashish effects, fails to block and even synergizes this action of THC (131, 215). The mechanism of this action is not known but probably involves a central relationship to biogenic amine changes rather than a peripheral effect on heat conservation (1).

Gastrointestinal Function

The overall effect of marihuana on gastrointestinal tract function is a tendency toward hypermotility upon chronic administration, especially when the drug is eaten (22). This may be due in part to recycling and intestinal excretion of THC metabolites by the enterophepatic system (114). However, the directly measured effects of THC on the isolated jejunum are inhibitory, although the drug is not a potent antispasmodic (54). Moreover, the propulsion of charcoal meal is slightly delayed; this effect is similar to, but much less potent than that of morphine (54). Further studies of this system will be needed for complete assessment of marihuana effects.

Drug Interactions

Some interactions of THC with drugs other than CNS drugs have had an obvious basis in the conjoint metabolism of the drug and THC by microsomal monooxygenases (see section on Metabolism). In other cases the interaction may be related to synergistic or antagonistic neural actions (see section on Central Nervous System). Other interactions with less obvious mechanisms have been noted. The acute toxicity of physostigmine in the rat is augmented by Δ^9-THC and is prevented by atropine or scopolamine (193). This is suggestive of cholinergic action, but others have identified an anticholinergic action for THC based on behavioral tests (24), pharmacological studies with isolated intestinal muscle (54, 124), and vagolytic or salivary blocking effects in dogs (37).

The compound 3-(hexahydro-1-*H*-azepin-1-yl)-3-nitropropriophenone-

HCl (phenitrone) has been reported in the Russian literature as an antagonist of the depressant effects of marihuana in dogs (120). This antagonism has not been confirmed with respect to marihuana-induced hypothermia (131, 215) and behavior (11, 215). The possibility that a more specific structural antagonist might be found among the nonpsychoactive cannabinoid components is suggested by the reported antagonism between THC and cannabinol in mice (115). This needs further exploration.

5. SUMMARY AND CONCLUSIONS

Summarizing the current status of preclinical marihuana research is a particularly difficult task. Some persons active in the general field of drug abuse have watched this area hopefully looking for "solutions" to the problem of marihuana abuse based upon data indicative of possible dangers to health. Others knowledgeable in the difficulties of extrapolating animal data to humans have been less optimistic and more critical.

An extensive amount of data has now been acquired concerning the cannabinoid chemical constituents of the plant and its variability. The principal components of marihuana smoke have been identified and quantitated. Although much work is in progress on the characterization of other noncannabinoid smoke components, the publication of these data must be awaited.

The metabolic fate of the cannabinoids has now been traced through three or four stages of enzymatic reaction. The large number of metabolites now identified make it difficult to select any one in particular as characteristic of cannabis use, but a group of products with a carboxyl derivative at position 9** appearing in the urine and feces in free or conjugated states may form the basis of tests for detection of marihuana consumption. The hypothesis that 11-hydroxy-THC metabolites represent the active species within the body has been strengthened by recent evidence.

Acute and subacute studies have shown Δ^9-THC to be a drug with relatively low physical risk, and its effects on operant behavior and pharmacological functions have been found to be reversible.

Tolerance to some pharmacological actions of THC has been demonstrated, but it is not yet known whether this is metabolic (distributional) or functional (neural change). Many pharmacological effects of THC have been identified; these include analgesic, anticonvulsant, hypotensive, antiglaucomic and antiasthmatic actions. However, none of these has received adequate therapeutic evaluation in animals or humans in comparison to standard therapy.

** According to a benzopyran-based numbering system. Also given as position 7 in a terpene derivation.

REFERENCES

1. Abel, E. L., Comparative effects of Δ^9-THC on thermoregulation, in *Cannabis and its Derivatives; Pharmacology and Experimental Psychology,* W. D. M. Paton and J. Crown (Eds.), Oxford University Press, London, 1972.
2. Agurell, S. and K. Leander, Metabolism of cannabis, VIII. Stability, transfer, and absorption of cannabinoid constituents of cannabis (hashish) during smoking, *Acta Pharm. Suec.,* **8,** 391 (1971) (abstract).
3. Agurell, S., I. M. Nilsson, A. Ohlsson, and F. Sandberg, Elimination of tritium-labelled cannabinols in the rat with special reference to the development of tests for the identification of cannabis users, *Biochem. Pharmacol.,* **18,** 1195 (1969).
4. Agurell, S., I. M. Nilsson, A. Ohlsson, and F. Sandberg, On the metabolism of tritium-labeled Δ^1-tetrahydrocannabinol in the rabbit, *Biochem. Pharmacol.,* **19,** 1333 (1970).
5. Agurell, S., I. M. Nilsson, J. L. G. Nilsson, A. Ohlsson, M. Widman, and K. Leander, Metabolism of 7-hydroxy- Δ^1(6)-THC and CBN, *Acta Pharm. Suec.,* **8,** 698 (1971) (abstract).
6. Agurell, S., J. Dahmen, B. Gustafsson, U-B, Johansson, K. Leander, I. Nilsson, J. L. G. Nilsson, M. Norqvist, C. H. Ramsay, A. Ryrfeldt, F. Sandburg, and M. Widman, Metabolic fate of tetrahydrocannabinols, in *Cannabis and its Derivatives: Pharmacology and Experimental Psychology.* W. D. M. Paton and J. Crown (Eds.), Oxford University Press, London, (1972).
7. American Medical Association, Council on Mental Health and Committee on Alcoholism and Drug Dependence, Dependence on cannabis, *JAMA,* **201,** 368 (1967).
8. H. Aramaki, N. Tomiyasu, H. Yoshimura, and H. Tsukamoto, Forensic chemical studies on marihuana, II. Application of a new detection method for marihuana constitutents to the practical identification of marihuana, *Eisei Kagaku,* **14,** 262 (1968).
9. Barry, H. III, and Kubena, R. K., Effects of Δ^1-tetrahydrocannabinol on avoidance by rats and monkeys, *Proc. 78th Ann. Conv. Am. Psychol. Assoc.,* **5,** 805 (1970).
10. Ben-Zvi, Z., R. Mechoulam, and S. Burstein, Identification through synthesis of an active Δ^1(6)-tetrahydrocannabinol metabolite, *J. Am. Chem. Soc.,* **92,** 3468 (1970).
11. Berger, H. J. and J. C. Krantz, Phenitrone: Ineffective blockade of (-)-trans-Δ^9-tetrahydrocannabinol in mice and dogs, *J. Pharm. Pharmacol.,* **24,** 491 (1972).
12. Bicher, H. I. and R. Mechoulam, Pharmacological effects of two active constituents of marijuana, *Arch. Int. Pharmacodyn. Ther.,* **172,** 24 (1968).
13. Birmingham, M. K., J. T. Oliver, G. J. Possanza, Y. T. Langlois, and P. B.

Stewart, Reduction in blood pressure of hypertensive rats by marijuana extract and tetrahydrocannabinol, *Fed. Proc.,* **31,** 39 (1972) (abstract).

14. Black, M. B., J. H. Woods, and E. F. Domino, Some effects of (-)- Δ^9-trans-tetrahydrocannabinol and other cannabis derivatives on schedule-controlled behavior, *Pharmacologist,* **12,** 258 (1970) (abstract).

15. Bloomquist, E. R., *Marijuana: The Second Trip,* Glencoe Press, Beverly Hills, Calif., 1971.

16. Bose, B. C., A. G. Saifi, and A. W. Bhagwat, Observations on the pharmacological actions of *Cannabis indica.* Part II., *Arch. Int. Pharmacodyn. Ther.,* **147,** 285 (1964).

17. Bose, B. C., A. G. Saifi, and A. W. Bhagwat, Observations on the pharmacological action of *Cannabis indica, Arch. Int. Pharmacodyn. Ther.,* **147,** 291 (1964).

18. Boyd, E. S. and D. A. Meritt, Effects of thiopental and a tetrahydrocannabinol derivative on arousal and recovery cycles in the cat, *JPET,* **149,** 138 (1965).

19. Boyd, E. S., E. H. Boyd, and L. E. Brown. Effects of tetrahydrocannabinols on evoked responses in polysensory cortex, *Ann. N.Y. Acad. Sci.,* **191,** 100 (1971).

20. Boyd, E. S., E. H. Boyd, J. S. Muchmore, and L. E. Brown, Effects of two tetrahydrocannabinols and of pentobarbital on cortico-cortical evoked responses in the squirrel monkey, *JPET,* **176,** 480 (1971).

21. Braude, M. C., Toxicology of cannabinoids, in *Cannabis and its Derivatives: Pharmacology and Experimental Psychology,* W. D. M. Paton and J. Crown (Eds.), Oxford University Press, London, 1972, pp. 88–100.

22. Braude, M. D., R. Mansaert, and E. B. Truitt, Jr., Some pharmacological correlates to marihuana use, *Semina. Drug Ther.,* **1,** 229 (1971).

23. Brawley, P. and J. C. Duffield, Pharmacology of hallucinogens, *Pharmacol. Rev.,* **24,** 31 (1971).

24. Brown, H., Anticholinergic-like behavioral effects of trans-(-)- Δ^8-tetrahydrocannabinol, *Psychopharmacologia,* **21,** 294 (1971).

25. Bueno, O. F. A. and E. A. Carlini, Dissociation of learning in marijuana-tolerant rats, *Psychopharmacologia,* **25,** 49 (1972).

26. Burstein, S. H. and D. Kupfer, Hydroxylation of trans- Δ^1-tetrahydrocannabinol by hepatic microsomal monooxygenase, *Chem. Biol. Interactions,* **3,** 317 (1971).

27. Burstein, S., J. Rosenfeld, and T. Wittstruck, Isolation and characterization of two major urinary métabolites of Δ^1-tetrahydrocannabinol, *Science,* **176,** 422 (1972).

28. Canada, Commission of Inquiry into the Non-Medical Use of Drugs (LeDain Commission), *Interim Report of the Commission of Inquiry Into the non-Medical Use of Drugs,* (1970). *Cambis: A Report of the commis-*

sion of Inquiry Into the Non-Medical Use of Drugs, Information Canada, Ottawa, Canada, 1972.

29. Carder, B. and J. Olson, Marihuana and shock induced aggression in rats, *Physiol. Behav.*, **8**, 599 (1972).

30. Carlini, E. A., Tolerance to chronic administration of *Cannabis sativa* (marihuana) in rats, *Pharmacology,***1**, 135 (1968).

31. Carlini, E. A. and J. Masur, Development of fighting behavior in starved rats by chronic administration of (-)- Δ^9-trans-tetrahydrocannabinol and cannabis extracts, *Commun. Behav. Biol.*, **5**, 57 (1970).

32. Carlini, E. A. A. and C. Gonzalez, Aggressive behavior induced by marihuana compounds and amphetamine in rats previously made dependent on morphine, *Experientia*, **28**, 542 (1972).

33. Carlini, E. A., A. Hamaoui, and R. M. Martz, Factors influencing the aggressiveness elicited by marihuana in food-deprived rats, *Br. J. Pharmacol. Chemother.*, **44**, 794 (1972).

34. Cartwright, L. G., *Cannabis sativa* (hemp), *Australas. J. Pharm.*, **51**, S33 (1970).

35. Cavero, I. and B. S. Jandhyala, Hemodynamic effects of Δ^9-tetrahydrocannabinol, *Fed. Proc.*, **31**, 505 (1972) (abstract).

36. Cavero, I., R. K. Kubena, J. Dziak, J. P. Buckley, and B. S. Jandhyala, Certain observations on interrelation between respiratory and cardiovasuclar effects of (-)- Δ^9-trans-tetrahydrocannabinol, *Res. Commun. Chem. Pathol. Pharmacol.*, **3**, 483 (1972).

37. Cavero, I., J. P. Buckley, and B. S. Jandhyala, Parasympatholytic activity of (-)- Δ^9-trans-tetrahydrocannabinol in mongrel dogs, *Eur. J. Pharmocol.*, **19**, 301 (1972).

38. Chesher, G. B., S. Hasleton, D. M. Jackson, and G. A. Starmer, Studies of a possible cumulative effect of cannabis extracts, *Proc. 30th Int. Cong Alcoholism and Drug Abuse*, Amsterdam (1972).

39. Chesher, G. B., S. L. Hasleton, D. M. Jackson, and G. A. Starmer, The effect of repeated administration of a cannabis extract on operant behavior in the rat, *Proc. 5th Int. Cong. Pharmacol.*, San Francisco, Calif., **41** (1972).

40. Christensen, W., B. Best, and A. Herin. Effects of Δ^9-tetrahydrocannabinol on limbic electrical activity and heart rate in the rat, *Proc. Ann. Rocky Mt. Bioeng. Smyp.*, **163** (1971).

41. Christensen, H. D., R. I. Freudenthal, J. T. Gidley, R. Rosenfeld, G. Boegli, L. Testino, D. R. Brine, C. G. Pitt, and M. E. Wall, Activity of Δ^8 and Δ^9-tetrahydrocannabinol and related compounds in the mouse, *Science*, **172**, 165 (1971).

42. Claussen, U. and F. Korte, Haschisch, XV. Comments on the behavior of hemp and of Δ^9-6α-trans-tetrahydrocannabinol during smoke, *Liebig's Ann. Chem.*, **713**, 162 (1968).

43. Cohen, G. M., D. W. Peterson, and G. J. Mannering, Interactions of Δ^9-tetrahydrocannabinol with the hepatic microsomal drug metabolizing system, *Life Scie.,* **10,** 1207 (1971).
44. Cohn, R. A., E. Barrett, and J. Pirch, Differences in behavioral responses of male and female rats to marihuana, *Proc. Soc. Exp. Biol. Med.,* **140,** 1136 (1972).
45. Colasanti, B. and N. Khazan, Changes in EEG voltage output of the sleep-awake cycle in response to tetrahydrocannabinols in the rat, *Pharmacologist,* **13,** 246 (1971).
46. Cole, J. M., W. A. Pieper, and D. M. Rumbaugh, Effects of Δ^9-tetrahydrocannabinol on spaced responding in great apes, *Commun. Behav. Biol.,* **6,** 285 (1971).
47. Conrad, D. G., T. F. Elsmore, and F. J. Sodetz, Δ^9-tetrahydrocannabinol: Dose-related behavior in chimpanzee, *Science,* **175,** 547 (1972).
48. Cottrell, J. C., S. S. Sohn, and W. H. Vogel. Toxic effects of marihuana tar on mouse, *Nature,* 1973 (in press).
49. Coutselinis, A. S. and C. J. Miras, The effects of the smoking process on cannabinols, *U.S. Secretariat Report* ST/SGA/SER/24, Nr 23 (1970).
50. DeRopp, R. S., L. H. Kastl, and L. Balbus, Acute effects of marihuana smoke in mice, *Proc. Western Pharmacol. Soc.,* **15,** 21 (1972).
51. Dewey, W. L., L. R. Yonce, L. S. Harris, W. M. Reavis, E. D. Griffin, Jr., and V. E. Newby, Cardiovascular effects of trans- Δ^9-tetrahydrocannabinol (Δ^9-THC), *Pharmacologist,* **12,** 259 (1970) (abstract).
52. Dewey, W. L., T. C. Peng, and L. S. Harris, The effect of 1-trans-delta-^{9}-tetrahydrocannabinol on the hypothalamo-hypophyseal-adrenal axis of rats, *Eur. J. Pharmacol.,* **12,** 382 (1970).
53. Dewey, W. L., J. Jenkins, T. O'Rourke, and L. S. Harris, The effects of chronic administration of trans- Δ^9-tetrahydrocannabinol on behavior and the cardiovascular system of dogs, *Arch. Int. Pharmacodyn.,* **198,** 118 (1972).
54. Dewey, W. L., L. S. Harris, and J. S. Kennedy, Some pharmacological and toxicological effects of 1-trans- Δ^8 and 1-trans- Δ^9-tetrahydrocannabinol in laboratory rodents, *Arch. Int. Pharmacodyn. Ther.,* **196,** 133 (1972).
55. Dewey, W. L., D. E. McMillan, and L. S. Harris, Blood levels of H^3- Δ^9-tetrahydrocannabinol (H^3 Δ^9-THC) and its metabolites in tolerant and non-tolerant pigeons, *Proc. 5th Int. Cong. Pharmacol.,* San Francisco, Calif., 56 (1972).
56. Dingell, J. B., H. G. Wilcox, and H. A. Klausner, Biochemical interactions of Δ^9-tetrahydrocannabinol, *Pharmacologist,* **13,** 296 (1971).
57. Domino, E. F. Neuropsychopharmacologic studies of marijuana. Synthetic and natural tetrahydrocannabinol (THC) derivatives in animals and man, *Ann. N.Y. Acad. Sci.,* **191,** 166 (1971).
58. Drew, W. G., L. L. Miller, and A. Wikler, Effect of delta-9-THC on the open-field activity of the rat, *Psychopharmacologia,* **23,** 289 (1972).

59. Durandina, A. I. and V. A. Romasendko, Functional and morphological changes in experimental acute posoining by resinous substances prepared from Yujnochuisk cannabis (Part 1), *Bull. Narcotics*, **23**, 1 (1971).
60. Durandina, A. I. and V. A. Romasenko. Functional and morphological disorders in chronic poisoning by resinous substance from Yujnochuisk cannabis resin (Part 2), *Bull. Narcotics*, **24**, 31 (1972).
61. Elsmore, T. F. and G. V. Fletcher, Δ^9-Tetrahydrocannabinol aversive effects in rat at high doses, *Science*, **175**, 911 (1972).
61a. Fehr, K. O. and H. Kalant, Analysis of cannabis smoke obtained under different combustion conditions, *Can. J. Physiol. Pharmacol.*, **50**, 761 (1972).
62. Ferraro, D. P., D. M. Grilly, and W. C. Lynch, Effects of marihuana extract on the operant behavior of chimpanzees, *Psychopharmacologia*, **22**, 333 (1971).
63. Ferraro, D. P. and D. K. Billings, Comparison of behavioral effects of synthetic (-) Δ^9-trans-tetrahydrocannabinol and marihuana extract distillate in chimpanzees, *Psychopharmacologia*, **25**, 169 (1972).
64. Foltz, R. L., A. F. Fentiman, Jr., E. G. Leighty, J. L. Walter, H. R. Drewes, W. E. Schwartz, T. F. Page, Jr., and E. B. Truitt, Jr., Metabolite of (-)-trans- Δ^8-tetrahydrocannabinol: Identification and synthesis, *Science*, **168**, 844 (1970).
65. Foltz, R. L., G. W. Kinzer, R. I. Mitchell, and E. B. Truitt, Jr., The fate of cannabinoid components of marihuana during smoking, forthcoming (1973).
66. Ford, R. D. and D. E. McMillan, Further studies on the behavioral pharmacology of 1- Δ^8- and 1- Δ^9-tetrahydrocannabinol (Δ^8- and Δ^9-THC), *Fed. Proc.*, **31**, 506 (1972) (abstract).
67. Forney, R. B. Toxicology of marihuana, *Pharmacol. Rev.*, **23**, 279 (1971).
68. Forney, R. B. and G. F. Kiplinger, Toxicology and pharmacology of marijuana, *Ann. N.Y. Acad. Sci.*, **191**, 74 (1971).
68a. Frank, I. M., Hepler, R. S., Epps, L., Ungerleidel, J. T. Szara, S. Marihuana and Δ^9-THC: Effects on intraocular pressure in young adults. *Fifth Int. Congr. Pharmacol., Abstr. Vol. Papers*, **426**, 71 (1972).
69. Frankenheim, J. M., D. E. McMillan, and L. S. Harris, Effects of 1- Δ^9- and 1- Δ^8-transtetrahydrocannabinol and cannabinol on schedule-controlled behavior of pigeons and rats, *JPET*, **178**, 241 (1971).
70. Freudenthal, R. I., J. Martin, and M. E. Wall, Distribution of Δ^9-tetrahydrocannabinol in the mouse, *Br. J. Pharmacol.*, **44**, 244 (1972).
71. Fujimori, M., D. M. Trusty, and H. E. Himwich, Electroencephalographic analysis of delta-9-transtetrahydrocannabinol (THC) in the rabbit, *Fed. Proc.*, **31**, 250 (1972) (abstract).
72. Fuxe, K. and Jonsson, G. The effect of tetrahydrocannabinols on central monoamine neurons, *Acta Pharm. Suec.*, **8**, 695 (1971).
73. Gallager, D. W., E. Sanders-Bush, and F. Sulser, Dissociation between

behavioral effects and changes in metabolism of cerebral serotonin (5-HT) following Δ^9-tetrahydrocannabinol (THC), *Pharmacologist,* **13,** 296 (1971).

74. Gamage, J. R. and E. L. Zerkin, *A Comprehensive Guide to the English-Language Literature on Cannabis (Marihuana),* Stash Press Inc., Beloit, Wisc., 1969.

75. Gerber, W. F. Effect of marihuana extract on fetal hamsters and rabbits, *Toxicol. Appl. Pharmacol.,* **14,** 276 (1969).

76. Gerber, W. and L. Schramm, Teratogenicity of marihuana extract as influenced by plant origin and seasonal variation, *Arch. Int. Pharmacodyn. Ther.,* **177,** 224 (1969).

77. Gershon, S., On the pharmacology of marihuana, *Behav. Neuropsychiat.,* **1,** 9 (1970).

78. Gill, E. W. and G. Jones, Brain levels of Δ^1-tetrahydrocannabinol and its metabolites in mice-correlation with behavior and the effect of the metabolic inhibitors SKF-525A and piperonyl butoxide, *Biochem. Pharmacol.,* **21,** 2237 (1972).

79. Gjerstad, G., Naturally occurring hallucinogens, III. *Q. J. Crude Drug Res.,* **12,** 1849 (1972).

80. Gonzalez, S. C. and E. A. Carlini, Extinction of operant responses by rats under the effects of *Cannabis sativa* extract, *Psychon. Sci.,* **24,** 203 (1971

81. Gonzalez, S. C., V. K. R. Matsudo, and E. A. Carlini, Effects of marihuana compounds on the fighting behavior of Siamese fighting fish,*Pharmacology,* **6,** 186 (1971).

82. Gonzalez, S. C., I. G. Karniol, and E. A. Carlini, Effects of *Cannabis sativa* extract on conditioned fear, *Behav. Biol.,* **7,** 83 (1972).

83. Great Britain, Lewis, A., Chairman Advisory Committee on Drug Dependence: Cannabis (The Wootton Report), *Cannabis: A Review of the International Clincial Literature,* Her Majesty's Stationery Office, London, 1968.

84. Grinspoon, L., Marihuana, *Sci. Am.,* **221,** 17 (1969).

85. Grinspoon, L., *Marihuana Reconsidered,* Harvard University Press, Cambridge, Mass., 1971.

86. Grunfeld, Y. and H. Edery, Psychopharmacological activity of the active constituents of hashish and some related compounds, *Psychopharmacologia,* **14,** 200 (1969).

87. Gurney, O., D. E. Maynard, R. G. Pitcher, and R. W. Kierstead, Metabolism of (-)-Δ^9-and (-)-Δ^8-tetrahydrocannabinol by monkey liver, *J. Am. Chem. Soc.,* **94,** 7928 (1972).

88. Haley, S. L., P. L. Wright, J. B. Plank, M. L. Keplinger, M. C. Braude, and J. C. Calandra, The effect of natural and synthetic delta-9-tetrahydrocannabinol on fetal development, *Toxicol. Appl. Pharmacol.,* 1973 (in press).

89. Harbison, R. D. and B. Mantilla-Plata, Prenatal toxicity, maternal distribution and placental transfer of tetrahydrocannabinol, *JPET,* **180,** 446 (1972).

90. Hardman, H. F., E. F. Domino, and M. H. Seevers, General pharmacological actions of some synthetic tetrahydrocannabinol derivatives, *Pharmacol. Rev.*, **23**, 295 (1971).
91. Harris, L. S., General and behavioral pharmacology, *Pharmacol. Rev.*, **23**, 285 (1971).
92. Harris, R. T., W. Waters, and D. McLenden, Behavioral effects in Rhesus monkeys of repeated intravenous doses of Δ^9-tetrahydrocannabinol, *Psychopharmacologia*, **26**, 297 (1972).
93. Heath, R. G., Personal communication, 1972.
94. Henriksson, B. G. and T. Jarbe, Effect of two tetrahydrocannabinols, (Δ^9-THC and Δ^8-THC) on conditioned avoidance learning in rats and its transfer to normal state conditions, *Psychopharmacologia*, **22**, 23 (1971).
95. Ho, B. T., G. E. Fritchie, L. F. Englert, W. M. McIssac, and J. E. Idänpään-Heikkilä, Marihuana: Importance of the route of administration, *J. Pharm. Pharmacol.*, **23**, 301 (1971).
96. Ho, B. T., R. An, G. E. Fritchie, L. F. Englert, W. M. McIsaac, B. MacKay, and D. H. W. Ho, Marijuana, Pharmacological studies, *J. Pharm. Sci.*, **60**, (1971).
97. Ho. B. T., D. Taylor, L. F. Englert, and W. M. McIsaac, Neurochemical effects of 1-Δ^9-tetrahydrocannabinol in rats following repeated inhalation, *Brain Res.*, **31**, 233 (1971).
98. Ho, B. T., V. Estevez, L. F. Englert, W. M. McIsaac, Δ^9-Tetrahydrocannabinol and its metabolites in monkey brains, *J. Pharm. Pharmacol.*, **24**, 414 (1972).
99. Ho, B. T., D. Taylor, G. E. Fritchie, L. F. Englert, and W. M. McIsaac, Neuropharmacological study of Δ^9- and Δ^8-1-tetrahydrocannabinols in monkeys and mice, *Brain Res.*, **38**, 163 (1972).
100. Hockman, C. H., R. G. Perrin, and H. Kalant, Electroencephalographic and behavioral alterations produced by Δ^1-tetrahydrocannabinol, *Science*, **172**, 968 (1971).
101. Hollister, L. E., E. Moore, S. Kantena, and E. Noble, Delta-1-tetrahydrocannabinol, synhexyl and marihuana extract administered orally in man: Catecholamine excretion, plasma cortisol levels and platelet serotonin content, *Psychopharmacologia*, **17**, 354 (1970).
102. Hosko, M. I. and H. F. Hardman, Effect of Δ^9-THC on cardiovascular responses to stimulation of vasopressor loci in the neuraxis of anesthetized cats, *Pharmacologist*, **13**, 296 (1971).
103. Idänpään-Heikkilä, J., G. E. Fritchie, L. F. Englert, B. T. Ho, and W. M. McIsaac, Placental transfer of tritiated-1-Δ^9-tetrahydrocannabinol, *New Eng. J. Med.*, **281**, 330 (1969).
104. Isbell, H., C. W. Gorodetzsky, D. Jasinski, U. Claussen, F. V. Spulak, and F. Korte, Effects of (-)-Δ^9-trans-tetrahydrocannabinol in man, *Psychopharmacologia*, **11**, 184 (1967).

105. Jacobsen, E., *Hallucinogens. Psychopharmacol.: Dimensions Perspect.*, Tavistock Publications, London, England, 1968, p. 175.
106. Jaffe, P. G. and M. Baum, Increased resistance-to-extinction of an avoidance response in rats following the administration of hashish resin, *Psychopharmacologia*, **20**, 97 (1971).
107. Joyce, C. R. B. and S. H. Curry, Eds., *The Botany and Chemistry of Cannabis*, J. & A. Churchill, London, 1970.
108. Kalant, O. J., *An Interim Guide to the Cannabis (Marijuana) Literature*, Addiction Research Foundation, Toronto, 1968.
109. Kennedy, J. S. and W. J. Waddell, Whole-body autoradiography of the pregnant mouse after administration of ^{14}C-delta-9-THC (tetrahydrocannabinol), *Toxicol. Appl. Pharmacol.*, **22**, 252 (1972).
110. Keplinger, M. L., P. L. Wright, S. L. Haley, J. B. Plank, M. C. Braude, and J. C. Calandra, The effect of natural and synthetic delta-9-THC on reproductive and lactation performance in albino rats, *Toxicol. Appl. Pharmacol.*, (1973) (in press).
111. Kilbey, M., M. R. Farmer, D. McLendon, and K. M. Johnson, Time course of Δ^9-tetrahydrocannabinol inhibition of frog killing behavior in the rat, *Proc. 19th Ann. Conf. Southwest. Psychol. Assoc.*, Oklahoma City, April (1972).
112. Kilbey, M. M., G. E. Fritchie, D. M. McLendon, and K. M. Johnson, Attack behavior in mice inhibited by Δ^9-tetrahydrocannabinol, *Nature*, **238**, 463 (1972).
113. Killam, K. F. and E. K. Killam, The action of tetrahydrocannabinol on EEG and photomyoclonic seizures in the baboon, *Proc. 5th Int. Cong. Pharmacol.*, San Francisco, Calif., July 23–28, 124 (1972).
114. Klausner, H. A. and J. V. Dingell, The metabolism and excretion of Δ^9-tetrahydrocannabinol in the rat, *Life Sci.*, **10**, Pt. 1, 49 (1971).
115. Krantz, J. C., Jr., J. J. Berger, and B. L. Welch, Blockade of (-)-trans-Δ^9-tetrahydrocannabinol depressant effect of cannabinol in mice, *Am. J. Pharm.*, **143**, 149 (1971).
116. Krasnegor, N. H., The effects of Δ^9-THC on auditory stimulation, *Proc. Eastern Psychol. Assoc.*, (Boston), (1972).
117. Krasnegor, N. A. and T. F. Elsmore, The effects of chronic administration of Δ^9-tetrahydrocannabinol on Sidman avoidance performance in Rhesus monkeys, *Proc. 80th Ann. Conv. Am. Psychol. Assoc.*, 819 (1972).
118. Kubena, R. K., J. L. Perhach, and H. Barry, III, Corticosterone elevation mediated centrally by delta-1-tetrahydrocannabinol in rats, *Eur. J. Pharmacol.*, **14**, 80 (1971).
119. Kubena, R. K. and H. Barry, III, Stimulus characteristics of marihuana components, *Nature*, **235**, 397 (1972).
120. Kudrin, A. N. and O. N. Davydova, Elimination of hashish intoxication with phenitrone in dogs, *Farmakol. Toksikol.*, **31**, 549 (1968).

121. Lachine, E. E., A. M. Zohdy, and S. A. Tawab, Effect of a combination of the alcoholic extract of *Cannabis sativa* and hyoscine hydrobromide (Manzoul) on the EEG (electroencephalogram) patterns in rabbits, *Drug Res.,* **1,** 94 (1968).
122. Lahiri, P. K., A. R. Laddu, and H. F. Hardman, Effect of Δ^9-tetrahydrocannabinol (THC) on the heart rate (HR) of the dog, *Fed. Proc.,* **31,** 505 (1972).
123. Lapa, A. J., C. A. Sampaio, C. Timo-Iaria, and J. R. Valle, Blocking action of tetrahydrocannabinol upon transmission in the trigeminal system of the cat, *J. Pharm. Pharmacol.,* **20,** 373 (1968).
124. Layman, J. M. and A. S. Milton, Actions of Δ^1-tetrahydrocannabinol and cannabidiol at cholinergic junctions, *Br. J. Pharmacol.,* **41,** 379P (1971).
125. Layman, J. M. and A. S. Milton, Distribution of tritium labeled Δ^1-tetrahydrocannabinol in the rat brain following intraperitoneal administration, *Br. J. Pharmacol.,* **42,** 308 (1971).
126. Leighty, E. G., Metabolism and distribution of cannabinoids in rats after different methods of administration, *Biochem, Pharmacol.,* **22,** 1613 (1973).
127. Lemberger, L., The metabolism of the tetrahydrocannabinols, *Adv. Pharmacol. Chemother.,* **10,** (1972).
128. Lipparini, F., A. Scotti deCarolis, and V. G. Longo, Neuropharmacological investigation of some trans-tetrahydrocannabinol derivatives, *Physiol. Behav.,* **4,** 527 (1969).
129. Lomax, P., Acute tolerance to the hypothermic effect of marihuana in the rat, *Res. Commun. Chem. Pathol. Pharmacol.,* **2,** 159 (1971).
130. Lomax, P., Effect of marihuana on pituitary-thyroid activity in the rat, *Ag. Actions,* **1,** 252 (1970).
131. Lomax, P. and G. Campbell. Phenitrone and marihuana-induced hypothermia, *Experientia,* **27,** 1191 (1971).
132. Magus, R. D. and L. S. Harris, Carcinogenic potential of marihuana smoke condensate. *Fed. Proc.,* **30,** 279 (1971) (abstract).
133. Maitre, L., M. Staehelin, and H. J. Bein, Effect of an extract of cannabis and some cannabinols on catecholamine metabolism in rat brain and heart, *Ag. Actions,* **1,** 136 (1970).
134. Manning, F. J., J. H. McDonough, T. F. Elsmore, C. L. Saller, and F. J. Sodetz, Inhibition of normal growth by chronic administration of delta-9-tetrahydrocannabinol, *Science,* **174,** 424 (1971).
135. Manning. F. J. and T. F. Elsmore, Shock-elicited fighting and delta-9-tetrahydrocannabinol, *Psychopharmacolgia,* **25,** 218 (1972).
136. Manno, J. E., G. F. Kiplinger, N. Scholz, R. B. Forney, and S. E. Haine, Influence of alcohol and marihuana on motor and mental performance, *Clin. Pharmacol. Ther.,* **12,** 202 (1971).
137. Mantilla-Plata, B. and R. D. Harbison, Phenobarbital and SKF-525-A effect

on Δ^9-tetrahydrocannabinol (THC) toxicity and distribution in mice, *Pharmacologist,* **13,** 297 (1971) (abstract).
138. Marks, B. H., Delta-9-tetrahydrocannabinol and luteinizing hormone secretion, in *Progress in Brain Research, Drug Effects on Neuroendocrine Regulation,* B. H. Marks, D. DeWied, W. Gispen, and E. Zimmerman (Eds.), Elsevier, Amsterdam, 1973.
139. Martinez, J. L., S. W. Stadnicki, and U. H. Schaeppi, Δ^9-Tetrahydrocannabinol: Effects on EEG and behavior of Rhesus monkeys, *Life Sci.,* **11,** Pt. 1, 643 (1972).
140. Masur, J. and N. Khazan, Induction by *Cannabis sativa* (marihuana) of rhythmic spike discharges overriding REM sleep electrocorticogram in the rat, *Life Sci.,* **9,** Pt. 1, 1275 (1970).
141. Masur, J., R. M. W. Martz, and E. A. Carlini, Effects of acute and chronic administration of *Cannabis sativa* and (-)-Δ^9-*trans*-tetrahydrocannabinol on the behavior of rats in an open-field area, *Psychopharmacologia,* **19,** 388 (1971).
142. Masur, J., R. M. W. Martz, and E. A. Carlini, Behavior of worker and nonworker rats under the influence of (-)- Δ^9-trans-tetrahydrocannabinol, chlorpromazine, and amylobarbitone, *Psychopharmacologia,* **25,** 57 (1972).
143. Maynard, D. E., O. Gurny, R. G. Pitcher, and R. W. Kierstead, (-)-Δ^8-Tetrahydrocannabinol: Two novel *in vitro* metabolites, *Experientia,* **27,** 1154 (1971).
144. McDonough, J. H., Jr., F. J. Manning, and T. F. Elsmore, Reduction of predatory aggression of rats following administration of Δ^9-tetrahydrocannabinol, *Life Sci.,* **11,** Pt. 1, 103 (1972).
145. McGlothlin, W. H., and L. J. West, The marihuana problem: An overview, *Am. J. Psychiatr.,* **125,** 126 (1968).
146. McIsaac, W. M., G. E. Fritchie, J. Idänpään-Heikkilä, B. T. Ho, and L. F. Englert, Distribution of marijuana in monkey brain and concomitant behavioral effects, *Nature,* **230,** 593 (1971).
147. McMillan, D. E., L. S. Selig, J. M. Frankenheim, and J. S. Kennedy, (l)-Δ^9-Trans-tetrahydrocannabinol in pigeons: Tolerance to the behavioral effects *Science,* **169,** 501 (1970).
148. McMillan, D. E., W. L. Dewey, and L. S. Harris, Characteristics of tetrahydrocannabinol tolerance, *Ann. N.Y. Acad. Sci.,* **191,** 83 (1971).
149. McMillan, D. E., R. D. Ford, J. M. Frankenheim, R. A. Harris, and L. S. Harris, Tolerance to active constituents of marihuana, *Arch. Int. Pharmacodyn. Ther.,* **198,** 132 (1972).
150. McMillan, D. E., W. L. Dewey, R. F. Turk, and L. S. Harris, Distribution of radioactivity in brain, liver, and lung of tolerant and non-tolerant pigeons treated with ^{3}H-Δ^9-tetrahydrocannabinol (^{3}H-Δ^9-THC), *Proc. 5th Int. Cong. Pharmacol.,* San Francisco, Calif., July 23–28, 154, (1972).
151. Mechoulam, R., Marihuana chemistry, *Science,* **168,** 1159 (1970).

REFERENCES

152. Mechoulam, R. (Ed.), *Cannabis-Chemical, Pharmacological and Clinical Aspects*, Academic Press, New York, 1972.
153. Merkus, F. W. H. M., M. G. J. Jaspers-van Wouw, and J. F. C. Roovers-Bollen, Introduction to the analysis of cannabis constituents, especially in smoke and body fluids, *Pharm. Weekbl.*, **7**, 98 (1972).
154. Mikes, F. and P. G. Waser, Marihuana components. Effects of smoking of Δ^9-tetrahydrocannabinol and cannabidiol, *Science*, **172**, 1158 (1971).
155. Milzoff, J. R., R. B. Forney, C. J. Stone, and D. O. Allen, The cardiovascular effects of Δ^9-THC in vagotomized rats, *Pharmacologist*, **13**, 247 (1971) (abstract).
156. Milzoff, J. R., R. Martz, and R. N. Harger, Evaluation of the depressor response of Δ^9-tetrahydrocannabinol in the rat, *Fed. Proc.*, **31**, 505 (1972) (abstract).
157. Miras, C. J., The effect of hashish on noradrenaline concentration and uptake in the brain, *Acta Pharma. Suec.*, **8**, 694 (1971) (abstract).
158. Miras, C. J., Hashish, its chemistry and pharmacology, G. E. W. Wolstenholme and J. Knight (Eds.), Little, Brown and Co., Boston, 1965, pp.37.
159. Moore, L. A., Jr., *Marihuana (Cannabis) Bibliography, 1960-1968*, Bruik Humanist Forum, Los Angeles, Calif., 1969.
160. Moreton, J. E. and W. M. Davis, Effects of Δ^9-tetrahydrocannabinol on locomotor activity and on phases of sleep, *Pharmacologist*, **12**, 258 (1970) (abstract).
161. Nahas, G. G., *Cannabis sativa*. The deceptive weed, *N.Y. State J. Med.*, **72**, 856, (1972).
162. Nahas, G. G., *Marijuana—Deceptive Weed*. Raven Press, New York, 1973
163. Nahas, G. H. Toxicology and pharmacology of *Cannabis sativa* with special reference to delta-9-THC, *Bull. Narcotics*, **24**, 11 (1972).
164. Nakazawa, K. and E. Costa, Metabolism of Δ^9-tetrahydrocannabinol by lung and liver homogenates of rats treated with methylcholanthrene, *Nature (London)*, **234**, 48 (1971).
165. National Institute of Mental Health, U.S. Department of Health, Education and Welfare, *Marihuana and Health*, U. S. Government Printing Office, Washington, D.C., First Annual Report, 1971; Second Annual Report, 1972; Third Annual Report, 1973.
166. Navratil, J., A. Medek, J. Hrbek, Z. Krejci, S. Komenda, and M. Dvorak, Effect of cannabis on the conditioned alimentary motor reflex in cats, *Activ. Nerv. Super.*, **14**, 109 (1972).
167. Neto, J. Palermo and E. A. Carlini, Aggressive behavior elicited in rats by *Cannabis sativa*. Effects of *p*-chlorophenylalanine and DOPA, *Eur. J. Pharmacol.*, **17**, 215 (1972).
168. Neumeyer, J. L. and R. A. Shagoury, Chemistry and pharmacology of marihuana, *J. Pharm. Sci.*, **60**, 1433 (1971).

169. Newman, L. M., N. P. Lutz, M. H. Gould, and E. F. Domino, Δ^9-Tetrahydrocannabinol and ethyl alcohol. Evidence of cross-tolerance in the rat, *Science*, **175**, 1022 (1972).
170. Nilsson, I. M., S. Agurell, K. Leander, J. L. G. Nilsson, and M. Widman, Cannabidiol: Structure of three metabolites formed in the liver, *Acta Pharm. Suec.*, **8**, 701 (1971).
171. Orsingher, O. A. and S. Fulginiti, Effects of *Cannabis sativa* on learning in rats, *Pharmacology*, **3**, 337 (1970).
172. Oskoui, M., Effect of Δ^1-tetrahydrocannabinol (Δ^1-THC) on cardiovascular respiratory systems, vasomotor center (VC), sympathetic and vagus nerve discharge activities and mocardial function, *Fed. Proc.*, **31**, 505 (1971) (abstract).
173. Pace, H. B., M. W. Davis, and L. A. Borgen, Teratogenesis and marihuana, *Ann. N.Y. Acad. Sci.*, **191**, 123 (1971).
174. Pal, B. and J. J. Ghoah, 1- Δ^8-Tetrahydrocannabinol. Effects on the urinary excretion of 5-hydroxyindoleacetic acid, *Biochem. Pharmacol.*, **21**, 263 (1972).
175. Park, Y. Y. and B. E. Tilton, Effects of marihuana smoke on avoidance response in rats, *Proc. West. Pharmacol. Soc.*, **13**, 151 (1970).
176. Paton, W. D. M. and J. Crown, *Cannabis and Its Derivatives: Pharmacology and Experimental Psychology*, Oxford University Press, London, 1972.
177. Paton, W. D. M. and R. G. Pertwee, Effect of cannabis and certain of its constituents on pentabarbitone sleeping time and phenazone metabolism, *Br. J. Pharmacol.*, **44**, 250 (1972).
178. Paton, W. D. M. and D. M. Temple, Effects of chronic and acute cannabis treatment upon thiopentone anesthesia in rabbits, *Br. J. Pharmacol.*, **44**, 346P (1972).
179. Persaud, I. and A. Ellington, Cannabis in early pregnancy, *Lancet*, **2**, 1306 (1967).
180. Persaud, I. and A. Ellington, Teratogenic activity of cannabis resin, *Lancet*, **2**, 406 (1968).
181. Peterson, D. W., G. M. Cohen, and S. B. Sparber, Delay of the behavioral effects of Δ^9-tetrahydrocannabinol in rats by 2-diethylaminoethyl 2,2-diphenylvalerate hydrochloride (SKF 525-A), *Life Sci.*, **10**, 1381 (1971).
182. Phillips, R. N., D. J. Brown, and R. B. Forney, Enhancement of depressant properties of alcohol or barbiturate in combination with aqueous suspended Δ^9-tetrahydrocannabinol in rats, *J. Forensic Sci.*, **16**, 152 (1971)-A.
183. Phillips, R. N., M. A. Neel, D. J. Brown, and R. B. Forney, Enhancement of caffeine or methamphetamine stimulation in mice with aqueous-suspended Δ^9-tetrahydrocannabinol, *Pharmacologist*, **13**, 297 (1971) (abstract).
184. Phillips, R. N. R. F. Turk, and R. B. Forney, Acute toxicity of Δ^9-terahydrocannabinol in rats and mice, *Proc. Soc. Exp. Biol. Med.*, **136**, 260 (1971).

185. Phillips, R. N., D. J. Brown, R. Martz, J. Hubbard, and R. B. Forney, Subacute toxicity of aqueous-suspended delta-9-tetrahydrocannabinol in rats, *Toxicol. Appl. Pharmacol.*, **22**, 45 (1972).
186. Pillard, R. C., Marihuana, *New Engl. J. Med.*, **283**, 294 (1970).
187. Pirch, J. H., P. R. Barnes, and E. Barratt, Tolerance to EEG effects of marihuana in rats, *Pharmacologist*, **13**, 246 (1971) (abstracts).
188. Pirch, J. H., R. A. Cohn, P. R. Barnes, and E. S. Barratt, Effects of acute and chronic administration of marihuana extract on the rat electrocorticogram, *Neuropharmacology*, **11**, 231 (1972).
189. Pradhan, S. N., P. T. Bailey, and B. Ghosh, Some behavioral effects of Δ^9-tetrahydrocannabinol in rats, *Res. Commun. Chem. Pathol. Pharmacol.*, **3**, 197 (1972).
190. Price, P. J., W. A. Suk, G. J. Spann, and A. E. Freeman, Transformation of Fischer rat embryo cells by the combined action of murine leukemia virus and (-)-trans-delta-9-tetrahydrocannabinol, *Proc. Soc. Exp. Biol. Med.*, **140**, 454 (1972).
191. Razdan, R. D., Hallucinogens, *Ann. Rept. Med. Chem.*, **1970**, 24.
192. Rickles, W. H., Jr., B. Chatoff, and C. Whitaker, *Marihuana: A Selective Bibliography, 1924-1970*, Brain Research Institute Publications Office, Los Angeles, Calif., 1970.
193. Rosenblatt, J. E., D. S. Janowsky, J. M. Davis, and M. K. El-Yousel, Augmentation of physostigmine toxicity in the rat by Δ^9-tetrahydrocannabinol, *Res. Commun. Chem. Pathol. Pharmacol.*, **3**, 479 (1972).
194. Rosenkrantz, H., G. R. Thompson, and M. C. Braude, Oral and parenteral formulations of marihuana constituents, *J. Pharm. Sci.*, **61**, 1106 (1972).
195. Salustiano, J., K. Hashino, and E. A. Carlini, Effects of *Cannabis sativa* and chlorpromazine on mice as measured by two methods used for evaluation of tranquilizing agents, *Med. Pharmacol. Exp.*, **15**, 153 (1966).
196. Sampaio, C. A., Influence of cannabis, tetrahydrocannabinol and pyrahexyl on the linguomandibular reflex of the dog, *J. Pharm. Pharmacol.*, **19**, 552 (1967).
197. Santos, M., M. R. P. Sampaio, N. S. Fernandez, and E. A. Carlini, Effects of *Cannabis sativa* (marihuana) on the fighting behavior in mice, *Psychopharmacologia*, **8**, 437 (1966).
198. Scheckel, C. L., E. Boff, P. Dahlen, and T. Smart, Behavioral effects in monkeys of racemates of two biologically active marihuana constituents, *Science*, **160**, 1467 (1968).
199. Schildkraut, J. J. and D. J. Efron, Effects of Δ^9-tetrahydrocannabinol on the metabolism of norepinephrine in rat brain, *Psychopharmacologia*, **20**, 191 (1971).
200. Schultes, R. E., The plant kingdom and hallucinogens, Part I, *Bull. Narcotics.* **21**, 3 (1969).

201. Segal, M. and A. F. Kenney, Δ^1- and $\Delta^1 6$-Tetrahydrocannibinol: Preliminary observations on similarities and differences in central pharmacological effects in the cat, *Experientia,* **28,** 816 (1972).
202. Siegel, R. K., Effects of *Cannabis sativa* and lysergic acid diethylamide on a visual discrimination task in pigeons, *Psychopharmacologia,* **15,** 1 (1969).
203. Siegel, R. K., Effects of *Cannabis sativa* and LSD on pigeons in three visual environments, *Perceptual and Motor Skills,* **30,** 510 (1970).
204. Siegel, R. K. and J. Poole, Psychedelic induced social behavior in mice, A preliminary report, *Psychol. Rep.,* **25,** 704 (1969).
205. Silva, M. T. A., E. A. Carlini, U. Claussen, and F. Korte, Lack of cross-tolerance in rats among (-)-delta-9-trans-tetrahydrocannabinol (Delta-9-THC), cannabis extract, mescaline and lysergic acid diethylamide (LSD-25), *Psychopharmacologia,* **13,** 332 (1968).
206. Singer, A. J. (Ed.), Marihuana: Chemistry, pharmacology and patterns of social use, *Ann. N.Y. Acad. Sci.,* **191,** 1 (1971).
207. Skinner, R. F., Analysis of marihuana, *Proc. West. Pharmacol. Soc.,* **14,** 4 (1971).
208. Snyder, S. H., *Uses of Marihuana,* Oxford University Press, New York, 1971.
209. Sofia, R. D., A paradoxical effect for delta-1-tetrahydrocannabinol in rats. *Res. Comm. Chem. Path. Pharmacol.,* (1973) (in Press).
210. Sofia, R. D., The lethal effects of delta-1-tetrahydrocannabinol in aggregated and isolated mice following single dose administration, *Eur. J. Pharmacol.,* **20,** 139 (1972).
211. Sofia, R. D. and H. Barry, III, Depressant effects of Δ^1-tetrahydrocannabinol enhanced by inhibition of its metabolism, *Eur. J. Pharmacol.,* **13,** 134 (1970).
212. Sofia, R. D., R. J. Ertel, B. N. Dixit, and H. Barry, III, Effect of Δ^9 tetrahydrocannabinol on the uptake of serotonin by rat brain homogenates, *Eur. J. Pharmacol.,* **16,** 257 (1971).
213. Sofia, R. D., B. N. Dixit, and H. Barry, III, Effect of Δ^1-tetrahydrocannabinol on serotonin metabolism in the rat brain, *Life Sci.,* **10,** 425 (1971).
214. Sofia, R. D., T. A. Solomon, and H. Barry, III, The anticonvulsant activity of Δ^1-tetrahydrocannabinol in mice, *Pharmacologist,* **13,** 246 (1971) (abstract).
215. Spaulning, T. C., R. D. Ford, D. E. McMillan, and L. S. Harris, Some pharmacological effects of phenitrone and its interaction with Δ^9-THC, *Eur. J. Pharmacol.,* **19,** 310 (1972).
216. Sperling, F. and A-A. O. Coker, Response of isolated rat lungs to Δ^9-tetrahydrocannabinol, *Fed. Proc.,* **31,** 505 (1972) (abstract).
217. Sprague, R. A., H. Rosenkrantz, G. R. Thompson, and M. C. Braude, Monkey brain and lung respiration after chronic i.v. treatment with delta-9-tetrahydrocannabinol, *Fed. Proc.,* **31,** 909 (1972).

217a. Thompson, G. R., H. Rosenkrantz, U. H. Schaeppi and M. C. Braude, Comparison of Acute Oral Toxicity of Cannabinoids in Rats, Dogs and Monkeys. *Toxicol. Appl. Pharmacol.* **25,** 363 (1973).

218. Thompson, G. R., H. Rosenkrantz, R. W. Fleischman, and M. C. Braude, Toxicity of delta-9-tetrahydrocannabinol (delta-9-THC) in Rhesus monkeys treated per os or intravenous for 28 days, *Proc. 5th Int. Cong. Pharmacol.,* San Francisco, Calif., July 23–28, 232 (1972).

219. Truitt, E. B., Jr., Pharmacological activity in a metabolite of 1-trans-Δ^8-tetrahydrocannabinol, *Fed. Proc.,* **29,** 619 (1970) (abstract).

220. Truitt, E. B., Jr., Biological disposition of tetrahydrocannabinols, *Pharmacol. Rev.,* **23,** 273, (1971).

221. Truitt, E. B., Jr., Evaluation of an active metabolite hypothesis for 11-hydroxytetrahydrocannabinols, *Proc. 30th Int. Cong. on Alcoholism and Drug Dependence,* Amsterdam 1972 (to be published).

222. Truitt, E. B., Jr., and S. M. Anderson, Biogenic amine alterations produced in the brain by tetrahydrocannabinols and their metabolites, *Ann. N.Y. Acad. Sci.,* **191,** 68 (1971).

223. Truitt, E. B., Jr., and S. M. Anderson, The role of biogenic amines in the central action of tetrahydrocannabinols and their metabolites, *Acta Pharm. Suec.,* **8,** 696 (1971) (abstract).

224. Ueki, S., M. Fujiwara, and N. Ogawa, Mouse killing behavior induced by Δ^9-tetrahydrocannabinol in the rat, *Proc. 5th Int. Cong. Pharmacol.* San Francisco, Calif. July 23–28, 238 (1972).

225. U.S. National Commission of Marihuana and Drug Abuse, *Marihuana: Signal of Misunderstanding.* First Report, Government Printing Office, Washington, D.C., March (1972).

226. Wall, M. E., D. R. Brine, G. A. Brine, C. G. Pitt, R. I. Freudenthal, and H. D. Christensen, Isolation, structure and biological activity of several metabolites of Δ^9-tetrahydrocannabinols, *J. Am. Chem. Soc.,* **92,** 3466 (1970).

227. Wall, M. E., D. Brine, M. Perez-Reyes, and M. Lipton, Studies on the *in vitro* and *in vivo* metabolism of Δ^9-tetrahydrocannabinol, *Acta Pharmacol. Seuc.,* **8,** 702 (1971).

228. Wallach, M. B. and S. Gershon, The effects of delta-8-tetrahydrocannabinol on the electroencephalogram (EEG), reticular formulation multiple unit activity (RUA) and sleep of the cat, *Fed. Proc.,* **31,** 250 (1972).

229. Waller, C. W. and J. J. Denny, *Annotated Bibliography of Marihuana, 1964–1970,* The Research Institute of Pharmaceutical Sciences, University of Mississippi, 1971.

230. Way, E. L. and H. Isbell, Chairmen, Symposium: Marihuana and Its Surrogates, *Pharmacol. Rev.,* **23,** 263 (1971).

231. Webster, C. D. M. D. Willinsky, B. S. Herring, and G. C. Walters, Effects of 1-delta-9-tetrahydrocannabinol on temporally spaced responding and discriminated Sidman avoidance behavior in rats, *Nature,* **232,** 498 (1971).

232. World Health Organization, *The Use of Cannabis: Report of a WHO Scientific Group*, WHO Technical Report Series No. 478, World Health Organization, Geneva, 1971.
233. Zimmerberg, B., S. D. Glick, and M. E. Jarvik, Impairment of recent memory by marihuana and Δ^9-tetrahydrocannabinol in rhesus monkey, *Nature,* **233,** 343 (1971).

Chapter Five*

CLINICAL PHARMACOLOGY OF MARIHUANA

LEO E. HOLLISTER, *Veterans Administration Hospital and Department of Medicine, Stanford University School of Medicine, Palo Alto, California*

A number of excellent reviews or collations of papers dealing with recent work with marihuana now have appeared. Since few single reviews can cover this immense field, and each reviewer tends to have his own prejudices about what data are important, the reader may be well advised to sample several (6, 24, 43, 44, 60, 68).

1. HUMAN EXPERIMENTATION WITH MARIHUANA

Legal and Regulatory Constraints

Although some investigators had initial problems in attempting marihuana research in man, these have largely been overcome (70). Attempts have been made by the regulatory bodies involved to facilitate research with marihuana and related substances. In addition to making it as easy as possible for qualified investigators to study marihuana, these bodies give further encouragement by an increasing amount of funding through grant and contract mechanisms.

Problems in Dosing

Dosage has remained a persistent problem in clinical pharmacological studies. First, even synthetic delta-1-tetrahydrocannabinol (THC) may vary somewhat, depending on its handling following its chemical synthesis. Any deterioration of this material between its time of synthesis and administration to man may result in doses less than putative. Use of such material as

---

* Work cited as having been done by the author was supported in part by PHS grant MH-03030.

a standard for assay of THC content of native materials perpetuates the error. Second, the GLC (gas-liquid chromatographic) assay of THC, because of the high temperatures used, decarboxylates the THC acids that are present to varying degrees in natural materials. As the THC acids may be pharmacologically inactive unless decarboxylated, any failure to do so may lead to a falsely high estimate of the dose of active material. Finally, natural marihuana tends to deteriorate over time unless it is properly stored (limited access to air, light, and heat). We have obtained samples of varying ages that have shown very little THC content. Unless one is careful to analyze the content of these materials frequently, one is likely to give smaller doses than believed. At least one prominent investigator acknowledged this difficulty, and it seems likely that others have fallen victim to this source of error without realizing it (58). Problems in the delivery of doses are mentioned in a later section.

Problems in Selecting Subjects

Most subjects selected for experiments with marihuana are experienced smokers. The reasons for choosing such subjects are the following:

1. They are more readily available (and eager).
2. One does not bear the moral risk of initiating someone into drug use.
3. They do not have to be taught the technique of smoking.
4. They may be sophisticated drug "tasters."

Naive subjects can still be found, but these days they may best be saved for doing metabolic studies, or some other purpose that makes better use of their uncontaminated state.

One runs a few risks in selecting experienced drug users. If their use has been too high or too long, they may have altered their metabolism of the drug. Further, the learned effects of drug use may spread to the experimental situation, so that a relatively high level of placebo response may occur.

Difficulties in Maintaining Blind Controls

Although the double-blind controlled study has become a shibboleth of clinical pharmacological research, it is not especially applicable to drugs of this sort. With higher doses of drug, it is virtually impossible for the subject or experimenter not to know when an active drug is being given. Lower doses, especially those at threshold levels, give more difficulty, although the objective changes they produce may often tip-off the investigator. As there are many reasons for wanting to continue to use this technique, it should be recognized that its conditions are only partly met in most clinical studies.

2. CONSTITUENTS, METABOLITES, AND HOMOLOGS

Natural Cannabinoids

The three major natural cannabinoids are Δ^1-THC, cannabinol (CBN), and cannabidiol (CBD). Of these, only the first has been extensively studied in man. The latter two are presumed to be inactive on the basis of tentative studies (52). The Δ^6 isomer of THC, which accounts for only a minute portion of the THC, content of natural marihuana, has been found to be active in animal studies and may be presumed to be active in man. Methyl and propyl side chain homologs of THC have been isolated from certain types of marihuana, but they have not yet been tested in man (47). It would appear reasonable that a seven carbon side chain homolog might also be found. Other possible active materials present in marihuana are alkaloids (31). At the moment, however, it would appear that Δ^1-THC accounts for the major activity of marihuana.

Metabolites

Increasing evidence suggests that the action of THC is mediated in large part, if not totally, through the formation of an active 7-hydroxy metabolite. This is only one of the several monohydroxy metabolites, as shown in Fig. 1. It is likely that this particular metabolite is further metabolized to an acid form. The dihydroxy metabolites are thought to be inactive. Administration of 1 mg of labeled 7-hydroxy-Δ^1-THC intravenously produced in man an almost instant onset of a clinical syndrome similar to that from the parent compound (38). The drug and its metabolites were excreted in urine and feces for more than a week. Whether or not the activity of THC is solely in this metabolite remains to be determined.

Homologs

For many years it was thought that the naturally occurring THC was Δ^3-THC. This material, as well as its amyl side chain homologs, synhexyl or pyrahexyl, was synthesized many years ago. The latter, in particular, has been extensively studied. In comparison to Δ^1-THC, it has similar clinical effects but is both less potent and slower in onset of action (18). Although the Δ^3-THC had been thought to be inactive, recent evidence suggests otherwise. As in the case of synhexyl, its potency is somewhat weaker than Δ^1-THC, in the ratio of approximately 1:3 to 1:6 (22). A great many synthetic homologs of THC are possible, including some that are water soluble. These will doubtless be studied in man over the next several years.

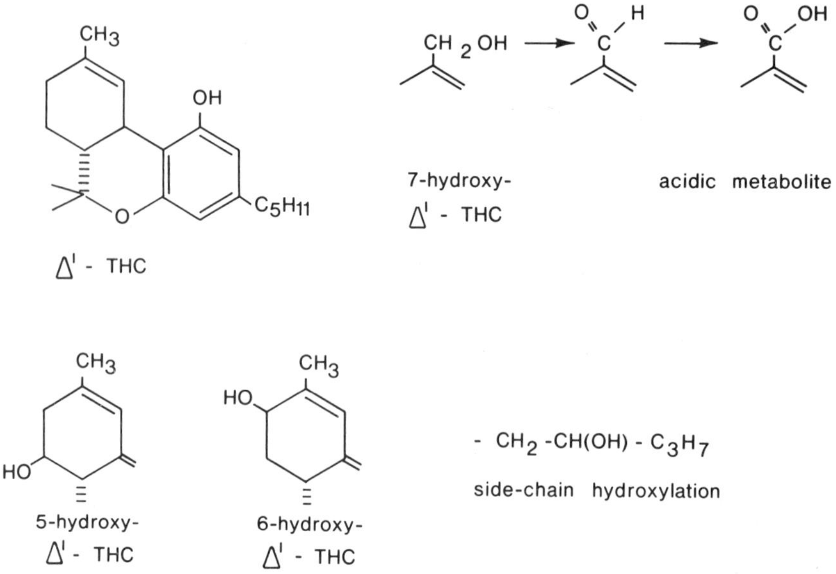

Fig. 1. Postulated metabolic pathway of THC. 7-hydroxy metabolite is active in man. Dihydroxy metabolites are presumed to be inactive.

3. PHARMACOKINETICS

Absorption

Smoking It has long been known that cannabis materials are more potent when smoked than when taken orally, and a clinical estimation of relative potency by these two routes indicates a roughly threefold difference (27). One would expect the lipoprotein surfactant lining of the alveoli to be a superb vehicle for the absorption of such a lipid-soluble material as THC. That this is the case is supported by clinical experience of an extremely rapid onset of effects of smoked hashish or other potent preparations. The slang word "toke" denotes the usual large, deep inhalation of marihuana smoke and may be used as a unit of measurement: one-toke, two-toke, and so on, "grass". The conversion of THC to an active metabolite must occur rapidly in the lung, where enzymes suitable for this reaction are found.

Measurement of the kinetics of THC following smoking of labeled material supports the notion that the lung affords rapid absorption. In many respects, these kinetics are similar to those following intravenous injection (37). It has been estimated that the smallest amount of THC in cigarettes that produces reliable clinical reactions is 5 mg (17). One must assume that probably only 20% of this dose is actually absorbed, so that THC is a more potent material than would appear at first.

Oral Doses From what is known of the high-lipid solubility of THC, it is reasonable to assume that it is absorbed in the upper intestine. Absorption is facilitated when the material is given in a lipid medium. Estimates are that 95% of an oral dose is absorbed, but the rate of absorption is highly variable, depending on gastrointestinal motility, position, and the presence of other materials in the stomach or small intestine. Measurement of label following oral administration of labeled THC revealed a steady increase in plasma concentration to a peak at 3 hr followed by a slower fall over the next 7 hrs (35). The correlation of amount of label in plasma with clinical symptoms reported in another study was remarkably good. Such findings indicate that plasma concentrations of this drug are well correlated with clinical effects.

Distribution, Biotransformation, and Excretion

By use of small intravenous tracers doses of ^{14}C-labeled Δ^1-THC (5.6 to 7.9 μg/kg, approximately 0.5-mg total dose) the disposition of THC was studied in man. A two-phase plasma disappearance curve was found, the rapid phase having a half-life of about 30 min during which redistribution of the drug occurred, followed by a slow phase with a half-life of about 56 hr. Since the rapid phase correlated reasonably well with the expected span of clinical effects of THC similarly administered, pharmacologically active doses of the drug might be handled in a similar fashion. Metabolites of THC appeared in plasma within 10 min, but during the first hour most THC in plasma was unchanged. The 7-hydroxy metabolite constituted only a relatively small fraction of material in plasma, but other presently unidentified materials might represent further metabolites derived from it. Less than 1% of THC was excreted in urine unchanged (34). A later study by the same group used chronic smokers of marihuana rather than naive subjects. The same kinetic pattern was found, but the respective plasma half-lives were reduced by about 50% (36). Such findings suggest enzyme induction following repeated exposure to marihuana with increased rate of metabolic disposition of the drug. *In vitro* studies showed that THC is bound to lipoproteins in human plasma to the extent of 80 to 95%. Thus prolonged binding in tissues, as indicated by the prolonged half-life following redistribution of the drug, is quite reasonable (65).

The prolonged excretion of metabolites of marihuana constituents has been confirmed by others. Marihuana metabolites were observed in urine for several days following single doses (26). No unchanged THC could be detected, although unchanged CBD and CBN were found, suggesting that the metabolism of these compounds is less rapid than that of THC. Repeated doses of marihuana usually showed no evidence of buildup of marihuana metabolites in urine.

The 7-hydroxy metabolite of THC was first described in animals (53). Increasing evidence indicates that it is present in man as well and may prove to be the principal source of THC activity (38). This compound is metabolized in turn along the same pathways as THC itself (see Fig. 1). Whether other metabolites are also active remains to be seen. It is tempting to speculate that some of the phasic aspects of the clinical action of marihuana may be temporally related to the peaks of various metabolites in the body.

4. CLINICAL SYNDROMES

General Considerations

The pattern of clinical syndromes produced by marihuana or synthetic Δ^1-THC at various doses and by various routes of administration has been extensively detailed elsewhere (3, 7, 9, 18, 22, 27, 30, 41, 58, 67, 69). The dose is of crucial importance, with syndromes varying from a mild and brief "high" when low doses are smoked to a prolonged hallucinogenic experience when high doses are taken orally. The onset of symptoms may be delayed by more than 2 hrs after oral administration, but symptoms may appear within minutes when materials are smoked. Thus the time course, but not the symptoms, is altered greatly by the route of dosing. As with most drugs, the larger the dose taken, regardless of route, the longer the action.

Specific Effects

Marihuana has a biphasic clinical action, with an initial period of stimulation (anxiety, heightened perceptions, euphoria) followed by a later period of sedation (relaxation, sleepiness, dreamlike states). Overlying these phenomena, which are observed to some extent from any effective dose, are definite psychotomimetic effects. These are seldom noted at small doses, but they become increasingly severe with large doses. The hallmark of a psychotomimetic effect is a change in time perception (see Section 7). Other prominent symptoms are paresthesias; altered perceptions; difficulty in thinking, concentrating, speaking, or remembering; depersonalization; visual illusions and pseudohallucinations; and various subjective phenomena peculiar to each individual.

The usual dose to obtain mild clinical effects is 5 mg smoked in a cigarette or 10 mg taken orally. Doses of 20 mg smoked or over 70 mg taken by mouth are liable to produce severe and unsettling effects. Sometimes these can unsettle the investigator: One of our subjects developed a severe tachycardia and markedly elevated blood pressure in response to his adverse psychological reaction to a cigarette containing a 19-mg dose.

Although qualitative differences between the effects of natural marihuana products and synthetic or isolated THC may exist, the latter compound is generally used as the basis for dosage of all preparations. Comparisons between the effects of THC itself and those of natural preparations usually do not show much difference, although one has the clinical impression that euphoria is more predictable from THC. Expert users of marihuana are said to be able to distinguish between lots of materials that have predominant euphoric or sedative effects, but it remains to be seen if there is a chemical or pharmacological basis for such distinctions.

Relevance of Clinical Effects in Laboratory to Social Use

It is rather heartening that the clinical syndromes described for marihuana in the laboratory correspond closely to those reported by street users (with the exception of those which are too personal or metaphysical to be measured). With a questionnaire technique and a sampling method that allowed distribution of the questionnaire until it reached a respondent who was a user of marihuana, clinical aspects of the social use of the drug were described (61). The most common symptoms and signs reported are paresthesia, floating sensations, and depersonalization; weakness and relaxation perceptual changes (visual, auditory, tactile); subjective slowing of time; flight of ideas, difficulty in thinking, and loss of attention; loss of immediate memory; euphoria and silliness; sleepiness. Other common symptoms not verifiable in the laboratory are claims of increased insight and perception, as well as increased sexual desire, performance, and enjoyment.

Placebo Effects

People who should know better sometimes state that marihuana is really a placebo, a kind of ritual by which its devotees attain whatever experiences they desire. To be sure, many do that, but very likely only when they have taken no active materials or subthreshold doses. As we have seen, THC is one of the more potent mind-altering drugs. The vagaries in determining dosage have probably led many investigators astray in their estimate of the dose given to their subjects.

The effects of suggestion may be quite strong with a drug of this type. Many frequent users of the drug find it difficult to distinguish between a placebo and an active preparation, or at least the distinction is less strictly based on subjective effects than one might expect (29). On the other hand, objective changes in these users are usually more evident and allow distinctions to be made fairly accurately. One must assume that some conditioning to the marihuana "high" occurs. The influence of individual and group expectations from the drug undoubtedly augments and alters its effects. In this regard, one might hope that the present tendency to use mild preparations of the drug and strong elements of suggestibility will continue.

5. PHYSIOLOGICAL EFFECTS

General

Cardiovascular

Tachycardia is a frequent concomitant of almost any marihuana preparation by any route of administration. Although severe degrees may be attributable to anxiety about the experiences from the drug, it is not that alone. Quite possibly it is due to a transient release of epinephrine early in the course of drug action (23). Some evidence suggests that tolerance to the tachycardic action develops with repeated doses of the drug. Effects on blood pressure are generally far less predictable, some investigators finding slight changes in either direction. Orthostatic hypotension is more serious and, like tachycardia, is not explained solely as a reaction to psychological stress. The electrocardiogram is generally normal, but premature ventricular contractions have been reported (only after smoking) and rare instances of T wave abnormalities occur.

Eyes

Suffusion of the conjunctivae, like tachycardia, tends to parallel the clinical course. Conjunctival injection occurs following oral doses of drug and is thus not due to irritation from smoke. It may be part of a general mucous membrane response, for changes in the membranes of the mouth and throat have also been described. The most interesting, and unexpected, effect from marihuana has been lowering of intraocular pressure (15). Lowering occurs in subjects with initially normal pressures as well as in patients with glaucoma. No satisfactory mechanism for this action has been discovered yet.

Neuromuscular

Incoordination, tremor, and ataxia are more often subjective complaints than objectively demonstrable, but even the La Guardia Commission study demonstrated an impairment of static equilibrium (45). Muscle weakness is also a subjective complaint, which in one of our studies was demonstrated objectively by use of a finger ergometer (21). Deep tendon reflexes are generally unaltered.

Miscellaneous Effects

Although body temperature is reduced in animals regularly, it is far more difficult to document this in man. Salivation is regularly reduced, somewhat more by smoking than by other forms of administration. Appetite and hunger are said to be increased by users, but single doses given in an experimental situation led to an increased food intake in only 7 of 12 subjects both in fed and in fasting conditions (25).

Much of marihuana use occurs because of its reputation as a sexual stimulant or its ability to enhance sexual pleasure. Not much experimental evidence is at hand for either assertion, but that does not necessarily mean they are not valid. One thing seems likely: People who smoke marihuana are more likely to be sexually free (13).

Neurophysiological

Electroencephalographic Studies

Increased alpha activity correlated with feelings of euphoria were noted in the La Guardia Commission report (45). Six of ten subjects showed a slight tendency toward a less persistent alpha rhythm following 4 to 7 grains of marihuana of unknown composition. One subject who took an overdose (48 grains) completely lost alpha activity previously present (3). Single doses of synhexyl had no effect on the EEG, but slowing of dominant frequencies occurred during chronic ad libitum dosage (72). Following smoking of cigarettes thought to contain about 9 mg of THC, slight slowing was noted in the alpha band with more peaking of frequencies (58). A later study by the same group, using smoked doses of up to 36 mg of THC, revealed inconsistent and minimal 0.3 to 0.6 Hz slowing of the alpha frequency (12). Similar changes were noted in subjects receiving oral doses of marihuana extract equivalent to 32 mg of THC. Flattening of anterior lead tracings, synchronization of posterior lead tracings, and occasional paroxysmal slowing of the alpha rhythm were noted. These changes were not readily distinguishable from those which occurred when the same subjects were treated with placebo; in both conditions subjects were practically immobile and frequently drowsing (20).

Doses of 9 mg of THC in smoked material or 90 mg taken orally produced increased low-voltage fast activity, decreased alpha activity, and slight slowing of alpha frequencies (30). Acute doses of smoked marihuana equivalent to 7.5 and 22.5 mg of THC produced a transitory increase in the percentage of alpha time and a reduction in the theta and beta bands. Daily smoking of marihuana for periods of 10 to 22 days produced synchronization of the EEG (73). These differences in EEG effects from marihuana are no less confusing than those reported for many other centrally acting drugs. The consensus seems to be for slightly increased alpha activity, minimal slowing of rhythm, and tendency toward synchronization.

Sleep Studies

Data obtained from questionnaires indicated that marihuana users find that low doses have sedative effects but that high doses are stimulating and interfere with induction of sleep (62). As with most studies involving the effects of drugs on sleep, the timing of the dose prior to sleep may be of critical importance, especially when a drug has the biphasic effect of marihuana. Sleep laboratory studies, using doses of 61 to 258 μg/kg of THC given orally just prior to beginning sleep recording, showed an increased total sleep time, increments in stage-4 sleep, decrements in REM sleep, and at highest doses, reduced wake time and stage 1 sleep. After REM deprivation, doses of 250 μg/kg of THC and 750 μg/kg of synhexyl reduced the amount of REM "rebound" and increased stage 4 sleep (55).

Studies in chronic smokers of marihuana revealed a slightly increased amount of REM sleep in the latter third of the night, with further increase in REM sleep during the first third of the night when the drug was withdrawn. Acute effects of marihuana under baseline conditions were to suppress briefly the amount of REM sleep with evidence of rebound on discontinuation (71). Although it seems clear that the acute effect of marihuana is to decrease REM sleep, the chronic effects may be to increase it. Whether increased REM sleep during chronic use is part of a continuing rebound phenomenon is not yet clear, but in this regard, the effect of marihuana is somewhat different from that of hypnotics.

Evoked Potentials

The contingent negative variation (CNV), a negative surface potential evoked by the pairing of two stimuli, is believed to be a measure of "expectancy" or anticipation, with some relationship to attention or arousal. Oral doses of marihuana extract calibrated for THC content were given in doses of 350 μg/kg 1 hr before recording and compared with doses of 0.7 ml/kg of 95% ethanol and placebo. THC selectively enhanced the CNV amplitude as compared with placebo, whereas ethanol depressed it (33). Enhancement has previously been reported for dextroamphetamine and depression of CNV amplitudes from pentobarbital sodium. Timing may be of crucial importance, for this early effect, obtained during the "high" stage, could be reversed later on. Lysergic acid diethylamide, with which marihuana shares some hallucinogenic effects, also augments CNV amplitudes (66). Subjects receiving marihuana have smaller averaged evoked potentials in response to irrelevant stimuli than those receiving placebo(59). Both these findings suggest that at least at one point in the marihuana-induced state, the ability to focus attention without distraction may be increased.

6. BIOCHEMICAL EFFECTS

Plasma free fatty acid levels remained unchanged after marihuana, whereas sharp elevations are observed after days of the LSD type. Blood glucose values were also unchanged, despite claims in the older literature that marihuana produces hypoglycemia. The lack of change in plasma glucose values has now been verified on numerous occasions. Both creatinine and phosphorus clearance were temporarily decreased, a phenomenon that has been observed with LSD. Plasma cortisol levels, platelet concentrations of serotonin, and urinary excretion of catecholamines are essentially unchanged by moderate doses of drugs. In general, these data in man have contributed little to our understanding of the drug (18, 23).

7. PSYCHOLOGICAL TESTS

Cognitive Functions

Most cognitive functions can be impaired by doses of marihuana, but there are many variables that influence the results. The dose of drug is a paramount consideration, and with higher doses one can be fairly certain to

TABLE 1   COGNITIVE TESTS

Test	Dose/Route[a]	Results	Reference
Serial 7 subtraction		Slowed	
Finger labyrinths	8, 12, 16 (O)[b]	Impaired	56
Sentence reproduction		Impaired	
Serial 7 subtraction		Unimpaired	46
Goal-directed alternation	20, 40, 60 (O)	Impaired	46
Digit spans		Impaired	64
Digit spans		Unimpaired	
Counting backward	10 (O)	Unimpaired	67
Saying alphabet		Unimpaired	
Serial additions		Slight decrease in accuracy	
Digit coding	45 (O)	Impaired	9
Reading comprehension		Impaired	
Word recognition	? (S)	Impaired	1
Digit-symbol substitution	4, 18 (S)	Impaired (naive)	69
	27 to 39 (O)	Unimpaired	21
	9 (S), 90 (O)	Unimpaired	29

[a] Doses based on milligrams of THC.
[b] (O) oral; (S) smoked.

show impairment in most tests. The complexity of the test will determine the likelihood of showing impairment, those which are most complex also being most likely to show deterioration of performance. Differences in types of subject, either in terms of the normal variation between subjects from one experiment to the next, or in terms of "naive" or "casual" users of marihuana versus "chronic" users, also influence the results obtained. Thus one need not be overly disturbed to find different results reported for different tests; it would be strange if such variations did not occur. Many of the commonly used cognitive tests in various experiments with man are summarized in Table 1.

Tests involving immediate memory functions are most sensitive to impairment, whereas those that rely primarily on long-term memory are little changed. Tests which require that the subject reproduce specific information from memory reveal distortions in memroy, suggesting the process of confabulation, which would not be unexpected with immediate memory disorders. Clinically, the loss of immediate memory is easily ascertained simply by talking to the subjects: "I can't remember what I was just talking about," "My mind wanders and thoughts rush in," "What was that you wanted me to do?," and so forth.

Perceptual Tests

The most consistently demonstrated perceptual alteration is a distortion in time sense (Table 2). To some extent, this perceptual change is the hallmark of hallucinogenic drugs, being seen dramatically with LSD. The distortion in time sense must be measured against the degree of total toxicity,

TABLE 2 PERCEPTUAL TESTS

Test	Dose/Route	Results	Reference
Time estimation	4.5, 18 (S)	Prolonged	69
	45 (O)	Prolonged	9
	9 (S), 90 (O)	Prolonged	29
Time production	1.5–5.1 (S)	Shortened	48
	9 (S), 90 (O)	Unchanged	29
Time production/ Estimation	27–39 (O)	Improved	21
Smell threshold		Unchanged	
Tactile sensation	60 (O)	Unchanged	72
Two-point discrimination		Unchanged	
Vibratory sense		Unchanged	
	4 (S)	Increased	58
Light intensity	7–8 (S)	Unchanged	50
Tone discrimination		Unchanged	
	60 (O)	Unchanged	72
Auditory frequency		Unchanged	
Depth perception	? (O)	Impaired	8
Archimedes spiral		Shortened	
Musical (Seashore)	60 (O)	Subjectively improved Objectively unchanged	72
Rod-frame test	9 (S), 90 (O)	Unchanged	29
	27–39 (O)	Unchanged	21

TABLE 3 MOTOR TESTS

Test	Dose/Range	Results	Reference
Reaction time, simple	27–39 (O)	Impaired	21
Reaction time, complex	45 (O)	Impaired	9
Flexibility of closure	30–70 (O)	Impaired	18
Continuous	4.5, 18 (S)	Unchanged	69
performance test	1.6–5.1 (S)	Decreased (casual)	48
Pursuit rotor	4.5, 18 (S)	Decreased (naive)	69
Driving simulation	? (S)	Unchanged	10
	12, 16 (O)	Decreased	56
Hand-steadiness	45 (O)	Reduced	9
Bender-Gestalt	4 (S)	Impaired	58

for undoubtedly one can get time sense distortions with severe degrees of intoxication with nonhallucinogenic drugs such as alcohol.

Subjective time is slowed, which creates a paradox in the various tests used. Estimates of time are prolonged, for with slowing of subjective time, an absolute amount of time seems longer. Productions of time are shortened, for here the slowing of the internal clock is reflected in a feeling that more time has elapsed than actually has. Once again, these distortions are common clinical phenomena: "Time seems either to stand still or rush by," "So many things are happening inside me that I can't keep track," "I thought it was much later in the day than it really was," and so forth.

The single reported study on depth perceptions showed impairment, which again is consistent with clinical descriptions of either lengthening or shortening of visual perspectives. Most sensory modalities seem to be unchanged. The increase in vibratory sensation is difficult to explain and is not reflected in clinical experience. One clinical experience that has never been tested in the laboratory is that pain sensation in skin is increased under marihuana. We get many more complaints about the skill of technicians in drawing blood samples when people are under the drug than when they are not.

Motor Tests

These tests seem to be most sensitive to deterioration under the influence of drug, perhaps representing the summation of mental impairment as well as motor incoordination (Table 3). Since motor incoordination, unsteadiness, and tremors are common clinical signs, this would possibly explain the great vulnerability of motor tests to being adversely affected by the drug.

The most complex motor task, and the one with the greatest consequences for the individual and others, is the ability to operate a motor vehicle. In the case of marihuana, the answer is not yet at hand; it appears that it may take a number of studies to arrive at some kind of consensus. Further, the situation prevailing in the testing laboratory may not be comparable to that on the highway, much as we might like to believe that to be the case. It seems logical to believe, on the basis of other data available, that some socially used doses of marihuana could make driving unsafe. Unfortunately, we lack a reliable forensic test for determining the doses that cause such impairment. Even the most ardent proponents of marihuana as a legal drug would not insist that it be treated preferentially to alcohol, where forensic tests are widely applied.

8. THERAPEUTIC USES

Marihuana has been used therapeutically in the past and one may expect to see a revival of interest. The past uses of the drug have been well reviewed elsewhere (49).

Hypnotic

One of the most plausible uses of marihuana is as a hypnotic drug. The reports of many subjects that they had dreamlike states even suggested the possibility that the drug might be unlike other hypnotics in not suppressing dreaming (rapid eye movement, or REM) sleep. Such is not the case. Sleep time is prolonged, as it should be with a hypnotic drug, but REM sleep is suppressed to a degree comparable to that found with conventional hypnotics (55). Further, the initial stimulant action of the drug may impair sleep for some persons especially susceptible to these effects.

Analgesia

Although simple screening tests for analgesic action in animals suggest that marihuana may be useful, it has not been subjected to any clinical trial. The difficulty in giving parenteral doses as well as the considerable delay in effect when the drug is given orally suggest that it would not fare well in comparison to existing analgesics. Persons who employ the drug for sexual purposes report an increased sensitivity of skin. We have observed some degree of hyperesthesia of skin and subcutaneous tissues in subjects from who blood was being drawn during experiments.

Withdrawal from Other Drugs

Despite some superficial similarity of the effects of marihuana to those of barbiturates or opiates, it is likely that this drug is not a pharmacological equivalent of either. Thus it seems to be an unlikely candidate for treating withdrawal reactions to alcohol, barbiturates, or opiates. Clinical trials for this purpose were undertaken a number of years ago, but despite some initially favorable reports, this use did not catch on (16). In view of the present abundance of drugs which are satisfactory for treating withdrawal reactions, marihuana is not likely to offer any compelling advantages.

Antidepressant

The sedative and euphoriant effects of marihuana might seem valuable for treating depression, in which anxiety and sadness are often the rule. Past attempts to treat depression with marihuana did not attract much interest, but it could be that the times were prejudicial to its wider use (54). Since sedative drugs may be of value in treating common types of depression mixed with anxiety, marihuana could be useful, but it probably is no more so than the conventional sedatives so widely available. The actions of tricyclic antidepressants, which are clearly the drugs of choice for endogenous or retarded depressions, are quite different from those of marihuana, which would not supplant these agents in these more severe depressive syndromes. Nonetheless, marihuana deserves a careful therapeutic trial for this possible indication.

Appetite Stimulant

Street lore has long had it that one's appetite becomes ravenous and one's appreciation of food sublime after use of marihuana. A recent attempt to study this appetite-stimulating effect in the laboratory gives some support to this idea, although it is by no means a constant phenomenon (25). It has not been studied in patients whose appetite is poor, but only in subjects with normal appetite, thus one cannot draw conclusions about its clinical utility. Further, to be useful in the clinic, this effect would have to be sustained over time. The combination of euphoriant and appetite stimulating effects might be useful in one of the most serious psychiatric disorders, anorexia nervosa. It would seem that these individuals would be the most likely candidates for therapeutic trials.

Antihypertensive

The hypotensive effects both of THC and especially of homologs such as the dimethylheptyl derivative have engendered hopes that some derivative might be a useful therapeutic agent for essential hypertension. Hypotensive effects have been attainable only with doses of THC which have severe mental effects. Although the mechanism of its hypotensive action has not been worked out, it may be due to blocking of compensatory mechanisms for maintaining blood pressure in the erect posture. Since this mode of action is perhaps the least desirable mechanism for lowering blood pressure of the several available, and many other available drugs work in this way, the possible therapeutic use of some THC derivative as an antihypertensive drug is doubtful.

Anticonvulsant

Early pharmacological studies indicated that marihuana abolished electrically induced seizures in mice but not those produced by metrazol, and that it acted synergistically with diphenylhydantoin (40). An early clinical report in five epileptic children also indicated favorable results (11). On the other hand, chronic administration of marihuana has been reported to cause temporal spikes in users and aggravate seizures in some with known epilepsy. Since new approaches to the control of seizures are desirable, this line of investigation should be pursued.

Other Uses

When a new psychotropic drug is said to be useful for treating migraine or menstrual disorders (and virtually all share this claim sooner or later), it has arrived. Such a claim has been made for marihuana. As the present prophylaxis of migraine attacks leaves much to be desired, this use bears scrutiny.

9. ADVERSE EFFECTS

Somatic

In general, marihuana must be reckoned as one of the safest drugs known, at least in regard to lethality. One fatality has been ascribed to excessive smoking of marihuana and cannabinol was found in the urine, but the circumstances of death were not at all clear (14). Respiratory tract changes, such as those suffered by smokers of tobacco, might be expected in marihuana smokers as well. Pharyngitis, sinusitis, and bronchitis have been found in heavy smokers of hashish among American soldiers in Germany (63). Carinal biopsies showed changes similar to those seen in heavy smokers, principally epithelial metaplasia. The most serious complication reported to date has been cerebral atrophy in young drug users who might be considered "potheads." Their ventricles appeared to be dilated on pneumoencephalograms, but it was not certain that marihuana alone was the cause (5). This study, as well as other clinical studies of adverse reactions, has been severely criticized by purists who demand the same rigorous scientific controls as those used in experiments with rats in the laboratory. Clinical data are just not that susceptible to controls. Yet it may be stated with some degree of confidence that most serious side effects of drugs are first discovered in the clinic rather than in the laboratory. Rather than disavow such reports, it might be more prudent to take them under advisement.

Allergy to marihuana may be manifested by urticaria and angioneurotic edema, or, rarely, by anaphylactoid reactions. In the latter instance, the subject was positive to scratch-testing with THC (39). Cirrhosis and abnormal hepatic tests have been described in marihuana users, but it seems doubtful that they are related to the drug. Although marihuana, like most other drugs, passes the placenta readily, and, if given in enough doses to enough species, will show some teratogenic effects, it seems unlikely that this is a hazard in humans. Chromosomal changes have not been demonstrated (51).

Psychiatric

The number of young patients admitted to psychiatric hospitals who are drug users is rising rapidly, but such a relationship does not necessarily imply causality. Many clinicians are of the opinion that marihuana is more likely to exacerbate an underlying psychiatric disorder than it is to cause one.

The most common acute reactions are "bad trips" and toxic-confusional states. The former resemble the acute panic reactions seen with other hallucinogenic drugs and may possibly be due to inadvertent overdose (70). These are usually self-limiting. Many clinicians prefer not to use drug treatment but rather to "talk the patient down." Doses of sedatives, such as diazepam or secobarbital, may be useful. Toxic states are accompanied by disorientation, paranoid ideation, and sometimes by hallucinations (4). These also rather quickly subside and are usually best treated with conventional sedatives. Paranoia also occurs in subjects in laboratory experiments. Schizophreniform psychoses and depression are less frequent sequelae of marihuana use. The latter have led to suicidal attempts (32). It is worth considering whether the alarming increase in suicides among young people may be related to the rapid expansion of drug use.

Many persons are concerned about the more subtle long-term effect of the "amotivational syndrome." Personality changes manifested by emotional lability, loss of interest and ambition, lack of self-esteem and personal hygiene, and pansexuality have been attributed to prolonged use of marihuana. It may be argued that these are also attributes of many who accept voluntarily a new life style, which includes not only these changes in personality but also the taking of drugs. Thus drug-taking would be the consequence rather than the cause of the change in life style. Nonetheless, clinical evidence suggests that for many young people it works the other way and that they do not voluntarily choose the kind of existence they often achieve by drug-taking. "Flashbacks," or recrudescent symptoms of an earlier hallucinogenic drug experience, have been attributed to marihuana. If they occur during marihuana use they are not true flashbacks, but simply a milder form of hallucinogenic experience. True flashbacks following marihuana are said to occur only in subjects with prior experience with stronger hallucinogens.

10. MARIHUANA AND OTHER DRUGS

Comparisons

LSD

The Lexington group compared effects of smoked Δ^9-THC with those of LSD given intramuscularly. Subjective effects of the two drugs were not readily distinguished, but objective differences were marked: LSD increased body temperature, increased both systolic and diastolic blood pressures, increased deep tendon reflexes, and dilated pupils, whereas THC had none of these effects (28). Our own retrospective comparison of the effects of orally administered Δ^9-THC and LSD came to similar conclusions regarding objective differences. We thought that in terms of subjective effects, Δ^9-THC produced less total impairment of function with more euphoria and dreamlike states than LSD at comparable doses. Sedation, which was not a characteristic of LSD effect, was a prominent feature with THC, most subjects falling asleep (19).

Dextroamphetamine and Ethanol

We compared doses of marihuana extract, calibrated to provide 0.5 mg/kg of Δ^9-THC, with doses of 950 mg/kg of ethanol and 0.2 mg/kg of dextroamphetamine, all taken orally. A marihuana placebo control was also used, against which changes from the other drugs were measured (21). Despite the fact that marihuana is considered to have a biphasic clinical action with initial stimulation and euphoria followed later by sedation, clinically there was little resemblance to the stimulant properties of dextroamphetamine. It does, however, have ethanol-like sedative properties.

Ethanol

Another comparison of ethanol and marihuana used two doses of the latter, one smoked and one taken orally. The subjects, who were all heavy users of marihuana, showed little effect from the rather large acute dose of ethanol, and were scarcely able to distinguish active smoked marihuana from placebo (30). They uniformly distinguished the active oral dose, which was considerably stronger than the active smoke, as measured by symptom reports.

Interactions

Marihuana cigarettes were smoked either alone or in combination with oral intake of 15 g of ethanol per 50 lb of body weight (42). Addition of alcohol increased impairment as compared with marihuana alone, an effect which was appreciated subjectively as well. One might expect similar additive effects between marihuana and other sedatives, particularly those of the barbiturate type.

REFERENCES

1. Abel, E. L., Retrieval of information after use of marihuana, *Nature,* **231,** 58 (1971).
2. Aldrich, C. K., The effect of a synthetic marihuana-like compound on musical talent as measured by the Seashore test, *Pub. Health Rep.,* **59,** 431–433 (1944).
3. Ames, F., A clinical and metabolic study of acute intoxication with *Cannabis sativa* and its role in the model psychoses, *J. Ment. Sci.,* **104,** 972–999 (1958).
4. Baker, A. A. and E. G. Lucas, Some hospital admissions associated with cannabis, *Lancet,* **1,** 148 (1969).
5. Campbell, A. M. G., M. Evans, J. L. G. Thomason, and M. J. Williams, Cerebral atrophy in young cannabis smokers, *Lancet,* **2,** 1219–1225 (1971).

6. *Cannabis. A report of the Commission of Inquiry into the Non-Medical Use of Drugs,* Information Canada, Ottawa, 1972. Catalogue No. H 1-5370/4.
7. Clark, L. D. and E. N. Nakashima, Experimental studies of marihuana, *Am. J. Psychiat.,* 125, 379-384 (1968).
8. Clark, L. D. and E. N. Nakashima, Experimental studies of marihuana, *Science,* **164,** 851 (1969).
9. Clark, L. D., R. Hughes, and E. N. Nakashima, Behavioral effects of marihuana. Experimental studies, *Arch. Gen. Psychiatr.,* **23,** 193-198 (1970).
10. Crancer, A., Jr., J. M. Dille, J. C. Delay, J. E. Wallace, and M. D. Haykin, Comparison of the effects of marihuana and alcohol on simulated driving performance, *Science,* **64,** 851-854 (1969).
11. Davis, J. P. and H. H. Ramsey, Antiepileptic action of marihuana-like substances, *Fed. Proc.,* **8,** 284-285 (1949).
12. Domino, E. F., Neuropsychopharmacologic studies of marihuana: Some synthetic and natural THC derivatives in animals and man, *Ann. N.Y. Acad. Sci.,* **191,** 166-191 (1971).
13. Goode, E., Sex and marihuana, *Sexual Behav.,* **2,** (5), 45-51, May (1972).
14. Hendrickx, A., C. Scheiris, and P. Schepens, Toxicological study of a fatal intoxication in man due to cannabis smoking, *J. Pharm. Belg.,* **24,** 371-375 (1969).
15. Hepler, R. S. and I. M. Frank, Marihuana smoking and intraocular pressure, *JAMA,* **217,** 1392 (1971).
16. Himmelsbach, C. K., Treatment of the morphine-abstinence syndrome with a synthetic cannabis-like compound, *South. Med. J.,* **37,** 26-29 (1944).
17. Hochman, J. S. and N. Q. Brill, Marihuana intoxication: Pharmacological and psychological factors, *Dis. Nerv. Syst.,* **32,** 676-679 (1971).
18. Hollister, L. E., R. K. Richards, and H. K. Gillespie, Comparison of tetrahydrocannabinol and synhexyl in man, *Clin. Pharmacol. Ther.,* **9,** 783-791 (1968).
19. Hollister, L. E. and H. K. Gillespie, In *Drugs and Youth,* J. R. Wittenborn, H. Brill, J. P. Smith and S. A. Wittenborn (Eds.) Chas. C Thomas, Springfield, Ill., 1969, pp. 208-211.
20. Hollister, L. E., S. L. Sherwood, and A. Cavasino, Marihuana and the human electroencephalogram, *Pharmacol. Res. Comm.,* **2,** 305-308 (1970).
21. Hollister, L. E. and H. K. Gillespie, Marihuana, ethanol and dextroamphetamine. Mood and mental function alterations, *Arch. Gen. Psychiat.,* **23,** 199-203 (1970).
22. Hollister, L. E., Tetrahydrocannabinol isomers and homologs: Contrasted effects of smoking, *Nature,* **227,** 968-969 (1970).
23. Hollister, L. E., F. Moore, S. L. Kanter, and E. Nobel, Δ^1-Tetrahydrocannabinol, synhexyl and marihuana extract administered orally in man: Catecholamine excretion, plasma cortisol levels and platelet serotonin concentration, *Psychopharmacologia (Berl.),* **17,** 354-360 (1970).

24. Hollister, L. E., Marihuana in man: Three years later, *Science*, **172**, 21–28 (1971).
25. Hollister, L. E., Hunger and appetite after single doses of marihuana, ethanol and dextroamphetamine, *Clin. Pharmacol. Ther.*, **12**, 44–49 (1971).
26. Hollister, L. E., S. L. Kanter, F. Moore, and D. E. Green, Marihuana metabolites in urine of man, *Clin. Pharmacol. Ther.*, (in press).
27. Isbell, H., G. W. Gorodetsky, D. Jasinski, U. Claussen, F. V. Spulak, and F. Korte, Effects of (-)- Δ^9-trans-tetrahydrocannabinol in man, *Psychopharmacologia (Berl.)*, **11**, 184–188 (1967).
28. Isbell, H. and D. Jasinski, A comparison of LSD-25 with (-)- Δ^9-transtetrahydrocannabinol (THC) and attempted cross tolerance between LSD and THC, *Psychopharmacologia*, 14, 115–123 (1969).
29. Jones, R. T., Marihuana-induced "high": Influence of expectation, setting and previous drug experience, *Pharmacol. Rev.*, 23, -369 (1971).
30. Jones, R. T. and G. C. Stone, Psychological studies of marihuana and alcohol in man, *Psychopharmacologia*, **18**, 108-117 (1970).
31. Klein, F. K., H. Rapoport, and H. W. Elliott, Cannabis alkaloids, *Nature*, **232**, 258–259 (1971).
32. Kolansky, H. and W. T. Moore, Effects of marihuana on adolescents and young adults, *JAMA*, **216**, 486–492 (1971).
33. Kopell, B. S., J. R. Tinklenberg, and L. E. Hollister, Contingent negative variation amplitudes: Marihuana and ethanol, *Arch. Gen. Psychiat.* (in press).
34. Lemberger, L., S. D. Silberstein, J. Axelrod and O. J. Kopin, Marihuana. Studies on the disposition and metabolism of Δ-9-tetrahydrocannabinol in man, *Science*, **170** 1320–1322 (1970).
35. Lemberger, L., J. Axelrod, and I. J. Kopin, Metabolism and distribution of Δ^9-tetrahydrocannabinol in man, *Pharmacol. Rev.*, **23**, 371–380 (1971).
36. Lemberger, L., J. Axelrod, and I. J. Kopin, Metabolism and disposition of tetrahydrocannabinols in naive subjects and chronic marihuana users, *Ann. N.Y. Acad. Sci.*, **191**, 142–154 (1971).
37. Lemberger, L., J. L. Weiss, A. M. Watanabe, I. M. Galanter, R. J. Wyatt, and P. V. Cardon, Δ9-tetrahydrocannabinol. Temporal correlation of the psychological effects and blood levels after various routes of administration, *N. Eng. J. Med.*, **286**, 685–688 (1972).
38. Lemberger, L., R. E. Crabtree, and H. M. Row, 11-Hydroxy-Δ-9-tetrahydrocannabinol. Pharmacology, disposition and metabolism of a major metabolite of marihuana in man. *Science,.*
39. Liskow, B., J. L. Liss, and C. W. Parker, Allergy to marihuana, *Ann. Int. Med.*, **75**, 571–573 (1971).
40. Loewe, S. and L. S. Goodman, Anticonvulsant action of marihuana-like substances, *Fed. Proc.*, **6**, 352 (1947).

41. Manno, J. E., G. F. Kiplinger, I. F. Bennett, S. Haine, and R. B. Forney, Comparative effects of smoking marihuana and placebo on human motor and mental performance, *Clin. Pharmacol. Ther.,* **11,** 808–815 (1970).
42. Manno, J. E., G. F. Kiplinger, N. Scholz, R. B. Forney, and S. E. Haine, The influence of alcohol and marihuana on motor and mental performance, *Clin. Pharmacol. Ther.,* **12,** 202–211(1971).
43. *Marihuana: A Singal of Misunderstanding.* First Report of the National Commission on Marihuana and Drug Abuse. Supt. of Documents, U.S. Govt. Printing Office, Washington, D.C. 20402, Stock #5266–0001.
44. *Marihuana and Health.,* Second Annual Report to Congress. U.S. Govt. Printing Office, 75–724 O. Washington, D.C., 1972.
45. Mayor's Committee on Marihuana. *The Marihuana Problem in the City of New York—Sociological, Medical, Psychological and Pharmacological Studies.* Cattell Press, Lancaster, Pa., 1944.
46. Melges, F. T., J. R. Tinklenberg, L. E. Hollister, and H. K. Gillespie, Marihuana and temporal disintegration, *Science,* **168,** 1118–1120 (1970).
47. Merkus, F. W. H. M. Cannabivarin and tetrahydrocannabivarin, two new constituents of hashish, *Nature,* **232,** 579–580 (1971).
48. Meyer, R. E., R. C. Pillard, L. M. Shapiro, and S. M. Mirin, Administration of marihuana to heavy and casual marihuana users, *Am. J. Psychiat.,* **128,** 198–204 (1971).
49. Mikuriya, T. H. Marihuana in medicine: Past, present and future, *Calif. Med.,* **110,** 34–40 (1969).
50. Myers, S. A. and D. F. Caldwell, The effects of marihuana on auditory and visual sensation. A preliminary report, *New Phsyician,* **18,** 212–215 (1969).
51. Neu, R. L., H. O. Powers, S. King, and L. I. Gardner, Δ^8-and Δ^9-Tetrahydrocannabinol: Effects on cultured human leukocytes, *J. Clin. Pharmacol.,* **10,** 228–230 (1970).
52. Neumeyer, J. L. and R. A. Shagoury, Chemistry and pharmacology of marihuana, *J. Pharm. Sci.,* **60,** 1433–14t7 (1971).
53. Nilsson, I. M., S. Agurell, J. L. G. Nilsson, A. Ohlsson, F. Sandberg, and M. Wahlquist, Δ^1-Tetrahydrocannabinol: Structure of a major metaolite, *Science,* **168,** 1228–1229 (1970).
54. Parker, C. S. and F. Wringley, Synthetic cannabis preparations in psychiatry, I. Synhexyl, *J. Ment. Sci.,* **96,** 276–279 (1950).
55. Pivik, R. T., V. Zarcone, W. C. Dement, and L. E. Hollister, Δ-9-tetrahydrocannabinol and synhexyl: Effects on human sleep patterns, *Clin. Pharmacol. Ther.,* **13,** 426–435 (1972).
56. Rafaelsen, O. J., P. Bech, J. Christiansen, H. Christrup, B. Kofod, J. Nyboe, and L. Rafaelsen, Cannabis and alcohol: Effects on simulated driving, Paper presented at 5th World Congress on Psychiatry, Mexico, Dec. 1 (1971).
57. Rafaelsen, L., P. Bech, H. Christrup, and O. J. Rafaelsen, Cannabis and

alcohol: A comparison of psychological effects, presented at V World Congress on Psychiatry, Mexico, Dec. 1 (1971).
58. Rodin, E. A., E. F. Domino, and J. P. Porzak, The marihuana-induced "social high." Neurological and electroencephalographic concomitants, *JAMA*, **213**, 1300–1302 (1970).
59. Roth, W. T., M. Galanter, H. Weingartner, T. B. Vaughn, and R. J. Wyatt, The effect of marihuana and the synthetic Δ-9 THC on the auditory evoked response and background EEG in humans. Submitted for publication.
60. Singer, A. J. (Ed.), *Marihuana: Chemistry, Pharmacology, and Patterns of Social Use, Ann. N.Y. Acad. Sci.,* **191**, 1971.
61. Tart, C. T., Marihuana intoxication; common experiences. *Nature*, **226**, 701–704 (1970).
62. Tart, C. T. and H. J. Crawford, Marihuana intoxication: Reported on effects on sleep, *Psychophysiology*, **7**, 348 (1970).
63. Tennant, F. S., M. Preble, T. J. Prendergast, and P. Ventry, Medical manifestations associated with hashish, *JAMA*, **216**, 1965–1969 (1971).
64. Tinklenberg, J. R. F. T. Melges, L. E. Hollister, and H. K. Gillespie, Marihuana and immediate memory, *Nature*, **226**, 1171 (1970).
65. Wahlquist, M., I. M. Nilsson, F. Sandberg, and S. Agurell, Binding of Δ^1-THC to human plasma proteins, *Bicohem. Pharmacol.*, **19**, 2579–2584 (1970).
66. Walter, W. G., The contingent negative variation: An electro-cortical sign of significant association in the human brain, *Science*, **146**, 434 (1964).
67. Waskow, I. E., J. E. Olsson, C. Salzman, and M. M. Katz, Psychological effects of tetrahydrocannabinol, *Arch. Gen. Psychiat*, **22**, 97–107 (1970).
68. Way, E. L. and H. Isbell, (Chairmen), *Symposium: Marihuana and Its Surrogates, Pharmacol. Rev.*, **23**, 263–389 (1971).
69. Weil, A. T., N. E. Zinberg, and J. M. Nelson, Clinical and psychological effects of marihuana in man, *Science*, **162**, 1234–1242 (1968).
70. Weil, A. T., Adverse reactions to marihuana. Classification and suggested treatment, *New England J. Med.*, **282**, 997–1000 (1970).
71. West, L. J., Psychophysiology of marihuana in humans, in *Fourth Ann. Rpt. to Legislature. Drug Abuse Information Proj.*, D. E. Smith and D. J. Bentel (Eds.), Dept of Pharmacology, UCSF Med. Cen., San Francisco, CA. 1970.
72. Williams, E. G., C. K. Himmelsbach, A. Wikler, D. C. Ruble, and B. J. Lloyd, Studies on marihuana and pyrahexyl compound, *Pub. Health Rep.*, **61**, 1059 (1946).
73. Volavka, J., R. Dornbush, S. Feldstein, G. Clare, A. Zaks, M. Fink, and A. M. Freedman, Marihuana, EEG and behavior, *Ann. N.Y. Acad. Sci.*, **191**, 206–215 (1971).

Chapter Six

TREATMENT AND REHABILITATION OF NARCOTIC ADDICTION

GEORGE M. HENRY, *Department of Psychiatry, University of Kentucky College of Medicine, Lexington, Kentucky*

The treatment of narcotic addiction has involved almost every conceivable approach to patients. Psychoanalysis, maintenance on opioids, incarceration, religious conversion, a variety of psychoactive drugs, hypnosis, frontal lobotomy, electroconvulsive therapy, pharmacologic blockade, legal coercion, group therapy, aversive conditioning, socioeconomic and welfare support, sleep therapy, education, isolation into long-term therapeutic communities—all have been tried. Unfortunately most of these treatments have not proven successful in long-term rehabilitation of addicts, and the problems of addiction seem to grow each year. Few outcome studies indicate any treatment approach to be overwhelmingly effective. In fact, we do not know whether most of them are better than no treatment at all. Nevertheless, it is important to review the major therapeutic modalities currently available and to draw conclusions about their relative efficacy and the implications for the future.

This chapter considers the treatment of the addict, beginning with methods of detoxification and then discussing opioid maintenance, the antagonist drugs, institutional and community-based psychosocial approaches to treatment, the results of outcome studies, and finally concluding recommendations. Although the various clinics, hospitals, and other rehabilitation centers often make use of a variety of approaches to treatment, the discussion focuses more on different rationales of therapy than on the detailed programs of individual centers.

1. DETOXIFICATION

The first step in treatment involves manipulating the drugs to obtain necessary evaluative information and to achieve pharmacologic control of the patient's habit. Unless it is known that the patient will be maintained chronically on opioids, he should be withdrawn from all drugs before proceeding with other phases of treatment. The safest and probably most widely used method for achieving withdrawal is that developed by the U. S. Public Health Service Hospital, Lexington, Kentucky (100).

Patients who are addicted to narcotics are frequently dependent on drugs of the barbiturate type such as alcohol, minor tranquilizers, and other hypnotics as well as barbiturates themselves (20). Since the barbiturate abstinence syndrome is more dangerous than opioid abstinence, and since opioid abstinence can mask the early signs of barbiturate withdrawal, it is important to determine whether barbiturate dependency exists. Administering a test dose of a moderately long-acting barbiturate (e.g., pentobarbital 200 mg by mouth) can be helpful. If the patient becomes intoxicated with this dosage (dysarthria, ataxia, nystagmus, positive Romberg sign), then it can be assumed that he is not significantly dependent on barbituratelike drugs, and withdrawal from opioids can proceed. However, if he does not show signs of intoxication, the degree of his barbiturate tolerance must be determined (e.g., by giving pentobarbital 200 mg by mouth every 6 hr until intoxication is produced). The combined barbiturate-opioid addict should be stabilized on the determined dose schedule of pentobarbital while opioids are withdrawn. Then the barbiturate can be decreased at a rate of about 100 mg/day (56, 104). A dependence on cocaine, amphetamine, or cannabis does not cause concern in the detoxification phase of treatment since these drugs can be discontinued abruptly.

For detoxifying opioid-dependent patients in a hospital, the principles stated by Blachly are often followed (12). The patient is allowed to begin acute narcotic withdrawal for the purpose of diagnosis. However, the treatment drug is prescribed before the syndrome intensifies greatly (i.e., beyond grade 2; see Table 1). Although any opioid drug can be used for the withdrawal, methadone is frequently chosen because it is readily absorbed in the oral form, is easily standardized, and its own abstinence syndrome is relatively milder than that of many other narcotics (1, 12). Blachly has given the following equivalents for 1 mg methadone: 1 mg heroin, 3 mg morphine, 0.5 mg dihydromorphinone (Dilaudid), 20 mg meperidine (Demerol), 30 mg codeine, 4 mg Pantopon (hydrochlorides of opium alkaloids), 7 to 8 ml paregoric, 0.3 ml laudanum, 1 mg racemorphan (Dromoran), and 0.5 mg levorphanol (Levodromoran) (12). If the patient is addicted to meperidine, then it may be necessary to use meperidine itself to effect a smooth withdrawal (103).

Some physicians prefer to treat before grade 2 (25), but grade 1 signs are relatively easy to feign. If there is doubt about the diagnosis of opioid dependence, a nalorphine or naloxone test may be used (see Section 2).

It is rarely necessary to administer more than 40 mg of methadone daily to cover a patient's level of addiction in the United States; in other countries, where more potent heroin is available, a larger dose may be necessary (11, 25). An initial dose of 10 to 15 mg will often suffice. Frequently a second dose of about 20 mg is needed around 12 hr later. Since the drug is long-lasting, a single daily dose may be prescribed thereafter. However, many physicians prefer to prescribe it on a 6- or 12-hr basis since the patient on heroin is accustomed to taking his drug several times daily and the more frequently prescribed regimen does not cause him to become unduly anxious about "waiting so long" for the drug. The methadone dosage is kept constant for a 2- to 3-day stabilization period before a schedule of reduction (about 20% each day) is instituted. When the total daily dose has reached 20 mg, the methadone can then be reduced by 50% for the next 1 to 3 days before being discontinued altogether. About 3 or 4 days later the patient may begin to complain of vague aches and pains, weakness, loss of appetite, and disturbed sleep. These symptoms can last several weeks. Small doses of codeine or aspirin for the pains and barbiturate for sleep may be helpful. Chlorpromazine or other psychotropic drugs are occasionally used for symptom relief, and one or two small doses of methadone may be prescribed to make the patient more comfortable if the symptoms are severe. Warm continuous-flow baths often decrease the muscle aches and restlessness. A more prolonged withdrawal program should be used for patients who are older, physically ill, or otherwise unable to tolerate this schedule.

On the other hand, a shorter routine detoxification program is preferred by some investigators (e.g., by giving 60, 40, and 20 mg of methadone daily and then discontinuing the drug). Much has been said and written about the terrors of opioid abstinence, and indeed several theories concerning the development of addiction center around the conscious or unconscious operations of the patient to avoid experiencing withdrawal. Unpleasant as it is, however, the abstinence syndrome can be withstood by most addicts without major complications. A careful review of the literature by Glaser and Ball in 1970 revealed no conclusively documented cases of death due to opioid withdrawal (42). This "cold turkey" experience, the unmodified opioid abstinence syndrome, consists of a progression of symptoms like those listed in Table 1. It reaches a maximum after about 36 hr for heroin addiction (48 hr for morphine) and begins gradually to subside over the next week or more. A number of long-term treatment facilities (9, 114), many correctional institutions, and a great many addicts on their own (52) do not use methadone or any other narcotic at all.

Other important functions of detoxification programs are establishing good nutrition, correcting vitamin deficiencies, diagnosing and treating

TABLE 1 ABSTINENCE SIGNS[a] IN SEQUENTIAL APPEARANCE AFTER LAST DOSE OF NARCOTIC IN PATIENTS WITH WELL-ESTABLISHED PARENTERAL HABITS

Grades of Abstinence	Signs (observed in cool room, patient uncovered or under only a sheet)	Morphine	Heroin	Meperidine	Dihydro-morphinone	Codeine	Methadone
Grade 0	Craving Anxiety	6[b]	4	2–3	2–3	8	12
Grade 1	Yawning Perspiration Lacrimation Rhinorrhea "Yen" sleep	14	8	4–6	4–5	24	34–48
Grade 2	Increase in above signs plus: Mydriasis Gooseflesh (piloerection) Tremors (muscle twitches) Hot and cold flashes Aching bones and muscles Anorexia	16	12	8–12	7	48	48–72
Grade 3	Increased intensity of grade 2 signs plus: Insomnia	24–36	18–24	16	12	—	—

	Increased blood pressure Increased temperature Increased respiratory rate and depth Increased pulse rate Restlessness Nausea				
Grade 4	Increased intensity of above plus: Febrile facies Position—curled up on hard surface Vomiting Diarrhea Weight loss (5 lb daily) Spontaneous ejaculation or orgasm Hemoconcentration leucocytosis, eosinopenia, increased blood sugar	36–48	24–36	—	16	—

Note: Racemorphan (Dromoran) and levorphanol (Levodromoran), although three and six times as strong as morphine sulfate, show same time curve as morphine sulfate. Similarly do paregoric, laudanum, and hydrochlorides of opium alkaloids (Pantopon), depending on their relative content of morphine.
a Not all signs are necessary to diagnose any particular grade.
b Hours after last dose of narcotic.
From Blachly (12).

intercurrent diseases, and offering kind and reassuring support. The "hustler" and other low-ranking members of the addict subculture (54), who frequently have spent all their money and other resources in the pursuit of heroin, often present serious health problems. Cherubin, Nelson, and others list the most common medical complications of narcotic addiction as serum hepatitis, venereal diseases, skin infections and scars, superficial venous thromboses, tetanus, bacterial endocarditis, pulmonary emboli, malaria, malnutrition, periodontal disease, dental caries, adrenal and gonadal dysfunction, and psychosomatic disorders (23, 24, 71, 83). Clinicians have noted for a long time that addicts often seem to have endured physical illness while on the streets, as if holding it in check with the analgesic and tranquilizing opioid drugs, only to experience full-blown disease when they are hospitalized.

The patient's complaints concerning genuine physical illness should be distinguished from his complaints of symptoms not related to identifiable medical disease. The addict is often somatically oriented.* The doctor treating an addict during the detoxification phase must be alert to those physical complaints which are aimed at getting more narcotics (1, 69). In the hospital one cannot "hustle" for "bread" with which to "cop" heroin from a "pusher." There the source of opioids is not the pusher but the doctor, and the way to get them is by pursuading the doctor to prescribe them. Since doctors prescribe narcotics for such findings as severe pain, congestive heart failure, and symptoms and signs of a major withdrawal syndrome, the patient can be expected to behave as if he is in such distress. The doctor should look for such objective and difficult-to-feign signs as mydriasis and piloerection before prescribing further opioid drugs. One valuable source of information is the other hospital staff, whom the patient will be less likely to try to impress since they do not hold the key to his desired goal. Therefore, if the patient is noted to be rather quiescent around other patients, to complain mildly around the nursing aide or the nurse, but to writhe in pain with severe muscle cramps in the presence of the doctor, he may be suspected of engaging in drug-seeking behavior just as he would do on the outside. However, this behavior may also indicate a conditioned abstinence phenomenon (Section 2). Just as the physician does not like to be "conned" by the patient's drug-seeking behavior, he also does not want to overlook distress in his patients.

* Until the last few decades most opioid addicts obtained their drugs from doctors and other legitimate sources of supply for the purpose of alleviating pain or other somatic complaints. Even now the so-called southern addict (typically a white, middle-aged opioid addict from the rural areas of the southeastern United States) can be expected to obtain drugs from legitimate or quasi-legitimate sources, using them for "pain" or "suffering" (5, 86).

In summary, the acute detoxification process is relatively easy to accomplish. The patients are usually admitted to a hospital, but many workers recommend that they not be intermixed with nonaddicted patients because of concern that other patients may be proselytized, the need to enforce strict limits to insure that addicted patients not obtain nonprescribed drugs, and the disquieting influence which manipulative patients have on a ward milieu. Addicts are increasingly being evaluated and detoxified as outpatients (43, 45). Most clinicians would regard this as undesirable, however, because the patient may not have a smooth withdrawal and may more easily be lost to treatment. Regardless of where detoxification is carried out, the most important factors are: (1) diagnosing the class(es) of drugs and the extent of the habit; (2) withdrawing the drugs after a short stabilization period, first withdrawing from opioids and then pentobarbital if barbiturate-type tolerance is present; (3) evaluating and treating medical illnesses; (4) initiating good nutrition and hygiene; and (5) making optimal plans for continued treatment and followup.

One must bear in mind that some of the primary abstinence symptoms (e.g., vague discomforts and symptoms of physiologic arousal) last for several weeks, and that the patient can gain relief by self-administering an opioid drug. Another source of difficulty which may play a role in relapse after detoxification is the phenomenon of protracted or secondary abstinence. Himmelsbach demonstrated in 1941–1942 that patients previously addicted to opioids had greater autonomic reactivity (49) and incomplete recovery of blood pressure, basal metabolic rate, body weight, hematocrit, sedimentation rate, and specific gravity of the blood (50) for 4 to 6 months following withdrawal from morphine. [Martin and co-workers showed similar reactions in rats (78) and spinal dogs (76).] These effects may cause the patient to experience the discomforts of physiologic arousal, thereby influencing him to return to drugs.

Thus under no circumstances can treatment be considered finished when an addicted patient has been detoxified. Even the most aggressive, supportive, and far-reaching approaches fail much too often. It is a certainty that the addict who has been rendered drug-free and has regained his health will return to addiction shortly after release from the detoxification center unless, when he returns, something is radically different about the environment or his own response to it (92).

2. MAINTENANCE ON OPIOID DRUGS

If one assumes that the availability of narcotic drugs is not likely to change substantially or that the socioenvironmental factors predisposing to drug use cannot be significantly improved in the near future—and indeed both assumptions have been borne out by our experiences in the past—then effective treatment of addiction logically focuses on a manipulation of the drugs themselves. One major and popular treatment approach is to furnish the addict with a supply of opioid drugs. The rationale is that he is already dependent, already tolerant, and already a victim of the recurrent abstinence experience, at least at an unconscious physiological level. Thus to satisfy the "need" for which he chose his drug in the first place, to prevent the "drug hunger" or physiological abstinence syndrome, and to keep him free from the illicit narcotic market and the criminal life which attends it, many would prefer to provide the addict with a sufficient amount of drugs to satisfy his craving safely.

Examples of the Maintenance Approach

Morphine

Within five years after passage of the Harrison Narcotic Act in 1914 there sprang up a number of clinics and dispensaries for the treatment of narcotic addiction by maintenance on morphine (9, 82, 85). Although the total number of such clinics is unknown, the estimate is often given of 40 or more (85, 93). The clinics were not operated in any standard way. Most were not registered. Many apparently kept no records. Although a number of the clinics were run ethically and efficiently, it is widely acknowledged that a great deal of abuse took place in some. A number led to the diversion of narcotic drugs into illicit channels (82). The background mood of the country concerning temperance and abstinence during this period also played a role in the conclusion by many observers that the clinics were wrong in principle (14). They were declared illegal in 1923 and closed down, largely because of actions by the American Medical Association's Council of Mental Health (85).

Heroin

The medical profession's next major experiment with the provision to addicts of opioid drugs was the "British System" (93). The proportionate problem of narcotic addiction in Great Britain had never been anywhere near that of the United States, and no law comparable to the Harrison Act was passed in England. Heroin remained a legal prescription drug. The physician was not prohibited from providing it "to gratify the habit" of an addicted patient. Since the available figures for assessing the magnitude of narcotic addiction in Britain had not indicated an alarming increase by 1958, when a report was issued by the first Interdepartmental Committee on Drug Addiction (the First Brain Committee Report), it was widely assumed that the system was working.

Very soon after this report, however, attention in England focused upon a rapid increase in the figures for addiction. For instance, in 1958 there were only 62 known heroin addicts, but by 1968 there were 2240 (95). In addition, it became apparent that there was an alarming rate of increase in the use of narcotics among healthy young people. By 1964, when the geometrically increasing curve had been observed, a Second Brain Committee was called, with the result that drastic changes were recommended (72). It was clearly established that a few practitioners were responsible for a significant diversion of heroin supplies to the illicit market and that many addicts were selling at least part of their daily supply to new users.

New regulations came into law in The Dangerous Drugs (Notification of Addicts) Regulations 1968 and The Dangerous Drugs (Supply to Addicts) Regulations 1968. They included central registration of all addicts, special treatment facilities, licensing of a relatively few practitioners to prescribe heroin, establishing an agency to monitor the physician's work, setting up special regulations and procedures for treatment, and establishing ongoing review. Now an addict can get his legal supply of opioid drugs only by attending the special facilities and by having his prescriptions mailed to an approved retail pharmacy from which he gets his drug every day (72).

Recently there has been a minor revival of interest in the United States for a maintenance program using heroin (29).

Methadone

In 1965, Drs. Vincent Dole and Marie Nyswander reported the use of methadone for maintaining addicts on a legal drug which is cross-tolerant with heroin (30). The early criteria for inclusion of a subject in the experimental treatment program were rather strict. The recipient of methadone had to be a person who was 20 to 50 years of age, had used heroin for at least 4 years, showed evidence of several relapses after withdrawal treatment, was currently addicted, and had no major medical complications. It was the aim of the program to maintain the addict on a safe level of methadone for the purpose of ridding him of the "hunger" for heroin, thereby making unnecessary the drug-seeking behavior which included participation in criminal activities. Whereas it was hoped initially that addicts maintained on methadone could ultimately be withdrawn, the greatest practical emphasis in the program has become long-term maintenance.

The addict qualifying for and wanting maintenance treatment with methadone is either hospitalized or seen daily at the clinic. Once the fact of addiction is established and the pharmacologic extent of the habit is determined, a sufficient amount of methadone is prescribed to cover the abstinence symptoms. Usually about 30 to 40 mg a day will suffice. The methadone is dissolved in fruit juice and administered orally in the presence of a staff member to make it unavailable for parenteral injection (10). Since the drug has a long duration of action, the entire daily dose may be given at one time. If the patient prefers, however, a divided dose regiment may be used initially. The amount of drug is increased at a rate of about 5 mg daily every 2 to 3 days until the desired dosage is achieved. In general, investigators distinguish between "low-level" methadone maintenance up to about 50 mg a day and "high-level" maintenance between 80 and 120 mg a day. Several outcome studies indicate a slightly better chance for staying in treatment, being abstinent from heroin, and remaining employed when subjects are maintained on the higher levels (59, 110). When the patients come for their methadone they are often checked by urine testing (e.g., thin layer chromatography) for the presence of morphine derivatives. They are also asked for evidence of employment status and are involved in group therapy.

Since 1963 the methadone maintenance approach to treatment has achieved great popularity (21). It does not require elaborate facilities and the cost of administering it is relatively low (61). An estimated 85,000 addicts were reported being treated in some 450 methadone programs by the summer of 1972 (73). There have been many reports of the advantages of such treatment over other approaches. National and international meetings and symposia have dealt with the use and study of methadone treatment (89, 90). Several governmental regulations and laws have been passed for control and standardization. In the United States at the present time it is necessary to have authorization from the Food and Drug Administration to operate such a clinic. Strict regulations for handling, prescribing, and dispensing the drugs must be followed.

The American Medical Association's Council on Mental Health and the Committee on Alcoholism and Drug Dependence have stated guidelines for the proper medical use of methadone in maintenance programs (2). The guidelines include criteria for admission, which are considerably broadened since the early days of methadone maintenance. Patients who are admitted to the program must be voluntary. A specific medical diagnosis based on history, physical examination, and laboratory tests must establish the fact of current addiction, unless the patient is to be started on methadone after a period of institutionalization in a hospital or prison. Patients who require special consideration are those with serious intercurrent physical or psychiatric illness, who require comprehensive treatment; adolescents younger than 18, who should have other treatment modalities if possible; patients needing to transfer from one maintenance program to another, who need priority in gaining admission; and pregnant patients.

According to the guidelines, methadone should be administered daily in a noninjectable oral form, in the presence of the physician or his designated agent, at a dose level just enough to prevent withdrawal symptoms. It should be continued under close observation until there is evidence of "adherence to the program and progress toward rehabilitation." This usually takes at least 6 months, at which time the physician may consider prescribing a 2- or 3-day supply and having the patient attend clinic only twice weekly. Caution must be taken to protect children from having access to the patient's methadone and to keep the addict from selling a part of his supply. The facilities should include medical and psychiatric services with the possibility of hospitalization. Valid urine testing methods and direct observation of the urine collection are necessary for checking random specimens at least once a week. Tests should be made for methadone, morphine, quinine (a "cutting" agent for heroin), cocaine, barbiturates, amphetamines, and glutethimide. There should be social, vocational, and educational supportive services and a trained staff. Satellite clinics and private services are to be used only when conditions are stabilized and when allied supportive needs are minimal. Permanent, accurate, and detailed records are a must (2).

The results of treating addicts with methadone maintenance are reported to be relatively good from the standpoint of several usual outcome measures. When addicts seeking treatment are given the choice among alternative programs, a high percentage choose methadone maintenance (68). Chappel and co-workers report that 75% of addicts will volunteer for long-term methadone when asked to choose among abstinence with supportive measures, abstinence with institutionalization, abstinence with total living and working arrangements, abstinence with cyclazocine or other narcotic antagonists, and methadone programs (21). The patients on methadone are reported to remain in treatment a relatively long time (57). Assessments of the percentage of eligible patients who are gainfully employed, who are free of morphine derivatives on random urine testing, and who are not apprehended for criminal behavior are also claimed to be good (110, 40).

Other Narcotic Drugs

Almost any other opioid drug could be used to maintain an addicted patient. One such agent which has received attention is levomethadyl, a drug with morphinelike effects which last up to 72 hr (35). It has been tried either alone (57, 116) or as the Friday drug for methadone-maintained patients who must be away from the clinic over the weekend (60). When used in doses of 80 mg three times weekly, it protected against the euphoric and physiologic effects of a challenge injection of 50 mg heroin 24 to 48 hr following the last dose in the five patients who were tested (117). There were no withdrawal effects 48 hr after the final dose. Lower doses of levomethadyl (30 to 40 mg three times weekly) were less effective. Anxiety, irritability, and jerking movements during sleep were found as secondary side effects (57, 116).

Inherent Problems in Opioid Maintenance

It is unfortunate that the term "blockade" has been applied to the effects of methadone (30, 39). This drug is a potent opioid itself, with typical opioid agonistic effects. It does not "block" neuronal receptors to the effects of opioids as do the true opioid antagonists (Section 3). The so-called "heroin blockade" in methadone maintenance is merely an example of opioid cross-tolerance.

There are a number of significant drawbacks to the treatment of addicts by long-term opioid maintenance. First, Baden and Gearing reported mortality rates of 30/2500 and 28/2205, respectively, in methadone-maintained patients, which is far in excess of the death rate for the general population in the comparable age range and is as high as the rate for heroin users (3, 40).

Second, the continuance of opioid addiction, whether self-administered by the heroin addict on the street or prescribed by the doctor in the clinic, keeps the addict in a chronic state of altered physiologic function, with decreased responsivity to a wide range of stimuli (47, 48).

Third, as with any opioid drug, methadone use is associated with the development of tolerance, necessitating a continued increase in dosage to produce the same net effect. Martin has expressed concern that some of the primary and secondary drug effects may be dangerous, especially as the higher dose schedules are attained (75).

Fourth, the large-scale distribution of narcotic drugs has in every other known instance led to a significant diversion of the supplies into illicit channels and a subsequent increase in the prevalence of addiction. Reports are now coming forth to indicate that this phenomenon is being seen in the case of methadone (116). For instance, *The New York Times* reported on August 13, 1972, that several physicians and clinic directors were being indicted or at least enjoined from further use of methadone, since evidence of abuse was accumulating (73).

Fifth, if an addicted woman is pregnant, her newborn will also be addicted. Although the clinical problems of treatment and withdrawal of the addicted infant usually are not great, we certainly do not know very much about the long-range and subtle developmental effects of opioid drugs on the vulnerable organism.

Sixth, from a philosophical standpoint, there are many clinicians and a number of laymen alike who abhor the ethical implications of keeping someone "slavishly dependent" on a drug and having him return to "establishment" settings for daily handouts and checks on his "good behavior." As Lennard, Epstein, and Rosenthal point out (68), to use potent drugs for the long-term solution of adaptive problems necessitates a careful consideration of the internal and external ecological costs.

3. OPIOID ANTAGONISTS

If the patient can be kept abstinent, rehabilitative efforts may be directed toward helping him cope better without incurring the risks of such adverse effects. The most promising method for maintaining abstinence is the use of specific narcotic antagonists, drugs which compete with opioids at neuronal receptor sites.

Examples of Specific Antagonists

Nalorphine (N-allylnormorphine) and levallorphan (1, 3-hydroxy-N-allylmorphinan) are highly effective in reversing the euphoric, respiratory depressant, and other agonistic effects of acutely administered morphine, and of precipitating a full-blown abstinence syndrome when injected into an animal or human subject who is tolerant to morphine or other opioids. Nalorphine also has weak agonistic effects of its own (analgesia, respiratory depression, lowering of body temperature, depression of nociceptive reflexes, prevention of release of acetylcholine by the gut, miosis, slowing of heart rate, and nausea) and is capable of producing psychotomimetic symptoms. It is rather short-acting, having a peak action in 45 to 60 min and a duration of only about 2 hr (108). Nevertheless, the drug can be used beneficially to counteract the effects of opioid overdosage and to diagnose opioid addiction by producing an abstinence syndrome. As little as 2 to 3 mg of nalorphine will precipitate withdrawal signs almost immediately in patients addicted to opioids (108).

The longer-acting antagonists such as naloxone (N-allylnoroxymorphone) and the benzomorphan compound cyclazocine have been proposed for use in keeping addicts free of the effects of opioids (77). Whereas naloxone has very weak agonistic effects and does not produce psychtomimetic symptoms, its duration of action (about 10 hr) is still too short to be practical in treating most outpatients.* It must be administered parenterally because of a noxious taste and poor gastrointestinal absorption. Furthermore, it is expensive and difficult to supply in large quantities (46). Cyclazocine, which is readily absorbed in the oral form and effective for about 24 hr, produces hallucinations in some patients, particularly if used in amounts two or three times the normal treatment dosage. Since chronic administration of antagonistic drugs for many months or years has not been reported, the possibility of long-term negative effects is not known. Nevertheless, these drugs have been found useful in the short-term treatment of some addicts (33, 34, 36–39, 58, 77).

Cyclazocine blocks morphine-accepting receptors at a dose ratio of 4 mg cyclazocine to 60 mg morphine (or 15 mg heroin), with a peak drug effect in 6 hr and a duration of 24 hr. After the patient is off drugs for a week, cyclazocine is begun at 0.2 mg/day and the dose is gradually increased over a few weeks period to about 4.0 mg daily. In this way the side effects of somnolence, dizziness, headaches, nausea, "fuzzy thinking," constipation, and sometimes hallucinations are lessened or absent (38). If the patient omits his daily dose, mild symptoms of withdrawal may be experienced: headaches, paranoid or depressed feelings, and "electric shocks" in the neck and back. In spite of this slight degree of physical dependence, the drug does not lead to opioid-seeking behavior. Most importantly, tolerance does not develop to the opioid blocking effects (74). A subject on cyclazocine who is challenged with heroin experiences no euphoric or other agonistic effects, unless he receives such large amounts of the opioid that the blockade is overcome (21, 58). This is an important qualification, however, since it may give the addict an incentive for the self-administration of very large doses of a narcotic.

A great deal of work is being done to develop and study other drugs which are effective receptor blockers, long-lasting, absorbed by the oral route, and free of significant agonistic effects. One such drug, EN–1639 (*N*-cyclopropylmethylnoroxymorphone) is now under final testing in humans at the Addiction Research Center, Lexington, Kentucky 46). Like naloxone to which it is closely related, EN-1639 is derived from thebine, a chemical present in small amounts in opium. It is over twice as potent as naloxone, and since it can be administered orally it costs about 20 times less. The side effects are less frequent and less intense than those of cyclazocine. The

---

* The treatment program of the Connecticut Mental Health Center makes use of naloxone by administering the drug at the end of each day-treatment session after a full program of therapy and vocational training (43, 46).

duration of action is about 24 hr. It may soon be available in sustained-release or implantable forms (46).

Therapeutic Uses of Opioid Antagonists

Nalorphine and naloxone are approved in the United States by the Food and Drug Administration only for the diagnosis and treatment of opioid intoxication and overdosage. To determine whether a person has used opioid drugs within the past 48 to 72 hr, 2 to 5 mg of nalorphine can be injected subcutaneously. Within 30 min the symptoms and signs of an acute abstinence syndrome will appear if the patient is tolerant to opioids (108). Pupillary dilatation is often measured as a subtle indicator of narcotic abuse, but one must be careful to avoid overinterpreting this sign, which can also be related to anxiety and other nonspecific factors. Naloxone (0.16 mg by intramuscular injection, followed in 30 min by 0.24 mg intravenously if necessary) is being proposed as an alternative to the nalorphine test, for the purpose of precipitating acute withdrawal signs in dependent subjects by means of a drug without significant agonistic effects of its own (13). The use of such a test is important when methadone maintenance is considered for patients who do not have a documented history of relapse following previous detoxification and treatment.

For respiratory depression or coma in which opioid toxicity is suspected, 2 to 5 mg of nalorphine is injected intramuscularly or intravenously and a 5- to 15-mg dose is repeated every 15 min until respiratory stimulation occurs; then the drug may be repeated every 3 hr until the patient is relatively stable (79).

The use of antagonists for treatment of addiction has been limited to approved experimental programs, and the number of addicts who have been treated with these drugs is relatively small (46). Yet they are receiving increasing attention in both medical and governmental circles as a mainstay in the treatment of drug dependence. An example of such attention is the proposal by Hammond (46) for three different therapeutic and preventive uses for the narcotic antagonists: the rehabilitation of addicts who do not want, or are not selected for, methadone maintenance; the treatment of the "casual user" of heroin who has not yet become fully addicted; and the prophylactic treatment of populations at high risk for developing addiction, such as teenagers in a school where a heroin epidemic has broken out and members of the armed forces where high use rates of heroin are found.

The opioid antagonists have a central role in that approach to treatment which is formulated according to the conditioned-response hypothesis for the mechanism of drug dependence. In his 1965 paper on the role of conditioning factors in addiction and relapse, Wikler presented the foundations of this hypothesis (102). The pre-addict is initially influenced to choose his favorite class of drugs (e. g., opioids, alcohol, amphetamines) by certain effects of the drugs which he values (109). For opioids these include a number of "primary reinforcers" of which the subject may or may not be consciously aware, such as the ability to produce euphoria; to decrease aggression, hunger, pain, fatigue, sexual drive, and fantasy (98); and to reduce the sensitivity to changes in behavioral incentives (47, 48). In the subculture to which many pre-addicts feel a strong "need to belong," a requisite for membership is the "mainlining of dope" and the affirmation that it produces a "high," "pep," "kick," or "drive." This process may be seen as a form of operant conditioning in which the "secondary reinforcers" of language play a significant role (79, 107). Once the drug choice is made, these exogenous factors take over to further the process of conditioning. The abstinence phenomena which begin within a few hours after each dose can be relieved by taking the subsequent dose, thus defining the terms of *operant* or instrumental conditioning.

Furthermore, since the aversive withdrawal phenomena occur repetively in the same physical and social environment, the experience of abstinence becomes *classically* conditioned to the environment itself (e.g., the addict's room or the street corner where he makes his contact for heroin) (99, 102). Both these conditioning factors then lead to continuance of the self-administration of opioid drugs. Three observations—the development of tolerance to the euphorigenic effect of narcotics, the addict's obvious state of misery and remorse (even with drugs), and the fact that full-blown "cold turkey" withdrawal is tolerated by many addicts—all contribute evidence to the position that motivations for continuing addiction are unconscious (102). Similarly, the relapse to opioid abuse following withdrawal can be understood in terms of incomplete extinction of some of these operantly and classically conditioned responses (102, 106).

The innovative treatment program suggested for this complex conditioning situation is one which leads to extinction of all the previously conditioned responses. A drug that blocks the "primary" reinforcing effects of opioid drugs should be employed together with appropriate techniques for hastening extinction of drug-seeking behavior (106). The narcotic antagonists are proposed to prevent the operantly conditioned abstinence-suppressing effects of the opioid drug and stop the classically conditioned reinforcement of correlated behaviors (105). For extinction to occur, it is necessary for the patient repeatedly to experience "no effect" (no "high" and no suppression of abstinence symptoms) when he goes through the actions of acquiring and using his drugs. After the new patient is detoxified in a standard manner, he is brought up to a dosage of the antagonist great enough to block his usual amount (or more) of the addicting drug. A challenge injection of morphine or heroin may be used to help him learn the effect of the blockade. "Experimental extinction" should be begun before he is discharged to outpatient status. Then, while maintained on the antagonist, the patient is sent out into the community, where experience has proven that he is likely to "get some stuff" and try it out. Only by repeating the usually risky and harrowing experiences of "hustling," obtaining the drug, preparing it, "shooting it up," and feeling no effect can the addicted patient begin to undergo the extinction of the heretofore reinforced behaviors.

While the addict is still being seen very frequently (e.g., in a long-term therapeutic community, a detoxification center, a day hospital, or perhaps even an often visited clinic), attention should be given to principles of "positive reconditioning" (102). For example, monetary reward for the production of socially useful work should be provided. If the addict responds positively to specific social interactions, they too should be used to reinforce responsible behavior.

In view of the potential promise of such a scientifically based treatment regimen, it is surprising that no carefully designed study has tested its efficacy.

4. PSYCHOSOCIAL MANAGEMENT

Obviously the task of treatment involves more than withdrawing, maintaining, or rendering ineffective the pharmacologic agents addicts abuse. Rarely is physiologic addiction the only problem. For those narcotic users with a "needle" habit" (psychological dependence only) the psychosocial problems predominate overwhelmingly. Many clinicians hold that the major problem in treating all drug addicts is not their dependence on the drug per se but their dependence upon the drug-addict way of life (22, 32, 88). Such a life offers them a constant source of excitement, challenge, and adventure. There is a ready-made group of companions, an in-group "argot" (79), and the opportunity to thwart authority, avoid responsibility, and dull emotional pain. Any treatment program that hopes to accomplish long-term gains must make provision for grappling with these problems.

As Ball points out (6), the term "rehabilitaion" may be a misnomer when applied to the treatment of most addicts, since the life style of deviancy, criminality, and identification with a drug-using subculture often begins by midadolescence. They have never lived in other than an antisocial way.

Studies attempting to assess the personality patterns and the prevalance of diagnosable psychiatric illnesses in narcotic addicts have found a great amount of psychopathy and a scattering of different neurotic and psychotic states (80, 111). A majority of the addicts treated in the U. S. Public Health Service Hospitals at Lexington and Ft. Worth were found to be antisocial before their addiction began (65). The many personality problems of addicted patients were listed by Jurgensen to include inappropriate anger, distrust, disbelief in "real" relationships, immaturity, passivity, dependency, the inability to tolerate discomfort, unwillingness to postpone gratification, and the ability to influence the behavior of others to meet their own ends (65). Cassel describes four characterologic mechanisms of interpersonal relatedness which cause difficulty in treating addicts: manipulation, corruption, wedging (provoking disagreement among others), and infuriation (feeling gratified when another person has been provoked to anger) (18). Levine and Stephens discuss these interpersonal "games" from the standpoint of therapeutic attempts to change them (69).

An effective treatment program therefore must include methods not only for coping with dependence on the process of drug-taking but also for treating psychopathy and psychiatric conditions and for dealing with fundamental socioenvironmental problems. In short, the addict needs massive support to achieve independence and confidence, maintain freedom from overwhelming anxieties, and establish a more adaptive life style.

Most narcotic treatment centers today employ a number of therapeutic modalities, including preintake preparatory services, intake evaluation, detoxification, methadone maintenance or administration of opioid antagonists, and group therapy [group therapy was found far more effective than individual therapy by psychiatric residents in a methadone maintenance program (66)]. They also include a number of supportive measures which coordinate such services as vocational rehabilitation, school, welfare, parole, job training, and living arrangements. Almost all programs use former addicts as counselors, as group therapists or co-therapists, and sometimes as administrators (26). The rationale for this practice involves an attempt to overcome cultural ad experiential gaps between the addicts and professional staffs from medical, psychiatric, psychologic, social work, theological, and nursing backgrounds. Many utilize institutional settings, some away from the addict's home area but an increasing number in the community itself (43). Representative of the former types are the National Institute of Mental Health's Clinical Research Center in Lexington, the chronic addict centers in Sweden (9), and such self-contained organizations as Synanon, Daytop Village, and the Phoenix Houses. The latter types are represented by community-based services like parts of the Illinois Drug Abuse Program and the Washington Heights Rehabilitation Center in New York.

The Clinical Research Center, which occupies the facilities of the old U.S. Public Health Service Hospital in Lexington, has four inpatient units, three of which are for men from different large geographic areas and one for women from all parts of the United States. There are now about 500 patients in residence. The units are NARA (Narcotic Addict Rehabilitation Act) services (see below), to which patients are admitted under civil commitment, kept for about 6 months, and transferred for aftercare to outpatient treatment facilities in their home communities. Therapy programs consist of psychotherapy (largely in groups), social services, occupational therapy, recreational therapy, vocational assignments, special training, academic and nonacademic education, and general medical, surgical, and dental care (70). Adequate outcome studies of hospitalization using the NARA approach to treatment are not yet available. Studies concerning the older methods are summarized in Section 5.

Both Synanon (18, 51, 114), which developed in California, and Daytop Village (8, 43), which originated in New York, accept into residency certain addicts who are highly motivated to remain abstinent. Each center insists that a new resident admit his condition to be a weakness that must be overcome by following the strict requirements of the longer term residents and staff. Under the threat of rejection from the organization and the rule of strict abstinence, the new member participates openly in confrontation groups and works hard at menial tasks within the community. Only when he openly acknowledges his insecurities and interpersonal "hangups" and demonstrates consitent responsibility in his work tasks is he rewarded with increased status, more responsibility, or better working and living conditions. Glaser, in describing the Daytop-originated program in Philadelphia called Gaudenzia House, points out that these systems incorporate principles of operant conditioning by reinforcing "responsible" behaviors with social rewards (41). Failure to submit to the organization's rules brings about a reduction in the prestige of the work assignment, public criticism, the requirement of public apology, or shaming (e.g., "haircutting"). Dismissal, either temporary or permanent, is the ultimate threat. These sanctions may be viewed as negative reinforcement.

In Synanon it is expected that a successful addict will remain permanently within the organization, the implication being that addicts have already proven their fundamental incompatibility with society at large. In Daytop, although many staff positions are filled by former addicts who have "worked themselves up," there is provision for most of the residents to progress through different phases, including reentry into the outside community. In view of two considerations—the avowed wish of Synanon's leaders not to release outcome data because they believe the publication of information about failures would discourage others in their program, and the recent internal struggles within the Daytop organization which led to the loss of many of their records (43)—accurate determinations of effectiveness are not known for these treatment methods. Although their proponents claim very great success with the addicts who are able to stay within the program (18, 43, 114), Holzinger reported in 1965 that his visit to Synanon provided him with a figure of "over 30%" for the recovery rate of those addicts who stay in the program (51).

The Washington Heights Rehabilitation Center study involved a far-reaching community-based treatment program founded on the concept of "rational authority" (15). The addicts were all under court order to stay in the program as a condition of their probation. Each participant had to agree to abide by the following principles:

1. Accept the services of the tratment program for an indeterminant period and "to the extent necessary" to effect rehabilitation.
2. Attend and use the medical and hospital services of the program when indicated.
3. Submit to random and on-demand urine testing.
4. Agee to the usual conditions of probation: report to the probation officer; follow the advice and direction of the court and the officer; do not leave the jurisdiction of the court without permission; notify the probation office of any expected changes; attend school or work regularly; do not "indulge in unlawful, disorderly, injurous, immoral, or vicious habits of conduct"; and "avoid undesirable persons and places."

With this backing of enforcement and continual free communication with the probation officer, the staff of the clinic could use the hospital or jail, be assured of mandatory continuance in treatment, and obtain direct evidence concerning behavior from urine testing, job reports, and police records. The addict in the treatment program was provided medical care, family counselling, group therapy, job training, and home visits. For the study, the investigators had difficulty obtaining a sufficiently large experimental group within the geographical boundaries they had established. For this reason they altered their method of comparing a group of addicts in the treatment program with a matched group of addicts in the usual program of probation plus various community services. They wound up with an experimental group more widely scattered, older, and with a larger proportion of whites than the control group. This biased their results in their favor since the last two factors are usually associated with more favorable outcome. Using a followup period of 1 year within the program, the investigators found no differences of statistical significance between the experimental and control groups when looking at the extent of heroin usage, illegal activity, work, and measures of adopting socially conventional behaviors (e.g., going to parties, visiting with friends who do not take drugs or participating in sports). Some 86% of the addicts in the experimental group ($n = 86$) showed success on two or more of these measures of outcome, as compared to 73% of the control group of addicts ($n = 73$).

Although addicts at other community-based treatment centers are frequently under pressure of legal authority to obtain treatment, it is unusual for the authority structure to be utilized so directly in an outpatient program. One example of a less direct use of civil authority is the Narcotic Addict Rehabilitation Act (NARA) program which has been employed widely since its establishment in 1966 (18, 94, 115). Under NARA, regardless of whether he is charged with a legal offense, a person known to abuse narcotics can be sent on civil commitment to an inpatient center for 30 days evaluation and 6 months of hospital treatment, and then to a community-based outpatient treatment program for 36 months. Individualized professional services are procured on contract with the NARA organization, with a case load limitation of 20 patients at one time for an individual professional worker. NARA provides for individual or group psychotherapy, medical services, job training and counselling, and monetary assistance. Determinations are made for the urinary excretion of opioid substances.

When civil authority is not included as a necessary part of treatment, the program has to accept a higher proportion of early dropouts. This occurs because many addicts enter treatment primarily for the purpose of decreasing their drug tolerance (so they can return to heroin use at a smaller, less expensive dose level), and many others cannot tolerate abstinence or the anxieties of trying to develop a new identity and life style (92). Yet these persons represent important subgroups of the drug-abusing population which cannot be ignored if the problems are to be met adequately. Even if it could be assumed (112) that all these persons would eventually come to the attention of law enforcement authorities and therefore be included under the jurisdiction of an authority-treatment system, they have needs for help before they are apprehended or committed, and society would benefit from having fewer crimes to suffer if they could be identified and helped earlier.

Work is now being done to study methods for controlling and preventing heroin outbreaks by the use of epidemiologic field methods and active recruitment of identified addicts into treatment programs. Hughes and his colleagues from the Illinois Drug Abuse Program have attempted to halt an epidemic by dentifying new heroin users early and involving every known user in treatment (53). They interviewed the entire "friendship group" of each addict, removed by enforcement or treatment one or more key members of the network's distribution system when possible, and went into the community ("outreach" approach) to persuade newly identified addicts to enter treatment. The treatment available in the IDAP includes detoxification on an outpatient basis unless serious intercurrent medical problems coexist; "pretreatment" with methadone maintenance; methadone maintenance or cyclazocine treatment in conjunction with ongoing group therapy; Daytop-type therapeutic communities called Gateway Houses with an 18- to 24-month residential program; other residential facilities which provide a highly structured environment to a mixed population of narcotic and non-narcotic drug abusers for 1 to 6 months; a combined outpatient and inpatient unit within the inner city where patients may stay for a few days or up to several months; and other outpatient clinics with special attention to certain problem categories like pregnancy and psychosis (43).

Hughes and Crawford found that heroin usage was most contagious in the ealy stages. Frequently the initiate happened to meet his friend, a new heroin user, just as he was about to obtain or use the drug. The friend, still not having an expensive habit to support, would encourage him to share his supply. This finding, also observed by others (16, 118), challenges the opinion (17) that heroin initiates are not proselytized, but rather actively seek out the drug themselves. Thus it is important to identify and treat new addicts early. Since the spread is most often to close friends and relatives, identification of the immediate friendship group is necessary. The authors used a monetary payment of up to $10 as reinforcement for participation. Finally, because the addicts in a community tend to associate with one another, the identification of one may lead to the finding of others. In larger heroin outbreaks, Hughes and his group are making use of multimodality treatment programs within the neighborhood, offering immediate treatment, employing an epidemiologic field team to bring in the less motivated addicts, and engaging community leaders to help involve the remaining hard-core addicts (53).

Another approach to treatment which provides a great deal in the way of support and opportunity for adopting a new life style, but does not include medication and does not tolerate any but the most strongly motivated young male addicts, is the Teen Challenge organization with centers in San Francisco, Los Angeles, Chicago, Pennsylvania, Little Rock, and Fort Worth. The 9- to 12-month residential programs are focused around the religious beliefs of the Assemblies of God, which founded and administer them. The new resident is reinforced for "acquiring self-discipline" (including abstinence from drugs, alcohol, smoking, and homosexuality), gaining insight into himself and his problems, attending chapel, and studying the Bible. He is aided by vocational training and placement. He is expected to graduate to a "sponsor family" outside the residential house where it is hoped he will develop close ties to older male models. Sometimes a subsistence allowance is provided. Some 22% of the approximately 600 to 700 men who entered during the first six years are estimated to have completed and left the program drug-free; the annual success rate is now given as 31% (43). No followup figures are known.

5. RESULTS OF TREATMENT FOR NARCOTIC ADDICTION

Perhaps it is obvious from the very multiplicity of approaches to treatment that results have been generally disappointing. It should also be obvious that no single or simple approach could possibly satisfy all the complexities contributing to narcotic addiction, including the serious socioeconomic problems of poverty, unemployment, lack of opportunities, and an inadequate educational system; personality disturbances of major proportions involving conditioning to antisocial behaviors and difficulties in tolerating anxiety and frustration; the ingenuity of organized crime, reinforced by enormous profits; the rigidity of legislative and judicial structures; and the powerful pharmacologic effects and adaptive biological and psychological responses to the opioid drugs themselves.* One therefore might not expect overwhelming success in treatment outcome. This point was made by Vogel, who felt that Knight and Prout need not apologize for a 36% abstinence rate after hospital treatment of New York patients addicted to narcotics (67).

Studies of treatment outcome use a number of parameters for measuring the degree of success. Since the rate of relapse is notoriously high for patients who leave therapy early (96), one basic measure is the percentage of patients who remain in treatment. A second frequent measure of outcome is abstinence. To establish that a patient is not abstinent is relatively easy; one can believe him if he says he is using drugs, and the substances can be detected in urine. However, to establish abstinence requires proof beyond an addict's proclamation and a single negative urine determination (86). A third measure is the patient's employment status. If he has a job the likelihood of criminality is felt to be less and he is in a better position to respond positively to such conventional reward systems as money and social reinforcement. A fourth measure is the absence of a court record. If

---

* Perhaps a great deal of the horror of the public, the "dope-fiend" image of the addict, and the overkill approach of our laws concerning sanctions for drug possession can be attributed to this awareness of the power of the drugs.

the patient has been able to avoid arrest, a gross indicator of his participation in antisocial behavior, this may be evidence of a positive change in his personality pattern.

Several followup studies from the U. S. Public Health Service Hosptal in Lexington are frequently cited as evidence that treatment which consists of detoxification, hospitalization, and various standard therapies is not successful. Pescor reported only 14% known abstinence but 40% known relapses in 4766 male patients discharged from 1936 to 1940 (87). Hunt and Odoroff studied 1912 patients discharged from Lexington between 1952 to 1955 and reported less than 7% abstinence (55). Duvall and co-workers confirmed Hunt and Odoroff's findings with 453 of their patients, observing that only 3% remained abstinent throughout a 5-year followup period (31). Vaillant reported 10% abstinence in 100 patients during the first 2 years following their discharge (96). Such figures are bleak indeed if taken at face value. However, Pescor's study (87) involved only 60% of the patients who had been chosen for the original sample. Sufficient evidence to determine the addiction status of the remaining 40% could not be found. Since abstinent patients are more likely to avoid identification in the methods used by the investigator, the 14% abstinence figure may be an underestimation. A recalculation of the abstinence rate using Pescor's data for the known patints indicates that 19% were abstinent at the 6- to 48-month followup.

All these Lexington studies contained a large proportion of patients who were "voluntary" admissions and who typically left the program very early. For those who had to have longer treatment (or imprisonment) plus parole, the results were much better. Vaillant found that only 4% of the patients who later sought voluntary hospitalization remained abstinent for the first year, whereas 67% of those who were imprisoned for 8 months or longer and then paroled for a year or more were abstinent (96). In a study of California physician addicts who were placed on probation as a part of treatment, Jones observed a 92% success rate (completion of the probation period and return to medical practice) when the patients had to present continual evidence of abstinence (62, 63).

Furthermore, for all the voluntary and involuntary patients together there is evidence that the abstinence figures improved as time out of the hospital increased. Duvall and co-workers found 49% of their patients abstinent by the fifth year of followup (31) and Vaillant found 41% of his patients abstinent and living in the community by 12 years (96). Altogether 30% of the patients in the latter study had "good outcomes," characterized by abstinence by all available evidence for at least 3 years and no conviction for theft or drugs in 4 years. O'Donnell found a similar positive outcome (43% abstinence) over time in a study of 122 white male addicts from

Kentucky (86). Such improvement over time may represent the natural course of addiction and not relate to the treatment in any way. However, this hypothesis is not proven, and it certainly does not tell the whole story to quote 10% abstinence figures for the results of hospital treatment.

Winick has advanced the thesis that by their mid-thirties most addicts spontaneously become abstinent (112, 113). His "maturing out" theory states that addiction begins in late adolescence when the person is faced with multiple inner drives and major decisions, and it burns out when his life becomes more stabilized through "some process of emotional homeostasis." The evidence for Winick's notion came from the dropout of about two-thirds of the "active addicts" from Federal Bureau of Investigation files. Although it is now known that a significant proportion of addicts die (3, 23, 71, 86) and others learn to adapt more successfully without coming to the attention of legal authorities (86), the maturing-out theory may be true for as many as one-third of addicted persons (7). The fundamental problem is that we do not know the natural course of opioid addiction for the vast majority of heroin users on the street. Therefore we do not have a reliable baseline with which to compare the results of treatment.

The methadone maintenance programs are claimed to yield promising results and certainly they are receiving the kind of emphasis that should accrue to the treatment of choice. Yet there is a notable paucity of objective controlled studies comparing this increasingly popular approach to any other approach, including placebo or no-treatment (76). Therefore one has difficulty in giving perspective to published figures concerning the outcome of patients treated with methadone. There are reports of 68 to 82% employment, 60 to 87% continuance in treatment, and 54 to 90% abstinence rates for patients treated for 2 to 24 months with a high-dose regimen (100 mg daily) of methadone; when a low-dose schedule (30 to 40 mg daily) was used, 64% employment, 52% "in-treatment," and 70% abstinence were found (57, 98, 110). None of these studies compares the findings to a control group who received some other approach to therapy. One exception is the study of Joseph and Dole (64), in which arrest rates were compared between a group of patients on methadone and a group of control patients who were discharged from the detoxification unit of the Beth Israel Medical Center and were matched for age, ethnic background, and month of admission to the program. Although the two groups had had approximately the same arrest rates prior to being admitted to treatment (20 and 21%, respectively), the first year arrest rate after treatment for the 1530 methadone patients was 6%, whereas the rate for the 100 control patients was 25%; by the third year of followup the arrest rates were 2 and 19%, respectively, for the 367 methadone patients and the 95 control patients who were followed (64).

Chappel and co-workers reported a threefold increase in the percentage of 33 cyclazocine-treated patients who remained in treatment for 14 months when compared to 153 control patients managed only with the "supportive" measures of the clinic program (21). They also observed a 68% employment figure in the 19 patients who completed 20 months of treatment. Fink indicated a 40% rate for continued treatment in over 450 cyclazocine-treated patients of whom he had knowledge during 2 years of studies (33). However, he reported only 20% rehabilitation (abstinent from opioids and in school or working) and a 65% rate of return to heroin use 5 to 16 months following discharge to outpatient status of 74 patients who could be traced (34). Still not tested in a systematic way is the approach to long-term treatment advocated by Wikler, in which patients stabilized on opioid antagonists would be subjected to deconditioning procedures for the extinction of drug acquisatory behavior (see Section 3).

Vaillant's 12-year followup study showed that relatively long imprisonment followed by parole was associated with at least a year of abstinence in 67% of 26 addicts (96, 97). Diskind and Klosky found 32% of 344 addicts to be abstinent for at least a year after parole (27). Pescor, in the study comparing 109 paroled prison addicts with 4766 Lexington discharges of all types over a 6- to 48-month period, found 31% of the paroled patients to be abstinent in contrast to only 19% of the total known sample (87).

6. CONCLUSIONS

Of all the existing approaches to treatment and rehabilitation, three seem best in terms of what we know: abstinence, narcotic antagonists, and the use of authority.

In spite of the difficulties in achieving it, abstinence is preferable to continued opioid maintenance. The continued use of an opioid drug, whether heroin from a "pusher" (31), morphine from a physician (86), or methadone from a maintenance clinic (3, 40), is associated with a mortality rate at least two to three times greater than that of general population in the same age range. Chronic use of the drugs significantly alters the "internal ecology" (68) in ways we do not fully understand (75). Tolerance develops and continues as long as the drugs are used.

In addition to these problems, which pertain to the individual addict, there are other reasons for which society needs the opioid user to be abstinent, even if the individual wants to take the drugs and accepts the risks of increased morbidity and mortality. It has not been possible in previous times to control legal supplies of opioid drugs, as the morphine clinics and the "British System" have shown, and methadone programs now seem to have increasing difficulties controlling the drugs (in spite of orange juice and large-volume soluble "Diskettes"). Stolen methadone, the selling of prescribed doses, and ingestion by children are serious problems to which society must attend. In the long run, such consequences resulting from opioid maintenance probably far outweigh the arguments raised on the other side—that illegal addiction is costly through crime and maintenance offers the best means of avoiding that cost.

However, it is recognized that the ideal goal of abstinence has heretofore been very difficult to achieve for most narcotic addicts. A high percentage of addicted persons coming to treatment are reported to prefer methadone maintenance, and few more impressive improvement rates have been found with other approaches to treatment. Practically, therefore, opioid maintenance should be considered a delaying action with the patient being transferred to a treatment program that leads to abstinence as soon as possible.

The antagonist drugs, which prevent the agonistic effect of opioids, provide the pharmacologic foundation required to extinguish the conditioned responses that are thought to maintain drug addiction—conditioned abstinence and conditioned drug-seeking behavior (102). The development of potent new opioid antagonists which have few agonistic actions and can be administered in long-lasting depot forms holds promise. Patients who have received them can be sent into the community where they probably will revert to drug-seeking behavior but will no longer be reinforced to continue it because the opioids will have no effect. It is of prime importance to continue treating these patients, not only with the antagonist drugs but also with multiple supportive and rehabilitative services for helping them to live without their drugs. There will be an increased risk of dependence on other classes of drugs like alcohol, amphetamines, barbiturates, and cannabis. Patients will need reinforcement for such socially approved and constructure behaviors as employment, maintaining relationships with nonaddicted persons, delaying gratification, and participation in lawful activities.

Authority in some form sufficient to get the addict in treatment and maximize the probability of his staying there is necessary for most opioid-dependent patients. The followup studies of Vaillant (96), the experiences of the California Civil Addict Program (43), the findings of the British (72), the Swedish (9), and the Japanese (81) who dealt with drug dependence, and the rationale behind the NARA program all point to the need for authority. Relatively few addicts seem to have the motivation and strength to finish a Synanon, Teen Challenge, voluntary hospital, or clinic program.

Experience has shown that those who cannot be recruited and persuaded to complete treatment will relapse unless forced to continue in the program (97).

Finally, answers must be found for many of the unresolved questions concerning treatment and rehabilitation. For all the elegant studies which have brought us to the present state of knowledge concerning the mechanism of action of opioids and opioid antagonists and their effects on behavior, and for all the money and energy we have spent on treating the addict, we still do not know what happens to drug-dependent persons who are not treated or incarcerated. Because we do not know the effect of "no treatment," there is no baseline for comparing the results of existing treatment programs. Most of the outcome studies are not contrasted with control groups, and there are so many uncontrolled variables between different studies that it is impossible to compare the results with each other.

Perhaps the most obvious conclusion resulting from this review is that adequate treatment and rehabilitation of the narcotic addict will have to await the development of new techniques and new conceptualizations in the future.

ACKNOWLEDGMENTS

The author is grateful to Dr. Arnold M. Ludwig for guidance, suggestions, and helpful criticism in the writing of this chapter, and to Dr. Abraham Wikler for ideas and comments regarding the manuscript.

REFERENCES

1. American Medical Association Council on Mental Health and Committee on Alcoholism and Drug Dependence, Treatment of morphine-type dependence by withdrawal methods, *JAMA*, **219**, 1611 (1972).
2. American Medical Association Council on Mental Health and Committee on Alcoholism and Drug Dependence, Oral methadone maintenance techniques in the management of morphine-type dependence, *JAMA*, **219**, 1618 (1972).
3. Baden, M. M. Methadone related deaths in New York City, *Int. J. Addict.*, **5**, 489 (1970).
4. Bailey, W. C., Nalline control of addict-probationers, *Int. J. Addict.*, **3**, 131 (1968).
5. Ball, J. C., Two patterns of opiate addiction, in *The Epidemiology of Opiate Addiction in the United States*, J. C. Ball and C. D. Chambers (Eds.), Charles C Thomas, Springfield, Ill., 1970, Chap. 5.

6. Ball, J. C., On the treatment of drug dependence, *Am. J. Psychiat.*, **128,** 873 (1972).
7. Ball, J. C., and R. W. Snarr, A test of the maturation hypothesis with respect to opiate addiction, *U.N. Bull. Narcotics.*, **21** (4), 9 (1969).
8. Bassin, A., Daytop Village, *Psychol. Today,* **2,** 48 (1968).
9. Bejerot, N., *Addiction and Society*, Charles C Thomas, Springfield, Ill., 1970.
10. Bennett, I. F., Development of a newly formulated tablet for methadone maintenance programs, in *Proceedings of The Third National Conference on Methadone Treatment,* Publ. Health Ser. Publ. 2172, 143 (1970).
11. Bewley, T. H., The diagnosis and management of heroin addiction, *Practitioner,* **200,** 215 (1968).
12. Blachly, P. H., Management of the opiate abstinence syndrome, *Am. J. Psychiat.*, **122,** 742 (1966).
13. Blachly, P. H., Naloxone for diagnosis in methadone programs, *JAMA*, in press (1973).
14. Brill, H., Drug addiction and dependence in New York State: A programme for prevention and control, in *Modern Trends in Drug Dependence and Alcoholism,* R. V. Phillipson (Ed.), Appleton-Century-Crofts, New York, 1970, Chap. 1.
15. Brill, L. and L. Lieberman, *Authority and Addiction,* Little, Brown & Co., Boston, 1969.
16. Brown, B. S., S. K. Gauvey, M. B. Meyers, and S. D. Stark, In their own words: Addicts' reasons for initiating and withdrawing from heroin, *Int. J. Addict.,* **6,** 635 (1971).
17. Cameron, D., Youth and drugs: A world view, in *Drug Dependence, A Guide for Physicians,* American Medical Association, Chicago, 1969.
18. Cassel, R. H., *Drug Abuse Education,* The Christopher Publishing House, North Quincy, Mass., 1971.
19. Cassidy, W. J., Maintenance methadone treatment of drug dependency, *Can. Psychiat. Assoc. J.,* **17,** 107 (1972).
20. Chambers, C. D. and M. Moldestad, The evolution of concurrent opiate and sedative addictions, in *The Epidemiology of Opiate Addiction in the United States,* J. C. Ball and C. D. Chambers (Eds.), Charles C Thomas, Springfield, Ill., 1970, Chap. 8.
21. Chappel, J. H., J. Jaffe, and E. C. Senay, Cyclazocine in a multimodality treatment program: Comparative results, *Int. J. Addict.*, **6,** 509 (1971).
22. Chein, I., D. L. Gerard, R. S. Lee, and E. Rosenthal, *The Road to H*, Basic Books, New York, 1964.
23. Cherubin, C. E., The medical sequelae of narcotic addiction, *Ann. Int. Med.,* **67,** 23 (1967).
24. Cherubin, C. E., A review of the medical complications of narcotic addiction, *Int. J. Addict.,* **3,** 163 (1968).

25. Connell, P. H., Treatment of narcotic and non-narcotic drug dependence: The need for research, in *Modern Trends in Drug Dependence and Alcoholism*, R. V. Phillipson (Ed.), Appleton-Century-Crofts, New York, 1970, Chap. 2.
26. Deitch, D. and D. Casriel, The role of the ex-addict in treatment of addiction, *Fed. Prob.*, **31(4)**, 45 (1967).
27. Diskind, M. H. and G. Klonsky, A second look at the New York State Parole drug experiment, *Fed. Prob.*, **28 (4)**, 34 (1964).
28. Dole, V. P., Research on methadone maintenance treatment, *Int. J. Addict.*, **5**, 59 (1970).
29. Dole, V., Comments on "Heroin Maintenance," *JAMA*, **220**, 1493 (1972).
30. Dole, V. P. and M. Nyswander, A medical treatment for diacetylmorphine (heroin) addiction, *JAMA*, **193**, 646 (1965).
31. Duvall, H. J., B. Z. Locke, and L. Brill, Followup study of narcotic drug addicts five years after hospitalization, *Pub. Health Rep.*, **78**, 185 (1963).
32. Epstein, S., The narcotics dilemma: Who is listening to what?, *Int. J. Addict.*, **1**, 1 (1966).
33. Fink, M., Narcotic antagonists in opiate dependence, *Science*, **169**, 1005 (1970).
34. Fink, M. and A. M. Freedman, Antagonists in the treatment of opiate dependence, in *Modern Trends in Drug Dependence and Alcoholism*, R. V. Phillipson (Ed.), Appleton-Century-Crofts, New York, 1970.
35. Fraser, M. F. and H. Isbell, Actions and addiction liabilities of alpha-acetylmethadols in man, *JPET*, **105**, 458 (1952).
36. Freedman, A. M. and M. Fink, Basic concepts and use of cyclazocine in the treatment of narcotic addiction, *Br. J. Addict.*, **63**, 59 (1968).
37. Freedman, A. M., M. Fink, R. Sharoff, and A. Zaks, Cyclazocine and methadone in narcotic addiction, *JAMA*, **202**, 191 (1967).
38. Freedman, A. M., M. Fink, R. Sharoff, and A. Zaks, Clinical studies of cyclazocine in narcotic addiction, *Am. J. Psychiat.*, **124**, 1499 (1968).
39. Freedman, A. M., A. Zaks, R. Resnick, and M. Fink, Blockade with methadone, cyclazocine, and naloxone, *Int. J. Addict.*, **5**, 507, (1970).
40. Gearing, F. R., Evaluation of methadone maintenance treatment program, *Int. J. Addict.*, **5**, 517 (1970).
41. Glaser, F. B., Gaudenzia, Incorporated; HIstorical and theoretical background of a self-help addiction treatment program, *Int. J. Addict.*, **6**, 615 (1971).
42. Glaser, F. B. and J. C. Ball, Death due to withdrawal from narcotics, in *The Epidemiology of Opiate Addiction in the United States*, J. C. Ball and C. D. Chambers (Eds.), Charles C Thomas, Springfield, Ill., 1970, Chap. 5.
43. Glasscote, R. M., J. N. Sussex, J. H. Jaffe, J. Ball, and L. Brill, *The Treatment of Drug Abuse*, Joint Information Service of the American Psychiatric

Association and the National Association for Mental Health, Washington, 1972.
44. Gorodetzky, C. W., J. D. Sapira, D. R. Jasinski, and W. R. Martin, Liver disease in narcotic addicts, I. The role of the drug, *Clin. Pharmacol. Ther.,* **9,** 720 (1968).
45. Guy, G. R., A. D. Matzger, W. Bathurst, and D. E. Smith, Short-term heroin detoxification on an outpatient basis, *Int. J. Addict.,* **6,** 241 (1971).
46. Hammond, A. L., Narcotic antagonists: New methods to treat heroin addiction, *Science,* **173,** 503 (1971).
47. Hill, H. E., R. E. Belleville, and A. Wikler, Studies on anxiety associated with anticipation of pain, II. Comparative effects of pentobarbital and morphine, *A. M. A. Arch. Neurol. Psychiat.,* **73,** 602 (1955).
48. Hill, H. E., R. E. Belleville, and A. Wikler, Motivational determinants in modification of behavior by morphine and pentobarbital, *A. M. A. Arch. Neurol. Psychiat.,* **77,** 28 (1957).
49. Himmelsbach, C. K., Studies on the relation of drug action to the autonomic nervous system: Results of cold pressor tests, *JPET,* **73,** 91 (1941).
50. Himmelsbach, C. K., Clinical studies on drug addiction. Physical dependence, withdrawal and recovery, *Arch. Intern. Med.,* **69,** 766 (1942).
51. Holzinger, R. Synanon through the eyes of a visiting psychologist, *Q. J. Stud. Alcoholism,* **26,** 304 (1965).
52. Hughes, H. M., *The Fantastic Lodge,* Houghton Mifflin, Boston, 1961.
53. Hughes, P. H. and G. A. Crawford, A contagious disease model for reasearching and intervening in heroin epidemics, *Arch. Gen. Psychiat.,* **27,** 149 (1972).
54. Hughes, P. H., G. A. Crawford, N. W. Barker, S. Schumann, and J. A. Jaffe, The social structure of a heroin copping community, *Am. J. Psychiat.,* 128, 551 (1971).
55. Hunt, G. H. and M. E. Odoroff, Follow-up study of narcotic drug addicts after hospitalization, *Pub. Health Rep.,* **77,** 41 (1962).
56. Isbell, H., Addiction to barbiturates and the barbiturate abstinence syndrome, *Ann. Int. Med.,* **33,** 108 (1950).
57. Jaffe, J. H., Further experience with methadone in the treatment of narcotics users, *Int. J. Addict.,* **5,** 375 (1970).
58. Jaffe, J. H. and L. Brill, Cyclazocine, a long acting narcotic antagonist: Its voluntary acceptance as a treatment modality by narcotics abusers, *Int. J. Addict.,* **1** (1), 99 (1966).
59. Jaffe, J. H., C. R. Schuster, B. B. Smith, and P. H. Blachley, Comparison of acetylmethadol and methadone in the treatment of long-term heroin users, *JAMA,* **211,** 1834 (1970).
60. Jaffe, J. H. and E. C. Senay, Methadone and l-methadyl acetate: Use in management of narcotic addicts, *JAMA,* **216,** 1303 (1971).

61. Jaffe, J. H., M. S. Zaks, and E. N. Washington, Experience with the use of methadone in a multi-modality program for the treatment of narcotics users, *Int. J. Addict.,* **4,** 481 (1969).
62. Jones, L. E., How 92% beat the dope habit, *Bull. Los. Angeles Co. Med. Assoc.,* **19,** 37 (1958).
63. Jones, L. E., Experiences with probation in California, *Fed. Bull.,* **45,** 165 (1958).
64. Joseph, H. and V. Dole, Methadone patients on probation and parole, *Fed. Prob.,* **34** (1), 42 (1970).
65. Jurgensen, W. P., Problems of inpatient treatment of addiction, *Int. J. Addict.,* **1** (2), 62 (1966).
66. Kleber, H. D., The New Haven methadone maintenance program, *Int. J. Addict.,* **5,** 449 (1970).
67. Knight, R. G. and C. T. Prout, A study of results in hospital treatment of drug addictions, in *Management of Addictions*, E. Podolsky (Ed.), Philosophical Library, New York, 1955, Chap. 29.
68. Lennard, H. L., L. J. Epstein, and M. S. Rosenthal, The methadone illusion, *Science,* **176,** 881 (1972).
69. Levine, S. and R. Stephens, Games addicts play, *Psychiat. Q.,* **45,** 582 (1971).
70. *Lexington, The Clinical Research Center—Addiction Research Center,* U. S. Department of Health, Education and Welfare, Public No. (HSM) 71-9071, 1971.
71. Louria, D., B. S. Hessle, and J. Rose, The major medical complications of heroin addiction, *Ann. Int. Med.,* **67,** 1 (1967).
72. Mahon, T. A., The British system, past and present, *Int. J. Addict.,* **6,** 627 (1971).
73. Markham, J. M., Methadone abuse rapidly becoming major drug problem, *The New York Times,* August 13, 1972.
74. Martin, W. R., Opioid antagonists, *Pharmacol. Rev.,* **19,** 463 (1967).
75. Martin, W. R., Commentary on the Second National Conference on Methadone Treatment, *Int. J. Addict.,* **5,** 545 (1970).
76. Martin, W. R. and C. G. Eades, A comparison between acute and chronic physical dependence in the chronic spinal dog, *JPET.* **146,** 385 (1964).
77. Martin, W. R., C. W. Gorodetzky, and T. K. McLane, An experimental study in the treatment of narcotic addicts with cyclazocine, *Clin. Pharmacol. Ther.,* **7,** 455 (1966).
78. Martin, W. R., A. Wikler, C. G. Eades, and F. T. Pescor, Tolerance to and physical dependence on morphine in rats, *Psychopharmacologia,* **4,** 247 (1963).
79. Maurer, D. W. and V. H. Vogel, The argot of narcotic addicts, in *Narcotics and Narcotic Addiction,* 3rd ed., Charles C Thomas, Springfield, Ill., 1967, Chap. 10.
80. Monroe, J. J., W. F. Ross, and J. I. Berzins, The decline of the addict as

"psychopath": Implications for community care, *Int. J. Addict.,* **6,** 601 (1971).
81. Nagahama, M., A review of drug abuse and counter measures in Japan since World War II, *Bull. Narcotics,* **20** (3), 19 (1968).
82. *Narcotic Addiction: Offical Actions of the American Medical Association.* American Medical Association, Chicago, Ill., 1963.
83. Nelson, A. S., Medical problems associated with addiction to opioid drugs, *Int. J. Addict.,* **1** (1), 50 (1966).
84. O'Donnell, J. A., A follow-up of narcotic addicts, *Am. J. Orthopsychiat.,* **34,** 948 (1964).
85. O'Donnell, J. A. and J. C. Ball, *Narcotic Addiction,* Harper & Row, New York, 1966.
86. O'Donnell, J. A., *Narcotic Addicts in Kentucky,* National Institute of Mental Health, Chevy Chase, Md., 1969.
87. Pescor, M. J., Follow-up study of treated narcotic addicts, *Pub. Health Rep.,* Suppl. No. 170, 1 (1943).
88. Preble, E. and J. J. Casey, Jr., Taking care of business—The heroin user's life on the street, *Int. J. Addict.,* **4,** 1 (1969).
89. *Proceedings of the First National Conference on Methadone Treatment,* The Rockefeller University, New York, 1968.
90. *Proceedings of the Third National Conference on Methadone Treatment,* Publ Health Ser. Publ. 2172, 1970.
91. Rayport, M., Experience in management of patients medically addicted to narcotics, *JAMA,* **156,** 684 (1954).
92. Scher, J., Patterns and profiles of addiction and drug abuse, *Arch. Gen. Psychiat.,* **15,** 539 (1966).
93. Schur, E. M., *Narcotic Addiction in Britain and America,* Indiana University Press, Bloomington, 1962.
94. Simrell, E. V., History of legal and medical roles in narcotic abuse in the U. S., in *The Epidemology of Opiate Addiction in the United States,* J. E. Ball and C. D. Chambers (Eds.), Charles C Thomas, Springfield, Ill., 1970, Chap. 2.
95. Spear, H. B., The growth of heroin addiction in the United Kingdom, *Br. J. Addict.,* **64,** 245 (1969).
96. Vaillant, G. E., A twelve-year follow-up of New York narcotic addicts, I. The relation of treatment to outcome, *Am. J. Psychiat.,* **122,** 727 (1966).
97. Vaillant, G. E. and R. W. Rasor, The role of compulsory supervision in the treatment of addiction, *Fed. Prob.,* **30,**(2), 53 (1966).
98. Wieland, W. F. and C. D. Chambers, Two methods of utilizing methadone in the outpatient treatment of narcotic addicts, *Int. J. Addict.,* **5,** 431 (1970).
99. Wikler, A., Recent progress in research on the neurophysiologic basis of morphine addiction, *Am. J. Psychiat.,* **105,** 329 (1948).

100. Wikler, A., Rationale of the diagnosis and treatment of addictions, *Conn. State Med., J.*, **19,** 560 (1955).
101. Wikler, A., Narcotics, in *The Effect of Pharmacologic Agents on the Nervous System, Proc. Ass. Res. Nerv. Ment. Dis.* **37,** Williams & Wilkins, Baltimore, Md., 1959, Chap. 20.
102. Wikler, A., Conditioning factors in opiate addiction and relapse, in *Narcotics,* D. M. Wilner and G. G. Kassebaum, (Eds.), McGraw-Hill, New York, 1965, Chap. 6.
103. Wikler, A., Opioid addiction, in *Comprehensive Textbook of Psychiatry,* A. M. Freedman and H. I. Kaplan (Eds.), Williams & Wilkins, Baltimore, Md., 1967, Chap. 27.
104. Wikler, A., Diagnosis and treatment of drug dependence of the barbiturate type, *Am. J. Psychiat.*, **125,** 758 (1967).
105. Wikler, A., Interaction of physical dependence and classical and operant conditioning in the genesis of relapse, in *The Addictive States,* Association for Research in Nervous and Mental Disease, Vol. 46, Williams & Wilkins, Baltimore, Md., 1968, Chap. 21.
106. Wikler, A., Some implications of conditioning theory for problems of drug abuse, in *Drug Abuse; Data and Debate,* P. H. Blachly (Ed.) Charles C Thomas, Springfield, Ill., 1970, pp. 104-113.
107. Wikler, A., Present status of the concept of drug dependence, *Psychol. Med.*, **1,** 377 (1971).
108. Wikler, A., H. F. Fraser, and H. Isbell, *N*-allylnormorphine: Effects of single doses and precipitation of acute "abstinence syndromes" during addiction to morphine, methadone, or heroin in man (postaddicts), *JPET,* **109,** 8 (1953).
109. Wikler, A. and R. W. Rasor, Psychiatric aspects of drug addiction, *Am. J. Med.*, **14,** 566 (1953).
110. Williams, H. R., Low and high methadone maintenance in the outpatient treatment of the hard core heroin addict, *Int. J. Addict.*, **5,** 439 (1970).
111. Willis, J. H. Drug dependence: Some demographic and psychiatric aspects in U. K. and U. S. subjects, *Br. J. Addict.*, **64,** 135 (1969).
112. Winick, C., Maturing out of narcotic addiction, *U. N. Bull. Narcotics*, **14**(1), 5 (1962).
113. Winick, C., The life cycle of the narcotics addict and of addiction, *U. N. Bull. Narcotics*, **16,**(1) 1 (1964).
114. Yablonsky, L., *The Tunnel Back,* Macmillan, New York, 1965.
115. Yolles, S. F., The narcotic addict rehabilitation act of 1966 and its implications, in *Modern Trends in Drug Dependence and Alcoholism,* R. V. Phillipson (Ed.), Appleton-Century-Crofts, New York, 1970, Chap. 6.
116. Zaks, A., M. Fink, and A. M. Freedman, Levomethadyl in maintenance treatment of opiate dependence, *JAMA*, **220,** 811 (1972).

117. Zaks, A., T. Jones, M. Fink, and A. M. Freedman, Naloxone treatment of opiate dependence, *JAMA*, **215,** 2108 (1971).
118. Zimmering, P., Heroin addiction in adolescent Boys, *J. Nerv. Ment. Dis.*, **114,** 19 (1951).

Chapter Seven

THE EPIDEMIOLOGY OF PSYCHOACTIVE AND HALLUCINOGENIC DRUG USE

G. W. MERCER, *Department of Psychology, York University, Toronto, Canada*

R. G. SMART, *Addiction Research Foundation, Toronto, Canada*

Between 1967 and 1972 there has been an explosion of research on the epidemiology of drug use. Opiate and alcohol use have been under investigation for many years, but the epidemiologic study of psychoactive and hallucinogenic drugs was relatively new.

Psychoactive and hallucinogenic drug use has previously been examined from a number of viewpoints. Reasons for this drug use have been hypothesized and examined (31, 150). Users (35, 51, 183) and use patterns (2) have been classified. Many writers have felt that drug use was part of a larger attitudinal and value structure. Some approached the subject from a purely philosophical perspective (104, 167, 217), whereas others used empirical approaches, which linked drug use to conceptual systems (116), the general propensity to use chemical agents for personal change (42), stimulus seeking (43), political values (3, 110, 161), the desire to belong to a group (208), the need for ritual (14), and many personality variables (32).

However, this sort of causal hypothesization is outside the scope of this chapter. This is by and large a descriptive essay. Its purpose is simply to attempt to make some coherent sense out of the literature of recent years on the use of psychedelics such as marihuana and LSD and psychoactives such as amphetamines, tranquilizers, and barbiturates. More specifically, the writers have considered the methodological difficulties associated with this kind of research; the reported morbidity and mortality associated with the use of these drugs; the reported nature, extent, and trends of the use and the characteristics of the users of these drugs; and, finally, any overall conclusions and research directions that can be drawn from these studies. The majority of the reports drawn on were of an empirical nature, as opposed to the philosophical approaches. However, as a word of caution, the studies examined and the conclusions drawn here should not be construed as a necessarily accurate representation of the actual epidemiology of drug use as it existed in the world; they are only interpretations based all too often on scattered and incomplete data. Also, although an effort was made to include most of the relevant English-language literature, this review is probably not exhaustive, especially where European and Asian studies were concerned.

Because often many different aspects of drug use and users are dealt with in the same paper, the present writers have attempted to organize and group these various aspects and findings wherever possible. The organizational framework used has the following form. Initially, the general methodological difficulties inherent in epidemiological research are discussed; then there is a brief overview of drug-related morbidity and mortality; after this the epidemiological literature itself (1967–1972) is examined; finally, overall conclusions are drawn with a summary and suggestions for further research.

The studies which examined epidemiology are grouped according to geographical areas, since it was assumed that the drug use studies done in one part of the world did not necessarily apply to other parts of the world. These groupings are the Americas (Canada and the United States, Mexico, Chile); Britain and Europe (Britain, France, Scandinavia, Switzerland, Holland, Germany, Czechoslovakia); Africa; Asia and Asia Minor (Mideast, India); and Australia. Because of the large number of studies done in the United States and Canada, this subsection is further divided into sections covering secondary school studies, university and college studies, and studies sampling other population groups (i.e., normal adults, hippies, soldiers in Vietnam, and miscellaneous adult populations). The Canadian and United States studies which dealt with school samples are each considered with separate regard to the relationships between drug use and drug use trends, year of study, geographical variables, gender, multiple drug use, grade average, social variables, and the user's personality.

Before beginning, perhaps the illicit drug use discussed in this paper should be put into some perspective. Every study examined which had data on alcohol and tobacco use found that the use of these drugs far outweighed the use of any other drug. High school student rates of 50 to 60% use of alcohol and 30% use of tobacco were not uncommon (5, 26, 254, 255). University studies found between 58 and 100% alcohol use and 34 to 60% tobacco use (4, 30, 137, 228, 259). Both high school and university studies reported that illicit drug use correlated positively with alcohol and tobacco use (4, 30, 137, 228, 259). Further, it has been noted (253, 255, 273) that students' use of alcohol, tobacco, tranquilizers, and stimulants related positively to parental use of these drugs. As Smart and Fejer put it (253, p. 12): "Any successful effort to reduce drug abuse will mean that most people in the population will have to use fewer drugs such as alcohol, tobacco and psychoactives." (see also ref. 258).

Finally, it should be noted at this point that, for stylistic reasons and unless specified otherwise by means of a comment referring to current or present use, the terms "drug use" and "drug user" will be used in the sense of having used a drug, as opposed to presently using the drug.

1. GENERAL METHODOLOGICAL DIFFICULTIES IN EPIDEMIOLOGICAL DRUG RESEARCH

Methodological problems in epidemiological research and indeed in all social science research generally derive from two basic areas: reliability and validity. Concerns of reliability have to do with the question of whether the measuring instrument being used can be relied on to measure the same thing every time it is used. Is it a reliable measure? Concerns of validity have to do with what the instrument is measuring and deal with the question of whether the instrument is actually measuring what it is presumed to be. Is it a valid measure of the phenomenon under consideration? Further refinements of problems of validity have to do with the questions "With how much precision does the instrument measure the phenomenon under consideration?" and "How generalizable are any conclusions that can be drawn from the data gathered by the measure; that is, to what degree do the data reflect the rest of the world which was not measured with regard to this phenomenon?" These in turn lead to the technical aspects of the measure design, sampling techniques, and data analysis techniques.

With specific regard to drug use epidemiology, the questions of measure reliability and validity have often been mentioned but have seldom been examined in any systematic way. The most commonly used method of data collection has been the distribution and collection of self-reports of drug use. The majority of these self-reports have been anonymous in the hope that the respondents would more readily admit to the use of illicit substances if they thought that this admission could not be associated with them personally. Only a very few studies of the validity and reliability of this data collection method have been attempted (213, 288).

One such study by Whitehead and Smart (288) considered reliability in two different ways. The first consisted of questioning young drug users in a treatment center about their drug use and comparing their responses with their responses to the same questions gathered at a later date (test-retest reliability). They found that out of a total of 180 responses, 86% were reliable; that is, the same person gave the same responses to the same questions on both test dates. Although these data shed some light on the reliability of drug use histories taken from young drug users in a treatment center, they did not illuminate the question of the reliability of anonymous questionnaires distributed to persons not in a treatment center. To do this Whitehead and Smart compared the anonymous drug use reports of high school students who were tested in different cities at the same time with basically the same form of self-report questionnaires. They found that the use rates were similar in comparable populations, and they came to the conclusion that "if the students are lying (i.e., the reports are invalid) they are doing so in a fairly reliable way in widely separated communities."

Concerning validity, in the same paper Whitehead and Smart found that within the studies they examined, only a small proportion of the respondents admitted to having used nonexistent drugs (e.g., they were asked if they had used "MOT," which is actually a fictitious drug name). Whitehead and Smart also reported that the tabulated figures gathered by self-report questionnaire as to the proportion of users in the group were similar to the figures based on estimates of the proportion of users in the group given by the respondent's peers. Thus the data gathered through the use of anonymous self-report questionnaires appeared to have some validity inasmuch as there appeared to be little indiscriminate overrepresenting of drug use and the figures gathered more or less corresponded to the independent measure of peer group reports.

Turning to the question of measure design, King (156) studied the validity of the "obvious" notion that coded identifiable questionnaires would yield fewer returns and fewer admissions of illegal drug use than would anonymous questionnaires. No support was found for this notion since coded and anonymous returns showed similar rates of marihuana and LSD use.

Further, the precision of many studies could have been much greater than it was in terms of delineating drug use figures within some time-bound context. To elaborate, caution should be used in interpreting "drug use" figures, not only because of the different populations and sampling methods used in different studies, but also because the majority of studies reported only the numbers who have "ever used" a drug. Thus if a certain percentage of students experimented with marihuana and stopped using it —say 5% per year—after 4 years of high school and 3 years of college, there would be an increase from 5% "ever used" in the first year of high school to 35% "ever used" by the last year of university. This point can be further demonstrated by the Lipp et al. study (173) of medical students, where they reported 52% of the sample had "ever used" marihuana while only 30% were "currently using." If one were to assume studies employing the "ever used" category to be properly representing the percentage of those actually using the drug, one would probably have a considerable error factor (about 60% in this example). The problem could easily be rectified by differentiating between "ever used" and "current use" or "use in the last 6 months," and so on. (These writers hope that more researchers will use time-explicit drug use categories in the future.)

Problems of sampling cannot be extensively reviewed here; however, a few brief points must be mentioned. First, the majority of drug surveys found were done in North America and most used college and high school samples. Not only does this make generalization to broader populations tenuous, but it also tends to create the impression that drug use is centered in these groups. This sampling bias can be shown by examining Berg's (23) excellent 1970 overview of the nonmedical use of dangerous drugs in the United States: of the 52 surveys cited dealing with cannabis and hallucinogen use, over 90% sampled students and less than 2% used a random sample of the general population. Similarly, only three of the 25 references in Smart and Fejer's (250) 1971 review of illicit drug use in Canada dealt with a population out of school. The generalizability of much of the literature was further reduced through the frequent use of availability rather than random sampling, and the lack of similarity between the types of sampling tools (e.g., interview, anonymous questionnaire, various categorization and duration of use questions) made comparisons of most studies difficult indeed. Some surveys, because of poor sampling technique, could not even be generalized to the rest of the immediate population from which they were taken.

Second, concerning sampling methods, some studies employed random samples of classes (e.g., 237, 286, 287) or accidental samples of students (e.g., 131, 151, 207, 283) or mailed questionnaires (e.g., 48, 93, 142, 262), although some (e.g., 95, 125) used all students at school on a particular day. Occasionally nonquestionnaire techniques such as urinalysis (e.g., 15, 44) were used in determining epidemiology rates. However, drug use data gathered by urinalysis will, by and large, only detect use within the 24- to 48-hr period prior to testing and thus this technique probably underestimates the overall use rates.

Little was known about drug use among refusals or how various accidental samplings affected results. Haberman et al. (123) did show, however, that students who were absent from school on the day of a survey reported rates of marihuana use twice as high as those who participated. This suggests that, with 8 to 10% absenteeism rates in high schools, drug use surveys could be substantially underestimating the numbers of users.

The source of the sample affects the generalizability of the study's conclusions as much as how the sample was taken. Thus studies which examined drug users sampled from police records, prisons, psychiatric hospitals, and the like, can hardly be generalized to the whole population of drug users. Moreover, with regard to use rates determined by the examination of police records, changes in arrest rates over the years could be as much as function of police sensitivity to drug use and their enforcement or lack of enforcement of laws as to any changes in actual use rates. [As an aside, it is interesting to note how much more flattering of users were studies dealing with a more or less random sample of college students than were studies dealing with student drug users in, for example, psychiatric hospital settings (8, 13, 40). See refs. 190 and 191 for further details.]

Another data collection problem worth mentioning occurs in the study of drug use of native or clandestine populations. Three problems are associated with attempting an epidemiological analysis of drug use by these groups: (1) particularly for primitive populations, there are few competent researchers willing to go into the area and investigate; (2) the standard technique of questionnaires is of little use in an illiterate population; and (3) obtaining reliable information from a group that does not want to be investigated is a particularly difficult task.

Analytic methods are less a problem in this kind of research, except to note that data on social and demographic characteristics were usually examined one or two at a time. Some multivariate, multiple regression, or correlational analyses have been performed (e.g., 252), but they were not commonly used. The lack of such techniques makes it difficult to specify the independent contribution of each of a set of variables to the prediction of drug use.

2. AN OVERVIEW OF MORBIDITY AND MORTALITY

To come to a fuller appreciation of the implications of the trends and rates of psychoactive and hallucinogenic drug use, it might be appropriate to first briefly examine some of the psychological and physiological consequences of the use of these drugs in terms of morbidity and mortality (see also 191).

A consideration that must be kept in mind pertaining to morbidity studies on drug use is the difficulty in establishing any casual relationship. Such a relationship is straightforward in terms of mortality, where an autopsy can tell if a person died from an overdose. However, whether the use of a drug caused a psychosis or simply precipitated it is more difficult to determine. Further, although drug-related disease such as viral hepatitus caused from using dirty hypodermics and purely transitory toxic reactions are included in the count of the ills induced by a drug, they fit only loosely within a strict definition of morbidity.

Cannabis

A number of purely physical maladies have been reported in connection with the heavy use of cannabis, particularly in Eastern countries. In India, where cannabis was reported as being usually smoked with tobacco, two early studies reported that users complained of chronic bronchitis (58, 143). Between 33 and 50% of Chopra and Chopra's (58) and Soueif's (264) samples reported that cannabis use had caused some harm to their health, and there have been other reports of liver dysfunction (154), temporary conjugate deviation of the eyes (199), lack of muscle tone (1), psychic deterioration (60, 61, 232), and even death from overdose (38, 39, 136). On the other hand, some studies which used drug administration with control groups (99, 100, 182) found no permanent physical effects from cannabis use. A point to keep in mind here is that although a sample of cannabis users might show signs of physical deterioration, this deterioration could well be caused not directly by the drug but rather by their overall life style. This applies particularly to studies done in countries where disease and malnutrition rates are high.

Transitory panic reactions, particularly among naive users (11, 120, 217, 272, 284), and short-term depressive reactions (284) have been noted, as have longer lasting anxiety reactions (73, 180, 292).

Short-term toxic psychosis with remittance between 1 and 7 days has also been reported (11, 73, 120, 145).

Residual amnesia (75) and bouts of manic, even violent behavior (232) were noted in a few Eastern studies of heavy cannabis users, although these findings were very rare.

Although a number of writers felt that cannabis use may simply precipitate a psychosis rather than cause one *de novo* (73, 195, 202, 265, 280), the use of this drug, especially in the context of multiple drug use, was widely felt to be a contributing factor in the etiology of psychosis among drug users (133, 153, 162, 195, 216, 276). On the other hand, it has been argued (202) that cannabis use could protect a person from psychosis.

LSD

With regard to purely physiological results from LSD ingestion, while no reports of death from overdose were found, there were a few scattered reports of convulsions (12, 63), which might be considered toxic reactions. Psychologically, LSD use has resulted in panic reactions (101, 278), depression (278), transitory psychotic reactions (134, 187, 214), the precipitation of psychosis in prepsychotics (233, 274), prolonged psychotic reactions (64, 159, 229, 233), and "flashbacks" or seeming recurrences of the drug effect without using the drug (101, 169, 175). On the other hand, several authors (34, 101, 274) found that the majority of those who had a psychotic reaction to the drug were already psychotic or prepsychotic. Glickmal and Blumenfield (105) have even argued that "psychosis, suicides and homicides which have been reported as LSD reactions would have occurred without LSD ingestion and in fact may have been temporarily controlled by the fantasy of a cure through LSD." (See also ref. 248.)

Amphetamines

The use of amphetamines has been connected with malnutrition and weight loss (130, 141, 234), rashes, skin abcesses, hepatitus (6, 141), and possible liver damage (260). Dependence upon the drug has been noted (155) and a withdrawal syndrome was hypothesized by one author (260).

Amphetamine use was also linked with the precipitation of psychosis in prepsychotics, particularly susceptible being those with the potential for paranoid schizophrenic reaction. Finally, a transitory toxic paranoid schizophrenic-like psychosis has also been associated with amphetamine use (66, 67, 70, 87, 119).

Barbiturates and Tranquilizers

Both barbiturates and nonbarbiturate hypnotics have been found to cause physical dependence, although with barbiturates the dependence was much more severe (91, 212). Psychological dependence has also been noted, especially among those with an abnormal psychological disposition such as psychoneurotics and those with personality disorders (115, 146). Examinations of drug overdose and suicide figures (84, 168, 290) have shown that of all drugs, barbiturate use, often accompanied by alcohol ingestion, accounted for the majority of drug overdoses and appeared to be the drug of choice in suicides from overdose.

Overall Considerations

The literature on drug use morbidity and mortality was particularly unsatisfactory. The authors suspect that the majority of toxic or psychotic reactions caused by illegal drugs were not reported to the authorities and, of those reported, only a few found their way into the literature. Those that did were largely in the form of case studies or small samples of users, and they gave little or no indication of the overall rates of morbidity connected with drug use. Further, some types of damage are virtually impossible to assess accurately; these include overall change in life style, eating and sleeping habits, and so on, which might occur when a person enters, say, an amphetamine-using subculture. Accidents that might not have occurred had the person not been using drugs are another aspect of mortality. For example, one study (257) showed amphetamine users tended to have an uncommonly large number of traffic accidents.

Admittedly, a few studies have attempted to get at overall barbiturate dependence rates (115, 146) and adverse reactions to LSD, marihuana, and other psychoactives (279); however, their results were somewhat limited. Research in this area is imperative.

3. EPIDEMIOLOGY IN THE AMERICAS

Canada and the United States

Because of the large numbers of studies carried out in Canada and the United States, these reports have been grouped for clarity into those dealing with high school samples, those dealing with university and college samples, and those dealing with nonschool population groups.

Secondary School Drug Use

Drug Use Trends. The majority of the studies examined seem to indicate that drug use in high schools was increasing. For example, in 1968 in Toronto, Ontario, Smart and Jackson (256) found 6.7% of their student sample reported marihuana use, 2.5% LSD, and 7.3% amphetamines; two years later, Smart, Fejer, and White (255) pointed out a 200% increase in the use of marihuana and a 300% increase in the use of LSD within the same population. Interestingly, the rate of amphetamine use had remained virtually the same. In his two surveys of Halifax, Nova Scotia, students, Whitehead (286, 287) noted an increase in marihuana use from 6.6% in 1969 to 17.3% in 1970, while LSD use increased from 2.4 to 8.1%. Amphetamine use showed only a 0.5 percentile point increase from 6.4 to 6.9%.

Surveys conducted in the San Mateo, California, high schools in 1967 (148), 1968 and 1969 (29, 79) indicated an increase in marihuana use from 13.5% in 1967 to 32.0% in 1968 to 39.6% in 1969. Likewise, LSD use increased from 6.3 to 10.7 to 15.1% over these years. Amphetamine use also increased from 16.3% in 1968 to 20.8% in 1969. It should be noted here that these American figures referred to drug use "within the past year," whereas the Canadian figures referred to use "within the past 6 months." As was previously mentioned, the latter format gives a better estimate of present epidemiology than the former.

Drug Use and Year of Study. Generally, the studies reviewed here indicated that drug use increased with grade level. For example, the San Mateo Department of Public Health and Welfare study (79) reported an 11.1% marihuana use rate for seventh- and eighth-grade students and a 39.6% use rate for high school students, while LSD use increased from 2.4 to 15.1% and amphetamine use from 5.6 to 20.8% between these two groups.

Other studies have also reported an increase in drug use rates in higher grades (5, 26, 89, 95, 193, 254, 286, 287). Smart and Fejer noted in their 1971 review of trends in illicit drug use that marihuana use increased in the later grades, while LSD use increased around grade 11. Comparing 1968 and 1970 data, they stated:

> Drug use then has changed from an activity involving primarily young students in the early years of high school to include an older population of students. It should be pointed out that this does not indicate that the crest of a wave is passing into higher and higher grades later to disappear and hence produce lower drug rates. The percentage of students using illicit drugs is higher in grade 9 and 11 in 1970 than it was for any grade in 1968. The use of illicit drugs is higher in all grades in 1970 than in 1968. There is no sign that the movement of the crest will be associated with less drug use. (253, p. 4)

Geographical Variables and Drug Use. Drug use rates seem to differ from geographical area to geographical area. Two major trends can be noted.

First, within the United States, the highest rates of drug use within high school populations have been reported as being on the west coast, particularly in California. For example, in 1969 39.6% of the San Mateo, California (79), students reported marihuana use as opposed to 12.2% in Utah (114), 22.6% in Wisconsin (277), and 18.7% in Maryland (147). In Canada there appeared to be little difference between the east and the west: 19.7% of a Vancouver, British Columbia, sample (237) and 18.3% of a Toronto sample (255) reported marihuana use.

Second, a more important overall relationship can be seen: most types of drug use increased with proximity to large metropolitan areas. To illustrate, in their 1968 survey of Michigan public schools Bogg et al. (36) indicated that the rates of marihuana, LSD, and amphetamine use in central city schools were 12.3, 0.5, and 2.1%, respectively, whereas use in small town public schools was reported as 6.4, 1.8, and 1.0% for these drugs. Studies done in Ontario also tended to show an increase in drug use in larger communities. For example, in largely rural Lincoln and Welland counties (254) the 1970 drug use pattern reported for "used in last 6 months" was 12.4% for marihuana while in the Metropolitan Toronto area (255) it was 18.3%. Further, in 1971 in the relatively sparsely populated Haldimand County (95) marihuana use was reported as 10.4% in the high schools, as opposed to 21.2% in the city of North Bay (94). Similar urban/rural drug use relationships can be found between other studies (e.g., 81 and 224). However, there was at least one exception to this rule: marihuana use in 1970 in Timmins, a large mining town (5), was higher than in Toronto (255).

Gender and Frequency of Drug Use. With respect to marihuana and LSD use, the majority of the studies found that more males were users than were females, although some recent studies have shown that this difference has been diminishing. For example, in Toronto in 1968 (256), 8.6% of the males and 4.1% of the females reported using marihuana "within the last 6 months"; in 1970 (255) 16.9% of the males and 12.0% of the females reported marihuana use "within the last 6 months"—an increase of 100% for the males and 200% for the females. Similarly, in 1968 5.6% of the males and 1.3% of the females reported LSD use while the 1970 figures were 8.4 and 5.9%, respectively—a 50% increase in the number of males and a 353% increase in the number of females who were using LSD.

As with marihuana and LSD, studies generally indicate that more males than females use stimulants, although the difference was not as great as for the previously mentioned drugs. The largest difference noted was for a sample of public, parochial, and private high school students (79), where 17.0% of the males and 12.0% of the females reported having ever used amphetamines. Interestingly, the proportion of amphetamine users in many high school populations remained relatively stable, hovering around the 5% level (5, 26, 36, 94, 122, 131, 132, 147, 165, 237, 255, 256, 269, 277, 286, 287), as opposed to the previously mentioned drastic increases in marihuana and LSD use. Some notable exceptions were two California studies (79, 261), one Utah study (114), and a Toronto sample of drop-in center participants (193) which reported overall rates between 10 and 23%. (See also refs. 7, 246.)

The difference between male and female barbiturate use was less again, with seldom more than a 2 percentile point difference between the number of males using the drug and the number of females using the drug (33, 255,

256, 261). Overall barbiturate use was low, hovering around 3 to 5% of the sample (165, 254, 255, 256, 287), although more recent studies (5, 26, 94, 95) brought the figure closer to 8%. On the other hand, Smith's (261) 1967 California sample reported 14.1% barbiturate use. The male/female relationship was reversed for tranquilizers: generally, as many or more females than males reported the use of tranquilizers (5, 95, 165, 255, 256). However, overall tranquilizer use seemed relatively stable and hovered around the 7 to 10% level (5, 26, 94, 95, 165, 254, 255, 256, 286).

Multiple Drug Use. The bulk of the research reviewed indicated that the majority of illicit users of LSD, stimulants, tranquilizers, and barbiturates fell into the "experimenter" category—those who have used the drugs only once or, at most, a few times. The exception to this rule appears to have occurred with marihuana use: as many as 50% of those who tried it continued in its use (5, 18, 26, 29, 94, 95, 114, 122, 148, 193, 254, 255, 277).

It has been widely reported (5, 26, 50, 94, 95, 111, 193, 251, 254, 255, 256, 289) that the more a student used any given drug, the more likely he was to use other drugs. Whitehead et al. in their review of multiple drug use wrote "rates of drug use among marihuana smokers are considerably higher than the rates of drug use among those who have not smoked marihuana . . . 9 times as many have used stimulants . . . the rate of LSD use is 62 times greater among marihuana smokers than among those who have not taken marihuana" (289, p. 6539). Smart et al. pointed out that "marihuana use is more closely related to the use of LSD than any other drug" and differentiated three use patterns:

> While the use of each drug is significantly related to the use of every other drug, three sub-groups appear to exist among drug using students. The first sub-group is made up of students who use alcohol, tobacco and marihuana. The second group uses barbiturates, opiates, speed and stimulants. The third group consists of those who use glue and solvents. (255, p. 40)

Other writers have also reported a close connection between amphetamine and barbiturate use (97, 118), barbiturates possibly being used to allow the amphetamine user to relax and sleep after getting "strung out."

Grade Average and Drug Use. Generally, it has been reported that students with lower grade averages used drugs more than did those with higher averages. This can be seen in the high use rate found in Hayashi's (132) study of failing students as well as in more comprehensive surveys (5, 26, 36, 94, 165, 209, 254, 255, 256, 269). An interesting variation in this pattern was found by Smart et al. (255), who reported a slightly higher rate of marihuana use for students with an A average or over, as well as for failing students.

Social Variables and Drug Use. Studies have indicated that students coming from middle, upper-middle, and professional class homes tended to report the highest overall drug use rates (33, 36, 79, 94, 95, 254, 255, 256).

With regard to religion and drug use, Jewish students and students with no religion seemed to have the highest proportion of drug users, followed by Protestants, and finally Catholics (26, 33, 94, 193, 243, 254, 256).

Family environment also appeared to affect drug use. Broken homes, homes with only one parent, and situations where the student was not living at home have been more closely associated with drug use than a more stable, two-parent home environment (26, 254, 255, 256, 273). For example, Tec (273) in his study of 1700 suburban youths found that the degree of involvement with illicit drugs was negatively related to availability and quantity of parental models, high evaluation and recognition received by the child from the parents, perceptions of the family as warm and not simply rigidly controlling and/or indifferent, and subjective feelings of satisfaction and involvement with, as well as the ability to rely upon, the family as a unit.

Peer groups have been reported as the most important source of drug information, especially from drug users (247, 249) and for alienated students (245), whereas nonusers (96) and younger students (244) were found to rely more strongly on the mass media for information than did users.

Without being exhaustive or going into detail, a few other characteristics of high school drug users ought to be mentioned. Drug use has been found to correlate positively with having friends who use drugs (26, 193), sibling drug use (255, 256), high anxiety scores (94, 95), past psychological treatment (95), feelings of alienation (255), trouble with police authorities (193, 221), a positive feeling toward drug use and its legalization (193, 209, 269), and leisure time pursuits away from home but not in formal organizations (26, 209). Curiosity was most often cited as the principal reason for commencing drug use (26, 193).

University and College Studies

It should be noted at this point that although there were more studies dealing with college drug use than with secondary school drug use, the basis of comparison among college studies was not nearly as strong as the basis of comparison among the high school studies due to the lack of similarities in sampling, data collection instruments, and analysis found among the college studies. Thus the validity of conclusions drawn from comparing these college studies was consequently less than that of comparing high school studies.

Drug Use Trends. In 1969 Mauss (181) found that college-oriented high school students regarded marihuana use as part of college life and that they were more likely to have used marihuana than students not expecting to go to college. Thus colleges might have enrolled a higher proportion of drug users than would have been expected by chance. In any case, overall college drug use rates were generally higher than high school rates. For example, in 1970 Becker Associates (18) found that in their sample of Massachusetts high school students, 21% reported marihuana use and 6% LSD use, while they found the reported use rates for their university sample were 48% for marihuana and 11% for LSD.

With the exception of tranquilizer and barbiturate use, which remained stable, the studies reviewed indicated that drug use and multiple drug use in the colleges were increasing, although perhaps not as drastically as in the high schools. For example, McKenzie (186) reported that the use of cannabis had risen at the University of Maryland from 15% in 1967 to 23.9% in 1968 to 35.6% in 1969—an increase of over 100%—while Goldstein (109) reported a 10% increase in cannabis use from 1968 to 1969. Similarly, the nationwide United States sample gathered by *Reader's Digest* in 1967 (80) showed considerably less drug use than nationwide samples gathered in 1969 (103, 206). In California, two surveys completed in 1967 (33, 86) reported cannabis use levels of 18.1 and 13.7%, while two surveys done in 1969 (68, 200) reported levels of 31.4 and 23.3%. Campbell also reported an increase in the number of users at Bishop's University, Lennoxville, Québec, between 1968 and 1969 (48, 49).

Drug Use and Year of Study. Within undergraduate samples, Morrison (200), Anker et al. (4), Kohn and Mercer (161), Greenwald and Luetgert (117), and Harris (128) found that upper years of undergraduate programs had a higher proportion of drug users than did lower years of study.

On the other hand, most graduate student samples reported less drug use than even the previously examined high school students (4, 86, 179, 185, 200). For example, McGlothlin and Cohen (185) indicated that of their sample of 121 male California graduate students, only 10.7% had tried marihuana, whereas Anker et al. (4) found the graduate students in their study reported 29.0% marihuana use, 2.6% LSD use, 12.0% amphetamine use, and 4.4% barbiturate use, as opposed to their undergraduate sample which reported use rates of 44.0, 3.9, 10.3, and 3.9%, respectively, for those drugs. On the other hand, a slightly higher proportion of the graduate students reported amphetamine and barbiturate use than did the undergraduates. However, inasmuch as the question was in an "ever used" category, these higher rates of use might be confounded by the previously mentioned time factor. The only report of high drug use by graduate students came from Lipp's (173) survey of four medical schools where he found a range of 17 to 70% marihuana use with an overall mean of 52% use.

Geographical Variables and Drug Use. Possibly because universities and colleges tend to be located in urban areas, and because many students were not brought up in the same area as the college they are attending, the previously mentioned rural/urban continuum for drug use was not as strong for colleges as it was for high schools. DeFleur and Garrett (76) noted that there was a smaller proportion of drug users among students who came from less populated areas than among students from more heavily populated areas, although Kohn and Mercer (161) reported that this relationship did not hold for their sample. However, with regard to the college the student was attending, as opposed to his point of origin, the more rural colleges tended to have fewer drug-using students than their urban counterparts. To illustrate, in 1970 DeFleur and Garrett (76) surveyed students in a rural western United States College and found 12.8% marihuana use. In the same year Brady et al. (41) surveyed a university in a more populated region and found 23.2% marihuana use, while Becker Associates (18) found 48.0% use for students in the Boston, Massachusetts, area.

The tendency that has been noted in reviewing the high school studies for west coast United States students to use drugs more than students in other areas could not be found for the college studies, although this might be due to the lack of comparability between studies rather than the nonexistence of such a trend.

Place of residence has also been predictive of drug use: Greenwald and Luetgert (117) found users to be more likely to live in city centers than in the suburbs, and they and others (4, 186) reported that students living with their families tended not to use drugs. Cohabitation (4) and not living in a university residence (186) have also been cited as correlating positively with drug use. On the other hand, Eells (86) found considerably less drug use in his sample of on-campus graduate students than in his off-campus graduate students, although there was little reported difference for his undergraduates along this dimension. Whereas a university residence may immunize a student from drug use, fraternities appeared to have the opposite effect (139, 268). On the other hand, some studies found no relationship between place of residence and illicit drug use (92, 259). As would be expected of a social phenomenon, users reported having large numbers of friends who are also users (48, 161), a circumstance that could be seen as a reinforcement of further use (238).

Gender and Frequency of Drug Use. In the university and college studies, as was shown in the high school studies, more males than females used cannabis (4, 18, 80, 128, 137, 157, 186, 188, 220, 267, 291). However, later studies indicate that this trend was diminishing due to an increase in female drug use (71, 76, 161, 259).

LSD and other hallucinogen use also seems to have been increasing, again with more males having reported use of these drugs than have females. For example, in 1968 in a northeast United States sample, Wolk (291) found that 3.2% of the males and 0.9% of the females reported LSD use, whereas in the same area in 1970 Becker Associates (18) found 12.0% of the males and 8.0% of the females used LSD.

Except for two Canadian studies (41, 161), every study reviewed which examined amphetamine use found higher rates of use for these drugs than for any illicit or prescription drug other than marihuana. However, because of poor comparability between studies and because relatively few studies included any information on amphetamine use, it was difficult to discern whether or not any real trends existed. From the available data one can get the impression that the use of amphetamines among college students remained relatively stable, with a slight increase between 1968 and 1969 and a slight drop between 1970 and 1971. To illustrate, the Blaine et al. (30) study of medical students reported 16.6% amphetamine use in 1966; four studies (85, 137, 179, 291) reported amphetamine use of 11.1, 18.0, 8.5, and about 8%, 1967; three studies (71, 109, 220) found 18.0, 12.3, and about 10% use in 1968; there were reports (49, 98, 103, 198, 200, 206) of 3.3, 24.7, 10.0, 14.4, 6.8, and 13.5% in 1969; the figures for two 1970 studies (41, 259) were 4.1 and 4.9%; and for 1971 the only available statistics (4, 161) were 10.3 and 10.7%. Perhaps the apparent drop in amphetamine use in 1970 and 1971 may have been in response to the "speed kills" publicity in those years. One other study with 1968 data (15) examined a sample of students in a dormitory in a women's college by urinalysis and found an 8.3% use rate. However, as was mentioned earlier, caution must be used in interpreting overall use rates from urinalysis data.

Males using amphetamines outnumbered females using amphetamines in earlier studies (220, 291), although later studies indicated a trend away from this pattern (4, 161).

As was previously mentioned, a positive relationship was found between amphetamine use and barbiturate and tranquilizer use. Thus it is not surprising that the trends in barbiturate and tranquilizer use appeared similar to the trends in amphetamine use, with a peak around 1969 and a later decline. For example, in 1967 Wolk's (291) sample of Connecticut university undergraduates reported about 5.7% overall tranquilizer use and Marra's (179) sample of New York University undergraduates reported 3.7% barbiturate use. By 1969 Francis and Patch's (98) Michigan college students reported 12.1% tranquilizer use and *Newsweek* (206) indicated that 11.7% of the students in a sample which covered 57 colleges reported barbiturate use. However, by 1971 there were reports of 3.9 and 3.0% barbiturate use (4, 161) and 4.4% tranquilizer use (4) in undergraduate populations.

More women than men were found to use tranquilizers (228, 291). On the other hand, there has been some indication (e.g., 220) that more men used barbiturates (possibly in conjunction with amphetamines, where men were the heavier users) than did women, although later studies (4, 161, 259) have found no significant difference in use rates between the sexes for these drugs. By and large, within the studies reviewed the use rates for tranquilizers and barbiturates were closer for men and women than for any other drug use category.

Multiple Drug Use. Most of the college studies examined which dealt with the relationship between cannabis experimentation and continued use (4, 16, 18, 33, 49, 71, 85, 86, 92, 98, 109, 121, 137, 139, 157, 158, 161, 179, 186, 195, 196, 198, 291) and between cannabis use and the use of other drugs came to the conclusion that about half of those who tried cannabis continued to use it and that continued cannabis use correlated highly with multiple drug use, particularly with the use of LSD. To illustrate, Cross and Keir (71) reported that 29.0% of their sample of Connecticut and Massachusetts college students used marihuana, and of these, 38% reported multiple drug use; Mizner et al. (198) in their sample of Colorado students reported 26.0% marihuana use, and of these users 34.8% were multiple drug users. Thus if about half of those who try marihuana go on to use it again, about 60% of those who use it again will try other drugs, particularly LSD. Should these approximations hold true, the extent of multiple drug use in a population could be estimated from marihuana use figures alone. (This does not necessarily imply cannabis use directly causes the use of other drugs—the writers feel the relationship is more probably one of heavy use of illicit drugs within a drug-oriented subculture facilitating the use of other illicit drugs.)

As in the high school studies reviewed, it has been noted in some college studies (4, 30, 68, 157) that illicit drug use related positively to the use of legal drugs such as tobacco, alcohol, and medications. Moreover, student drug use correlated with parental drug use where it was examined (68, 255). The point here is that student drug use should be kept in a societal perspective.

Drug Use, Grade Average, and Academic Program. Concerning drug use and academic achievement, Anker et al. (4) found drug-using graduate students tended to receive lower grades than their nonusing peers, although for undergraduates there was no significant difference between users and nonusers in regard to this dimension. On the other hand, Sadava (238) linked drug use to academic frustration and Steffenhagen (267) found users had a higher academic standing than nonusers in his University of Vermont sample.

Both Blum (33) and Mizner (198) reported that drug use was least at small denominational and technical colleges and highest at private colleges and state universities. Many medical students tended to be users (30, 173, 198), especially of amphetamine drugs (30, 198). The faculty or department a student belonged to also appeared to be predictive of his drug use patterns: Blum et al. (33), King et al. (158), Hinckley (137), and Greenwald and Luetgert (117) found that majors in the social sciences and/or liberal arts showed the highest proportion of drug users, whereas physical science and/or education students had the least proportion of users.

Social Variables and Drug Use. A number of studies have reported that student drug use correlated positively with above-average parental education and income (4, 33, 48, 117, 128, 267). Subscribing to the Jewish religion (4, 137), religious noninvolvement, and lack of church attendance also have been cited to relate positively to college student drug use (33, 117, 137, 161). As would be expected, drug users tended to be permissive about drug use and favored the legalization of marihuana (48, 71, 76, 86, 152, 157, 161). The user's sociopolitical attitudes have been described as being rebellious (139, 161), in opposition to traditional values (33, 271), liberal (157, 172), and tending toward general alienation and involvement with protest movements (103, 128).

Having poor relations with parents (4, 117), not being married, selling drugs (4), and having a good knowledge of drugs (76, 259) have all been related positively to drug use. Further, curiosity and enjoyment have been universally cited as the major reasons for drug use (71, 86, 149, 158, 161, 172, 198, 259, 291). As with high school students, university students have reported that peer groups were the most important sources of drug information (173).

Since drug use has been linked with liberal sociopolitical values and ethics, it was not surprising that drug users had more liberal sexual attitudes than their nonusing counterparts (157, 251). They also seemed to practice what they preached, as both Campbell (48) and Anker et al. (4) found that users reported more sexual experiences than nonusers, Anker et al. pointing out that this included dating and homosexual encounters as well as heterosexual coitus.

Drug Use and Personality. Without going into detail, psychological findings associated with students drug users include the following: they were less dogmatic (33), more socially poised, more pleasure seeking, less inflexible (139), more opposed to external control (157), more self-accepting (201), more concerned with philosophical problems involving themselves and their environment (172), more introspective (33), and more creative, thoughtful, and independent than their nonusing peers (228). On the other hand, they have been noted to perceive their mental health as unsure (137), have less purpose in life (241), and be more likely to have had a history of contact with psychiatrists (4) than nonusers. (This might have to do with the observation that more users seemed to come from families with higher incomes and these are the people who generally seek professional help for problems.) It has also been reported that female drug users saw this use as part of a general configuration of independence and expectation of independence (238), an observation which, if true, could be used to explain recent higher use rates for females, and to predict, with the spread of equality for women, even higher female drug use rates in the future.

Other Population Groups

Few studies dealt with drug use in nonschool populations. The research was scarce and scattered and often sampled only societal subgroups—hippies, American soldiers in Vietnam, high school dropouts, hospital and psychotherapy patients, and so on. Because of these limitations, some of the studies examined had considerably less methodological rigor than the previously examined research. However, they did allow the depiction of a broader picture than could have been achieved by using only rigorous epidemiological papers.

Normal Adult Populations Studies. Studies dealing with North American samples from the normal adult population will now be considered.

Between 1965 and 1966, Robins and Murphy (230) interviewed 221 Negro men selected from public school records, thus making their selection completely arbitrary and predating any drug use. The men at the time of interview were between 30 and 35 years of age, all had a normal IQ, and all lived in their city of birth, St. Louis, Missouri. It was found that 47% of the sample had used marihuana, 17% amphetamines, and 14% barbiturates, and 50% of the marihuana users had tried other drugs. While socioeconomic status and grade school marks were no predictors of drug use, it was found that more high school dropouts used drugs than those who had graduated.

Some four years later Becker Associates (18) reported a 45% marihuana use rate for the males in their sample of 372 young, full-time employees of five major Boston, Massachusetts, firms. Females in the sample reported only 22% marihuana use, while LSD use was 18% among males and only

4% among females. The majority of the cannabis users had tried it more than once—only 4% of the sample were one-time experimenters. It should be pointed out that this rate of use was not very much different from the rates reported at many colleges, although it was somewhat less than Becker Associates reported for a sample of Boston University students (18) taken concurrently.

Between 1967 and 1968 drug use rates for a representative sample of the San Francisco population over 19 years of age were collected and analyzed (176, 188). It was found that 9% of the females and twice as many males had tried cannabis and that 3% of the sample had tried LSD. Use rates for both amphetamines and tranquilizers were around 8% for men and 13% for women. Drug use was found to relate positively to age; absence of traditional religious commitment; heavy use of tobacco and alcohol; and, for women only, living away from home. Although there was no significant difference for the entire sample between student and nonstudent marihuana use rates, it was found that high school dropouts were more likely to have used marihuana than those who stayed in school. It was further noted that not only did more women than men in the sample use amphetamines and barbiturates, but more women than men used prescription drugs of all categories. On the other hand, more young persons, particularly men, used prescription drugs illicitly than did older people.

With regard to the use of mood-modifying prescription drugs, Cooperstock and Sims (69) analyzed a sample of 6989 prescriptions which covered two 1-week periods (one in October 1965 and one in April 1966) in Toronto, and they found that 40% of the prescriptions were for psychotherapeutic agents such as major and minor tranquilizers, 16% were for respiratory and cerebral stimulants such as amphetamines and amphetamine-barbiturate compounds, and 44% were for sedatives and hypnotics, largely of the barbiturate type. They also found that 69% of these prescriptions were written for women and noted that, when the projected figures were compared to the population figures for Metropolitan Toronto, it averaged out to about one mood-modifying prescription for every person over 15 years of age per year. [In the United States Levine (1970) found that 67% of the prescriptions for psychotropic drugs were written for women.] Cooperstock and Sims also reported that more of those in the suburbs received prescriptions than did those in the city center, the figures being 58 and 42%, respectively. However, since only 35% of the area inhabitants lived in the city center, the overall drug use pattern was higher for city center residents. Further, they found that socioeconomic level did not relate to the number of prescriptions received.

In 1971 in Toronto, Smart and Fejer (252) interviewed a random, stratified sample of 1200 adults and found a cannabis use rate of 12.2% for the men and 5.5% for the women and an LSD use rate of 2.6% for the overall population. Marihuana use related negatively to age and related positively to being well educated, having a history of psychiatric contacts, being single, and being male. They pointed out that it must not be assumed that the schools are the centers of drug use: whereas 28% of the adults between the ages of 20 and 25 reported marihuana use, the corresponding figure for the Toronto high school sample was only 18%.

In 1969 Gallup (102) did a nationwide (U.S.) survey of adults over 21 years of age and found an overall cannabis use rate of 4%. The findings indicated that younger persons were more likely to have used marihuana than were older persons: 12% of those between the ages of 21 and 29, 3% of those between the ages of 30 and 49, and only 1% of those 50 or over reported the use of this drug. More men reported marihuana use (6%) than did women (2%), and more of those with a college background (9%) reported use than did those with either high school (3%) or grade school only (1%). Those in western states had the highest use rate at 9%, eastern states came next with 5%, while in the midwest and south only 2% of the sample reported any marihuana use.

Hippies. The hippies and their 1968 Chicago Democratic Convention counterparts, the yippies, have been written about at length by their own and by "establishment" writers (50, 138, 205, 223, 235, 236, etc.). One thing, perhaps the only thing, that these writers agreed upon is that hippies use copious amounts of drugs, particularly marihuana and LSD. Without getting into a broad discussion of yippie-hippie philosophy or even the meanings of terms, it is possible to examine a number of studies that dealt with so-called hippies (126, 239, 240, 263, 294).

Overall, the drug use rates for hippies were found to be high, ranging from 100% for cannabis, 88% for LSD, and 61% for amphetamines in a New York City sample (263), to 70.3% cannabis use, 22.2% LSD use, and 33.2% amphetamine use for a midwestern sample (126). New York (263) and San Francisco (126, 240) samples showed considerably more drug use than a Denver, Colorado, sample (126), while the sample of "yippies" at the 1968 Democratic Convention (294) showed a drug use pattern somewhere between the two extremes, possibly because it consisted of hippies indigenous to the area as well as those having traveled from areas having more (e.g., west coast) and less (e.g., midwest) drug use.

Shick et al. (239) reported an extremely high use of oral and intravenous amphetamines (87%) in their sample of San Francisco hippies; however, the majority of those interviewed were seen in connection with the free health clinic in Haight-Ashbury, which is a sampling bias that might account for this high figure. Various researchers have also noted that the mean age for those hippies interviewed was about 20 years (126, 240, 294); they were mostly white, middle-class youths (126, 240) with parents who had a higher than average education and income (126, 294); they reported no traditional religious convictions (294); they used marihuana instead of alcohol (240, 294); about half had been to college or were in school (240, 294); and more hippie women used amphetamines than did hippie men, although there was no significant difference found between hippie male and hippie female use of cannabis (263, 294). Zaks et al. (294) found that 50% of their hippie sample was comprised of firstborns, 37% lived with their families, and 68% reported that they had permissive parents. Shick et al. (240) found that LSD was their drug of choice, while Hamburger (126) noted that hippies seemed repulsed by the idea of using narcotic drugs. Hippies were reported to take drugs in groups as opposed to using them alone (126), and curiosity and peer pressure were cited as the major reasons for initiating use (294). Multiple drug use was common, particularly combinations of marihuana and LSD (240, 294). It has also been reported that many hippies sold small amounts of cannabis in connection with using it (126).

If part of the hippie philosophy is "turn on, tune in, drop out," it might be appropriate here to discuss the "turning on" of high school dropouts and the "tuning in" at music festivals. Concerning dropouts, in 1969 the Utah Governor's Citizen Advisory Committee (113) sent questionnaires to high school dropouts and received a 32% return ($n = 180$). More male dropouts reported drug use than did female dropouts, while the overall drug use rates were 49.7% cannabis use, 32.7% LSD use, 28.5% amphetamine use, and 31.2% barbiturate use. The committee hypothesized that since less than a third of the questionnaires were returned and since it was probably only the cooperative people who returned questionnaires, the actual drug use rates for dropouts were probably considerably higher. If this hypothesis is true, it would put the proportion of dropouts using drugs within the drug use rates reported by hippies and it well might be that those dropouts had indeed joined the hippie subculture (50, 112, 235). In any case, it was reported that these rates were considerably higher than for Utah students who stayed in school. Robins and Murphy (230) also reported high drug use rates for high school dropouts (see above).

Regarding "tuning in," high rates of public illicit drug use by young people have been reported at music festivals (192, 210) with more drug use at "acid rock" festivals than at those offering more traditional or "country" forms of music (192).

Soldiers in Vietnam. Surveys of United States soldiers in Vietnam found marihuana use rates ranging from 23.0 (28) to 68.0% (275). The only rates for LSD and amphetamine use found were supplied by Black et al. (28) at 7.0 and 10.0%, respectively (about 62% of those were heavy users). Cannabis use rates for soldier psychiatric patients have been reported as around 54%, while rates for dispensary and surgery patients are around 33% (54, 219).

Concerning the question of whether being stationed in Vietnam leads to drug use, Treanor and Skripol (275) reported that the majority (88%) of the cannabis users in their sample had used marihuana previous to coming to Vietnam. However, Roffman and Sapol (231) found only 38.9% of their subjects had used the drug before. As would be expected from previously mentioned studies of drug users, Roffman and Sapol found cannabis users subscribed to no religious beliefs, came from large urban centers, and used large amounts of alcohol. They also noted that heavy use related to having used cannabis before coming to Vietnam and to multiple drug use. Users tended to have a lower rank than nonusers. Evidently drug use in the army has been an increasing problem: Baker (12) indicated that 20% of the 1968 and 25% of the 1969 admissions to an east coast psychiatric hospital were related to drugs, while in 1967 4.8% of all the cases received at the army criminal investigative repository were drug cases, but by 1969 the figure had risen to 37.4%.

Miscellaneous Adult Populations. North American epidemiological studies of interest—although they have no broad, generalizable sample base and they were taken from limited populations—will be discussed here in terms of their relationships to previously introduced variables.

Devenyi and Wilson (82) found that barbiturate abuse was significantly more widespread for younger persons, and particularly for females, in their sample of an adult alcoholic population.

McGlothlin et al. (184) studied 247 white middle-aged adults who had taken LSD in conjunction with psychotherapy or in controlled experimental conditions and found that 44% had used marihuana. The marihuana users were reported as being socioculturally alienated but personally secure. They were more likely to have been in the fine arts or professions than their nonmarihuana-using counterparts.

Goode (111) interviewed 200 young, largely Caucasian marihuana smokers and concluded that marihuana use is largely a social phenomenon, and that heavy use correlated positively with having friends who also used the drug. Within this group there seemed to be no single "pusher": 47% of the sample had sold marihuana at one time or another. About half of the marihuana users had tried LSD, 43% had tried amphetamines, and 24% had tried barbiturates.

In a sample of 74 ghetto youths in a work training program, Lipscomb

(174) found that 54% had used marihuana, 5% LSD, 20% amphetamines, and 4% barbiturates. Alcohol was the most widely used drug at 84%. (It is interesting to note here that the drug use rates for these ghetto youths were not significantly higher than some of the rates reported in this paper for college students.) In 1968, Klein and Phillips (160) reported a trend away from "hard" drugs such as heroin and cocaine toward "softer" drugs such as marihuana in their 11-year study of working-class street gang members.

Goldberg (108), in his examination of court and youth center records, found an interesting relationship between marihuana and heroin use: in a sample of 259 cases of juvenile drug abusers in a New York City probation office, he found 20% marihuana use and 39% heroin use; in a sample of 165 juvenile drug abusers at a juvenile center, he reported 11% marihuana use and 42% heroin use; and in a sample of 219 drug abusers at a juvenile center, he found 3% marihuana use and 72% heroin use. Thus it would seem that, for his samples in any case, there was an inverse relationship between current marihuana use and current heroin use.

With regard to LSD use in particular, using the MMPI Smart and Fejer (251) compared 100 volunteer illicit users of LSD (largely drawn from a hippie area in Toronto) with a matched control group of 45 persons. They reported that users of LSD were generally single, male, multiple drug users from the two highest social classes. Although LSD use correlated positively with conduct disorders and psychoses, they noted that much of the psychopathology predated LSD use.

Although no systematic studies of drug use by native and religious cult populations could be found, it has been noted by a number of writers (55, 56, 167, 242) that American Indian populations, particularly those in the southwestern United States (as well as in Mexico and South America), use psychedelic substances such as peyote, psilocybin, and the like, for spiritual reasons. Some of this cult use has even been formalized in the Native American Church and Leary's League for Spiritual Discovery.

Some Noteworthy Overviews

Yolles (293), in his testimony before the U. S. Senate Judiciary Subcommittee to investigate juvenile delinquency, stated that there were 8 to 12 million persons in the United States who had tried marihuana, and that its use was increasing. He estimated that about 10% of all users were chronic users, 25% occasional users, and the rest experimenters or one-time users.

In terms of literature reviews, Berg's (23) review was probably the most complete for the United States, and Smart and Fejer's (250) review was similarly thorough for Canadian studies. Cox and Smart (70) discussed the nature and extent of "speed" use in North America in a competent but incomplete literature review, and Richards and Carroll (227) briefly considered some of the literature in their paper on illicit drug use and addiction in the United States.

Hammond (127) examined arrest figures in his attempt to estimate drug abuse in Canada and noted that there were drastic increases in arrest rates for marihuana and LSD possession and trafficking. He also considered the problems in overprescribing of psychotropics.

Mexico

Cabildo (47) studied 3096 minors and juveniles in Mexico City and found that the overall cannabis use rate was 4.0% and that overall drug use increased with grade level. De la Fuente (77) found similar cannabis use rates for his two preparatory school samples, whereas Carranza Acevedo (52) reported a slightly higher cannabis use rate (7.6%) for his sample of 7800 secondary school students. In a study of adult factory workers (21), 2.5% of the males admitted to cannabis use within the month previous to the questionnaire administration. The same study reported that 3.0% of the males and 4.2% of the females had used barbiturates up to six times within the previous month. Barbiturate use was reported as 4.7% for a sample of 233 preparatory school youths early in the school year, and as 5.9% for a later sample of 393, while amphetamine use was reported as 3.0 and 5.5%, respectively (77). Carranza Acevedo's secondary school sample (52) reported amphetamine use rates of 0.9%.

See Belsasso et al. (22) for a more detailed analysis of Mexican studies.

Chile

The only Chilean study available was by Richard et al. (226), who examined 1304 students from four Chilean colleges (subject age range 14 to 19) by questionnaire. They found an overall marihuana use rate of 34.7%, with 48.2% of the males and 20.7% of the females admitting to having used the drug. It was also reported that more females of higher socioeconomic status used marihuana than did those of middle socioeconomic status (23.9 versus 17.3%). Marihuana use correlated positively with age, seeming to peak at around 16 years; 19.7% of the 14-year-olds reported use of the drug, 40.3% of the 16-year-olds reported use, and 35.6% of the 18- and 19-year-olds reported use. It was estimated that about 16% of the users were habitual users and that 23% were multiple drug users with experience with hallucinogens and/or stimulants and/or tranquilizers and/or barbiturates. When asked whether or not they intended to continue marihuana use,

42.7% of the multiple drug users and 23.6% of the "marihuana only" users said that they would. About 35% of the users thought that marihuana smoking was beneficial or neutral, whereas only 4.3% of the nonusers agreed with them. Interestingly, over the whole sample, only 0.3% thought smoking tobacco was beneficial and only 0.7% thought drinking alcohol was beneficial, whereas 5.6% thought smoking marihuana was beneficial. Students with poor parental relationships, particularly with the father, were likely to have used drugs.

Marihuana use was seen as a social phenomenon, with 70.4% of the users reporting group use, especially at parties (64.8%) and within groups of close friends (21.7%).

4. EPIDEMIOLOGY IN BRITAIN AND EUROPE.

Britain

Most of the studies found for Britain dealt primarily with the prevalence of narcotic use, and usually used hospital or prison samples. Since there was very little comparability between there studies, they are generally considered individually.

Four studies dealing with heroin addicts, all conducted in connection with hospitals, clinics, and day centers (6, 163, 197, 270), reported high rates of cannabis use, ranging from 86 to 100%, while psychedelic drug use ranged from 46 to 74%. All four reported that the addicts were multiple drug users. Anumonye and McLure (6) dealt with the youngest sample of addicts (mean age 17 years) and reported somewhat less drug use than the other three studies, which dealt with older addicts (mean age 24 years). To illustrate, Anumonye and McClure reported cannabis and LSD use rates as 86 and 46%, respectively, while the corresponding rates reported by Mitcheson et al. (197) were 99 and 74%. There were more male than female addicts in all four papers. Two of the studies reported a high incidence of parental separation and disharmony (6, 270). Mitcheson et al. (197) studied heroin users in a small town and found, like Stimson and Ogborne (270) and Anumonye and McClure (6), that many came from the higher socioeconomic classes and were multiple drug users.

Two papers dealt with amphetamine use. Hawks et al. (130) interviewed 74 regular users of methylamphetamine injections (4 males to 1 female) in a number of settings including clinics and a general practice. They found that the users were generally single, under 25, and had a history of parental separation, poor education, and a high rate of police charges. Concerning multiple drug use, beside amphetamines, 45% regularly used cannabis, 24%

tranquilizers, and 15% hallucinogens. [Interestingly, there was a high rate of female homosexuality (50%), a finding that has previously (20) been related to amphetamine use.] The other paper on amphetamine use was by Cockett and Marks (62), who found by urinalysis a use rate of 6.9% in their sample of 972 juveniles at a London remand center.

Backhouse and James (10) interviewed 290 delinquent boys aged 14 to 16 at a detention center in southeast England and they found that they reported 7.2% cannabis use, 8.2% amphetamine use, and 2.1% barbiturate use. There was also a positive relationship between alcohol use, tobacco use, and the use of other drugs. The majority of the subjects were multiple drug users.

Linken (171) reported 12.7% cannabis use, 9.9% amphetamine use, and 2.4% LSD use in his sample of 252 young patients at a clinic for venereal disease. He also found that the majority were multiple drug users with stable, heterosexual relationships, although the users tended to have earlier sexual experiences than the nonusers. Male drug users outnumbered the female users by only 8%.

Two college surveys (27, 282) which were unpublished and unavailable at the time of this writing were, however, reviewed in Hawks (129). He reported that Binnie and Murdock (27) found 10% of their student sample had used cannabis and, unlike many American studies, only 9% of the cannabis users had tried LSD. Both Binnie and Murdock and Webb et al. (27, 282) noted that the cannabis users in their student samples tended to be more radical and permissive in their political and social attitudes than nonusers, were enrolled in nonscience subjects more often than nonusers, and seldom took any other illicit drugs, with the single exception of amphetamines. Webb et al. also reported that cannabis users tended to seek medical and psychiatric advice more, as well as drink alcohol and smoke tobacco more than student nonusers.

Two papers (115, 146) dealt with the prescription use of tranquilizers and barbiturates in urban medical practices. Johnson and Clift (146) found that only 1.3% of the patients within a total of 7500 reported that they used these drugs regularly. The majority of the users were older people (mean age 62.7 years). Grant (115) reported that 1.1% of his sample of 2998 patients used barbiturates regularly. Again the majority of users were over 60 years of age.

If the extent of use of any given drug can be inferred by the number of court charges involving the drug, then cannabis and amphetamines were the illicit drugs most in use. In 1967 Hallam et al. (124) examined court charges records in Middlesex and found that of 202 drug offences, 91 involved cannabis, 90 amphetamines, 4 barbiturates, and 1 LSD. They also found that two-thirds of the offenders were under 25 years of age, educated, most were unmarried, and the males outnumbered the females 6 to 1. Although multiple drug use was reported, they found that 74% of the cannabis users and 83% of the amphetamine users had not tried heroin.

Two reviews of drug use in Britain are of note, one by Bewley (25) and one by Hawks (129). Bewley estimated that there were 30 to 60 regular users of cannabis, 200 users of amphetamines, and 1 to 5 users of hallucinogens per 100,000 persons. Hawk's review is considerably more comprehensive than Bewley's and therefore cannot be gone into in detail.

France

Virtually no epidemiological works on drug use could be obtained for France, possibly because, until recently, there was thought to be very little "drug problem" in that country (65). Defer et al. (74), in a paper on the history of marihuana use in France, reported that in 1967 they examined three adolescents who smoked hashish, two of whom were diagnosed as psychopathic and one as hebephrenic. They also wrote that cannabis users have a taste for other drugs and come from many diverse backgrounds including students, apprentices, and fraternity members. Curiosity, self-insight, rebellion, and existential depression were listed as reasons for drug use, and the writers saw the situation as a sociocultural phenomenon.

A French magazine, *Réaltiés* (90), reported that the I.F.O.P. estimated that 8% of the French population had tried marihuana, and that in the 20- to 34-year-old group, perhaps 15% had tried the drug. It was also noted that of all those arrested for drug offences in 1969, 66% were male and 25% were students. Again, drug use was seen as a social problem.

Scandinavia

In 1968 the Copenhagen health department administered 8600 questionnaires to Danish secondary school students (225). The findings indicated that 11.5% of the sample had used cannabis, 1% had used LSD, and multiple drug use patterns (including amphetamine use) were exhibited by the 1% of the sample who were frequent cannabis users. More males reported drug use than did females, and there were twice as many drug users in technical schools as there were in general high schools. The majority of users were in the 17- to 19-year age bracket, although technical school students and apprentices were found to have the highest proportion of users in the 14- to 16-year age bracket. Drug use rates were highest in and around urban areas, especially Copenhagen, where an earlier health department publication dealing with the same study (222) indicated that cannabis was used by 30% of the Copenhagen youths who participated in the survey. Overall use was reported as increasing, as indicated by both police records and a comparison of the present data with a 1966 survey. Another survey (178) done in 1968 reported that 17% of Copenhagen youth between the ages of 15 and 20 years had tried hashish.

In Göteborg, Holmberg and Jansson (140) interviewed 73 patients seen at an outpatient department for drug addicts (mean age 22 years) and found that although the ratio of male to female patients was 4 to 1, female cannabis, LSD, and amphetamine use did not differ significantly from male drug use (the overall use rates for these drugs were 34.2, 5.5, and 72.6%, respectively). However, four times as many females had used barbiturates and tranquilizers than had the males (28.6 versus 6.8%). Amphetamine taken by injection was the drug of choice. Concerning reasons for drug use, "mental disease" was listed first, followed by peer pressure, high-grade environmental risk (e.g., lack of job security), curiosity, and in order to increase artistic powers.

There were a number of overviews of Swedish drug abuse worth noting (24, 106, 107, 215). With regard to amphetamine use, Perman (215) estimated in 1970 that about 0.5% of Sweden's population was addicted, although no references were cited. Goldberg (106, 107), in a two-part article, reviewed Swedish drug surveys done up to 1967 and came to the conclusion that drug abuse was on the rise. The factors he cited as relating positively to drug use were largely social ones: an unstable home environment, having friends who use drugs, and belonging to a drug-using subculture. He noted that at that time more young people than in the past were using drugs, and that in recent years the drugs used had changed from opiates to amphetamines, then cannabis, and finally hallucinogens, entered the scene. Bewley (24), in his comparison of recent trends in British and Swedish drug use, also noted an overall increase in drug abuse.

In their recent review of drug use and attitudes in Norway, Irgens-Jensen and Brun-Gulbrandsen (144 pointed out that drug use in this country was considerably lower than in other Scandinavian countries. They argued that this was because of Norway's strong antidrug propaganda, puritan traditions, and the largely rural and thinly populated character of the country. For example, they compared three studies done in 1969, one in Stockholm (203), one in Copenhagen (204), and one in Oslo (266). The cannabis use rates were about three times higher in Copenhagen and Stockholm than the 8% use rates in the Oslo sample. Concerning trends in use, they referred to another study (45) which found an increase from 5% cannabis use in 1968 to 8% in 1969, with 1% LSD use and 2% amphetamine use in 1969 among a sample of 800 Oslo youths between the ages of 15 and 20 years. They also noted that drug use seemed to be connected with a bad home environment, broken homes, dropping out of school, and maladjustment.

Switzerland

Two Swiss studies of interest were found. In the first Ladewig (164) interviewed 30 "juvenile drug abusers" (taken from the ranks of psychiatric patients and prisoners) and found that the majority were psychologically dependent on stimulants. Hashish had also been used in conjunction with amphetamines, especially by the 41% of the group judged to be neurotic. Drug use was interpreted as a reaction to an identity crisis.

Bätig (17), on the other hand, using a sample of 307 paid university and technical school volunteers, found that 18.6% had used cannabis, 5.2% LSD, and 12.4% stimulants, and that multiple drug use was common. Cannabis use correlated positively with overall multiple drug use, while alcohol and amphetamines were reported as being often used together as were tranquilizers and sleeping pills. No significant differences were found between the sexes in regard to drug use; however, the sample could have been better, since only 7.2% were females. Those who had used cannabis were underrepresented in the natural sciences but overrepresented in the humanities group. Curiosity was listed by 63% of those who had taken LSD and 44% of those who had taken cannabis as the reason for initial use. It was also reported that 50% of the sample volunteered to be in the study in hopes of being allowed to try drugs, a fact that may well have biased the sample.

Holland

In the autumn of 1967 a questionnaire was circulated to drug users within drug-using subcultures in Holland (63). It had a 64% return rate ($n = 958$), estimated to represent about 20% of the drug-using subculture in Holland. The study reported that the male to female ratio of "drug users" was about 3 to 1, and that females used smaller quantities and numbers of drugs than did the males. The mean age of the sample was 23 years, and the upper and middle classes were overrepresented. The educational level of the users was high—54% were university students—although heavy use was connected with deficient social orientation and with being out of school and work. LSD and hashish were the drugs of choice as opposed to opium or alcohol, and 51% of those who had tried hashish had also sold the drug. The majority (75%) of the sample were multiple drug users.

Germany

The only German paper available on drug use (83) estimated that there were perhaps 200 to 250 "hard-core" drug users in the city of Belfield and another 800 to 1500 occasional hashish users. Of the sample of 100 hard-core hashish and LSD users examined in the study, 25% were high school students and the mean age of the sample was about 17 years.

Czechoslovakia

The only available Czechoslovakian paper is by Vondráček et al. (281), who reported in 1968 that the prescription of both stimulants and barbiturates had increased drastically in that country: from 1958 to 1965 the use of barbiturates increased from 7.6 million tablets to 15.1 million tablets, and the use of stimulants increased from 0.2 million tablets to 19.1 million tablets. With regard to illicit drug use, 40% of all the addicts seen in a Prague clinic were addicted to stimulants, while the number of psychiatric patients addicted to drugs was reported to be on the increase.

5. EPIDEMIOLOGY IN AFRICA

Although a 1966 article by Boroffka (37), based on an examination of African hospital admissions, stated that cannabis habituation was a problem of the middle classes in Nigeria, other writers (9, 166) have felt that Nigerian cannabis use was generally by men from the lower classes and was found particularly in the urban areas among the unemployed.

In North Africa, cannabis smoking was depicted as a leisure activity for the lower classes and was not considered a particularly dangerous pursuit (88, 218). A paper from Southern Rhodesia (72) pointed out that cannabis was used by north European teenagers in the area as well as by indigenous populations. The Europeans used the drug for euphoric purposes and the Africans used it to increase their endurance and to work better.

6. EPIDEMIOLOGY IN ASIA AND ASIA MINOR

Mideast

In 1967 Soueif (264) compared 240 hashish users in Cairo with 49 hashish users from semi-urban and rural upper Egypt. As controls he used 115 appropriately matched Cairo nonusers and 40 upper Egypt nonusers. All the subjects were male paid volunteers and were examined using a standardized interview schedule. The majority of both using groups had started to take the drug before they were 20 years of age with their peak usage between 17 and 18 years of age. The urban group ranked social pressure and the search for euphoria followed by curiosity as the major reasons for initial hashish use, whereas the rural group ranked euphoria first, curiosity second, and social pressure third. Both ranked "feeling like men" and "sexual thrill" as the fourth and fifth reasons for initial use. The urban group used hashish, on the average, five or more times a month; the rural group used the drug slightly less, averaging three or more times a month. Both groups indicated that hashish was used mostly in small groups, although more persons in the rural group used the drug alone (12 as opposed to 2%). Compared to the controls, users scored higher on some items on the Taylor Manifest Anxiety scale and were more likely to have fathers that used the drug.

Osaka et al. (211) interviewed the first 100 patients at a Cairo psychiatric clinic and reported that 0.9% of the sample were addicts of opium, barbiturates, and meprobamate.

Miller (194), in his commentary on drug abuse in Israel, noted that according to police reports, juvenile drug use had increased since the six-day war largely due to the influence of Western tourists and Arabs. Foreign students at universities were said to be the main student consumers of drugs, particularly of hashish and LSD, although there were reports of a few Israeli delinquents turning to drug use.

India

No recent epidemiological studies on India could be located. However, earlier references (53, 57, 59) pointed out that cannabis use in India has had a long tradition in both social and religious contexts. Chopra and Chopra (59) went into detail on the use of cannabis as a household remedy.

The Chopras (57) divided cannabis users in India into four groups: the poor classes, who used it in small amounts to relieve tension; the idle and mentally below average, who used it in larger quantities for its narcotic effects; the rich and idle pleasure seekers; and the priests and religious mendicant class who used it to help them to meditate. The same study noted that heavy use can lead to physical and mental deterioration.

7. EPIDEMIOLOGY IN AUSTRALIA

In Australia, juvenile drug use of all types seems to have been increasing, according to a report by Le Fevre (168) based on Department of Health and police records. Multiple drug use was common among 2182 drug offenders in his sample, while barbiturate and alcohol use predominated. Concerning stimulant use in Australia, Bell (19) noted that addiction to stimulants was increasing, particularly among delinquents, "Bohemians," and truck drivers.

Rosenberg (234) interviewed 50 "addicts," aged 30 years or less, from hospitals and a prison in the Sydney area and reported that 92% had used amphetamines and 90% had used barbiturates. Psychotic symptoms were noted in 82% of the subjects. Most had grown up under adverse conditions, had done poorly in school, and had unstable work records.

Briscoe and Hinterberger (44) examined a total of 1577 urine samples for amphetamine use taken from college (4.1% use), private school (0% use), prison admission (8.1% use), welfare center (5.5% use), psychiatric hospital admission (12.3% use), and general medical practice (3.7% use) populations. The overall amphetamine use rate was 5.6%. More females reported amphetamine use than did males (9.2% as opposed to 5.0%) and more older females used amphetamines than did younger females. None of the subjects knew they were to be tested beforehand.

Wheeler and Edmonds (285) studied 100 "drug-dependent" young persons (60% under 21 years of age) at a drug referral center in Sydney. The majority (89%) were multiple drug users. The figures for the use of each drug are 59% marihuana, 44% hallucinogens, 80% stimulants, and 42% sedatives. Half of the sample had had trouble with the police and half had received psychiatric treatment. Although the educational achievement of the sample paralleled the general population, 63% were unemployed. Only 15% lived with their families, and 80% were either single, separated, or divorced.

8. WORLD EPIDEMIOLOGY: SUMMARY WITH SUGGESTIONS FOR FURTHER RESEARCH

The following summary only covers the most common and generalizable conclusions that can be drawn from the epidemiological literature reviewed. The reader is referred to the preceding sections for the examination of more contentious or detailed aspects.

Overall, use rates of psychoactive and hallucinogenic drugs increased between 1967 and 1972, with cannabis use having had the largest overall increase and the largest overall proportion of users, especially in North America. Generally, more males were reported to use these drugs than were females, except for barbiturates and tranquilizers, where this relationship was reversed. However, later studies indicated that female drug use rates have been increasing for the hallucinogens, and this increase may account for a good portion of the overall increase in the number of persons using drugs. The majority of illicit users seemed to fall into the "experimenter" category, but cannabis users appeared to be most likely to continue in the use of the drug. Heavy cannabis use correlated highly with multiple drug use, especially with the use of LSD. European and Australian rates of cannabis and LSD use seemed lower than North American rates, but there was less of a difference among these areas in terms of amphetamine and barbiturate use. It also appears that the use rates for legally prescribed psychoactives have increased over the years covered by this review. The data on Indian and African drug use rates were sparse, but it would seem that LSD, amphetamine, barbiturate, and tranquilizer use were not as much of a problem as chronic heavy cannabis use by a small proportion of the lower classes, especially in urban areas.

Within the high school surveys it was reported that there was an increase in drug use in the higher grades, but this relationship was not as strong in the university studies. Within the student surveys the lowest drug use rates were found among graduate students, then came high school students, and college students had the highest use rates.

Within all the studies examined, there appeared to be a definite increase in drug use rates with proximity to urban areas. In the United States drug use rates appeared to be highest on the west coast.

High rates of drug use (especially cannabis) in North America were also related to having parents with above average income and education (i.e., middle, upper-middle, and professional class), having only one parent, the user having a poor relationship with his parents, living away from home, cohabitation, not being married, having been in trouble with the authorities, being a dropout, having no religion, and with having friends who use drugs. Further, drug-using students generally received lower academic marks than did their nonusing peers.

Users were also reported to have more liberal attitudes toward sex, drugs, and politics than nonusers and also to indulge in sexual activities more than nonusers. Peer groups seemed the most important source of drug information for users, whereas curiosity was most often cited as the major reason for initial drug use.

Illicit drug use correlated highly both with reported parental drug use and with the use of socially sanctioned drugs such as alcohol, tobacco, and analgesics. Illicit drug use itself was by no means restricted to school or ghetto populations, although that impression could be gained from the decided lack of studies that dealt with the general adult population. Nevertheless, some groups such as hippies, high school dropouts, correctional and psychiatric institution inmates, and possibly soldiers in Vietnam seemed to have a higher proportion of users, especially for cannabis drugs, than the majority of the rest of the population.

In terms of further research, there are a number of pressing needs.

Initially, it is imperative that research be done on the reliability and validity of various drug use measures, questionnaire formats and administration, and so on. Once reasonably valid and reliable measures have been constructed, they should be used in a series of broad epidemiological studies covering representative samples of the overall population. These broad samplings should be repeated on a regular basis every two or three years in order to obtain a growing and comprehensive picture of drug use rates and changes in these rates. Further, there should be coordination of research activities, not only so that there would be less unnecessary replication of populations studied and variables examined, but also so that standardized extent and duration of use categories could be employed, thus allowing some basis for reasonably accurate interstudy comparisons.

Various methodologies other than the one-shot anonymous self-report questionnaires also need to be employed. Longitudinal studies using an anthropological approach, complete with day-to-day field notes gathered by persons living within the drug-using subculture, might shed more light on the etiology of drug use than the cut-and-dried questionnaire approach. A variant on this theme might involve having subjects keep a daily diary or record of their drug use behavior over the period of a few years. For example, this could be done with a group of freshmen who would be paid to keep this kind of record over their years in university. Another worthwhile longitudinal approach would be the administration of drug use and attitudinal questionnaires to the same subjects at various times during the year for a few years. This would allow not only for the collection of data on how drug use patterns and attitudes change over the years and in different social and physical environments, but also could yield data on measure reliabilities. Biological drug use measures such as urine and blood analysis might also be employed to determine absolute use rates and to gather postquestionnaire reliabilities. Other approaches might involve the administration of intensive, broad, and systematic personality inventories to persons exhibiting various levels and types of drug use behavior, or the detailed study of social milieux and physical environments where heavy drug use is found.

All of these could be greatly facilitated through the establishment of a central funding agency responsible for the direction and coordination of drug use research.

Overall, the data analysis techniques used in this area need improvement. Analysis of variance, factor analysis, and even simple correlational analysis are sadly lacking. Data need to be interpreted as well as reported.

On the other hand, more examination of police records would probably yield little or no useful information in terms of epidemiology, since such data deal only with those users who have been caught, and it seems from the high reported use rates in many surveys that those who are caught are in the minority.

Finally, one gets the impression from the literature that much of the drug use research has been almost random with no fixed goal or even direction. Emphasis on theory or at least an attempt at the beginning of a theory dealing with drug use rates, patterns, and the reasons for these rates and patterns is desperately needed, even if the theory has to be abandoned later.

In conclusion, although there have been many valuable and worthwhile studies in the field, there is a desperate need for improvement in design and coordination between studies at this point in time. Theory and the examination of populations in terms of theory are presently of paramount importance if epidemiological studies are ever going to be able to predict drug use behavior instead of simply describing it.

ACKNOWLEDGEMENTS

The authors wish to thank Ms. C. D. Rogers and Ms. S. Snook for their assistance in the preparation of this manuscript, and Ms. I. Jaunzemis and Mr. E. Madsen for their assistance in the translating of some of the non-English titles.

REFERENCES

1. Abdulla, A., Cannabis indica als Volksseuche in Aegypten, *Schweiz. Med. Wochenschr.*, **83**, 541 (1953).
2. Ahmed, S., Patterns of juvenile drug use, *Diss. Abstr.*, **28**, 4703 (1968).
3. Allen, J. R. and L J. West, Flight from violence: Hippies and the Green Rebellion, *Am. J. Psychiat.*, **125**, 364 (1968).
4.* Anker, J. L., D. H. Milman, S. A. Kahan, and C. Valenti, Drug usage and related patterns of behavior in university students, I. General survey and marihuana use, *J. Am. Coll. Health Assoc.*, **19**, 178 (1971).
5.* Annis, H. M., R. Klug, and D. Blackwell, *Drug use among high school students in Timmins,* Addiction Research Foundation, Toronto, 1971.
6.* Anumonye, A. and J. L. McClure, Adolescent drug abuse in a North London suburb, *Br. J. Addict.*, **65**, 25 (1970).

* Drug use rates for all asterisked (*) references have been compiled in tabular form. Copies of these tables may be obtained by requesting *Tables of Psychoactive and Hallucinogenic Drug Use: A Compendium of Recent Epidemiological Studies* by G. W. Mercer, from the Addiction Research Foundation of Ontario, 33 Russell Street, Toronto 4, Ontario.

7. Archibald, H. D., *The non-medical use of drugs in Canada: The contemporary situation*, Paper presented at the International Institute on the Prevention and Treatment of Drug Dependence, Lausanne, Switzerland, 1970.
8. Askevold, F., The occurrence of paranoid incidents and abstinance delerium in abusers of amphetamine, *Acta Psychiatr. Scand.*, **34,** 145 (1959).
9. Asuni, T., Socio-psychiatric problems of cannabis in Nigeria, *Bull. Narcotics*, **16,** 17 (1968).
10.* Backhouse, C. I. and I. P. James, The relationship and prevalence of smoking, drinking and drug taking in (delinquent) adolescent boys, *Br. J. Addict.*, **64,** 75 (1969).
11. Baker, A. A. and E. G. Lucas, some hospital admissions associated with cannabis, *Lancet,* **1,** 148 (1969).
12. Baker, S. L., Drug abuse in the United States Army, *Bull. N. Y. Acad. Med.*, **47,** 541 (1971).
13. Bakewell, W. E. and A. Wikler, Symposium: Non-narcotic addiction: Incidence in a university hospital ward, *JAMA,* **196,** 710 (1966).
14. Ballante, A., Marijuana: The symbol and the ritual, *J. Secondary Educ.*, **43,** 218 (1968).
15.* Barber, J. M. and R. K. Means, *Amphetamine use among college women,* Paper presented to the Research Council of the American School Health Association 44th Annual Meeting, Houston, Texas, Oct. 24, 1970.
16. Barter, J. T., G. L. Mizner, and P. H. Werme, *Patterns of Drug Use Among College Students: An Epidemiological and Demographic Survey of Student Attitudes and Practices,* Department of Psychiatry, University of Colorado Medical School, Boulder, 1970.
17.* Bättig, K., Konsum psychoaktiver Pharmaka und illegaler Drogen bei Zürcher Hochschulstudenten, *Schweiz. Med. Wochenschr.*, **100,** 1887 (1970).
18.* Becker associates, Survey Plan, *The Boston Globe,* March, 1970.
19. Bell, D. S., Addiction to stimulants, *Med. J. Aust.*, **1,** 41 (1967).
20. Bell, D. S. and W. H. Trethowan, Amphetamine addiction and disturbed sexuality, *Arch. Gen. Psychiatr.*, **4,** 74 (1971).
21.* Belsasso, G. and R. Rosenkranz, Incidencia del uso de tabaco, alcohol, y drogas psicotrópicas (Marihuana, Substancias Volátiles, Barbitúricos, Estimulantes, Tranquilizantes, Opiateos, Substancias Alucinógenas) en obreros de la zona metropolitana de la Ciudad de México, *Rev. Inst. Nac. Neurol.*, **6,** (1972).
22. Belsasso, G., R. Rosenkranz, E. Blum, and R. Blum, Estado actual do los estudios médicos sobre Marihuana, *Gac. Med. Mex.*, **70,** 3 (1972).
23. Berg, D. F., The non-medical use of dangerous drugs in the United States: A comprehensive view, *Int. Addict.*, **5,** 777 (1970).
24. Bewley, T. H., Drug dependence—Recent changes in England and Sweden, in *Drugs and Youth,* proceedings of the Rutgers Symposium on Drug Abuse,

J. R. Wittenborn, H. Brill, J. P. Smith, and S. A. Wittenborn (Eds.), Chas. C. Thomas, Springfield, Ill., 1969.

25. Bewley, T. H., Recent changes in the incidence in all types of drug dependence in Great Britain, *Proc. R. Soc. Med.,* **61,** 175 (1968).
26.* Bilodeau, L., *Drug Use Among the Students in the Secondary Schools and CEGEP's on Montreal Island in 1969 and 1971,* Research Division, Office for the Prevention and Treatment of Alcoholism and other Toxicomanias, Québec, 1971.
27. Binnie, H. L. and G. Murdock, *The Attitudes to Drugs and Drug Takers of Students at the University and Colleges of Higher Education in an English Midland City* (unpublished report), 1969.
28.* Black, S., K. L. Owens, and R. P. Wolff, Patterns of drug use: A study of 5,482 subjects, *Am. J. Psychiatr.,* **127,** 420 (1970).
29. Blackford, L. S., Trends in student drug use in San Mateo County, *California's Health,* **27,** 3 (1969).
30.* Blaine, J. D., C. M. Lieberman, and J. Hirsch, Preliminary observations on patterns of drug consumption among medical students, *Int. J. Addict.,* **3,** 399 (1968).
31. Blum, R. H., Drugs and personal values, Paper presented at the National Association of Student Personnel Administrators Drug Education Conference, Washington D. C., November 1966.
32. Blum, R. H. and Associates, *Society and Drugs,* Jossey-Bass, San Francisco, 1969.
33. Blum, R. H. and Associates, *Students and Drugs,* Jossey-Bass, San Francisco, 1969.
34. Blumenfield, M., Ten months experience with LSD users admitted to County Psychiatric Receiving Hospital, *N. Y. State J. Med.,* **67,** 1849 (1967).
35. Blumer, H., *The World of Youthful Drug Use,* A.D.D. Project Report, School of Criminology, University of California, Berkeley, 1967.
36.* Bogg, R. A., R. G. Smith, and S. D. Russell, *Drug Dependence in Michigan, Part III. A Study of Attitudes and Actions of the Young People of Michigan,* Dept. of Public Health, Michigan, 1968.
37. Boroffka, A., Mental illness and Indian hemp in Lagos, *East Afr. Med. J.,* **43,** 377 (1966).
38. Bouquet, J., Cannabis, Part I, *U. N. Bull. Narcotics,* **2,** 14 (1950).
39. Bouquet, J., Cannabis, Part II, *U. N. Bull. Narcotics,* **2,** 22 (1951).
40. Bowers, M. B., A. Chipman, A. Schwartz, and O. T. Dan, Dynamics of psychedelic drug abuse, *Arch. Gen. Psychiatr.,* **16,** 560 (1967).
41.* Brady, J. F., D. R. Ross, C. F. Grindstaff, and E. F. Ryan, *Non-Medical Drug Use Among Students at the University of Western Ontario,* University of Western Ontario, London, 1970.
42. Brehm, M. L. and K. W. Black, Self image and attitudes towards drugs, *J. Pers.,* **36,** 299 (1968).

43. Brill, N. Q., E. Crumpton, and H. M. Grayson, Personality factors in marihuana use, *Arch. Gen. Psychiatr.*, **24**, 163 (1971).
44.* Briscoe, O. V. and H. Hinterberger, A survey of the usage of amphetamines in parts of the Sydney community, *Med. J. Aust.*, **1**, 480 (1968).
45.* Brun-Gulbrandsen, S. and B. B. Lind, *Marihuana og hasjisj—holdninger og bruk* (Marihuana and hashish—Attitudes and use), Oslo, 1970.
46.* Byles, J. A., *Alienation and Social Control,* Interim Research Project on Unreached Youth (Phase I), Toronto, Ontario, 1967.
47.* Cabildo, H., Investigación sobre el uso de substancias intoxicantes entre menores y jóvenes del Distrito Sanitario XVI, *Rev. Salud Púb. Méx.*, **19**, (1972).
48.* Campbell, I. L., *Marijuana Use at Bishop's University (A Preliminary Statistical Report),* Bishop's University, Lennoxville, Québec, January 11, 1969.
49.* Campbell, I. L., *Marijuana Use at Bishop's University (A Second Preliminary Statistical Report),* Bishop's University, Lennoxville, Québec, 1969.
50. Carey, J. T., *College Drug Scene,* Prentice-Hall, Englewood Cliffs, N.J., 1968.
51. Carey, J. T., Marijuana use among the New Bohemians, *J. Psychedelic Drugs*, **2**, 79 (1968).
52.* Carranza Acevedo, J., Trastornos Conductuales Producidos por la Administración Crónica de anfetaminas, *Arch. Invest. Méx.* (Revista del Depto. de Investigación Cientifica del I.M.S.S.), **1**, 221 (1970).
53. Carstairs, G. M., Daru and Bhang, *Q. J. Stud. Alcohol,* **15**, (1954).
54.* Casper, E., J. Janecek, and H. Martinelli, Marijuana in Vietnam, *U.S. Army Vietnam Med. Bull.*, **40**, 60 (1968).
55. Castaneda, C., *The Teachings of Don Juan: A Yaqui Way of Knowledge,* Ballantine, New York, 1969.
56. Castaneda, C., *A Separate Reality,* Simon and Schuster, New York, 1971.
57. Chopra, I. C. and R. N. Chopra, The use of the cannabis drugs in India, *Bull. Narcotics,* **9**, 4 (1957).
58. Chopra, R. N. and G. S. Chopra, The present position of hemp-drug addiction in India, *Indian Med. Res. Mem.*, **31**, 1 (1939).
59. Chopra, R. N. and I. C. Chopra, Treatment of drug addiction: Experience in India, *Bull. Narcotics,* **9**, 21 (1957).
60. Christozov, C., L'aspect Marocain de l'intoxication cannabique d'après des études faites dans les conditions d'un hôpital psychiatrique de malades chroniques, 1ère partie, *Maroc. Med.*, **44**, 630 (1965).
61. Christozov, C., L'aspect Marocain de l'intoxication cannabique d'après des études sur des malades mentaux chroniques, 2ème partie, *Maroc. Med.*, **44**, 866 (1965).
62.* Cockett, R. and V. Marks, Amphetamine taking among young offenders, *Br. J. Psychiatr.*, **115**, 1203 (1969).

63. Cohen, H., Principal conclusions from the report: Psychology, social-psychology and sociology of illicit drug use, *Br. J. Addict.*, **65**, 39 (1970).
64. Cohen, S. and K. S. Ditman, Prolonged adverse reactions to lysergic acid diethylamide, *Arch. Gen. Psychiatr..,* **8,** 475 (1963).
65. Collins, L. and D. LaPierre, The French connection—In real life, *The New York Times Magazine,* February 6, 1972, p. 14.
66. Connell, P. H., *Amphetamine Psychosis,* Chapman and Hall, London, 1958.
67. Connell, P. H., Amphetamines, 2, *Med. World,* **96,** 106 (1962).
68.* Coopersmith, S. and L. Dick, Attitudes towards alcohol and other drugs, expressed by college students and their parents, Paper delivered at the International Congress on Alcohol and Alcoholism, Washington D.C., September 18, 1969.
69. Cooperstock, R. and M. Sims, Mood-modifying drugs prescribed in a Canadian city: Hidden problems; *Am. J. Pub. Health,* **61,** (1971).
70. Cox, C. and R. Smart, The nature and extent of speed use in North America, *Can. Med. Assoc. J.,* **102,** 724 (1970).
71.* Cross, H. J. and R. G. Keir, Drug usage and attitude toward drugs among college students, *College Student Survey,* **5,** 1 (1971).
72. Dagga smoking in Rhodesia, *Cent. Afr. J. Med.,* **12,** 215 (1966).
73. Dally, P., Undesirable effects of marijuana, *Br. Med. J.* **3,** 367 (1967).
74. Defer, B., K. Billiard-Grasser, and M.-L. Diehl, A propos de L'épidémiologie du Cannabisme en France, *Ann. Med. Psychol. (Paris),* **128,** 113 (1970).
75. Defer, B. and M.-L. Diehl, Les Psychoses Cannabiques Aiguës (à propos de 560 observations), *Ann. Med. Psychol. (Paris),***126,** 260 (1968).
76.* DeFleur, L. B. and G. R. Garrett, Dimensions of marijuana usage in a land-grant university, *J. Counseling Psychol.,* **17,** 463 (1970).
77.* De la Fuente, R. *Encuesta sobre el Consumo de Drogas por los estudiantes universitarios,* Escuela Nacional Preparatoria, Mexico City (unpublished manuscript), 1971.
78.* Demos, G. and J. W. Shainline, *Drug Use on the College Campus: A Pilot-Study Survey,* California State College, Long Beach, (unpublished manuscript), 1967.
79.* Dept. of Public Health and Welfare, *Five Mind-Altering Drugs,* San Mateo, Calif., 1969.
80.* Dickenson, F., Drugs on campus: A Gallup poll, *Reader's Digest,* November 1967, 48.
81.* Division of Alcoholism, Alberta Dept. of Health, Survey reveals frequency and use of alcohol, drugs among students, *Concept,* **2,** (1968).
82.* Devenyi, P. and M. Wilson, Abuse of barbiturates in an alcoholic population, *Can. Med. Assoc. J.,* **104,** 219 (1971).
83. Ebel, E., *Drogenkonsum Jugendlicher in Bielefeld,* Johannes Hospital, Bielefeld, West Germany, 1971.

84. Edwards, J. E. and F. A. Whitlock, Suicide and attempted suicide in Brisbane, *Med. J. Aust.,* **1,** 932 (1968).
85.* Eells, K., Marijuana and LSD: A survey of one college campus, *J. Counseling Psychol.,* **15,** 459 (1968).
86. Eells, K. *A Survey of Student Practices and Attitudes with Respect to Marijuana and LSD.* California Institute of Technology, Pasadena, 1967.
87. Ellinwood, E. H., Amphetamine psychosis, 1. Description of individuals and process, *Seminars Psychiatr.,* **1,** 208 (1969).
88. Elsarrag, M. E., Psychiatry in the Northern Sudan: A study in comparative psychiatry, *Br. J. Psychiatr.,* **114,** 945 (1968).
89. Entwistle, M., Student's questionnaire, *The First Edition,* (Sutton District High School, Ontario), **5,** (1972).
90. Escoffier-Lambiotte and G. Mendel, La drogue chez les jeunes: révolte ou suicide?, *Réalités,* **288,** 72 (1970).
91. Essig, C. F., *Clin. Pharmacol. Ther.,* **5,** 334 (1964).
92. Ewing, J. H., *Why Students "Turn On", Marijuana and Other Drug Use in an Undergraduate Male Population,* Paper presented at the 2nd International Congress of Social Psychiatry, London, August 4-9, 1969.
93.* Faircloth, E., News release of the preliminary results of a survey of students enrolled in Florida's private and public universities and junior colleges, Office of the Attorney General, Florida, 1969.
94.* Fejer, D. *Drug Use Among High School Students in North Bay Ontario,* Addiction Research Foundation, Toronto, Ontario, 1971.
95.* Fejer, D. and R. G. Smart, *Drug Use and Psychological Problems Among Adolescents in a Semi-Rural Area of Ontario: Haldimand County,* Addiction Research Foundation, Toronto, Ontario, 1971.
96. Fejer, D., R. G. Smart, P. Whitehead, and L. LaForest, *Drug Information Sources: Which Ones are Most Informative and Most Influential for High School Students?,* Addiction Research Foundation, Toronto, Ontario, 1970.
97. Fischmann, V. S., Stimulant users in the California rehabilitation centre, *Int. J. Addic.,* **3,** 113 (1968).
98.* Francis, J. B. and D. J. Patch, *Student Attitudes Toward Drug Programs at the University of Michigan,* University Committee on Drug Education, University of Michigan, September 1969.
99. Freedman, H. L. and M. J. Rockmore, Marihuana, a factor in personality evaluation and army maladjustment, I. *J. Clin. Exp. Psychopathol.,* **7,** 765 (1946).
100. Freedman, H. L. and M. J. Rockmore, Marihuana, a factor in personality evaluation and army maladjustment, II. *J. Clin. Exp. Psychopathol.,* **8,** 221 (1946).
101. Frosch, W. A., E. S. Robbins, and M. Stern, Untoward reaction to LSD resulting in hospitalization, *N. Engl. J. Med.,* **273,** 1235 (1965).

102.* Gallup, G. H., Gallup poll, *The Washington Post,* October 26, 1969.
103.* Gallup, G. H. and J. O. Davies, *The Washington Post,* May 20, 1969.
104. Ginsberg, A., The great marijuana hoax: First manifesto to end the bringdown, *Atl. Mon.,* **218,** 106 (1966).
105. Glickmal, L. and M. Blumenfield, Psychological determinants, *J. Nerv. Ment. Dis.,* **145,** 79 (1967).
106. Golderg, L., Drug abuse in Sweden, Part I. *Bull. Narcotics,* **20,** 1 (1968).
107. Goldberg, L., Drug abuse in Sweden, Part II. *Bull. Narcotics,* **20,** 9 (1968).
108.* Goldberg, M., Problem of drug abuse in juvenile court population, *N. Y. State J. Med.,* **71,** 1623 (1971).
109.* Goldstein, J. W., *The Social Psychology of Student Drug Usage: Report on Phase One,* Report of the Carnegie-Mellon University Drug Research Project, June 1970.
110. Goode, E., Marijuana and the politics of reality, *J. Health Soc. Behav.,* **10,** 83 (1969).
111.* Goode, E., Multiple drug use among marijuana smokers, *Soc. Probl.,* **17,** 48 (1969).
112. Goodman, P., *Growing Up Absurd,* Random House, New York, 1956.
113.* Governor's Citizen Advisory Committee on Drugs, Drug Use Among High School Drop-Outs in the State of Utah, in *Advisory Committee Report on Drug Abuse,* Utah, 1969.
114.* Governor's Citizen Advisory Committee on Drugs, Drug Use Among High School Students in the State of Utah, in *Advisory Committee Report on Drug Abuse,* Utah, 1969.
115.* Grant, I. N., Drug habituation in an urban general practice, *Practitioner,* **202,** 428 (1969).
116. Greaves, G., Level of conceptual system functioning in experience with sex and drugs, *Psychol. Rep.,* **28,** (1971).
117. Greenwald, B. S. and M. J. Leutgert, A comparison of drug users and nonusers on an urban commuter college campus, *Int. J. Addict.,* **6,** 63 (1971).
118. Griffith, J. A., A study of illicit amphetamine drug traffic in Oklahoma City, *Am. J. Psychiatr.,* **123,** 560 (1966).
119. Griffith, J. K., J. H. Cavanaugh, and J. A. Oates, International Symposium on Amphetamines and Related Compounds, in *Experimental Psychosis Induced by the Administration of D-Amphetamine,* E. Costa and S. Garattini (Eds.), Raven Press, New York, 1970.
120. Grossman, W., Adverse reactions associated with cannabis products in India, *Ann. Intern. Med.,* **70,** 529 (1969).
121.* Haagen, C. H., *Social and Psychological Characteristics Associated with the Use of Marijuana by College Men,* Office of Psychological Services, Wesleyan University, Middletown, Conn., 1970.

122.* Haake, B. F., *Memorandum to the Board of Education*, Mamaroneck, N.Y., 1967.
123. Haberman, P. W., E. Josephson, A. Zanes, and J. Elinson, High school drug behavior: A methodological report on pilot studies, Paper presented to the 1st International Conference on Student Drug Surveys Newark, N.J., September 1971.
124. Hallam, A. G., E. C. Murphy, T. Burke, P. J. Ely, D. T. Fane, and J. Walters, Report on a Drug Survey, 1967, *Br. J. Addict.*, **64**, 257 (1969).
125. Halpern, G. and G. Mori, *Drug Use and Drug Education*, Ottawa Board of Education and Addiction Research Foundation, Ottawa, Ontario, 1970.
126.* Hamburger, E., Contrasting the hippie and junkie, *Int. J. Addict.*, **4**, 121 (1969).
127. Hammond, R. C., Drug abuse in Canada, *Appl. Ther.*, **12**, 7 (1970).
128. Harris, E. M., A measurement of alienation in college student marijuana users and non-users, *J. Sch. Health*, **41**, 130 (1971).
129. Hawks, D. V., The dimensions of drug dependence in the United Kingdom, *Int. J. Addict.*, **6**, 135 (1971).
130.* Hawks, D., M. Mitcheson, A. Ogborne, and G. Edwards, Abuse of methylamphetamine, *Br. Med. J.*, **2**, 715 (1969).
131.* Hayashi, T., *The Nature and Prevalence of Drug and Alcohol Usage in the Fort William Schools*, Addiction Research Foundation, Fort William, Ontario, 1968.
132.* Hayashi, T., *The Nature and Prevalence of Drug and Alcohol Usage in the Port Arthur Board of Education Summer School, 1968*, Addiction Research Foundation, Fort William, Ontario, 1968.
133. Hekimian, L. G. and S. Gershon, Characteristics of drug abusers admitted to a psychiatric hospital, *JAMA.*, **205**, 125 (1968).
134. Hensala, J. D., L. J. Epstein, and K. H. Blacker, LSD and psychiatric inpatients, *Arch. Gen. Psychiar.,.*, **16**, 554 (1967).
135.* Herz, S., Behavioral patterns in sex and drug use on three campuses: implications for education and society, *Psychiatr. Q. (suppl)*, **42**, 258 (1968).
136. Heyndrickx, A., Toxicological study of a fatal intoxication by man due to cannabis smoking, *J. Pharm. Belg.*, **24**, 371 (1969).
137.* Hinckley, R. G., Nonmedical drug use and the college student, *J. Am. Coll. Health Assoc.*, **17**, 35 (1968).
138. Hoffman, A., *Revolution for the Hell of It.*, Dial Press, New York, 1968.
139.* Hogan, R., D. Mankin, J. Conway, and S. Fox, Personality correlates of undergraduate marijuana use, *J. Consult. Clin. Psychol.*, **35**, 58 (1970).
140.* Holmberg, M. B. and B. Jansson, Experiences from an out-patient department for drug addicts in Göteborg, *Acta Psychiatr. Scand.*, **44**, 172 (1968).
141. *Idem., Clinical Toxicology*, **2**, 99 (1969).

142.* Imperi, L. L., H. D. Kleber, and J. S. Davie, Use of hallucinogenic drugs on campus, *JAMA*, **204,** 1021 (1968).
143. Indian Hemp Drugs Commission (1894), Indian Hemp Drugs Commission Report, 1893–1894. Republished in *Marijuana*, (Introduction by J. Kaplan), Thos. Jefferson Publishing Co., Silver Spring, Md., 1969.
144. Irgens-Jensen, O. and S. Brun-Gulbrandsen, Drugs in Norway—Attitudes and use, *Int. J. Addict.*, **6,** 109 (1971).
145. Isbell, H., Studies on tetrahydrocannabinol in man, *Psychopharmacologia*, **11,** 184 (1967).
146.* Johnson, J. and A. D. Clift, Dependence on hypnotic drugs in general practice, *Br. Med. J.*, **4,** 613 (1968).
147.* Joint Committee on Drug Abuse, *A Survey of Secondary School Student's Perceptions of and Attitudes toward Use of Drugs be Teenagers*. Final Report, II, Montgomery County, Md., March 10, 1970.
148.* Juvenile Justice Commission, A survey of all students in one San Mateo, California, High School, 1967. Referenced in (23).
149. Keeler, M. H., Motivation for marijuana use: Acorrelate of adverse reaction, *Am. J. Psychiatr.*, **125,** 142 (1968).
150. Keniston, K., Heads and seekers: Drugs on campus, counter-cultures and American society, *Ment. Health Dig.*, **1,** 8 (1968).
151.* Kerner, K., Those who do—Drug survey, Part I, *Hunter College Envoy*, Hunter College, New York, March 1968.
152. Kerner, K., On and off—Drug survey, Part II, *Hunter College Envoy*, Hunter College, New York, March 1968.
153. Keup, W., Psychotic symptoms due to cannabis abuse, *Dis. Nerv. Syst.*, **31,** 119 (1970).
154. Kew, M. C., Possible hepatotoxicity of cannabis, *Lancet*, **1,** 578 (1969).
155. Kiloh, L. G. and S. Brandon, Habituation and addiction to amphetamines, *Br. Med. J.*, **2,** 40 (1962).
156. King, F. W., Anonymous vs. identifiable questionnares in drug usage surveys, *Am. Psychol.*, **25,** 982 (1970).
157.* King, F. W., Marihuana and LSD among male college students: Prevalence rate, frequency and self-estimates of future use, *Psychiatry*, **32,** 265 (1969).
158.* King, J., D. McDonald, and H. Salloum, *A Survey on the Use of Marijuana and LSD in the University of Saskatchewan, Regina Campus, and in Regina High Schools*, University of Saskatchewan, Regina, 1969.
159. Kleber, H. D., Prolonged adverse reactions from unsupervised use of hallucinogenic drugs, *J. Nerv. Ment. Dis.*, **144,** 308 (1967).
160. Klein, J. and D. Phillips, From hard to soft drugs: Temporal and substantive changes in drug usage among gangs in a working-class community, *J. Health Soc. Behav.*, **9,** 139 (1968).
161.* Kohn, P. M. and G. W. Mercer, Drug use, drug-use attitudes, and the authoritarianism-rebellion dimension, *J. Health Soc. Behav.*, **12,** 125 (1971).

162. Kolansky, H. and W. T. Moore, Effects of marihuana on adolescents and young adults, *JAMA*, **216**, 486 (1971).
163.* Kosviner, A., M. C. Mitcheson, K. Myers, A. Ogborne, G. V. Stimson, J. Zacune, and G. Edwards, Heroin use in a provincial town, *Lancet*, **1**, 1189 (1968).
164. Ladewig, D., Neuere Suchttrends bei Jugendlichen, *Schweiz, Med. Wochenschr.*, **99**, 781 (1969).
165.* LaForest, L., *The Incidence of Drug Use Among High School and College Students of the Montreal Island Area*, Office de la Prévention et du Traitement de l'Alcoolisme et des Toxicomanies, Québec, 1969.
166. Lambo, T. A., Medical and social problems of drug addiction in West Africa, *Bull. Narcotics*, **17**, 3 (1965).
167. Leary, T., The politics, ethics, and meaning of marijuana, in *The Marihuana Papers*, D. Solomon (Ed.), Bobbs-Merrill, Indianapolis, Ind., 1966.
168. Le Fevre, C. G., The coordinated data: A factual study of drug dependence and drug abuse during 1965-1969 in New South Wales: A summary, *Med. J. Aust.*, **1**, 395 (1971).
169. Leuner, H., Present state of psycholytic therapy and its possibilities, in *The Use of LSD in Psychotherapy and Alcoholism*, H. A. Abramson (Ed.), Bobbs-Merrill, Indianapolis, Ind., 1967.
170. Levine, J., The Nature and Extent of Psychotropic Drug Usage in the United States, Statement before the Subcommittee on Monopoly of the U.S. Senate Committee on Small Business, Washington D.C., 1969.
171.* Linken, A., A study of drug-taking among young patients attending a clinic for venereal diseases, *Br. J. Vener. Dis.*, **44**, 337 (1968).
172.* Linn, L. S., Social identification and use of marijuana, *Int. J. Addict.*, **6**, 79 (1971).
173.* Lipp, M., S. Benson, J. Tinkleberg, F. Melges, Z. Taintor, and M. Peterson, Marijuana and medical students: A study of four U. S. medical colleges, Paper presented at the American Association of Medical Colleges, Los Angeles, October 31, 1970.
174.* Lipscomb, W. R., Drug use in a black ghetto, *Am. J. Psychiatr.*, **127**, 1166 (1971).
175. Louria, D. B., Lysergic acid diethylamide, *N. Engl. J. Med.*, **278**, 435 (1968).
176. Manheimer, D. I., G. D. Mellinger, and M. B. Balter, Marijuana use among urban adults, *Science*, **166**, 1544 (1969).
177.* Manheimer, D. I., G. D. Mellinger, and M. B. Balter., Use of marijuana in an urban cross-section of adults, in *Communication and Drug Abuse*, Proceedings of the 2nd Rutgers Symposium on Drug Abuse, J. R. Wittenborn, J. P. Smith, and S. A. Wittenborn (Eds.), Chas. C Thomas, Springfield, Ill., 1970.
178.* Manniche, E. and E. Høegh, Hasjbrug blant dansk storbyungdom (Use of cannabis, by the youth of Copenhagen), *Sociol. Medd.*, **12**, (1967-1968).

179.* Marra, E. F., *Intoxicant Drugs: Survey of Student Use, Roles and Policies of the University,* University Committee on Drugs and the Campus, State University of New York, Buffalo, 1968.
180. Marten, G. W., Case report, adverse reaction to the use of marijuana, *J. Tenn. Med. Assoc.,* **62,** 627 (1969).
181. Mauss, A. L., Anticipatory socialization toward college as a factor in adolescent marijuana use, *Soc. Probl.,* **16,** 357 (1969).
182. Mayor's Committee on Marihuana, *The Marihuana Problems in the City of New York,* Cattell Press, New York, 1944.
183. McAree, C. P., R. A. Steffenhagen, and L. S. Zheutlin, Personality factors in college drug users, *Int. J. Soc. Psychiatr.,* **15,** 102 (1969).
184.* McGlothlin, W. H., D. O. Arnold, and P. K. Rowan, Marijuana use among adults, *Psychiatry,* **33,** 433 (1970).
185.* McGlothlin, W. H. and S. Cohen, The use of hallucinogenic drugs among college students, *Am. J. Psychiatr.,* **122,** 572 (1965).
186.* McKenzie, J. D., *Trends in Marijuana Use Among Undergraduate Students at the University of Maryland,* Counseling Center, University of Maryland, College Park, 1969.
187. Medical Society of the County of New York, Public Health Committee, Subcommittee on Narcotics Addiction, *N.Y. Med.,* **22,** 241 (1966).
188.* Mellinger, G. D., D. I. Manheimer, and M. B. Balter, *Patterns of Psychotherapeutic Drug Use Among Adults in San Francisco,* Family Research Center, Langley Porter Neuropsychiatric Institute (Mellinger and Manheimer), Berkeley, Calif.; and the Psychopharmacology Research Branch, National Institute of Mental Health (Balter), Chevy Chase, Md., 1969.
189.* Menard, L. C., Paper presented at the Loyola Conference on Student Use and Abuse of Drugs, Loyola College, Montreal, Québec, 1968.
190. Mercer, G. W., *The Role of Personality in Determining Reactions to Non-Narcotic Drugs,* Addiction Research Foundation, Toronto, Ontario, 1971.
191. Mercer, G. W., *Non-Alcholic Drugs and Personality: A Selected Annotated Bibliography,* Addiction Research Foundation, Toronto, Ontario, 1972.
192. Mercer, G. W. and K. Goshulak, *Comparisons of Two Festivals: Rockhill and Mariposa,* Addiction Research Foundation, Toronto, Ontario, 1971.
193.* Mercer, G. W., *Youth Centre Study, Report to the Borough of York,* York University, Toronto, Ontario, 1971.
194. Miller, L., *Drug Abuse in Israel,* World Federation for Mental Health International Symposium on Drug Abuse, Jerusalem, August 10–12, 1970.
195. Milman, D. H., The role of marihuana in patterns of drug abuse by adolescents, *J. Pediatr.,* **74,** 283 (1969).
196. Mirin, S. M., L. M. Shapiro, R. E. Meyer, R. C. Pillard, and S. Fisher, Casual versus heavy use of marijuana: A redefinition of the marijuana problem, *Am. J. Psychiatr.,* **127,** 1134 (1971).

197.* Mitcheson, M., D. Hawks, J. Davison, L. Hitchens, and S. Malone, Sedative abuse by heroin addicts, *Lancet,* **1,** 606 (1970).
198.* Mizner, G. L., J. T. Barter, and P. H. Werme, Patterns of drug use among college students: A preliminary report, *Am. J. Psychiatr.,* 127, 15 (1970).
199. Mohan, H. and G. C. Sood, Conjugate deviation of the eyes after *Cannabis indica* intoxication, *Br. J. Ophthalmol.,* **48,** 160 (1964).
200.* Morrison, R. L., *Preliminary Report on the Incidence of the Use of Drugs at Sacramento State College,* Sacramento State College, Sacramento, Calif., May 15, 1969.
201. Mukergee, B. N. and S. E. Scherer, A multivariate study of self-ideal congruence among drug users and non-users when social desirability factor is controlled, *Int. J. Pers.,* **3,** 333 (1971).
202. Murphy, H. B. M., The cannabis habit: A review of recent psychiatric literature, *U. N. Bull. Narcotics,* **15,** 15 (1963).
203.* *Narkotikamisbruk hos inskrivningsskyldiga, 1968–69* (Drug-taking among draftees, 1968–69), Militaerpsykologiska instituttet, Stockholm, 1969.
204. *Narkotikaproblemet, del III,* Betänkande avgivet av Socialstyrelsens narkomanvardkomite (The Narcotics Problem, Part III. Report issued by the Special Narcotics Committee appointed by the Board of Health and Welfare), Stockholm, 1969.
205. Neville, R., *Playpower,* Paladin, London, 1971.
206.* *Newsweek,* A survey of full-time college students on 57 campuses in the U.S. conducted by the Gallup Organization, December 29, 1969, p. 42.
207.* *New York Post,* Student referendum sponsored by U.C.L.A. Student Legislative Council, December 8, 1967.
208. Norton, W. A., The marijuana habit: Some observations of a small group of users, *Can. Psychiatr. Assoc., J.,* **13,** 163 (1968).
209.* Noyes, M. E., Great Neck North Senior High School Drug Survey, Statement for a press conference detailing some findings, Great Neck North Senior High School, New York, 1967.
210. Oki, G., *Rock Hill Visited,* Addiction Research Foundation, Toronto, Ontario, 1970.
211. Osaka, A., M. Kamel, and A. H. Hassan, Preliminary psychiatric observation in Egypt, *Br. J. Psychiatr.,* **114,** 949 (1968).
212. Oswald, I. and R. G. Priest, Registrar General (1954–1964) statistical review, England and Wales, *Br. Med. J.,* **2,** 1093 (1965).
213. Parry, H. J., M. B. Balter, and I. H. Cisin, Primary levels of underrepresenting psychotropic drug use, *Pub. Opin. Q.,* **34,** 582 (1971).
214. Pauk, X. D. and C. Shagass, Some test findings associated with susceptability to psychosis induced by LSD, *Compr. Psychiatr.,* **2,** 188 (1961).
215. Perman, E. S., Speed in Sweden, *N. Engl. J. Med.,* **283,** 760 (1970).

216. Perna, D., Psychotogenic effect of marihuana, *JAMA*, **209,** 1085 (1969).
217. Perskyo, I., Marihuana psychosis, *JAMA*, **212,** 1527 (1970).
218. Pfeiffer, W. M., *Transcultural Aspects of Cannabis Consumption*, C.I.N.P. 7th Congress, Prague, August 11-15, 1970.
219.* Postel, W. B., Marijuana use in Vietnam: A preliminary report, U.S. Army *Vietnam Med. Bul.*, **40,** 56 (1968).
220.* Rand, M. E., A survey of drug use at Ithaca College, Paper presented at the American College Health Association Annual Convention, May 1968.
221. Randall, H. B., Patterns of drug use in school-age children, *J. Sch. Health*, **40,** 296 (1970).
222.* *Rapport fra Sundhedsstyrelsens arbejdsgruppe vedrørende misbrug av euforiserende stoffer blandt ungdommen* (Report issued by the Working Committee of the Board of Health on abuse of euphoriants by young people), Copenhagen, 1968.
223. Reich, C. A., *The Greening of America*, Random House, New York, 1970.
224.* Renfrew County School Board, Pembroke Police Department and Pembroke R.C.M.P. Detachment, *Secondary School Drug Survey*, Pembroke Ontario, 1969.
225. Resume af rapport fra Sunhedsstyrelsens arbejdsgruppe vedrørende misbrug af euforiserende stoffer blandt ungdommen, *Fra Sundhedsstr.*, **5,** 13 (1969).
226.* Richard, P., A. M. Viveros, and L. Ortiz, La Marihuana tras La Cortina de Humo, *Rev. Domingo*, October 24, 7 (1971).
227. Richards, L. G. and E. E. Carroll, Illicit drug use and addiction in the United States, *Pub. Health Rep.*, **85,** 1035 (1970).
228. Robbins, E. S., L. Robbins, W. A. Frosch, and M. Stern, College student drug use, *Am. J. Psychiatr.*, **126,** 1743 (1970).
229. Robbins, E., Further observations on untoward reactions to LSD, *Am. J. Psychiatr.*, **124,** 393 (1967).
230.* Robins, L. N. and G. E. Murphy, Drug use in a normal population of young Negro men, *Am. J. Pub. Health*, **57,** 1580 (1967).
231* Roffman, R. A. and E. Sapol, Marijuana in Vietnam, *Int. J. Addict.*, **5,** 1 (1970).
232. Roland, J. L. and M. Teste, Le Cannabisme au Maroc, *Maroc. Med.*, **387,** 694 (1958).
233. Rosenberg, C. M., LSD psychosis, *Med. J. Aust.*, **1,** 129 (1968).
234.* Rosenberg, C. M., Young drug addicts: Addiction and its consequences, *Med. J. Aust.*, **1,** 1031 (1968).
235. Roszak. T., *The Making of a Counter Culture*, Anchor Books, New York, 1969.
236. Rubin, J., *We Are Everywhere*, Harper and Row, New York, 1971.
237.* Russell, J., *Survey of Drug Use in Selected British Columbia Schools*, Narcotic Addiction Foundation of British Columbia, Vancouver, 1970.

238.* Sadava, S. W., A field-theoretical study of college student drug use, *Can. J. Behav. Sci./Rev. Can. Sci. Comp.*, **3**, 337 (1971).
239.* Shick, J. F. E., D. E. Smith, and F. H. Meyers, Use of amphetamines in the Haight-Ashbury subculture, *J. Psychedelic Drugs*, **2**, 139 (1968).
240.* Shick, J. F. E., D. E. Smith, and F. H. Meyers, Use of marijuana in the Haight-Ashbury subculture, *J. Psychedelic Drugs*, **2**, 49 (1968).
241. Shean, G. D. and F. Fechtmann, Purpose in life scores of student marijuana users, *J. Clin. Psychol.*, **27**, 112 (1971).
242. Shonle, R., Peyote, the giver of visions, *Am. Anthropol.*, **27**, 53 (1925).
243.* Sinnott, C. F., Teens, *Am. J. Cath. Youth Work*, **9**, 11 (1968).
244. Smart, R. G., *Age and Sex Differences in the Most Influential Source of Drug Information*, Addiction Research Foundation, Toronto, Ontario, 1971.
245. Smart, R. G., *Alienation Among Adolescents and Source of Drug Information*, Addiction Research Foundation, Toronto, Ontario, 1970.
246. Smart, R. G., Illicit drug use in Canada: A review of current epidemiology with clues for prevention, *Int. J. Addict.*, **6**, 383 (1971).
247. Smart, R. G., *Most Influential Source of Drug Information and Extent of Use.*, Addiction Research Foundation, Toronto, Ontario, 1971.
248. Smart, R. G. and K. Bateman, Unfavourable reactions to LSD: A review and analysis of the available case reports, *Can. Med. Assoc. J.*, **97**, 1211 (1967).
249. Smart, R. G. and D. Fejer, *Credibility of Sources of Drug Information for High School Students*, Addiction Research Foundation, Toronto, Ontario, 1971.
250. Smart, R. G. and D. Fejer, The extent of illicit drug use in Canada: A review of current epidemiology, in *Critical Issues in Canadian Society*, C. L. Boydell, C. F. Grindstaff, and P. C. Whitehead (Eds.), Holt, Rinehart, and Winston, Toronto, 1971.
251. Smart, R. G. and D. Fejer, Illicit LSD Users: Their social backgrounds, drug use and psychopathology, *J. Health Soc. Behav.*, **10**, 297 (1969).
252.* Smart, R. G. and D. Fejer, *Marijuana Use Among Adults in Toronto*, Addiction Research Foundation, Toronto, Ontario, 1971.
253. Smart, R. G. and D. Fejer, Recent trends in illicit drug use among adolescents, *Can. Ment. Health Suppl.*, **68**, (1971).
254.* Smart, R. G., D. Fejer, and E. Alexander, *Drug Use Among High School Students and Their Parents in Lincoln and Welland Counties*, Addiction Research Foundation, Toronto, Ontario, 1970.
255.* Smart, R. G., D. Fejer, and J. White, *The Extent of Drug Use in Metropolitan Toronto Schools: A Study of Changes from 1968 to 1970*, Addiction Research Foundation, Toronto, Ontario, 1970.
256.* Smart, R. G. and D. Jackson, *A Preliminary Report on the Attitudes and Behaviour of Toronto Students in Relation to Drugs*, Addiction Research Foundation, Toronto, Ontario, 1969.

257. Smart, R. G., W. Schmidt, and K. Bateman, Psychoactive drugs and traffic accidents, *J. Safety Res.*, **1**, 67 (1969).
258. Smart, R. G., P. Whitehead, and L. LaForest, The prevention of drug abuse by young people: An argument based on the distribution of drug use, *Bull. Narcotics*, **23**, 11 (1971).
259.* Smith, B. C. Drug use on a university campus, *J. Am. Coll. Health Assoc.*, **18**, 360 (1970).
260. Smith, D. E., Speed kills: Patterns of high dose methamphetamine abuse, Paper presented at Discussion on Current Problems of Drug Abuse, San Francisco, 1968.
261.* Smith, M. E., *Report to Parents of Students in Castro Valley Unified School District*, Castro Valley School Board, Castro Valley, Calif., 1967.
262. Smith, S. N. and P. H. Blachly, Amphetamine usage by medical students, *J. Med. Educ.*, **41** (1966).
263.* Solomon, T., *A Pilot Study Among East Village "Hippies,"* Associated YM-YWHA's of Greater New York, New York, March 1968.
264. Soueif, M. I., Hashish consumption in Egypt, with special reference to psychosocial aspects, *Bull. Narcotics*, **19**, 1 (1967).
265. Spencer, D. J., Cannabis induced psychosis, *Br. J Addict.*, **65**, 369 (1970).
266. Stang, J., *Narkotikamisbruk blant sesjonsinnkalte i Oslo-omradet* (Drug taking among draftees in the Oslo area) (unpublished manuscript).
267. Steffenhagen, R. A., C. P. McAree, and L. S. Zheutlin, Social and academic factors associated with drug use on the University of Vermont campus, *Int. J. Soc. Psychiatr.*, **15**, 92 (1969).
268. Steffenhagen, R. A., C. P. McAree, and L. S. Zheutlin, Some social factors in college drug use, *Int. J. Soc. Psychiatr.*, **15**, 97 (1969).
269.* Stennett, R. G., H. J. Feenstra, and C. H. Aharan, *Tobacco, Alcohol and Drug Use Reported by London Secondary Schools*, Addiction Research Foundation and London Board of Education, London, Ontario, 1969.
270.* Stimson, G. V. and A. C. Ogborne, A survey of a representative sample of addicts prescribed heroin at London clinics, *Bull. Narcotics*, **22**, 13 (1970).
271.* Suchman, E. A., The hang-loose ethic and the spirit of drug use, *J. Health Soc. Behav.*, **9**, 146 (1968).
272. Talbott, J. A. and J. W. Teague, Marihuana psychosis, acute toxic psychosis associated with the use of cannabis derivatives, *JAMA*, **210**, 299 (1969).
273. Tec, N., Family and differential involvement with marihuana: A study of suburban teenagers, *J. Marriage Fam.*, **32**, 656 (1970).
274. Tietz, W., Complications following ingestion of LSD in a lower class population, *Calif. Med.*, **107**, 396 (1967).
275.* Treaner, J. J. and J. N. Skripol, Marijuana in a tactical unit in Vietnam, *U. S. Army Med. Bull.*, July-August, 29 (1970).

276. Tylden, E. and D. Wild, A case for Cannabis?, *Br. Med. J.*, **3**, 556 (1967).
277.* Udell, J. G. and R. S. Smith, *Attitudes, Usage and Availability of Drugs Among Madison High School Students*, Bureau of Business Research and Service, University of Wisconsin, Madison, July 1969.
278. Ungerleider, J. T., D. D. Fisher, and M. Fuller, The dangers of LSD, *JAMA*, **197**, 389 (1966).
279. Ungerleider, J. T., D. D. Fisher, S. R. Goldsmith, M. Fuller, and E. Forgy, A statistical survey of adverse reactions to LSD in Los Angeles County, *Am. J. Psychiat.*, **125**, 352 (1968).
280. Vierth, G., Psychopathologicische Syndrome nach Haschisch-Genuss, Beobachtungen aus Marokko, *Munch. Med. Wochenschr.*, **109**, 522 (1967).
281. Vondráček, V., J. Prokupek, R. Fischer, and M. Ahrenbergová, Recent patterns of addiction in Czechoslovakia, *Br. J. Psychiatr.*, **114**, 285 (1968).
282. Webb, M., D. V. Hawks, and A. Kosviner, Cannabis Use in a Student Population (unpublished report), 1969.
283.* Webster, C. D., *Marihuana Use Among Freshmen at the University of Toronto: Preliminary Survey*, Addiction Research Foundation, Toronto, Ontario, 1968.
284. Weil, A. T., Adverse reactions to marihuana, *N. Engl. J. Med.*, **282**, 997 (1970).
285* Wheeler, L. and C. Edmonds, A profile of drug takers, *Med. J. Aust.*, **2**, 291 (1969).
286.* Whitehead, P. C., The epidemiology of drug use in a Canadian city at two points in time: Halifax, 1969-70, Paper presented to the National Research Council, Committee on Problems of Drug Dependence, Toronto, Ontario, February 1971.
287.* Whitehead, P. C., The incidence of drug use among Halifax adolescents, *Br. J. Addict.*, **65**, 159 (1970).
288. Whitehead, P. C. and R. G. Smart, Validity and reliability of self-reported drug use, *Can. J. Criminol. Correct.*, **14**, 1 (1972).
289. Whitehead, P. C., R. G. Smart, and L. LaForest, Multiple drug use among marihuana smokers in Eastern Canada, *Committee of Problems of Drug Dependence, Report of the 32nd Meeting, February 16-18*, 6535 (1970).
290. Whitlock, F. A., The epidemiology of drug overdose, *Med. J. Aust.*, **1**, 1195 (1970).
291.* Wolk, D. J., Marijuana on the campus: A study at one university, *J. Am. Coll. Health Assoc.*, **17**, 144 (1968).
292. Wurmser, L., Chronic paranoid symptoms and thought disorders in users of marihuana and LSD as observed in psychotherapy, *Proc. Comm. Probl. Drug Depend.*, National Research Council, National Academy of Science 1969.

293. Yolles, S. F., *U. S. Senate Committee on the Judiciary: Hearings Before the Subcommittee to Investigate Juvenile Delinquency,* Government Printing Office, Washington, D. C., 1969.
294.* Zaks, M. S., P. Hughes, J. Jaffe, and M. B. Dolkart, Young people in the park: Survey of socio-cultural and drug use patterns of yippies in Lincoln Park, Chicago Democratic Convention, 1968, Paper presented at the American Orthopsychiatric Association 46th Annual Meeting, New York, March 30-April 2, 1969.

Chapter Eight

VALIDITY OF SURVEY DATA ON ALCOHOL USE

KAI PERNANEN, *Addiction Research Foundation, Toronto, Canada*

The field of alcohol and drug surveys is sorely in need of validity checks and validation studies. Not until recently, however, has any interest been shown in validating survey findings in this field.

This chapter is concerned with one crude indicator of aggregate validity* of central dependent variables in surveys of alcohol use, coverage estimates for total alcohol consumption and consumption of the different types of alcoholic beverage. These estimates can be arrived at by a comparison of yearly sales figures with survey estimates of annual consumption. With the help of some scattered validation findings I will try to pinpoint reasons for the lack of aggregate validity found in many surveys. The coverage figures for alcohol consumption are interesting not only as indicators of validity but also for the basis they form for further analyses into sampling difficulties, normative determinants of drinking in the population, and factors affecting recall of life events (10).

The validity of variables typically included as independent variables in alcohol surveys is not discussed here. Measurement errors of some of these variables have been studied in connection with other types of surveys, nota-

---

* *Aggregate validity* in a survey is measured by a comparison of the value obtained on a variable for the total sample (such as the mean) with the true value for the sample. Since the true sample value is seldom available, the true value for the population is substituted where independently available. *Coverage* is an example of aggregate validity. It designates the proportion of the average value on a variable over the units in a sample and the true average value. This paper discusses the coverage arrived at by comparing sample estimates of mean alcohol consumption over a time period to the independent "true" value of consumption as shown in alcohol sales statistics.

bly the U. S. Census and connected surveys. Among variables that have been studied are education, occupation, and personal income (e.g., 43). Suffice it to say in this connection that the validity of alcohol survey findings naturally depends on the validity of both the independent and the dependent variables, although only the aggregate validity of some dependent variables will be discussed here.

1. DATA FROM FAMILY EXPENDITURE SURVEYS

It has long been known to conductors of family expenditure surveys (i.e., surveys studying the buying habits of households) that there is considerable lack of coverage of purchases of alcohol, most often measured in terms of money value of purchases. This is true regardless of data collection methods and length of reference period for which information on purchases was asked. Information on this type of discrepancy is available for England, Finland, the United States, Norway, Sweden, and Canada (3).

Prais and Houthakker (38) present data from two parallel family budget surveys carried out in England in the 1950s which show a coverage of about 20% of the alcohol consumption shown in sales statistics.

Nyberg (33) estimates that family budget studies carried out in Finland in the 1955 and 1956 period at the most covered 50% of the purchases. It is likely that the coverage was close to 25% (48). Bruun refers to the Finnish family budget survey of 1966 where coverage was 24% (5). He also mentions that a family budget survey in Norway yielded similar results in 1958. In Sweden a survey of this type in the same year covered 56% of wine, 51% of beer, and 34% of liquor consumption (5).

Room (40) quotes the 1960–1961 Survey of Consumer Expenditures in the United States analyzed by Houthakker and Taylor (16), where the survey estimate of expenditures on alcohol was 42% of actual sales, lower than any other of the 42 categories covered. He also refers to a study by Lamale (23) comparing four different methods of data collection in the U.S. 1950 Survey of Consumer Expenditures, which showed that a weekly diary method covered 33%, a weekly recall method covered 35%, an annual consumption estimate covered 38%, and a "date-of-last-purchase" estimate covered 51% of sales.

In view of the foregoing studies it is surprising to find that a budget survey conducted in Sweden in 1952 shows a coverage of 71% of expenditures on wine and liquor (32). This can be explained partly by the fact that the "Bratt system" of rationing alcohol purchases was still in effect in Sweden (it was abolished in 1955).

Thus it seems that there is a wide range of coverage in the different types of family expenditure surveys that have been undertaken. They range from approximately 20 to 70%.

Surveys asking for actual drinking behavior generally have had coverages ranging from 40 to 60% (12, 30, 32)—the range probably being smaller because of the lower variability in the methods used. These surveys encounter specific problems of their own, in some ways different from those of the family expenditure surveys. The coverage figures of these surveys and family expenditure surveys are not strictly comparable, since the latter typically measure money expenditure and alcohol and the former measure consumption of alcohol.

2. DATA FROM THE ONTARIO DRINKING SURVEY

A survey of the drinking patterns of a probability sample of the Ontario population 15 years of age and over was carried out on the behalf of the Addiction Research Foundation in the spring of 1969 (12). The period chosen for the survey was such that the consumption typically is close to the yearly average for all of the alcoholic beverages, and thus this should not have any influence on the coverage figures. Of the 1891 interviews, 1752 were carried out in April and May, 13 in March, and 126 in June. The survey estimates are based on a day-to-day listing of drinking occasions, number of drinks, and size of drinks for the 7 days immediately preceding the interview.

The sales of beer for each person 15 years and over in Ontario in 1969 were 4.818 liters of absolute alcohol. The corresponding figures for spirits and wine were 3.773 and 0.819 liters, respectively (2). However, sales statistics do not provide information on the considerable amount of homemade wine in Ontario; 152 households out of the 1891 had manufactured wine during 1 year preceding the interview. (Thus the estimates of wine making from the survey are not strictly for the year 1969 as the sales figures are. Compared to sampling errors this fact probably has negligible consequences.) The estimate of wine produced at home which we have arrived at in our survey is 0.599 liters of absolute alcohol per person aged 15 or over. The 95% confidence limits, assuming a simple random sample, are 0.569 and 0.629 liters. The true standard error is probably somewhat greater and the confidence interval consequently wider, since the sample is geographically stratified and wine making probably tends to be clustered in certain areas.

The figures for consumption estimated in our survey should therefore be

TABLE 1 SALES, SURVEY ESTIMATES AND COVERAGE OF ALCOHOL CONSUMPTION IN ONTARIO—1969[a]

Beverage	Sales	Survey Estimates of Homemade Alcohol	Total Apparent Consumption	Survey Estimates of Consumption	Coverage (%)
Beer	4.818	0.012	4.830	2.350	48.7
Spirits	3.773	—	3.773	1.629	43.2
Wine	0.819	0.599	1.418	0.793	56.0
Total	9.410	0.611	10.021	4.772	47.6

[a] Annual consumption per person aged 15 and over in liters of absolute alcohol. The sales figures are based on ref. 2. The survey estimates of home made alcohol are based on respondents' estimates for one year preceding the interview in the Ontario Drinking Survey (12). The survey estimates of consumption are based on a question in the same survey asking the respondent to list all drinking occasions day-by-day for the seven days immediately preceding the interview.

compared with 4.830 liters for beer, 3.773 liters for spirits, and 1.418 liters for wine, corresponding to sales plus estimated home manufacture. The total amount of alcohol purchased plus that manufactured at home in 1969 rises to 10.012 liters per person over 15 years of age. Table 1 summarizes these data and gives the survey estimates for consumption of the alcoholic beverages and their coverage percentages.

It should perhaps be pointed out that with longer retention periods the probability of recall failures naturally increases. Home manufacture and its concomitant activities are, however, such laborious and extended activities that forgetting these occasions is much less probable than forgetting purchasing and consumption occasions and quantities. Moreover, there is another factor at play in the opposite direction, toward overreporting with increasing length of the reference period—forward telescoping. This designates the tendency to include into the reference period activities that occurred before the beginning of the period. This has been shown to be of considerable importance in connection with certain forms of consumer behavior (31). How relevant it is for production, purchases, and consumption of alcoholic beverages is anybody's guess and would depend on the length of the reference period.

There are also survey estimates available on *purchases* in the Ontario survey. These are for a reference period of 1 month and are thus not comparable with the figures for consumption. For wine the coverage of purchases compared with sales data is 51.6%, for beer 29.8%, and for spirits 31.6% (Table 2). The overall coverage of alcohol purchases is 32.4%.

3. FACTORS AFFECTING COVERAGE

The factors responsible for a less than perfect coverage in typical drinking surveys and family expenditure surveys seem to be the following: imperfect sampling frames and cluster effects, nonresponse, forgetting, and lying. The discussion below concerns mainly surveys measuring *actual* drinking behavior during a specific reference period, and to a lesser extent alcohol surveys asking for "typical" drinking behavior (i.e., "How often do you drink wine?" and auxiliary questions) or surveys asking for money expenditures on alcohol by households.

Sample Frames and Cluster Effects

In area samples (and often other types of sample which are based on an incomplete sampling frame, such as city directories) certain nonhousehold residences are typically left out. Some of these, for example, hotels, flop-

TABLE 2 SALES, SURVEY ESTIMATES AND COVERAGE OF ALCOHOL PURCHASES IN ONTARIO—1969[a]

Beverage	Sales	Survey Estimates of Purchases	Coverage (%)
Beer	4.818	1.435	29.8
Spirits	3.773	1.195	31.6
Wine	0.819	0.423	51.6
Total	9.410	3.053	32.4

[a] Annual purchases per person aged 15 and over in liters of absolute alcohol. The sales figures are based on ref. 2. The survey estimates of purchases are based on the responses to questions in the Ontario Drinking Survey (12) asking for purchases of wine, beer, and spirits by the household during one month immediately preceding the interview.

houses, and military installations, in all probability contain heavy drinkers to a disproportionate degree, and these thus have a zero probability of being included in the sample. On the other hand, certain other institutions are left out where low consumers are concentrated; these include hospitals, old age homes, and prisons. Naturally, prisons and hospitals may also contain disproportionately large numbers of high consumers of alcohol if overall consumption (e.g., "typical" drinking) is asked for, but for recent drinking behavior the impact would be toward an underestimate of aggregate consumption. The net effect of this noncoverage of sampling elements is not known, although estimation seems possible.

At least in the larger cities in North America there is a clustering of heavy consumers into certain districts, such as "skid row." As for any other single district, the probability of such areas being included in an area sample is very low. Thus for a large proportion of samples such areas are left out, which again means that they are biased in favor of lighter drinkers. Furthermore, low-status heavy drinkers are less likely to have fixed addresses, which also makes them fall outside the sampling frames. In countries where population registers can be used as sampling frames, and simple random sampling is more feasible, the listings are sometimes inaccurate for subpopulations where predominantly heavy consumers can be found, due to missing information on the most recent address.

The relative influence of these factors on the coverage figures is not known, since no satisfactory effort has been made to assess the effects of different factors causing incomplete coverage. Mäkelä (30) with a 96.7% response rate in a sample based on the Finnish population register gets a 38% coverage and he concludes that the elements not covered cannot explain the large discrepancy between sales statistics and survey results.

Nonresponse

With lower response rates the effect of nonresponse cannot be overlooked. It seems probable that heavier drinkers are *harder to locate* for an interview, even when they are within the sampling frame ("not-at-homes"). It is also probable that they are more likely to *refuse* an interview, especially if they know beforehand that their drinking behavior will be the subject of questioning.

Indications of the combined effect of these two forms of nonresponse are available from a Swedish survey (32) on alcohol use with four mailings of questionnaires and a response rate of about 80%. (The consumption coverage, based on questions of typical drinking, was approximately 50%.) By a check of the police registers it was shown that nonrespondents were approximately three times more likely to have been registered for drunkenness offences than were the respondents. Moreover, survey experience in general shows that subpopulations which typically have higher proportions of relatively heavy drinkers in alcohol surveys are overrepresented among nonrespondents (see, e.g., ref. 21).

This factor cannot explain a large part of the discrepancy in Mäkelä's study (30) with a 96.7% response rate and only 38% coverage. However, with response rates of 75 to 80%, which are fairly typical for North American studies, the coverage could become considerably smaller due to this factor.

Response Error

There are other types of purchasing behavior that tend to be underreported in family expenditure surveys, and for which incomplete sampling frames, cluster effects, and nonresponse cannot have as great an influence as for purchases and consumption of alcoholic beverages.

One of these is buying tobacco. Calculations based on Prais and Houthakker's expenditure survey in England (38) show that approximately 60% of tobacco consumption was covered. In the Finnish family expenditure surveys of 1955 and 1956 the coverage of tobacco purchases was also approximately 60% (48). In a Danish national morbidity survey reported by Gadourek (14) the coverage was 79% for all tobacco products and 70% for cigarettes.

Family expenditure surveys have used reference periods and methods of data collection that are different from most surveys of alcohol use, some of which have included questions on smoking. This, and the fact that one person in the household, typically the housewife, serves as informant for all the purchases made by the members of the households, makes comparisons with alcohol surveys rather unreliable. This is shown by the fact that Klaus Mäkelä in his interview survey gets a coverage of 94.3% of cigarette consumption (30).

Since the factors affecting response error appear to be similar for some other commodities and characteristics, I shall list a few of the results of validity checks and validity studies for these in the discussion below. They have necessarily been limited to attributes of the respondents for which there are independent validation data available, and not by practical or theoretical significance.

The most obvious and perhaps most important forms of response error are forgetting and lying. It is evident that the line between these forms is hard to define since motivational factors partly determine the extent and nature of retention. It has, for example, been proposed that cognitive dissonance theory could explain part of the lack of validity of survey findings (8). For this reason I have decided to refer to the other form or response error as selective reporting, implying that the selectiveness can be either conscious or subconscious.

Forgetting

The effect of *forgetting* depends on the type of question asked—whether it asks for typical behavior, such as "How often do you drink wine?" or for past actual behavior during a specified period.

Questions of *typical drinking behavior* have their own problems of measurement, and there is some indication that they also have their specific biases. Preliminary indications from an unpublished small-scale study at the Finnish Foundation for Alcohol Studies suggest that people tend to underestimate the frequency of their drinking, but, on the other hand, they tend to overestimate the quantities consumed on a "typical" drinking occasion (47). The amount of bias arising from this could very well depend on the drinking patterns of the individual and may affect the relationships with other variables. Much would depend, of course, on what type of measures or indices are built up from the replies to these questions. Alternative formulations of questions should be experimented with in the same survey—the "split ballot technique" [see Payne (36)]—and cross-validation perhaps attempted by using different measures and indices of drinking behavior in the same study.

In connection with questions on *recent actual drinking behavior*, the reference periods have varied from survey to survey; the last 24 hours (41), the past 7 days and last 24 hours in the Ontario survey (12), reference periods ranging from 1 week to the last 30 days depending on the typical drinking frequency (30), and so on. In addition, many studies have asked for the time distance to the most recent or the two most recent drinking occasions either for any type of beverage or for the different types of beverage separately (e.g., 6, 22, 42).

In *family expenditure studies* the reference periods have ranged from 1 or 2 weeks to a full year, and the methods of recording have ranged from an interview estimate of the sum spent on alcohol over a year to recording every purchase in a diary during a 2-week period.

These variations in procedure make comparisons of coverage figures very difficult due to the differential probabilities of forgetting and telescoping. The possibility also exists that certain factors vary in degree from one country to another, mainly depending on frequency and regularity of drinking.

Not many survey investigators have looked into the effect of forgetting on reporting alcohol use (or any other type of behavior for that matter). One first attempt was made by Kuusi (22). A recent study that has dealt with the problem extensively is that by Mäkelä (30). He shows that, compared to the number of reported *drinking occasions* during the 7 days preceding the interview, 76% is remembered to days 8 to 14 preceding the interview. After that the loss in retention is slower. During a 2-month interval the lowest retention rate, compared with the first week, is approximately 60%.

The overall *quantity of alcohol consumed* over the week shows a lesser degree of "extinction." This is connected with the fact that occasions during which comparatively small amounts of alcohol were consumed are more easily forgotten. (This may, in fact, explain the tendency noted in connection with typical drinking to underestimate the frequency of drinking and to overestimate the quantity consumed.)

Another interesting finding is that frequent drinkers forget their drinking occasions at a more pronounced rate than infrequent drinkers. This probably is an interference phenomenon and would lead to a somewhat biased consumption distribution based on survey estimates, and to an attenuation of relationships between consumption and other variables. It is important to note that these findings pertain to Finnish drinking patterns, where drinking occasions are less frequent and average amounts consumed per drinking occasion probably greater than those in North America, for example.

For drinking patterns as they exist in Ontario it seems that one cannot make the assumption that no forgetting occurs during the first week after the drinking occasion. Table 3 shows the percentage of users of alcohol reporting drinking occasions by time distance from the occasion.

If we assume total recall for the day preceding the interview, calculations based on the distribution in the table show that males remember 84% and females 83% of their drinking occasions during the preceding 7 days. (It must be emphasized that the percentages in Table 3 are subject to considerable random errors, especially the percentages of drinking occasions remembered.)

The percentages in Table 3 pertain to drinking occasions and since there is a greater probability for drinking occasions to be forgotten if small amounts were consumed, it is probable that the percentage figures for total amounts remembered would be higher.

It is clear that the largest proportion of forgetting over the 7 days occurs during the time interval between 1 and 2 days preceding the interview. Retention of wine-drinking occasions seems to be least affected by time (or intervening stimuli), at least among males. This probably has much to do

TABLE 3 PERCENTAGES OF DRINKERS REPORTING CONSUMPTION OF ALCOHOL BY TIME INTERVAL TO DRINKING OCCASION (12)

Time Interval to Drinking Occasion (days)	Wine		Beer		Spirits		Any Alcohol	
	M (N = 750)	F (N = 758)	M (N = 750)	F (N = 758)	M (N = 750)	F (N = 758)	M (N = 750)	F (N = 758)
1	12	13	34	10	18	15	50	32
2	10	9	26	9	14	14	42	29
3	12	9	25	7	14	14	43	27
4	10	10	23	10	13	10	41	26
5	12	9	23	9	12	13	40	24
6	12	9	23	7	13	10	41	23
7	12	10	24	8	12	11	38	24
Drinking occasions remembered over the 7 days[a]	95%	76%	75%	86%	76%	83%	84%	83%

[a] These percentages have been calculated by comparing the average number of respondents reporting drinking occasions during the seven days preceding the interview with the number of respondents reporting a drinking occasion during the day immediately preceding the interview (time interval = 1 day). This assumes total recall for the day immediately preceding the interview.

with the regularity of wine drinking with meals and perhaps also daily alcoholic drinking of cheap wines. The other distributions in the table show a clear trend of diminishing retention except for beer drinking among women.

One simple model that suggests itself in explaining the finding that occasions at which smaller amounts are consumed are less easily recalled is the number of memory cues connected with the situation in which drinking occurred. The number of cues would be related to factors such as the length of the drinking occasion, the location of the occasion, whether it is connected with other cues such as being one's birthday, and the activities connected with the occasion before, during, and after the occasion. This quantitative model could probably serve as a basis for further analyses into the problem. Suffice it to say now that there probably is in any alcohol survey a comparative overrepresentation of certain types of occasions due to selective recall failures. [Casey et al. (10) have established that recall of life events (such as vacation, marriage, change in residence) is positively related to the "saliency" of the event. This seems close to the preceding simple model.]

The comparative regularity of tobacco use makes it seem improbable that forgetting can explain the whole discrepancy between survey estimates and sales figures mentioned earlier. (Note, however, Mäkelä's (30) surprisingly high coverage.) Investigators of family expenditure behavior have explained part of the missing coverage by the prevailing norms and values regarding tobacco use in the population which led to underreporting. For alcohol use, selective reporting has also been adduced as a significant factor.

Selective Reporting

The effect of forgetting is difficult to separate from the effect of selective reporting in survey research. However, there are a few indications in the literature of the effect on reporting of the interview situation, the characteristics of the interviewer, and certain characteristics of the interviewer and the respondent.

A study by Hochstim (15) found more drinkers among women via mail and telephone interviews than in a personal interview (Table 4). This indicates a greater amount of deliberate underreporting in a face-to-face interview situation.* Of course, the figures in Table 4 do not tell us anything

---

* Hochstim also found that the respondents' rating their own health as "excellent" was affected by the type of interview conducted; in the personal interview 44%, in the telephone interview 37%, and in the mail inquiry 30% rated their health as excellent (15).

TABLE 4 FEMALE RESPONDENTS REPORTING ALCOHOL USE UNDER THREE DIFFERENT SURVEY DATA COLLECTION STRATEGIES (13)

Women Saying They ...	Mail (N = 507)	Telephone (N = 282)	Personal (N = 157)
... never drink wine	46%	44%	55%
... never drink beer	51%	49%	59%
... never drink whiskey or liquor	36%	34%	47%

about the absolute magnitude of selective reporting in any of the interview situations.

Room found great differences in coverage between different regions of the United States (Table 5). He attributes these differences in a large part to a "greater tendency for respondents to deny or underestimate drinking in milieux where drinking is not publicly accepted" (39). He bases this interpretation on the fact that regions having the lowest coverage have lower consumption (and presumably less acceptance of drinking) and have been strongholds of temperance sentiments both historically and currently.

The differential coverage of different types of alcoholic beverage also indicates the effect of selective reporting. The low-status drinks, such as fortified wine in Finland (21% coverage, compared to the overall coverage

TABLE 5 INDICES OF COVERAGE OF ALCOHOL CONSUMPTION IN GEOGRAPHICAL REGIONS OF THE UNITED STATES (37)

Region	Index of Coverage (total U.S. = 100)
New England	107
Middle Atlantic	133
East North Central	104
Pacific	94
South Atlantic	77
East South Central	69
West South Central	85
West North Central	81
Mountain	62

of 38% in Mäkelä's study) tend to be underreported to a greater degree than other types of alcoholic beverages. Canadian results are less conclusive in this respect. Part of the difficulty is that the predominant low-status drink is cheap domestic wine, which in the statistics is lumped together with all other types of wine, for which coverage is better than average. The coverage for wine is actually surprisingly high considering this fact. Sims, in a study based on annual surveys conducted by Canadian Facts Company over the period 1960–1968 in Ontario and Canada, showed that reporting of wine is more complete than reporting of beer and spirits (44). The rank order in coverage was the same as that found in our Ontario survey: wine, beer, and spirits. Room indicates that the coverage of wine in United States national samples is somewhat higher than the coverage of beer and distilled spirits (39).

Low-status (and cheap) drinks are, of course, consumed by low-status drinkers who, due to incomplete sampling frames and nonresponse, may be underrepresented among the respondents of most surveys, and this may partly explain the selective noncoverage. Several plausible hypotheses may explain the relatively good coverage of wine consumption and purchases. People who drink wine may be less reluctant to give truthful information on their drinking in general, perhaps because of their ethnic culture or other cultural influences coinciding with wine drinking. We should also note that about 40% of the wine consumed in Ontario is manufactured at home and this may also be connected with factors that facilitate truthful reporting of alcohol consumption.

Retention factors may also be at play. The *regularity* of wine consumption facilitates recall of recent drinking or estimates of typical drinking. Table 3 showed that at least for male drinkers there was no recall failure over the 7 days preceding the interview. With regular consumption valid estimates by the respondents are possible without an actual recall of every drinking occasion.

For another segment of the population wine consumption could be reserved for more festive occasions than the other types of alcoholic beverage and these occasions could provide more memory cues to aid recall. Further speculation should perhaps be halted until empirical data are available to test these hypotheses.

Mäkelä draws the conclusion that the largest single factor responsible for the low coverage figure is conscious underreporting (30). His conclusion, however, is partly based on the premise that there is no forgetting of drinking occasions and amounts over the last 7 days preceding the interview.

Comparisons of coverage rates between surveys carried out in different countries or regions within a country are central in comparisons of the survey findings themselves. They also can tell us something about the prevailing norms in the countries. However, the variations in the methods are so great that it is difficult to draw any conclusions from the variations in coverage rates of available surveys. It seems, however, that coverage figures for French surveys are comparatively close to 100%, at least for wine. For example, Bressard in a survey of the city of Saint-Etienne conducted in May-August, 1956, got a per capita consumption of 183 liters of wine for his sample of adults age 21 and over, whereas statistics of the alcohol control board of Saint-Etienne showed a per capita consumption of 160 liters for persons aged 16 and over (4). The survey estimate was based on a question about typical daily drinking. Swiecicki reports a total coverage rate of between 90 and 95% in a mail questionnaire survey carried out in Poland in 1962-1963 (46).

It is again possible that these differences between countries can be explained partly by the regularity of drinking occasions and amounts, which makes forgetting less probable and estimations of typical drinking more accurate than in other countries.

The *interview situation* is, of course, very important in eliciting truthful responses. A difficulty in measuring interviewer effects in regional alcohol surveys based on probability samples is that random assignment (or systematic assignment, from a theoretical point of view) of interviewers is not economically feasible. There are, however, some scattered findings available from alcohol surveys. Mulford and Miller noted interviewer effects in two Iowa studies. Male interviewers found more drinkers among female respondents (53%) than did female interviewers matched as to drinking habits and quota assignments (41%). Correspondingly, female interviewers found more drinkers among male respondents (71%) than did the male interviewers (54%) (27). In a later survey Mulford and Miller found that "marginal" drinkers—those who had no commitment to the use or nonuse of alcohol—were the ones most easily affected by characteristics of the interviewer (28). These and other tentative methodological findings are, however, limited, since the studies were based on quota samples, and the differences could be due to respondent selection by the interviewers, as the authors point out.

In a probability sample in a small Middle-Atlantic city Cosper found that interviewers who were light drinkers had 24% of the respondents reporting that they drank three or more drinks on an occasion, whereas moderate drinkers among interviewers had 49% of their respondents reporting that they drank that amount. There also was a clear tendency for light drinkers among the interviewers to receive vague or noncommittal responses to the questions on typical drinking. The sex combination of interviewer-respondent did not have an effect on the proportions of respondents reporting to be drinkers, but when interviewed by females more males said they preferred frequent drinking of small amounts, whereas when they were interviewed by males they reported a comparatively greater preference for more infrequent drinking with larger amounts per occasion (11). Kirsch et al. made a similar finding in a prestudy of the American Drinking Practices survey. They found that female interviewers tended to elicit a more moderate picture of the drinking and drinking history of patients at an alcoholism clinic than did male interviewers (20).

Cahalan in analyzing data from the Denver Validity Survey (see below) found a greater validity of responses when respondents of lower socioeconomic status were interviewed by interviewers of the same status than when they were interviewed by higher status interviewers (8).

These findings show the effect on the actual responses of the respondents' perceptions of the interviewer's expectations, and perhaps also the effects of the interviewer's values in determining his perception of the responses and thus his recording of replies. Explanations of this kind come to mind regarding selective reporting of consumption and purchases of alcohol. It is helpful to review some of the studies made on the validity of reports of other activities. They show the influence of the perceived self-interest of the respondent and the stigma or prestige accorded some attribute or form of behavior.

In many studies it has been found that people tend to report having a higher *education* than they actually have (34). *Voting and registration for voting* in national and municipal elections tend to be overreported in the United States. Parry and Crossley (34) in a 1949, validation study in Denver, Colorado, found that 13% of the respondents ($N = 920$) reported having voted, whereas records showed they had not. For other elections further back in time the overreporting was even more pronounced, on the average well over 20%. Similarly, a check showed that 34% of the respondents reported giving *Community Chest contributions* in the 1948 drive, although in fact they had not. *Possession of driver's license and library card* was overreported by 10 and 9%, respectively.

One has to remember that lack of coverage of alcohol consumption and purchases due to selective reporting does not mean that there is no overreporting. It is conceivable that some people overreport their consumption, perhaps selectively for different types of drinking. It also has been observed that at least in certain interview situations (e.g., when seeking treatment) some alcoholics report daily consumption figures which are physiologically impossible and would result in death (49). [Summers has seriously questioned the reliability of pretreatment and posttreatment data on drinking behavior as provided by alcoholics (45)].

In connection with alcohol consumption the main problem, however, is still the underreporting due presumably to the stigma connected with use of alcohol and behavior connected with alcohol use. In addition to (and in conjunction with) selective underreporting of different types of alcoholic beverage, there may also be underreporting of certain types of drinking occasions if they are generally connected with other activities that are normatively regulated and would give rise to response errors by themselves. This could be true, for example, of sexual and of criminal behavior (e.g., violence).

For many purposes it is important to know whether there is an underreporting of quantities consumed per occasion as well as occasions. This information is central in estimating the number of drunkenness events in a population, and in constructing quantity-frequency indices of alcohol use. Also in this respect there are probably differences in selective reporting between different cultures.

4. POSSIBLE CONSEQUENCES OF NONCOVERAGE

The consequences of aggregate noncoverage depend on the use made of the information, the type of index constructed from the reported data, and how the lack of coverage of drinking is distributed in the sample.

Noncoverage due to incomplete sampling frames, or due to clustering of high consumers into certain areas, or selective nonresponse of high consumers will lead to a biased distribution of consumption and attenuated or perhaps even spurious relationships between drinking variables and other variables. If the aim is a description of the modal drinking patterns of a country or region, this type of discrepancy is not as serious. In all surveys using drinking frequency or amount (or some index based on these), the implicit assumption has been that inferences may be extrapolated from the population covered to the heavy drinkers who probably are underrepresented in surveys. Considering the continuous character of drinking distributions, this seems at the moment a safe premise.

The effects of noncoverage due to forgetting are harder to speculate about. There seems to be no reason to assume that there are subgroups in the population where forgetting (or the drinking patterns that make forgetting more probable) is so significantly different that it would have an effect even on the distribution of consumption. (Mäkelä's finding that more frequent drinkers forget at a faster rate shows, however, that attenuation of relationships is possible because of this factor.)

Selective reporting is the most serious factor affecting coverage. Considering the different norm sets and role definitions applying to different subgroups of the populations as to their drinking and other behavior, it would be surprising if some of these did not underreport to a larger extent than others. [Herbert Hyman has pointed out that questions of prestige character have low validity and the extent of invalidity varies between different population groups (18).] It also seems unlikely (but is tacitly assumed) that selective reporting is independent of a respondent's actual consumption. Popham (37) pointed out that experience at the Addiction Research Foundation in Ontario, Canada, has shown that extremely heavy drinkers are prone to greatly underreport their drinking in a regular interview situation.

Aggregate coverage figures are still too crude a measure of validity of survey findings to allow any further speculation about the consequences. Studies based on validation of each individual's drinking would be needed, but the practical difficulties are so great that no known attempts have been made. There are no records available that would show an individual's actual alcohol consumption over a period of time. The only feasible approach at present is to experiment with alternative methods of data collection and alternative questions and question wording. Estimates of the effects of sampling inadequacies and nonresponse are possible and analysis of aggregate retention curves can help in deciding on an optimal reference period. For questions on typical drinking frequency and amounts, the simple technique of probing for how the respondent arrived at his estimate could form the beginnings of a more satisfactory approach.

The difficulties of *drug surveys* are in some ways different. Mostly the prevalence figures of drug use have been limited to very specific populations, such as university or high school students, for which there are no great problems in obtaining probability samples. (Although many drug surveys seem to have little regard for sampling procedures and let sheer numbers of respondents substitute for accuracy of estimates.) Memory errors are perhaps less likely for frequency of use, because of the amount and type of activity connected with (illicit) drug use situations. The reference periods are, however, typically much longer than in alcohol surveys, and telescoping may thus be a greater factor. Selective reporting still is a problem overlooked by most drug use surveys. Checks are possible to a much greater extent than has been attempted previously. With sample sizes of 10,000 respondents or more, experimentation with alternative methods and questions can also be carried out. The methodological problems of drug surveys deserve a more extensive treatment than is possible here.

The efforts outlined should be made to improve the coverage and to assess the effects of noncoverage. As mentioned, the study of selective reporting in surveys is an interesting subject in itself and can yield insights into the norms pertaining to drinking behavior in the population and different subpopulations. In addition to determining expression of information on drinking, these norms in part determine actual drinking behavior.

REFERENCES

1. Allen, G. I., L. Breslow, A. Weissman, and H. Nisselson, Interviewing versus diary keeping in eliciting information in a morbidity survey, *Am. J. Pub. Health,* **41,** 917 (1954).
2. Appendices to the Annual Report of the Addiction Research Foundation, 1971.
3. Asimakopulos, A., Analysis of Canadian consumer expenditure surveys, *Can. J. Econ. Polit. Sci.*, **31,** 222 (1965).
4. Bressard, M., Présentation d'une enquête sur la consommation des boissons en France, *Bull. Inst. Int. Hyg.,* **13,** 267 (1968).
5. Bruun, K., *Alkoholi: käyttö, vaikutukset ja kontrolli* (Alcohol: Its Use, Effects and Control), Tammi, Helsinki, 1972.
6. Bruun, K. and R. Hauge, *Drinking Habits Among Northern Youth*, The Finnish Foundation for Alcohol Studies, Helsinki, 1963.
7. Bueker, K., Reactions to a questionnaire survey, *J. Psychiatr. Nurs.,* **7,** 315 (1969).
8. Cahalan, D., Correlates of respondent accuracy in the Denver validity survey, *Pub. Opin. Q.,* **32,** 607 (1968–1969).
9. Cannell, C. F. and F. J. Fowler, Comparison of a self-enumerative procedure and a personal interview: A validity study, *Pub. Opin. Q.,* **27,** 250 (1963).
10. Casey, R. L., M. Masuda, and T. H. Holmes, Quantitative study of recall of life events, *J. Psychosom. Res.,* **11,** 239 (1967).
11. Cosper, R., Interview bias in a study of drinking practices, *Q. J. Stud. Alcohol,* **30,** 152 (1969).
12. de Lint, J., W. Schmidt, K. Pernanen, The Ontario Drinking Survey: A Preliminary Report, Addiction Research Foundation. Toronto, Substudy No. 1–10 & 4 & 37–70, 1970.
13. Fowler, R. F. and L. Moss, The continuous budget survey in the United Kingdom; in *Family Living Studies: A Symposium,* International Labour Office, Geneva, 1961, p. 40.
14. Gadourek, I., *Riskante Gewoonten en Zorg voor eigen Welzijn*, Wolters, Groningen, 1963.
15. Hochstim, J. R., Comparison of three information-gathering strategies in a population study of sociomedical variables. *Proc. Soc. Stat. Sect.—Am. Stat. Assoc.*, 154 (1962).
16. Houthakker, H. S. and L. Taylor, *Consumer Demand in the United States*, 2nd ed., Harvard University Press, Cambridge, Mass., 1970.
17. von Hofsten, E., A budget survey in Sweden, in *Family Living Studies: A Symposium*, International Labour Office, Geneva, 1961.
18. Hyman, H., Do they tell the truth, *Pub. Opin. Q.,* **8,** 557 (1944).
19. Kalimo, E., *Haastattelijain vaikutus haastattelutuloksiin (Interviewers'*

Effect on Interview Results), Finnish Foundation for Alcohol Studies, Helsinki, 1962.
20. Kirsch, A. D., C. H. Newcomb, and I. H. Cisin, An Experimental Study of Sensitivity of Survey Techniques in Measuring Drinking Practices, Report No. 1, Social Research Project, George Washington University, Washington, D.C., 1965.
21. Kish, L., *Survey Sampling,* John Wiley & Sons, New York, 1965.
22. Kuusi, P., *Alcohol Sales Experiment in Rural Finland,* The Finnish Foundation for Alcohol Studies, Helsinki, 1957.
23. Lamale, H., *Study of Consumer Expenditures, Incomes and Savings: Methodology of the Survey of Consumer Expenditures in 1950,* University of Pennsylvania Press, Philadelphia, 1959.
24. Lansing, J. B., G. Ginsburg, and K. Braaten, *An Investigation of Response Error,* Bureau of Economic and Business Research, University of Illinois, Urbana, 1961.
25. Manheimer, D. and H. Hyman, Interviewer performance in area sampling, *Pub. Opin. Q.*, **13**, 83 (1949).
26. Maynes, E. S., The anatomy of response errors: Consumer saving, *J. Mark. Res.*, **2**, 378 (1965).
27. Mulford, H. A. and D. E. Miller, Drinking in Iowa, I. Sociocultural distribution of drinkers, *Q. J. Stud. Alcohol,* **20**, 704 (1959).
28. Mulford, H. A. and D. E. Miller, The prevalence and extent of drinking in Iowa, 1961; A replication and an evaluation of methods, *Q. J. Stud. Alcohol,* **24**, 39 (1963).
29. Mulford, H. A., Drinking and deviant drinking, U.S.A., 1963, *Q. J. Stud. Alcohol,* **25**, 634 (1964).
30. Mäkelä, K., *Measuring the Consumption of Alcohol in the 1968–1969 Alcohol Consumption Study,* Social Research Institute of Alcohol Studies, Helsinki, 1971.
31. Neter, J. and J. Waksberg, A study of response errors in expenditure data from household surveys, *J. Am. Stat. Assoc.*, **54**, 18 (1964).
32. Nilsson, T., and P. -G. Svensson, Svenska folkets alkoholvanor och alkohollattityder—RUS (Riksundersökningen) (The Alcohol Habits and Alcohol Attitudes of the Swedish People), in *Svenska Folkets Alkoholvanor (Alcohol Habits of the Swedish People),* Statens offentliga utredningar, Finansdepartementet, Stockholm, 1971.
33. Nyberg, A., *Alkoholijuomien kulutus ja hinnat (The Consumption and Price of Alcoholic Beverages),* The Finnish Foundation for Alcohol Studies, Helsinki, 1967.
34. Parry, H. J. and H. M. Crossley, Validity of responses to survey questions, *Pub. Opin. Q.*, **14**, 61 (1950).
35. Partanen, J., K. Bruun, and T. Markkanen, *Inheritance of Drinking Behavior,* The Finnish Foundation for Alcohol Studies, Helsinki, 1966.

36. Payne, S., *The Art of Asking Questions*, Princeton University Press, Princeton, N.J., 1951.
37. Popham, R., Validity in survey questions on drinking, *The Drinking and Drug Practices Surveyor*, **1,** 7 (1970).
38. Prais, S. J. and H. S. Houthakker, *The Analysis of Family Budgets*, Cambridge University Press, Cambridge, Mass., 1955.
39. Room, R. Survey vs. sales data for the U.S., *The Drinking and Drug Practices Surveyor*, **3,** 15 (1971).
40. Room, R., Validity of alcohol expenditures data in consumer expenditure surveys, *The Drinking and Drug Practices Surveyor*, **4,** 8 (1971).
41. Sadoun, R., G. Lolli, and M. Silverman, *Drinking in French Culture*, Rutgers Center of Alcohol Studies, New Brunswick, N.J., 1965.
42. Sariola, S., *Drinking Patterns in Finnish Lapland*, The Finnish Foundation for Alcohol Studies, Helsinki, 1956.
43. Siegel, P. M. and R. W. Hodge, A causal approach to the study of measurement error, in *Methodology in Social Research*, H. M. Blalock, Jr., and A. B. Blalock (Eds.) McGraw-Hill, New York, 1968, p. 28.
44. Sims, M., Comparison of Sales Figures of Alcoholic Beverages with Types and Amounts Reported by Canadian Facts Company, Limited, in a Market Survey, Addiction Research Foundation, Toronto, Substudy No. 1-29-69, 1969.
45. Summers, T., Validity of alcoholics' self-reported drinking history, *Q. J. Stud. Alcohol.*, **31,** 972 (1970).
46. Swiecicki, A., Alkohol: *Zagadnienia polityki spotecznej (Alcohol: Problems of Social Policy)*, Warsaw, 1968.
47. Bruun, K., Finnish Foundation for Alcohol Studies, Helsinki, personal communication.
48. Marjamaa, K., Central Bureau of Statistics, Helsinki, personal communication.
49. Schmidt, W., Addiction Research Foundation, Toronto, personal communication.

INDEX

Absinthe
  ketone intoxication,
    alcoholic beverages
      wormwood (Artemisia absinthium)
      wormwood oil
        thujone (thanaceton) 166
Absinthism
  cancer of the esophagus and cardia in France
    carcinogenic substances
      alcoholic beverages 165
Absorption
  of ethanol
    congeneric substances
      alcoholic beverages 157
  of marihuana 202
  of THC
    clinical pharmacology of marihuana
      smoking
      oral doses 246-247
Abstinence
  alcohol intake 116
  liver pathology 119
  organic pathology related to alcohol use 145-147
Abstinence, abstinence syndrome
  treatment of narcotic addiction
    barbiturates 268
    opiods 269
    conditioned 272
    secondary 273
    results of treatment 289-292
    "maturing out" theory 291
Acetaldehyde
  congeneric substances
    alcoholic beverages
      blood concentrations 154
      acetaldehyde dehydrogenase 154
Acetylmethadol
  in gas chromatography
    derivative formation 47

INDEX

Acquired Predisposition
  see constitutional predisposition
Acute Alcoholic Hepatitis
  drinking patterns, alcohol abuse 143
Acute alcoholism
  from alcohol consumption 94
Acute Toxicity, in rats of distilled spirits
  congeneric substances
    alcoholic beverages 152
Adaptive Ultrastructural changes
  liver pathology, alcohol abuse 126
Addiction
  to alcohol
    in alcohol consumption 95
  narcotic
    treatment and rehabilitation of 267-294
      see Narcotic addiction
ADH, Liver
  typical/atypical
    in alcohol elimination 104
Adreno-cortical insufficiency
  alcohol intake 108
Adults
  drug use epidemiology 321-323, 325-326
Adverse effects, THC
  clinical pharmacology of
    marihuana 249, 259-261
    psychiatric 260-261
    somatic 259-260
      respiratory 260
      allergy 260
Aflatoxin
  carcinogenic substances
    alcoholic beverages 165
Africa
  drug use epidemiology 333
Age
  liver pathology, alcohol abuse 123
Aggregate validity
  validity of survey data
    on alcohol use 355
Aggression
  marihuana 221
Alcohol, *see also* Ethanol, Ethyl Alcohol
  daily caloric intake
    in alcohol consumption 96
Alcohol Abuse
  duration of
    liver pathology, alcohol abuse 124
  intensity of

    liver pathology, alcohol abuse 120
  influence of duration and dose of
    see "Duration and Dose of Alcohol Abuse"
  metabolic effects of
    liver pathology, alcohol abuse 139
Alcohol (Ethanol)
  in study of drug abuse
    drug self-administration 7, 9
Alcohol Gastritis
  drinking patterns, alcohol abuse 143
Alcohol Hypoglycemia
  alcohol intake 108
Alcohol Intake
  in Chilean alcoholics
    liver pathology, alcohol abuse 126
  see "Quantitative Effect of Alcohol Intake"
Alcohol Metabolism
  in alcohol elimination 103
Alcohol, Purified laboratory
  congeneric substances
    alcoholic beverages 155
Alcohol and THC
  marihuana and other drugs 262
Alcohol Use
  organic pathology related to volume
    and pattern of 93-167
Alcoholic Beverages
  congeneric substances
    alcoholic beverages 151
  in organic pathology related to alcohol use 93
  price of,
    in relation to liver cirrhosis mortality 94
Alcoholic Beverages, Commercial
  congeneric substances
    alcoholic beverages 155
Alcoholic Cardiomyopathy
  alcohol abuse 141
Alcoholic Cirrhosis
  drinking pattern, alcohol abuse
    in Australia 162
    in Chile 142
    in France 142
    among Hopi and Navajo Tribes 144
      drinking habits 144
    in Italy 142
    in Poland 142
    in Portugal 142
    in Russia 142
    in Scandinavia 142
    in South Germany 162

INDEX

in Switzerland 142
Alcoholic Heart Disease
  alcoholic abuse 141
Alcoholic Hepatitis
  alcohol intake 114
Alcoholic Hepatitis, Acute
  drinking patterns, alcohol abuse 143
Alcoholic Hepatitis, Chronic
  liver pathology, alcohol abuse 140
Alcoholic Myopathy
  from beer
    congeneric substances
      alcoholic beverages 162
Alcoholic Psychoses
  from alcohol consumption 94
Alcoholism
  association with cancer
    carcinogenic substances
      alcoholic beverages 165-166
  delta-type
    drinking pattern, alcohol abuse 142
Aldehydes
  congeneric substances
    alcoholic beverages 151
Allergy, to THC
  adverse effects
    marihuana 260
Amberlite XAD-2 Resin, nonionic
  in drug cleanup procedures 36, 37, 38, 39
Americas
  drug use epidemiology
    Canada and the United States 311-327
    Chile 327-328
    Mexico 327
Aminophenazone
  N-demethylation of, inhibitory effect of alcohols
    congeneric substances
      alcoholic beverages 154
Amobarbital
  in study of drug abuse
    drug self-administration 7
Amphetamines
  in cation exchange technique 35
  in direct extraction procedures 35
  drug use epidemiology
    morbidity and mortality 310
  in gas chromatography
    detectors 41, 42, 49, 50, 51
    derivative formation 47, 48, 49, 50, 51
  in gas chromatography/mass spectrometry 62, 64, 65

in mass fragmentography	66
in mass spectrometry	59
in mixed-bed ion-exchange resins	36
in nonionic resin	37, 38
in spectrofluorometry	53, 55, 57
in spin immunoassay	71
in thin layer chromatography	40

d-Amphetamine
   in cleanup procedures, nonionic resin 37
   in study of drug abuse
      drug self-administration 7

n-Amyl alcohol
   congeneric substances
      alcoholic beverages 151

Analgesia, THC
   therapeutic uses
      marihuana 257-258

Animal Experiments, Rats
   liquid diets with alcohol
      drinking pattern, alcohol abuse 144, 145
      special feeding techniques 145

Animal Models
   predisposition and susceptibility
      alcohol abuse 148
   for the study of drug abuse 1-26

Anlagefaktor, Chvostek
   predisposition and susceptibility
      alcohol abuse 148

Annual Consumption of Alcohol
   in organic pathology related to alcohol use 94

Antagonists, opioid
   see Opioid antagonists

Anticonvulsant, THC
   therapeutic uses
      marihuana
         metrazol
         synergism with diphenylhydantoin 259

Antidepressant, THC
   therapeutic uses
      marihuana 258

Antihypertensive, THC
   therapeutic uses
      marihuana 259

Appetite, THC
   physiological effects
      marihuana 251

Appetite Stimulant, THC
   therapeutic uses
      marihuana 258-259

Araq, mastic

380 INDEX

congeneric substances
  alcoholic beverages 155
Aromatic hydrocarbons, polycyclic
  carcinogenic substances
    alcoholic beverages
      bourbon, Scotch,
      Japanese whiskey 165,166
Arsenic
  British statutory limits
    wines 162
Arsenic (As_2O_3) Intoxication
  in pesticides
    alcoholic beverages
      chronic arsenic intoxication
        German winegrowing 162
Arsenical Cirrhosis
  Chronic arsenic intoxication
    alcoholic beverages 162
Artemisia Absinthium (wormwood)
  ketone intoxication
    alcoholic beverages
      thujone (thanaceton) 166
Asia and Asia Minor
  drug use epidemiology
    India 334
    Mideast 333-334
Ataxia
  congeneric substances
    alcoholic beverages 157
  from THC
    neuromuscular effects
      marihuana 251
Atropine
  in GC/MS 61
Australia
  drug use epidemiology 334-335
Australian alcoholics
  liver pathology, alcohol abuse 136
Authority
  psychosocial management
    treatment of narcotic addiction 286, 287, 292, 293
Autopsy, Chileans
  liver pathology, alcohol abuse 125
Average Cirrhogenic Dose
  liver pathology, alcohol abuse 123

Bantu Beer
  fusel oil content
    congeneric substances
      alcoholic beverages 156

siderosis
   iron content
      alcoholic beverages 163
Barbital
   in radioimmunoassay 69
Barbiturates
   drug detection and measurements
      in cleanup procedures
         ion-exchange resins 35, 36
         nonionic resin 38
      in gas chromatography
         derivative formation 44, 45, 46
      in gas chromatography/mass spectrometry 63, 65
      in GC/MS single ion monitoring 67
      in mass spectrometry 59, 60
      in radioimmunoassay 69
      in spectrofluorometry 56
      in spin immunoassay 71
   drug use epidemiology
      morbidity and mortality 310
   study of drug abuse
      drug self-administration
         patterns 9
   and THC
      marihuana and other drugs 262
Barbiturate Abstinence Syndrome
   treatment of narcotic adeliction 268
Beer
   congeneric substances
      alcoholic beverages 157
      alcoholic myopathy, cardiomyopathy 162
      liver damage, alcoholic cirrhosis 161, 162
   liver pathology, alcohol abuse 128
Behavioral
   indices of Toxicity
      in study of drug abuse
         consequences of drug self-administration 26
Behavioral dependence
   in study of drug abuse
      definition of 1-2
Behavioral Effects
   marihuana 219
Behavioral Tolerance
   marihuana 221
Benactyzine
   in spectrofluorometry 53
   in mass spectrometry 59
Beth Israel Medical Center
   treatment of narcotic addiction
      results 291

INDEX

Bilirubin
  alcohol intake 115
Binding, THC
  distribution, biotransformation
    and excretion of marihuana 247
Biochemical
  indices of Toxicity
    in study of drug abuse
      consequences of drug self-administration 26
Biochemical Effects
  of THC, LSD
    Clinical pharmacology of marihuana
      blood glucose
      creatinine and phosphorous clearance
      plasma cortisol
      plasma free fatty acids
      platelet serotonin
      urinary catecholamines 253
Biopsies, liver
  alcohol intake 112
Biotransformation
  of marihuana 203
  of THC
    clinical pharmacology of marihuana 247-248
Biphasic clinical action of THC
  clinical syndromes
    marihuana 248
Bitters
  oil of vermouth
    alcoholic beverages 166
Blood Acetaldehyde
  congeneric substances
    alcoholic beverages 154
Blood Alcohol Concentration (BAC)
  in alcohol consumption 97
Blood Glucose, THC
  LSD
    biochemical effects
      marihuana 253
Body Weight
  liver pathology, alcohol abuse 130
Body Temperature, THC
  physiological effects
    marihuana 251
Bone Marrow
  conversion from Normoblastic to Megaloblastic 115
  vacuolization 116
Bourbon Whiskey
  congeneric substances
    alcoholic beverages 153

Bouts
 in alcohol consumption 102
Bowen's Disease
 chronic arsenic intoxication
  alcoholic beverages 162
Brewery Workers
 beer consumption
  congeneric substances
   alcoholic beverages 162
Britain
 drug use epidemiology 328-330
Bromisoval
 in gas chromatography, detectors 41
 in mass spectrometry 60
Bromosulfalein – retention
 alcohol intake 106
Bronchial System
 malignant tumors of
  chronic arsenic intoxication
   alcoholic beverages 162
Buffer Capacity, of beverages
 congeneric substances
  alcoholic beverages 157
n-Butyl Alcohol
 congeneric substances
  alcoholic beverages 151

Caffeine
 in gas chromatography/mass spectrometry 66
Calcifying Pancreatitis, chronic
 alcohol abuse 140
 Czechoslovakia 141
Californian Wine
 iron content 163
Calorie Intake
 daily alcohol
  in alcohol consumption 96
Cancer
 Association with alcoholism
 Carcinogenic substances, alcoholic beverages
  cancer of the mouth, pharynx and esophagus 165
  carcinogenic agents 165-166
   syncarcinogenic effect
    alcohol
     dimethylnitrosamine 165
Cancerogenic Effect
 congeneric substances
  alcoholic beverages 156
Cane Sugar
 congeneric substances

384   INDEX

    alcoholic beverages 152
Cannabidiol (CBD)
    constituents of marihuana 245
    in gas chromatography, derivative formation 52
    in gas chromatography/mass spectrometry 62
    in mass spectrometry 59
    in spectrofluorometry 58
Cannabigerol
    in mass spectrometry 59
Cannabinoids
    in gas chromatography, derivative formation 52
    in gas chromatography/mass spectrometry 62
    in mass spectrometry 59
    in radioimmunoassay 70
    in spectrofluorometry 58
Cannabinol (CBN)
    constituents of marihuana 245
    in gas chromatography, derivative formation 52
    in gas chromatography/mass spectrometry 62
    in GC/MS mass fragmentography 67
    in mass spectrometry 59
    in spectrofluorometry 58
Cannabis, *see* Marihuana, THC
    drug use epidemiology
        morbidity and mortality 309
Carbohydrate, in diets
    alcohol intake 115
Carcinogenic effect
    carcinogenic substances
        alcoholic beverages 165
Carcinogenic Substances
    alcoholism, alcoholic beverages 165, 166
Carcinoma
    of the esophagus and forestomach
        congeneric substances
            alcoholic beverages 156
Cardiac Index
    alcohol intake 110
Cardiomyopathy
    alcoholic
        alcohol abuse 141
    from beer
        congeneric substances
            alcoholic beverages 162
    chronic beer drinkers in Canada
    United States and Belgium
        cobalt intoxication
            alcoholic beverages 164-165
Cardiovascular Effects
    of marihuana 223

INDEX 385

of THC
   clinical pharamacology of marihuana
     electrocardiogram (ECG)
      orthostatic hypertension
       tachycardia 250
Cardiovascular Phenomena
   Alcohol intake 109
Catecholamines, urinary excretion of, THC
   LSD
   biochemical effects
     marihuana 253
CBD
   see Cannabidiol
CBN
   see Cannabinol
Cell Membranes
   Pharmacologic effect of alcohols
     congeneric substances
       alcoholic beverages 152
Cellulose
   congeneric substances
     alcoholic beverages 152
Central Nervous System (CNS)
   alcohol intoxication, effect of 105
   marihuana, effects of 212
   in organic pathology related to alcohol use 93
Charcoal
   Toxicity of commercial spirits
     congeneric substances
       alcoholic beverages 153
Chile
   Alcoholic cirrhosis
     drinking pattern, alcohol abuse 142
     drug use epidemiology in the Americas 327-328
     liver pathology, alcohol abuse 120
Chilean alcoholics
   liver pathology, alcohol abuse
     drinking patterns 120
     alcohol intake 126
   intermittent/inveterate drinkers 126
Chloral Hydrate
   in gas chromatography, detectors 41
Chlordiazepoxide
   in gas chromatography/mass spectrometry 62
   in GC/MS, mass frugmentography 67
   in mass spectrometry 60
   in spectrofluorometry 56
   in study of drug abuse
     drug self-administration 7
Chlorphentermine

    in gas chromatography
        derivative formation 50
    in study of drug abuse
        drug self-administration 7
Chlorpromazine
    in gas chromatography, detectors 41
    in GC/MS, mass grugmentography 66
    in study of drug abuse
        drug self-administration 7
Cholesterol
    alcohol intake 112
Choline
    alcohol intake 114
Chronic Alcoholic Hepatitis
    liver pathology, alcohol abuse 140
Chronic Arsenic Intoxication
    German winegrowers
        alcoholic beverages 162
Chronic Calcifying Pancreatitis
    alcohol abuse 140
        Czechoslovakia 141
Chronic Toxicity of higher alcohols
    congeneric substances
        alcoholic beverages 154
Chvostek
    predisposition and susceptibility
        alcohol abuse 148
        Anlagefaktor 148
Cider
    congeneric substances
        alcoholic beverages 157
Cirrhogenic Dose
    liver pathology, alcohol abuse 123
Cirrhosis
    alcoholic, *see* alcoholic cirrhosis
    arsenical
        chronic arsenic intoxication
            alcoholic beverages 162
    in children
        liver pathology, alcohol abuse 140
    liver
        alcohol intake 111
    morbidity
        liver pathology, alcohol abuse 136
    portal
        abstinence, alcohol abuse 146
Classical conditioning
    opioid antagonists
        treatment of narcotic addiction 282
Clinical Pharmacology

INDEX 387

of Marihuana 243-262
   see Marihuana, Clinical Pharmacology of
Clinical Syndromes of THC
   clinical pharmacology of marihuana 248-250
      placebo effects 249-250
      relevance of clinical effects in laboratory to social use 249
      routes of administration 248
     specific effects
        adverse effects 249
        biphasic clinical action 248
        dose 249
        time course 248
CNV
   see contingent negative variation
Cobalt Intoxication
   chronic beer drinkers in Canada, United States, and Belgium
      alcoholic beverages 164-165
Cocaine
   in cleanup procedures
      nonionic resin 37
   in spin immunoassay 71
   in spectrofluorometry 55
   in study of drug abuse
      drug self-administration 7
Codeine
   in cleanup procedures
      nonionic resin 37
   in gas chromatography
      derivative formation 46, 47
   in spectrofluorometry 53, 54, 55
Cognitive Functions, THC
   psychological tests
      marihuana 253-255
        immediate memory 254
Color Blindness
   predisposition and susceptibility
      alcohol abuse 148
Collagen Biosynthesis
   congeneric substances
      alcoholic beverages 153
Collagen Formation
   liver pathology, alcohol abuse 139
Commercial alcoholic beverages
   congeneric substances
      alcoholic beverages 155
Comparisons
   marihuana and other drugs
      THC and alcohol, sedatives, barbiturates 262
      THC and dextroamphetamine 262
      THC and ethanol 262

388   INDEX

THC and LSD	261
Competitive Inhibition of Breakdown	
congeneric substances	
alcoholic beverages	156
Conditioned abstinence	
treatment of narcotic addiction	272
Conditioned reinforcers	
in operant conditioning	
study of drug abuse	5
Conditioning	
opioid antagonists	
treatment of narcotic addiction	
classical conditioning	282
extinction of conditioning	282, 293
operant conditioning	282
Congeneric Substances	
organic pathology and alcoholic beverages	151-162
Congeners	
congeneric substances	
alcoholic beverages	151
Conjunctival infection, THC	
effect on the eyes	
marihuana	250
Consequences of Drug Self-administration	
in study of drug abuse	23-26
indices of toxicity	
behavioral	26
biochemical	26
morphological	26
physical dependence	23
Constituents of marihuana	
clinical pharmacology of marihuana	
cannabidiol (CBD)	
cannabinol (CBN)	
Δ^1-THC	
Δ^6-THC	245
CBN, CBD in urine	248
Constitution	
predisposition and susceptibility	
alcohol abuse	148
Constitutional (Acquired) Predisposition	
predisposition and susceptibility	
alcohol abuse	147
Contaminations/Impurities	
congeneric substances	
alcoholic beverages	151
Contingent Negative Variation (CNV), THC	
neurophysiological effects	
evoked potentials, marihuana	253
Continuous Drinking	

drinking pattern, alcohol abuse 142
Continuous vs. Intermittent Drinkers
   drinking patterns, alcohol abuse 143
Continuous Reinforcement (CRF)
   in schedule of reinforcement
      study of drug abuse 5
Corn
   distillation of vodka
      congeneric substances
         alcoholic beverages 156
Coverage
   validity of survey data
      on alcohol use 355
         cluster effects on 359
         comparisons of coverage 362, 367
         consequences of noncoverage 370
         of consumption of alcohol 358
         of different alcoholic beverages 366
         effects of sample frames on 359
         factors affecting coverage 359
         in family expenditure surveys 356, 361
         in Ontario Drinking Survey 357
         of purchases of alcohol 356, 359
Creatinine and phosphorus
   clearance, THC
      LSD
         biochemical effects
            marihuana 253
Critical Dose
   drinking pattern, alcohol abuse 142
Cumulation
   due to competitive inhibition
      congeneric substances
         alcoholic beverages 156
Cyclazocine
   opioid antagonists
      treatment of narcotic addiction 279-280, 288, 292
N-cyclopropylmethylnoroxymorphone (EN-1639)
   opioid antagonists
      treatment of narcotic addiction 280
Czechoslovakia
   chronic calcifying pancreatitis
      alcohol abuse 141
      drug use epidemiology 333

Daily Alcohol Calorie Intake
   in alcohol consumption 96
Daily Alcohol Consumption
   Maximal
      in alcohol elimination 104

INDEX

in West Germany 1971	94
Daily Elimination	
Maximal	
in alcohol elimination	103
Daytop Village	
psychosocial management	
treatment of narcotic addiction	284, 285
Deep Tendon Reflexes, THC	
neuromuscular effects	
marihuana	251
Delirium Tremens	
congeneric substances	
alcoholic beverages	161
N-Demethylation	
of aminophenazone, inhibitory effect of alcohols	
congeneric substances	
alcoholic beverages	154
Denmark	
alcohol consumption	94
Dependence	
Behavioral	
in study of drug abuse	1-2
Physical	
in study of drug abuse	1, 23
Detoxification	
treatment of narcotic addiction	267-273
barbiturate abstinence syndrome	268
cold turkey	269
conditioned abstinence	272
medical complications	272
nalorphine/naloxone test	268
opioid abstinence syndrome	269
secondary abstinence	273
Dextroamphetamine and THC	
marihuana and other drugs	262
Diazepam	
in gas chromatography/mass spectrometry	62
in GC/MS, mass fragmentography	67
in mass spectrometry	60
in spectrofluorometry	56
Diet, Low-Fat	
alcohol intake	113
Dietary Histories	
Chilean alcoholics	
liver pathology, alcohol abuse	126
N,N-Diethyltryptamine (DET)	
in mass spectrometry	59
in spectrofluorometry	53
Dihydromorphinone	
in gas chromatography	

derivative formation	46
Dimethoxyamphetamines (DMA)	
in gas chromatography/mass spectrometry	49, 62
in mass spectrometry	59
Dimethylnitrosamine	
carcinogenic substances	
alcoholic beverages	165
N,N-Dimethyltryptamine (DMT)	
in spectrofluorometry	53
in mass spectrometry	59
Diphenylhydantoin	
in gas chromatography	
derivative formation	44
synergism with marihuana	
seizures in mice	259
Direct Toxic Effect	
alcohol intake	113
Discriminative Stimulus	
in operant conditioning	
study of drug abuse	5
Distillation Procedures	
congeneric substances	
alcoholic beverages	151
Distilled Spirits, acute toxicity in rats	
congeneric substances	
alcoholic beverages	
commercial spirits, rectified spirits, neutral spirits, spirit blends, purified spirits, whiskey, applejack, cognac, gin	152
Distortion in Time Sense, THC	
psychological tests	
marihuana	255
Distribution	
of marihuana	202
of THC	
clinical pharmacology of marihuana	247-248
Ditran	
in mass spectrometry	59
Diuresis	
alcohol elimination	
congeneric substances	
alcoholic beverages	157
Dogs, Mongrel	
alcohol intake	114
Dosage, THC	
clinical pharmacology of marihuana	243, 247, 248, 249
Dose –	
effect relationship	
liver pathology, alcohol abuse	135
time-product	

INDEX

liver pathology, alcohol abuse ... 135
Dose/Duration Dependence
    alcohol intake ... 111
Drinkers
    continuous vs. intermittent
        drinking patterns, alcohol abuse ... 143
    intermittent, Chilean
        liver pathology, alcohol abuse ... 126
    inveterate, Chilean
        liver pathology, alcohol abuse ... 126
    periodical
        liver pathology, alcohol abuse ... 119
    steady
        liver pathology, alcohol abuse ... 119
Drinking
    continuous
        alcohol abuse ... 142
    intermittent
        alcohol abuse ... 142
    moderate and heavy ... 95-102
    social
        alcohol consumption ... 96
    spree
        alcohol abuse ... 128
    weekend
        alcohol intake ... 113, 128
Drinking Habits
    in alcohol consumption ... 96
Driving and THC
    psychological tests
        marihuana ... 257
Drug Abuse, the study of
    use of animal models ... 1-26
Drug Abuse, definition of ... 2
Drug Detection and measurement
    chemical and biochemical methods ... 33
Drug-detoxifying Enzyme Systems, Induction of
    liver pathology, alcohol abuse ... 126
Drug Maintenance, opioids
    see Maintenance
Drug Metabolizing Systems
    in alcohol elimination ... 105
Drug Research, epidemiological
    general difficulties ... 305-308
Drug Self-Administration
    consequences of self-administration ... 23-26
    effect of environmental variables ... 21-23
    effect of pharmacological variables ... 17-22
    patterns ... 8, 9
    for preclinical assessment of a drug's abuse liability ... 10-16

INDEX 393

psychomotor stimulants 9
in study of drug abuse
  alcohol, amobarbitol
  d-amphetamine, chlordiazepoxide
  chlorphentermine, chlorpromazine
  cocaine, hexobarbital
  magnesium pemoline, mescaline
  methamphetamine
  methylphenidate, morphine
  nicotine, pentobarbital
  phenmetrazine, pipradrol
  secobarbital, SPA 6, 7
  barbiturates, ethanol, opiates 8, 9, 17
Drug Use
  epidemiology in Africa 333
  epidemiology in the Americas
    Chile 327-328
    Mexico 327
    Other population groups
      adults, hippies, soldiers in Vietnam 321-326
    Overviews, noteworthy 326-327
    Secondary Schools 311-315
    see Secondary School Drug Use
    University and College 315-321
    see University and College Studies
  epidemiology in Asia and Asia Minor
    India 334
    Mideast 333-334
  epidemiology in Australia 334-335
  epidemiology in Britain and Europe
    Britain 328-330
    Czechoslovakia 333
    France 330
    Germany 333
    Holland 332
    Scandinavia 330-332
    Switzerland 332
  psychoactive and Hallucinogenic,
    epidemiology of 303-338
  see Epidemiology, drug use
Duration of Alcohol Abuse
  liver pathology, alcohol abuse 124
Duration and Dose of Alcohol Abuse, influence of
  in organic pathology related to alcohol use 118-141
  liver pathology 118-140
  other organic lesions 140-141

ECG
  see Electrocardiogram
EEG

see Electroencephalography
EEG Effects
    of marihuana 214
EEG Studies
    see Electroencephalographic Studies
Electrocardiogram (ECG), THC
    cardiovascular effects,
        marihuana 250
Electroencephalography
    congeneric substances
        alcoholic beverages 157
Electroencephalographic (EEG) Studies, THC
    neurophysiological effects
        marihuana 251-252
Electron Microscopy
    liver pathology, alcohol abuse 127
EN-1639
    opioid antagonists
        treatment of narcotic addiction 280
Environmental variables affecting
    Drug Self-administration
        in study of drug abuse 21-23
            schedules of reinforcement 22
            stressful conditions 21
Enzyme Induction, drug-detoxifying
    liver pathology, alcohol abuse 126
Enzyme Induction, THC
    distribution, biotransformation and excretion of marihuana 247
Ephedrine
    in gas chromatography
        detectors 42, 51
        derivative formation 48
Epidemiology
    Drug Use
        psychoactive/hallucinogenic drugs 303-338
            epidemiology in Africa 333
            epidemiology in the Americas: Canada, U.S. 311-327
                noteworthy overviews 326-327
                other population groups 321-326
                secondary schools 311-315
                university and college 315-321
                    Chile 327-328
                    Mexico 327
            epidemiology in Asia and Asia Minor
                India 333-334
                Mideast 333
            epidemiology in Australia 334-335
            epidemiology in Britain and Europe
                Czechoslovakia, France,
                Germany, Holland, Scandinavia,

INDEX 395

Switzerland	328-333
morbidity and mortality	308-311
research difficulties	305-308
world epidemiology summary	
suggestion for further research	335-338

Epidemiology
   of alcohol beverage use
      in organic pathology related to alcohol use 93

Epidemiological Drug Research
   general methodological difficulties 305-308

Epitheliomata, multiple
   chronic arsenic intoxication
      alcoholic beverages 162

Erythropoiesis, suppression of
   alcohol uptake 115

Esophageal Cancer
   carcinogenic substances
      alcoholic beverages

France	165
South Africa	165

Esophageal Varices
   abstinence, alcohol abuse 147

Esophagoscopy
   abstinence, alcohol abuse 147

Eskimos
   in alcohol elimination 104

Esters
   congeneric substances
      alcoholic beverages 151

Ethanol
   see Alcohol

Ethanol Elimination, capacity of
   in organic pathology related to alcohol use 102-106

alcohol metabolism	103
drug metabolizing systems	105
effect of intoxication on CNS	105
Eskimos	104
ethanol oxidation	102
hourly elimination	103
Indians	104
intoxication	104
liver ADH, typical/atypical	104
maximal daily alcohol consumption	104
maximal daily elimination	103
nutritional factors	105
protein malnutrition	105
racial differences	104
microsomal ethanol-oxidizing system (MEOS)	106

Ethanol Oxidation

396   INDEX

in alcohol elimination 102
Ethanol and THC
   marihuana and other drugs 262
Ethchlorvynol
   in gas chromatography
      detectors 41
Ethers
   congeneric substances
      alcoholic beverages 151
Ethyl Alcohol
   congeneric substances
      alcoholic beverages 151, 157
   see also Alcohol, Ethanol
Europe
   drug use epidemiology
      Czechoslovakia 333
      France 330
      Germany 333
      Holland 332
      Scandinavia 330-332
      Switzerland 332
Evoked Potentials, THC
   neurophysiological effects
      marihuana
         contingent negative variation (CNV) 253
Excretion
   of marihuana 205
   of THC
      clinical pharmacology of marihuana 247-248
Excretory Pancreatic Function
   alcohol abuse 141
Executive Drinker
   in alcohol consumption 96
Extinction
   in operant conditioning
      study of drug abuse 6
Extinction of conditioning
   opioid antagonists
      treatment of narcotic addiction 282, 293
Eyes, effect of THC
   clinical pharmacology of marihuana
      conjunctival infection
      lowering of intraocular pressure 250-251

Fat Consumption
   alcohol abuse 140
Fatty infiltration
   alcohol intake 107
Fatty Metamorphosis
   alcohol intake 113

Fenfluramine
  in gas chromatography
    derivative formation 50
Fermentation Processes
  congeneric substances
    alcoholic beverages 151
Ferrous Radio-Iron, absorption in rats
  iron content
    alcoholic beverages 164
Fibrosis
  liver pathology, alcohol abuse 120
Fibrosis, portal
  abstinence, alcohol abuse 146
Filtration Procedures
  congeneric substances
    alcoholic beverages 151
Flurazepam
  in mass spectrometry 60
Folic Acid
  alcohol intake 114
Fractional Rectification
  congeneric substances
    alcoholic beverages 151
France
  alcoholic cirrhosis
    drinking pattern, alcohol abuse 142
    drug use epidemiology 330
    liver pathology, alcohol abuse 121
France/French
  in alcohol consumption 97
Free Fatty Acids
  alcohol intake 112
Free Fatty Acids, plasma, THC
    LSD
  biochemical effects
    marihuana 253
Function Tests, liver
  alcohol intake 113

Gas Chromatography (GC)
  in cleanup procedures
    liquid phases 39, 46, 47, 61
  specific GC methods
    derivative formation 44-52
      amphetamines and related compounds
        acetylation, dithiocarbomate,
        isothiocyanate, Schiff's base, ... 47-51, 62, 64, 67
      barbiturates
        methylation 44-46
        silylation 65

cannabinoids
  acetylation,
  methylation,
  silylation 52
 narcotic analgesics
  acetylation,
  silylation 46-47
 detectors 41-44
  electron capture (ECD) 41, 49-52, 66
  flame ionization (FID) 41, 49-52, 64
  fluorescence 43
  fluorine-sensitive 41
  infrared spectra 42-43
  mass spectrometer 44
  nitrogen specific 42
  nuclear magnetic resonance (NMR) 43
  thermionic 41
Gas Chromatography/mass spectrometry (GC/MS)
 in drugs detection and measurement 40-41, 49, 61-67
Gas Liquid Chromatography (GLC)
 assay of THC 244
Gas Liquid Chromatography with Mass Spectrography
 congeneric substances
  alcoholic beverages 156
Gastrectomy
 congeneric substances
  alcoholic beverages 157
Gastritis, alcohol
 drinking patterns, alcohol abuse 143
Gastrointestinal Disturbances
 alcohol intake 114
Gastrointestinal Function, effects on marihuana 225
Gateway Houses
 psychosocial management
  treatment of narcotic addiction 288
Gaudenzia House
 psychosocial management
  treatment of narcotic addiction 285
Genetic Predisposition and Susceptibility
 organic pathology related to alcohol use 147-150
Germany
 drug use epidemiology 333
Gerontology, gerontologic
 predisposition and susceptibility
  alcohol abuse 147
Gin, manufacture of
 alcoholic beverages
  oil of juniper,
  ketone intoxication 166-167
Gluconeogenesis

alcohol intake 108
Glucose Intolerance
    alcohol intake 108
Glucosuria
    alcohol intake 112
Glutethimide
    in cleanup procedures, nonionic resin 38
    in mass spectrometry 60
Glycogen Storage Disease
    predisposition and susceptibility
        alcohol abuse 149
Grain
    congeneric substances
        alcoholic beverages 152, 156
Grain Alcohol
    alcohol intake 111

Half-life, of THC
    distribution, biotransformation and excretion of marihuana 247
Hallucinogenic/Psychoactive drug use
    epidemiology of 303-338
    see Epidemiology, drug use
Hangover
    congeneric substances
        alcoholic beverages 157
Haustrunk
    home-made wine
    chronic arsenic intoxication
        alcoholic beverages 162
Heart Disease, Alcoholic
    alcoholic abuse 141
Heart Failure
    alcohol intake 117
Hemodynamic Alterations
    alcohol intake 109
Hemorrhage
    abstinence, alcohol abuse 147
Hemosiderosis
    liver pathology, alcohol abuse 121
Hepatic Enlargement
    liver pathology, alcohol abuse 120
Hepatic Iron Content
    sudden death of alcoholics
        iron content
            alcoholic beverages 164
Hepatic Lipid Accumulation
    alcohol intake 107
Hepatic Parenchyma, regenerative capacity of
    liver pathology, alcohol abuse 139
Hepatic Triglyceride Accumulation

alcohol intake 108
Hepatitis, alcoholic
   alcohol intake 114
Hepatomegaly, Chilean alcoholics
   liver pathology, alcohol abuse 126
Heptyl Alcohol
   congeneric substances
      alcoholic beverages 152
Heroin
   in gas chromatography
      derivative formation 46-47
   in gas chromatography/mass spectrometry 61, 65
   in spectrofluorometry 54-55
Heroin maintenance
   treatment of narcotic addiction
      British System 274-275
Hexobarbital
   in study of drug abuse
      drug self-administration 7
Hexyl Alcohol
   congeneric substances
      alcoholic beverages 151
Hippies
   drug use epidemiology 323-324
Histamine
   alcoholic beverages 166
Holland
   drug use epidemiology 332
Homologs, of ethanol (Fusel Oils)
   congeneric substances
      alcoholic beverages 151-152
         heptyl alcohol 152
         hexyl alcohol 151
         iso/n-amyl alcohol 151
         iso/n-butyl alcohol 151
         iso/n-propyl alcohol 151
Homologs, of THC
   clinical pharmacology of marihuana
      Δ^9-THC 261-262
      Δ^3-THC,
      pyrahexyl,
      synhexyl 245
Hopi Tribe
   alcoholic cirrhosis
      drinking patterns, alcohol abuse 144
Hourly Elimination
   in alcohol elimination 103
Hyaline Necrosis
   drinking patterns, alcohol abuse 143
Hydroxyproline

INDEX 401

congeneric substances
    alcoholic beverages 155
Hyperkeratosis
  chronic arsenic intoxication
    alcoholic beverages 162
Hyperuricemia
  abstinence, alcohol abuse 145
Hypnosis, THC
  therapeutic uses
    marihuana 257
Hypoglycemia, Alcohol
  alcohol intake 108
Hypomagnesemia
  alcohol intake 116
Hypoproteinemia
  liver pathology, alcohol abuse 129

Illinois Drug Abuse Program
  psychosocial management
    treatment of narcotic addiction 284, 287
Impurities/Contaminations
  congeneric substances
    alcoholic beverages 151
Incoordination, THC
  neuromuscular effects
    marihuana 251
India
  drug use epidemiology 334
Indians
  in alcohol elimination 104
Indices of Toxicity
  in study of drug abuse
    consequences of drug self-administration
      behavioral, biochemical, morphological 26
Infectious Hepatitis
  alcohol intake 107
Intensity of Alcohol Abuse
  liver pathology, alcohol abuse 120
Intensity Factor
  in intensity of alcohol use 95
Interactions
  with CNS drugs
    marihuana 222
  with other drugs
    marihuana 225
Interactions
  marihuana and other drugs
    THC and alcohol 262
    THC and sedatives, barbiturates 262
Interactions, Metabolic

402   INDEX

of marihuana	205
Intermittent Drinkers, Chilean	
liver pathology, alcohol abuse	126
Intermittent Drinking	
drinking pattern, alcohol abuse	142
Interval Schedule	
in schedule of reinforcement	
study of drug abuse	5
Intoxication	
in alcohol elimination	104
effect on CNS	105
Intraocular Pressure, lowering of, THC	
effect on the eyes	
marihuana	250
Intravenous infusion	
alcohol intake	106
Inveterate Drinkers, Chilean	
liver pathology, alcohol abuse	126
Iron Binding Protein	
alcohol intake	116
Iron Content	
alcoholic beverages	
beer, gin, rum, stout, vodka, whiskeys, wines	163
Bantu alcoholic beverages	
siderosis	163
siderosis in alcoholics	163-164
Iron Content, Hepatic	
sudden death of alcoholics	
iron content	
alcoholic beverages	164
Iron, Ferrous radioisotope	
absorption in rats	
iron content	
alcoholic beverages	164
Isoamyl Alcohol	
congeneric substances	
alcoholic beverages	151
Isobutyl Alcohol	
congeneric substances	
alcoholic beverages	151
Isopropyl Alcohol	
congeneric substances	
alcoholic beverages	151
Isovaleraldehyde	
congeneric substances	
alcoholic beverages	153
Italy	
alcoholic cirrhosis	

INDEX 403

    drinking pattern, alcohol abuse 142

Juniper (Juniperus communis, Juniperus sabina)
  alcoholic beverages
    manufacture of gin
    oil of juniper
    ketone intoxication
      sabinene, sabinol, thujan,
      thujol, thujone 166, 167

Kachasu
  distilled spirit, Zambian
  carcinogenic substances
    alcoholic beverages
      dimethylnitrosamine 165
Kaffer Corn
  brewing of Bantu beer
  congeneric substances
    alcoholic beverages 156
Ketone Intoxication
  alcoholic beverages
    Absinthe,
    Juniperus sabina
      sabinene, sabinol, thujan,
      thujol, thujone,
    Oil of Juniper,
    Wormwood oil 166, 167
Ketones
  congeneric substances
    alcoholic beverages 151
Ketonuria
  alcohol intake 112
Kinetics
  of THC after smoking
    absorption of marihuana 246

Lead
  British Statutory limits
    wines 162
Lead Poisoning
  moonshine
  southeastern United States
    alcoholic beverages 162-163
Lesions, Precirrhotic
  liver pathology, alcohol abuse 135
Leukopoiesis, suppression of
  alcohol intake 115
Levallorphan
  opioid antagonists
    treatment of narcotic addiction 279

INDEX

in radioimmunoassay 68
Levomethadyl maintenance
  treatment of narcotic addiction 277-278
Lipid Accumulation, Hepatic
  alcohol intake 107
Liqueur d'absinthe
  liver pathology, alcohol abuse 124
Liqueurs
  congeneric substances
    alcoholic beverages 161
Liquid Diets, with alcohol for rats
  drinking pattern, alcohol abuse 144, 145
  special feeding techniques 145
Liver, *see also* Hepatic
  malignant tumors of
    chronic arsenic intoxication
      alcoholic beverages 162
  in organic pathology related to alcohol use 93-140
    alcoholic Hepatitis 114
    infectious Hepatitis 107
    lipid accumulation 107
    liver biopsies 112
    liver cirrhosis 111
    liver damage, severe 130
    liver dysfunction 129
    liver function tests 113
    liver pathology 118-140
    triglyceride accumulation 108
Liver ADH, typical/atypical
  in alcohol elimination 104
Long-chain Alcohols, membrane potential
  congeneric substances
    alcoholic beverages 152
Low-fat Diet
  alcohol intake 113
LSD and THC
  biochemical effects of
  comparisons
  see Biochemical effects of THC, LSD
    Comparisons, marihuana and other drugs
LSD, *see* Lysergic Acid
  drug use epidemiology
    morbidity and mortality 310
Lyophilization
  in cleanup procedures 39
Lysergic acid diethylamide (LSD)
  in gas chromatography/mass spectrometry 61
  in mass spectrometry 59
  in radioimmunoassay 70
  in spectrofluorometry 53, 55-56

Magnesium Pemoline
  in study of drug abuse
    drug self-administration 7
Maintenance, on opioid drugs
  treatment of narcotic addiction 273, 279, 292
    heroin maintenance 274-275
    levomethadyl maintenance 277-278
    methadone maintenance 275-277, 288, 291
    morphine maintenance 274
    problems in maintenance 278-279
Malignant Tumors
  liver and bronchial system
    chronic arsenic intoxication
      alcoholic beverages 162
Malnutrition
  alcohol intake 116
Marihuana
  clinical pharmacology of 243-262
    adverse effects 249, 259-261
      allergy 260
      psychiatric 260-261
      somatic 259-260
    biochemical effects 253
    clinical syndromes 248-250
      placebo effects 249-250
      relevance to social use 249
      specific effects 248-249
    constituents, metabolites, homologs 245
    human experimentation 243-244
      difficulties in maintaining blind controls 244
      legal and regulatory constraints 243
      problems in dosing 243
      problems in selecting subjects 244
    marihuana and other drugs 261-262
      comparisons
        detroamphetamine and ethanol 262
        ethanol 262
        LSD 261
      interactions
        alcohol, sedatives 262
    pharmacokinetics 246-248
      absorption 246-247
      distribution, biotransformation and excretion 247-248
    physiological effects 250-253
      appetite, sexual stimulant 251
      body temperature, salivation 251
      cardiovascular 250
      eyes 250-251
      neuromuscular 251
      neurophysiologica

INDEX

```
    EEG, sleep, evoked potentials ................................................  251-253
  psychological tests
    cognitive functions ...........................................................  253-255
    motor tests ...................................................................  256-257
    perceptual tests ..............................................................  255-256
  therapeutic uses ................................................................  257-259
    analgesia .....................................................................  257-258
    anticonvulsant ................................................................  259
    antidepressant ................................................................  258
    antihypertensive ..............................................................  259
    appetite stimulant ............................................................  258-259
    hypnotic ......................................................................  257
    migraine attacks ..............................................................  259
    withdrawal from other drugs ...................................................  258
preclinical pharmacology of .........................................................  199-226
  metabolism .....................................................................  201
    absorption ....................................................................  202
    biotransformation .............................................................  203
    distribution ..................................................................  202
    excretion .....................................................................  205
    metabolic interactions ........................................................  205
  pharmaceutics and routes of administration ......................................  200
  pharmacologic actions
    central nervous system effects ................................................  212
      behavioral effects ..........................................................  219
        aggression ................................................................  221
        behavioral tolerance studies ..............................................  221
        gross observational effects ...............................................  219
        operant behavior ..........................................................  220
          negative reinforcement studies ..........................................  220
          positive reinforcement studies ..........................................  220
      interactions with other CNS drugs ...........................................  222
      neurochemical effects .......................................................  213
      neuroendocrine effects ......................................................  219
      neuropharmacological and EEG effects ........................................  214
      possible therapeutic applications ...........................................  223
    cardiovascular effects ........................................................  223
    effects on other systems ......................................................  224
      drug interactions ...........................................................  225
      gastrointestinal function ...................................................  225
      respiratory function ........................................................  224
      thermal regulation ..........................................................  225
  toxicity studies ................................................................  206
    acute toxicity ................................................................  206
    chronic toxicity ..............................................................  208
    special toxicity studies
      perinatal studies ...........................................................  211
Mashing Methods
  congeneric substances
    alcoholic beverages ..........................................................  151
```

Mass Spectrography
  with Gas Liquid Chromatography
    congeneric substances
      alcoholic beverages 156
Mass Spectrometry (MS) 59-67
  direct inlet MS 59-60
  in gas chromatography 40-41, 44
    GC derivative formation 45, 49-50
  in gas chromatography/mass spectrometry 61-67
Mastic Araq
  congeneric substances
    alcoholic beverages 155
Maturing Out Theory
  abstinence, narcotic addiction 291
Maximal Daily Alcohol Consumption
  in alcohol elimination 104
Maximal Daily Elimination
  in alcohol elimination 103
Megaloblastic, Bone Marrow
  alcohol intake 115
Melanosis
  chronic arsenic intoxication
    alcoholic beverages 162
Membrane Potential
  effect of long/short-chain alcohols
    congeneric substances
      alcoholic beverages 152
Memory, THC
  psychological tests
    marihuana 254
Meperidine
  in gas chromatography
    derivative formation 47
  in GS/MS mass fragmentography 67
  in spectrofluorometry 54-55
Mephobarbital
  in gas chromatography
    derivative formation 45
Mescaline
  in gas chromatography/mass spectrometry 49
  in gas chromatography/mass spectrometry 62
  in GC/MS mass fragmentography 67
  in mass spectrometry 59
  in spectrofluorometry 53, 57
  in study of drug abuse
    drug self-administration 7
Metabolic Effects, of alcohol abuse
  liver pathology, alcohol abuse 139
Metabolic Pathways
  congeneric substances

    alcoholic beverages 153
Metabolism
    of marihuana 201
Metabolites, of THC
    clinical pharmacology of marihuana
        7-hydroxy-Δ^1-THC 245, 247-248
        metabolites in wine 248
Methadone
    in gas chromatography
        derivative formation 47
    in gas chromatography/mass spectrometry 65
    in mass fragmentography 67
    in radioimmunoassay 68
    in spectrophotoflourometry 54, 55
    in spin immunoassay and enzyme immunoassay 71, 72
    in thin-layer chromatography 35-36, 38
    methadone maintenance 34, 57
Methadone Maintenance
    treatment of narcotic addiction 275-277, 288, 293
        criteria for admission 276
        guidelines for treatment 277
        results 277, 291
Methamphetamine
    in cleanup procedures
        ion-exchange resins 36
    in gas chromatography
        derivative formation 48-51
        detectors 42
    in gas chromatography/mass spectrometry 64
    in GC/MS mass fragmentography 66
    in mass spectrometry 59-60
    in spectroflourometry 57
    in study of drug abuse
        drug self-administration 7
    in thin-layer chromatography 40
Methanol
    congeneric substances
        alcoholic beverages 151, 153-154
Methapyrilene
    in spectrofluorometry 55
Methaqualone
    in GC/MS mass fragmentography 67
    in spectrofluorometry 57
p-Methoxyamphetamine
    in gas chromatography
        derivative formation 51
4-Methyl-2,5-dimethoxyamphetamine (STP)
    in gas chromatography/mass spectrometry 61-62
    in mass spectrometry 59
    in spectrofluorometry 53

INDEX 409

N-Methyl-3-piperidylbenzilate (LBJ, JB-336)
   in mass spectrometry 59
   in spectrofluorometry 53
3,4-Methylene dioxyamphetamine (MDA)
   in mass spectrometry 59
   in spectrofluorometry 53
Methylphenidate
   in study of drug abuse
      drug self-administration 7
Methyprylon
   in gas chromatography
      detectors 41
   in spectrofluorometry 56
Metrazol, seizures in mice, THC
   therapeutic uses
      marihuana 259
Mexico
   drug use epidemiology
      in the Americas 327
Microsomal Ethanol-Oxidizing System (MEOS)
   in alcohol elimination 106
Mideast
   drug use epidemiology 333-334
Migraine Attacks, THC
   therapeutic uses
      marihuana 259
Moderate Drinking and Heavy Drinking
   in organic pathology related to alcohol use 95-102
      addiction to alcohol 95
      blood alcohol concentration (BAC) 97
      bouts 102
      daily alcohol calorie intake 96
      drinking habits 96
      executive drinker 96
      France/French 97
      social drinking 96
      spiced wine/brandy 95
      temperance societies 95
      terrain ethylique 101
Mongoloids/caucasoids
   predisposition and susceptibility
      alcohol abuse 148
Mongrel Dogs
   alcohol intake 114
Moonshine
   lead poisoning
      alcoholic beverages 162
Moonshine-Belt
   southeastern United States
      lead poisoning

INDEX

    alcoholic beverages 162-163
Morbidity and Mortality
  drug use epidemiology 308
    Amphetamines 310
    Barbiturates and Tranquilizers 310
    Cannabis 309
    LSD 310
    overall considerations 311
Morphine
  in cleanup procedures
    ion-exchange resins 36
    nonionic resin 37-38
    saltin-out for TLC 40
  in gas chromatography
    derivative formation 46-47
  in GC/MS mass fragmentography 67
  in hemiagglutination-inhibition test 68
  in radioimmunoassay 68-69
  in spectrofluorometry 53-55
    dansylation 57
  in spin immunoassay and homogenous enzyme immunoassay 70-72
  in study of drug abuse
    drug self-administration 6
Morphine Maintenance
  treatment of narcotic addiction
    Harrison Narcotic Act
    morphine clinics 274
Morphological, indices of Toxicity
  in study of drug abuse
    consequences of drug self-administration 26
Mortality and Morbidity
  drug use epidemiology
    Amphetamines, Barbiturates,
    Cannabis, LSD, Tranquilizers 308-311
Motor Tests, THC
  psychological tests
    marihuana 256-257
      driving 257
Multiple Epitheliomata
  chronic arsenic intoxication
    alcoholic beverages 162
Muscle weakness, THC
  neuromuscular effects
    marihuana 251
Must
  congeneric substances
    alcoholic beverages 157
Mutagenic effect
  congeneric substances
    alcoholic beverages 156

Myocardium
   in organic pathology related to alcohol use 93
Myopathy, alcoholic, from beer
   congeneric substances
      alcoholic beverages 162

NADH Accumulation, hepatic
   predisposition and susceptibility
      alcohol abuse 149
Nalorphine
   in cleanup procedures
      nonionic resin 37
   opioid antagonists
      treatment of narcotic addiction 279, 281
   in radioimmunoassay 68
Nalorphine Test
   treatment of narcotic addiction 268
Naloxone
   in cleanup procedures
      nonionic resin 37
   opioid antagonists
      treatment of narcotic addiction 279, 281
Naloxone Test
   treatment of narcotic addiction 268
Narcotic Addiction
   treatment and rehabilitation of 267-294
      detoxification 267-273
      maintenance on opioid drugs 273-279
      opioid antagonists 279-283
      psychosocial management 283-289
      results of treatment 289-292
Narcotic Addiction Rehabilitation Act (N.A.R.A.)
   psychosocial management
      treatment of narcotic addiction 285, 287, 293
Narcotic Analgesics (Narcotics)
   in cleanup procedures
      ion exchange resins 35-36
      nonionic resin 37
   in gas chromatography
      derivative formation 46-47
   in spectrofluorometry 53-55
National Institute of Mental Health (N.I.M.H.)
   treatment of narcotic addiction
      N.I.M.H. Addiction Research Center 280
      N.I.M.H. Clinical Research Center 284-285
Navajo Tribe
   alcoholic cirrhosis
      drinking patterns, alcohol abuse 144
Necrosis, hyaline
   drinking patterns, alcohol abuse 143

Negative reinforcer
  in reinforcers
    study of drug abuse 4
Neurochemical Effects
  of marihuana 213
Neuroendocrine Effects
  of marihuana 219
Neuromuscular Effects, of THC
  clinical pharmacology of marihuana
    ataxia, deep tendon reflexes,
    incoordination, muscle weakness, tremor 251
Neuropharmacological Effects
  of marihuana 214
Neurophysiological Effects, of THC
  clinical pharmacology of marihuana
    electroencephalographic (EEG) studies 251-252
    evoked potentials, contingent negative variation (CNV) 253
    sleep studies 252
Nicotine
  in study of drug abuse
    drug self-administration 7
N.I.M.H.
  see National Institute of Mental Health
Nonalcoholic Volunteers
  alcohol intake 115
Norcodeine
  in gas chromatography
    derivative formation 46
Norephedrine
  in gas chromatography
    derivative formation 51
Nonresponse
  validity of survey data on alcohol use 360
    "not-at-homes" 360
    refusals 360
Normoblastic, Bone Marrow
  alcohol intake 115
Nuclear Magnetic Resonance Spectroscopy (NMR)
  in gas chromatography
    derivative formation 45
    detectors 43
Nutritional Factors
  in alcohol elimination 105
Nystagmus
  congeneric substances
    alcoholic beverages 157

Occupational Disease, of wine growers
  chronic arsenic intoxication
    alcoholic beverages 162

Oil of Juniper
  manufacture of gin
    alcoholic beverages 166
Oil of Vermouth
  alcoholic beverages 166
Operant Behaviour
  marihuana 220
Operant Conditioning
  conditioned reinforcers 5
  discriminative stimulus 5
  extinction 6
  operant level 5
  opioid antagonists
    treatment of narcotic addiction 282
  stimulus control 5
  in study of drug abuse
    definition of 2
Operant Level
  in operant conditioning
    study of drug abuse 5
Opiates
  in cleanup procedures
    ion-exchange resins 35-36
  in gas chromatography
    derivative formation 46
  in homogeneous enzyme immunoassay 71
  opiate self-administration
    effect of other drugs 17
  in study of drug abuse
    drug self-administration patterns 8
Opioid Abstinence Syndrome
  treatment of narcotic addiction 269
Opioid Antagonists
  classical conditioning 282
  N-Cyclopropylmethylnoroxymorphone (EN-1639) 280
  extinction of conditioning 282, 293
  N.I.M.H. Addiction Research Center 280
  operant conditioning 282
  treatment of narcotic addiction 279-283
    cyclazocine 279-280, 288, 292
    levallorphan 279
    nalorphine 279, 281
    naloxone 279, 281
Opioid Maintenance
see Maintenance
Opium
  in gas chromatography
    derivative formation 46
Organic Acids
  congeneric substances

414 INDEX

alcoholic beverages	151
Organic Pathology	
related to Volume and Pattern of alcohol use	93-167
Organic Pathology and Alcoholic Beverages	
organic pathology related to alcohol use	151-167
congeneric substances	151-162
other ingredients	162-167
Orthostatic hypotension, THC	
cardiovascular effects	
marihuana	250
Oxazepam	
in gas chromatography/mass spectrometry	62
in spectrofluorometry	56
Pancreas	
in organic pathology related to alcohol use	93
Pancreatic Function, in alcoholics	
abstinence, alcohol abuse	147
Pancreatic Function, Excretory	
alcoholic abuse	141
Pancreatitis, chronic, calcifying	
alcohol abuse	140
Czechoslovakia	141
Patterns	
of drug self-administration	8-9
Pattern of Drinking	
organic pathology related to alcohol use	142-145
Pectoral Hair	
predisposition and susceptibility	
alcohol abuse	148
Pentazocine	
in spectrofluorometry	56
Pentobarbital	
in gas chromatography/mass spectrometry	65
in radioimmunoassay	69
in study of drug abuse	
drug self-administration	7
Perceptual tests, THC	
psychological tests	
marihuana	255-256
time-sense distortion	255
Periodical Drinkers	
liver pathology, alcohol abuse	119
Periostitis deformans	
sodium fluoride intoxication	
alcoholic beverages	165
Peripheral Muscles	
in organic pathology related to alcohol use	93, 115
Peritoneoscopy	
liver pathology, alcohol abuse	120

Pesticides, containing arsenic
  alcoholic beverages
    German winegrowing,
      chronic arsenic intoxication 162
Pharmacokinetics, of THC
  clinical pharmacology of marihuana 246-248
    absorption
      oral doses,
        smoking 246-247
      biotransformation,
      distribution,
        excretion 247-248
Pharmacologic Actions
  of marihuana 212
Pharmacological Variables
  affecting Drug Self-Administration
    in study of drug abuse 17-21
      opiate self-administration,
        effect of other drugs 17
      drug interaction,
        with psychomotor stimulants 19
Phencyclidine (PCP)
  in spectrofluorometry 53
Phenmetrazine
  in gas chromatography
    derivative formation 49, 50
  in gas chromatography/mass spectrometry 64
  in GC/MS mass fragmentography 66
  in study of drug abuse
    drug self-administration 7
Phenobarbital
  in cleanup procedures
    nonionic resin 38
  in gas chromatography
    derivative formation 45
  in GC/MS mass fragmentography 67
Phoenix Houses
  psychosocial management
    treatment of narcotic addiction 284
Phosphorus and Creatinin Clearance, THC
  LSD
    biochemical effects
      marihuana 253
Physical Dependence
  in study of drug abuse
    in consequences of drug self-administration 23
    definition of 1
Physiological Effects, of THC
  clinical pharmacology of marihuana 250-253
    cardiovascular

416 INDEX

electrocardiogram,
orthostatic hypertension,
  tachycardia 250
eyes
  conjunctival infection,
  lowering of intraocular pressure 250-251
  miscellaneous effects
    body temperature, appetite,
    alivation, sexual stimulant 251
  neuromuscular
    ataxia, deep tendon reflexes,
    incoordination, muscle weakness,
    tremor 251
  neurophysiological
    EEG studies 251-252
    evoked potentials 253
    sleep studies 252

Pipradrol
  in study of drug abuse
    drug self-administration 7

Pituitary-Adrenal Function
  alcohol intake 117

Plasma cortisol, THC
  LSD
    biochemical effects, marihuana 253

Plasma Cortisol Levels
  alcohol intake 117

Plasma Free Fatty Acids, THC
  LSD
    biochemical effects, marihuana 253

Platelet counts
  alcohol intake 108

Platelet serotonin, THC
  LSD
    biochemical effects, marihuana 253

Poisoning
  lead and arsenic
    alcoholic beverages 162-163

Poland
  alcoholic cirrhosis
    drinking pattern, alcohol abuse 142

Polycyclic Aromatic Hydrocarbons
  carcinogenic substances
    alcoholic beverages
      bourbon, Scotch, Japanese whiskey 165-166

Population Groups
  drug use epidemiology in the Americas 321-326
  hippies 323-324
  miscellaneous adult populations 325-326
  normal adult populations 321-323

soldiers in Vietnam	324-325
Portal cirrhosis	
abstinence, alcohol abuse	146
Portal Fibrosis	
abstinence, alcohol abuse	146
Portugal	
alcoholic cirrhosis	
drinking pattern, alcohol abuse	142
Positive reinforcer	
in reinforcers	
study of drug abuse	4
Potatoes	
congeneric substances	
alcoholic beverages	152
distillation of vodka	156
Precirrhotic lesions	
liver pathology, alcohol abuse	135
Preclinical pharmacology of marihuana	199-226
see Marihuana, Preclinical Pharmacology of	
Preclinical Assessment of a Drug's Abuse Liability	
self-administration procedures as a means for	
in study of drug abuse	10-16
preference procedures	14
substitution procedure	10
Predisposition, Constitutional (acquired)	
see constitutional Predisposition	
Predisposition and Susceptibility Genetic	
organic pathology related to alcohol use	147-150
Preference Procedures	
in study of drug abuse	
preclinical assessment of a	
drug's abuse liability	14
Primary Alcohols	
congeneric substances	
alcoholic beverages	
Acute Toxicity	
Mean Lethal Doses	152
Prodromal Phase	
liver pathology, alcohol abuse	128
Propoxyphene	
in gas chromatography	
derivative formation	47
in GC/MS mass fragmentography	67
in spin immunoassay	71
n-Propyl Alcohol	
congeneric substances	
alcoholic beverages	151
Prospective Studies	
alcohol intake	118
Protein Malnutrition	

        in alcohol elimination 105
Proteinuria
    alcohol intake 112
Pseudoephedrine
    in gas chromatography
        detectors 51
Pseudomorphine
    in spectrofluorometry 54
Psilocin
    in mass spectrometry 59
Psychiatric Effects, THC
    adverse effects
        marihuana 260-261
Psychoactive and Hallucinogenic Drug Use
    epidemiology of 303-338
    see Epidemiology, drug use
Psychological Tests, THC
    clinical pharmacology of marihuana
        cognitive functions 253-255
            immediate memory 254
        motor tests 256-257
            driving 257
        perceptual tests 255-256
        time-sense distortion 255
Psychomotor Stimulants
    in study of drug abuse
        drug self-administration
            patterns 9
        pharmacological variables
            drug interactions 19
Psychopathy
    psychosocial management
        treatment of narcotic addiction 284
Psychoses, alcoholic
    from alcohol consumption 94
Psychosocial Management
    treatment of narcotic addiction 283-289
        authority 286-287
        Daytop Village 283-285
        Gateway Houses 288
        Gaudenzia House 285
        Illinois Drug Abuse Program 284, 287
        Narcotic Addiction Rehabilitation Act (N.A.R.A.) 285, 287, 293
        N.I.M.H. Clinical Research Centre 284-285
        Phoenix Houses 284
        psychopathy 284
        rehabilitation 283
        synanon 284-285, 293
        Teen challenge 288-293
        U.S. Public Health Service Hospitals 284-285, 290

Washington Heights Rehabilitation Centre	284, 286

Purified Laboratory Alcohol
  congeneric substances

alcoholic beverages	155

Quantitative Effect of Alcohol Intake,
  controlled studies of the

in organic pathology related to alcohol use	106-118
Effects of controlled prolonged ethanol administration	111-118
Effect of single doses	106-110

Quinidine

in spectrofluorometry	55

Quinine

in spectrofluorometry	54-56

Racial Difference

in alcohol elimination	104

Radio-Iron, Ferrous
  absorption of in rats

iron content, alcoholic beverages	164

Ratio Schedule
  in schedule of reinforcement,

study of drug abuse	5

Rats
  administration of liquid diets with alcohol

drinking patterns, alcohol abuse	144-145
special feeding techniques	145

Rectification, Fractional
  congeneric substances

alcoholic beverages	151

Regenerative capacity, of hepatic parenchyma

liver pathology, alcohol abuse	139

Rehabilitation
  psychosocial management

treatment of narcotic addiction	283

Reinforcement
  continuous

in study of drug abuse	5

  schedule of

in study of drug abuse	5, 22

Reinforcement, negative

marihuana	220

Reinforcement, positive

marihuana	220

Reinforcers
  in study of drug abuse

definition of	2, 4
conditioned reinforcers	5
negative reinforcer	4
positive reinforcer	4

INDEX

Resins
  in cleanup procedures
    ion-exchange 35-36, 39
    nonionic 36-39
Respiratory Effects, THC
  adverse effects
    marihuana 260
Respiratory Failure, alcohol toxicity
  congeneric substances
    alcoholic beverages 153
Respiratory Function, effects on
  marihuana 224
Response Error
  validity of survey data on alcohol use 361
    effect of interview situation 368
    forgetting 362
    overreporting 369
    regularity 367
    selective reporting 365
    underreporting 370
Reticulocyte Response
  alcohol intake 116
Retrospective analyses
  alcohol intake 118
Rhabdomyolysis
  drinking patterns, alcohol abuse 144
Rhesus Monkeys, fatty liver
  alcohol intake 115
Rohrer Index
  predisposition and susceptibility
    alcohol abuse 148
Routes of Administration, of THC
  pattern of clinical syndromes
    marihuana 248
Roving Ocular Movements (ROM)
  congeneric substances
    alcoholic beverages 157, 161
Rumanian Wine
  iron contact 163
Russia
  alcoholic cirrhosis
    drinking pattern, alcohol abuse 142

Salivation, THC
  physiological effects
    marihuana 251
Samogon
  low-quality vodka
    congeneric substances
      alcoholic beverages 156

Salting-out
  in cleanup procedures,
    for chromatography ... 40
Sarcoma
  congeneric substances
    alcoholic beverages ... 156
Scandinavia
  alcoholic cirrhosis
    drinking patterns, alcohol abuse ... 142
  drug use epidemiology ... 330-332
Schedule of Reinforcement
  in study of drug abuse ... 5, 22
    continuous reinforcement (CRF) ... 5
    environmental variables affecting drug self-administration ... 22
    interval schedule ... 5
    ratio schedule ... 5
Scopolamine
  in GC/MS ... 61
Secobarbital
  in gas chromatography
    derivative formation ... 45
  in study of drug abuse
    drug self-administration ... 7
Secondary abstinence
  treatment of narcotic addiction ... 273
Secondary School Drug Use
  drug use epidemiology in the Americas ... 311-315
    drug use trends ... 311-312
    drug use and year of study ... 312
    gender and frequency ... 313-314
    geographical variables ... 312-313
    grade average and drug use ... 314
    multiple drug use ... 314
    social variables and drug use ... 315
Secretin-Pancreozymin Test
  alcohol abuse ... 141
Sedatives, and THC
  marihuana and other drugs ... 262
Self-administration, drug
  in study of drug abuse ... 6-9, 17
  see also Drug Self-Administration
    consequences of self-administration ... 23-26
    effect of environmental variables ... 21-23
    effect of pharmacological variables ... 17-22
    of opiates ... 17
  for preclinical assessment of a drug's abuse liability ... 10-16
Serotonin
  platelet concentration, THC, LSD
    biochemical effects,
      marihuana ... 253

Serum Enzymes
 SGOT, GLDH, SDH, SLDH,
 SICD, SOCT, SGPT
  alcohol intake 106-107
Serum Iron Content
 alcohol intake 116
Serum Uric Acid
 alcohol intake 112
Secual Stimulant, THC
 physiological effects
  marihuana 251
Short-chain Alcohols
 membrane potential
  congeneric substances
   alcoholic beverages 152
Short-term Experiments
 alcohol intake 118
Siderosis
 Bantus, guinea pigs, alcoholics
  iron content
   alcoholic beverages 163-164
Skid-row Type
 liver pathology, alcohol abuse 127
Skin lesions
 (hyperkeratosis, melanosis, multiple epitheliomata, Bowen's disease)
 chronic arsenic intoxication,
  alcoholic beverages 162
Sleep Studies, THC
 neurophysiological effects
  marihuana 252
Social Drinking
 in alcohol consumption 96
Sodium Fluoride Intoxication
 periostitis deformans
  alcoholic beverages 165
Soldiers in Vietnam
 drug use epidemiology 324-325
Somatic Effects, THC
 adverse effects, marihuana 259-260
  allergy 260
  respiratory 260
South Germany
 alcoholic cirrhosis
  congeneric substances
   alcoholic beverages 162
SPA
 in study of drug abuse
  drug self-administration 7
Specific Effects (clinical) of THC
 clinical syndromes

INDEX   423

    marihuana 248-249
Spectrofluorometry 52-58
    in gas chromatography, detectors 43
    for DET, DMT, MDA, psilocybin, STP, LSD, mescaline, PCP, benactyzine, LBJ... 53, 55-57
    for morphine, codeine, narcotine, papaverine, pseudomorphine, heroin,
        meperidine, methadone, quinine, quinidine, methapyrilene cocaine,
        amphetamine, methamphetamine 53-57, 60
    for chlordiazepoxide, diazepam, oxazepam, pentazocine, methyprylon,
        barbiturates, methaqualone 56-57
    for cannabinoids, THC, CBD, CBN 58
    dansylation 57-58
Spiced Wine/Brandy
    in alcohol consumption 95
Spirits
    liver pathology, alcohol abuse 128
Spirits, distilled
    see Distilled Spirits
Spree-drinking
    liver pathology, alcohol abuse 128
Steady Drinkers
    liver pathology, alcohol abuse 119
Steatonecrosis
    alcohol intake 114
Stimulus control
    in operant conditioning,
        study of drug abuse 5
Stone Fruit
    congeneric substances
        alcoholic beverages 152
Stressful conditions
    in study of drug abuse
        environmental variables 21
Stroke Index
    alcohol intake 110
Substitution procedure
    in study of drug abuse,
        preclinical assessment of a drug's abuse liability 10
Sugar Beet
    distillation of vodka
    congeneric substances
        alcoholic beverages 156
Sulfur dioxide, preservative
    alcoholic beverages 166
Superbourbon
    congeneric substances
        alcoholic beverages 157
Susceptibility
    to alcohol induced liver damage 135
Switzerland
    alcoholic cirrhosis

drinking pattern, alcohol abuse 142
alcohol consumption 94
drug use epidemiology 332
Synanon
  psychosocial management
    treatment of narcotic addiction 284-285, 293
Syncarcinogenesis
  of alcohol and dimethylnitrosamine in rats
  carcinogenic substances
    alcoholic beverages 165
    hepatic carcinoma 165

Tachycardia, THC
  cardiovascular effects
    marihuana 250
Tasters, distillery
  liver pathology, alcohol abuse 121
    hemosiderosis 121
    MAC values 121
    occupational hazard 121
Teen Challenge
  psychosocial management
    treatment of narcotic addiction 288, 293
Temperance Societies
  in alcohol consumption 95
Tendon Reflexes, THC
  neuromuscular effects
    marihuana 251
Terrain Éthylique
  in alcohol consumption 101
Tetrahydrocannabinolic Acids (THCA)
  in gas chromatography
    derivative formation 52
Tetrahydrocannabinol (THC)
  see Marihuana, THC
  clinical pharmacology of marihuana 243-262
    assay by GLC 244
  in gas chromatography
    derivative formation 52
  in GC/MS 61-62
  in GC/MS mass fragmentography 67
  in mass spectrometry 59
  in radioimmunoassay 70
  in spectrofluorometry 58
Thanaceton (thujone)
  ketone intoxication
    alcoholic beverages 166-167
Therapeutic Uses, THC
  clinical pharmacology of marihuana
    analgesia 257-258

anticonvulsant	
diphenylhydantoin, metrazol	259
antidepressant	258
antihypertensive	259
appetite stimulant	258-259
hypnotic	257
migraine attacks	259
withdrawal from other drugs	258
Therapeutic Applications	
marihuana	223
Thermal Regulation, effect on	
marihuana	225

THC
  see Adverse Effects
  Biochemical Effects
  Clinical Syndromes
  Constituents of Marihuana
  Half-life
  Homologs
  Marihuana
  Marihuana and Other Drugs
    barbiturates
    dextroamphetamine
    ethanol
    LSD
    sedatives
  Metabolites
  Pharmacokinetics
  Physiological Effects
  Tetrahydrocannabinol
  Therapeutic Uses

Thin layer chromatography (TLC)	
in cleanup procedures	35
ion-exchange resins	35-36
nonionic resin	37-39
salting-out	40
in immunoassay	71-72
in mass spectrometry	59-60
in spectrofluorometry	53-58
Thrombopoiesis, suppression of	
alcohol intake	115
Thujan	
ketone intoxication	
alcoholic beverages	167
Thujol	
ketone intoxication	
alcoholic beverages	167
Thujone (thanaceton)	
ketone intoxication	
alcoholic beverages	166-167

Time Course, of THC
  clinical syndromes
    marihuana 248
Tolerance, role of acetaldehyde
  congeneric substances
    alcoholic beverages 154
Tolerance, behavioral
  marihuana 221
Toxicity
  of marihuana 206
Toxicity, chronic
  of higher alcohols
    congeneric substances
      alcoholic beverages 154
Toxicity, indices of
  in study of drug abuse
    consequences of drug self-administration
      behavioral, biochemical,
        morphological 26
Tranquilizers
  drug use epidemiology
    morbidity and mortality 310
Treatment and Rehabilitation
  of Narcotic Addiction 267-294
  see also Narcotic Addiction
Tremor, THC
  neuromuscular effects
    marihuana 251
Triglyceride Accumulation, Hepatic
  alcohol intake 108
Trimethoxyamphetamine(s) (TMA)
  in gas chromatography
    derivative formation 49, 62

Ultrastructural Changes
  alcohol intake 113
Ultrastructural Changes, Adaptive
  liver pathology, alcohol abuse 126
University and College Studies
  drug use epidemiology in the Americas 315-321
    drug use and personality 320-321
    drug use trends 316
    drug use and year of study 316-317
    gender and frequency 317-319
    geographical variables 317
    grade average and academic program 319-320
    multiple drug use 319
    social variables and drug use 320
Uric Acid, Serum
  alcohol intake 112

Urinary catecholamines, THC, LSD
  biochemical effects
    marihuana 253
U.S. Public Health Service Hospitals
  psychosocial management
    treatment of narcotic addiction 284-285, 290

Vacuolization
  Bone Marrow
    alcohol intake 115
Vermouth Wines
  oil of vermouth
    ketone content
      alcoholic beverages 166
Vitamins
  alcohol intake 114
Vitamin B_6
  alcohol intake 116
Vitamin B_{12}
  malabsorption
    alcohol intake 116
Vitamin Deficiencies
  liver pathology, alcohol abuse 129
Vodka, crude distillation of
  from grain corn, sugarbeets, potatoes
    congeneric substances
      alcoholic beverages 156

van der Waals' Forces
  hydrogen bonding, cell membranes
    congeneric substances
      alcoholic beverages 152
Washington Heights Rehabilitation Center
  psychosocial management
    treatment of narcotic addiction 284-286
Weekend Drinking
  alcohol intake 113
West Berlin alcoholics
  drinking patterns
    liver pathology, alcohol abuse 120
West Berlin
  liver pathology, alcohol abuse 120
West Germany
  alcohol consumption 94
Whiskey
  congeneric substances
    alcoholic beverages 152
Wine
  liver pathology, alcohol abuse 124, 128
Wines

arsenic/lead in wines,
  British statutory limits 162
congeneric substances
  alcoholic beverages 154, 161
effect on rats
  (sherries, muscatels, white and red wine) 154
Wine Growers, German
chronic arsenic intoxication
  alcoholic beverages 162
Withdrawal, from other drugs, THC
  therapeutic uses
    marihuana 258
Withdrawal
  liver pathology, alcohol abuse 127
World epidemiology, drug use
  summary
    suggestions for further research 335-338
Wormwood, wormwood oil
  ketone intoxication
    alcoholic beverages
      thujone (Thanaceton) 166

Xylose
  congeneric substances
    alcoholic beverages 152